Patterns of Psychological Research

Readings for General Psychology

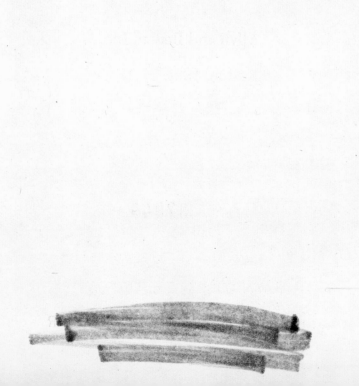

Patterns of Psychological Research

Readings for General Psychology

edited by

Jerome E. Singer *and* Francis L. Whaley

The Pennsylvania State University

Allyn and Bacon, Inc.

Boston, 1966

37044

Library of Congress Catalog Card Number: 66–16735

PRINTED IN THE UNITED STATES OF AMERICA

Preface

We believe that a student's best introduction to psychology is learning what kinds of questions psychologists ask and how they seek answers. This book is an attempt to provide such an experience. Fifty-one articles have been arranged in ten sections (learning set formation, brightness constancy, short-term memory, physiological aspects of hunger, visceral components of emotion, the development of conservation of numbers, the constancy of IQ, clinical versus actuarial prediction, social reinforcement in therapy, and conformity and commitment). Obviously, this does not cover all of the important topics, but it does provide a sampling within the range of psychology. The articles in each section deal with a single strand of research, thus demonstrating how each succeeding investigation builds upon, challenges, and clarifies previous ones.

No one selection of topics or studies can be universally pleasing. Many excellent reports have not been included; some studies stand alone and consequently fail to show the continuity of research; some represent the work of only one man or group. We found some articles too technical for an introductory course, others simply too long. What we have done is to select the ones we wanted to use in our own classes.

We have chosen to reprint the original reports rather than abridge or rewrite them. The first chapter provides an orientation for studying the articles; the introduction to each section provides an overview of the topic, explains the relationship between the component articles, and gives a list of discussion questions as a study guide. Since the articles within each section deal with the same line of investigation, the repetition of terminology, concepts, procedures, and results reduces the level of difficulty while permitting the student to acquire an intensive understanding of these topics. Some of the work is technical and challenging; most students could not be expected to master these fifty-one articles without help. We expect that the book will not be a totally independent reading assignment, but that an instructor will be available for clarification or discussion as needed.

Two articles are not reprinted as they were first published. At the request of the senior author, the Warren and Baron report on learning set corrects errors in the original report. These changes are footnoted in the article. The Mayer paper on hunger is a self-contained abstract—the first six pages—of a longer article. The bibliography has been selectively abridged.

The academic affiliations shown for the authors of the reports have been reprinted as they were in the original publication. In many of the cases they are no longer appropriate or accurate.

We wish to express our appreciation to the publishers who have permitted us to use their material; they are individually cited at the beginning of each article. As a token of our gratitude to the authors for permitting us to reprint their work, we have contributed one half of the royalties in their names to the American Psychological Foundation.

Jerome E. Singer
Francis L. Whaley

Contents

vii

PART EIGHT   The Constancy of Intelligence

PART NINE   Clinical and Actuarial Prediction

PART TEN   Operant Conditioning in Therapy

PART ELEVEN   *Commitment and Conformity*

PART ONE

Introduction

Metaphors enrich our speech. Fred Allen's remark that a certain dancer sounded like a demented woodpecker in a lumberyard paints a clearer picture than would several paragraphs of nonfigurative prose. But the same figures of speech that serve the poet and the wit so well often contain difficulties for the technical writer. No one has ever come out in favor of jargon; writers use technical words only because they are precise and carry no extra meaning. Some scientific metaphors have clarity and parsimony, and describe a vivid picture, but they are inaccurate—the atom is not built like a tinkertoy, nor is the brain a telephone switchboard. Recognizing the danger that metaphors pose, we shall use two of them to describe the aims of this book. We shall modify Toynbee's theory of the historical process and suggest that psychology, too, proceeds by a series of challenges and responses. And we shall reassert the old adage that the whole is greater than the sum of its parts.

CHALLENGE AND RESPONSE

Challenge and response, argument and rebuttal, theory and critique—all of these convey the flavor of the controversies that have characterized much of scientific thought, including psychology. To be sure, many times members of a discipline may be working together in a concerted attack on a particular problem or a search for a particular discovery. But the workaday process of the investigator and theorist is one in which he conducts an experiment to discriminate between two theories, collects normative data to counter a colleague's claims, or offers a new theoretical mechanism to account for a fellow psychologist's data. Although the controversy may become heated at times, please note that we are not suggesting that the basic impetus is one of antagonism or acrimony. Rather, what we are suggesting is that psychologists tend to channel their interests and endeavors. They become concerned and expert in specific areas. They marshal the data, read relevant articles, and organize their thoughts; they believe in and value the conclusions and the structure they bring to bear in a particular subfield. It is not surprising, then, that a new discovery, suggestion, or experiment should excite their interest, disorganize their theory, or pique their curiosity. It is their professional responses—practical, experimental, and theoretical—to these challenges which provide the bulk of scientific advances. (If the word "challenge" is replaced by "stimulus," a more psychologically flavored metaphor—stimulus and response—will emerge.) The response need not be a rechallenge; in fact, challenge and response may act as an organizing principle in several different ways. We can illustrate this by looking at the principles that bind the articles in three of the parts of this book.

The discovery of uranium in Canada was a challenge. It was stimulating but not controversial. Instead of trying to prove that it wasn't uranium, people rushed to the area to participate in its exploitation. Harlow's conceptualization of the learning set, reproduced in our initial reading, served a similar function.

Although black and white television is a recent invention in historical perspective, it is "old hat" to most Americans. Recently, when a manufacturer produced a color television set, it served as a challenge to other producers who marketed competing sets. This competition benefited all makers; it increased the market for color television and hastened technological improvements. At the same time, these improvements may also refine the existing black and white techniques. The study by Peterson and Peterson is analogous to color television: it stimulated work on short-term memory which has already made that area a productive field, and it seems likely to enhance our knowledge of long-term memory.

Almost every day there are advertisements in metropolitan newspapers about the relative advantages of gas and oil heat. If the ads are to be taken at face value, each fuel is cheaper, cleaner, healthier, safer, and more convenient than the other. While it is difficult for a consumer to assess the validity of these arguments, he can, nevertheless, understand the issues and the basis of the claims. Many people who are not plumbers or heating specialists buy houses and heating plants. The challenges issued by one fuel system to another may benefit the consumer. An argument in favor of gas heat may alert a customer to a flaw in the oil system and simultaneously bring about corrective changes on the part of the oil heat industry. When announcing these changes, the oil heat people may rebut with one of the failings of gas heat. These successive rechallenges alert people to the central problems and refine the methods of the competitors. An academic counterpart of this is found in our section on clinical prediction, where two different systems are presented successively.

THE SUM OF THE PARTS

The first metaphor, "challenge and response," was related to the creation of articles; the second, "the whole is greater than the sum of its parts," is related to the reading and understanding of articles. The great number and wide variety of journals staggers the most rapid readers; not even the most avid and dedicated psychologist can hope to read more than a small fraction of their contents. Most psychologists select their professional reading by giving their attention to articles that deal with a few problems of interest to them. By restricting the number of topics they follow, these psychologists save time and effort—not just because they don't attempt to read everything, but also because the reading they do is interrelated.

A psychological article does more than present new data or conclusions. It also summarizes previous work in its area and reinterprets it in light of its presentation. The reader who is familiar with an area does not have to reacquaint himself with the background and can easily comprehend the changes in perspective or additions to the field proposed by an author. If a psychologist reads an article in an unfamiliar field, he must concentrate on some novel terminology, bypass some unfamiliar references, and read some of the conclusions several times before grasping all of their implications. In short, he has an easier task and gets more from an article in a familiar rather than an unfamiliar area. Like the psychologist, the student will get more out of and find it easier to read articles in a familiar field. But what technical field is familiar to a typical student? If he reads thirty psychological reports, each in a different problem area, the odds are that he will be reading articles in thirty unfamiliar fields.

This book is a collection of fifty-one psychological articles. However, they are arranged in ten parts, so that only the first article in each set need be a novel experience, and this article is quoted as a reference by many later ones. Within each set, the readings are arranged so as to concentrate on a topic. Thus the metaphor, "the whole is greater than the sum of its parts," because a student expends less effort yet receives more insight from reading a set of five related articles than from reading five equivalent but unrelated articles. Reading several articles in a specific area will not qualify the reader as an expert or specialist in that field; but it will give him knowledge and insight into the development of an area which he might not otherwise get.

There is a price to be paid for these benefits. Five related articles cover one area; five unrelated articles cover five areas. The attainment of some depth is at the expense of breadth. Perception, for example, is one of the basic areas in psychology, cutting across a variety of topics and problems. Yet we have included only one set of readings that is perceptual. We have no illusions about these articles being representative of the whole area. Understanding them in great detail will not add at all to your specific knowledge of other aspects of perception. But understanding the logic and philosophy with which the investigators approach their problems will be useful as a background and will clarify these other aspects when they are encountered. If a text seeks to survey an entire discipline, its representativeness is an important factor. The articles in this book were not selected to provide a wide panorama of subject matter; they are intended, rather, to represent some of the methods, concerns, and modes of integration used by practicing psychologists.

THE NATURE OF PSYCHOLOGICAL KNOWLEDGE

At this point a more general question might be asked. Why should a student or any other nonspecialist in an area read technical articles? If he goes on to further work in psychology, he will develop his own interests and select his own articles; if he doesn't go on, wouldn't he be better off putting his curiosity to work absorbing the knowledge contained in textbooks?

The answer can be found in the table of contents of an introductory textbook. There will be chapters dealing with statistics, methodology, and perhaps the philosophy of science or the history of psychology. The rationale for their inclusion in a general text is the same as the purpose of this book. One of the basic points to be made in psychology is that results cannot be evaluated without considering how they were obtained. Facts are elusive. Today, A is right; tomorrow, B is right. Today, A is wrong; tomorrow, B is wrong. And so, as if recorded in a Gilbert and Sullivan patter song, knowledge is contravened, changed, channeled, and corrected. What remains relatively fixed are the procedures and criteria by which fact-modifying studies are evaluated. Knowledge of a discipline based upon a set of facts or theories is dated and is apt to change in time. Knowledge of a discipline based upon its methodology may not only retain the student's level of competence, it may also permit its expansion. Such knowledge of procedures may be obtained from two complementary sources. One is by reading a textbook describing the techniques; the other is by reading articles in which psychologists practice these techniques. This book is obviously one way of providing the second source.

It may be that all your life you have heard and believed the adage, "Spare the rod and spoil the child." You feel appropriate physical discipline is an aid in child-training. However, one introductory psychology text describes several experiments showing the effects of punishment on learning in rats and concludes, "Punishment momentarily suppresses a habit but does not weaken it." Both these statements about the effects of punishment cannot be right, yet both are made by intelligent, well-meaning people—the first by parents looking for a guide in raising their children, the second by psychologists interpreting a controlled study. How do you decide which to accept? If you know nothing about the basis of these results, you are forced to rely on the prestige of the spokesman in assessing the statement. If, however, you understand the procedures and the circumstances of the studies, the conclusions are qualified, and the apparent differences are often more a reflection of different circumstances than of contrasting belief. Knowledge composed only of facts and summaries cannot be easily adapted to new and different conclusions. Knowledge based on procedure and qualification may often modify the phrasing of the original question in new and more productive ways.

Instead of simply asking if punishment works, it becomes more fruitful to inquire, "Under what conditions does punishment have effects and why?" It would not be paradoxical to find that a psychologist who believed that punishment *usually* doesn't eliminate a response also spanked his child on appropriate occasions. Knowing which occasions are appropriate requires a sophisticated understanding of the research methodology used to investigate the issue. Twenty years ago students learned that intelligence was inherited; today, these former students, now parents, may see books offering methods of raising their children's IQ's. This is another apparent contradiction, but one that is bothersome only to those who had memorized conclusions. The students who also learned how the general conclusion was inferred from specific evidence need not be perplexed by new evidence modifying the older generalization. The section in this book on the constancy of the IQ presents in detail the case in point.

Most of the readings in this book describe experiments, since most published psychological literature *is* experimental. The flow is ever increasing. While commercial magazines sometimes falter and cease publication, professional journals are bigger and more frequently published than ever despite the fact that new ones are being constantly founded. And the established journals have long publication lags—any given issue may consist of articles submitted as much as two years earlier. They had to wait their turn that long to see the light of day. This growing tide of experimental evidence does not mean that psychology is all experimental. Experimentation is a method of advancing knowledge—a powerful and useful one—but like all methods it can only be used where applicable. Where it is not applicable, other methods, such as case studies, correlational studies, and critiques also play their parts in the psychological process; they challenge and stimulate some psychologists and are the appropriate products of others.

THE ELIMINATION OF ALTERNATIVES

The major goal of all scholarly inquiry is to discover relationships, whether they are between forces in an atom's nucleus or between systems of medieval religious belief. Psychologists reasonably seek to find relationships among psychological or behavioral variables. Their major problem is that for any one set of observations there are always a host of possible explanations or causes. How can the right one, if any, be isolated from the specious ones? This reduction or elimination of plausible alternatives is the objective of the sometimes complicated techniques that are employed in psychological investigation.

One advantage of the experimental method is that control groups (whose results may enable the investigator to discard an alternative) can be built into the study. Control groups are but one kind of experimental control; all sorts of controls have similar aims. If several different factors work together, or if there is just the possibility that they are working together, a good design may enable the investigator to untangle the variables. A sports example may illustrate this. An amateur golfer may find his game going sour and make several drastic changes: a new stance, a different club, a shifted grip. After these revisions, his game improves. In order to determine which changes were the effective ones, he would have to try them out in all possible combinations. If he sets up a system to try out these combinations efficiently, he will have grasped the essence of experimental design. It does more than enable the researcher to find something out; by weeding out false claims, it makes it possible for him to be specific about the cause.

Statistics serve a similar function. Consider again our golfer. Even though he does things in the same manner (the familiar other things being equal) he has good days and bad days. If he used grip A on a good day, and grip B on a bad one, he might conclude that grip A improved his game. If every time he used A his score was lower than when he used B, his conclusion might be correct; if A resulted in improvement only once, his conclusion might be erroneous. How often does A have to result in improvement to validate the statement, "Grip A is better than grip B?" This is one of the basic statistical questions: "When is a result due to chance and when can it be attributed to the factors being investigated?"

Probability theorists and statisticians have provided methods for accurately determining the likelihood that chance factors could have caused the result. In the case of the golfer, they may be able to compute that there is a 4 percent likelihood that chance factors, rather than grip A, resulted in his improved score. Even though this is an accurate estimate of chance effects, the golfer must still decide whether he should change his grip. If our golfer is also a psychologist, he may employ the term "significance." He may claim that grip A makes a significant difference in his score only if chance could account for the drop in scores less than 5 percent of the time. In this case, chance is so unlikely an alternative that he is willing to discard it as an explanation in favor of the "grip" hypothesis.

There are two related processes involved here. One is the computation of chance likelihood by standardized statistical tests, some of which you will encounter in the articles—Chi-square, correlation coefficient, t-test, analysis of variance. They all serve the same function under different circumstances; they all assess how likely it was that chance, rather than some hypothesized factor, caused the relationship. Usually they report this as a "p" value. The comment "$p = .04$" means that chance is likely to account for effects this great only about 4 percent of the time; similarly, "$p > .70$" means that chance is likely to account for results as large as those obtained 70 percent of the time. These definitions, of course, are grossly oversimplified and not at all rigorous. Greater sophistication in statistics can be achieved even from the chapters in an introductory psychology text.

Statistics, however, are only the first step. Our golfer must decide whether to change his grip or not; psychologists must decide whether one factor influences another or not. By an arbitrary but widely accepted convention, chance is discarded as an alternative explanation, and a relationship is deemed significant when chance factors could have accounted for the relationship 5 percent of the time or less, that is, when "$p < .05$."

NOTE ON STUDY QUESTIONS

The editors of this book of readings are convinced that beginning students need something more than the typical text, which gives an overview of many topics and only short references to the supporting literature. It is important that students learn how psychologists go about getting answers to questions. We believe that it is more beneficial, and more exciting, to view a topic as though it were a "whodunit." Given a certain problem or question, how does the psychologist begin to look for the culprit (in this case, the factor or factors that influence a certain event or behavior)? As in well-written mysteries, there are a profusion of clues, conflicting testimony, and a number of suspects. It is not easy to absorb, sift, and integrate all of the material in a series of studies, and, unfortunately, psychological studies are seldom resolved as easily as mysteries are solved.

These reports require a different study technique than does a novel, a chapter of a history text, or a chapter in an introductory psychology text. Based on our own teaching experience, we predict that many of you will ignore this advice, and you will continue to use the same study techniques that have given you your good grades so far. Again on the basis of our experience, we predict that many of you who don't adapt to this relatively new situation will shortly find yourselves in difficulty.

In an attempt to forestall this, we have included a set of study questions for each section. They are placed after the introduction to each set of readings, but before the articles. The introduction serves as an overview of the topic: it gives you a cognitive map of where you're going, and by what route. The study questions serve to indicate other points of interest, to sensitize you to certain aspects. We think that you should read the questions before you read the articles so that you can work out the answers as you read. Many of you will find it imperative, at least at first, to write out the answers and then go back to verify them. They are not intended as busy work, but as real aids to learning.

One final suggestion. Even professionals find it difficult to assimilate a complex article or set of articles without conscious "studying" and note-taking. We have found it useful to try to summarize each article in the form of four questions:

1. What question was the investigator trying to answer? Often, of course, there is more than one question. It is useful to have some understanding of the origin of the question, too. That is, why did the problem arise?
2. What procedure did the investigator use to get an answer?
3. What did he find?
4. How does this study relate to other work in the same area? In the case of the articles in this book, the selections within a section have been chosen precisely because they are related. Unless you can see this interrelationship you have only accrued isolated, independent information. And, as we have pointed out before, this is insufficient to understand the full implication of the studies.

PART TWO

Comparative Learning

Set Formation

Students often ask why psychologists spend so much time studying animals; in his introductory textbook, Donald Hebb[1] has provided a concise, pertinent answer. Psychologists study animals for three reasons: (1) animals are interesting in their own right and are, by themselves, the legitimate object of scientific investigation; (2) it is possible to experiment with animals using variables not as completely available when experimenting with humans, such as genetic control, environmental control, brain lesions, etc.; and (3) studies of animals provide a comparison for studies of man. This third, or comparative, function is the one that is utilized as the organizing principle for this section of the book.

Psychologists are not all of one mind as to how their efforts are to be directed. Some are clinical psychologists, others industrial, still others experimental. Even within the ranks of the experimentalists, there are different focuses of interest—some study humans, others study animals. And within the groups that engage in animal experimentation, additional breakdowns are possible.

Harlow, in the first paper in this section, points to a distinction between two views of learning. One, the so-called "S-R" or "connectionistic" position, emphasizes the learning of specific response acts to specific stimuli, an extreme form of which suggests that an organism is merely a living bundle of conditioned responses.

The other extreme position holds that learning is mainly a process of achieving insight. That is, the organism responds not to just one and then to another specific stimulus, but rather to some organization of these, and, when this organization is adequate, the person sees the proper relationship among them and responds appropriately.

Harlow's article represents a frontal attack on the first of these positions. The traditional procedure had been (and frequently still is) to con-

[1] Donald O. Hebb, A Textbook of Psychology (Philadelphia: W. B. Saunders Company, 1958).

front the subject with a task to learn and measure the learning of that task (up to some criterion such as a given frequency of correct responses) over a series of trials, disregarding entirely, or in large part, the history of the organism. Harlow, however, was primarily concerned with the differences in behavior across a series of tasks rather than with just focusing on the learning within any one task. If an organism learned the fiftieth task more easily than any one of the first five, that would be evidence that the subject had not only learned the specific task, but that in learning he had learned how to learn. Harlow documents this in several figures in his article. While the data are conventional in that they show the increase in percent of correct responses on the ordinate (vertical axis) as a function of successive trials on the abscissa (horizontal axis), they are unconventional in that they show this curve for successive series of tasks. Thus, in Figure 2, there are eight separate curves showing one learning curve for the first eight problems, another for the next eight problems, and, in the last curve, performance on problems 257–312. This figure demonstrates that the subjects not only learned each set of problems; it became increasingly easier for them to learn one task as they learned others.

Having demonstrated the existence of this "learning set," Harlow asks how general it is. Does it operate in children as well? (He shows that it does.) Does it operate in complex as well as in simple tasks? To test this, he went beyond the simple discrimination problem (in which the subject merely learns which of several objects is the "correct" one) to a reversal problem, in which the rules are changed in mid-game so that the formerly correct response has become wrong, and the subject must learn which one is now correct. Again, he demonstrated that learning sets also operate here for both monkeys and children.

This aspect led, within the next decade, to an intriguing series of investigations that, unfortunately, cannot be included here. A significant paper by Kendler and Kendler[2] revives the argument for S-R learning by including a process of "mediation." They document this by differences in rats, children, and adults in learning to solve various kinds of reversal discrimination problems. Harlow demonstrated an effect and used it in support of a particular learning theory; the Kendlers augment this effect and show that it can be interpreted as support for an S-R theory as well.

Harlow also speculates that most of our behavior reflects learning sets, suggesting that developmental studies could demonstrate their importance in all of our adaptive behavior. Certainly formal education becomes more meaningful in light of his study. Our society would find it hard to justify four or more years of college on the basis of specific content learning. As you will see in a later section ("Short-Term Memory"), and as you already know, an inordinately large amount of the specific facts you learn are promptly forgotten. Corporations that spend large amounts of money recruiting college graduates are too sophisticated to believe that these students will bring to their positions the thousands of details on which they've been tested in the thirty or forty courses they've taken. Instead, they're depending on the fact that the college education has produced some learning sets—that

[2] H. H. Kendler and T. S. Kendler, "Vertical and Horizontal Processes in Problem Solving," *Psychological Review*, 1962, 69, 1–16.

the college graduate will have learned how to learn and how to solve problems.

It is difficult to overemphasize the importance of Harlow's contribution in this area. Shortly after the publication of his paper, investigators were reporting learning set results for many additional species. The papers in this section are arranged not in the chronological order of their publication, but in a rough phylogenetic scale, ranging upward from the rat, cat, horse and raccoon, and marmoset to preschool children and adults.

We call this a "rough" phylogenetic ordering because cross-species comparisons are difficult to make. For one thing, geneticists have demonstrated amply that intraspecies differences are significant enough to warrant real caution.

In addition to intraspecies differences, there are other difficulties in assessing cross-species differences in "intelligence" or problem solving. Any such measure depends not only upon "intelligence," but upon the *kinds* of responses an organism can make. Porpoises, rats, horses, and primates do not have the same behavioral responses available to them. A task that is easy for one may be virtually impossible for another, not because of the mental ability required, but because the eye, ear, paw (or hand or fin) does not respond in the same way.

Another complication is due to the fact that tasks that apparently call for similar abilities turn out not to. For example, one study[3] compared "bright" and "dull" rats. A large number of rats were run in a maze. Those who made few errors were selected as the "bright" group, and those who made the greatest number of mistakes were categorized as the "dull" group. Rats were mated within their own groups, and their progeny were tested, categorized, selectively mated, and so on, through many generations. The resulting selected groups were significantly different from each other in their ability to learn the maze, which suggested that maze-brightness was a genetic characteristic. However, when these two extremely different groups were tested on other (and apparently similar) problems, the groups were not significantly unlike each other.[4] Thus, what appear to be comparable tasks for different groups (either strains or species) may really be tapping different abilities, so that conclusions about group differences may be confounded with task differences.

With these general precautions in mind, we present a series of studies, all of which deal with learning sets, but with a variety of subjects. Koronakas and Arnold attempted to extend learning set data from Harlow's monkeys and children "down" to the rat. Following Harlow's procedure, they trained the twenty rats on discrimination problems in which a door bearing a certain symbol was "correct," allowing the rat to proceed ultimately to a chamber where he found food. Their measure was the progress the rat showed in learning during successive problems in which the symbol was changed but the task was comparable, and which required the subject to learn the one symbol that was different from the other four—hence the name "oddity problem."

[3] R. C. Tryon, "Genetic Differences in Maze-Learning Ability in Rats," *National Society for the Study of Education Thirty-ninth Yearbook.* (Bloomington, Illinois: Public School Publishing Company, 1940), Part I, 111–119.

[4] L. V. Searle, "The Organization of Hereditary Maze-Brightness and Maze-Dullness," *Genetic Psychological Monographs,* 1949, 39, 279–325.

Warren and Baron used cats as their subjects in investigating the formation of learning sets. They tested four cats on tasks requiring them to dislodge the "correct" one of two wooden figures to get a food reward (there was no food under the "wrong" one, obviously). This was the object discrimination (OD) task. A second group of cats was trained on sign differentiated position (SDP) problems, which required the subjects to distinguish between colors and then select the correct position (left or right) depending upon the color. A third group was trained on both tasks to see whether the learning set generalized to another kind of problem.

The Warren and Warren paper illustrates a point about sample size as well as about learning set. In a study of rats (or of college sophomores) we expect that an experimenter will use large samples so as to minimize the possibility of chance errors. If, however, the investigator is studying the elephant or the black rhinoceros we must be satisfied with results from fewer cases. And so it is that we accept a report based upon one raccoon and two horses.

The Warrens also point to another advantage of learning set studies. While virtually any subject is able to learn some simple task if given enough trials, fish and invertebrates were not able to develop the learning set. The mammals tested (rats, cats, raccoon, horses, and humans) did so, however, even though this ability is not correlated (within mammals) with phylogenetic position.

In addition to providing more information on this ordering of learning ability within mammals, the Miles and Meyer paper provides an interesting sidelight. Meyer, writing in 1955, saw no evidence from his work with a raccoon that this species developed learning sets; but the Warrens' paper, which appears earlier in this series although written in 1962, does find support for this ability in the raccoon. This illustrates again the dangers in generalizing to a species from one animal or even from one subspecies, and of the necessity of considering both the subjects and procedures in comparing studies.

Miles and Meyer agree with the Warrens' conclusion that these complex tasks provide a better measure of phylogenetic groups than do simpler learning tasks. They point out that people sometimes separate the ordering of species at the primate level, regarding monkeys and apes differently from the other mammals. Since marmosets have characteristics of both primates and of lower mammals, using them as subjects helps restore the perspective of continuity.

Small children occupy a somewhat higher position in this continuum. Although Harlow's paper presented some comparisons of children and monkeys on simple discrimination tasks, Shepard provided her subjects with a much more difficult task. (We have already seen that the difficulty of the tasks in learning sets provides a basis for species comparisons.) Although her subjects did show improvement after the first set of problems, this improvement leveled off and even dropped instead of continuing toward the ceiling of near-perfect performance. Shepard must account for this as well as for the relatively fast learning of her subjects compared with those reported in the Harlow paper.

Shepard refers to the last paper in this section, the work of Adams on complex learning in adults. Adams raises an interesting problem about the most effective method of inducing the learning set. He compares two groups, one of which is trained in the conventional way (that is, on a number of different tasks), the other on repeated presentations of the same problems. The test is how well they learn a new task. Under his conditions (very complex problems to be solved very quickly) the latter group performs better.

Placing the section dealing with learning sets as the first block of readings was not determined by the flip of a coin; this is its logical place. The studies included demonstrate that humans become progressively more efficient as they work on a series of similar tasks. By analogy and extrapolation we can make the reasonable estimate that more complicated human learning tasks also benefit from learning set formation. Reading technical articles is a skill, but one that can be learned, and, we believe, one that will benefit from a learning set. The more articles you read, the easier they will become. You can get some idea of how and why the reading proceeds more smoothly by reading those in this section first.

STUDY QUESTIONS

1. How is the learning set defined by Harlow different from a practice effect?
2. What are the differences between the problem learning, the discrimination learning, and the discrimination reversal learning used by Harlow?
3. How does Harlow relate his findings to theories of "increments" and "connectionist" learning? to theories of "insight" and "hypothesis" learning?
4. Compare the learning sets formed by the rats in the Koronakos and Arnold study with those formed by Harlow's monkeys; are there differences in the ability of individual animals to form such sets? individual species?
5. Of what importance is the finding by Warren and Baron that a learning set for one type of problem transfers to a second kind? How do they relate this to training for difficult types of problems?
6. What considerations do Warren and Warren suggest about accepting the ability to form learning sets as a general measure of intelligence?
7. To what general factor do Miles and Meyer ascribe the difference in ability to form learning sets by marmosets as contrasted with macaques?
8. Consider two aspects of Shepard's study: Some children could not solve the first problem at all; the performance drop between the second and the third problem was attributed to boredom. Do these imply any limitations on the explicit use of a learning set as a teaching technique with children?
9. In Adams' study, what were the advantages of single problem set training? The advantage of multiple problem training?

The Formation of Learning Sets [1,2]

Harry F. Harlow

University of Wisconsin

In most psychological ivory towers there will be found an animal laboratory. The scientists who live there think of themselves as theoretical psychologists, since they obviously have no other rationalization to explain their extravagantly paid and idyllic sinecures. These theoretical psychologists have one great advantage over those psychological citizens who study men and women. The theoreticians can subject their sub-human animals, be they rats, dogs, or monkeys, to more rigorous controls than can ordinarily be exerted over human beings. The obligation of the theoretical psychologist is to discover general laws of behavior applicable to mice, monkeys, and men. In this obligation the theoretical psychologist has often failed. His deductions frequently have had no generality beyond the species which he has studied, and his laws have been so limited that attempts to apply them to man have resulted in confusion rather than clarification.

One limitation of many experiments on subhuman animals is the brief period of time the subjects have been studied. In the typical problem, 48 rats are arranged in groups to test the effect of three different intensities of stimulation operating in conjunction with two different motivational conditions upon the formation of *an isolated* conditioned response. A brilliant Blitzkrieg research is effected—the controls are perfect, the results are important, and the rats are dead.

If this *do and die* technique were applied widely in investigations with human subjects, the results would be appalling. But of equal concern to the psychologist should be the fact that the derived general laws would be extremely limited in their application. There are experiments in which the use of naive subjects is justified, but the psychological compulsion to follow this design indicates that frequently the naive animals are to be found on both sides of the one-way vision screen.

The variety of learning situations that play an important rôle in determining our basic personality characteristics and in changing some of us into thinking animals are repeated many times in similar form. The behavior of the human being is not to be understood in terms of the results of single

Reprinted from *Psychological Review*, 1949, 56, 51–65.

[1] This paper was presented as the presidential address of the Midwestern Psychological Association meetings in St. Paul, May 7, 1948.

[2] The researches described in this paper were supported in part by grants from the Special Research Fund of the University of Wisconsin for 1944–48.

learning situations but rather in terms of the changes which are affected through multiple, though comparable, learning problems. Our emotional, personal, and intellectual characteristics are not the mere algebraic summation of a near infinity of stimulus-response bonds. The learning of primary importance to the primates, at least, is the formation of learning sets; it is the *learning how to learn efficiently* in the situations the animal frequently encounters. This learning to learn transforms the organism from a creature that adapts to a changing environment by trial and error to one that adapts by seeming hypothesis and insight.

The rat psychologists have largely ignored this fundamental aspect of learning and, as a result, this theoretical domain remains a *terra incognita*. If learning sets are the mechanisms which, in part, transform the organism from a conditioned response robot to a reasonably rational creature, it may be thought that the mechanisms are too intangible for proper quantification. Any such presupposition is false. It is the purpose of this paper to demonstrate the extremely orderly and quantifiable nature of the development of certain learning sets and, more broadly, to indicate the importance of learning sets to the development of intellectual organization and personality structure.

The apparatus used throughout the studies subsequently referred to is illustrated in Fig. 1. The monkey responds by displacing one of two stimulus-

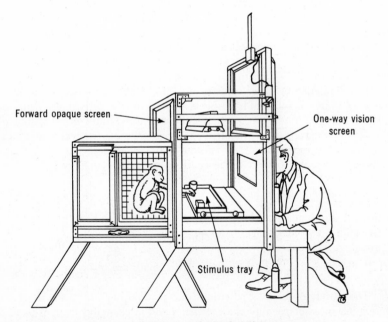

Forward opaque screen

One-way vision screen

Stimulus tray

FIG. 1. Wisconsin general test apparatus.

objects covering the food-wells in the tray before him. An opaque screen is interposed between the monkey and the stimulus situation between trials and a one-way vision screen separates monkey and man during trials.

The first problem chosen for the investigation of learning sets was the object-quality discrimination learning problem. The monkey was required to choose the rewarded one of two objects differing in multiple characteristics and shifting in the left-right positions in a predetermined balanced order. A series of 344 such problems using 344 different pairs of stimuli was run on a group of eight monkeys. Each of the first 32 problems was run for 50 trials; the next 200 problems for six trials; and the last 112 problems for an average of nine trials.

In Fig. 2 are presented learning curves which show the per cent of

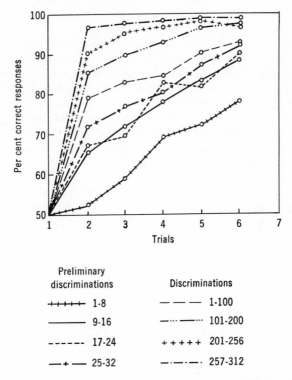

FIG. 2.   Discrimination learning curves on successive blocks of problems.

correct responses on the first six trials of these discriminations. The data for the first 32 discriminations are grouped for blocks of eight problems, and the remaining discriminations are arranged in blocks of 100, 100, 56, and 56 problems. The data indicate that the subjects progressively improve in their ability to learn object-quality discrimination problems. The monkeys *learn how to learn* individual problems with a minimum of errors. It is this *learning how to learn a kind of problem* that we designate by the term *learning set*.

The very form of the learning curve changes as learning sets become more efficient. The form of the learning curve for the first eight discrimination problems appears S-shaped: it could be described as a curve of 'trial-and-error' learning. The curve for the last 56 problems approaches linearity after Trial 2. Curves of similar form have been described as indicators of 'insightful' learning.

We wish to emphasize that this *learning to learn,* this *transfer from problem to problem* which we call the formation of a learning set, is a highly *predictable, orderly* process which can be demonstrated as long as controls are maintained over the subjects' experience and the difficulty of the problems. Our subjects, when they started these researches, had no previous laboratory learning experience. Their entire discrimination learning set history was obtained in this study. The stimulus pairs employed had been arranged and their serial order determined from tables of random numbers. Like nonsense syllables, the stimulus pairs were equated for difficulty. It is unlikely that any group of problems differed significantly in intrinsic difficulty from any other group.

In a conventional learning curve we plot change of performance over a series of *trials;* in a learning set curve we plot change in performance over a series of *problems.* It is important to remember that *we measure learning set in terms of problems* just as *we measure habit in terms of trials.*

Figure 3 presents a discrimination learning set curve showing progres-

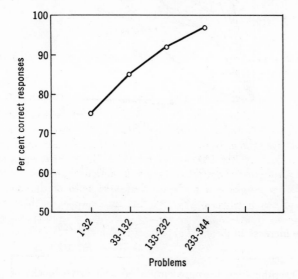

FIG. 3.   Discrimination learning set curve based on Trial 2–6 responses.

sive increase in the per cent of correct responses on Trials 2–6 on successive blocks of problems. This curve appears to be negatively accelerated or possibly linear.

Discrimination learning set curves obtained on four additional naive normal monkeys and eight naive monkeys with extensive unilateral cortical lesions, are shown in Fig. 4. Brain-injured as well as normal monkeys are seen to form effective discrimination learning sets, although the partial hemidecorticate monkeys are less efficient than the normal subjects. Improvement for both groups is progressive and the fluctuations that occur may be attributed to the small number of subjects and the relatively small number of problems, 14, included in each of the problem blocks presented on the abscissa.

Through the courtesy of Dr. Margaret Kuenne we have discrimination learning set data on another primate species. These animals were also run

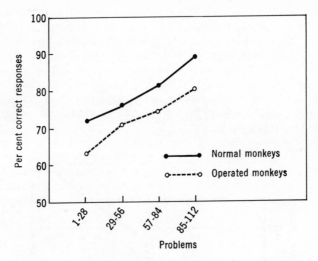

FIG. 4. Discrimination learning set curves based on Trial 2–6 responses: normal and operated monkeys.

on a series of six-trial discrimination problems but under slightly different conditions. Macaroni beads and toys were substituted for food rewards, and the subjects were tested sans iron-barred cages. The data for these 17 children, whose ages range from two to five years and whose intelligence quotients range from 109 to 151, are presented in Fig. 5. Learning set curves are plotted for groups of children attaining a predetermined learning criterion within differing numbers of problem blocks. In spite of the small number of cases and the behavioral vagaries that are known to characterize this primate species, the learning set curves are orderly and lawful and show progressive increase in per cent of correct responses.

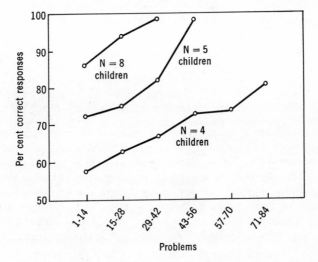

FIG. 5. Discrimination learning set curves based on Trial 2–6 responses: children.

Learning set curves, like learning curves, can be plotted in terms of correct responses or errors, in terms of responses on any trial or total trials. A measure which we have frequently used is per cent of correct Trial 2 responses—the behavioral measure of the amount learned on Trial 1.

Figure 6 shows learning set curves measured in terms of the per cent correct Trial 2 responses for the 344-problem series. The data from the first 32 preliminary discriminations and the 312 subsequent discriminations have been plotted separately. As one might expect, these learning set curves are similar to those that have been previously presented. What the curves show

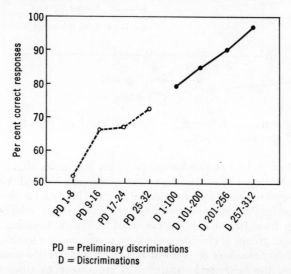

PD = Preliminary discriminations
D = Discriminations

FIG. 6.   Discrimination learning set curve based on Trial 2 responses.

with especial clarity is the almost unbelievable change which has taken place in the *effectiveness of the first training trial*. In the initial eight discriminations, this single paired stimulus presentation brings the Trial 2 performance of the monkeys to a level less than three per cent above chance; in the last 56 discriminations, this first training trial brings the performance of the monkeys to a level *less than three per cent* short of perfection. Before the formation of a discrimination learning set, a single training trial produces negligible gain; after the formation of a discrimination learning set, *a single training trial constitutes problem solution*. These data clearly show that *animals can gradually learn insight*.

In the final phase of our discrimination series with monkeys there were subjects that solved from 20 to 30 consecutive problems with no errors whatsoever following the first blind trial—and many of the children, after the first day or two of training, did as well or better.

These data indicate the function of learning set in converting a problem which is initially difficult for a subject into a problem which is so simple as to be immediately solvable. The learning set is the mechanism that changes the problem from an intellectual tribulation into an intellectual triviality and leaves the organism free to attack problems of another hierarchy of difficulty.

For the analysis of learning sets in monkeys on a problem that is ostensibly at a more complex level than the discrimination problem, we chose the discrimination reversal problem. The procedure was to run the monkeys on a discrimination problem for 7, 9, or 11 trials and then to reverse the reward value of the stimuli for eight trials; that is to say, the stimulus previously correct was made incorrect and the stimulus previously incorrect became correct.

The eight monkeys previously trained on discrimination learning were tested on a series of 112 discrimination reversal problems. Discrimination reversal learning curves for successive blocks of 28 problems are shown in Fig. 7. The measure used is per cent of correct responses on Reversal Trials

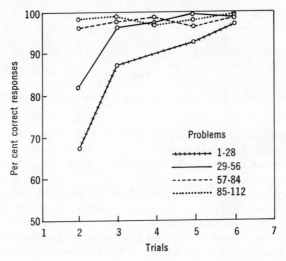

FIG. 7. Discrimination reversal learning curves on successive blocks of problems.

2 to 6. Figure 8 presents data on the formation of the discrimination reversal learning set in terms of the per cent of correct responses on Reversal Trial 2 for successive blocks of 14 problems. Reversal Trial 2 is the first trial following the 'informing' trial, i.e., the initial trial reversing the reward value of the stimuli. Reversal Trial 2 is the measure of the effectiveness with which the single informing trial leads the subject to abandon a reaction pattern which has proved correct for 7 to 11 trials, and to initiate a new reaction pattern to the stimulus pair. On the last 42 discrimination reversal problems the monkeys were responding as efficiently on Reversal Trial 2 as they were on complementary Discrimination Trial 2, i.e., they were making over 97 per cent correct responses on both aspects of the problems. The eight monkeys made from 12 to 57 successive correct second trial reversal responses. Thus it becomes perfectly obvious that at the end of this problem the monkeys possessed sets both to learn and to reverse a reaction tendency, and that this behavior could be consistently and immediately elicited with hypothesis-like efficiency.

This terminal performance level is likely to focus undue attention on the one-trial learning at the expense of the earlier, less efficient performance

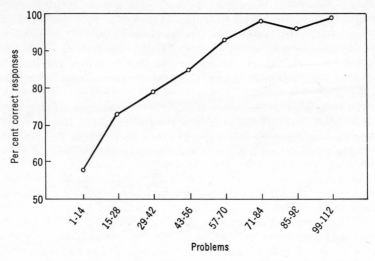

FIG. 8.   Discrimination reversal learning set curve based on Trial 2 responses.

levels. It should be kept in mind that this one-trial learning appeared only as the end result of an orderly and progressive learning process; insofar as these subjects are concerned, the insights are only to be understood in an historical perspective.

Although the discrimination reversal problems might be expected to be more difficult for the monkeys than discrimination problems, the data of Fig. 9 indicate that the discrimination reversal learning set was formed more rapidly than the previously acquired discrimination learning set. The explanation probably lies in the nature of the transfer of training from the discrimination learning to the discrimination reversal problems. A detailed analysis of the discrimination learning data indicates the operation through-

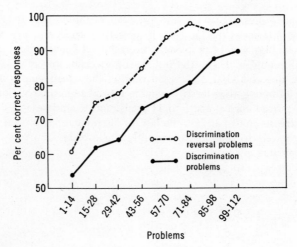

FIG. 9.   Discrimination reversal and discrimination learning set curves based on Trial 2 responses.

out the learning series of certain error-producing factors, but with each successive block of problems the frequencies of errors attributable to these factors are progressively decreased, although at different rates and to different degrees. The process might be conceived of as a learning of response tendencies that counteract the error-producing factors. A description of the reduction of the error-producing factors is beyond the scope of this paper, even though we are of the opinion that this type of analysis is basic to an adequate theory of discrimination learning.

Suffice it to say that there is reason to believe that there is a large degree of transfer from the discrimination series to the reversal series, of the learned response tendencies counteracting the operation of two of the three primary error-producing factors thus far identified.

The combined discrimination and discrimination reversal data show clearly how the learning set delivers the animal from Thorndikian bondage. By the time the monkey has run 232 discriminations and followed these by 112 discriminations and reversals, he does not possess 344 or 456 specific habits, bonds, connections or associations. We doubt if our monkeys at this time could respond with much more than chance efficiency on the first trial of any series of the previously learned problems. But the monkey does have a generalized ability to learn *any* discrimination problem or *any* discrimination reversal problem with the greatest of ease. Training on several hundred specific problems has not turned the monkey into an automaton exhibiting forced, stereotyped, reflex responses to specific stimuli. These several hundred habits have, instead, made the monkey an adjustable creature with an *increased capacity* to adapt to the ever-changing demands of a psychology laboratory environment.

We believe that other learning sets acquired in and appropriate to the monkey's natural environment would enable him to adapt better to the changing conditions there. We are certain, moreover, that learning sets acquired by man in and appropriate to his environment have accounted for his ability to adapt and survive.

Before leaving the problem of discrimination reversal learning we submit one additional set of data that we feel merits attention. Nine of the children previously referred to were also subjected to a series of discrimination reversal problems. The outcome is partially indicated in Fig. 10 which shows the per cent of correct Reversal Trial 2 responses made on successive blocks of 14 problems. It can be seen that these three- to five-year-old children clearly bested the monkeys in performance on this series of problems. Trial 2 responses approach perfection in the second block of 14 discrimination reversal problems. Actually, over half of the total Trial 2 errors were made by one child.

These discrimination reversal data on the children are the perfect illustration of set formation and transfer producing adaptable abilities rather than specific bonds. Without benefit of the monkey's discrimination reversal set learning curves we might be tempted to assume that the children's data indicate a gulf between human and subhuman learning. But the *extremely rapid* learning on the part of the children is not unlike the *rapid* learning on the part of the monkeys, and analysis of the error-producing factors shows that the same basic mechanisms are operating in both species.

Following the discrimination reversal problem the eight monkeys were

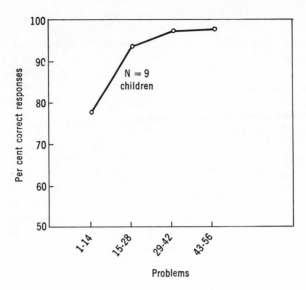

FIG. 10. Discrimination reversal learning set curve based on Trial 2 responses: children.

presented a new series of 56 problems designed to elicit alternation of unequivocally antagonistic response patterns. The first 7, 9, or 11 trials of each problem were simple object-quality discrimination trials. These were followed immediately by ten right-position discrimination trials with the same stimuli continuing to shift in the right-left positions in predetermined orders. In the first 7 to 11 trials, a particular object was correct regardless of its position. In the subsequent 10 trials, a particular position—the experimenter's right position—was correct, regardless of the object placed there. Thus to solve the problem the animal had to respond to object-quality cues and disregard position cues in the first 7 to 11 trials and, following the failure of reward of the previously rewarded object, he had to disregard object-quality cues and respond to position cues.

The learning data on these two antagonistic tasks are presented in Fig. 11. It is to be noted that the object-quality curve, which is based on Trials 1 to 7, begins at a very high level of accuracy, whereas the position curve, plotted for Trials 1 to 10, begins at a level little above chance. This no doubt reflects the operation of the previously well-established object-quality discrimination learning set. As the series continues, the object-quality curve shows a drop until the last block of problems, while the position curve rises progressively. In the evaluation of these data, it should be noted that chance performance is 50 per cent correct responses for the object-quality discriminations and 45 per cent for the position discriminations, since each sequence of 10 position trials includes an error "informing" trial. It would appear that the learning of the right-position discriminations interferes with the learning of the object-quality discriminations to some extent. In spite of this decrement in object-quality discrimination performance for a time, the subjects were functioning at levels far beyond chance on the antagonistic parts of the problems during the last half of the series. We believe that this

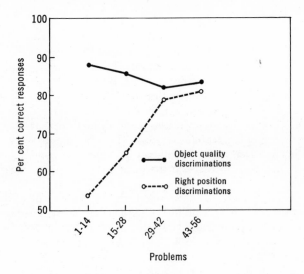

FIG. 11.   Learning set curves for problem requiring shift from object-quality discrimination to right-position discrimination.

behavior reflects the formation of a right-position learning set which operates at a high degree of independence of the previously established object-quality discrimination learning set.

The precision of the independent operation of these learning sets throughout the last 14 problems is indicated in Fig. 12. Since the right-position part of the problem was almost invariably initiated by an error trial, these data are limited to those problems on which the first trial object-quality discrimination response was incorrect. The per cent of correct Trial 7 responses to the 'A' object, the correct stimulus for the object-quality discriminations, is 98. The initiating error trial which occurs when the

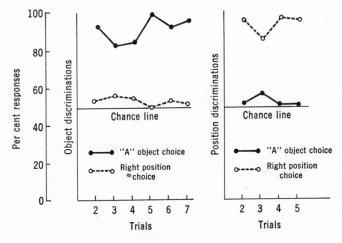

FIG. 12.   Object and position choices following initial errors on both phases of object-position shift series, based on problems 42–56.

problem shifts without warning to a right-position problem, drops this per cent response to the 'A' object to 52—a level barely above chance. The per cent of Trial 7 responses to the right position during the object-quality discriminations is 52. The single error trial initiating the shift of the problem to a right-position discrimination is followed by 97 per cent right-position responses on the next trial. In other words, *it is as though* the outcome of a single *push of an object* is adequate to switch off the 'A'-object choice reaction tendency and to switch on the right-position choice reaction tendency.

The cue afforded by a single trial produces at this point almost complete discontinuity of the learning process. The only question now left unsettled in the controversy over hypotheses in subhuman animals is whether or not to use this term to describe the behavior of a species incapable of verbalization.

Again, it should be remembered that both the object-quality discrimination learning set and the right-position discrimination learning set developed in a gradual and orderly manner. Only after the learning sets are formed do these phenomena of discontinuity in learned behavior appear.

Further evidence for the integrity of learning sets is presented in an additional experiment. Six monkeys with object-quality discrimination learning experience, but without training on reversal problems or position discriminations, were given seven blocks of 14 problems each, starting with a block of 25-trial object-quality discriminations, followed by a block of 14 25-trial positional discriminations composed of right-position and left-position problems presented alternately. The remaining five blocks of problems continued the alternate presentation of 14 object-quality discrimination problems and 14 right-left positional discrimination problems. Figure 13 presents curves showing the per cent of correct responses on total trials on these alternate blocks of antagonistic discriminations. The complex positional dis-

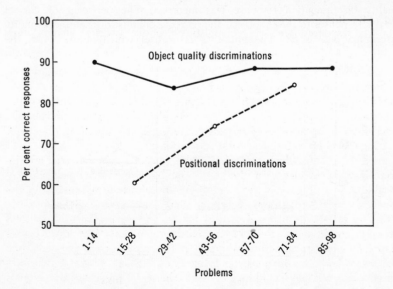

Fig. 13. Learning set curves for problem series with alternating object-quality and positional discriminations, based on total trial responses.

crimination learning set curve shows progressive improvement throughout the series, whereas the object-quality discrimination curve begins at a high level of accuracy, shows decrement on the second block, and subsequently recovers. By the end of the experiment the two basically antagonistic learning sets had 'learned' to live together with a minimum of conflict. These data are the more striking if it is recalled that between each two blocks of object-quality discriminations there were 350 trials in which no object was differentially rewarded, and between each two blocks of 14 positional discriminations there were 350 trials in which no position was differentially rewarded.

In Fig. 14 we present additional total-trial data on the formation of

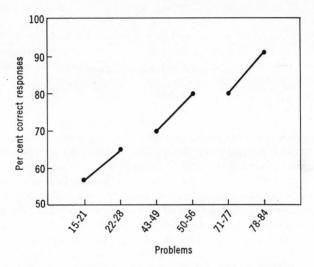

FIG. 14. Right-left positional discrimination learning set curve based on total trial responses. (Data on antagonistic object-quality discrimination problems omitted.)

the positional learning set. These data show the change in performance on the first and last seven positional discriminations in each of the three separate blocks of positional discriminations. The interposed object-quality discrimination problems clearly produced interference, but they did not prevent the orderly development of the positional learning sets, nor the final attainment of a high level of performance on these problems.

We have data which suggest that the educated man can face arteriosclerosis with confidence, if the results on brain-injured animals are applicable to men. Figure 15 shows discrimination learning set curves for the previously described groups of four normal monkeys and eight monkeys with very extensive unilateral cortical injury. The upper curves show total errors on an initial series of 112 six-trial discriminations. The lower curves show total errors on an additional group of 56 discriminations presented one year later. In both situations the full-brained monkeys make significantly better scores, but one should note that the educated hemidecorticate animals are superior to the uneducated unoperated monkeys. Such data suggest that half a brain is better than one if you compare the individuals having appropriate learning sets with the individuals lacking them.

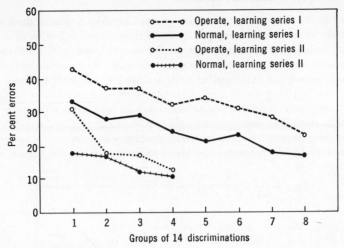

FIG. 15. Discrimination learning set curves based on total error responses: normal and operated monkeys.

More seriously, these data may indicate why educated people show less apparent deterioration with advancing age than uneducated individuals, and the data lend support to the clinical observation that our fields of greatest proficiency are the last to suffer gross deterioration.

Although our objective data are limited to the formation of learning sets which operate to give efficient performance on intellectual problems, we have observational data of a qualitative nature on social-emotional changes in our animals. When the monkeys come to us they are wild and intractable but within a few years they have acquired, from the experimenter's point of view, good personalities. Actually we believe that one of the very important factors in the development of the good personalities of our monkeys is the formation of social-emotional learning sets organized in a manner comparable with the intellectual learning sets we have previously described. Each contact the monkey has with a human being represents a single specific learning trial. Each person represents a separate problem. Learning to react favorably to one person is followed by learning favorable reactions more rapidly to the next person to whom the monkey is socially introduced. Experience with additional individuals enables the monkey to learn further how to behave with human beings, and eventually the monkey's favorable reactions to new people are acquired so rapidly as to appear almost instantaneous.

The formation of social-emotional learning sets is not to be confused with mere stimulus generalization, a construct applied in this field with undue freedom. Actually a learning set once formed determines in large part the nature and direction of stimulus generalization. In the classic study in which Watson conditioned fear in Albert, the child developed a fear of the rat and generalized this fear, but failed to develop or generalize fear to Watson, even though Watson must have been the more conspicuous stimulus. Apparently Albert had already formed an affectional social-emotional learning set to people, which inhibited both learning and simple Pavlovian generalization.

Our observations on the formation of social-emotional learning sets have been entirely qualitative and informal, but there would appear to be no reason why they could not be studied experimentally.

The emphasis throughout this paper has been on the rôle of the historical or experience variable in learning behavior—the forgotten variable in current learning theory and research. Hull's Neo-behaviorists have constantly emphasized the necessity for an historical approach to learning, yet they have not exploited it fully. Their experimental manipulation of the experience variable has been largely limited to the development of isolated habits and their generalization. Their failure to find the phenomenon of discontinuity in learning may stem from their study of individual as opposed to repetitive learning situations.

The field theorists, unlike the Neo-behaviorists, have stressed insight and hypothesis in their description of learning. The impression these theorists give is that these phenomena are properties of the innate organization of the individual. If such phenomena appear independently of a gradual learning history, we have not found them in the primate order.

Psychologists working with human subjects have long believed in the phenomenon of learning sets and have even used sets as explanatory principles to account for perceptual selection and incidental learning. These psychologists have not, however, investigated the nature of these learning sets which their subjects bring to the experimental situation. The determining experiential variables of these learning sets lie buried in the subjects' pasts, but the development of such sets can be studied in the laboratory as long as the human race continues to reproduce its kind. Actually, detailed knowledge of the nature of the formation of learning sets could be of such importance to educational theory and practice as to justify prolonged and systematic investigation.

In the animal laboratory where the experiential factor can be easily controlled, we have carried out studies that outline the development and operation of specific learning sets. We believe that the construct of learning sets is of importance in the understanding of adaptive behavior. Since this is our faith, it is our hope that our limited data will be extended by those brave souls who study *real* men and *real* women.

The Formation of Learning Sets in Rats

Chris Koronakos and William J. Arnold

University of Nebraska

The ability of primates to form learning sets has been clearly demonstrated by Harlow and his associates (4). Work done with rats seems to indicate that at least some of these animals may have the ability to form similar learning sets. In an early study of the formation of a triangularity concept

Reprinted from *Journal of Comparative and Physiological Psychology*, 1957, 50, 11–14.

in rats, Fields (2) found that the rats exhibited very limited initial generalization, but that after training was given on a wide variety of triangularity problems, they showed effective positive transfer to all subsequent problems. Marx (5) obtained evidence for cumulative transfer during training with rats on a series of simple water mazes. In a recent report on the solution of oddity problems by the rat, Bitterman and Wodinsky (1) present fragmentary data for two rats which seem to indicate that these rats formed learning sets.

The present study was designed to investigate the formation of learning sets in rats and thereby provide further data for phylogenetic comparisons of the ability to form learning sets.

METHOD

SUBJECTS AND APPARATUS

The Ss used were 20 experimentally naive pied rats, 10 males and 10 females. All Ss were approximately 150 days old at the beginning of the experiment.

FIG. 1. Discrimination learning apparatus.

Figure 1 presents a photographic view of the modified Fields's serial multiple visual discrimination apparatus (3), which was used in this experiment. As can be seen, five doors opened off the discrimination chamber. These doors were suspended on a rod and were designed to swing freely in the direction of the goal as soon as the rat pushed against them. The rat was released from the starting box into the first discrimination chamber; there it was required to push through the "correct" door in order to gain entrance into the second discrimination chamber, where it was again required to select the correct door. This door led into the alley containing the food reward. The rat was allowed to enter only the correct door in each unit. All other doors were locked by the insertion of a rod behind each of the incorrect doors.

The three principal sections of the apparatus, i.e., the starting box and the two discrimination chambers, were separated by two guillotine-type doors. Entrance into each discrimination chamber was controlled by E's manually operating the sliding doors.

A preliminary training apparatus was also used. This single-alley straightaway was essentially the same in design as one alley of the discrimination box.

PROCEDURE

The general experimental procedure was divided into two parts:

Preliminary training. On days 1 through 4 the rat was placed on a 22-hr. food deprivation schedule. Water was always present in the individual home cage. During this period the rat was handled for several minutes each day.

On days 5 through 7 the rat was given preliminary training in the straightaway. Each animal was given three rewarded trials on each of the three days. After a rat completed a day's training session, it was returned to its home cage, where it was fed a wet mixture of Purina Chow for 20 min.

Preliminary training in the discrimination apparatus was begun on the eighth day. The rat was given eight training trials: the first three trials were with the doors partially open; the remaining five trials were conducted with all doors locked but the one door in each section designated as the "correct" one. The position of the correct door was varied over the five trials according to a predetermined sequence, with each of the five doors being correct only once. No stimulus cards were used during these trials.

Discrimination training. This portion of the training was begun on the ninth day. The stimuli to be discriminated were sets of black and white figures or patterns that were photographed and pasted on 3- by 5-in. cards. Figure 2 shows the eight discrimination problems and their order of presentation. Two sets of each of the eight problems were made. One set of cards was clipped to the five doors of each discrimination chamber. The one unlocked door in each unit carried the "odd" or correct stimulus figure. For half the animals (five males and five females) problem 1 was the first problem in the series and problem 8 was the last problem. For the remaining half of the animals, problem 8 was presented first and problem 1 last in the series. The order of presentation of problems 2 to 7 was the same for all animals.

Each animal was given ten trials each day. A trial was defined as the traversal of the apparatus from starting box to goal. Thus, each trial involved two discrimination choices. The position of the correct door of each discrimination chamber was varied according to a sequence balanced for position effects and subject to the following conditions: (*a*) each door carried

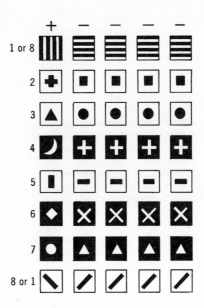

Fig. 2. Oddity problems and the order of their presentation.

the "odd" stimulus figure an equal number of times (two) within a set of ten trials per day; (b) the correct door never appeared in the same position twice in succession, and it never appeared in the same position in both units at the same time. The rat was allowed to remain in the goal area for 30 sec., after which it was returned to its home cage. Three minutes later it was given the second trial.

When an animal reached a criterion of 80 per cent correct responses, i.e., when it made 16 errorless choices out of 20, not necessarily in succession, it was given the next problem. However, if the rat was not able to attain this criterion, it was trained to a maximum of 80 trials, i.e., 160 discrimination choices, and then shifted to a new problem on the following day.

RESULTS

Of the 20 rats only 5 reached the criterion on all eight problems. The remaining 15 rats varied in both the number of problems learned and in the pattern of problems learned (that is, two rats each learning four problems may have learned a different group or selection of the eight problems).

Figure 3 shows a composite performance curve for the five animals which reached the criterion on all eight problems. It can be seen that there is a trend of accelerated learning of successive problems similar to that found in learning-set studies with primates.

Figure 4 illustrates the differences between rats in their ability to form learning sets. Three animals were selected whose performances were categorized as "good," "intermediate," and "poor" in order to demonstrate the different degree of interproblem improvement. Each of the curves shows the same general direction of interproblem improvement, but the clearest example of learning set is evident in the performance of the "good" rat.

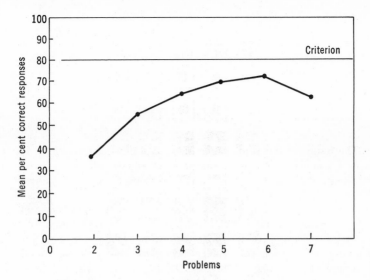

FIG. 3. Composite per cent correct response curve of the five animals which reached the 80 per cent criterion of learning on all problems. Each point represents the mean performance on the first ten trials of problems 2 through 7.

Problems 1 and 8 were analyzed separately in order to determine whether there was evidence of more rapid learning when either problem was presented first in the series as compared with the same problem presented last. Only those rats in each group were included which reached

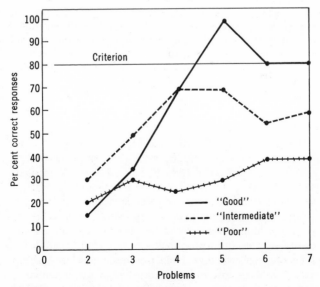

FIG. 4. Comparison of the interproblem performance curves of three animals of different levels of learning ability. Each point represents the first block of ten trials on each of the oddity problems (not including problems 1 and 8).

the learning criterion on both problems. Problem 1 required, on the average, 43.0 and 28.5 trials, respectively, to reach the criterion when presented first and last in the series. Problem 8 required means of 50.0 and 30.0 trials, respectively, to reach the learning criterion. Neither difference, however, was stable.

DISCUSSION

The results of this study seem to indicate that some rats form learning sets in a manner similar to primates. It should be recognized that there is one basic difference in methodology between the present study of rats and the several studies of primates conducted by Harlow and his associates. This experiment utilized only eight discrimination problems, with the rats having a considerable amount of training on each of the problems. In his studies Harlow gave his primates several hundred similar problems but relatively few trials per problem. His data usually demonstrated gradual improvement of performance on the initial problems, but as training on successive problems progressed, the percentage of correct responses on the second or third trial reached a very high level. The same kind of performance change on successive problems was found in some of the Ss in the present study, but equally high levels were not demonstrated, perhaps because of differences in methodology.

One qualification of the results of this investigation must be mentioned. It is possible that some problems may have been easier to learn than others. If the problems were arranged in order of decreasing difficulty, this condition could account for the empirical demonstration of apparent improvement of performance on successive problems without positing the formation of learning sets. It can be said that an effort was made to select problems of comparable difficulty, and the position of each problem in the series (except 1 and 8) was randomly determined. Several of the problems were drawn from other experiments and were known to be discriminable by rats. Although there was no independent verification that each problem was as difficult as every other problem, it does not appear reasonable to believe that the results obtained were due entirely to the variable of interproblem difficulty.

SUMMARY

A study was designed to investigate the formation of learning sets in rats. Following a period of preliminary adaptation to a modified Fields serial multiple-choice discrimination apparatus, 20 rats were trained on eight successive oddity problems. Each animal was given 20 discrimination choices per day. Training on a new problem was initiated after the S reached or exceeded a criterion of 16 errorless choices out of 20. If the criterion measure was not attained, the animal was given a maximum of 160 choices and then shifted to a new problem on the following day.

Analysis of individual and group performance curves pointed to a considerable amount of variability in the capacity of rats to form this kind of organized pattern of response. Five of the 20 rats demonstrated quite clearly the formation of learning sets. The remaining animals varied in the extent to which a learning set appeared, with some animals not reaching the criterion on any of the problems.

REFERENCES

1. BITTERMAN, M. E., & WODINSKY, J. The solution of oddity problems in the rat. *Amer. J. Psychol.*, 1953, **66**, 137–140.
2. FIELDS, P. E. Studies in concept formation. I. The development of the concept of triangularity by the white rat. *Comp. psychol. Monogr.*, 1932, **9**, 1–70.
3. FIELDS, P. E. The efficiency of the serial multiple visual discrimination apparatus and method with white rats. *J. comp. physiol. Psychol.*, 1953, **46**, 69–76.
4 HARLOW, H. F. The formation of learning sets. *Psychol. Rev.*, 1949, **56**, 51–65.
5. MARX, M. H. The effects of cumulative training upon retroactive inhibition and transfer. *Comp. psychol. Monogr.*, 1944, **18**, 1–62.

The Formation of Learning Sets by Cats [1,2]

J. M. Warren and Alan Baron

University of Oregon

There have been no systematic investigations of generalized interproblem transfer in discrimination learning by subprimate forms comparable to the extensive studies of learning sets in primates (2, 4, 5, 8, 9). The two experiments reported in this paper were designed to determine: (*a*) whether cats can form a discrimination learning set when tested under conditions in which rhesus monkeys show marked interproblem transfer, and (*b*) whether cats can concurrently form independent learning sets for solving two different kinds of discrimination problems.

METHOD

SUBJECTS

The Ss were 16 young experimentally naive house cats. Eight animals (no. 1 through 4 and 13 through 16) served in experiment 1, and 8 cats (no. 5 through 12) served in experiment 2.

Reprinted from *The Journal of Comparative and Physiological Psychology*, Vol. 49, No. 3, June, 1956.

[1] This investigation was supported (in part) by research grant M-835 from the National Institute of Mental Health, of the National Institutes of Health, Public Health Service.

[2] The authors wish to express their appreciation to L. J. Nidorf for his help in collecting the data.

APPARATUS

All the testing was conducted in the Wisconsin General Test Apparatus (4, Fig. 1).

The stimulus objects were pairs of wooden figures which varied randomly in multiple visual dimensions (e.g., form, brightness, surface area, and thickness). The series of objects was similar to, but rather more homogeneous than, the sets of objects employed by Harlow in his studies with monkeys.

PROCEDURE

The cats were housed in small rooms where they had continuous access to water and Purina Laboratory Chow. Liver and kidney were used as incentives during testing.

Experiment 1. One group of four cats was tested on a series of 340 object discrimination (OD) problems. On each trial S was required to displace one of two dissimilar (+ and −) objects presented on the retractable tray. Choice of the arbitrarily designated correct (+) object was rewarded with a small piece of meat; there was no punishment for errors. The spatial position of the correct object was varied from trial to trial according to a balanced, irregular sequence, and the noncorrection technique was used throughout.

Differing amounts of training per problem were given at various stages of the experiment. Testing on the first four problems was continued until S attained a criterion of 20 correct out of 25 consecutive responses. Problems 5 to 80 were presented for 50 trials each, and problems 81 to 140 for 25 trials each. The final 200 problems (141 to 340) were 10-trial problems. Each cat was tested 50 trials a day, usually five days a week, throughout the experiment.

A second group of four cats was trained on a series of 128 sign-differentiated position (SDP) discriminations (3). The S's task on these problems was to choose the stimulus on the left when confronted with one of two pairs of identical objects (e.g., white squares), and to displace the stimulus on the right when presented the other pair of identical objects (e.g., black triangles).

The Ss were trained to a criterion of 20 correct out of 25 consecutive trials on the first four problems. Problems 5 to 96 were presented for 50 trials each; the cats were trained to the criterion of 20 correct out of 25 responses on problems 97 to 112, and given 50 trials on problems 113 to 128.

Experiment 2. The Ss in this experiment were tested on 64 object and 64 sign-differentiated position discriminations, a total of 128 problems.

The Ss were trained to a criterion of 20 correct out of 25 consecutive responses on the first and last four problems; all the remaining problems were presented for 50 trials. As in the first experiment, the cats were given 50 noncorrection trials per day, usually five days a week.

The SDP and OD problems were alternated according to counterbalanced ABBA or BAAB order, i.e., each pair of objects was presented to half the Ss in a SDP problem, and to half the Ss in an OD problem, in order to avoid confounding the comparison of SDP and OD problem-tasks with possible differences in the discriminability of stimulus pairs.

RESULTS

EXPERIMENT 1

The course of learning-set formation by the group tested on OD problems is shown in Figures 1 and 2. In the upper panels of Figure 1 the percentages of correct responses on trials 2 to 10, 11 to 25, and 26 to 50 are

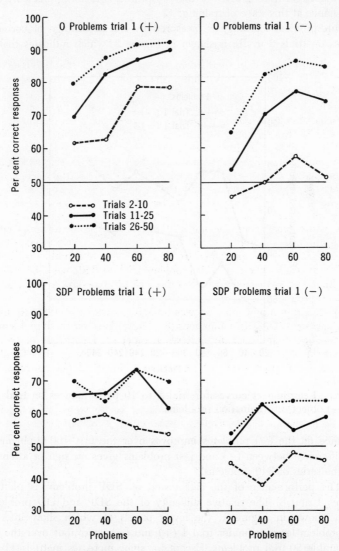

FIG. 1. Interproblem learning curves for trials 2 to 10, 11 to 25, and 26 to 50 performances of each group on trial 1 (+) and (−) problems.[3]

[3] The curve for trials 26 to 50 on the 0-problems presented in the original paper was inaccurately drawn. The correct mean values are presented here.

plotted against successive blocks of 20 problems separately for those problems on which S's response on trial 1 was rewarded (+) or nonrewarded (−).
These functions show that interproblem transfer is essentially complete after
testing on 60 problems, and that both the rate and final level of inter- and
intraproblem learning are greatly retarded when the cats are required to
respond to the initially nonpreferred object. Indeed, the percentage of correct responses on trials 2 to 10 of the trial 1 (+) problems is approximately
the same as the percentage correct on trials 26 to 50 of the (−) problems.[4]
Performance on trials 2 to 10 of the (−) problems is not appreciably better
than chance at this stage of training.

Interproblem learning, as measured by the percentage of correct responses on trials 2 to 10, is shown in Figure 2, which indicates that per-

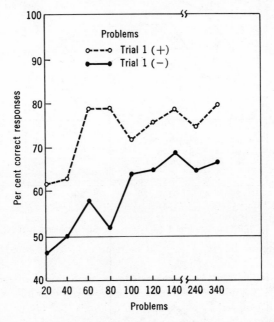

FIG. 2.   Learning-set curves for trial 2 to 10 performances on trial 1 (+)
and (−) object discrimination problems.

formance on the (−) problems improves over the first 100 problems, but
the difference between (+) and (−) problems gives no sign of attenuation
over the series of 340 problems.

The performance of the cats tested on SDP problems is plotted in
Figures 1 and 3. The relative difficulty of the SDP and OD problems is
clearly shown in Figure 1, the lower panels of which show inter- and
intraproblem learning under trial 1 (+) and (−) conditions over the set of
comparable 50-trial problems. Except for some increases in trials 11 to 25
and 26 to 50, in correct responses between the first and second problem

---

[4] This statement is untrue and was based on the inaccurate drawing published
in the original paper.

blocks of the (−) function, there is no indication of consistent gains in inter-problem learning. All the SDP curves are markedly lower than the comparable OD curves, and there is obviously less intraproblem learning.

The group's performance over the entire series of problems is presented in Figure 3, in which interproblem learning, as measured by the percentage of correct responses on trials 2 to 50 on the (+) and (−) problems, is plotted against successive blocks of 32 problems. There is no improvement on the (+) problems over the entire experiment, but the (−)

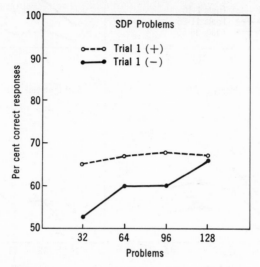

FIG. 3.   Learning-set curves for trial 2 to 50 performance on trial 1 (+) and (−) sign-differentiated position problems.

function rises from 53 to 67 per cent correct, and virtual equality with the (+) curve.

Because minimal evidence of learning set formation had been obtained by problem 96, the animals were trained to criterion on problems 97 to 112; Hayes *et al.* (2) reported that training to criterion on early problems facilitated the formation of learning sets in chimpanzee. The data from these problems yielded the best evidence of interproblem transfer: the group learned the first four problems to criterion with an average of 95 errors and 242 trials to criterion; the mean errors and trials to criterion on problems 97 to 112 were 34 and 101, respectively. The difference is significant at the .02 level of confidence (Mann-Whitney $U = 0$).

Experiment 2. Intra- and interproblem learning on (+) and (−) problems by the cats which were tested on both OD and SDP problems is shown in Figure 4, in which per cent correct responses on trials 2 to 10, 11 to 25, and 26 to 50 are plotted against successive problem blocks for the OD (+), OD (−), SDP (+), and SDP (−) problems. These functions indicate that a greater degree of interproblem learning occurs on the OD (−) and SDP (−) problems than on the comparable (+) problems, this datum suggesting that the suppression of perseverative tendencies is an important component of learning set formation in cats.

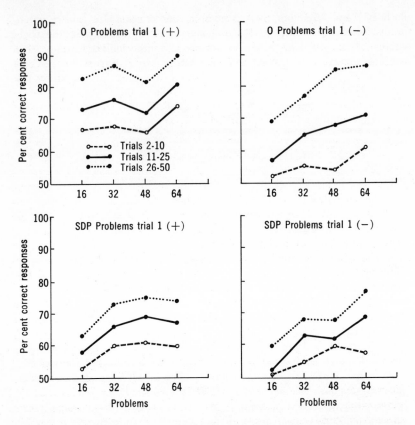

FIG. 4. Interproblem learning curves for trial 2 to 10, 11 to 25, and 26 to 50 performance on object and sign-differentiated position problems with (+) and (−) first trials.

Figure 4 also shows that performance on the OD problems (except for the first 10 trials of OD [−]) is consistently superior to performance on the comparable trials of SDP problems. Analysis of variance indicates that the difference in total errors between OD and SDP problems is significant at the 0.1 per cent level of confidence ($F = 168.5$, 1/21 df).

Inspection of Figure 4 also reveals that, at all stages of learning and on both trial 1 (+) and (−) problems, more intraproblem learning occurs on the OD than on SDP problems. For example, if one compares the OD and SDP (+) problems, it may be seen that trial 2 to 10 performance on the OD problems is superior to performance on trials 11 to 25 of the SDP problems. It should also be pointed out that the difference between the (+) and (−) functions for the SDP problems is much smaller than for the OD problems.

Direct comparisons between this group which was tested on both OD and SDP problems with the groups trained exclusively on either type must be made with caution because of the differences in procedure, but comparison of Figures 1 and 4 reveals that the group trained on only the OD problems performs at higher levels of efficiency than the group trained on both OD and SDP problems. However, the performance curves of the group tested on SDP problems exclusively are markedly lower than the curves for the group tested on both types, and only the latter group shows consistent improvement in interproblem learning over the first 60 problems.

DISCUSSION

The results of these experiments demonstrate that cats can form learning sets and can respond appropriately in terms of two independent learning sets. Although the data presented here show that the capacity for acquiring learning sets is not restricted to the order *Primates,* it is clear that the learning-set curves for cats quickly reach an asymptotic level of performance which is much lower than for monkeys.

The data also indicate one significant factor contributing to the inferior performance by cats, namely, the persistence of stimulus perseveration errors even after training on over 300 problems. It has been reported by a number of workers that both learned (9) and unlearned (5, 8) stimulus preferences are readily suppressed by monkeys at much earlier stages in learning set formation.

The performance of the cats tested exclusively on SDP problems suggests a hitherto unreported phenomenon, *latent* learning-set formation. It will be recalled that this group gave only minimal sign of interproblem learning over an extended series of 50-trial problems, but when trained to criterion on a set of 16 problems, they required only 36 per cent as many errors and 58 per cent as many trials as were made in learning the first four problems to criterion.

Comparisons within and between the two experiments yield unambiguous evidence of the greater difficulty of sign-differentiated position discriminations. Not only is there strikingly less efficient intra- and interproblem learning on these problems than on the object discriminations, but the data also indicate that training on a homogeneous series of SDP problems has detrimental effects on OD learning-set formation. The group tested on both OD and SDP problems was inferior to the group trained only on OD problems but consistently superior to the group trained only on SDP problems. Indeed, the latter group only in 128 problems attained a level of performance on SDP problems equivalent to that reached by the former after 64 problems, this finding suggesting that the alternation of easy OD and difficult SDP problems may prevent the development of unfavorable emotional or motivational states which would be more likely in those cats tested exclusively on SDP problems. This speculation is supported by the fact that one cat from the SDP group subsequently failed to learn a simple black-white discrimination in 600 trials. To considerable extent, the Ss in the SDP-only group seemed to have learned *not* to learn and to content themselves with periodic reinforcement.

The persistent difference in difficulty between OD and SDP discriminations is contradictory to results obtained by Bitterman (1), who reports that, for rats, the decline in the relative difficulty of "successive" discrimination, i.e., sign-differentiated position, problems is "so rapid in some situations that the difference in difficulty disappears entirely after a single preceding problem" (1, p. 240).

The results of experiments with primates indicate that children (6) and rhesus monkeys (7) require two to three times as many trials to solve SDP problems as to master OD problems. These findings are consonant with those obtained in the present investigation and suggest that the reported ease of SDP problem learning by rats may be a peculiar function of the perceptual organization of *Mus* or the use of the Lashley jumping stand with punishment for errors.

SUMMARY

EXPERIMENT 1

Four cats were tested on 340 object discrimination (OD) problems and four cats on 128 sign-differentiated position (SDP) discriminations. Both groups manifested significant interproblem transfer; interproblem and intraproblem learning of the SDP problems was markedly inferior to performance on the OD problems at all comparable stages of practice.

EXPERIMENT 2

Eight cats were tested on 64 OD and 64 SDP discriminations. Significant interproblem learning was observed, and performance on the OD problems was significantly superior to performance on the SDP discriminations.

It was concluded that cats show less interproblem transfer and reach an apparently asymptotic level of performance much sooner than monkeys. The final level of attainment is much lower in cats, largely because of the persistence of marked stimulus perseveration, even after very prolonged training.

REFERENCES

1. BITTERMAN, M. E., TYLER, D. W., & ELAM, C. E. Simultaneous and successive discrimination under identical stimulating conditions. *Amer. J. Psychol.*, 1955, **68**, 237–248.

2. HAYES, K. J., THOMPSON, R., & HAYES, CATHERINE. Discrimination learning set in chimpanzees. *J. comp. physiol. Psychol.*, 1953, **46**, 99–104.

3. HARLOW, H. F. Responses by rhesus monkeys to stimuli having multiple sign-values. In Q. McNemar & M. A. Merrill, *Studies in personality.* New York: McGraw-Hill, 1942.

4. HARLOW, H. F. The formation of learning sets. *Psychol Rev.*, 1949, **56**, 51–65.

5. HARLOW, H. F. Analysis of discrimination learning by monkeys, *J. exp. Psychol.*, 1950, **40**, 26–39.

6. PERKINS, M. J., BANKS, H. P., & CALVIN, A. D. The effect of delay on simultaneous and successive discrimination in children. *J. exp. Psychol.*, 1954, **48**, 416–418.
7. PRIBRAM, K. H., & MISHKIN, M. Simultaneous and successive visual discrimination by monkeys with inferotemporal lesions. *J. comp. physiol. Psychol.*, 1955, **48**, 198–202.
8. RIOPELLE, A. J., FRANCISCO, E. W., & ADES, H. W. Differential first-trial procedures and discrimination learning performance. *J. comp. physiol. Psychol.*, 1954, **47**, 293–297.
9. WARREN, J. M. Reversed discrimination as a function of the number of reinforcements during pretraining. *Amer. J. Psychol.*, 1954, **67**, 720–722.

Reversal Learning by Horse and Raccoon[1,2]

J. M. Warren and Helen B. Warren

Pennsylvania State University

A. THE PROBLEM

When rats (Dufort, Guttman and Kimble, 1954) and cats (Cronholm, Warren and Hara, 1960) are tested on serial reversals of the same discrimination habit, they show a progressive reduction in the number of errors per reversal. The purpose of the present experiment was to investigate the performance of two less frequently studied species, raccoon and horse, on similar series of discrimination reversals.

B. METHOD

1. SUBJECTS

The single raccoon studied, aged one year at the time of testing, had been hand fed during infancy and was quite tame and well adapted to the laboratory. He had previously served in an experiment on *umweg* learning in a closed field maze (Warren and Warren, 1959). During this experiment he had continuous access to water and dry dog food in his living cage and re-

Reprinted from *The Journal of Genetic Psychology*, 1962, 100, 215–220.

[1] This research was supported by Research Grants NSF-G3278 from the National Science Foundation, and M-1364 from the National Institute of Mental Health, U.S. Public Health Service.

[2] The authors are grateful for Kim Firestone's assistance in testing the horses.

ceived pork kidney, a highly preferred food, as a reward for correct responses during the test sessions.

Two horses were not laboratory subjects; to emphasize this fact we refer to them by their names, Pancho and Rag Mop. They lived in and were tested at a riding stable, and throughout the experiment were ridden during the morning by students. The horses were tested in the early afternoon, approximately seven hours after their morning feeding.

2. APPARATUS

The raccoon was tested in the Wisconsin General Test Apparatus (Harlow, 1949). A black object was always presented on the right, and a white object on the left, on a grey tray containing two food wells 12 inches apart, so that both brightness and positional cues were constant and relevant.

The horses, tested in a large paddock, were released at the entrance gate and required to choose between two boxes, 40 feet from the entrance and 20 feet from one another. The box on the right was black and the one on the left white, so that brightness and spatial cues were combined in the same fashion for the horses as for the raccoon. It was impossible for humans, and presumably horses, to tell which of the boxes, 30 inches deep, contained hay until approached within one or two feet.

3. PROCEDURE

On the first training trial neither stimulus was rewarded. S was required on subsequent trials to choose the initially non-preferred stimulus and training was continued until the criterion of 11 correct out of 12 responses, with the last eight all correct, was attained. Upon completion of the preliminary discrimination, S was required to select the previously incorrect stimulus. Thereafter, the two stimuli became alternately correct and incorrect as the criterion was satisfied. The animals were trained to criterion on one problem per day with minimal intervals between trials. The raccoon completed 20 reversals; circumstances beyond our control prevented training the individual horses on more than six and nine reversals. The non-correction method was used throughout.

C. RESULTS

The results for the raccoon are presented in Figure 1, which shows that this S made a striking improvement in performance over the series of reversal tasks. This animal never on subsequent reversals made as many errors as on the first reversal. Indeed, on only four occasions did he commit as many errors on reversal learning as in solving the original discrimination (Reversal 0). The average number of errors on Reversals 1 through 4 was 8.75, and on Reversals 17 through 20, 2.25.

Learning curves for the two horses are shown in Figure 2. Both animals learned the successive reversal problems very quickly; Pancho solved all the reversals more quickly than he mastered the original discrimination, and averaged fewer than two errors per reversal over the series of nine on which he was tested. Rag Mop made the same number of errors on the first reversal as on the original discrimination, and averaged two errors per problem over six reversals.

D. DISCUSSION

The raccoon and the horses all showed a rapid reduction in the number of errors made in learning successive reversals of a positional discrimination. Qualitatively similar results have been obtained in comparable experiments with cats (Cronholm, Warren and Hara, 1960), human imbeciles (House and Zeaman, 1959) and rats (Dufort, Guttman and Kimble, 1954). Within this series of mammals, proficiency in interreversal learning is not related to capacity for solving more complex problems. Rats and imbeciles approach the limit of one error per reversal most rapidly, cats

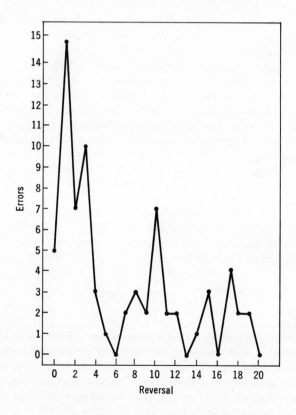

FIG. 1.   Reversal learning by a raccoon.

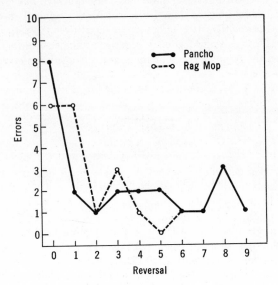

FIG. 2.   Reversal learning by two horses.

and raccoons most slowly. Yet imbeciles (House and Zeaman, 1958) do not form learning sets for non-spatial visual discriminations, and rats (Koronakos and Arnold, 1957) form such sets far less efficiently than either cats (Warren and Baron, 1956) or raccoons (Shell and Riopelle, 1957).

The serial reversal task, however, does clearly differentiate between higher vertebrates, and fish and invertebrates. Chickens (Warren, Brookshire, Ball and Reynolds, 1960), in addition to the mammals just listed, show a marked reduction in errors on consecutive habit reversals. The results obtained from several species of fish (Adkins and Fields, 1957; Bitterman, Wodinsky and Candland, 1958; Warren, 1960), crabs (Datta, Milstein and Bitterman, 1960) and sowbugs (Thompson, 1957) have been consistently negative. In fact, in some studies a progressive *deterioration* in performance has been observed (e.g., Adkins and Fields).

The findings just discussed clearly support the supposition that major stages in the evolution of the nervous system are correlated with the emergence of new capacities for solving complex problems, rather than with increases in the rate of simple learning.

E. SUMMARY

A raccoon and two horses were tested on serial reversals of a positional discrimination. A rapid decline in the number of errors made on consecutive reversals was observed in all three animals. Improvement in the rate of interreversal learning on simple discriminations does not correlate with taxonomic status or ability to solve more complex problems within the series of mammals studied. However, all mammals tested on this task "learn to learn," but fish and invertebrates do not.

REFERENCES

1. ADKINS, R. J., & FIELDS, P. E. Conditioning young steelhead trout to colored lights. *U. Wash. Sch. Fish. Tech. Rep.*, 1957, No. 33.
2. BITTERMAN, M. E., WODINSKY, J., & CANDLAND, D. K. Some comparative psychology. *Amer. J. Psychol.*, 1958, **71**, 94–110.
3. CRONHOLM, J. N., WARREN, J. M., & HARA, K. Distribution of training and reversal learning by cats. *J. Genet. Psychol.*, 1960, **96**, 105–113.
4. DATTA, L., MILSTEIN, S., & BITTERMAN, M. E. Habit-reversal in the crab. *J. Comp. Physiol. Psychol.*, 1960, **53**, 275–278.
5. DUFORT, R. H., GUTTMAN, N., & KIMBLE, G. A. One-trial discrimination reversal in the white rat. *J. Comp. Physiol. Psychol.*, 1954, **47**, 248–249.
6. HARLOW, H. F. The formation of learning sets. *Psychol Rev.*, 1949, **56**, 51–65.
7. HOUSE, B. J., & ZEAMAN, D. Reward and non-reward in the discrimination learning of imbeciles. *J. Comp. Physiol. Psychol.*, 1958, **51**, 614–618.
8. ———. Position discrimination and reversals in low-grade retardates. *J. Comp. Physiol. Psychol.*, 1959, **52**, 564–565.
9. KORONAKOS, C., & ARNOLD, W. J. The formation of learning sets in rats. *J. Comp. Physiol. Psychol.*, 1957, **50**, 11–14.
10. SHELL, W. F., & RIOPELLE, A. J. Multiple discrimination learning in raccoons. *J. Comp. Physiol. Psychol.*, 1957, **50**, 585–587.
11. THOMPSON, R. Successive reversals of a position habit in an invertebrate. *Science*, 1957, **126**, 163–164.
12. WARREN, J. M. Reversal learning by paradise fish (*Macrapodus opercularis*). *J. Comp. Physiol. Psychol.*, 1960, **53**, 376–378.
13. WARREN, J. M., & BARON, A. The formation of learning sets by cats. *J. Comp. Physiol. Psychol.*, 1956, 49, 227–231.
14. WARREN, J. M., & WARREN, H. B. Interspecies differences in learning by carnivores? *Percep. & Motor Skills*, 1959, **9**, 346.
15. WARREN, J. M., BROOKSHIRE, K. H., BALL, G. G., & REYNOLDS, D. V. Reversal learning by white leghorn chicks. *J. Comp. Physiol. Psychol.*, 1960, **53**, 371–375.

Learning Sets in Marmosets [1]

Raymond C. Miles[2] and Donald R. Meyer

The Ohio State University

The common marmoset, genus *Callithrix,* has perhaps more features to command the attention of the student of animal behavior than any other relative stranger to the laboratory. Although it is scarcely larger than a full-grown albino rat, this diminutive primate has a brain that is as large in proportion to its body size as any in the animal kingdom. Unlike its close relatives, however, the marmoset has claw-like nails, and in a manner more typical of lower mammals than of primates, gives birth to either twins or triplets. The possibilities that this species affords to studies of brain organization and of developmental factors are thus both striking and obvious.

From a comparative standpoint, the marmoset is in a phylogenetic position of more than passing interest. Standing as it does at the transition between major subdivisions of its order (1, 7), this most primitive of monkeys affords a reference point at which tests of behavioral capacity have unusual significance. This experiment has been designed to perform one such evaluation, to study the ability of marmosets to form discrimination learning sets.

Learning sets develop, as Harlow (3) first established through extensive studies with macaques, if the Ss are trained on successive discriminations between objects that differ in several stimulus dimensions. One can trace an orderly transition, by this method, from performances in which little evidence of learning is manifest after six trials, to those in which solutions are obtained by the animals within a single trial (9).

Harlow (5) has proposed that an evaluation of such phenomena will undoubtedly reveal systematic differences between groups of animals that all learn simple habits readily. The data for a test of this hypothesis are largely nonexistent at present, but several years ago the junior author had an opportunity to study learning-set formation in a single raccoon. This animal, which served in lieu of a badger as mascot of the local football team, had excellent use of its paws and a singular fondness for raisins. It was tested in the same apparatus that had been used in the initial work by Harlow, but extensive presentations of discrimination problems revealed very little indication of a trend toward interproblem improvement. Since raccoons have been traditionally held in relatively high esteem by com-

Reprinted from *Journal of Comparative and Physiological Psychology,* 1956, 49, 219–22.

[1] Supported by funds allocated by the University Advisory Committee on Research Grants.

[2] Now at the University of Wisconsin.

parative psychologists, the E concluded that this capacity is at best rudimentary in infraprimate mammals. Thus, the evidence is clearly in keeping with the contention that tests of interproblem transfer provide the most discriminative complex indices that we have for assessing behavioral evolution.

That such tests will separate, on a quantitative basis, some species within the primate order has been known from the inception of the program. Thus M. K. Harlow (cited in 3), while emphasizing similarities, found that preschool children are clearly superior to monkeys if both are studied under conditions as comparable as it is possible to make them. Whether monkeys differ as much within themselves, or at all, is the question asked by the present experiment. Unless we are willing to disregard completely the comparative anatomy, expectations are that the marmosets will be inferior to *Macaca mulatta*. Efforts have been made, despite our human tendencies to make each new study *new*, to duplicate the conditions under which the learning set phenomenon was first introduced.

METHOD

SUBJECTS

The Ss were three adult common marmosets and four adolescent rhesus monkeys. The latter were maintained and tested at the Primate Laboratory, University of Wisconsin, and the data obtained were kindly furnished by Professor Harry Harlow. The marmosets were from a colony established at The Ohio State University. All the macaques and one marmoset had not been tested prior to this experiment; two marmosets had learned three discriminations of differences in hue. These variations were not deemed important, apart from the adaptation standpoint, in view of the relatively large number of problems that one must present to marmosets before any evidence of transfer is forthcoming.

APPARATUS

The rhesus monkeys were studied in the form-board situation provided by the Wisconsin General Test Apparatus, which was used as a model for the smaller apparatus employed for the marmosets. The latter was a rectangular box 27 in. long, 13 in. wide, and 13 in. high. It was constructed of plywood, painted a uniform gray, and provided with an overhead light for interior illumination. Half the box served as a restraining cage, and this was separated from a test compartment by vertically arranged iron rods spaced 1 in. apart. An opaque screen, which could be raised or lowered through a cord and pulley arrangement, was installed between the cage and the compartment. The E watched the animals perform through a one-way-vision screen placed across the end of the compartment; this was of glass from the top of the box to a line halfway down and of cheesecloth beyond that level. Within the test compartment was a movable form-board tray, and carved into this tray were two 1-in. circular food wells spaced 8 in. apart. A supply of small, lightweight objects similar to those employed in prior experiments completed the marmoset equipment; there were 1,000 in all, and included were such things as aspirin tins, ladies' heels, and small jars.

PROCEDURE

The general procedure[s] for handling and testing rhesus monkeys have been repeatedly detailed (3, 4, 9), and were duplicated as far as possible in the work with the marmosets. The Ss were never handled by E, but were trained to enter cages for transport between their residence and the apparatus. Prior to the experiment proper, the rhesus monkeys and the naive marmoset were thoroughly adapted to their respective situations and given brief practice in displacing a neutral object that on each presentation covered one or the other food well. To make such responses, the animals reached through the bars of their restraining cages, and were reinforced by a small piece of food which they found in the underlying well. Peanuts or raisins were used in the work with macaques, while the marmosets were treated to small slivers of cooked white-of-egg or apple. Between presentations E lowered the opaque screen, retracted and arranged the tray, raised the screen in front of the monkey, and after a pause of 1 sec. returned the tray to its position in front of the bars. The same procedures were followed in setting up the problems for discrimination learning.

During the conduct of the formal tests, the marmosets were fed for 15 min. a day after each experimental session; their diet consisted of bananas, apples, oranges, and eggs, occasionally supplemented by a vitamin mixture spread on bread. Actually, the bulk of their diet was obtained in the test situation, for the daily series averaged about 120 trials. This extension beyond the session of 42 trials used in the procedure with macaques was deemed essential because of the prolonged training required to demonstrate the transfer phenomenon in the more primitive species.

The rhesus monkeys, which were being utilized as a control for still another study, encountered a series of 392 discrimination problems. In each of these problems, a pair of dissimilar stimulus objects was presented on the test tray for a total of six trials. A food reward was placed under one of these objects, and was obtained by the monkey if its choice was correct. The position of the object reinforced varied from trial to trial in counterbalanced sequences similar to those employed by Harlow (4) in his study of error factors in discrimination learning. Essentially the same conditions prevailed in tests with the marmosets, though it was soon discovered that they were often unable to move even the light objects used in their test. This was countered by assistance from E, who attached threads to the objects and withdrew them whenever they were touched by the monkey.

The rhesus monkeys learned 7 problems per day; the marmosets 14 to 20, depending upon their individual caprice. After 100 problems had been presented, however, all marmosets would work consistently for 20 problems per day. They encountered, in all, a total of 1,000 problems. The first 500 were arranged with novel test objects, and then these objects were rearranged at random for presentation in the last 500 problems.

RESULTS

The obtained data are summarized in Figure 1. The curves indicate per cent correct performances as a function of intraproblem practice. Each point is based upon the scores obtained in a given block of problems, and individual scores are combined. The first impression to be gained from these

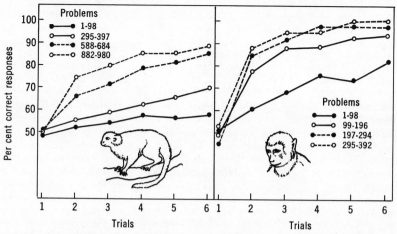

Fig. 1. Intraproblem learning curves based on selected blocks of inter-problem experience.

graphs is the formal similarity between the two sets of functions, one for macaques and the other for marmosets. Both show, for example, that rate of learning-set formation first accelerates and then decelerates. Both sets of curves can be interpreted in terms of a developing discontinuity between trials 1 and 2, though this point is one that must be judged primarily upon the basis of other evidence. Despite the similarities, however, the quantitative disparity between the two groups is enormous. Thus, the performances of marmosets with 500 problems behind them is scarcely better than that obtained from the naive rhesus monkey, and the rhesus macaques with prior experience of 98 problems are ahead of marmosets with 881.

Learning-set formation, in terms of trial 2 performance, is shown in Figure 2. One gains the impression from these graphs that marmosets approach an asymptote which is considerably below that for the rhesus mon-

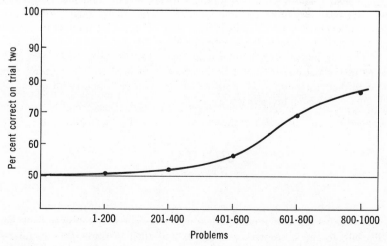

Fig. 2. Per cent correct responses for successive problem blocks in the marmoset.

keys. It would appear, in fact, that had the experiment continued, a persistent difference of about 20 per cent (which is a significant fraction of the possible range of improvement with this type of problem) would have been obtained.

With regard to statistical reliability, it seems sufficient to say that the dullest macaque was at all times better than the brightest marmoset, and that within-group differences were small compared with the difference between the species.

DISCUSSION

An outcome of this kind is in keeping with our preconceptions. The familial resemblances between our two species are revealed through the formal learning parallels; the differences between them, however, are as gross as those revealed through studies of structure. Harlow's contention, accordingly, has survived a critical test. There is every indication that the method will order different primate species in a series comparable to those that have been drawn by taxonomists. This, of course, has been attempted before, but with little success apart from that encountered in studies with delayed response tasks (6).

With regard to the classical dilemma of sensory-motor comparability, it may be said that unpublished experiments have shown that marmosets are capable of fine discriminations of brightness and have some form of color vision. Other work with South American groups (2, 8) would lead us to suspect that these animals are not trichromats, and it is not unreasonable to imply that this would be a handicap. But it is hard to maintain that the differences obtained can be assigned to such a factor alone, or even are largely a result of such a deficit. The motivational problem, similarly, while undoubtedly present, cannot be taken too seriously in view of the consistent and long test sessions employed. Thus, the major factor seems squarely to be an associative process, which makes good sense in view of the well-known trend in primate brain development.

The psychoneurologists who may have eyed the surgically convenient cortex of the marmoset should be heartened by these results, because they indicate that tests employed quite widely in ablative studies with macaques are suitable for such investigations.

SUMMARY

This experiment was designed to assess the capacity of marmosets, genus *Callithrix*, to form discrimination-learning sets. Three animals were trained according to the customary procedure, and their performances compared with those obtained from four rhesus monkeys. The results showed that macaques and marmosets are qualitatively alike, but that marmosets are grossy inferior on a quantitative basis. This conclusion is in keeping with the view that tests of interproblem transfer provide discriminative indices of phylogenetic status, and that marmoset behavior can be meaningfully assessed in psychoneurological studies with the same procedures that have been developed for higher members of the primate order.

REFERENCES

1. CLARK, W. E. L. *History of the primates.* London: Adlard, 1953.
2. GRETHER, W. F. Color vision and color blindness in monkeys. *Comp. psychol. Monogr.,* 1939, **15**, No. 4, 1–38.
3. HARLOW, H. F. The formation of learning sets. *Psychol. Rev.,* 1949, **56**, 51–65.
4. HARLOW, H. F. Analysis of discrimination learning by monkeys. *J. exp. Psychol.,* 1950, **40**, 26–39.
5. HARLOW, H. F. Primate learning. In C. P. Stone (Ed.), *Comparative psychology.* New York: Prentice-Hall, 1951.
6. HARLOW, H. F., UEHLING, H., & MASLOW, A. H. Comparative behavior of primates: 1. Delayed reaction tests on primates from the lemur to the orangoutan. *J. comp. Psychol.,* 1932, **13**, 313–343.
7. HOOTON, E. *Man's poor relations.* Garden City, New York: Doubleday, 1942.
8. MALMO, R. B., & GRETHER, W. F. Further evidence of red blindness (protanopia) in cebus monkeys. *J. comp. physiol. Psychol.,* 1947, **40**, 143–148.
9. MEYER, D. R. Intraproblem-interproblem relationships in learning by monkeys. *J. comp. physiol. Psychol.,* 1951, **44**, 162–167.

Learning Set in Preschool Children

Winifred O. Shepard

Iowa Child Welfare Research Station

There is ample evidence from the work of Harlow (2, 3, 4), North (6, 7), and Riopelle (8, 9, 10) that the learning-set phenomenon is a genuine one in animal discrimination learning behavior. There are, however, to the author's knowledge, only two recorded instances of this phenomenon with human beings. One is Kuennes study with preschool children mentioned by Harlow (2). The other is Adams' study with adult males (1). Furthermore, all but the last-mentioned study dealt with simple simultaneous discrimination tasks. Adams dealt with a fairly complex discrimination task in

Reprinted from *Journal of Comparative and Physiological Psychology,* 1957, 50, 15–17.

which Ss had to learn to associate each of four buttons with a different spatial arrangement of stimuli. The present study was designed to add to our knowledge of the learning set phenomenon by using conditional space discrimination tasks with preschool children.

METHOD

SUBJECTS

Twenty-six children between the ages of four and six from the Iowa Preschool Laboratories participated in the experiment. Six of these were dropped for failure to learn the first task.

STIMULI

The stimuli were 12 upper- and lower-case Greek letters randomly arranged in 6 pairs. Each symbol was cut from black construction paper and mounted on a white 4- by 4-in. cardboard square. These six pairs constituted the stimuli for six learning tasks.

APPARATUS

The apparatus consisted of a black wooden baseboard which measured 17½ by 5½ in. It had three 4½-in.-square shallow depressions in it. A red board 19½ by 9½ in. was hinged to this baseboard in such a manner that, between trials, it stood at right angles to the base, permitting E to manipulate the stimuli without being seen by S. During trials, it could be swung back, revealing the stimuli. There were also four black 4½-in.-square boxes, each with one open end. The boxes could be fitted, three at a time, into the depressions in the baseboard. Two boxes were always kept in place in the outside depressions. The E slipped a chip under one of them on each trial. The other two boxes were fitted with grooves on one face. A stimulus card could be slipped into these grooves. On each trial one of the stimulus presentation boxes was presented in the middle depression.

PROCEDURE

The Ss were randomly divided into two groups, one group getting pair 1 first and pair 6 last, and the other group getting pair 6 first and pair 1 last. On each task Ss had to learn to pick the left-hand box when presented with one stimulus and the right when presented with the other. Correct responses were set up in order A, RLRRRLLR, and order B, its reverse. During the first task orders A and B were alternated until S reached criterion or was eliminated. The second task consisted of one run through order A (eight trials); the third, one run through order B, and so on through the sixth task.

Each child was brought into the experimental room and seated at a low table in front of the apparatus. The E sat opposite him behind the apparatus. The S was first told that he had to win a large quantity of poker

chips in order to be able to select a prize. He was then told that every time
E pulled back the red board he would see three boxes and that the middle
one would have a picture on it. It was explained that he must look at the
picture carefully each time and then tip back one of the other boxes to see
if he could find a chip. Whenever S did tip back the right box, he was
allowed to take the chip and place it in a box he kept next to him. Whenever he tipped back the wrong box, he was merely told to look at the picture
again, but was not allowed to correct his response. The Ss were run on the
first task to a criterion of ten successive correct responses. The Ss who made
an incorrect response on trial 40 were eliminated, and Ss who made a correct response on trial 40 were continued until they either made an error or
reached criterion. If an S showed no signs of learning the first task by trial
10, verbal encouragement was given. He was reminded frequently to look
at the pictures carefully, because the picture would tell each time which
box to pick. The Ss who showed strong position preferences were told that
the chip was not always on the same side. All Ss who were not eliminated
on the first task received eight trials on each of the remaining five tasks.
No further verbal help was given. The entire experiment was run in one
session with a 5-min. rest period after the third task.

RESULTS AND DISCUSSION

As mentioned earlier, 6 Ss were eliminated from the experiment for failure to learn the first task. The trials to criterion for the remaining 20 Ss (excluding criterional trials) ranged from 0 to 32 with a mean of 16.2.

Figure 1 shows the mean number of correct responses on trials 2 to 8
made by the 20 Ss on each task. Trial 1 data were not considered since it
was always a purely chance affair. As can be seen from the figure, the major
facilitative effect took place from the first to the second task. The fact that
the curve dips down after the second task can probably be explained in
terms of boredom and consequent wandering of attention—phenomena quite
often observed in the members of this particular population after they have,
effectively, solved a learning problem.

The data on which this figure was based were subjected to treatments by subjects (5) analysis of variance which is summarized in Table 1.
It can be seen from this table that the task effect was significant at less
than the .001 level. When the simple effects of task were tested, it was

TABLE 1

SUMMARY OF ANALYSIS OF VARIANCE OF CORRECT RESPONSES
IN TRIALS 2 TO 8 FOR SIX TASKS

Source	df	MS	F
Tasks	5	8.85	5.36**
Subjects	19	2.85	1.73
Tasks × Subjects	95	1.65	

** $p < .001$.

found that performance on the first task differed from each of the others at less than the .01 level, but that none of the other intertask differences approached significance at this level, indicating that these Ss had "learned to learn" after successful completion of the first task.

Since half the Ss received the pairs in the order 1 to 6 and half in the order 6 to 1, it was possible to compare performance on each of these pairs when administered first and last. On pair 1 the mean number of correct responses on trials 2 to 8 for these ten Ss who received it first was 3.6 and for the ten who received it last 5.7. The probability of occurrence of this difference is less than .01. The mean number of correct responses on trials 2 to 8 for the ten Ss who received pair 6 first was 4.8. For those who received it last it was 5.7. This difference, while in the right direction, has a probability of occurrence between .1 and .2. It seems likely that both these differences were deflated by the boredom factor mentioned before.

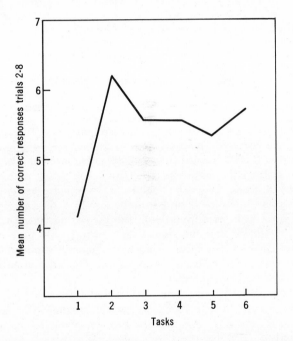

FIG. 1.   Mean number of correct responses in trials 2 to 8 on each task.

Finally, a word should be said about the difference in results reported here and those found by Kuenne (2), who found it took a much longer series of tasks to demonstrate learning set in preschool children. Several factors probably account for this discrepancy. The Ss in the present study were older than hers, were not experimentally naive, and were given verbal encouragement. Furthermore, in this study, due to the press of time, Ss who failed to learn the first task in a specified time were eliminated. In Kuenne's study, all problems were presented for six trials regardless of S's performance, and each S continued in the series of problems until he met a series criterion.

SUMMARY

Twenty preschool children were presented on one day, with six conditional space discrimination problems. There was a marked improvement in performance from the first to the second task and then a slight decline probably attributable to boredom.

REFERENCES

1. ADAMS, J. A. Multiple versus single problem training in human problem solving. *J. exp. Psychol.*, 1954, **48**, 15–18.
2. HARLOW, H. F. The formation of learning sets. *Psychol. Rev.*, 1949, **56**, 51–65.
3. HARLOW, H. F. Analysis of discrimination learning by monkeys. *J. exp. Psychol.*, 1950, **40**, 26–39.
4. HARLOW, H. F., & WARREN, J. M. Formation and transfer of discrimination learning sets. *J. comp. physiol. Psychol.*, 1952, **45**, 482–489.
5. LINDQUIST, E. F. *Design and analysis of experiments in psychology and education.* New York: Houghton Mifflin, 1953.
6. NORTH, A. J. Improvement in successive discrimination reversals. *J. comp. physiol. Psychol.*, 1950, **43**, 442–460.
7. NORTH, A. J. Performance during an extended series of discrimination reversals. *J. comp. physiol. Psychol.*, 1950, **43**, 461–470.
8. RIOPELLE, A. J. Transfer suppression and learning sets. *J. comp. physiol. Psychol.*, 1953, **46**, 108–114.
9. RIOPELLE, A. J., & COPELAN, E. L. Discrimination reversal to a sign. *J. exp. Psychol.*, 1954, **48**, 143–145.
10. RIOPELLE, A. J. Learning sets from minimum stimuli. *J. exp. Psychol.*, 1955, **49**, 28–32.

Multiple Versus Single Problem Training

in Human Problem Solving [1]

Jack A. Adams

Skill Components Research Laboratory, AF
Personnel and Training Research Center

Military training programs for maintenance technicians must be concerned
with methods of training proficient problem solvers who can quickly trouble-
shoot malfunctioning equipment. Harlow (1) has presented evidence to
show that highly effective problem-solving behavior can be acquired
through practice on a large number of problems where all problems have
the same general solution but differ in stimulus properties from problem to
problem. He has termed the learning of the ability to readily solve a new
problem of a specified class as the formation of a "learning set."

The study to be presented investigates the effectiveness of two different
training procedures in the formation of a learning set. Harlow's method of
training on a large number of problems may be only one of several possible
training techniques that might be used. One possibility is that repeated presentation of the *same* problem could also lead to considerable facility in the
solution of a new problem. This investigation evaluates the relative effectiveness of multiple problem and single problem training in the solution of
a simple discrimination problem by adult human Ss.

METHOD

Apparatus. Stimuli were on 2 × 2-in. slides and presented by a Selec-
troslide projector manufactured by Spindler and Sauppe of Los Angeles,
California. The Ss were seated between the projector and the screen and
were run four at a time. The table at which Ss were seated was partitioned
so that they could not see one another respond. In front of each S was a
small response box on which were mounted four horizontal and linearly

Reprinted from *Journal of Experimental Psychology*, 1954, 48, 15–18.

[1] The experimental work for this study was performed as part of the United
States Air Force Personnel and Training Research and Development Program. The
opinions or conclusions contained in this report are those of the author. They are
not to be construed as reflecting the views or indorsement of the Department of
the Air Force.

arranged plunger-type microswitches and a small frosted lamp. When a slide was presented, S pressed the one of the four buttons he judged correct. If the choice was correct, the lamp on the response box came on.

Subjects.—The Ss were 127 basic airmen trainees selected from the population available at Lackland Air Force Base, Texas. Subgroups of four Ss were randomly assigned to a multiple problem training group (M) and a single problem training group (S). The N was 68 in Group M and 59 in Group S.

Experimental procedure.—The basic unit of study was the *problem,* which was comprised of eight slides. These eight slides consisted of two slides each of four different spatial arrangements of a stimulus pair, and the particular arrangement of any given pair indicated which of the four buttons on S's response box was correct. For example, consider a problem involving two stimulus forms, A and B. The solution to this problem is: A to the left of B, Button No. 1; A to the right of B, Button No. 2; A above B, Button No. 3; and A below B, Button No. 4 (buttons numbered from left to right). These relationships were maintained throughout all problems regardless of the stimulus pair used. A sophisticated S who "understands" these relationships could conceivably respond 100% correct following the first slide of a new problem with Stimuli C and D. If the new pair is arranged in a horizontal pattern on the first slide, then S "knows" that either Button No. 1 or 2 is correct. If he chooses Button No. 1 and it is incorrect, then he knows that No. 2 must be correct, and correct responses for the other three pairs to be presented on the subsequent seven slides of the problem can be immediately deduced. Similarly, if the stimulus pairs are arranged vertically on the first slide, S knows that either Button No. 3 or 4 is correct, and the correct response for each of the remaining slides of the problem can be deduced from his choice on the first slide. This sophistication in the solution of this simple problem is, however, the type of behavior to be acquired, and the training method for maximizing it is the factor under investigation in this study.

Each S was presented 216 slides. There were 192 slides in the training series and 24 in the test series. Group M received 24 *different* problems in the training series and three presentations of the twenty-fifth problem for the test series. Group S received 24 presentations of the *same* problem in the training series and then received the same test series as Group M. The stimulus pair in the problem given Group S in the training series was a circle and a triangle. Problem 1 for Group M was also a circle and a triangle so that the equivalence of groups might be determined prior to differential treatment. Problems 2–24 for Group M involved abstract stimuli. The test problem given both groups also had abstract stimuli. Care was taken to minimize stimulus similarity within a problem and between problems. The eight slides were randomized separately for each problem with the restriction that no two identical slides follow one another.

Instructions were quite general and indicated only that a series of stimulus pairs would be presented and for each pair S had to learn to turn on the lamp on the response box by selecting the correct button. These initial instructions were the only instructions given and were the same for both groups.

A slide remained on the screen until all four Ss had responded. The Ss were under instruction to respond only once to each slide and to respond rapidly. Under this speed set, Ss typically responded within 3 sec. after the slide first appeared on the screen. In order that all Ss might have time to observe the lamp on the box and note correctness of their responses, a slide was not removed until 3 sec. after the last S had responded.

It could be contended that the speed set employed would not allow Ss sufficient time to fully consider all possible hypotheses before responding, with the result that maximum proficiency in problem solving may not be exhibited. Although there may be some merit in this contention, the purpose of this experiment was to compare two methods for training in problem solving, and there is no reason to believe that the speed set interacted with the variables studied.

A 2-min. rest was given between each block of six problems. All training was completed in a single practice session, and both groups took about the same amount of time to complete their respective slide series.

RESULTS

Figure 1 shows the percentage correct for each problem given Groups M and S. Problem 1 was the same for both groups and both have 27% correct. With chance response level at 25% (four possible responses), the obtained 27% does not exceed chance at the 5% level of confidence. Both groups steadily increase in proficiency over the training series. Group S, which was trained on repeated presentation of the same problem, is superior to Group M and shows a negatively accelerated acquisition curve. Group M, which was given multiple problem training, has an essentially linear increase in percentage correct as a function of number of training problems. It should be noted that the limit of the acquisition curves in the training series differs for the two groups. The limit is 100% for Group S but only 94% for Group M because at the asymptote Ss in Group M would average 50% correct on the first slide of a new problem.

In the test series, both groups were given three presentations of a new problem to evaluate their ability to solve it as a function of type of prior training. Figure 1 shows that both groups have the same value of 61% correct on the first presentation. For Group M this test problem is only another new problem, and 61% correct is consistent with the trend established in the training series. However, for Group S the test problem is the first new

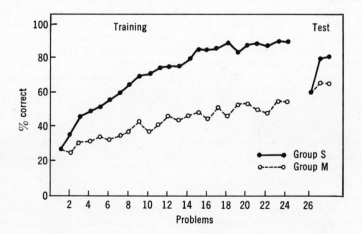

FIG. 1.   Performance of the multiple problem training group (M) and the single problem training group (S) on the training and test problems.

problem encountered and their level of 61% on the first presentation is a 30% reduction in proficiency from the level on the final training problem. On the second and third presentations of the test problem, Group S recovers most of this loss and is clearly superior to Group M. A test of the null hypothesis for the difference between the two groups gives a probability of .06 for the second presentation and .02 for the third presentation.

To examine test series performance more closely, Fig. 2 represents a detailed enlargement of the three test series values shown in Fig. 1 and gives the percentage correct for each group on each of the 24 slides presented in the test series. The important feature to note in this graph is that Group S undergoes a brief period of adjustment to the new problem during which performance level is below that of Group M. On Slide 1, Group S's level of 34% is not significantly above the chance level of 25% ($p = .12$). A test of the null hypothesis for the difference between the two groups on Slide 1 yields significance at the 6% level of confidence. On Slide 2, the difference between the two groups is significant at the 2% level. By Slide

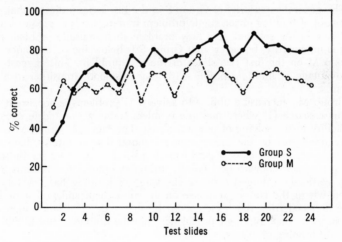

Fig. 2.   Performance of Groups M and S on each slide of the test series.

3 there is negligible difference between them and, on subsequent slides, Group S displays consistent superiority.[2]

The data for both groups were examined for individual differences in problem-solving ability. Group S was divided into low- and high-ability groups of 17 Ss each; these were compared for their ability to solve the new problem in the test series. The high- and low-ability designation was on the basis of number of presentations of the training problem required be-

[2] It could be contended that performance of Group S on the test problem was influenced by the sudden change from conventional symbols used in the training series (circle and triangle) to abstract forms used as test problem stimuli. To evaluate this possibility, Group S was replicated ($N = 56$), with the exception that abstract forms were used as stimuli in *both* training and test series. Performance trends of Group S and the replicate group were found to be essentially the same. A test of the null hypothesis was made for the difference between these two groups on each of the three presentations of the test problem. None of the obtained differences was significant at the 5% level.

fore solution was obtained. The high-ability group solved the problem in 2–7 presentations and the low-ability group required 14–23 presentations. On presentations 1, 2, and 3 of the test problem the high-ability group had 57%, 85%, and 84% correct, and the low-ability group had 60%, 73%, and 79% correct. It is evident that ability differences in single problem solution are not importantly reflected in the solution of a new problem of the same class. Group M revealed no important information with respect to ability differences. The Ss who acquired solution of the problem class in the training series also readily solved the test problem since it was merely another problem of the same class. Those Ss who failed to achieve complete solution at the end of the training series also failed in the test series.

DISCUSSION

The general superiority of Group S in the test series indicates that, with the amount of training given, single problem training leads to greater over-all proficiency in the solution of a new problem than multiple problem training. It is noteworthy, however, that Group S is below the performance level of Group M on the first two slides of the test problem. This suggests that one advantage of multiple problem training is smooth transition to a new problem.

Group M's increasing ability to solve new problems is consistent with previous research (1) where multiple problem training resulted in considerable facility in the solving of new problems. The fact that Group M is only slightly above 50% by the end of training shows that an intermediate stage in the solution to this class of problems has been attained where Buttons 1 and 2 are associated with horizontally arranged stimuli, and Buttons 3 and 4 with vertically arranged stimuli. The stage of learning has not yet been reached where the correct response on all subsequent slides of a problem can be deduced from the response on the first slide. The linear increasing trend suggests that this high proficiency may be attained after a sufficient number of training problems.

SUMMARY

Under investigation were two methods of training Ss in the solution of problems of a specified class. The problem class under consideration was a simple discrimination where the general solution was the same for all problems but the stimulus characteristics could vary from problem to problem. It was found that a group trained on repeated presentations of the same problem was more proficient in solving a new problem of the class than a group trained on a number of different problems.

REFERENCES

1. HARLOW, H. F. The formation of learning sets. *Psychol. Rev.*, 1949, **56**, 51–65.

PART THREE

The Perception
of Constant Brightness

Psychology has existed as a separate academic discipline for only some 100 years. Present-day psychologists often place psychology's birth at 1879, the year Wilhelm Wundt opened his laboratory at the University of Leipzig. Professor Wundt's new "child" came supplied with a considerable inheritance of subject matter; for "psychological" questions existed centuries before psychology did. These questions concerned the problems of interpreting complicated aspects of human functioning, and often they involved sensory issues. How do we see? Hear? Taste? Touch? In the decades before the establishment of Wundt's laboratory, it was not unusual to pose these questions in terms of physiological interests; for example, how does the eye react to light? Even today, despite the enormous knowledge we have gained, we still cannot give definitive answers to these physiological questions. But, after the birth of psychology, it was soon realized that physiological processes alone were unlikely to be able to completely explain certain characteristics of the ways in which humans perceive their environment.

We have all seen diagrams that compare the human eye with a camera: they both have lenses; the camera has film, the eye a retina for its light-sensitive, image-capturing surface. But this resemblance is not a complete one. Imagine that you are looking through the viewfinder of a camera with your right eye (for simplicity's sake, let the viewfinder be a wire frame rather than an optical device). Imagine the further unlikely condition that the camera's lens is the same size and shape as your right eye's and that the camera's film is the same size and shape as your right retina. With the camera focused upon an object, that object yields the same image, roughly speaking, upon the retina as on the film. Suppose the object being photographed is a man sitting in an easy chair with his feet propped up on a hassock in front of him. After the photograph is taken, the developed picture will show a distorted man with large feet and a small head. Given that his feet are closer to the camera than his head, the laws of optics dictate that the man's feet make a relatively larger image on the film, and, hence, that

his picture reflect this fact. But note: although the man's feet made a similarly larger image than his head did on your right retina, you did not "see"
a man with large feet and a small head—you "saw" a normal man. What
you "saw" was not a faithful reproduction of the image on your retina. This
lack of correspondence between the retinal image and the perception is the
key issue in this section. If the image on our retina does not entirely determine what we see, what else does?

The illustration concerned the phenomenon of size constancy; under
certain circumstances, our perception of the size of objects—people or things
—is relatively invariant of those objects' retinal projections. But the size of
objects is not their only attribute exhibiting constancy. The shape of an
object has a similar effect—that is, our perception of it is not always determined by its retinal image. If we look at a window from an angle, the
window appears rectangular although the projection on the retina is
trapezoidal. In an analogous fashion, our perception of an object's brightness
does not correspond to that object's actual "brightness."

Any discussion of vision will, of necessity, be somewhat complicated,
involving considerations of the physics of light and optics, and of sensory
physiology as well as of psychology. The topic of brightness is no exception.
Newton's experiments with sunlight and prisms in the seventeenth century
demonstrated that white light is a mixture of all the spectral wavelengths.
When white light strikes an object, it is reflected. If only a few of the constituent wavelengths of the white light are reflected, the object has a particular hue, such as red; if all of the wavelengths are reflected, the object
is "white," a mixture of all hues (wavelengths). Thus, a red object is one
that reflects only (or, more accurately, primarily) red wavelengths. In ac-
tuality, there are few pure red objects; most red objects reflect not only red
light but some of all wavelengths (white light) as well. The relative amount
of the red reflection to the white reflection determines another characteristic, the purity of the color. A completely pure color is monochromatic:
it is a reflection or emission of only one wavelength; it is perceived as being
saturated. A completely impure color is a mixture of all wavelengths—that
is, it is "white." It is perceived as being unsaturated. However, the two
characteristics, hue and saturation, are not alone sufficient to describe colors.
The characteristic of brightness is also needed.

The brightness of a source of light is a function of the energy it emits.
The brightness of an object is dependent on two factors—the energy of the
light striking the object and the energy it reflects. The more light that
strikes an object, the more it will reflect and the brighter it will seem.
Similarly, if two objects are struck by the same amount of light, the one
that reflects more will appear the brighter. Unfortunately, the picture we
have painted (no pun intended) is not quite this simple, and we shall have
to take cognizance of three complicating factors. Although we need three
dimensions (hue, brightness, and saturation) to describe our perception of
color, these are not dimensions in the same sense as other physical dimensions. Imagine a wooden block. If we want to describe its volume, we need
to state its length, width, and height. More important, we can change the
block's volume by changing each of its dimensions independently; that is,
we change the length and leave the height and width unaffected. If we want
to describe the block's color, we can do so by describing its hue, brightness,
and saturation. But if we wish to modify the color, we find that a change in

one dimension also changes the others; if we change the block's saturation, its brightness also changes. Thus, two objects of equal saturation and reflecting equal energy will appear differentially bright if they are of different hues. As will be shown below, this problem can be avoided by using only the achromatic colors—black, white, and grey.

The second complication is one of black and white. White is not a single wavelength—it is typically a mixture of all hues; by definition it is completely unsaturated. If we have an object that reflects all wavelengths, the "color" of the object will, in general, depend on the energy of the light it reflects. If this energy is high, the object is white; if the energy is moderate, the object is grey; if the energy is low, the object is black. The crux of this set of readings is that the perception of greyness (including blackness and whiteness) at times remains independent of the light energy reflected. Under some conditions, a "black" object will reflect more light than a "white" one. The fact that our *perception* of an object's luminance (its brightness) sometimes remains independent of its *actual* luminance is what is known as brightness constancy. The *why* of this seemingly contradictory state is first approached by Wallach's article.

In Part I of his article, Wallach introduces the third additional factor to our brightness, hue, and saturation description of colors. The color of light *reflected* from an opaque object (called a surface color) looks subjectively different from a light *source* of equal hue, brightness, and saturation. For example, a grey picture on a television tube is not perceived in the same way as the television set's cabinet, which, physically, is just as grey. Wallach describes a situation in which two slide projectors are focused on the same screen and project a disc of one luminance surrounded by a ring of a different luminance. (Remember, since Wallach is dealing with white light, both light sources are of equal hue and both are unsaturated; therefore, differences between them are ones of brightness only.) He points out that the perception of the disc's color (in this case, brightness) depends on the level of illumination in the room and the brightness of the surrounding field, as well as on the amount of light coming from the disc itself. Moreover, these very factors also help decide whether the disc is seen as a surface color or as a luminous patch.

In Part II of his paper, Wallach sets forth his hypothesis concerning brightness constancy. He proposes that the ratio of the brightnesses of two objects always stays constant. If a grey object abuts a white one that reflects four times as much light, increasing the light that shines on these objects increases the amount *both* reflect. Therefore, greater illumination on the grey does not whiten it, for this grey object reflects one fourth as much light as the adjoining white object. Wallach describes four experiments that test this hypothesis by having subjects perform a matching task. A ring (Ring I) of known illumination surrounds a disc (Disc I) of known illumination. Another ring (Ring II) of known illumination surrounds a disc (Disc II). Subjects adjust the illumination of Disc II until it matches Disc I in brightness. If brightness were determined by the amount of illumination of the disc alone, at the matching point the illumination of Disc II would equal that of Disc I. However, this does not occur, for at the matching point the ratio, illumination of Disc II to the illumination of Ring II, equals the ratio, illumination of Disc I to the illumination of Ring I. Subjects are matching, not luminance, but luminance ratios.

The experiments described by Wallach are straightforward. But understanding them depends upon understanding an episcotister, a device with a rotating opaque circle and a variable wedge, which controls the amount of light projected upon the screen by the slide projector. If a slide projector were set up to produce a circle of light upon the screen, an opaque circle covering the lens would reduce the illumination on the screen (from the projected source) to zero. If a 90° wedge were cut from the (360°) opaque circle, the screen would be illuminated with one quarter of the original illumination. By varying the size of the wedge from 0° (an opaque circle) to 360° (no circle), we can vary the amount of light illuminating the screen. An opaque circle with a 90° wedge will provide only half the light of one with an 180° wedge, but unfortunately the patterns of their projected light may no longer be circular. This difficulty is a minor one, for if our opaque circles are rotated rapidly, they still screen out light, yet the patterns are again circular. If the lights of two projectors are matched in intensity, they will illuminate a screen in proportion to the sizes of their episcotister wedges.

The experiments performed by Wallach were done within a particular setting, which in itself may have had an influence on the subjects' performance. Wallach discusses two variables present in his setting—the width of the surrounding ring and the illumination of the experimental room. The article by Hochberg and Beck explores the effects on brightness perception due to light placement. Their studies show that when an object is perceived as perpendicular to a light source it appears brighter than when it is perceived as parallel to that source. Contrary to predictions from Wallach's hypothesis, the ratio of the brightness of the object to its surroundings is also changing. Hochberg and Beck discuss some of the theoretical issues in brightness constancy: they are seeking for an explanation that will encompass both their results and Wallach's. A later study by Beck[1] explores the brightness–illumination effect in considerably greater detail.

Dunn and Leibowitz are also concerned (albeit implicitly) with the specific effects of Wallach's arrangement—a disc of a given intensity surrounded by an adjoined ring of a different intensity. They suggest that this two-intensity visual field may be related to the phenomenon of simultaneous contrast, wherein a bright visual field makes an abutting less luminous one seem even duller than usual. One of the factors affecting simultaneous contrast is the separation between the brighter (inducing) field and the duller (test) field. Using an experimental strategy similar to Wallach's, they find that brightness constancy is affected in much the same way as simultaneous contrast by field separation. They suggest that the two phenomena may have the same underlying mechanism and point to work by Ratliff, Miller, and Hartline which demonstrates a correspondence of simultaneous contrast effects and the interaction of retinal elements.

Brightness constancy is one of the classic problems in the field of visual perception. The experimental work of Hess and Pretori was published in 1894; it is likely that if there were a simple explanation for the effect, it would have been discovered since. Jameson and Hurvich show that all of the complicated explanations thus far advanced also are not completely

[1] J. Beck, "Apparent Spatial Position and the Perception of Brightness," *Journal of Experimental Psychology*, 1965, 69, 170–179.

adequate. In an ingenious experimental procedure, they inserted into a surrounding field five test fields of differing brightness. When subjects matched the brightness of these five fields, the matches were different for each field, and only one of them exhibited brightness constancy.

Jameson and Hurvich refine their measures further by correcting for the effects of psychophysical judgments at differing intensities. The striking of a match in a darkened room makes a great change in our perceived illumination, but striking the match in a lighted room makes little change. This illustrates that our perception of changes in brightness (or brightness itself) is not a simple linear function of the amount of light energy changed. Even when perceived (rather than physical) illumination levels are used, Jameson and Hurvich can demonstrate their results. They use these results to rule out several previous constancy explanations, and although they offer no complete alternative explanation, they point out that a theory of general color vision, that of opponent processes, does seem to bring some order into the experimental data.

If we review the ordering of the papers in this section, we can see a general pattern. Wallach proposes a new explanation to an old problem. His explanation triggers off other studies and a new mass of knowledge results. At the end we cannot say definitely what the explanation is for brightness constancy, but we can say what is *isn't* and under what circumstances any given explanation fails to hold up. We begin to comprehend the general visual mechanisms by an attrition of the incorrect and partial explanations, as well as by verification of the correct and complete ones.

STUDY QUESTIONS

1. What are the differences between the wavelength, purity, and luminance of a color, on the one hand, and its hue, saturation, and brightness, on the other?
2. The data collected by Wallach supported his hypothesis of matching brightness ratios, that is, his subjects behaved in accord with "the law of brightness constancy." For each of his tables, what would the data have been if his subjects had behaved in accord with "the law of retinal stimulus?"
3. Exactly how do Hochberg and Beck change from parallel to perpendicular illumination of a test field within any one of their three experiments? Why is an experimental technique of this sort an important aspect of testing Wallach's conclusions?
4. How does separation of test and inducing fields affect brightness constancy in the Dunn and Leibowitz study? What is gained by relating this finding to simultaneous contrast?
5. Why do Jameson and Hurvich use surfaces of five different reflectances in their test field? What variables are they investigating by doing this?
6. In the Jameson and Hurvich study, what has been gained by graphing (in logarithmic units) test luminance against apparent brightness (Figure 9) instead of graphing test luminance against matching luminance (Figure 7)?
7. Jameson and Hurvich state that their results are incompatible with both the "correction" and the "constant ratio" theories of brightness constancy. How do they support this claim and what do they offer as an alternative?

Brightness Constancy and the Nature

of Achromatic Colors

Hans Wallach

Swarthmore College

PART I

The problem of brightness constancy arises through the following circumstances. The amount of light which is reflected by an opaque object and which stimulates the eye depends not only upon the color of the object but just as much upon the amount of light which falls on the object, that is upon the illumination in which the object is seen. When in spite of this, the seen colors are in agreement with the object colors, when a given object appears to have the same color in various illuminations, we speak of brightness constancy.

The majority of investigators who aim at all at functional explanations understand this problem to mean: How is illumination registered and in what way is it taken into account so that the experienced colors remain constant when the illumination is varied? In this version the problem is a difficult one at the outset, for illumination is never directly or independently given but is represented in stimulation only in as much as it affects the amount of light which is reflected by the objects. To be sure, we perceive illumination as well as surface color; a spot of light here, a shadow there, a brightly lighted region near the window or the dim light of dusk on everything. But the fact remains that both variables, object color and objective illumination, affect the eye through the same medium, the varying amount of reflected light. If the seen illumination were found to be in agreement with the objective illumination, in principle the same problem would arise which we face regarding the surface colors. There is only one stimulus variable to represent two objective variables each of which seems to have its counterpart in experience. Under these circumstances investigation has largely consisted in the study of factors by which illumination could be recognized and in the demonstration of their effectiveness in bringing about constancy.

The following observations suggested a radically different approach

Reprinted from *Journal of Experimental Psychology*, 1948, 38, 310–324.

to the writer. They concern some variations of an experiment by A. Gelb which demonstrated brightness constancy in a most impressive way. Gelb's experiment[1] is most conveniently performed by opening the door of a dimly lighted room and by suspending in the frame a piece of black paper. This paper is illuminated by a strong projection lantern which stands on the floor or on a low table and is tilted upwards so that the part of its beam which is not intercepted by the black paper passes through the open door onto the ceiling of the adjacent room where it is invisible to the observer. In the light of the strong lantern the paper may look white instead of black. When a white piece of paper is held up in front of the black paper so that it too reflects the strong light of the lantern, the black paper assumes a black color. According to the usual interpretation it looks first white because no cues for the special strong illumination are available when this illumination affects only one visible surface. With the introduction of the white paper into the beam a special brilliant illumination becomes visible and constancy is restored: the two papers are perceived with their real color.

The arrangement of Gelb's experiment lends itself to a still more impressive demonstration. When the black paper is presented alone, reducing the intensity of the lantern light by small steps to zero causes the perceived color of the paper to vary all the way from white through gray to black. Every change in illumination is accompanied by a corresponding change in the perceived color. However, when a larger white paper is fastened behind the black paper so that the latter is seen surrounded by white, the same changes in illumination do not at all affect the seen colors which remain white and black throughout. Paired in this way the colors are immune to changes in illumination and remain 'constant.' It is rather a change in the perceived illumination which now accompanies the change in the objective illumination.

The question arises: what determines the color with which the black paper is seen at a given intensity of the lantern light when the paper is presented alone? Do we deal in this situation with an absolute relation between the intensity of the light which stimulates a portion of the retina and the resulting perceived color? In considering this question we have to remember that there is another variable in the situation, the dim general illumination of the room. When this is varied it becomes immediately clear that this general illumination also affects the color of the black paper. When, with a high intensity of the lantern light, the general illumination is raised, the color of the black paper changes from white to gray, and this in spite of the fact that the paper too now reflects light of a somewhat higher intensity than before. Only *relatively*, that is in relation to the light which comes from other surfaces, has the light reflected by the black paper become less intense.

Such dependence of the perceived color on the *relative* intensity of the perceived light should be demonstrable in a much simpler form, and this is the case.

In a dark room a white screen is illuminated by the light of two slide projectors. In one of the projectors an opaque card with a circular hole of

[1] Described in W. D. Ellis, *A source book of gestalt psychology*. New York: Harcourt, Brace, 1939, p. 207.

½ in. diameter is inserted, and the bright image of the hole is focused on the screen. The slide for the other projector consists of a blank glass covered with an opaque card with a circular hole of one in. diameter and with a ½ in. cardboard disk which is pasted concentrically into the hole. Focused on the screen this slide produces a bright ring. The two projectors are so adjusted that this ring surrounds the image of the ½ in. hole so that the edge of the latter coincides with the inner edge of the ring. The light intensity of the projectors can be changed by running them on variable transformers or by letting their beams pass through episcotisters.

We have then on the screen a circular region (disk) and surrounding it a ringshaped region which reflect light intensities that can be separately controlled. When the intensity of the disk is kept constant and that of the ring is widely varied, the color of the disk may change all the way from white to dark gray. The disk looks dark gray when the light reflected from the ring is of high intensity and it becomes white when the brightness of the ring is greatly lowered. When the light intensity of the disk is varied and that of the ring is kept constant, the color of the disk, of course, undergoes similar changes. Again it is quite clear that the color which appears in one region, namely in that of the disk, depends on the relation of the light intensity of this region to that of its surroundings. This is true also of the ring. It can be shown in corresponding fashion that its color depends on the relation of the intensity of the ring to that of the disk.

When the ring is altogether omitted so that the disk is seen in completely dark surroundings, it ceases to look white or gray and assumes instead a luminous appearance similar to that of the moon at dusk. Lowering the intensity of the disk greatly does not change this mode of appearance, provided the rest of the room is really dark; the disk looks merely dimmer. The same observation can be made with the ring when it is presented without the disk, or with both the ring and the disk when they are placed far from each other on the screen. Opaque colors which deserve to be called white or gray, in other words 'surface colors,' will make their appearance only when two regions of different light intensity are in contact with each other, for instance when the ring surrounds the disk or when two oblongs have the longer edges as their common border.

The importance of a close contact for the emergence of surface colors becomes strikingly clear in the following observation. The intensity of the disk is adjusted to be one quarter that of the ring, which makes the color of the disk a medium gray. An opaque object is moved from the side into the beam of the lantern which projects the ring so that part of it is blotted out by the shadow of that object. When this happens the gray color disappears almost simultaneously from that part of the disk which is adjacent to the shadow. It looks as if the dense gray there were dissolving leaving the screen transparent to let a light behind it shine through. Brought about in this fashion, the change from surface color to a luminous appearance is quite impressive. That side of the disk which is still well surrounded by a brighter ring continues to show the gray color, and between it and the luminous side the disk shows a steady gradient in the density of the gray.

These observations make it clear that, at least under these conditions, surface colors occur in our experience when regions of different light intensity are in contact with each other and that the particular surface colors which come about depend on the relation of these light intensities. They are apparently the product of nervous processes of limited scope, for close spatial contact between the regions of different light intensity is required for their emergence. Moreover, the degree to which surface color is present in a certain region depends on the intimacy of the contact between this region and its partner. This is easily demonstrated by the following observations.

No matter what the brightness relation between ring and disk be, the ring will always show a less dense surface color and have more of a luminous appearance than the disk. This becomes quite clear when two pairs of such regions are presented for comparison which are so chosen that the intensity of the ring in one pair equals that of the disk in the other one, and vice versa. Even the region of lower light intensity in each pair, which is perceived as a gray, has a more luminous appearance where it occurs in the ring than where it occurs in the disk. The most obvious explanation for this difference in the mode of appearance is that the disk is more under the influence of the ring than vice versa, in as much as the disk is completely surrounded by the ring, whereas the ring is in contact with the disk only on one side. This explanation agrees well with the observation reported earlier that the elimination of part of the ring rendered that part of the disk more luminous which was then no longer enclosed by a region of different light intensity.

This influence under which surface colors emerge is clearly a mutual one. Though less so, the ring does display surface color. There is a great difference in the mode of appearance between a ring which surrounds, for instance, an area of higher intensity and an equal ring presented in an otherwise dark field. Whereas the latter looks merely luminous, the former shows in addition to some luminosity a distinct gray.

The mutual influence on which the emergence of surface colors depends must also account for the fact that the particular colors which come about depend on the relation of the stimulating light intensities. It is probably best conceived of as some kind of interaction which takes place as part of the nervous process which underlies color perception.

It will be remembered that the dependence of the perceived colors on the relative intensities of the stimulating light was also evident in the variations of Gelb's experiment which were first reported. It remains to be added that the transition from surface color to a luminous mode of appearance can be demonstrated with Gelb's set-up in the following way. At first the special illumination of the black paper and the general illumination of the room are so adjusted that the black paper looks white. When now the general illumination is further reduced, the paper becomes more and more luminous, and it ceases altogether to look white when the rest of the room is completely dark. Luminosity of the paper can also be produced by excluding the general illumination from its immediate neighborhood. By such measures a rather luminous gray, not unlike that appearing in the ring, may also be achieved. Thus it is not only in projected rings and disks that luminosity appears as an alternative to surface colors when adequate differences in intensity are lacking or when the contact between those regions is diminished. Clearly discernible segregated objects as for instance a suspended piece of black paper function in the same fashion.

PART II

So far, we have become acquainted with the way in which surface colors come into existence and with the manner in which they depend on the stimulus situation. They depend on the relation of stimulus intensities on the retina which are so located with regard to each other that the subsequent nervous processes interact. Now the question arises what bearing this has on the problem of brightness constancy.

In order to answer this question, some clarification of the nature of brightness constancy is needed. One may say that brightness constancy prevails when a perceived color is in agreement with the corresponding object color. Object color is a persistent physical characteristic of a surface, the property to reflect a certain proportion of the light which falls on that surface. For instance, a surface which looks black under constancy conditions reflects about four percent of the illuminating light, and a white one about 80 percent. This property, called reflectance, is not conveyed to the eye as such. It is rather represented to the eye by light of a given intensity. This fact constitutes the problem of brightness constancy, for the intensity of the reflected light depends to the same degree on the color of the reflecting surface as on the strength of the illumination. If in our environment illumination were always and everywhere the same, the fact that our visual sense is not directly affected by reflectances but only by the reflected light intensities would not raise a problem in perception, for the reflected light could represent the object colors unequivocally. But illumination varies widely, even between different parts of the same visual field, and often very different light intensities come to represent the same reflectance to the eye and, in constancy, produce the same color in the observer's experience. When, for instance, a medium gray which reflects 20 percent of the illuminating light is presented once in an illumination of an intensity 100 and again under light of an intensity 300, the intensities of the reflected light are 20 and 60 respectively; if complete constancy prevails, both stimulus intensities lead to perception of the same medium gray. Similarly the white background on which the gray samples are shown will reflect light of the intensity 80 in the weaker illumination and of the intensity 240 where it is in the stronger illumination, and the two differently illuminated parts of the background will probably both be judged as white. At first glance no orderly connection between stimulus intensity and perceived color seems to exist.

There is, however, one feature in the stimulus situation which remains the same when the illumination is varied. The intensity of the light reflected by the gray in the weaker illumination (20) stands in a ratio of 1:4 to that reflected by the white in the weaker illumination (80), and the same ratio exists between the intensities reflected by the gray and the white in the stronger illumination (60 and 240). It is easy to see that in the case of any given set of object colors the *ratios* of the intensities of the reflected light remain the same for any change in illumination which affects all of them.[2] Thus, if the perceived colors were to depend on the *ratios* of the intensities of the reflected lights, they would remain unchanged when a given set of object colors were presented in changed illumination, and con-

[2] This is a simple consequence of the fact already mentioned that object colors reflect a constant *fraction* of the illumination.

stancy would be assured. A medium gray may serve again as an example. Although it affects the eye with different light intensities when the illumination is changed, it would be perceived as the same color because the ratio of the intensity that it reflects to the intensity of the light reflected by the surrounding white would remain the same, for a change in illumination affects the latter in the same proportion.

At this point we have to consider the observations reported in Part I. They suggested that the perceived surface colors depend on the relation, not yet quantitatively defined, of the light intensities in interacting regions. But we now find that constancy would result, if our visual perception functioned in such a fashion that the perceived colors depended on the *ratios* of the intensities of the reflected light.

Thus, we merely have to make the assumption that the relation on which surface colors depend is one of simple proportionality to give the observations of Part I a direct bearing on the problem of brightness constancy. If this assumption were correct brightness constancy would find its explanation in the very process by which surface colors come about.

This assumption can be tested by simple experiments. If it is correct, the particular colors which are perceived in a pair of ring and disk should depend on the ratio of the intensities of the two regions, and only on that ratio. In other words, no matter what the absolute intensities of ring and disk may be, the same colors should be seen in the case of any pair of intensities which happen to stand in the same ratio to each other. This is, in close approximation, the case, as the following report of quantitative experiments[3] shows.

Two pairs of ring and disk were used, in order to permit simultaneous comparison. The intensity of each of these four regions could be varied independently.

Four identical projections lanterns equipped with 500 watt bulbs were used for this purpose. They were arranged in two groups and each group produced on the screen a pair of ring and disk as described in Part I. They were all so adjusted that they gave their respective regions the same light intensity. This was done in the following way. First a pair of ring and disk was formed with one lantern from group I and one from group II, and the intensity of one of them was varied until the contour between the ring and the disk disappeared because of brightness equality. Then these two lanterns were restored to their respective groups and similar adjustments were made within each group by varying the light intensities of the not yet equated lanterns.

The intensity variations required by the experiments were brought about with the help of episcotisters through which the lantern beams had to pass before reaching the screen. This technique has the advantage that the episcotister apertures are a direct measure of the relative intensities in the various regions.

Measurements were made by the method of limits. Ring and disk of one pair and the ring of the other pair were kept at constant intensities, and the intensity of the remaining disk was varied in suitable steps until the S judged the colors of the two disks as equal.

[3] These experiments were performed by the students of various seminars in Perception and classes in Experimental Psychology at Swarthmore College under the author's supervision.

In the first experiment one of the rings was given the full illumination of its lantern and the disk inside it received half of the intensity, for its light beam passed through an episocotister of 180 degrees aperture. The light for the ring of the other pair was cut down to one-eighth of full intensity by passing it through an episcotister of 45 degrees aperture. The aperture for the disk of the latter pair was varied in steps of two degrees. The following are the means of one upper and one lower limit for each of five Ss: 24, 26, 24, 23, 24 degrees with a total mean of 24.2 degrees. This result means that, on the average, a light intensity in a disk corresponding to an episcotister aperture of 24.2 degrees when it is surrounded by a ring of an intensity of 45 degrees aperture brings about in the S's experience the same gray as does a disk of an intensity of 180 degrees aperture inside a ring of an intensity of 360 degrees aperture. There is only a small deviation from the value of 22.5 degrees which with 45 degrees forms the same ratio as does 180 degrees with 360 degrees. Comparing the grays in the two disks was not difficult for the Ss. The great difference in absolute intensity between the two pairs of ring and disk (8:1) made the less intense pair look much dimmer, but that did not affect the distinctness of the disks' color. However, it made the rings look very different; though both were white, the more intense one was by far more luminous. This latter observation which was also made in most of the following experiments seems to be important, for it corresponds to a fact which can be observed in real constancy situations. When identical sets of object colors are placed in different illuminations and appear approximately the same, the set in the stronger objective illumination is often also *seen* to be more strongly illuminated. Perceived illumination and the different degree of luminous appearance which was frequently observed in our experiments seem, functionally speaking, to be closely related experiences. A detailed discussion will be presented in a later publication.

In another experiment a disk of 90 degrees intensity was shown in a ring of 360 degrees intensity. This combination which forms an intensity ratio of 4:1 brings about a much darker gray in the disk. In the other pair, the disk whose intensity was varied was surrounded by a ring of 180 degrees intensity. The proportionate value for the disk is here 45 degrees. The averages of two upper and two lower limits for each of four Ss were 46, 52, 45, 44 degrees with a mean of 47 degrees.

In the following experiment the disk of the brighter pair was varied and a ratio of 3:1 between ring and disk was used. In the darker pair, the ring had an intensity of 180 degrees and the ring one of 60 degrees, and the variable disk was surrounded by a ring of 360 degrees intensity. Five upper and five lower limits were determined for each of three Ss. The means were 113, 115, 121 degrees. The proportionate value is here 120 degrees.

It will be noted that so far all deviations from the proportionate values were in one direction. They all imply that, where they occur, a disk of proportionate intensity in the dimmer pair looks darker than the disk in the pair of higher intensity; *viz.*, in the first two experiments the disk in the less intense pair had to be given a slightly higher than proportionate intensity to give a color match and in the last experiment the disk in the more intense pair had to be made objectively darker. Thus, although these deviations are small, they deserve our attention. Experiments with an improved technique were made to find out how significant they are.

To facilitate measuring a variable episcotister[4] was used for the determination of the limits. This device permits changing the aperture by definite amounts while it is spinning. Only when the Ss had given a judgment of equality was the episcotister stopped and its angle measured with a protractor.

It has been described above how the intensities of the four lanterns were equated at the outset of the experiments. These equations are likely to contain subliminal errors which could affect our measurements. In the experiments which follow the episcotisters were interchanged between the groups of lanterns after half the number of limits had been determined for a given S, so that the group which during the first half of an experiment produced the brighter pair of ring and disk were made to produce the dimmer pair during the second half, and vice versa. Thus, any error in the original lantern adjustment which would affect the measurements during the first half of the experiment in one direction would in the second half affect it in the opposite direction. In this manner such an error will appear in the scatter of the limit values but will not affect their mean.

The first experiment (I) done with this improved technique was one with a small difference between the brighter and the dimmer pair. The former had a ring of 360 degrees intensity and a disk of 180 degrees, and the other pair had a variable disk in a ring of 180 degrees. Four Ss took part in the experiment. For each one four upper and four lower limits were determined. Table I presents the means of these limits. The proportionate value is here 90 degrees. It will be noted that the small deviations from this value are in a direction opposite to those previously reported, for they would imply that a disk of proportionate intensity in the dimmer pair is perceived as a slightly lighter gray than the disk in the more intense pair.

TABLE I

EPISCOTISTER SETTINGS IN DEGREES FOR DISK WITHIN RING OF
180 DEGREES IN COMPARISON WITH DISK OF 180 DEGREES
WITHIN RING OF 360 DEGREES

Subjects	Ad.	McN.	Ba.	Cl.	
Upper limit	88	86	85.5	90	
Lower limit	84	84	79.5	84.5	
Mean	86	85	82	86	Grand mean: 85

TABLE II

EPISCOTISTER SETTINGS IN DEGREES FOR DISK WITHIN RING OF
90 DEGREES IN COMPARISON WITH DISK OF 240 DEGREES
WITHIN RING OF 360 DEGREES

Subjects	Mo.	Cr.	Ke.	Cy.	
Upper limit	61	62	73	74	
Lower limit	62	64	68	67	
Mean	61.5	63	70.5	70.5	Grand mean: 66.4

[4] Designed and built by R. Gerbrands, Emerson Hall, Cambridge, Mass.

This is not so with the results of the following experiment (II) in which a still lighter gray was produced and in which the intensity of the dimmer ring was only one quarter of that of the brighter one. In the dimmer pair the ring had an intensity of 90 degrees and the disk was variable, while in the brighter pair the ring had 360 degrees and the disk 240 degrees of light. The results are given in Table II. With the Ss Mo. and Cr., 10 upper and 10 lower limits were determined, with Ke. and Cy. only six. Individual differences are larger in this experiment. For two of the Ss there was a marked deviation from the proportionate value of 60 degrees, which implied that for them a disk of 60 degrees intensity in the dimmer pair showed a slightly darker gray than the disk in the brighter pair.

Ten Ss were employed in an experiment (III) in which the variable disk was surrounded by a ring of 360 degrees of light and the dimmer pair consisted of a ring of 90 degrees and a disk of 30 degrees intensity. Six upper and lower limits were determined for each S, except for Ss Mo. and Cr., who again supplied 10 pairs of limits each. The average of the individual means as shown in Table III was 106 degrees, a clear deviation from the proportionate value of 120 degrees. It implies that the gray in the disk of low intensity looks somewhat darker than a disk of proportionate value in the brighter pair.

TABLE III

EPISCOTISTER SETTINGS IN DEGREES FOR DISK WITHIN RING OF 360
DEGREES IN COMPARISON WITH DISK OF 30 DEGREES
WITHIN RING OF 90 DEGREES

Subjects	Ca.	Ga.	Hs.	Ht.	Lu.	Ro.	Mo.	Cr.	Ke.	Cy.	
Upper limit	104.5	91	117.5	116.5	113	130	128	107.5	105	113	
Lower limit	92.5	91	99.5	98.5	103	112	100	103	97	95	
Mean	98.5	91	108.5	107.5	108	121	114	105	101	104	Grand mean: 106

The direction of the deviations from proportionate values encountered in the last two experiments was such that they could be regarded as the effect of a slight influence of the absolute stimulus intensities on the color process which otherwise could be conceived as functioning according to a proportional law. The question arose whether these deviations reflected intrinsic properties of the color process or whether they were introduced by incidental experimental conditions. An answer cannot yet be given and must be left to further detailed investigation. However, an experiment which was performed with this question in mind will be reported below, because it will add the data of still another combination of intensities.

It was suspected that the presence of the brighter pair of ring and disk in the visual field when the gray in the disk of the dimmer pair developed was responsible for the fact that this gray looked a trifle too dark. If the high intensities of the brighter pair had an influence across the spatial interval on the colors which emerged in the dimmer pair, this is what should have happened. Such an influence can be avoided by presenting the pairs successively. This was done in the following experiment (IV). The intensities in the brighter pair were 360 and 180 degrees, the ring in the dimmer pair was 90 degrees and the disk was varied. Table IV shows for four Ss the means of four upper and four lower limits. Ordinarily, with an intensity ratio of 4:1 between the rings the deviation under discussion was to be expected. It did not appear. The slight deviation from the proportionate value of 45 degrees was in the opposite direction.

In another experiment, however, successive presentation failed to eliminate completely the deviation under discussion. Experiment III was repeated with three further Ss who did the experiment twice, once with successive and once with simultaneous presentation. The limits listed in Table V are the averages of four determinations each. Although successive presentation reduces the deviation from the proportionate value of 120 degrees, it does not eliminate it.

TABLE IV

EPISCOTISTER SETTINGS IN DEGREES FOR DISK WITHIN RING OF 90 DEGREES IN COMPARISON WITH DISK OF 180 DEGREES WITHIN RING OF 360 DEGREES

Subjects	Ad.	McN.	Ba.	Cl.	
Upper limit	43	42	41	44	
Lower limit	41	40	42	44	
Mean	42	41	41.5	44	Grand mean: 42

TABLE V

EPISCOTISTER SETTINGS IN DEGREES FOR DISK WITHIN RING OF 360 DEGREES IN COMPARISON WITH DISK OF 30 DEGREES WITHIN RING OF 90 DEGREES

Subjects Presentation	Cl.		He.		Be.	
	Sim.	Succ.	Sim.	Succ.	Sim.	Succ.
Upper limit	110.5	121	99	108.5	104	112
Lower limit	99.5	99	97.5	99	94	104
Mean	105	110	98	104	99	108

These deviations from proportionate values appear rather insignificant when one compares them with the remaining effect of the proportional law. For example, in experiment III which showed the largest deviation, a disk of an intensity of 30 degrees aperture had on the average the same color as one of an intensity of 106 degrees aperture, that is, an intensity 3.5 times as high. The deviation from the proportionate value of 120 degrees amounts only to 12 percent.

It should be mentioned at this point that such experiments can also be done with a less elaborate set-up. Two color mixers and one projection lantern suffice for a crude demonstration of the proportional law. With the help of a large color wheel of black and white disks and a small one fastened on top of it to the same mixer one can obtain a ring-shaped and a circular region in which the intensities of the reflected light can be varied independently. On one mixer, e.g., the large wheel can be set to show a sector of 90 degrees white and the small one a sector of 45 degrees white.

To the other mixer are fastened a small wheel with a white sector of 180 degrees and a large wheel of 360 degrees white. When the mixers spin in general room illumination, one sees a dark gray disk surrounded by a medium gray ring on one mixer and a light gray disk in a white ring on the other one. However, when the mixers are placed in separate strictly local illumination they look quite different. That illumination can be provided by a lantern equipped with an opaque slide which has two circular holes a good distance apart. It projects two narrow beams of light of equal intensity. When the mixers are placed each in one of the beams at such a distance from the projector that their wheels are covered by the light almost to the outer rim and the rest of the room is entirely dark, both color mixers show a white ring and a light gray disk much alike in color. The reason for this change is easy to understand. Under local illumination the two color mixers provide exactly the same pattern of stimulus intensities as the set-up in experiment IV, and thus the same colors develop as in that experiment. In general illumination, on the other hand, the pairs of ring and disk are surrounded by regions of other intensity, e.g., the light reflected by the wall of the room, which cooperate in determining the colors which come about in the pairs. If, for instance, light reflected by a white wall forms the stimulus intensity of the surrounding region, that intensity stands to the intensity of the dimmer ring in a ratio of 4:1, and in this relation the ring should assume a medium gray color, as indeed it did.

It was explained above how the assumption that the achromatic colors depend on the ratios of the pertinent stimulus intensities accounts for brightness constancy. On that occasion complete constancy was shown to follow from this assumption. However, complete constancy has hardly ever been demonstrated experimentally. An object color presented in reduced illumination usually looks somewhat darker than another sample of that color in full illumination, though not as much darker as the difference of the reflected light intensities would warrant if there were no constancy. Yet complete constancy would follow from a direct application of the proportional law. Deviations from proportionality which occurred in our experiments are by far too small to account for the usual lag in constancy. The difficulty resolves itself when it is realized that the proportional law cannot be applied so simply to this situation. Here the two pairs of regions, the sample and its background in full illumination and the other sample with background in reduced illumination, are not as completely separated from each other as the corresponding regions in our experiments, for the regions of different illumination are in contact with each other and the brighter one can have an influence on the dimmer one. In other words, we have here a case where three or more regions of different intensity interact. Such processes have not yet been sufficiently investigated, and no report can be made at this time. It seems, however, quite likely that a full investigation will furnish the rules for the prediction of the lag in constancy in individual experiments.

This report may so far have given the impression that, apart from the small deviations discussed, the proportional law permits prediction of color equations if the pertinent stimulus intensities are known. However, this is so only with important qualifications. To a certain extent also the geometrical arrangement of the regions of different intensity has an influence on what colors come about in these regions. Some brief experiments which permit a first appraisal of the importance of these conditions will be reported below.

In the measuring experiments so far reported the width of the ring was ⅘ of the diameter of the disk so that the area of the ring was four times as large as the area of the disk. A reduction of the width of the ring to ¼ of the diameter of the disk so that its area was about the same as that of the disk did not affect the color in the disk as the following experiment shows, in which the colors in two disks were compared which were surrounded by rings of different width. Both rings were given the same intensity of 120 degrees aperture; the disk in the narrow ring had an intensity of 15 degrees and appeared as a very dark gray; the disk in the ring of standard width was variable. The mean of two upper and two lower limits for a single S was also 15 degrees. A number of other observers were satisfied with that equation.

The width of the narrow ring was further reduced so that it amounted to only 1/16 of the diameter of the disk. The same constant intensities as in the last experiment were used. The averages of two upper and two lower limits for each of two Ss were 37 and 37 degrees. This result means that a disk of 15 degrees intensity inside the very narrow ring looked as light as a disk of 37 degrees intensity inside a ring of standard width. The outcome of this experiment was so striking that we repeated it with another combination of intensities. The intensity of the two rings remained the same, but the disk in the very narrow ring had an intensity of 60 degrees. Again a higher intensity was needed for an equation in the disk inside the standard ring. The averages of two upper and two lower limits for the same two Ss were 87 and 86 degrees. However, with this intensity ratio of 120:60, which produces a light gray, the effect of making the ring very narrow was not so great. It amounted only to 45 percent, whereas in the case of a ratio of 120:15 which normally produces a very dark gray the disk in the standard ring had to be made 145 percent more intense. On the whole it looks as if the very narrow ring which has only one-quarter of the area of the disk cannot make the disk color as dark as does a ring of sufficient width.

As just reported, no difference in the effect of a ring which has about the same area as the disk and of one which has four times the area of the disk has been found. Two further measurements were made with a much wider ring. Its width was 1.5 the diameter of the disk and its area 15 times that of the disk. In one experiment the intensity ratio between the wide ring and its disk was again 120:15. In the disk of the standard pair the averages of four upper and four lower limits for the two Ss were 17 and 16 degrees. When a ratio of 120:60 was used, averages for two pairs of limits were 66 and 63 degrees. The deviations from 15 and 60 degrees respectively are probably incidental. At any rate, they are not in the direction which would indicate an enhancement in the effectiveness of the ring with increased width. It seems that, once the ring has an area equal to that of the disk, any further increase in its width does not affect the resulting color of the disk.

It was reported in Part I that a ring looks more luminous than a disk of the same intensity in another pair in which the intensities of ring and disk are the same as in the first pair but interchanged. The question arises whether such a reversal of intensities also causes a color difference in the regions of equal intensity. Two pairs of disk and ring in which the area of the ring was the same as that of the disk were presented and the lights were so arranged that in one pair the lower intensity was in the ring and in the other pair in the disk. The two higher intensities in the two pairs amounted both to 360 degrees, the ring of lower intensity was kept at 45 degrees, and the disk of lower intensity was variable. Measurements were made with four Ss. The means of three upper and three lower limits were 54, 71, 83, 86 degrees. These figures indicate that for the same intensity ratio the lower intensity appears as a lighter gray when it is given in the ring than when it is given in the disk. A rather dark gray results from a ratio of 360:45 degrees. In the case of smaller ratios which give rise to lighter grays the differences in color which result when the intensities of ring and disk are interchanged are very much smaller. For an intensity ratio of 2:1 only a difference in luminosity can be discerned.

SUMMARY

It was found that opaque achromatic surface colors are perceived when light of different intensity stimulates adjacent areas on the retina. The achromatic color which is seen in a particular region must be regarded as the result of stimulation received from that region *and* of stimulation from neighboring regions. Although these colors are qualities which are perceived in a given region, they are products of an interaction process, which depends on difference in stimulation in at least two areas. In the absence of a suitable difference in stimulation a color of an entirely different mode of appearance is seen. A single bright region in an otherwise dark field, for instance, looks luminous instead of white, and reducing the light intensity in that region fails to make it look gray; it continues to appear luminous and merely becomes dimmer.

The first steps were taken to investigate quantitatively the rules of this dependence in the simplest case, that of two regions of different intensities of stimulation where one region surrounds the other. The colors which come about under these circumstances depend in close approximation on the *ratios* of the intensities involved and seem independent of the absolute intensity of local stimulation. The region of higher intensity will assume the color white and that of lower intensity will show a gray (or a black) which depends on the intensity ratio of the two regions. The greater the difference in intensity the darker will be the gray which appears in the region of the lower intensity.

It can be shown that a dependence of perceived colors on the ratios of stimulus intensities accounts for the constancy of achromatic colors under varying illumination. Complete constancy would follow from this rule of interaction of two intensities. The fact that measurements of brightness constancy rarely give results which denote complete constancy presents no difficulty for this explanation. These experiments involve interaction between more than two regions of different stimulus intensity.

Apparent Spatial Arrangement

and Perceived Brightness

Julian E. Hochberg and Jacob Beck

Cornell University Yeshiva College

The problems of brightness constancy (e.g., the constancy of perceived object color under different illumination conditions), and of the perceptual constancies in general, arise from the fact that changed sensory stimuli frequently elicit unchanged responses (and vice versa) which follow more closely the variations of distal stimuli (objects) than of the sensory-surface stimulus distributions. This raises difficulties for any formulation of a one-to-one correspondence between stimulus and experience (confusingly called the "constancy hypothesis," [5, p. 86]), which at first sight would seem essential to psychological prediction.

Such findings have been used in attempted ("nativistic") refutation of the constancy hypothesis and its associated stimulus-sensation units of analysis (5), and to demonstrate the importance of nonstimulus organizational "forces." Empiricist "inferential" explanations, on the other hand, retain the constancy hypothesis in *sensation,* and ascribe the obtained discrepancies to the effects of past experience in *perception.* Objections to the nativistic position are: (*a*) some evidence suggests that the accuracy of the perceptual constancies depends on past experience (1); (*b*) no well-defined analytic units have been presented to supplant the old "sensations," and in their absence precise prediction is difficult despite the considerable heuristic value of the more or less intuitive Gestalt "laws." General objections to the empiricist positions have been: (*a*) it is not possible to distinguish between "sensation" and "perception"; (*b*) there is some awkwardness involved in the doctrine of "unconscious inference" and its derivatives, especially when referred to the lower animals in which the constancies appear (7, pp. 605–607); (*c*) any attempt at precise prediction from this viewpoint must await as yet unperformed "ecological surveys" to determine what the past experiences of an organism are likely to have been; (*d*) the constancies also appear to exist without opportunity for past experience (3), and while demonstrated effects of past experience on the constancies do not necessarily refute the Gestalt position, evidence of the reverse seriously injures a thoroughgoing empiricist explanation.

An alternative formulation is appealing: responses may occur in one-to-one correspondence not to what we had previously taken to be the stimuli but to their relationship, without regard to central factors, whether

Reprinted from *Journal of Experimental Psychology,* 1954, 47, 263–266.

of association or organization. In considering this possibility, we do not have to postulate innate knowledge; we need only seek new dimensions for analyzing the physical stimuli which *are* in correspondence with experience (or response). Gestaltists most frequently sought such invariant relationship not in the stimulus distribution, but in the as yet largely unmeasurable psychophysiologically isomorphic cortical processes; however, one may instead direct attention to the reanalysis of the proximal stimulus pattern as do Gibson (2), Helson (4), and Wallach (6).

Thus, Wallach (6) suggests that we may understand brightness percep-

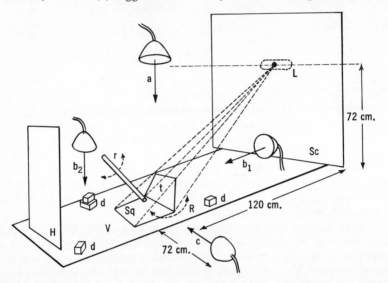

FIG. 1. Apparatus for presenting the same target at different apparent slants and illumination conditions.

tion by taking as the stimulus not the intensity of illumination falling on a given retinal region, but the relationship of the intensities of illumination falling on adjacent regions. The relationship approximated a *ratio* of intensities in the situations he studied; i.e., the stimuli in the perception of brightness appeared to be the ratios of illumination intensities on adjacent areas, rather than the illumination intensities themselves. Thus, if Ss viewed a variable disk surrounded by a ring of 180 illumination intensity units—degrees of episcotister opening—and were asked to match the variable disk to a disk of 90 units surrounded by a ring of 360 units, they set the variable disk to a mean value of 47 units, only 2 units away from the proportionate 4:1 intensity ratio, which would here be $90 \div 360 \times 180$, or 45 units. If this redefinition of the stimulus will explain all of brightness constancy, we can again effect a one-to-one psychophysical formulation of perceived brightness.

The constancy hypothesis was shaken since the same *absolute* stimulus intensities aroused different brightness responses (and vice versa); can conditions also be found in which the same *distributions* or relationships of stimulus intensity arouse different brightness responses? The object of the present experiments was to determine whether a change in the apparent

TABLE 1

RELATIVE APPARENT BRIGHTNESSES OF THE TARGET WITH DIFFERENT
APPARENT POSITIONS AND ILLUMINATION CONDITIONS

| | | | Light Source (Fig. 1) | Ss' Responses | |
| | | | | Trapezoid Brighter | Square Brighter |
Exp.	Group	N			
I	A	6	a	5	0
	B	6	a	6	0
II	C	15	a	14	0
			b_1	0	14
III	D	5	a	5	0
	E	5	b_1	0	5
	F	5	c	0	0

position of a target surface relative to an illumination source results in a change in the perceived brightness of that surface (cf. 7, pp. 600, 612), even though the actual illumination conditions remain constant.

EXPERIMENT I

The apparatus[1] is shown in Fig. 1: the main illumination (100 w.) came from above (a), this being "indicated" to Ss by the shadow distribution on several cubes (d). These "cues" are of considerable importance since, in preliminary experiments, little or no success was achieved without them. The Ss looked monocularly through a reduction screen (Sc) at an upright cardboard trapezoid target (t), covered with Number 8 Hering gray paper, cut so that its retinal image would be the same as that of a square (Sq) lying flat on the black cloth surface (V). All Ss ($N = 13$) reported seeing a horizontal square, whose brightness they were then (Judgment I) asked to match quickly and unanalytically to a scale (H) of Hering gray paper patches (Nos. 1, 3, 5, . . . 19). A round rod, r, ¾ in. in diameter, 22 in. long, painted white for Group A and black for Group B, was then waved behind the target (trying to avoid any cast shadows visible to S). This was kept up for some seconds, as it was difficult not to "see" the horizontal square (Sq) instead of the upright trapezoid (t); indeed, one S was dropped at this point, unable to see the target as upright. The Ss again compared the target's brightness with the gray scale (Judgment II).

The results (Table 1) indicate that the target when apparently upright is reported as brighter than when apparently horizontal. Two questions may, however, be asked: First, while illumination of the rod is not likely to have been responsible for the brightness change since it was black for some Ss and white for others, might not inadvertently cast shadows, or even the motion itself, have been the important factor? Second, if a stimulus is perceived as parallel to the line of regard, it should have a greater apparent area than when perceived as perpendicular to the line of regard (Fig.

[1] Modified from one devised by Professor J. J. Gibson to study the relationship between perceived slant and perceived form.

1); may not the lower reported brightness in the former case be due to the smaller amount of *retinal* illumination per unit of *perceived* surface? The next two experiments were undertaken to test the first question by varying the means whereby the apparent shift in the target position is brought about, and to test the second by changing the direction of illumination while, of course, holding the apparent size change constant.

EXPERIMENT II

The procedure of Exp. I was modified here in three ways: (*a*) When attempting to make the target appear upright, it was moved through short horizontal arcs (*R*) instead of having a rod (*r*) waved behind it. (*b*) The 15 Ss (Group C) of this experiment ran through the procedure with the illumination coming from above (*a*), and then repeated the experiment with the illumination coming horizontally from in front of the trapezoid (*b₁*, Fig. 1), with a concealed supplementary source (*b₂*) to remove the shadow of the target (*t*) from the cues. (*c*) The Ss were alternated in each part of the experiment as to the condition to which they were first subjected, the upright target or the horizontal square.

The results (Table 1) under illumination from above are the same as those in Exp. I: when seen upright, the target appears brighter than when seen flat. Under illumination from in front (*b₁*), the results are the reverse: with horizontal illumination, the target appears less bright when seen as upright than when flat. Since the change in perceived area consequent upon the change in perceived target position would be the same both when illumination comes from above and from the front, we can reject the amount-of-illumination-per-perceived-surface-area as a determining factor. This suggests that the brightness changes are due either largely or solely to the perceived change in target position with respect to the direction of illumination; this is supported by the results of the next experiment.

EXPERIMENT III

Two changes were here made in the procedures of Exp. I: (*a*) The target was changed from flat to upright appearance by shifting from monocular vision to binocular vision (through a larger hole, *L*). (*b*) Illumination was maintained from above (*a*) as in Exp. I, for Group D (*N* = 5), from in front horizontally (*b₁*) as in the second part of Exp. II, for Group E (*N* = 5), and horizontally from the side (*c*), for Group F (*N* = 5).

The results of Groups D and E show the same changes in brightness as were found in Exp. II. There is no evidence of any perceived brightness changes in Group F, in which there is no change in perceived orientation of the target with respect to the illumination, since the illumination is parallel to the target surface in either of the two perceived positions. These results again suggest that the brightness changes are obtained due to the change in the relationship of the perceived direction of illumination and the perceived position of the surface it falls upon.

DISCUSSION

In general, the results of these experiments suggest that when a surface of a given illumination is perceived as being perpendicular to the direction of illumination, it appears less bright than when the same surface, with the same illumination, seems parallel to the direction of illumination. How does this fit the various approaches to brightness constancy?

A simple one-to-one correspondence of illumination and perceived brightness must as usual be rejected, since the same stimulus arouses different responses. Likewise, any attempt to bring the perception of brightness into one-to-one correspondence with illumination *ratios* is inadequate, since differing responses are here obtained with the same illumination relationships. Either we must view Wallach's ratio formulation (or, for that matter, Helson's "adaptation level" explanation) as incomplete, or hold that there are at least two different kinds of brightness constancy, one bound to the illumination conditions and the other not, an unparsimonious position. The general viewpoint may, however, be retained (as may also a Gestalt organizational one) if the determinants of perceived brightness include not only the peripheral illumination relationships but the "cues" to spatial position and the illumination direction (cf. 7, p. 612). The empiricist or "inferential" position, disconcertingly enough, seems well able to explain the findings, at least by hindsight: thus, to reflect a given amount of light to the eye, a surface parallel to the incident illumination would have to have a higher albedo or brighter object color than would a surface perpendicular to the incident illumination, and would therefore be "inferred" to be brighter.

SUMMARY

In order to determine whether perceived brightnesses can be brought into one-to-one correspondence with stimulus illumination *relationships* any more than with absolute illumination intensities, Ss made judgments of the brightness of a target which, under constant or controlled conditions of illumination, was made to appear to be either perpendicular or parallel to the apparent direction of illumination. Since substantially the same illumination distributions produced different perceived brightnesses, analyses of brightness constancy in terms of stimulus illuminations cannot at present be considered complete explanations.

REFERENCES

1. Brunswik, E. Über Farben-, Grossen- und Gestaltkonstanz in der Jugend. In H. Volkelt (Ed.), *Bericht über den XI. Kongress exp. Psychol.* Jena: Fischer, 1930. Pp. 52–56.

2. GIBSON, J. J. *The perception of the visual world.* Cambridge: Houghton Mifflin, 1950.
3. GOGEL, W. C., & HESS, E. H. A study of color constancy in the newly hatched chick by means of an innate color preference. *Amer. Psychologist*, 1951, **6**, 282. (Abstract)
4. HELSON, H. Adaptation-level as frame of reference for prediction of psychological data. *Amer. J. Psychol.*, 1947, **60**, 1–29.
5. KOFFKA, K. *Principles of Gestalt psychology.* New York: Harcourt, Brace, 1935.
6. WALLACH, H. Brightness constancy and the nature of achromatic colors. *J. exp. Psychol.*, 1948, **38**, 310–324.
7. WOODWORTH, R. S. *Experimental psychology.* New York: Holt, 1938.

The Effect of Separation Between Test and Inducing Fields on Brightness Constancy [1]

Bruce Dunn and H. Leibowitz

University of Wisconsin

Historically (Hering, 1920; Woodworth & Schlosberg, 1954), discussions of the mechanisms underlying brightness constancy have considered the possible role of simultaneous brightness contrast. Such analyses have been hindered, however, by the lack of an unequivocable specification of the conditions under which contrast occurs experimentally (Graham, 1934). More recently, a number of studies on contrast have appeared which provide a more precise specification of contrast and which permit consideration of the contribution of contrast to brightness constancy. Diamond (1953, 1955) and others (Heinemann, 1955; Leibowitz, Mote, & Thurlow, 1953) determined that the contrast effect between two simultaneously visible fields is primarily unidirectional. The brighter field (referred to as the inducing field) inhibits the dimmer (referred to as the test field), while the dimmer field has little if any effect on the brighter. Utilizing this specification, it has been determined that although some constancy is present in the absence of contrast as here defined, the presence of contrast markedly increases the tendency toward constancy. Such results support the assumption that contrast is indeed a major variable contributing to the phenomenon of brightness constancy. The feasibility of this assumption was strengthened

Reprinted from *Journal of Experimental Psychology* 1961, 61, 505–507.

[1] Supported in part by Grant M1090 from the National Institute of Mental Health of the National Institutes of Health, United States Public Health Service. Computations were aided by facilities supplied by the University of Wisconsin Numerical Analysis Laboratory with funds provided by the Wisconsin Alumni Research Foundation.

by two subsequent experiments in which reduction of exposure duration increased both contrast (Chinetti, 1957) and constancy effects (Leibowitz & Chinetti, 1957; Leibowitz, Chinetti, & Sidowski, 1956). The purpose of the present study is to provide a further test of the relationship between contrast and constancy by manipulation of the separation between test and inducing fields, a procedure which has previously been shown to result in a decrease in simultaneous brightness contrast (Leibowitz, Mote, & Thurlow, 1953).

APPARATUS AND PROCEDURE

The apparatus has previously been described in detail (Leibowitz, Myers, & Chinetti, 1955). The S is seated in front of the partition dividing two adjacent, equal sized chambers. In the left chamber a square "grey" test field of 36.2% reflectance (No. 12 Munsell Grey) subtending a visual angle of 1° at a viewing distance of 6 ft. is viewed under various levels of illuminance produced by sources not visible to S. In the right chamber, which is otherwise dark, S views a photometric field of the same dimensions and located in a position comparable to that of the test field. The S's task is to adjust the luminance of the photometric field so that it matches the test field. An inducing field is provided by an 86% reflectance "white" subtending 6° on each side and placed just above and contiguous to the test field (designated as 0° separation), and at separations of 6° and 12° between the nearest edges of the fields. The S observed binocularly at all times with unrestricted head and eye movements. The walls and floors of the chambers were painted "flat" black (reflectance 1.78%).

Data were obtained from 16 Ss, volunteers from elementary psychology classes, under three levels of illuminance (−1.75, −0.16, and 2.44 log

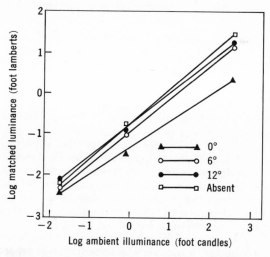

FIG. 1. Log matched luminance of the comparison field as a function of the log illuminance incident on the test stimuli with separation between test and inducing fields as parameter. (On this plot, a slope of unity indicates agreement with the "additivity law of luminance." A slope of zero represents the "law of brightness constancy.")

ft-c) in the absence of an inducing field, and with the inducing field present at three separations. Order of presentation of illuminance level and inducing field conditions was determined by counterbalanced squares.

RESULTS

The mean data for all Ss are presented in Table 1 and plotted as the log of the mean matched luminance as a function of the log ambient illuminance in Fig. 1. On this plot, a horizontal line represents a prediction in terms of brightness constancy which assumes that the same match would be obtained between the test and photometric fields at all levels of illuminance. At the other theoretical extreme the additivity law of luminance, under which perceived brightness is determined solely by the quantity of incident luminous energy, is here represented by a straight line of unit slope. As is typical in such studies, the matches lie between the two theoretical extremes. However, the extent to which the data approach the theoretical brightness constancy function is related to the separation between the test and inducing field. For adjacent test and inducing fields both contrast, as indicated by a shift of the entire function to lower matched luminance values, and constancy, as indicated by a lesser slope (0.67) are greatest. With increasing separation and in the absence of the inducing field, both contrast and constancy decrease. The slopes of the functions for 6° and 12° of separation and in the absence of the inducing field are 0.84, 0.85, and 0.88, respectively. The most marked effect of separation occurs when comparing the adjacent inducing field with 6° of separation. Separation beyond 6° as in the previous contrast study, has only a negligible effect. Analysis of variance indicated that both luminance and separation are significant at beyond the .001 level.

DISCUSSION

The results of the present experiment are in agreement with the assumption that simultaneous contrast can play a significant role in brightness constancy. This reasoning is based on the assumption that when two behavioral measures covary, their underlying mechanisms share common elements. It has previously been demonstrated that both contrast and constancy increase with reduction of exposure duration, and with an increase of the luminance of the inducing field relative to that of the test field. The present study represents another such measure of covariance, i.e., a decrease in both measures with separation between test and inducing fields.

Such results, however, imply only that simultaneous contrast is *one* of the variables contributing to constancy as some tendency toward constancy is observed in the absence of contrast, e.g., the condition in the present study in which the inducing field was absent. There are a number of possibilities. Changes in pupil diameter could be expected to decrease the difference in perceived brightness of objects viewed under different illuminance levels. This would tend to decrease the slopes of the matched lumi-

TABLE 1

MEAN LOG MATCHED LUMINANCE IN FOOT-LAMBERTS AS A FUNCTION
OF ILLUMINANCE LEVEL WITH SEPARATION BETWEEN TEST
AND INDUCING FIELD AS THE PARAMETER

Separation in Degrees of Arc	Log Ambient Illuminance (Foot-Candles)		
	−1.75	−0.16	2.44
0	−2.42	−1.45	0.44
6	−2.32	−0.99	1.24
12	−2.19	−0.92	1.26
Inducing field absent	−2.25	−0.78	1.41

nance-ambient illuminance functions, and to induce some tendency toward constancy. With familiar objects, especially outside of the laboratory, memory and context probably play an important role (Bolles, Hulicka, & Hanly, 1959; Hering, 1920; Woodworth & Schlosberg, 1954). The particular significance of contrast is due to the fact that it can be readily demonstrated in lower forms both behaviorally (von Buddenbrock, 1952) and electrophysiologically (Ratliff, Miller, & Hartline, 1958). Thus, contrast would appear, by virtue of its biological generality, to be a basic mechanism subserving the brightness constancy phenomenon.

SUMMARY

Luminance matches were obtained between a 1° square "grey" test field viewed under various levels of illuminance and a photometric field of the same size. Data were obtained with the test field viewed against a "black" background, and with a "white" inducing field introduced at various degrees of separation from the test field.

The tendency toward brightness constancy was observed under all experimental conditions, but increased markedly as the separation between test and inducing fields was decreased.

The results are interpreted as supporting the point of view that simultaneous brightness contrast is one of the important mechanisms underlying the phenomenon of brightness constancy.

REFERENCES

Bolles, R. C., Hulicka, I. M., & Hanly, B. Colour judgment as a function of stimulus conditions and memory color. *Canad. J. Psychol.*, 1959, **13**, 175–185.

Chinetti, P. J. The effect of reduced exposure duration on simultaneous brightness contrast. Unpublished doctoral dissertation, University of Wisconsin, 1957.

Diamond, A. L. Foveal simultaneous brightness contrast as a function of inducing and test-field luminances. *J. exp. Psychol.*, 1953, **45**, 304–314.

Diamond, A. L. Foveal simultaneous contrast as a function of inducing-field area. *J. exp. Psychol.*, 1955, **50**, 144–152.

GRAHAM, C. H. Vision: III. Some neural correlations. In C. Murchison
(Ed.), *Handbook of general experimental psychology*. Worcester, Mass.:
Clark Univer. Press, 1934.

HEINEMANN, E. G. Simultaneous brightness induction as a function of in-
ducing- and test-field luminances. *J. exp. Psychol.*, 1955, **50**, 89–96.

HERING, E. *Grundzüge der Lehre vom Lichtsinn*. Berlin: Springer, 1920.

LEIBOWITZ, H., & CHINETTI, P. Effect of reduced exposure duration on
brightness constancy. *J. exp. Psychol.*, 1957, **54**, 49–53.

LEIBOWITZ, H., CHINETTI, P., & SIDOWSKI, J. Exposure duration as a variable in perceptual constancy. *Science*, 1956, **123**, 668–669.

LEIBOWITZ, H., MOTE, F. A., & THURLOW, W. R. Simultaneous contrasts as a
function of separation between test and inducing fields. *J. exp. Psychol.*,
1953, **46**, 453–456.

LEIBOWITZ, H., MYERS, N. A., & CHINETTI, P. The role of simultaneous contrast in brightness constancy. *J. exp. Psychol.*, 1955, **50**, 15–18.

RATLFF, F., MILLER, W. H., & HARTLINE, H. K. Neural interaction in the
eye and the integration of receptor activity. *Ann. NY Acad. Sci.*, 1958,
74, 210–222.

VON BUDDENBROCK, W. *Vergleichende Physiologie*. Band I. *Sinnesphysi-
ologie*. Basel: Birkhäuser, 1952.

WOODWORTH, R. S., & SCHLOSBERG, H. *Experimental psychology*. (Rev. ed.)
New York: Holt, 1954.

Complexities of Perceived Brightness

Dorothea Jameson and Leo M. Hurvich[1]

It is quite generally recognized that if the amount of light falling on a
given surface is doubled, and the intensity of the retinal light image is
thereby doubled, the apparent brightness may be perceived to increase by
an amount that is quite different from the twofold increase in stimulus
luminance. The precise relation between perceived brightness and stimulus
luminance has been extensively investigated by the various experimental
procedures used to develop psychological scales of sensory attributes, and
on the basis of such studies, perceived brightness has come to be described
as a visual attribute that increases with the logarithm or with some power
(less than 1.0) of the stimulus luminance (1). This psychophysical relation
is of concern to psychophysicists, photometrists, colorimetrists, illuminating
engineers, and scientists interested specifically in sensory mechanisms.

Others, especially psychologists, who are primarily concerned with the
visual perception of real objects emphasize a different aspect of the problem of apparent brightness. They point to the relative constancy of apparent
brightness of visually perceived objects that is found in spite of tremendous changes in the intensity of retinal (proximal) stimulation: White snow

Reprinted from *Science*, 1961, 133, 174–179.

[1] D. Jameson is a research scientist in the department of psychology and Dr.
Hurvich is professor of psychology at New York University, New York.

continues to look bright and black coal continues to look dark even through a range of illumination so great that the coal in the high illumination may actually reflect more light to the eye than does the snow at the low extreme of illumination. Consequently we find a second group of investigations concerned not with the precise manner in which brightness increases with luminance but, rather, with the degree to which perceived brightness remains independent of stimulus luminance—that is, with the problem of brightness constancy (2).

BRIGHTNESS CONSTANCY

In experimental analyses of brightness constancy, brightness matches are usually made between a single test object viewed under various conditions of illumination and surround and a separate, continuously variable comparison, or matching, stimulus that is seen in a constant surround. Independent controls for test and surround stimulation may be provided, as in the classical experiments of Hess and Pretori (3) and those of Wallach (4), or test and surround may be varied together by a single control for the over-all level of field illumination. The results usually fall somewhere between two extremes: If a so-called "reduction screen" is used for viewing the test stimulus, so that only the focal area to be matched is visible in otherwise dark surroundings, apparent brightness increases with increase in illumination, and matching luminance is directly proportional to luminance of the test stimulus ("stimulus matches"); if, on the other hand, the reduction screen is removed and the total scene is made visible, brightness matches to the same focal area may then remain constant, or nearly so, in spite of increases in illumination of the over-all scene—that is, matching luminance remains constant and independent of test-stimulus luminance. This tendency away from stimulus matches and toward brightness constancy is sometimes described as a perceptual regression from the proximal stimulus toward the real object (5). Some investigators explain it by saying that perceived brightness is a judgment that is influenced both by the intensity of light stimulation reflected from the surface of the object to the retina and by a "correction factor" that takes into account the over-all level of illumination incident on the various objects in the visual field. This "correction factor" or "allowance for the illumination" presumably compensates for the changes in stimulus intensity, and the perception thus remains constant (6).

Another proposal that has been made to account for the tendency toward brightness constancy is the suggestion that perceived brightness is not a matter of interpretation, but a direct response controlled by the ratios of the various luminances in the total visual field rather than by the luminance of any given focal area (4). Since the reflectances (or transmittances) of all objects in the field remain constant, their luminance ratios relative to one another are also invariant as over-all scene illumination is increased, and consequently, in this view, the perceived brightnesses of the various objects in the field remain constant and independent of level of illumination.

A careful study of the earlier data suggests that neither the "interpretation" hypothesis nor the "constant-ratio" hypothesis can adequately explain the variety of brightness phenomena observed, and the experiments discussed below will make clear why this is so.

TABLE 1

LUMINANCE MATCHES TO INDIVIDUAL AREAS OF THE TEST PATTERN
FOR THREE LEVELS OF OVER-ALL ILLUMINATION. MEAN
LUMINANCE DATA AND VARIABILITY FOR
THREE SUBJECTS.

Focal area of test pattern	Log photometric luminance (mlam) of focal area	Mean log luminance (mlam) of matching field
Center	0.18	1.47 ± 0.10
	0.47	1.61 ± 0.20
	1.28	1.78 ± 0.10
Right	0.08	1.37 ± 0.08
	0.37	1.44 ± 0.14
	1.18	1.61 ± 0.14
Upper	$\bar{1}.78$	1.08 ± 0.14
	0.07	1.18 ± 0.17
	0.88	1.37 ± 0.17
Left	$\bar{1}.15$	0.54 ± 0.10
	$\bar{1}.44$	0.45 ± 0.20
	0.26	0.55 ± 0.10
Lower	$\bar{2}.74$	0.25 ± 0.17
	$\bar{1}.04$	$0.\overline{22} ± 0.20$
	$\bar{1}.85$	$\bar{1}.78 ± 0.33$

MATCHING APPARENT LUMINANCES

In our experiments (7), a pattern of squares of different luminances (see Fig. 1) comprised the visual scene, and each square differed from its neighbor and from the background by a constant ratio. The maximal ratio of focal-area luminances within the test pattern was 27:1 for the brightest (center) to the darkest (lower) of the square areas. The test pattern was projected on a screen 110 centimeters from the subject's eyes. The limiting boundaries of the rectangular illuminated test field subtended visual angles of 11°50′ by 10°20′, and each side of the individual squares of the test pattern subtended a visual angle of 3°. The over-all level of illumination of this scene was varied in three steps through a range of 1.1 log units.

With the total pattern visible, the subject matched the apparent brightness of each square area within the pattern at each of the three levels of illumination. He made these matches by successive inspection, by looking first at the designated focal area of the test pattern on the screen located to his right and then at the matching field contained within a shielded cubicle directly in front of him. The matching field was an illuminated

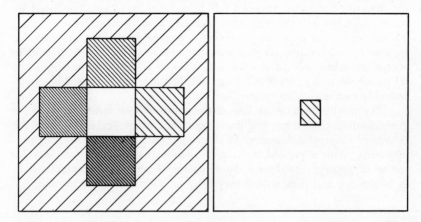

FIG. 1. Outline of test pattern (left) and matching field (right). Striations of test pattern are used in the figure only to illustrate density differences of different individual areas.

rectangle (1°45' by 2°24') of continuously variable luminance, located about 41 centimeters from his eyes and centered in an illuminated surround (tungsten illumination, 60 mlam) that subtended an angle of about 145° at the eyes. Matches to the individual focal areas were made in random sequence, and the over-all level of scene illumination was also randomized. Results were obtained for three subjects, each of whom repeated all matches in a second experimental session.

RESULTS

The averaged results for the luminance matches for both sessions and for all subjects are presented in Table 1 and in Figs. 2 through 6. The means are geometric averages—that is, averages of the logarithm of the luminance values. Each of the figures contains the mean data (open circles) for a single focal area of the test pattern and shows the relation between the calibrated luminance of that area of the test pattern (plotted as the abscissa) and its apparent luminance as measured by the matching luminance (plotted as the ordinate). Each figure also shows the alternative relations to be expected if (i) apparent brightness were constant and independent of increase in luminance (the law of brightness constancy), or (ii) apparent brightness increased according to some invariant law with the luminance of the retinal image in the focal area (the law of retinal stimulus). Figures 2, 3, and 4, for the center, right, and upper squares, respectively, show that for these three areas apparent brightness increases with increase in stimulus luminance but the matching luminance increases at a rate that falls between the rates predicted by the stimulus law and the constancy law. On the other hand, the mean data for the left square, shown in Fig. 5, closely approximate the function predicted by the law of brightness constancy. Finally, for the lower (and the darkest) test area, Fig. 6 shows that

the apparent-luminance matches fall below the luminances predicted by
the stimulus law and the brightness constancy law. Here we have the paradoxical result that apparent brightness *decreases* as stimulus luminance is
increased. Conservative skeptics who find the result of Fig. 6 difficult to
accept are asked only to observe, say, a bottle of india ink or a standard
telephone set under dim illumination and then note the increased blackness
when the overhead lights are switched on.

The results contained in Figs. 2 through 6 make it clear that no single
generalization concerning brightness constancy is applicable to all of the
objects of different reflectances in any single visual scene or stimulus configuration. With a general increase in illumination, light objects may increase in apparent brightness, intermediate objects may remain constant
in brightness, and dark objects may become still darker in appearance.

FINDINGS VERSUS HYPOTHESES

How do such results square with the explanations of brightness perception referred to above? If the experimentally determined luminance
matches depart from the law of simple stimulus proportionality because the
subject is applying a "correction" for level of illumination, then the data
of Figs. 2–4 imply that he is systematically under-correcting, and consequently perceiving some increase in brightness with the general increase
in illumination. The data of Fig. 5, however, imply, on such an analysis,
that the subject's "correction" is nearly perfect: the apparent brightness
shows almost perfect constancy as the level of illumination is increased.
But if we use Fig. 6 as an index, the subject is presumably applying an
over-correction for illumination, since this area of the test pattern appears
increasingly *darker* as the level of illumination is *increased*. When we remember that the subject is viewing a single test pattern, it hardly seems
likely that he is applying a different correction for illumination to each of
the different areas of the pattern. The concept obviously loses any usefulness it might have had as an explanatory principle once we recognize that

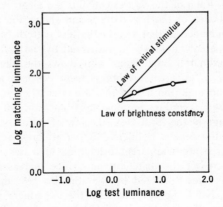

FIG. 2. Relation between photometric test luminance and matching luminance for center square of test pattern.

the "illumination correction" would have to be multivalued for a single scene.

We run into similar difficulties with the hypothesis that invariant luminance ratios yield constant perceived brightnesses. The luminances of the various areas within the test pattern used in our experiments maintain invariant ratios with respect to one another as the illumination of the whole field is varied, and yet only one of the five areas remains constant in perceived brightness.

Thus, the two most frequently cited explanations for brightness constancy phenomena fail in this situation: Both of these explanations require that all areas of the test pattern behave in the same way, and hence they do not account for the observed result that each individual area of the total scene shows its own characteristic and different dependence on stimulus luminance.

An important consequence of these characteristic variations can be seen from the combined data as plotted in Fig. 7. Here the graph shows the relation between the stimulus luminance and the apparent (matching) luminance for all five focal areas of the test pattern at each of the three levels

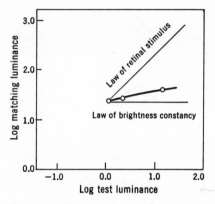

FIG. 3. Relation between photometric test luminance and matching luminance for right square of test pattern.

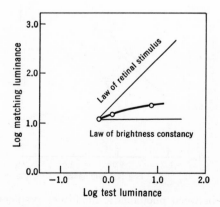

FIG. 4. Relation between photometric test luminance and matching luminance for upper square of test pattern.

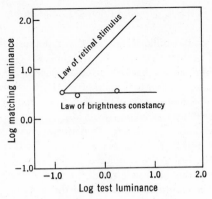

FIG. 5.   Relation between photometric test luminance and matching luminance for left square of test pattern.

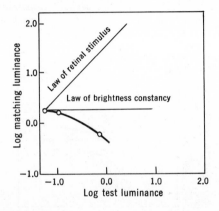

FIG. 6.   Relation between photometric test luminance and matching luminance for lower square of test pattern.

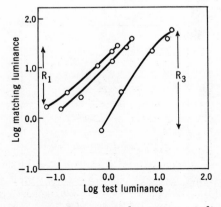

FIG. 7.   Relation between photometric luminance gradient of test pattern and apparent (matching) luminance gradient for three levels of general illumination.

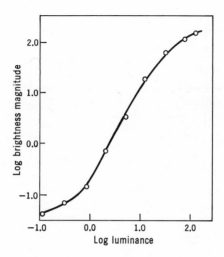

FIG. 8. Relation between luminance of matching field and estimations of perceived brightness magnitude.

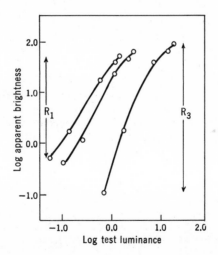

FIG. 9. Relation between photometric luminance gradient of test pattern and apparent brightness gradient for three levels of general illumination.

of general illumination. Although the calibrated photometric gradient of this stimulus pattern is identical for all three levels, the *apparent* luminance gradient increases with increase in the level of over-all illumination. This effect is obvious from the figure if one simply compares the extent labeled R_1 (the range of apparent luminance for the lowest level) with that labeled R_3 (the corresponding range when the over-all level has been increased by 1.1 log units). The photometric range of stimulus luminance is constant

TABLE 2

RELATION BETWEEN LUMINANCE AND MAGNITUDE OF PERCEIVED BRIGHTNESS
OF MATCHING FIELD WITH CONSTANT, UNIFORM LUMINANCE OF
THE SURROUND. MEAN RESULTS FOR THREE SUBJECTS.

Log luminance (mlam)	Mean log brightness magnitude
$\bar{1}.07$	$\bar{2}.6332$
$\bar{1}.51$	$\bar{2}.8554$
$\bar{1}.94$	$\bar{1}.1662$
0.30	$\bar{1}.8554$
0.70	0.5366
1.09	1.2796
1.51	1.7835
1.89	2.0538
2.11	2.1844

at all three levels of illumination: $\log L_{max}$ minus $\log L_{min}$ equals 1.44. For the apparent luminance matches, however, $\log L_{max}$ minus $\log L_{min}$ at the lowest level of illumination is less than the photometric range and equal to 1.22; at the intermediate level it is equal to 1.39; and at the highest level of illumination the apparent range exceeds the photometric range and $\log L_{max}$ minus $\log L_{min}$ equals 2.00.

Could these results simply be an artifact of the experimental conditions? Our yardstick for apparent luminance of the various areas of the test pattern is the matching luminance of the comparison field, and this field is itself seen in its own bright surround. We know that the relation between units of stimulus luminance and units of perceived brightness is not usually a simple one of direct proportionality. We also know that this relation is itself dependent upon the particular visual circumstances under which it is determined—that is, level of bright-adaptation, nature of surround illumination, and so forth (8, 9). Since our concern here is with apparent brightness per se, it becomes critical to determine directly the perceived brightnesses of the matching stimuli that were used to specify the apparent luminances of the various areas of the test pattern in these experiments.

PERCEIVED BRIGHTNESS AND LUMINANCE OF STIMULUS FIELD

Consequently, the relation between perceived brightness and the luminance of the matching stimulus field was determined, for the same three individuals who made the apparent luminance matches, by a method of subjective magnitude estimation. In this psychological scaling procedure, the apparent brightness of the illuminated surround (60 mlam), which remained constant, was assigned an arbitrary brightness magnitude value of 100. With this value for the surround as a standard of comparison, the subjects were required to assign estimates of numerical magnitude to the apparent brightness of the stimulus matching field as the luminance of this field was varied in a series of nine steps through a luminance range of three log units.

The geometric means ($n = 12$) of the magnitude estimates for the three individuals are given in Table 2, and the functional relation is plotted in logarithmic units in Fig. 8. The curve has been fitted by inspection to the plotted points representing the mean data obtained by the scaling procedure. The slope of the function is quite steep throughout most of the range, becoming less steep at the high levels where the stimulus luminance exceeds that of the surround, and also leveling off at the very low luminance levels at which an appearance of "maximal blackness" is approached.

With the subjective magnitude function of Fig. 8, we now have the means at hand for "calibrating" in units of apparent brightness the luminance units of the matching experiments, and Fig. 9, based on this conversion, shows the relation between the apparent brightness gradient of the scene and the photometric luminance. Correlative with Fig. 7, the extent labeled R_1 represents the range of apparent brightness from the darkest to the brightest area of the test pattern for the lowest level of over-all illumination, and R_3, the corresponding range for the highest of the three illumination levels. The expansion in range of perceived brightness is obvious, and it occurs because of a dependence on luminance that is opposite in sign for the different areas of the test pattern: Whereas the brightest area gets brighter as luminance is increased, with the same increase in illumination, the darkest area in the configuration becomes progressively blacker.

IMPLICATIONS

The data expressed in brightness units confirm the conclusion already drawn from the data on luminance matches. We cannot accept the suggestion that there is a simple equivalence between fixed ratios of stimulus luminance and fixed ratios of apparent brightness, with brightness constancy resulting when the stimulus ratios are invariant. The data of Fig. 9 are in direct conflict with such a hypothesis.

The results have some interesting implications for the alternative "interpretation" or "correction factor" hypothesis, which requires that an observer be able to take into account the level of illumination. The data of Fig. 9 make it clear that even in the absence of "secondary cues," such as penumbras, highlight flecks, and so on, there is indeed a perceptual basis for differentiating between high and low illumination levels in terms of the difference in brightness gradients at the different levels (10). But to assume that the gradient discrimination could serve as a correction factor for illumination level and yield a result of perceived brightness constancy would be both circular and absurd, since the difference in brightness gradients at the different levels is itself based upon departures from brightness constancy in both the brightening and darkening directions.

It is difficult, furthermore, to see how the different brightness ranges could be accounted for in terms of Helson's (11) quantitative formulation of adaptation-level theory, which states, in essence, that the zero of organic functions shifts with changing conditions, thereby preserving invariant relations between the stimulus field and the organism. Presumably, in the experiments reported here, the adaptation luminance was approximately equal to the luminance of the focal area for which complete brightness constancy was most closely approximated for the three levels of over-all illumination. Relative to this adaptation luminance for constant perceived brightness, however, the photometric luminances of the remaining areas of the test pattern and of the background remain in constant ratio with respect both to the adaptation level and to each other. Unless one resorts either to ad hoc manipulation of the constants in Helson's quantitative adaptation-level formulation or to a systematic exploration of what he calls the residual terms of his general formula, we do not see how consideration of "adaptation level" alone can account for the fact that both the lighter and darker focal areas depart from the adaptation level in apparent brightness by different amounts at the different levels of illumination.

The opponent-colors formulation that we ourselves have been exploring in comparable experiments concerned with the *chromatic* aspects of perceived color (9, 12) assumes that the perceptual response in any focal area will be a function of a number of variables: (i) the focal stimulation per se; (ii) the momentary sensitivity of the responding mechanism; and (iii) the ongoing physiological activities in the focal area that are not directly determined by the focal stimulation. These ongoing activities include spontaneous events, which would presumably be of significance at near-threshold stimulus levels, and usually also include induced activities that depend on immediately preceding stimulation of the focal area, or on induced activities dependent on simultaneous stimulation of the nonfocal, surround areas, or on both. The latter two factors are clearly involved in the ordinary brightness contrast and constancy situations, of which the experiments discussed here are an example. The general nature of induced effects has been shown to be one of antagonism and proportionality. Illumination of an area surrounding a focal area induces blackness in the focal area, and in proportion to the magnitude of the surround excitation. The relative effectiveness of a constant blackness increment (or brightness decrement) in a focal area is small where the direct response to the focal stimulus is large, and the induction increment becomes progressively more significant as the direct focal response decreases in magnitude. This concept of opponent spatial interaction at the physiological response level accounts for the perception of increasing blackness with increasing illumination of the surround—a phenomenon that cannot be accounted for in terms of adaptation or sensitivity changes alone. The physiological, opponent induction concept derives from both Hering (13) and Mach (14). The perceptual effects of such induced response activities have long been obvious in unusual phenomena such as Mach rings, as well as in the commonplace observation that dark objects definitely become "blacker" as the room illumination is increased from an initially "dim" level; and quantitative results of the sort reported here for a relatively complex stimulus pattern are actually predictable from the classical experiments with simple infield-surround field configurations of the sort first reported by Hess and Pretori (3) and from the shadowed illumination experiments of Helson (15). Direct evidence for the physiological basis or opponent induction processes is more recent, and is beautifully demonstrated in the work of Hartline and Ratliff (16) on the electrophysiological responses recorded from the eye of *Limulus*. The systematic, physiologically based, visual response relations involved in contrast and constancy situations need to be more fully explored and understood before we shall be able to deal with the nonspecific "judgmental" and "interpretive" processes that also influence our perceptions of real objects in the natural environment.

REFERENCES AND NOTES

1. S. S. Stevens and E. H. Galanter, *J. Exptl. Psychol.* **54**, 377 (1957); R. M. Hanes, *ibid.* **39**, 719 (1949).
2. D. Katz, *The World of Colour*, R. B. MacLeod and C. W. Fox, trans. (Routledge and Kegan Paul, London, 1935); K. Koffka. *Principles of Gestalt Psychology* (Harcourt Brace, New York, 1935).
3. C. Hess and H. Pretori, *Arch. Ophthalmol. Graef's* **40**, 1 (1894).
4. H. Wallach, *J. Exptl. Psychol.* **38**, 310 (1948).
5. R. H. Thouless, *British J. Psychol.* **22**, 1 (1931–32).
6. R. S. Woodworth and H. Schlosberg, *Experimental Psychology* (Holt, New York, 1954).
7. The research project of which this study forms a part is being supported by grants from the National Science Foundation and the National Institutes of Health.
8. J. C. Stevens and S. S. Stevens, *Office Naval Research Symposium Rep. No. ACR-30* (1958), p. 41; R. G. Hopkinson, *Nature* **179**, 1026 (1957).
9. D. Jameson and L. M. Hurvich, *J. Opt. Soc. Am.* **49**, 890 (1959).
10. A recent report by Beck in which he used pattern textures of two different lightnesses showed that subjects were able to make judgments of changes in illumination Beck was, however, unable to specify a stimulus correlate of the illumination judgment [J. Beck, *J. Exptl. Psychol.* **58**, 267 (1959)].
11. H. Helson, in *Psychology: Study of a Science*, S. Koch, Ed. (McGraw-Hill, New York, 1959), vol. 1, p. 565.
12. L. M. Hurvich and D. Jameson, *Psychol. Rev.* **64**, 384 (1957).
13. E. Hering, *Grundzüge der Lehre von Lichtsinn* (Springer, Berlin, 1920).
14. E. Mach, *Sitzber. Akad. Wiss. Wien, Math. naturw. Kl. Abt.* **II 52**, 303 (1865).
15. H. Helson, *J. Opt. Soc. Am.* **33**, 555 (1943).
16. H. K. Hartline and F. Ratliff, *J. Gen. Physiol.* **41**, 1049 (1958).

PART FOUR

Short-Term Memory

There is general agreement among psychologists that learning is a fundamental process in an organism's adjustment to his environment. Despite this basic position, learning remains the source of some of our most profound theoretical disagreements. It continues to be the proverbial elephant surveyed by the blind men, each inspecting a different aspect, and each conjecturing a beast of a different appearance. Unfortunate as this is, disagreement about the central processes of an area of inquiry is not unique to psychology; it is found from philosophy to physics, and from the arts to astronomy.

One factor contributing to this elephantine problem is the measurement of learning. Since we have no way of getting a direct measure of learning, we of necessity resort to the measurement of performance. That is, if a person emits a response that he was to have learned, we assume that he learned it. If he doesn't emit the response, we are left with the question of whether he did not learn it, learned it and forgot it, or learned it but is just not emitting it for some reason. Thus, if forgetting begins at once, the measure of performance underestimates the amount of learning that occurred.

Until recently there has been little understanding of the extent to which rapid forgetting does happen. Students are continually confronted with the fact that much of what they learn is unavailable at some later time, and since Ebbinghaus (in 1885) psychologists have accepted the conclusion that there is a sharp decline in retention over time. The interpretations of why this occurs vary, however, as they do for learning itself. Even elephants forget, and probably for much the same reasons we do.

One position (on human forgetting, at least) holds that, since we are less likely to remember something as it recedes into the past, forgetting is a function of time, and therefore there is some kind of decay, perhaps physiological or neurological, which accounts for it. Another position espouses an interference theory; that is, what we already know interacts and interferes with the retention of the newly learned material. Other things being equal (the objective of controlled experiments), the more one knows, the more likely this information is to interfere with remembering newly learned material. Thus, learning a list of 100 nonsense syllables decreases the probability of your remembering another 50 that are to be learned. This phenomenon bears the forbidding label of proactive inhibition (PI). The companion to this is a backward-working effect—that is, learning the extra 50 decreases the probability that you will remember the initial 100. This phenomenon bears the somewhat similar, hence the now less forbidding, label of retroactive inhibition (RI). The apocryphal lament of the Professor of Ichthyology at Stanford University illustrates this: every time he learned the name of a student in his class, he forgot the name of a fish.

If we are to discover how forgetting occurs, we need measures of what is remembered at various intervals after learning has happened. One problem in obtaining these measures has been the uncontrolled rehearsal by the subjects; that is, after having some item presented, the subject probably repeats it to himself (rehearses it) before he is tested for retention. These rehearsals act as additional learning trials, and either strengthen the learning (habit strength) or impede forgetting, or both. The Petersons, among others, found a resolution to this problem, and, as so often happens when a promising procedure is reported, sparked a series of studies, several of which are included here.

The first section of this book indicated that scientific writing is not easy to read. This section on memory is one of the most difficult: the procedures are involved, the distinctions fine, and virtually every word is essential. As information theorists would say, the redundancy is low. Accordingly, it may be advisable to go to the last selection (Melton's) and skim through this to get an overview of the series of investigations, and then to study the reports in sequence (Melton refers to and builds upon all of them). Similarly, it will be helpful to read the summary of each article both before and after reading the article itself.

The first article in this section presents the original study in which the Petersons systematically varied both the opportunity for rehearsal and the interval of time over which the subject was to remember the material. To prevent rehearsal, they presented the stimulus (a consonant syllable such as CHJ) and had the subject immediately begin to count aloud backward (by three's) from some three-digit number (506, 503, 500, etc.). This counting, which presumably prevented the subject from repeating the consonants to himself, was done for 3 seconds on some trials, and for 6, 9, 15, and 18 seconds on others. The Petersons were also interested in the latency of the responses—the length of time it took the subjects to emit the response *after* they were to do so. (This is different from the 3, 6, etc., seconds of counting; it is the time period between the end of the counting and the emission of the response.) Our principal concern here is the finding that the percentage of items remembered was related to the interval of time between the learning and the test of retention, even though this interval varied only from 3 to 18 seconds.

As a further check on the effect of rehearsal, they divided the same subjects into two groups for Experiment II. Half of these (vocal rehearsal group) were instructed to repeat the stimulus for a period of 0, 1, or 3 seconds between the presentation of the stimulus and the signal for them to start counting. The other half (silent) were given the same interval (0, 1, or 3 seconds) but were not given instructions on what to do during this time; they might or might not, then, rehearse, while *all* those in the vocal group would. In brief, in this second part of their report (Experiment II), the Petersons compare the performance of two groups: one (vocal) is forced to rehearse for an interval (0, 1, or 3 seconds) before counting; the other (silent) is given the equivalent intervals without any instructions. Again, the proportion of correct responses is measured over various intervals of counting (3, 9, and 18 seconds). Retention was related to the time spent rehearsing before counting.

We have all learned the classic steps in scientific methodology, and we recall that replication occupies a high status there. This requires that any investigator report not only his findings, but also the details of his methodology, so that others can replicate the study to determine whether the findings have any generality, or whether they reflect chance variation or only specific conditions. Thus, Murdock, before attempting to extend the Petersons' findings, first replicated their study, confirming their conclusion that forgetting increased with the duration of interpolated activity. In his first experiment, however, he measured the retention of not only the 3 consonants used by the Petersons (Murdock's Session 1), but also a single word (Session 2), and 3 words (Session 3). As Melton points out, the retention of 3 consonants is similar to that of 3 words over the same interval of time, suggesting that the number of "units" to be remembered is the important factor, whether these units are consonants, words, or, presumably, digits or facts, etc. Melton fills in this chart, showing that the retention curves over intervals of time for 1, 2, 3, 4, and 5 units support this conclusion.

So far, then, the evidence shows that retention drops quickly over time and is related to the number of units to be remembered. Murdock, however, still wonders about the effect of interference on this retention. To test this (Experiment II), he presented a number of words (0, 3, 6, 9, or 12) to a subject before presenting the to-be-remembered stimulus; then he used the same procedures as before. If proactive inhibition (PI) acts to interfere with the retention of the test stimulus, retention should decrease as the number of prior words is increased. There was less retention in those trials in which the stimulus was preceded by 3 words than when no words preceded the stimulus, but beyond that the results were in the other direction, leaving us puzzled about the effects of this previous learning on the short-term memory of new learning.

Murdock incidentally obtained confirmation of this result (the U-shaped effect of PI) in his third experiment. In this he was investigating still another factor. Given the effect on retention of an intervening activity, he now asks whether retention is affected by the rate at which one works during that time. To check this, he varied the rate at which subjects read the interpolated words, and concluded that this produced no differences.

At this point in the readings we face a diversion. Psychologists have long recognized that some words are more easily learned than others. For example, if such words as dog, table, mother, and green are used as stimuli in one condition of a study, while words such as chrysalis, fenestration, ambergris, and gonfalon are used in another, differences in rates of learning (or remembering) might be due to the words used, rather than to the independent variable. To avoid these effects, psychologists have resorted to nonsense syllables (JAV, KEL, etc.). Unfortunately, these also differ in the ease with which they're learned. Learnability relates to the syllables' meaningfulness, that is, the extent to which they can be associated with other words. Using measures of this meaningfulness (derived from prior studies by Glase and by Archer) Peterson, Peterson, and Miller question whether there will be differences in short-term memory between high- and low-association-value nonsense syllables. Their positive results serve to remind investigators that this factor must be controlled in studying short-term memory.

Meanwhile, we are still faced with the problem of how forgetting occurs. Thus far, we have seen evidence that forgetting occurs rapidly and as a function of time. But what of the interference theory? Keppel and Underwood point out that long-term memory (LTM) has been found to be influenced by proactive and retroactive inhibition—that is, material learned before and/or after the to-be-remembered material affects its retention. They ask whether these act on short-term memory (STM) in the same way, even though the effects of interference presumably increase as a function of the interval of time between the learning and testing for retention.

Thus, they reason that a subject should be better able to remember the item on his first test than to remember an item after he has learned (and been tested on) another 18 or 30 items. In short, each item he learns makes it more difficult for him to remember subsequent ones, and an analysis of performance by successive blocks of trials should show decreasing retention.

Again, however, behavior is seldom simple. The authors discuss two other factors that can reduce this effect. For one thing, PI may not increase directly with the amount of previous material; it may increase only up to some point and then only slightly beyond that. If only a few trials in STM produces this level, the effect will be difficult to detect.

The second factor is one familiar to you from the section on learning set. You have already seen that learning one set of material can make it easier to learn another set. To the extent that this "learning to learn" phenomenon operates in the STM material, we should observe better performance in subsequent blocks of trials. Again, however, this "practice" effect may also reach an asymptote quickly.

So we see that learning a set of material might interfere with learning (remembering) subsequent material as a function of proactive inhibition, but this same learning might be predicted, from learning set data, to facilitate the new learning (remembering). Keppel and Underwood grapple with the problem of ferreting out the relative effects of these opposing tendencies.

The last article in this set, Melton's, selects the common strands running through the other articles and weaves these fibers into the fabric of a general theory of memory. He first discusses memory in general, pointing to some of the theories of how memory is maintained and to the question of whether short-term and long-term memory may be processed differently. This leads him to review this series of investigations of short-term memory, and to conclude that further work in this area is likely to increase our knowledge of how and why forgetting occurs.

STUDY QUESTIONS

1. Peterson and Peterson had subjects count backwards to prevent rehearsal in two experiments. What hypothesis about rehearsal did their second experiment test? With what results?

2. How does Murdock measure the latency of his subjects' responses? Why is this variable important?
3. Murdock feels his results support, in part, both a time decay and an interference theory of forgetting. On what basis does he make this statement?
4. How do Peterson, Peterson, and Miller relate meaningfulness and very short-term memory (recall interval of 6 seconds or less)?
5. Keppel and Underwood list four ways in which they show similarities in LTM and STM. Which of their data provide support for each point?
6. Why does Melton wish to establish a general theory for both short-term and long-term memory? Why not two theories?
7. What are the arguments for and against the belief that there is a permanent memory trace established by a one-second exposure to a small unit of stimulus material (5 or fewer consonants)?
8. Melton's Figure 4 is a theoretical statement. On what evidence does he base the solid lines? The dashed lines?

Short-Term Retention of

Individual Verbal Items [1]

Lloyd R. Peterson and Margaret Jean Peterson

Indiana University

It is apparent that the acquisition of verbal habits depends on the effects of a given occasion being carried over into later repetitions of the situation. Nevertheless, textbooks separate acquisition and retention into distinct categories. The limitation of discussions of retention to long-term characteristics is necessary in large part by the scarcity of data on the course of retention over intervals of the order of magnitude of the time elapsing between successive repetitions in an acquisition study. The presence of a retentive function within the acquisition process was postulated by Hull (1940) in his use of the stimulus trace to explain serial phenomena. Again, Underwood (1949) has suggested that forgetting occurs during the acquisition process. But these theoretical considerations have not led to empirical investigation. Hull (1952) quantified the stimulus trace on data concerned with the CS-UCS interval in eyelid conditioning and it is not obvious that the construct so quantified can be readily transferred to verbal learning. One objection is that a verbal stimulus produces a strong predictable response prior to the experimental session and this is not true of the originally neutral stimulus in eyelid conditioning.

Reprinted from *Journal of Experimental Psychology*, 1959, 58, 193–198.

[1] The initial stages of this investigation were facilitated by National Science Foundation Grant G-2596.

Two studies have shown that the effects of verbal stimulation can decrease over intervals measured in seconds. Pillsbury and Sylvester (1940) found marked decrement with a list of items tested for recall 10 sec. after a single presentation. However, it seems unlikely that this traditional presentation of a list and later testing for recall of the list will be useful in studying intervals near or shorter than the time necessary to present the list. Of more interest is a recent study by Brown (1958) in which among other conditions a single pair of consonants was tested after a 5-sec. interval. Decrement was found at the one recall interval, but no systematic study of the course of retention over a variety of intervals was attempted.

EXPERIMENT I

The present investigation tests recall for individual items after several short intervals. An item is presented and tested without related items intervening. The initial study examines the course of retention after one brief presentation of the item.

METHOD

Subjects.—The Ss were 24 students from introductory psychology courses at Indiana University. Participation in experiments was a course requirement.

Materials.—The verbal items tested for recall were 48 consonant syllables with Witmer association value no greater than 33% (Hilgard, 1951). Other materials were 48 three-digit numbers obtained from a table of random numbers. One of these was given to S after each presentation under instructions to count backward from the number. It was considered that continuous verbal activity during the time between presentation and signal for recall was desirable in order to minimize rehearsal behavior. The materials were selected to be categorically dissimilar and hence involve a minimum of interference.

Procedure.—The S was seated at a table with E seated facing in the same direction on S's right. A black plywood screen shielded E from S. On the table in front of S were two small lights mounted on a black box. The general procedure was for E to spell a consonant syllable and immediately speak a three-digit number. The S then counted backward by three or four from this number. On flashing of a signal light S attempted to recall the consonant syllable. The E spoke in rhythm with a metronome clicking twice per second and S was instructed to do likewise. The timing of these events is diagrammed in Fig. 1. As E spoke the third digit, he pressed a button activating a Hunter interval timer. At the end of a preset interval the timer activated a red light and an electric clock. The light was the signal for recall. The clock ran until E heard S speak three letters, when E stopped the clock by depressing a key. This time between onset of the light and completion of a response will be referred to as a latency. It is to be distinguished from the interval from completion of the syllable by E to onset of the light, which will be referred to as the recall interval.

The instructions read to S were as follows: "Please sit against the back of your chair so that you are comfortable. You will not be shocked during this experiment. In front of you is a little black box. The top or green light is on now. This green light means that we are ready to begin a trial. I will

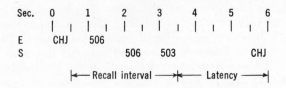

FIG. 1.   Sequence of events for a recall interval of 3 sec.

speak some letters and then a number. You are to repeat the number immediately after I say it and begin counting backwards by 3's (4's) from that
number in time with the ticking that you hear. I might say, ABC 309. Then
you say, 309, 306, 303, etc., until the bottom or red light comes on. When
you see this red light come on, stop counting immediately and say the letters that were given at the beginning of the trial. Remember to keep your
eyes on the black box at all times. There will be a short rest period and
then the green light will come on again and we will start a new trial."
The E summarized what he had already said and then gave S two practice
trials. During this practice S was corrected if he hesitated before starting
to count, or if he failed to stop counting on signal, or if he in any other way
deviated from the instructions.

Each S was tested eight times at each of the recall intervals, 3, 6, 9,
12, 15, and 18 sec. A given consonant syllable was used only once with
each S. Each syllable occurred equally often over the group at each recall
interval. A specific recall interval was represented once in each successive
block of six presentations. The S counted backward by three on half of the
trials and by four on the remaining trials. No two successive items contained
letters in common. The time between signal for recall and the start of the
next presentation was 15 sec.

RESULTS AND DISCUSSION

Responses occurring any time during the 15-sec. interval following signal
for recall were recorded. In Fig. 2 are plotted the proportions of correct
recalls as cumulative functions of latency for each of the recall intervals.
Sign tests were used to evaluate differences among the curves (Walker &
Lev, 1953). At each latency differences among the 3-, 6-, 9-, and 18-sec.
recall interval curves are significant at the .05 level. For latencies of 6 sec.
and longer these differences are all significant at the .01 level. Note that
the number correct with latency less than 2 sec. does not constitute a
majority of the total correct. These responses would not seem appropriately described as identification of the gradually weakening trace of a stimulus. There is a suggestion of an oscillatory characteristic in the events determining them.

The feasibility of an interpretation by a statistical model was explored
by fitting to the data the exponential curve of Fig. 3. The empirical points
plotted here are proportions of correct responses with latencies shorter than
2.83 sec. Partition of the correct responses on the basis of latency is required by considerations developed in detail by Estes (1950). A given
probability of response applies to an interval of time equal in length to the
average time required for the response under consideration to occur. The
mean latency of correct responses in the present experiment was 2.83 sec.
Differences among the proportions of correct responses with latencies
shorter than 2.83 sec. were evaluated by sign tests. The difference between

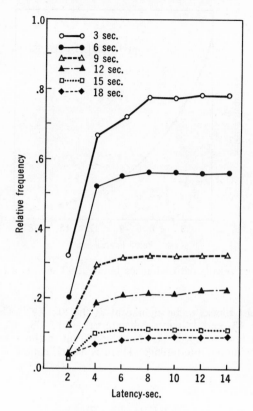

FIG. 2.   Correct recalls as cumulative functions of latency.

the 3- and 18-sec. conditions was found to be significant at the .01 level. All differences among the 3-, 6-, 9-, 12-, and 18-sec. conditions were significant at the .05 level.

The general equation of which the expression for the curve of Fig. 3 is a specific instance is derived from the stimulus fluctuation model developed by Estes (1955). In applying the model to the present experiment it is assumed that the verbal stimulus produces a response in S which is conditioned to a set of elements contiguous with the response. The elements thus conditioned are a sample of a larger population of elements into which the conditioned elements disperse as time passes. The proportion of conditioned elements in the sample determining S's behavior thus decreases and with it the probability of the response. Since the fitted curve appears to do justice to the data, the observed decrement could arise from stimulus fluctuation.

The independence of successive presentations might be questioned in the light of findings that performance deteriorates as a function of previous learning (Underwood, 1957). The presence of proactive interference was tested by noting the correct responses within each successive block of 12 presentations. The short recall intervals were analyzed separately from the long recall intervals in view of the possibility that facilitation might occur with the one and interference with the other. The proportions of correct responses for the combined 3- and 6-sec. recall intervals were in order of occurrence .57, .66, .70, and .74. A sign test showed the difference between

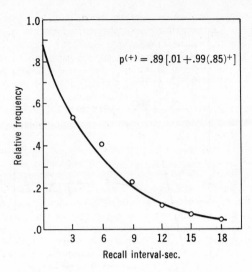

FIG. 3.   Correct recalls with latencies below 2.83 sec. as a function of recall interval.

the first and last blocks to be significant at the .02 level. The proportions
correct for the 15- and 18-sec. recall intervals were .08, .15, .09, and .12.
The gain from first to last blocks is not significant in this case. There is no
evidence for proactive interference. There is an indication of improvement
with practice.

EXPERIMENT II

The findings in Exp. I are compatible with the proposition that the after-
effects of a single, brief, verbal stimulation can be interpreted as those of
a trial of learning. It would be predicted from such an interpretation that
probability of recall at a given recall interval should increase as a function
of repetitions of the stimulation. Forgetting should proceed at differential
rates for items with differing numbers of repetitions. Although this seems
to be a reasonable prediction, there are those who would predict otherwise. Brown (1958), for instance, questions whether repetitions, as such,
strengthen the "memory trace." He suggests that the effect of repetitions of
a stimulus, or rehearsal, may be merely to postpone the onset of decay of
the trace. If time is measured from the moment that the last stimulation
ceased, then the forgetting curves should coincide in all cases, no matter
how many occurrences of the stimulation have preceded the final occurrence. The second experiment was designed to obtain empirical evidence
relevant to this problem.

METHOD

The Ss were 48 students from the source previously described. Half of the
Ss were instructed to repeat the stimulus aloud in time with the metronome
until stopped by E giving them a number from which S counted back-

ward. The remaining Ss were not given instructions concerning use of the interval between E's presentation of the stimulus and his speaking the number from which to count backward. Both the "vocal" group and the "silent" group had equated intervals of time during which rehearsal inevitably occurred in the one case and could occur in the other case. Differences in frequency of recalls between the groups would indicate a failure of the uninstructed Ss to rehearse. The zero point marking the beginning of the recall interval for the silent group was set at the point at which E spoke the number from which S counted backward. This was also true for the vocal group.

The length of the rehearsal period was varied for Ss of both groups over three conditions. On a third of the presentations S was not given time for any repetitions. This condition was thus comparable to Exp. 1, save that the only recall intervals used were 3, 9, and 18 sec. On another third of the presentations 1 sec. elapsed during which S could repeat the stimulus. On another third of the presentations 3 sec. elapsed, or sufficient time for three repetitions. Consonant syllables were varied as to the rehearsal interval in which they were used, so that each syllable occurred equally often in each condition over the group. However, a given syllable was never presented more than once to any S. The Ss were assigned in order of appearance to a randomized list of conditions. Six practice presentations were given during which corrections were made of departures from instructions. Other details follow the procedures of Exp. I.

RESULTS AND DISCUSSION

Table 1 shows the proportion of items recalled correctly. In the vocal group recall improved with repetition at each of the recall intervals tested.

TABLE 1

PROPORTIONS OF ITEMS CORRECTLY RECALLED IN EXP. II

Group	Repetition Time (Sec.)	Recall Interval (Sec.)		
		3	9	18
Vocal	3	.80	.48	.34
	1	.68	.34	.21
	0	.60	.25	.14
Silent	3	.70	.39	.30
	1	.74	.35	.22
	0	.72	.38	.15

Conditions in the silent group were not consistently ordered. For purposes of statistical analysis the recall intervals were combined within each group. A sign test between numbers correct in the 0- and 3-repetition conditions of the vocal group showed the difference to be significant at the .01 level. The difference between the corresponding conditions of the silent group was not significant at the .05 level. Only under conditions where repetition of the stimulus was controlled by instructions did retention improve.

The obtained differences among the zero conditions of Exp. II and the 3-, 9-, and 18-sec. recall intervals of Exp. I require some comment, since procedures were essentially the same. Since these are between S comparisons, some differences would be predicted because of sampling variability. But another factor is probably involved. There were 48 presentations in Exp. I and only 36 in Exp. II. Since recall was found to improve over successive blocks of trials, a superiority in recall for Ss of Exp. I is reasonable. In the case of differences between the vocal and silent groups of Exp. II a statistical test is permissible, for Ss were assigned randomly to the two groups. Wilcoxon's (1949) test for unpaired replicates, as well as a t test, was used. Neither showed significance at the .05 level.

The 1- and 3-repetition conditions of the vocal group afforded an opportunity to obtain a measure of what recall would be at the zero interval in time. It was noted whether a syllable had been correctly repeated by S. Proportions correctly repeated were .90 for the 1-repetition condition and .88 for the 3-repetition condition. The chief source of error lay in the confusion of the letters "m" and "n." This source of error is not confounded with the repetition variable, for it is S who repeats and thus perpetuates his error. Further, individual items were balanced over the three conditions. There is no suggestion of any difference in responding among the repetition conditions at the beginning of the recall interval. These differences developed during the time that S was engaged in counting backward. A differential rate of forgetting seems indisputable.

The factors underlying the improvement in retention with repetition were investigated by means of an analysis of the status of elements within the individual items. The individual consonant syllable, like the nonsense syllable, may be regarded as presenting S with a serial learning task. Through repetitions unrelated components may develop serial dependencies until in the manner of familiar words they have become single units. The improved retention might then be attributed to increases in these serial dependencies. The analysis proceeded by ascertaining the dependent probabilities that letters would be correct given the event that the previous letter was correct. These dependent probabilities are listed in Table 2. It is clear that with increasing repetitions the serial dependencies increase. Again combining recall intervals, a sign test between the zero condition and the three repetition condition is significant at the .01 level.

TABLE 2

DEPENDENT PROBABILITIES OF A LETTER BEING CORRECTLY RECALLED
IN THE VOCAL GROUP WHEN THE PRECEDING LETTER WAS CORRECT

Repetition	Recall Interval (Sec.)		
Time (Sec.)	3	9	18
3	.96	.85	.72
1	.90	.72	.57
0	.86	.64	.56

Learning is seen to take place within the items. But this finding does not eliminate the possibility that another kind of learning is proceeding concurrently. If only the correct occurrences of the first letters of syllables are considered, changes in retention apart from the serial dependencies can be assessed. The proportions of first letters recalled correctly for the 0-, 1-, and

3-repetition conditions were .60, .65, and .72, respectively. A sign test between the 0- and 3-repetition conditions was significant at the .05 level. It may tentatively be concluded that learning of a second kind took place.

The course of short-term verbal retention is seen to be related to learning processes. It would not appear to be strictly accurate to refer to retention after a brief presentation as a stimulus trace. Rather, it would seem appropriate to refer to it as the result of a trial of learning. However, in spite of possible objections to Hull's terminology the present investigation supports his general position that a short-term retentive factor is important for the analysis of verbal learning. The details of the role of retention in the acquisition process remain to be worked out.

SUMMARY

The investigation differed from traditional verbal retention studies in concerning itself with individual items instead of lists. Forgetting over intervals measured in seconds was found. The course of retention after a single presentation was related to a statistical model. Forgetting was found to progress at differential rates dependent on the amount of controlled rehearsal of the stimulus. A portion of the improvement in recall with repetitions was assigned to serial learning within the item, but a second kind of learning was also found. It was concluded that short-term retention is an important, though neglected, aspect of the acquisition process.

REFERENCES

BROWN, J. Some tests of the decay theory of immediate memory. *Quart. J. exp. Psychol.*, 1958, **10**, 12–21.

ESTES, W. K. Toward a statistical theory of learning. *Psychol. Rev.*, 1950, **57**, 94–107.

ESTES, W. K. Statistical theory of spontaneous recovery and regression. *Psychol. Rev.*, 1955, **62**, 145–154.

HILGARD, E. R. Methods and procedures in the study of learning. In S. S. Stevens (Ed.), *Handbook of experimental psychology*. New York: Wiley, 1951.

HULL, C. L., HOVLAND, C. I., ROSS, R. T., HALL, M., PERKINS, D. T., & FITCH, F. B. *Mathematico-deductive theory of rote learning: A study in scientific methodology.* New Haven: Yale Univer. Press, 1940.

HULL, C. L. *A behavior system.* New Haven: Yale Univer. Press, 1952.

PILLSBURY, W. B., & SYLVESTER, A. Retroactive and proactive inhibition in immediate memory. *J. exp. Psychol.*, 1940, **27**, 532–545.

UNDERWOOD, B. J. *Experimental psychology.* New York: Appleton-Century-Crofts, 1949.

UNDERWOOD, B. J. Interference and forgetting. *Psychol. Rev.*, 1957, **64**, 49–60.

WALKER, H., & LEV, J. *Statistical inference.* New York: Holt, 1953.

WILCOXON, F. *Some rapid approximate statistical procedures.* New York: Amer. Cyanamid Co., 1949.

The Retention of Individual Items [1]

Bennet B. Murdock, Jr.

University of Vermont

The present paper reports a study of the short-term retention of individual verbal items. A study by Peterson and Peterson (1959) provided the starting point for the present experiments. In this study a single consonant syllable was presented to S, then immediately followed by a three-digit number. The S had to repeat the number, count backward by 3's or 4's at a 1-sec. rate for anywhere from 3 to 18 sec., then recall the original syllable. The results showed that the probability of recall decreased exponentially with duration of interpolated activity and approached an asymptote very close to zero.

Three experiments will be reported. Experiment I both replicated the original Peterson and Peterson (1959) study and investigated the effect of varying the nature of the to-be-remembered item. Experiment II was a study of short-term proactive inhibition (PI) which investigated the effect of varying the number of items preceding the to-be-remembered item. Experiment III studied the effect of varying the rate of the interpolated activity.

EXPERIMENT I

METHOD

This experiment was conducted in four successive sessions spaced about 4 weeks apart. Session 1 was a replication of the Peterson and Peterson (1959) study. The procedure was identical to theirs except for the following conditions: (a) the duration of the interpolated activity (i.e., counting backward) was 0, 3, 6, 9, 12, or 18 sec.; thus, we substituted the 0-sec. interval for the 15-sec. interval; (b) the metronome was set at rate of 1 beat/sec. instead of 2 beats/sec.; (c) the zero point of the interpolated activity was considered to begin with the first beat of the metronome following the presentation of the nonsense syllable; and (d) all Ss were given sufficient preliminary practice on the interpolated activity to enable them to count backward accurately. As in the Peterson and Peterson (1959) study both latency and accuracy of response were recorded, the consonant syllables were selected

Reprinted from *Journal of Experimental Psychology*, 1961, 62, 618–625.

[1] This study was supported by a research grant, M-3330, from the National Institutes of Health. Cynthia Marvin conducted many of the experiments and helped in the analysis of the results.

from the same pool, and the same controls (counterbalancing of syllables among conditions and conditions among stages of practice) were employed.

Session 2 was an exact duplication of Session 1 except for the to-be-remembered items. Instead of consonant syllables the items were single, monosyllabic, nonhomophonic words selected from the Thorndike-Lorge (1944) list of the 1000 most common words in the English language.

To test whether the large differences obtained between the results of Sessions 1 and 2 could be attributed simply to the number of "chunks" of information (i.e., three unrelated letters in the first session or one common word in the second session; see Miller, 1956) Session 3 was an exact duplication of Sessions 1 and 2 except that the to-be-remembered items were word triads. That is, on each trial S was presented three monosyllabic nonhomophonic words from the same pool as above. In selecting the word triads the only stipulation was that the three words could be clearly spoken in the same length of time (i.e., 1 sec.) required to say the three letters of the consonant syllables of Session 1.

As both accuracy and latency of recall were used as dependent variables, Session 4 was conducted to determine whether the duration of the interpolated activity itself would affect response latency. No stimulus item other than the three-digit number was presented; S was merely required to say "stop" as quickly as possible after the interpolated activity (counting backward) was terminated.

The same Ss were used in all four sessions; they were students of both sexes from the introductory psychology course who were fulfilling a course requirement. There were 24 Ss in each of the first three sessions and 20 Ss in the fourth session.

RESULTS

The results of Session 1 clearly confirmed the results of Peterson and Peterson (1959). They presented their results in terms of the proportion of correct responses occurring with latencies less than 2.83 sec. (the overall mean latency for all correct responses). We analyzed our results in the same way and compared them with the values predicted by the formula given in Peterson and Peterson (1959, Fig. 3, p. 195). The differences between the results predicted by this formula and the results actually obtained in Session 1 were small and nonsystematic; the mean (algebraic) difference in proportion was $-.025$.

The mean proportion recalled at each retention interval is shown in Table 1. These results include all correct responses regardless of latency. To receive credit for a correct response in Sessions 1 and 3, S had to recall all three consonants or words in the correct order. Clearly, in all cases forgetting increased with the duration of interpolated activity, and with the longer retention intervals there was very little recall in Sessions 1 and 3.

As a simple statistical test, for each S we determined the total number of items recalled (maximum of 48) over all retention intervals. The mean values were 22.1, 44.3, and 23.0 items with SDs of 3.86, 1.99, and 5.98 for Sessions 1 to 3, respectively. The difference between Sessions 1 and 3 was not significant ($t = 0.94$), but the difference between Session 2 and the other two combined was highly significant ($t = 24.9$, $P < .001$).

An analysis of the latency data substantiated the above results. The mean latencies are shown in Table 2 and, in general, latencies increased with the duration of the retention interval. An analysis of variance of the results of Session 4 showed that the duration of the interpolated activity

TABLE 1

MEAN PROPORTION OF CORRECT RECALLS AT EACH
RETENTION INTERVAL: EXP. I

Retention Interval	Session 1 CCC Trigrams		Session 2 Words		Session 3 Word Triads	
	Mean	SD	Mean	SD	Mean	SD
0 sec.	.94	.11	.98	.04	.93	.10
3 sec.	.77	.15	.99	.03	.73	.21
6 sec.	.40	.18	.96	.07	.39	.23
9 sec.	.26	.19	.91	.10	.30	.21
12 sec.	.24	.14	.86	.11	.31	.22
18 sec.	.16	.12	.84	.14	.23	.16

TABLE 2

MEAN LATENCY OF CORRECT RECALLS AT EACH RETENTION INTERVAL: EXP. I

Retention Interval	Session 1 CCC Trigrams		Session 2 Words		Session 3 Word Triads		Session 4 Simple RT	
	Mean	SD	Mean	SD	Mean	SD	Mean	SD
0 sec.	1.91	0.97	1.13	0.30	1.63	0.28	1.06	0.26
3 sec.	2.01	0.64	1.32	0.31	2.02	0.67	0.85	0.17
6 sec.	2.45	1.01	1.51	0.55	2.32	0.74	0.86	0.18
9 sec.	3.16	1.21	1.61	0.58	2.40	0.72	0.90	0.18
12 sec.	2.49	0.91	1.59	0.62	2.63	1.06	0.92	0.19
18 sec.	3.04	1.18	1.69	0.65	2.79	1.20	0.92	0.25

TABLE 3

MEAN PROPORTION OF CORRECT RECALLS AT EACH
RETENTION INTERVAL: EXP. II

Retention Interval	Number of Prior Words					Mean
	0	3	6	9	12	
0 sec.	.995	1.000	.985	.985	.974	.988
3 sec.	1.000	.959	.927	.948	.969	.960
6 sec.	.953	.834	.896	.901	.865	.890
9 sec.	.938	.844	.860	.849	.875	.873
12 sec.	.938	.771	.834	.818	.860	.844
18 sec.	.907	.823	.802	.828	.823	.836
Mean	.955	.872	.884	.888	.894	

did have a significant effect ($F = 25.14$, $P < .001$), but most of the difference was due to the 0-sec. retention interval. Thus, the "true" values for
the 0-sec. interval for the first three sessions should be slightly lower than
those reported. The corrections for differences among the remaining retention intervals are probably too slight to bother with.

To summarize the results of Exp. I: (a) they confirm the previous findings of Peterson and Peterson (1959); (b) they show that, for three types of items, forgetting, whether measured by accuracy or latency, increased with the duration of the interpolated activity; and (c) they show little difference between the retention of three consonants and three words but marked differences between the retention of three "chunks" and one word. The possible confounding of intersession practice effects will be considered with the results of the next experiment.

EXPERIMENT II

METHOD

This experiment was a study of short-term PI. As in Session 2 of Exp. I the stimulus items were single monosyllabic nonhomophonic words. A given item was preceded by 0, 3, 6, 9, or 12 words, also from the Thorndike-Lorge list of the 1,000 most common words. The preceding words were read at a 1-sec. rate, but always S was asked to recall only the stimulus item. The interpolated activity was, as in Exp. I, counting backward for 0, 3, 6, 9, 12, or 18 sec. Each S was tested under all conditions. The 5 × 6 design (five levels of prior words, six retention intervals) required 30 trials (lists) for one replication, and there were eight replications in all. Thus, each S was given a total of 240 trials, 60 on each of 4 days. There were 24 Ss from the same population as before.

In all other respects the procedure was identical with that of Exp. I. There was complete counterbalancing of conditions within Ss and stimulus material across Ss. That is, there were eight blocks of 30 trials each so that the experimental conditions appeared equally often at all stages of practice. Within each block the order of the 30 trials was randomized. Each specific stimulus item was assigned equally often to each retention interval and, so far as possible, to each level of number of prior words. The specific words preceding the stimulus item were randomized by starting at a different place on the mimeographed word list for each S.

RESULTS

An analysis of intersession practice effects showed that the proportion of words correctly recalled over the 4 days were .87, .87, .92, and .93, respectively. Although the magnitude of the improvement was relatively slight, it was consistent enough to be highly significant ($F = 9.12$, $P < .001$). In Exp. I the proportion of correct recalls for the first session (consonant syllables) was .46, and the proportion of correct recalls for the third session (word triads) was .48. Since the slight improvement was about what would be expected by practice effects alone, the confounding of practice effects and stimulus items probably does not affect the conclusion that consonant syllables and word triads were equally well recalled.

The mean proportion of correct recalls, regardless of latency, at each retention interval in Exp. II is shown in Table 3 [above], and the mean latency of correct recalls is shown in Table 4 [below]. Analyses of variance showed that, for each measure, both variables (number of prior words and retention interval) were significant at at least the .01 level. As the retention interval

TABLE 4

MEAN LATENCY OF CORRECT RECALLS AT EACH RETENTION
INTERVAL: EXP. II

Retention Interval	Number of Prior Words					Mean
	0	3	6	9	12	
0 sec.	0.90	1.01	0.98	0.97	1.01	0.97
3 sec.	1.09	1.12	1.17	1.16	1.17	1.14
6 sec.	1.20	1.27	1.33	1.24	1.29	1.27
9 sec.	1.26	1.31	1.35	1.47	1.26	1.33
12 sec.	1.19	1.33	1.35	1.29	1.31	1.29
18 sec.	1.32	1.35	1.37	1.43	1.40	1.37
Mean	1.16	1.23	1.26	1.26	1.24	

increased, accuracy decreased and latency increased. As the number of
prior words increased, accuracy decreased from 0 to 3 words, then increased slightly but consistently from 3 to 12 words. As the number of
prior words increased, latency increased from 0 to 3 words but then stayed
relatively constant from 3 to 12 words.

When the control condition (0 prior words) is omitted, there were in
all 264 extralist intrusions, 161 intralist intrusions, and 81 omissions. Thus,
the number of extralist intrusions, intralist intrusions, and omissions occurred in approximately the ratio 3:2:1. An intralist intrusion was considered to be one of the words preceding the to-be-remembered stimulus
item, an extralist intrusion was any other word, and an omission was a
failure to respond. An analysis of the intralist intrusions showed that almost
half (74, or 46%) of these intrusions were the word immediately preceding
the to-be-remembered stimulus item, and in general the percentage decreased with increasing remoteness from the stimulus item.

If the control group is included, there were in all 324 extralist intrusions. Of these 324 intrusions 98 (30%) were words that had been correct on
one of the preceding trials, 86 were classified as having been mispronounced
by S, 10 were obvious associations or synonyms of the correct response, and
130 were unclassifiable. Of the 98 intrusions from previous trials 58 had
been correct on the immediately preceding trial, 13 on the preceding trial
once removed, and the number decreased regularly with increasing remoteness. Thus, in general the analysis of the errors showed marked recency effects for both intralist and extralist intrusions.

To summarize, the results of Exp. II showed that proactive inhibition
does occur in the short-term retention of individual items but (at least for
accuracy) appears to be a U shaped function of number of previous words.

EXPERIMENT III

METHOD

This experiment was a study of the effect of different rates of interpolated
activity on short-term retention of individual items. For this purpose counting backward did not seem to be a suitable type of interpolation; Ss could

not easily count faster than a 1-sec. rate, and a slower rate might allow rehearsal of the original item. Therefore, a new procedure was devised. A list of words of unknown length was read to S, and S was instructed to remember both the first and the last three words in the list. Requiring S to remember the last three words seemed to prevent rehearsal of the first word.

A preliminary experiment was conducted to test the feasibility of this method. There were lists of six different lengths: 4, 7, 11, 16, 21, and 31 words, all nonhomophonic words from the Thorndike-Lorge 1,000 most common. There were 10 counterbalanced replications of the six lengths for a total of 60 trials (or lists) in all. Group testing was used, and all words were read in time with an electric metronome beating at a rate of 1 beat/sec. After each list had been read Ss had 20 sec. in which to write down the first and last three words of the list. A "ready" signal preceded by 2 sec. the start of each list. There were 29 Ss from the same population as before, all tested in a single session.

An analysis of the results of this preliminary experiment showed that, with one reversal, the proportion of correct recalls of the first word decreased as list length increased. The minimum proportion was .841 for the 31 word list. Statistically, the effect of list length was highly significant ($F = 5.81$, $P < .001$) and, in general, the results were quite comparable to the analogous data on single words in Exp. I and II. Therefore, it was decided to use this method to study the effect of rate of interpolation on short-term retention.

The main experiment was conducted in three sessions and followed closely the procedure of the preliminary experiment. In Session 1 there were six list lengths: 4, 7, 10, 13, 16, and 19 words. The metronome was beating at a rate of 2 beats/sec.; starting with the second beat after the first word had been read the remaining words were read either at every beat, every other beat, or every fourth beat. Thus, in effect, the first word was presented for 1 sec. and the remaining words were read at a rate of either 2, 1, or 0.5 words/sec. List length and presentation rate were orthogonal to each other, and there were three replications for a total of 54 trials (or lists). The order of presentation was randomized within each replication.

In Session 2 (actually requiring 2 days to complete) there were three list lengths (7, 13, and 19 words) but five different rates. The metronome was set at a rate of 2.5 beats/sec., and starting with the second beat the remaining words were read at every beat, every other beat, every third beat, every fourth beat, or every fifth beat. Thus, the rates used ranged from 0.5 to 2.5 words/sec. There were eight replications for a total of 120 trials, 60 on each of the 2 days. The order of presentation was randomized within each replication.

In Session 3 there were six list lengths (4, 7, 10, 13, 16, and 19 words) but only two different rates. The metronome was set at a rate of 2.0 beats/ sec., and the entire list was read either at a rate of one word every beat or one word every third beat. Thus, the two rates were 2.0 and 0.67 words/sec. These two rates were selected on the basis of the results of Session 2 as those which should yield maximum differences. At the slower rate Ss would have more time to rehearse the first word before the rest of the list started; this confounding was deliberately introduced in a further attempt to maximize the differences between the two rates. There were five replications for a total of 60 trials, and the order of presentation was randomized within each replication.

Group testing was used throughout. The same Ss were tested in all three sessions (though not in the preliminary experiment). They were 27 students from the same population as before; however, only 21 were tested in Session 3.

RESULTS

In each of the three sessions the proportion of correct recalls decreased as the retention interval increased. Analyses of variance showed that the effect was statistically significant at beyond the .001 level in all three cases.

In Session 1, the proportions of correct recalls were .827, .860, and .829 for the rates of 0.5, 1, and 2 words/sec., respectively. An analysis of variance showed that the differences were not statistically significant ($F <$ 1.00). In Session 2, the proportions of correct recalls were .909, .940, .918, .963, and .946 for words read every 1, 2, 3, 4, and 5 beats, respectively. Again, the differences were not statistically significant ($F = 2.10$, $P > .05$). In Session 3, the proportions of correct recalls were almost identical for the two conditions (.894 and .895). Thus, there seems little doubt that, under the conditions of this experiment, the rate of interpolation is not an effective variable governing the short-term retention of individual items.

In Exp. III, Ss were asked to recall not only the first word but also the last three words. Since varying numbers of words preceded the last three words, an analysis of the recall data of the last three words as a function of number of preceding words can give further information about short-term proactive inhibition effects. The proportion of correct recall of the last three words is shown in Table 5. These results show exactly the same pattern as those of Exp. II (see Table 3): an initial drop followed by a gradual rise. The rise from 4 to 16 preceding words was reasonably linear, and the least-squares regression line of the means (bottom row of Table 5) had a slope significantly greater than zero ($t = 4.76$, $df = 3$, $P < .02$). Thus, these results confirm the conclusion of Exp. II; PI first increases but then decreases as the number of previous words increases.

An analysis of the errors showed omissions of 54%, 63%, and 64%; extralist intrusions of 28%, 25%, and 18%; and intralist intrusions of 18%, 12%, and 18%, each for Sessions 1, 2, and 3, respectively. Averaged across sessions the mean number of omissions, extralist intrusions, and intralist intrusions were 60%, 27%, and 12%, respectively. The corresponding values from Exp. II were 16%, 52%, and 32%, respectively. Thus, in Exp. III there were far

TABLE 5

MEAN PROPORTION OF CORRECT RECALLS OF THE LAST
THREE WORDS: EXP. III

Session	Number of Preceding Words					
	1	4	7	10	13	16
1	.938	.827	.846	.866	.863	.885
2	—	.874	—	.887	—	.898
3	.916	.867	.890	.895	.892	.905
Mean	.927	.856	.868	.883	.878	.896

more omissions and far fewer intrusions than in Exp. II. In Exp. II the interfering words preceded the to-be-remembered word while in Exp. III the interfering words followed the to-be-remembered word; this difference in procedure may have been responsible for the different ratios of omissions to intrusions found in the two experiments.

TABLE 6

MEAN PROPORTION OF CORRECT RECALLS OF EACH OF THE
LAST THREE WORDS: EXP. III

Session	Word		
	Last−2	Last−1	Last
Prelim. exp.	.784	.914	.977
1st Session	.761	.884	.966
2nd Session	.770	.916	.974
3rd Session	.801	.906	.974
Mean	.779	.905	.973

There was a definite serial position effect in the recall of the last three words. Table 6 shows the proportion of correct recalls of the first, second, and third of these last three words (the third word being the last word in the list). The data show the typical serial position effect of free recall (Deese & Kaufman, 1957); there appears to be rather little interexperiment variability.

To summarize, the results of Exp. III showed no effect of rate of interpolation on short-term retention but confirmed the PI findings of Exp. II (and also see Rouse, 1959).

DISCUSSION

The results of the present experiments substantiate and extend the previous word of Peterson and Peterson (1959). With an appropriate interpolated activity, the forgetting of an individual item will increase over a retention interval measured in seconds. Further, the interpolated activity evidently need not be highly similar to the to-be-remembered stimulus item; there would appear to be little formal similiarity between the three-digit numbers used in counting backward and the consonant syllables, single words, and word triads used in Exp. I and II.

Given this low similarity, it would seem unlikely that the interpolated activity would interfere with the retention of the stimulus item in the same sense that, for instance, an A-C list interferes with the retention of an A-B list in paired-associate learning. However, the interpolated activity presumably prevents rehearsal of the item, and the results consistently showed that the more time that elapsed without rehearsal the poorer the retention. Thus, the results of the various experiments using the counting backward as an interpolated activity would seem to be more compatible with a decay theory than with an interference theory of forgetting.

On the other hand, the results of Exp. III (using, of course, a quite different interpolated activity) showed that the rate of interpolation was not a significant variable determining forgetting. Given a constant number of interfering items, the total time required to present these items (and hence the time for decay to occur) could vary over a range of three or four to one and still produce the same amount of forgetting. Since in Exp. III it was the number of interpolated items and not their rate of presentation that was the critical variable, these results are more compatible with an interference theory than with a decay theory. Thus, taken as a whole, the present experiments do not provide unambiguous support for either a decay theory or an interference theory of forgetting.

The curvilinear PI function found in Exp. II and III may, at least partly, reflect the "behavioral strategy" (Pollack, Johnson, & Knaff, 1959) adopted by Ss. That is, in remembering the last word or words in a list of uncertain length, the more words that have been read the greater the probability that recall of the most recent word or words will be tested; Ss can react accordingly. Although such a possibility cannot be completely ruled out it seems unlikely for two reasons: (a) As Table 5 shows, the PI function in Exp. III was essentially the same in Session 2 as in Sessions 1 and 3. However, the uncertainty about list length was only half as great in Session 2 and, as Pollack, Johnson, and Knaff (1959) suggest, behavioral strategy would vary with degree of certainty. (b) During the course of each session Ss would gradually acquire a knowledge of the particular list lengths used, and this knowledge should facilitate the behavioral strategy. However, in Exp. III there was nothing approaching a significant practice effect, either in the preliminary experiment or in Sessions 1–3.

Finally, it is worth noting again the large differences in the retention of consonant syllables and word triads in one case, and individual words in the other case. Over the retention intervals studied, the proportion of correct recalls dropped to about .20 for the former and about .80 for the latter. It can be argued that the consonant syllables and word triads are three items to be remembered while an individual word is only a single item. If this is so, then, the number of items to be remembered would seem to be a significant variable in short-term retention.

SUMMARY

Three experiments were conducted on the short-term retention of individual items. Experiment I confirmed the findings of Peterson and Peterson (1959) and suggested that the number of items or "chunks" of information in the to-be-remembered stimulus item may be a significant variable in short-term retention. Experiment II demonstrated a significant proactive inhibition effect and suggested that the effect may be a U shaped function of number of preceding items. Experiment III showed that the rate of interpolated activity did not have a significant effect on short-term retention. The implications for a decay theory and an interference theory of forgetting were briefly discussed.

REFERENCES

DEESE, J., & KAUFMAN, R. A. Serial effects in recall of unorganized and sequentially organized verbal material. *J. exp. Psychol.*, 1957, **54**, 180–187.

MILLER, G. A. The magical number seven, plus or minus two: Some limits on our capacity for processing information. *Psychol. Rev.*, 1956, **63**, 81–97.

PETERSON, L. R., & PETERSON, M. J. Short-term retention of individual verbal items. *J. exp. Psychol.*, 1959, **58**, 193–198.

POLLACK, I., JOHNSON, L. B., & KNAFF, P. R. Running memory span. *J. exp. Psychol.*, 1959, **57**, 137–146.

ROUSE, R. O. Proactive inhibition as a function of degree of practice on the two tasks. *Amer. Psychologist*, 1959, **14**, 385. (Abstract)

THORNDIKE, E. L., & LORGE, I. *The teacher's word book of 30,000 words.* New York: Columbia University, Bureau of Publications, 1944.

Short-Term Retention and Meaningfulness [1]

Lloyd R. Peterson, Margaret Jean Peterson, and Arthur Miller

Indiana University

Retention has been found to decrease markedly within seconds after one presentation of a consonant syllable (Peterson & Peterson, 1959). Repetition of the item by the subject immediately after presentation was found to increase recall. Repetition was also accompanied by an increase in the sequential dependency of letters on the immediately preceding letter in the syllable. Repetition of the syllable was shown to constitute a serial learning task in which successive letters were in turn response and then stimulus.

Since frequency is related to meaningfulness (Underwood & Schulz, 1960, ch. 5) it was predicted that the short-term retention of items would vary as their meaningfulness. It was further predicted that sequential dependencies between letters at recall would vary with meaningfulness of items.

EXPERIMENT I

SUBJECTS

Eighteen students from introductory psychology courses at Indiana University served as subjects. Participation in experiments was a requirement of the course.

RETENTION MATERIALS

A low association value set of 16 items was originally selected from Glaze's 0 per cent nonsense syllables (1928), but was later found in Archer's more recent norms for trigrams (1960) to have a mean value of 13.1 per cent. Sixteen nonsense items in another set from Glaze's 100 per cent list had a mean Archer value of 84.9 per cent.

A set of 16 three-letter words was selected from Thorndike and Lorge's (1944) list of words occurring more than 100 times per million words of written English, and had a mean Archer value of 99.2 per cent.

Reprinted from *Canadian Journal of Psychology*, 1961, 15, 143–147.

[1] This research was facilitated by research grant G 12917 from the National Science Foundation.

APPARATUS

The items were presented on a memory drum set in a 3 by 4 ft. black screen. A sliding shutter permitted exposure of eight columns of items without change of tape. The drum was set to turn every 1.1 sec. during periods of activation. The drum motor was controlled by two decade interval timers.

PROCEDURE

A sequence started with the exposure of a three-letter item for 1.1 sec., while S spelled the item aloud. The drum then turned to a three-digit number and S began counting backward by three or four from the number. Six sec. after the removal of the letters from the aperture a bell rang and the drum turned to a blank space. S stopped counting and attempted to recall the item by spelling it aloud. Twelve sec. after the bell rang the drum turned to another blank space and then to a new item. S was given six practice presentations in which he was corrected for procedural errors.

The experiment proper consisted of 48 presentations in which S counted backward by three during half of the session and by four during the remainder. Instructions for change in the counting task were given during a short break after the twenty-fourth presentation. Each of the three types of item occurred equally often within each block of six presentations. Order of presentation within a block of six was randomized.

RESULTS AND DISCUSSION

Marked differences in recall directly related to association value are apparent in Table I. A treatment by subject analysis of variance of the number

TABLE I

RECALL IN EXPERIMENT I

Response class	Proportion of items recalled		Sequential letter probabilities		Proportion of first letters recalled	
	$\bar{X}$	$\sigma_{\bar{x}}$	$\bar{X}$	$\sigma_{\bar{x}}$	$\bar{X}$	$\sigma_{\bar{x}}$
Low N.S.	.58	.05	.83	.02	.77	.04
High N.S.	.64	.03	.92	.02	.73	.03
Words	.85	.03	.98	.01	.86	.03

of items correctly recalled resulted in an F of 28.4 for the treatment conditions. With 2 and 34 degrees of freedom this F is significant at the .001 level.

The serial dependencies within the items were analysed by calculating the conditional probabilities that a letter was correctly recalled given that the preceding letter was correct. Table I shows that the sequential letter probabilities were also directly related to association value. All comparisons of these dependent probabilities among the three conditions were significantly different at the .01 level by two-tailed sign test. It is clear that in the case of words, if the first letter was correctly recalled, it was very likely that the other letters would follow correctly.

Analysis of the mean frequencies of recall of the first letters showed no significant differences. An analysis of variance resulted in an F of less than one.

A check was made on the subjects' perception of the items by noting errors in reading the items from the drum. Three subjects made a total of six errors, two errors occurring in each of the experimental conditions. The positive relationship between association value and recall cannot be attributed to differences in perception of the items.

The predictions are confirmed by the data. The results of this experiment, together with the earlier study, are consistent with the hypothesis that frequency is a basic variable producing differences in association-value and letter-sequence habits as secondary phenomena (Underwood & Schulz, p. 44). It seems plausible that highly integrated units should be recalled better than poorly integrated items. Another possibility is that the associations evoked by items might facilitate recall either by stimulating correct responses or by providing a means for recognition of errors. Since mediating associations would require time to occur, the latency of correct recalls should vary with the association value of the item recalled. A second experiment was designed to compare latencies among sets of trigrams selected from the extremes of Archer's scale and tested at either a 1- or 6-sec. retention interval.

EXPERIMENT II

Sixteen students without previous experience in short-term retention experiments were drawn from the source previously described. Twenty-four nonsense syllables below 11 per cent on Archer's scale formed one set of items and 24 words of 100 per cent Archer value the other. A Standard Electric timer was wired into the apparatus previously described. It was automatically activated when the bell rang to signal recall and was stopped by E depressing a key after a third letter was spoken by S. The time from ringing of the bell to start of the next presentation was increased to 18 sec.

Recall intervals of 1 and 6 sec. were combined with the two types of items in a factorial design in which all comparisons were within subjects. The four experimental conditions were each represented in random order within each block of four presentations. In all other respects Experiment II followed the procedures of Experiment I.

RESULTS AND DISCUSSION

It is seen in Table II that differences in recall related to association value appeared only at the 6-second interval. An analysis of variance was contraindicated by the gross differences in variability between the 1- and 6-second conditions. A t test of the difference between words and nonsense syllables in number of items recalled at 6 seconds resulted in a t of 9.0, which with

TABLE II

RECALL IN EXPERIMENT II

Response class	Proportion of items recalled				Latency of items recalled			
	1 sec.		6 sec.		1 sec.		6 sec.	
	$\bar{X}$	$\sigma_{\bar{x}}$	$\bar{X}$	$\sigma_{\bar{x}}$	$\bar{X}$	$\sigma_{\bar{x}}$	$\bar{X}$	$\sigma_{\bar{x}}$
Low N.S.	.96	.02	.38	.05	2.05	.13	2.67	.18
Words	.98	.01	.82	.03	1.84	.10	2.63	.16

15 degrees of freedom is significant at the .001 level. The corresponding difference at 1 second is not significant. The amount of forgetting after 1 second is not appreciable for either condition. Differences in number of items recalled between 1 and 6 seconds are significant at the .01 level by two-tailed sign tests for both types of items.

The latencies were analysed by computing the mean latency of correct items in each of the four conditions for each individual. When examination of the distributions of these mean latencies showed no marked departures from normality nor any appreciable heterogeneity of variance, an analysis of variance was applied. The association value F was not significant ($F = 4.19$, df $= 1$ & 15). The hypothesis that mediating associations facilitate recall is not supported by the data. The rôle of mediating responses in learning may be limited to associative aspects and not be of any consequence in response recall.

A significant difference in latency was found for recall interval ($F = 24.8$, df $= 1$ & 15). However, interpretation of this finding is obscured by the fact that the intervening task was reading a number in the case of the 1-second interval, and counting backward in the 6-second interval. A further experiment was designed in which latency at short intervals was investigated.

EXPERIMENT III

Subjects were instructed to begin counting backward immediately at the start of the recall interval by speaking a number three units less than the number appearing in the drum. Thus, the task for the 1-sec. condition was the same as for the other conditions of the experiment. Recall intervals of 1, 2, 3, or 6 sec. were each tested 21 times with every S. The items were trigrams of Archer association value below 16 per cent. The interval from signal for recall to beginning of the next test was 15 sec. Other details were the same as in Experiment II.

RESULTS

Table III shows that recall at the 1-second interval did not differ appreciably from recall at that interval in Experiment II. Frequency of correct recalls after 1 second was slightly lower in the present experiment, but on the other hand the mean latency of correct recalls was somewhat shorter. Laten-

TABLE III

RECALL IN EXPERIMENT III

Response measure	Recall interval (sec.)			
	1	2	3	6
Proportion correct	.92	.88	.79	.51
Mean latency (sec.)	1.89	2.06	2.23	2.73

cies of correct recalls increased gradually with lengthening of the recall interval. Mean latencies of correct recalls at the 1-second recall interval were shorter than those at the 6-second interval for all 12 subjects. A Friedman two-way analysis of variance by ranks results in a χ^2_r of 26.7 which is significant at the .001 level (df $= 3$).

Examination of the frequency data and the latency data of individual subjects does not reveal any abrupt changes in the characteristics of recall over the first 6 seconds after presentation. Thus there is no evidence here to suggest that immediately after presentation retention is maintained by a mechanism different from that effective at 6-second intervals.

SUMMARY

Recall of individual trigrams after 6 sec. was found to vary with meaningfulness as measured by association value. At recall sequential dependencies between letters within the items were found to vary with association value. Frequency of occurrence in recall of initial letters did not vary with association value. It was concluded that letter-sequence habits may underlie differences in response recall related to meaningfulness. Mean latencies of correct responses at a 6-sec. recall interval were not different between sets of trigrams from the two extremes of Archer's scale, even though gross differences in recall were found. It was therefore considered unlikely that mediating responses had any significant role in response recall. Increases in latency and decreases in frequency of correct responses were found to be gradual over recall intervals of 1, 2, 3, and 6 sec. for low association value trigrams.

REFERENCES

ARCHER, E. J. A re-evaluation of the meaningfulness of all possible CVC trigrams. *Psychol. Mongr.*, 1960, **74**, no. 11.

EPSTEIN, W., ROCK, I., & ZUCKERMAN, C. B. Meaning and familiarity in associative learning. *Psychol. Mongr.*, 1960, **74**, no. 4.

GLAZE, J. A. The association value of nonsense syllables. *J. genet. Psychol.*, 1928, **35**, 255–67.

PETERSON, L. R., & PETERSON, M. J. Short-term retention of individual verbal items. *J. exp. Psychol.*, 1959, **58**, 193–8.

THORNDIKE, E. L., & LORGE, I. *The teacher's word book of 30,000 words.* New York: Bureau of Publications, Teachers College, 1944.

UNDERWOOD, B. J., & SCHULZ, R. W. *Meaningfulness and verbal learning.* New York: Lippincott, 1960.

Proactive Inhibition in Short-Term

Retention of Single Items[1]

Geoffrey Keppel and Benton J. Underwood

Northwestern University, Evanston, Illinois

In 1959 Peterson and Peterson developed a technique whereby a single verbal item was presented to S for a learning trial of approximately .5-sec. duration, with retention being measured over intervals of up to 18 sec. These procedures produced a very systematic relationship between length of retention interval and percentage of items correct at recall, with 78% correct after 3 sec., and 8% after 18 sec. Thus, forgetting of the single item is nearly complete after 18 sec. The reliability of this forgetting curve is demonstrated by the fact that Murdock (1961) has repeated the Peterson-Peterson experiment and obtained nearly identical results.

The present experiments were designed to obtain data which would aid in interpreting theoretically the extraordinarily rapid forgetting of the single items which has been observed in the above experiments. The nature of the interpretative problem and how it arises, requires some background discussion.

The first distinction which must be made is between short-term retention procedures and long-term retention procedures. The short-term studies, as exemplified by Peterson and Peterson, involve retention of *single* items over very short intervals, say, 60 sec. or less. The long-term retention studies involve retention of *lists* of items over much longer intervals, such as 20 min., although usually hours or days are employed. Clearly no dichotomy is possible between the two types of studies based on length of retention interval, but in actual practice a working distinction between the two exists. We may identify the short-term studies as measuring short-term memory (STM) and the long-term studies as measuring long-term memory (LTM) with the understanding that the present usage also involves memory for singly presented items versus memory for lists of items.

The critical issue is whether or not LTM and STM will require fundamentally different interpretative principles. The resolution of this issue rests primarily on determining the role which proactive inhibiton (PI) plays in STM. Interference theories of LTM use PI as a cornerstone paradigm (e.g., Postman, 1961); associations learned prior to the learning of associations

Reprinted from *Journal of Verbal Learning and Verbal Behavior,* 1962, 1, 153–161.

[1] This work was supported by Contract Nonr-1228(15), Project NR 154–057, between Northwestern University and the Office of Naval Research.

for which retention is being tested may interfere with recall. However, a secondary fact reported by Peterson and Peterson (1959) and by Peterson (1963) is that little or no evidence is found for PI in STM. In addition, since little or no retroactive inhibition (RI) is believed to be produced by the activity used to prevent rehearsal in the studies of STM, it would appear that an interference theory, based on PI and RI, is quite incapable of handling the extraordinarily rapid forgetting observed in the studies of STM. Thus, we are faced with a potential theoretical schism, with one set of propositions being used for LTM and another possibly wholly different set for STM. In the interests of theoretical continuity, such a schism should be avoided if possible.

As noted above, the critical issue involved is the role which PI plays in STM. If PI is operative in STM, the variables which govern magnitude of PI in LTM should also have counterparts in the laws of STM. Some of these more critical variables will now be discussed.

Number of Interfering Associations. In LTM the greater the number of previously acquired associations the greater the PI (Underwood, 1945; 1957). It is the reported failure to reproduce this law in studies of STM that has led to the conclusion that there is little, if any, PI in STM. Actually, the procedure used in these studies of STM would seem to be ideal for obtaining PI. For example, in the Peterson-Peterson study, a counterbalancing technique was used in which each S served eight times at each of six retention intervals. Thus, each S at the termination of his conditions had been presented 48 different items. The items presented late in the session should be subject to a greater number of potentially interfering associations than would those items presented early in the session. Yet there appears to be little difference in the retention of items presented early in the session and those presented late in the session (but see later discussion).

Degree of Learning. In LTM the higher the degree of learning of the list to be recalled the better the recall when the PI paradigm is used (Postman and Riley, 1959). This is not to say that the absolute PI is less with higher than with lower degrees of learning (when evaluated against a control group) of the list to be recalled, for according to Postman and Riley this relationship is complex. But, given a high degree of learning of a list, its recall will be higher than will the recall of a list with a low degree of learning when the proactive interference is constant on both lists. This fact has been used by Melton (1963) indirectly to suggest that PI is indeterminate in the available studies of STM. His reasoning is that as S proceeds through a series of conditions the learning-to-learn will serve to increase the degree of learning of items presented. This higher degree of learning, in turn, will counteract a decrement in retention which should occur as a function of the increasing number of potentially interfering associations which have been established as practice proceeds.

There is evidence that learning-to-learn does occur in STM studies (Peterson and Peterson, 1959). That it does occur requires a distinction between learning and retention in STM, a distinction which has not, in fact, been carefully maintained in the studies to date. Normally, we may use an immediate test (say, after 1 sec.) as a measure of degree of learning. Retention for longer intervals are assessed against the scores on the immediate test to determine the retention function. However, when percentage correct for immediate retention is essentially 100%, there is no way to derive a meaningful retention function. For, in a manner of speaking, the true degree of learning may be more than 100%. Thus, if STM of common words is to be compared with that of consonant syllables, and if the immediate test for words shows 100% correct recall and that for syllables 85%, comparison of the retention of the two materials at longer intervals may be both a function of underestimated differences in degree of learning and of differences in material. Latency measures at recall might be used as subsidiary indices of forgetting which occurs when the percentage correct remains near 100% for retention intervals of increasing length, but the moment recall falls substantially below 100% we have subject selection (those who do not get an item correct are not included in the measures) which may distort the mean of the natural distribution of latencies based on all Ss.

Length of Retention Interval. The logic of the PI situation demands an increase in PI as a function of the length of the retention interval (Underwood, 1948). So far as is known, no completely satisfactory test of this relationship has been made for LTM. Theoretically the increase in PI with increase in length of the retention interval may be accounted for by the recovery of extinguished interfering associations. Several studies strongly suggest such recovery (e.g., Briggs, 1954).

Interaction of Variables. If the facts and theory of PI in LTM hold for STM, certain interactions among the above variables will be expected. Most critical among these is the interaction between the number of potentially interfering associations and the length of the retention interval. Theoretically it is assumed that the longer the retention interval the greater the recovery of interfering associations. If there are few or none such associations little or no decrement will be observed as a function of length of retention interval (i.e., forgetting will be very slow). If there are many potential associations which could interfere proactively, the longer the retention interval the greater the forgetting, since the longer the interval the greater the number of interfering associations which will have recovered.

We may now focus on the fact that PI is said not to be involved in the rapid forgetting in STM. In the Peterson-Peterson study Ss were tested on 48 successive items following two practice items. It has been suggested that PI reaches some maximum level rather quickly as a function of the number of previous items and that a constant amount of PI may occur thereafter. Thus, two practice items may "throw in" the maximum amount of PI and additional items may have no further decremental effects (Postman, 1962; Melton, 1963). While it seems apparent that there must be a limit to the number of previous items which will contribute to interference in STM, it does not seem reasonable that all potential interfering associations would be established with only two items—the two practice items. It seems more reasonable to look at the Peterson-Peterson data from another point of view. If it is assumed that there is a practice effect in learning successive items, degree of learning for each successive item will be higher and higher. By principles of PI in LTM, the recall should also be higher and higher if amount of interference remains constant. But, of course, interference does not remain constant; more and more potentially interfering associations are acquired as testing continues. As noted earlier in the discussion, the question is how the positive effects of increased degree of learning with successive stages of practice balance out against the increased interference which accompanies the higher degree of learning. Some indication of the direction the answer may take is available in the Peterson-Peterson data.

These investigators divided the 48 experimental items into successive blocks of 12 items each so that Blocks 1 through 4 may reflect increasing degrees of learning of the items to be recalled and, simultaneously, increasing numbers of potentially interfering items. The percentage correct at recall by blocks was determined separately for two short intervals (3 and 6 sec.) and for two long intervals (15 and 18 sec.). The results are presented in Fig. 1. For the short retention intervals there is a consistent increase in recall

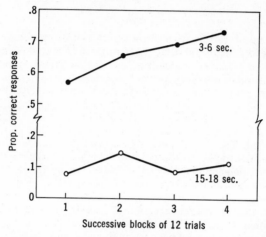

FIG. 1. Retention of single consonant syllables over short (3–6 sec.) and long (15–18 sec.) retention intervals as a function of number of preceding items. From Peterson and Peterson (1959).

from Block 1 to Block 4, the difference between the recall for the two extreme blocks being significant at the .02 confidence level. Peterson and Peterson identified this as a practice effect. Since there is no reason to believe that the practice effect occurs in the recall process it must mean that the degree of learning attained in the constant exposure period increases as trials proceed. For the longer retention interval there is no increase in recall. If only practice effects are involved, this curve should rise in exactly the same manner as the curve for shorter intervals. That it does not may indicate an increase in amount of PI as trials proceed. Thus, Fig. 1 gives indirect evidence for the critical interaction discussed earlier; that is, the interaction between amount of interference and length of the retention interval. With short retention intervals the practice effects more than compensate for increased interference; with long retention intervals the interference is of sufficient magnitude to mask the practice effects.

The evidence for the interaction between number of previous items and length of retention interval as inferred from Fig. 1 is not entirely satisfactory. Not only is the magnitude of the interaction small, but the failure to find a change in retention over blocks for the longer retention intervals must be interpreted as due to a balance between practice and interference effects. We believe it is possible to devise situations which will destroy this balance and thus give more direct evidence for the role of PI. Furthermore, studies are needed in which STM is examined for Ss without prior practice so that the rate of onset of PI as a function of 0, 1, 2, 3, etc., previous items is observed. The present experiments were designed to study these two issues.

EXPERIMENT 1

METHOD

Subjects. A total of 108 Ss from introductory psychology classes at North-western University served in Exp. 1. Most Ss had served in one or more verbal-learning experiments but in no case did an S have prior experience with the specific materials of the present experiment.

Procedure. Three retention intervals were used, namely, 3 sec., 9 sec., and 18 sec. A single consonant syllable was used for each retention interval. The procedure of Peterson and Peterson (1959) was followed, in which E spelled a syllable aloud and S attempted to recall it after the appropriate retention interval. The interval was timed from the moment the last letter of the syllable was spoken to the point at which S was instructed to recall. During the retention interval S counted backward by threes from a three-digit number spoken immediately after the presentation of the syllable, the rate of counting being one three-digit number per sec. Half the Ss were given a short practice period in counting backwards prior to being given the first syllable. However, since this practice had no discernible effect on the scores, the variable has not been maintained in presenting the results.

The three trigrams or consonant syllables were KQF, MHZ, and CXJ. Each has a 4% association value in the Witmer list (Underwood & Shulz, 1960). The retention for each S was measured over all three intervals with, of course, a different trigram being used for each interval. The three intervals were completely counterbalanced and three different orders of the trigrams were used such that each occurred equally often as the first, second, and third trigram presented. Thus 18 Ss are needed to fill the 18 different trigram-interval orders. Since 108 Ss were used, the design was replicated six times.

The design allows retention to be determined for the three retention intervals after 0, 1, and 2 prior trigrams. Recall for the first trigram will be referred to as Test 1 (T-1), that of the second T-2, and the third, T-3.

RESULTS

The results in terms of proportion of items correct for T-1, T-2, and T-3 for each retention interval are shown in Fig. 2. Each point is based on 36 Ss. Forgetting is apparent for all three tests. There is a large drop in proportion correct from T-1 to T-2, suggesting a severe proactive effect produced by a single prior item. There is no strong evidence that T-2 differs from T-3; thus, this may suggest a steady state or a constant amount of PI after the initial drop from T-1 to T-2. However, two facts relative to this point should be noted. First, at 3 sec. and at 18 sec., proportion correct is higher for T-2 than for T-3; only at 9 sec. is there a reversal. The fact that performance

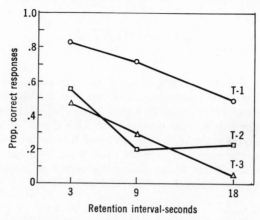

Fig. 2. Retention of single consonant syllables as a function of length of interval and number of prior syllables. Experiment 1.

is better at 18 sec. than at 9 sec. (forgetting decreases between 9 and 18 sec.) suggests the possibility that for some unknown reason the 9 sec. T-2 estimate of retention is too low. Secondly, it is noted that the absolute number of Ss recalling correctly at T-2 and T-3 for the 9- and 18-sec. intervals is very low. At none of these points is retention above 25% and on T-3 at 18 sec. forgetting is virtually complete. At these low levels of performance it may be very difficult to show consistent differences. Nevertheless, it must be concluded that there is no evidence for an increase in PI between T-2 and T-3. Furthermore, there is no evidence for an interaction between tests and retention intervals; the curves for T-1 and T-3 are essentially parallel, although here again it must be noted that on T-3 at 18 sec. forgetting is virtually complete, a situation which may preclude the appearance of an interaction. If, however, retention at 3 sec. is used as a base and if percentage of items lost between 3 sec. and 18 sec. is calculated, there is a 40% loss (from 30 items to 18 items) for T-1, and an 88% loss (from 17 to 2 items) for T-3. This method of evaluating the results clearly shows the expected interaction. While we do not believe that this response measure (proportion lost) can be judged inappropriate, it was our expectation that the interaction would be of such magnitude as to be measurable by the direct recall measures. Therefore, we will conclude only that the results are not unfavorable to the interaction hypothesis.

The retention exhibited on T-1 falls from 83% at 3 sec. to 50% at 18 sec. The difference between these two proportions is highly significant ($z = 3.00$). Only 83% of the Ss could correctly reproduce the trigram shown them 3 sec. later, and this was the first trigram shown. This suggests that degree of learning was low. However, to account for this we have no evidence to choose between failure to hear the letters and letter sequence correctly, as opposed to true forgetting over 3 sec. In any event, with a low degree of learning, STM should be easily interfered with. If interference via PI is responsible for the forgetting on T-1, it must come from associations acquired in previous laboratory experiments, from conflicting letter-sequence habits, or both.

EXPERIMENT 2

Except for one major change, Exp. 2 was very similar to Exp. 1. The change made was toward increasing the degree of initial learning by using a 2-sec. visual exposure of the items for learning. As previously noted in presenting the results for Exp. 1, recall was very poor for T-2 and T-3 for the 9- and 18-sec. retention intervals. With such low recall it is doubtful that any clear interaction between tests and intervals could have been observed. Therefore, it was believed that by increasing the degree of learning a greater range of forgetting could be observed for T-2 and T-3.

METHOD

A total of 216 Ss served in Exp. 2. Some had served in previous laboratory experiments on verbal learning and some had not. The three trigrams used in Exp. 1 also were employed in Exp. 2. However, each trigram was presented visually for a 2-sec. learning trial before the retention interval. Each trigram was printed with a lettering set on a 3 × 5-in. card, the letters being ½ in. high. Following the presentation of a card for 2 sec., E spoke a number as the card was removed and S counted backward by threes as in Exp. 1. Practice in number counting was given prior to presentation of the first trigram.

Each S again served in all three retention-interval conditions. Intervals were completely counterbalanced as were also the three trigrams; thus, 36 Ss were required for each possible interval-trigram order.

RESULTS

The proportions correct at each test for the three retention intervals are shown in Fig. 3. Each proportion is based on 72 Ss. It is apparent that the level of recall is appreciably higher than in Exp. 1. This is due, we believe,

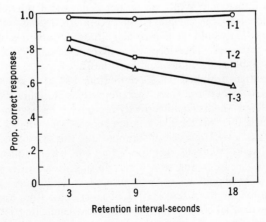

FIG. 3. Retention of single consonant syllables as a function of length of interval and number of prior syllables. Experiment 2.

to the longer exposure of the item on the learning trial. On T-1 only four responses (out of a possible 216) were incorrect; obviously, therefore, no forgetting is measurable across intervals on T-1. Proportion correct falls sharply from T-1 to T-2, with a continued but smaller decrease from T-2 to T-3. However, the drop from T-2 to T-3 is significant statistically. For each successive block of 18 Ss the interval order is perfectly balanced and each item has occurred equally often with each interval. Therefore, we may treat each group of 18 Ss as an independent experiment, thus giving 12 experiments. We may determine the total correct responses on T-2 and T-3 for each experiment separately, thus deriving two distributions of 12 entries each, one distribution representing number correct on T-2 and the other on T-3. The mean total items recalled per experiment for T-2 was 13.92, for T-3, 12.42. The mean difference (1.50 ± .54) gives a t of 2.78, which, with 11 df, is significant beyond the 5% level.

Although the forgetting over time for T-2 and T-3 is not as precipitous as in Exp. 1, it is clearly evident. Since there is no forgetting on T-1, it might appear that Fig. 3 shows the expected interaction between tests and intervals. However, such a conclusion is unwarranted. Whether or not forgetting "above" 100% correct occurred across intervals for T-1 is indeterminate from the correct-response measure. In recording the scores, note was made of all correct responses with latencies of 3 sec. or less. On T-1 almost all responses had latencies shorter than 3 sec. and there was no change in frequency of such responses with increasing intervals. This might be taken to indicate no forgetting across 18 sec. for T-1, hence that the interaction apparent in Fig. 3 is real. Experiment 3 would support such an interpretation.

The fact that Exp. 2 produced a difference between T-2 and T-3 in retention indicated that no "bottom" or steady state of PI had been reached. To test more fully the course of PI as a function of number of prior items, Ss in Exp. 3 were tested on six successive items.

EXPERIMENT 3

METHOD

A total of 96 Ss was used, divided into two subgroups of 48 each. Two retention intervals were employed, 3 sec. and 18 sec. One subgroup received the retention intervals in the order 3-18-3-18-3-18, and the other in the reverse order. This procedure permitted determination of retention after 3 sec. and after 18 sec. following 0, 1, 2, 3, 4, and 5 previous items.

Six new trigrams were chosen having a Witmer association value of 21%. This was the lowest association value from which six trigrams could be chosen so that no letter was duplicated among the 18 used. The six trigrams were: CXP, GQN, HJL, KBW, SFM, and ZTD. Six different orders of the trigrams were used such that each trigram occurred equally often on each successive test and, of course, equally often with each retention interval for each subgroup. None of the Ss used had served previously in laboratory experiments of verbal learning. The presentation procedures were exactly the same as in Exp. 2.

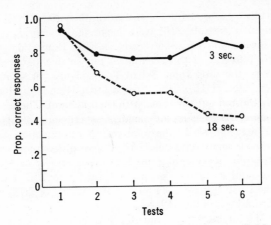

FIG. 4. Retention as a function of number of prior syllables and length of retention interval. Experiment 3.

RESULTS

The proportions of correct responses for both interval patterns are combined in Fig. 4. In this figure the six successsive tests are given along the abscissa, with one curve representing retention after 3 sec. and the other retention after 18 sec. The trend of proactive interference which was initiated by the three tests in Exp. 2 is extended and clarified by Fig. 4. It may be noted that retention on T-1 is lower than in Exp. 2 for the 3-sec. interval. Since the procedures were identical in the two experiments, the differences must arise from the samples of Ss and from differences in materials. Actually, the trigrams of Exp. 2 had lower association value than those of Exp. 3. Whatever the cause, it is clear that degree of learning is lower in Exp. 3 than in Exp. 2. This unexpected turn of events, however, produces the very desirable effect of removing any problem of a "ceiling" effect in response measurement, at least for Tests 2 through 6.

It may be noted first that the recall on the very first item presented Ss does not differ for the 3-sec. and the 18-sec. retention intervals. However, with each successive test the differences increase, thus demonstrating the interaction between tests (number of prior interfering associations) and length of retention interval. Severe PI builds up over 18 sec. with successive tests but this does not happen over 3 sec. For T-1 through T-6, the z's for the difference between proportions for 3 and 18 sec. are: .47, 1.17, 2.17, 2.17, 4.51, and 4.23.

Significant forgetting is shown for the 30-sec. interval between T-1 and T-4 ($z = 2.33$). The rise between T-4 and T-5 is not significant statistically but may indicate that practice effects are more than counteracting interference effects produced by prior tests (see later).

The question as to whether a steady state of a constant amount of PI is being approached in the 18-sec. curve is not clearly answered by Fig. 4. The question can be more easily answered by replotting Fig. 4 to separate the two independent groups. That is, the 3-sec. curve in Fig. 4 is based on two different groups of Ss, one having the 3-18-3-18-3-18 order of intervals, the other the reverse. We may, therefore, plot the 3- and 18-sec. curves separately for each group. This is done in Fig. 5. The solid lines represent the group given the 3-18 etc. order, the dotted lines representing the group given the reverse order. The filled circles represent the 3-sec. retention, the open circles the 18-sec. retention.

For the 18-sec. curves, the 3-18 Groups shows no evidence of leveling off and the 18-3 Group shows only slight evidence of negative acceleration. In short, it would appear that extrapolation of these curves beyond the six tests used would give further continued larger and larger decrements in recall over 18 sec. That this is not so apparent in Fig. 4 appears to be due to the fact that this figure combines two groups of slightly different ability levels. It also should be noted that for both groups there is a rise in reten-

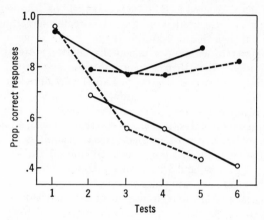

Fig. 5. Retention as a function of number of prior syllables and length of retention interval (solid circles, 3 sec.; open circles, 18 sec.) for Ss having intervals in the order 3-18-3-18-3-18 (solid lines) and in the reverse order (dotted lines). Experiment 3.

tion between the second and third tests for the 3-sec. interval. Although neither rise is significant statistically, the trend may be reliable in view of the Peterson-Peterson data shown in Fig. 1 where performance does systematically improve as a function of successive tests for short retention intervals.

DISCUSSION

The results of the present experiments give strong support to the presumption that short-term retention of single items and long-term retention of lists of items are subject to the same laws of proactive inhibition. The parallelism of the results for STM and LTM when common variables are manipulated may be briefly summarized.

(1) In LTM, number of potential interfering associations and amount of PI are directly related. The same relationship occurred in Exps. 2 and 3; reasons for the failure of the evidence from Exp. 1 to support the principle were discussed earlier.

(2) Length of retention interval and magnitude of PI are directly related in LTM given a constant amount of interference. This relationship was observed in all experiments except for T-1 in Exps. 2 and 3, where interference was presumed to be low, and degree of learning high.

(3) In LTM combining the effects of the above two variables leads to an interaction between number of potential interfering associations and length of retention interval. The interaction was clearly apparent in Exp. 3.

(4) In LTM, given constant interference, magnitude of PI decreases as degree of learning of list to be recalled increases. The degree of learning was not systematically manipulated in the present studies. However, since there is no reason to believe that auditory presentation intrinsically gives more PI than visual presentation, it may be inferred that the 2-sec. visual presentation in Exp. 2 produced a higher degree of learning than did the shorter auditory presentation in Exp. 1. Greater forgetting was observed in Exp. 1 than in Exps. 2 and 3. However, this is not a "clean" result, since the degree of learning of potentially interfering items in Exps. 2 and 3 would be higher than that of comparable items in Exp. 1. Nevertheless, the forgetting on T-1 over 18-sec. in Exp. 1 may be taken as an indication that the lower the degree of learning of the item to be recalled the more retention is influenced by proactive interference from sources outside the immediate experimental situation (associations developed in previous experiments or "natural" letter-sequence associations). It is a fact that on T-1 in Exp. 1 the intrusion of letters increased from 5% to 8% to 14% of all letters given for the 3-, 9-, and 18-sec. intervals, respectively. This suggests a recovery over time of interfering associations.

No data on letter intrusions occurring for tests beyond T-1 have been given. The reason for this is simply that by the nature of the designs used it is impossible to isolate variables which may be involved in producing intrusions. In the present studies, time between successive recalls differ; degree of learning of items given previously differ for different intervals; whether or not a previously presented item was correct or incorrect at recall should influence overt intrusions on subsequent items. If systematic laws concerning evocation of letter intrusions are to be derived, experiments must be explicitly designed for the purpose. For these reasons we have not presented intrusion data.

If the conclusion of the present experiments are sound, that is, the conclusion that the laws of proaction are the same for STM as for LTM, some economy in time may be gained by working out further laws of PI on STM rather than on LTM. For example, interitem similarity (e.g., letter duplication) should clearly influence STM. But there is reason to believe that this relationship may be complex. Specifically, in the present results it was noted that many intrusions consisted of a letter from a previous item replacing a letter at recall which occupied the same serial position, e.g., the middle letter. This suggests the operation of an A-B, A-C interference paradigm in which A is the common serial position. Such intrusions also represent the evidence needed to support the notion of spontaneous recovery of extinguished or partially extinguished associations over short intervals. If, however, serial position does constitute a common stimulus from item to item, identical letters in the same position for different items may produce a positive effect—i.e., proactive facilitation may result.

Finally, it may be noted that PI measured with a short recall interval

(2 sec.) in LTM may disappear with longer intervals (Underwood, 1950). In all the STM studies reported thus far, recall intervals of from 10 sec. to 14 sec. have been used. A reduction in the time allowed for recall may increase the apparent PI, thus allowing work with higher degrees of learning of single items than has been customary. With high degrees of learning and long recall intervals (as in Exp. 2), no measurement of forgetting is possible for initial items tested. Very short recall intervals might produce systematic evidence for forgetting for such degrees of learning.

SUMMARY

Three experiments were performed to determine the relationship between certain variables influencing proactive inhibition in long-term retention of lists of verbal items and the influence of these variables on short-term retention of single items. More particularly, retention of single items over 18 sec. should, if the laws of long-term retention are applied, decrease with number of previous items to which S has been exposed. In addition, amount of forgetting should be a direct joint function of number of previous items and length of the retention interval.

In Exp. 1 each S was presented consonant syllables singly, with retention being measured after 3, 9, and 18 sec. Forgetting of the first item presented (T-1) was less than for the second (T-2) or third (T-3) item, but forgetting of the latter (T-2 vs. T-3) did not differ. On all three tests forgetting was directly related to length of retention interval, but no interaction was evident between number of previous items and length of retention interval.

In Exp. 2 a higher degree of initial learning of the items was achieved. Forgetting increased directly as a function of number of previous items presented. The predicted interaction was indeterminate since retention was essentially 100% on T-1 for all retention intervals.

Experiment 3 tested retention of six successive items over 3- and 18-sec. intervals. Retention after 3 sec. showed an initial drop and then a rise over the six tests, the rise suggesting a practice effect. Forgetting over 18 sec. increased directly from T-1 to T-6 and there was no indication that a constant amount of proactive interference had been reached. The interaction between length of retention interval and number of potential proactively interfering items was very evident.

The results were interpreted to mean that proactive inhibition in short-term memory of single items follows the same laws as proactive inhibition in long-term memory of lists of items.

REFERENCES

BRIGGS, G. E. Acquisition, extinction and recovery functions in retroactive inhibition. *J. exp. Psychol.*, 1954, **47**, 285–293.

MELTON, A. W. Discussion of Professor Peterson's paper. In C. N. Cofer (Ed.) *Problems and processes in verbal behavior and learning.* New York: McGraw-Hill, 1963.

MURDOCK, B. B., JR. The retention of individual items. *J. exp. Psychol.*, 1961, **62**, 618–625.

PETERSON, L. R. Immediate memory: Data and theory. In C. N. Cofer (Ed.) *Problems and processes in verbal behavior and learning.* New York: McGraw-Hill, 1963.

PETERSON, L. R., AND PETERSON, M. J. Short-term retention of individual verbal items. *J. exp. Psychol.*, 1959, **58**, 193–198.

POSTMAN, L. The present status of interference theory. In C. N. Cofer (Ed.) *Verbal learning and verbal behavior.* New York: McGraw-Hill, 1961.

POSTMAN, L. Short-term memory and incidental learning. Paper read at ONR conference, Ann Arbor, Michigan, February, 1962.

POSTMAN, L., AND RILEY, D. A. Degree of learning and interserial interference in retention. *Univer. Calif. Publ. Psychol.*, 1959, **8**, 271–396.

UNDERWOOD, B. J. The effect of successive interpolations on retroactive and proactive inhibition. *Psychol. Monogr.*, 1945, **59**, No. 3.

UNDERWOOD, B. J. Retroactive and proactive inhibition after five and forty-eight hours. *J. exp. Psychol.*, 1948, **38**, 29–38.

UNDERWOOD, B. J. Proactive inhibition with increased recall time. *Amer. J. Psychol.*, 1950, **63**, 594–599.

UNDERWOOD, B. J. Interference and forgetting. *Psychol. Rev.*, 1957, **64**, 49–60.

UNDERWOOD, B. J., AND SCHULZ, R. W. *Meaningfulness and verbal learning.* Philadelphia: Lippincott, 1960.

Implications of Short-Term Memory for a

General Theory of Memory [1]

Arthur W. Melton

University of Michigan, Ann Arbor, Michigan

Memory has never enjoyed even a small fraction of the interdisciplinary interest that has been expressed in symposia, discoveries, and methodological innovations during the last five years. Therefore, it seems probable that

Reprinted from *Journal of Verbal Learning and Verbal Behavior*, 1963, 2, 1–21. Copyright © 1963 by Academic Press Inc.

[1] This paper comprises, in substance, the author's Vice-Presidential Address to Section I (Psychology) of the American Association for the Advancement of Science, 1962. The author is particularly indebted to the Center for Human Learning, University of California, Berkeley, where a research appointment during the Fall semester of 1962–1963 gave the freedom from academic routine and the stimulating discussions that led to the repetition of the Hebb experiment and also supported the preparation of this paper. Early exploratory studies on short-term memory and the experiment on the recall of different sized verbal units were supported by Project MICHIGAN under Department of the Army Contract DA-36-039-SC-78801, administered by the United States Army Signal Corps. Reproduction for any purpose of the United States Government is permitted.

the next ten years will see major, perhaps even definitive, advances in our understanding of the biochemistry, neurophysiology, and psychology of memory, especially if these disciplines communicate with one another and seek a unified theory. My thesis is, of course, that psychological studies of human short-term memory, and particularly the further exploitation of new techniques for investigating human short-term memory, will play an important role in these advances toward a general theory of memory. Even now, some critical issues are being sharpened by such observations.

The confluence of forces responsible for this sanguine prediction about future progress is reflected in this AAAS program on memory (see other articles in this issue of this Journal). Advances in biochemistry and neurophysiology are permitting the formulation and testing of meaningful theories about the palpable stuff that is the correlate of the memory trace as an hypothetical construct (Deutsch, 1962; Gerard, 1963; Thomas, 1962). In this work there is heavy emphasis on the *storage* mechanism and its properties, especially the consolidation process, and it may be expected that findings here will offer important guide lines for the refinement of the psychologist's construct once we are clear as to what our human performance data say it should be.

Within psychology several developments have focused attention on memory. In the first place, among learning theorists there is a revival of interest in the appropriate assumptions to be made about the characteristics of the memory traces (engrams, associations, bonds, $_sH_r$'s) that are the products of experiences and repetitions of experiences. Thus, Estes (1960) has questioned the validity of the widespread assumption (e.g., Hull, 1943; Spence, 1955) that habit strength grows incrementally over repetitions, and has proposed an all-or-none conception as an alternative. More recently, he has examined (Estes, 1962) in detail the varieties of the incremental and all-or-none conceptions and the evidence related to them. Already, some defenders of the incremental concept (Jones, 1962; Keppel and Underwood, 1962; Postman, 1963) have taken issue with Estes' conclusions, and it would appear that this fundamental question about memory will loom large in theory and experiments for some time to come. At a somewhat different level, the revival of experimental and theoretical interest in the notion of perseveration or consolidation of the memory trace (Glickman, 1961), and attempts to embody it in a general theory of learning (Hebb, 1949; Walker, 1958), have also focused attention on a theory of memory as a fundamental component of a theory of learning.

A second strong stimulus to research on memory from within psychology are several findings of the last few years that have forced major revisions in the interference theory of forgetting and consequently a renaissance of interest in it (Postman, 1961). First, there was the discovery by Underwood (1957) that proactive inhibition had been grossly underestimated as a source of interference in forgetting. Then, the unlearning factor as a component of retroactive inhibition was given greater credibility by the findings of Barnes and Underwood (1959). And finally, the joint consideration of the habit structure of the individual prior to a new learning experience, the compatibility or incompatibility of the new learning with that structure, and the unlearning factor (among others) led to the formulation of the interference theory of forgetting in terms that made it applicable to all new learning (Melton, 1961; Postman, 1961; Underwood and Postman,

1960). Thus, this development focuses attention on the interactions of memory traces during learning as well as their interactions at the time of attempted retrieval or utilization in recognition, recall, or transfer.

But perhaps the most vigorous force directing attention within psychology to the need for a general theory of memory is the spate of theorizing and research on immediate and short-term memory during the last five years. In 1958, and increasingly thereafter, the principal journals of human learning and performance have been flooded with experimental investigations of human short-term memory. This work has been characterized by strong theoretical interests, and sometimes strong statements, about the nature of memory, the characteristics of the memory trace, and the relations between short-term memory and the memory that results from multiple repetitions. The contrast with the preceding thirty years is striking. During those years most research on short-term memory was concerned with the memory span as a capacity variable, and no more. It is always dangerous to be an historian about the last five or ten years, but I venture to say that Broadbent's *Perception and Communication* (1958), with its emphasis on short-term memory as a major factor in human information-processing performance, played a key role in this development. Fortunately, many of the others who have made important methodological and substantive contributions to this analysis of short-term memory have presented their most recent findings and thoughts in these Meetings on Memory, and they thus adequately document my assessment of the vigor and importance of this recent development. Therefore I will refrain from further documentation and analysis at this point, since the impact of some of these findings on our theory of memory is my main theme.

THE DOMAIN OF A THEORY OF MEMORY

A theory of memory is becoming important for a number of different reasons, and somehow all of these reasons properly belong to a comprehensive theory of memory. Its storage mechanism is the principal concern of biochemists and neurophysiologists; the morphology of its storage—whether as a multiplexed trace system with one trace per repetition, or a single trace system subjected to incremental changes in "strength" by repetition—is becoming a principal concern of learning theorists; its susceptibility to inhibition, interference, or confusion both at the time of new trace formation and at the time of attempted trace retrieval or utilization is the concern of forgetting and transfer theorists; and the perhaps unique properties of its manifestation in immediate and short-term retention is the principal concern of psychologists interested in human information-processing performance. One knows intuitively that all of these different approaches emphasize valid questions or issues that must be encompassed by a general theory of memory, but nowhere—with perhaps the exception of Gomulicki's (1953) historical-theoretical monograph on memory-trace theory—will one find explicit systematic consideration of these several different facets of the problem of memory.

Since my present intention is to marshal some data relevant to one of the main issues in a general theory of memory—namely, the question of whether single-repetition, short-term memory and multiple-repetition, long-term memory are a dichotomy or points on a continuum—I feel compelled to discuss briefly what I believe to be the proper domain of a theory of memory and to differentiate it from a theory of learning.

After some exclusions that need not concern us here, learning may be defined as the modification of behavior as a function of experience. Operationally, this is translated into the question of whether (and, if so, how much) there has been a change in behavior from Trial n to Trial $n + 1$. Any attribute of behavior that can be subjected to counting or measuring operations can be an index of change from Trial n to Trial $n + 1$, and therefore an index of learning. Trials n and $n + 1$ are, of course, the presentation and test trials of a so-called test of immediate memory or they may be any trial in a repetitive learning situation and any immediately subsequent trial. By convention among psychologists, the change from Trial n to Trial $n + 1$ is referred to as a learning change when the variable of interest is the ordinal number of Trial n and not the temporal interval between Trial n and Trial $n + 1$, and the change from Trial n to Trial $n + 1$ is referred to as a *retention* change when the variable of interest is the interval, and the events during the interval, between Trial n and Trial $n + 1$. Learning and retention observations generally imply that the characteristics of the task, situation, or to-be-formed associations remain the same from Trial n to Trial $n + 1$. When any of these task or situation variables are deliberately manipulated as independent variables between Trial n and Trial $n + 1$, the object of investigation is *transfer* of learning, i.e., the availability and utilization of the memorial products of Trial n in a "different" situation.

Now, these operational definitions of learning, retention, and transfer are completely aseptic with respect to theory, and I think it is important to keep them so. In part, this is because it is useful to keep in mind the fact that *learning* is never observed directly; it is always an inference from an observed change in performance from Trial n to Trial $n + 1$. Furthermore— and this is the important point for theory—the observed change in performance is always a confounded reflection of three theoretically separable events: (i) the events on Trial n that result in something being stored for use on Trial $n + 1$; (ii) the storage of this product of Trial n during the interval between Trials n and $n + 1$; and (iii) the events on Trial $n + 1$ that result in retrieval and/or utilization of the stored trace of the events on Trial n. For convenience, these three theoretically separable events in an instance of learning will be called *trace formation, trace storage,* and *trace utilization.*

Obviously, a theory of learning must encompass these three processes. However, it must also encompass other processes such as those unique to the several varieties of selective learning and problem solving. Some advantages will accrue, therefore, if the domain of a general theory of memory is considered to be only a portion of the domain of a theory of learning; specifically, that portion concerned with the *storage* and *retrieval* of the residues of demonstrable instances of association formation. This seems to me to fit the historical schism between learning theories and research on memory and the formal recognition of this distinction may well assist in avoiding some misconceptions about the scope of a theory of memory. Historically, our major learning theories have not felt compelled to include consideration of the question whether storage of the residue of a learning experience (Trial n) is subject to autonomous decay, autonomous consolidation through reverberation, or to even consider systematically the memory-span phenomenon. On the other hand, much of the controversy between learning theorists surrounds the question of the necessary and sufficient conditions for association (or memory trace) formation. And even though most learning theories must say something about the conditions of transfer, or utilization of traces, they do not always include explicit consideration of the interference theory of forgetting or alternative theories. As for those who have been concerned with memory theory, they have, following Ebbinghaus (1885), employed the operations of rote learning, thus avoiding in so far as possible the problems of selective learning and insuring the contiguous occurrence of stimulus and response under conditions that demonstrably result in the formation of an association. Their emphasis has been on the storage and retrieval or other utilization of that association, i.e., of the residual trace of it in the central nervous system (CNS), and on the ways in which frequency of repetition and other learning affect such storage and retrieval.

The implication of this restriction on the domain of a theory of memory is that the theory will be concerned with post-perceptual traces, i.e., memory traces, and not with pre-perceptual traces, i.e., stimulus traces. It seems to me necessary to accept the notion that stimuli may affect the sensorium for a brief time and also the directly involved CNS segments, but that they may not get "hooked up," associated, or encoded with central or peripheral response components, and may not, because of this failure of being responded to, become a part of a memory-trace system. This view is supported by the recent work of Averbach and Coriell (1961), Sperling (1960), and Jane Mackworth (1962) which shows that there is a very-short-term visual pre-perceptual trace which suffers rapid decay (complete in .3 to .5 sec.). Only that which is reacted to during the presentation of a stimulus or during this post-exposure short-term trace is potentially retrievable from memory. While it is not necessary to my argument to defend this boundary for memory theory, because if I am wrong the slack will be taken up in a more inclusive theory of learning, it is of some interest that it is accepted by Broadbent (1963) and that it is consistent with a wealth of recent research on "incidental learning" in human subjects (Postman, in press).

What, then, are the principal issues in a theory of memory? These are about either the storage or the retrieval of traces. In the case of the storage of traces we have had four issues.[2] The first is whether memory traces should be given the characteristic of *autonomous decay* over time, which was dignified by Thorndike (1913) as the Law of Disuse and which recently has been vigorously defended by Brown (1958). The antithesis is, of course, the notion that associations, once established, are permanent—a position initially formulated by McGeoch (1932) and incorporated in a radical form in Guthrie's (1935) theory of learning.

[2] For the purposes of this discussion, I am ignoring the hypothetical property of autonomous, dynamic changes within memory traces in the directions specified by gestalt laws (Koffka, 1935). While the need for such an hypothetical property is not yet a dead issue (Duncan, 1960; Lovibond, 1958), it has had very little support since the classical treatment of the matter by Hebb and Foord (1945).

The second storage issue is again an hypothesis about an autonomous process, but one involving the *autonomous enhancement* (fixation, consolidation) of the memory trace, rather than decay. The hypothesis was first formulated in the perseveration theory of Müller and Pilzecker (1900), with emphasis on the autonomous enhancement, or strengthening, of a memory trace if it was permitted to endure without interruption. As such, the emphasis was on a property of automatic "inner repetition" if repetition and duration are given a trade-off function in determining the strength of traces. More recently, the hypothesis has been that the memory trace established by an experience *requires* consolidation through autonomous reverberation or perseveration if it is to become a stable structural memory trace in the CNS (Deutsch, 1962; Gerard, 1963; Glickman, 1961; Hebb, 1949). Presumably, the alternative view is that every experience establishes a structural memory trace without the necessity of consolidation through reverberation or perseveration, but also without denying that such reverberation or perseveration, if permitted, may strengthen the trace.

The third issue about storage is the one previously referred to as *morphological* (at the molecular level) in our brief reference to the current controversy about the all-or-none versus the incremental notions of association formation. The all-or-none notion implies that the increment in the probability of response on Trial $n + 2$ is a consequence of establishment of independent and different all-or-none trace systems on Trials n and $n + 1$; the incremental notion implies that the same trace system is activated in some degree on Trial n and then reactivated and strengthened on Trial $n + 1$. It is, of course, possible that both notions could be true.

The fourth issue about trace storage is actually one that overlaps the issues about retrieval or utilization of traces, and is perhaps the most critical current issue. This is the question whether there are two kinds of memory storage or only one. A duplex mechanism has been postulated by Hebb (1949), Broadbent (1958), and many others, and on a variety of grounds, but all imply that one type of storage mechanism is involved in remembering or being otherwise affected by an event just recently experienced, i.e., "immediate" or short-term memory for events experienced once, and that a different type is involved in the recall or other utilization of traces established by repetitive learning experiences, i.e., long-term memory or habit. Since a clean distinction between "immediate" memory and short-term memory is not possible (Melton, 1963), we shall henceforward refer to these two manifestations of memory as short-term memory (STM) and long-term memory (LTM).

Some principal contentions regarding the differences between the two memory mechanisms are that: (*a*) STM involves "activity" traces, while LTM involves "structural" traces (Hebb, 1949; 1961); (*b*) STM involves autonomous decay, while STM involves irreversible, non-decaying traces (Hebb, 1949); and (*c*) STM has a fixed capacity that is subject to overload and consequent loss of elements stored in it, for nonassociative reasons, while LTM is, in effect, infinitely expansible, with failure of retrieval attributable mainly to incompleteness of the cue to retrieval or to interference from previously or subsequently learned associations (Broadbent, 1958; 1963). On the other hand, the monistic view with respect to trace storage is one which, in general, accepts the characteristics of LTM storage as the characteristics of STM storage as well, and thus ascribes to the traces of events that occur only once the same "structural" properties, the same irreversibility, the same susceptibility to associational factors in retrieval, as are ascribed to LTM.

The bridge to the theoretical problems of trace retrieval and utilization as major components of a theory of memory is obviously wrought by the issue of memory as a dichotomy or a continuum. Those who accept a dichotomy do so on the basis of data on retention, forgetting, or transfer that suggest two distinct sets of conditions for retrieval and utilization of traces; those who accept a continuum do so on the basis of data that suggest a single set of conditions or principles.

The history of our thought about the problems of retrieval and utilization of traces reveals three main issues. The first is the question of the dependence of the retrieval on the completeness of the reinstatement on Trial $n + 1$ of the stimulating situation present on Trial n. Psychologists have formulated several principles in an attempt to describe the relevant observations, but all of them may be subsumed under a principle which asserts that the probability of retrieval will be a decreasing function of the amount of stimulus change from Trial n to Trial $n + 1$. Changes in directly measured and manipulated cue stimuli, like the CS in a classical conditioning experiment, that result in decrement in response probability are generally referred to a sub-principle of stimulus generalization (Mednick and Freedman, 1960); changes in contextual stimuli that result in forgetting are usually referred to a sub-principle of altered stimulating conditions or altered set (McGeoch and Irion, 1952); and stimulus changes that occur in spite of all attempts to hold the stimulating situation constant are referred to a sub-principle of stimulus fluctuation (Estes, 1955). Since these are all principles of transfer, when they are employed to interpret failure of retrieval on Trial $n + 1$, it is clear that all principles of transfer of learning, whether they emphasize the occurrence of retrieval in spite of change or the failure of retrieval in spite of some similarity, are fundamental principles of trace retrieval and utilization. At this moment I see no necessary difference between the dual- and single-mechanism theories of memory with respect to this factor of stimulus change in retrieval, but there may be one implicit and undetected.

The second issue relates to the interactions of traces. Here, of course, is the focus of the interference theory of forgetting which has, in recent years, led us to accept the notion that retrieval is a function of interactions between prior traces and new traces at the time of the formation of the new traces, as well as interactions resulting in active interference and blocking of retrieval. This theory was given its most explicit early expression in the attack by McGeoch (1932) on the principle of autonomous decay of traces, and has been refined and corrected in a number of ways since then (Postman, 1961). In its present form it accepts the hypothesis of irreversibility of traces and interprets all failures of retrieval or utilization as instances of stimulus change or interference. Therefore, it implicitly accepts a one-mechanism theory of memory. However, it has been recognized (Melton, 1961) that the principal evidence for the theory has come from the study of retrieval following multiple-repetition learning, and that the extension of the theory to STM is not necessarily valid. Since dual-mechanism theorists assert that retrieval in STM is subject to disruption through overloading, but not through associative interference, a prime focus of memory theory becomes the question of associative interference effects in STM.

A third important issue related to retrieval is the relationship between repetition and retrieval probability. While the fact of a strong correlation between repetition and probability of retrieval seems not to be questionable, there are two important questions about repetition that a theory of memory must encompass. The first of these is the question of whether repetition multiplies the number of all-or-none traces or whether it produces incremental changes in the strength of a trace. This has already been listed as a problem in storage, but it is obvious that the alternative notions about storage have important implications for the ways in which repetitions may be manipulated to increase or decrease probability of retrieval. The second is the question of whether there is a fundamental discontinuity between the characteristics of traces established by a single repetition and those established by multiple repetitions (or single repetitions with opportunity for consolidation). This appears to be the contention of the dual-mechanism theorists; whereas, a continuum of the effects of repetition in the establishment of "structural," permanent traces seems to be the accepted position of the single-mechanism theorists.

In summary so far, when the domain of a theory of memory is explicitly confined to the problems of the storage and retrieval of memory traces, it becomes possible to formulate and examine some of the major theoretical issues under the simplifying assumption that the formation of the associations or memory traces has already occurred. Then it becomes clear that the conflicting notions with respect to the properties of trace storage and the conflicting notions with respect to the principal determinants of trace retrieval, or failure thereof, converge on the more fundamental issue of the unitary or dual nature of the storage mechanism. My plan is to examine these alleged differences between STM and LTM in the light of some recent studies of human short-term memory, and then return to a summary of the implications these studies seem to have for the major issues in a general theory of memory.

STM AND LTM: CONTINUUM OR DICHOTOMY?

The contrasting characteristics of STM and LTM that have led to the hypothesis that there are two kinds of memory have not, to my knowledge, been considered systematically by any memory theorist, although Hebb (1949), Broadbent (1957; 1958; 1963), and Brown (1958) have defended the dichotomy.

The decay of traces in immediate memory, in contrast to the permanence, even irreversibility, of the memory traces established through repetitive learning, is the most universally acclaimed differentiation. For Hebb (1949) this rapid decay is a correlate of the non-structural, i.e., "activity," nature of the single perception that is given neither the "fixation" effect of repetition nor the opportunity for "fixation" through reverberation. For Broadbent (1957; 1958) and Brown (1958) this autonomous decay in time is a property of the postulated STM mechanism, and attempts have been made (e.g., Conrad and Hille, 1958) to support the notion that time per se is the critical factor in decay. Obviously, this autonomous decay can be postponed by rehearsal—recirculating through the short-term store (Broadbent, 1958)—and Brown (1958) has maintained that such rehearsal has no strengthening effect on the structural trace. However, the decay of a specific trace begins whenever rehearsal is prevented by distraction or overloading of the short-term store (Broadbent, 1957; 1958). A corollary of this last proposition is that the initiation of the decay process, by dislodging the trace from the short-term store, is not dependent on new learning and therefore not on the associative interference principles which account for most if not all of the forgetting of events that reach the long-term store through repetition, reverberation, or both (Broadbent, 1963).

These characteristics contrast sharply with those attributed to LTM by the interference theory of forgetting which has dominated our thinking since McGeoch's (1932) classical attack on the Law of Disuse and which has gained new stature as a consequence of recent refinements (Melton, 1961; Postman, 1961). This theory implies: (a) that traces, even those that result from single repetitions, are "structural" in Hebb's sense, and are permanent except as overlaid by either the recovery of temporarily extinguished stronger competing traces or by new traces; and (b) that all persistent and progressive losses in the retrievability of traces are to be attributed to such associative interference factors, and not to decay or to a combination of nonassociative disruption plus decay. And, as a consequence of these two implications, it is assumed that the effect of repetition on the strength of the single type of trace is a continuous monotonic process. On this basis a continuum is assumed to encompass single events or sequential dependencies between them when these events are well within the span of immediate memory and also complex sequences of events, such as in serial and paired-associate lists, that are far beyond the span of immediate memory and thus require multiple repetitions for mastery of the entire set of events or relations between them.

My discussion of the question: "STM or LTM; continuum or dichotomy?" will therefore examine some experimental data on STM to see (a) whether they are interpretable in terms of the interference factors known to operate in LTM, and (b) whether the durability of memory for sub-span and supra-span to-be-remembered units is a continuous function of repetitions.

The reference experiments that provide the data of interest are those recently devised by Peterson and Peterson (1959) and Hebb (1961), with major emphasis on the former. While a number of ingenious techniques for investigating STM have been invented during the last few years, I believe that the Petersons' method is the key to integration of retention data on immediate memory, STM, and LTM. This is because, as you will see, it can be applied to to-be-remembered units in the entire range from those well below the memory span to those well above it, and the control and manipulation of duration and frequency of presentation are essentially continuous with those traditionally employed in list memorization.

In what must have been a moment of supreme skepticism of laboratory dogma, not unlike that which recently confounded the chemist's dogma that the noble gases are nonreactive (Abelson, 1962), Peterson and Peterson (1959) determined the recallability of single trigrams, such as X-J-R, after intervals of 3, 6, 9, 12, 15, and 18 sec. The trigrams were presented auditorily in 1 sec., a 3-digit number occurred during the next second, and S counted backward by 3's or 4's from that number until, after the appropriate interval, he received a cue to recall the trigram. The S was given up to 14 sec. for the recall of the trigram, thus avoiding any time-pressure in the retrieval process. The principal measure of retention was the frequency of completely correct trigrams in recall.

The results of this experiment are shown in Fig. 1. It is noteworthy that the curve has the Ebbinghausian form, even though the maximum interval is only 18 sec., and that there is an appreciable amount of forgetting after only 3 and 6 sec. Other observations reported by the Petersons permit us to estimate that the recall after zero time interval, which is the usual definition of immediate memory, would have been 90%, which is to say that in 10% of the cases the trigram was misperceived, so that the forgetting is actually not as great as it might appear to be. Even with this correction for misperception, however, the retention after 18 sec. would be only about 20%, which is rather startling when one remembers that these trigrams were well below the memory span of the college students who served as Ss.

The rapid deterioration of performance over time is not inconsistent with the decay theory, nor is it necessarily inconsistent with the notion that traces from single occurrences of single items are on a continuum with traces from multiple items learned through repetition. However, additional data with the same method were soon forthcoming. Murdock (1961) first replicated the Peterson and Peterson experiment with 3-consonant trigrams, and then repeated all details of the experiment except that in one study he used single common words drawn from the more frequent ones in the Thorndike-Lorge word lists, and in another study he used word triads, i.e., three unrelated common words, as the to-be-remembered unit.

Murdock's results from these three experiments are shown alongside the Petersons' results in Fig. 1. His replication of the Petersons' study with trigrams gave remarkably similar results. Of considerable significance, as we will see later, is his finding that single words show less forgetting than did the trigrams, but that *some* forgetting occurs with even such simple units. Finally, the most seminal fact for theory in these experiments is his discovery that word triads act like 3-consonant trigrams in short-term retention.

Murdock's data strongly suggested that the critical determinant of the slope of the short-term retention function was the number of Millerian (1956) "chunks" in the to-be-remembered unit. Of even greater importance from my point of view was the implication that, other things being equal, the rate of forgetting of a unit presented once is a function of the amount of intra-unit interference, and that this intra-unit interference is a function of the number of encoded chunks within the item rather than the number of physical elements, such as letters, or information units.

The first of several projected experimental tests of this hypothesis has been completed.[3] The to-be-remembered units were 1, 2, 3, 4, or 5 consonants. The unit, whatever its size, was presented visually for 1 sec., and read off aloud by S. Then .7 sec. later a 3-digit number was shown for 1 sec.

[3] This study and a subsequent one are graduate research projects of David Wulff and Robert G. Crowder, University of Michigan, and will be reported under the title: Melton, A. W., Crowder, R. G., and Wulff, D., *Short-term memory for individual items with varying numbers of elements.*

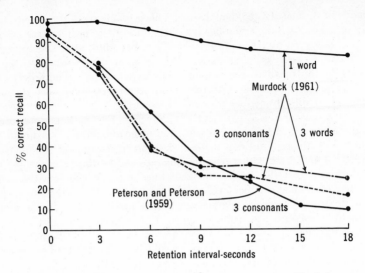

FIG. 1. Percentage frequency of completely correct recall of 3-consonant trigrams (Peterson and Peterson, 1959; Murdock, 1961), and 1-word and 3-word units (Murdock, 1961).

and removed. The S read off the number and then counted backward aloud by 3's or 4's until a visual cue for recall, a set of 4 asterisks, was shown. The delayed retention intervals were 4, 12, and 32 sec., and a fourth condition involved recall after only .7 sec., hereafter referred to as the zero interval. The Ss were given 8 sec. for the recall of each item. In the course of the experiment each S was tested four times at each combination of unit size and interval for a total of 80 observations. Every condition was represented in each of 4 successive blocks of 20 observations, and there was partial counterbalancing of conditions within the blocks and of to-be-remembered units between the blocks. Through my error, the to-be-remembered units of each specific size were not counterbalanced across the four retention intervals. Thanks only to the power of the variable we were investigating, this did not, as you will see, materially affect the orderliness of the data.

The results for the last two blocks of trials are shown in Fig. 2. Again, the measure of recall performance is the percentage of completely correct recalls of the to-be-remembered unit, i.e., the single consonant had to be correct when only one was presented, all five consonants had to be correct and in the proper order when the 5-consonant unit was presented. The same relationships hold when Ss are not as well-practiced in the task, i.e., in Blocks 1 and 2, although the absolute amounts of forgetting are greater. The data in Fig. 2 are to be preferred to those for the earlier stages of practice, because all five curves in this figure have their origin very near to 100% recall. That is, in all cases it is possible to assume that Ss had, in fact, learned the to-be-remembered unit during the 1-sec. presentation interval.

Aside from the self-evident generalization that the slope of the short-term forgetting curve increases as a direct function of the number of elements in the to-be-remembered unit, two features of these data are worthy of special attention. First, it should be noted that the slope of the curve for

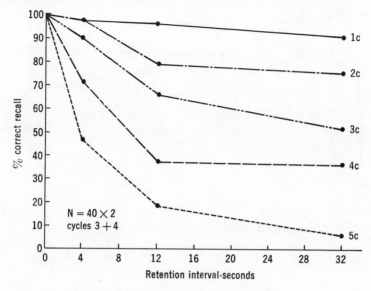

FIG. 2.   Percentage frequency of completely correct recall of units of 1 to 5 consonants with well-practiced Ss (Blocks 3 and 4).

the 3-consonant units is not as steep as was reported by both Peterson and Peterson (1959) and by Murdock (1961). We do not know why there is this discrepancy, although it occurs consistently in our work with the Petersons' method.

The other point of interest is the obvious forgetting of the one-consonant unit. This curve looks very much like the one obtained by Murdock for single words. Both findings have significance for theory because they represent instances of forgetting when the intra-unit interference is at a minimum for verbal units. But before giving additional consideration to this point, a further set of data from this experiment needs to be presented and a more general statement of the observed relationships deserves formulation.

If the increased slopes of the forgetting curves shown in Fig. 2 are attributed to an increase in intra-unit interference, it is of some importance to show that the more frequent breakdown of complete recall as one increases the number of letters in the to-be-remembered unit is not merely a breakdown in the sequential dependencies between the letters, but is also reflected in the frequency of correct recall of the first letter of the unit. In Fig. 3 are shown the percentages of first-letter recalls in the last two blocks of our experiment. Although they are lacking in the monotonic beauty of the curves for whole units correct, I am willing to accept the generalization that first-letter recall suffers interference as a function of the number of other letters in the to-be-remembered unit. Thus, what Peterson (1963) has called "background conditioning," and is measured by the recall of first letters, and what he has called "cue learning," and is represented by sequential dependencies in recall, are affected alike by the number of elements in the to-be-remembered unit. This is expected in so far as there is functional parallelism between "free" recall and serial or paired-associate

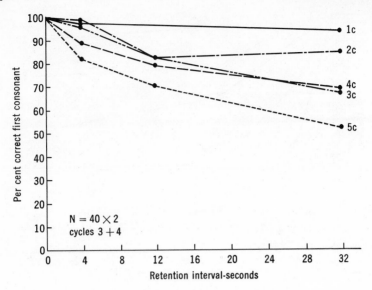

FIG. 3. Percentage frequency of correct recall of the first letter in 1- to 5-consonant units with well-practiced Ss (Blocks 3 and 4).

recall with respect to the effect of learning and interference variables (Melton, 1963).

In Fig. 4 the results obtained so far have been generalized and extrapolated. This set of hypothetical curves will be used as the conceptual anchor for three points that are related to the question whether short-term and long-term memory are a dichotomy or points on a continuum. The first, and most obvious, point about the figure is that it reaffirms the notion that intra-unit interference is a major factor in the short-term forgetting of subspan units, but now the parameter is the number of encoded chunks, instead of the number of physical elements or information units. This is consistent with Miller's (1956) cogent arguments for the concept of chunk as the unit of measurement of human information-processing capacities. It is also the unit most likely to have a one-to-one relationship to the memory trace. Obviously, it is also the concept demanded by the parallelism of the findings of Murdock with 1 and 3 words and our findings with 1 to 5 consonants, even though it cannot, of course, be asserted that the number of elements beyond one in these experiments, be they words or consonants, stand in a one-to-one relationship to the number of chunks. Even though the strings of consonants in our experiment were constructed by subtracting from or combining consonant trigrams of Witmer (1935) association values less than 60%, there were surely some easy-to-learn letter sequences and some hard-to-learn letter sequences. That such differences in meaningfulness are correlated with chunkability is well known (Underwood and Schulz, 1960). Also, Peterson, Peterson, and Miller (1961) have shown, although on a limited scale, that the meaningfulness of CVC trigrams is positively correlated with recall after 6 sec. in the Petersons' situation. But perhaps the greatest gain from the use of the chunk as the unit of measurement in formulating the otherwise empirical generalization is a suggestion this yields about how we may get a handle on that intervening variable. It sug-

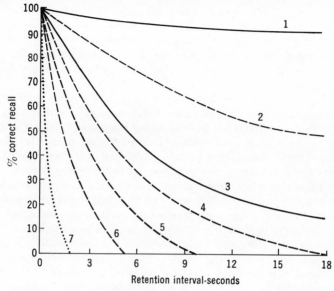

FIG. 4. The expected relationship between the number of recoded units ("chunks") in the to-be-remembered unit, the duration of the short-term retention interval, and the percentage frequency of completely correct recall, when each to-be-remembered unit is presented once, i.e., with just sufficient duration for one completely correct perceptual encoding. The solid-line curves represent some of the empirically determined functions; the dashed lines represent extrapolated functions; the dotted line represents the expected short-term memory function for a to-be-remembered unit that is at memory-span length for the individual S.

gests to me that we may be able to establish empirical benchmarks for 1, 2, 3, . . . , n chunks in terms of the slopes of short-term memory functions and then use these slopes to calibrate our verbal learning materials in terms of a chunk scale.

The evidence that the slope of the short-term forgetting curve increases dramatically as a function of the number of encoded chunks in the unit is evidence against autonomous decay being a major factor, but it does not deny that such decay may occur. It is evidence against decay as a major factor because: (a) a single consonant *was* remembered with very high frequency over a 32-sec. interval filled with numerical operations that surely qualify as overloading and disrupting activities (if one grants that the Petersons' method adequately controls surreptitious rehearsal); and (b) the major portion of the variance in recall is accounted for by intra-unit interference, rather than time. It does not deny that decay may occur, since there was *some* forgetting of even the single consonant (and of the single word in Murdock's experiment) even though only one "chunk" was involved, and intra-unit interference was at a minimum.

The reason for the forgetting of the single chunk is, I believe, to be found in the other sources of interference in recall in this type of experiment. In the first place, I presume that no one will argue that counting backward aloud is the mental vacuum that interference theory needs to insure the absence of retroactive inhibition in the recall of the to-be-remembered unit, nor is it necessarily the least interfering, and at the same time rehearsal-preventing, activity that can be found for such experiments. However, we must leave this point for future research, because we have none of the systematic studies that must be done on the effects of different methods of filling these short retention intervals, and we also have no evidence, therefore, on the extent to which retroactive interference and intra-unit interference interact.

On the other source of interference which may explain the forgetting of the single chunk—namely, proactive interference (PI)—we do have some evidence. Peterson (1963) has maintained, on the basis of analysis of blocks of trials in the original Peterson and Peterson (1959) study, that there is no evidence for the build-up of proactive inhibition in that experiment, only practice effects. However, this evidence is unconvincing (Melton, 1963) when practice effects are strong, and if it is assumed that proactive inhibition from previous items in the series of tests may build up rapidly but asymptote after only a few such previous items. Such an assumption about a rapidly achieved high steady-state of PI is given some credence by the rapid development of a steady-state in frequency of false-positives in studies of short-term recognition memory (Shepard and Teghtsoonian, 1961).

A second, and powerful, argument for large amounts of PI throughout the Peterson type of experiment is the frequency of overt intrusions from previous units in the series during the attempt to recall an individual unit. Murdock (1961) found such intrusions in his studies of short-term retention of words, and there was the strong recency effect among these intrusions that is to be expected if the steady-state notion is valid. The analysis of such intrusions in studies involving letters rather than words is limited by the identifiability of the source of the intrusions, but all who run experiments with letters become convinced that such intrusions are very common and usually come from the immediately preceding units.[4]

More systematic evidence for strong PI effects in STM in the Petersons' situation is given by Keppel and Underwood (1962). A representative finding is shown in Fig. 5. A three-consonant item which is the first item in the series is recalled almost perfectly after as long as 18 sec., and PI builds up rapidly over items, especially for the longer retention interval. These data support the notion that there is substantial PI in the Peterson and Peterson experiment on short-term memory for single verbal units. As such, they, as well as the other evidence cited, indicate that the small amount of forgetting of single consonants or single words over short intervals of time may be partly, if not entirely, attributable to the PI resulting from sequential testing of recall of such items. Keppel and Underwoods' results do not, however, support the view that the PI reaches a steady state in as few as five items, but this does not necessarily deny the steady-state notion. Also, a careful study of these data and the data on intra-unit interference suggests some strong interactions between PI, intra-unit interference (II), and the retention interval, all of which would support the interference interpretation, but discussion of these interactions would be tedious and unrewarding until properly designed experiments have been performed.

---

[4] Apparent intrusions from preceding to-be-remembered units were very common in the 1- to 5-consonant experiment reported here, but the experimental design did not counterbalance first-order sequence effects over conditions and nothing meaningful can be said about such intrusions except that they occur with substantial frequency.

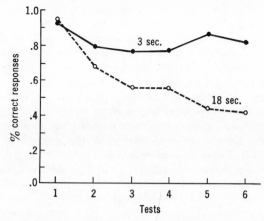

FIG. 5. Percentage frequency of completely correct recall of 3-consonant trigrams after 3 and 18 sec., as a function of the ordinal position of the test in a series of tests. The decline in recall reflects the buildup of proactive inhibition (Keppel and Underwood, 1962).

My conclusion from all this is that there is sufficient direct or inferential evidence for PI, RI, and II in the short-term retention of single subspan verbal units, and that the PI and potential RI may account for the observed forgetting of one-chunk units, that is, when II is minimal. So much for interference.

The other line of investigation that needs to be considered before the question of continuum versus dichotomy can be properly assessed has to do with the effect of repetition on the short-term memory for sub-span and just supra-span strings of elements or chunks.

The concept of the memory span is rather important in this discussion because it is the boundary between the number of elements, or chunks, that can be correctly reproduced immediately after a single repetition and the number of elements, or chunks, that require two or more repetitions for immediate correct reproduction. Interestingly enough, the short-term forgetting curve for a unit of memory-span length turns out to be the limiting member of the hypothetical family of curves that has been used to generalize the relationship between the slope of the forgetting curve and the number of chunks in the to-be-remembered unit. The extrapolated forgetting curve for a unit of memory-span length is shown as the dotted-line curve of Fig. 4.

The origin of this limiting curve on the ordinate will, of course, depend on the statistical definition of the span of immediate memory, but in order to be consistent I have placed it in Fig. 4 at or near 100% recall after zero interval. It is also assumed that the presentation time for this and all other smaller numbers of chunks is just sufficient for one perceptual encoding of each element, i.e., for one repetition. For a unit of span length it is not surprising that a precipitous decline of completely correct recall to zero is expected when only very short, but filled, delays are introduced before recall begins. No experiment in the literature fits exactly these operational requirements, but the prediction is a matter of common experience in looking up telephone numbers, and we also have Conrad's (1958) evidence that

Ss show a radical reduction in correct dialing of 8-digit numbers when required merely to dial "zero" before dialing the number.

At this point we are brought face to face with the question of the effects of repetition of sub-span and supra-span units on their recall. Such data are important for at least two reasons. In the first place, the argument for a continuum of STM and LTM requires that there be only orderly quantitative differences in the effects of repetition on sub-span and supra-span units. In the second place, if repetition has an effect on the frequency of correct recall of sub-span units, such as consonant trigrams, this must certainly have some significance for the conceptualization of the strength of a memory trace—whether it is all-or-none or cumulative.

The effect of time for rehearsal of a set of items before a filled retention interval was first studied by Brown (1958). His negative results led him to the conclusion that recirculation of information through the temporary memory store merely delays the onset of decay, but does not strengthen the trace. However, the original Peterson and Peterson (1959) report on the retention of consonant trigrams included an experiment which showed a significant effect of instructed rehearsal on short-term retention.

Fortunately, we now have available a report by Hellyer (1962) in which consonant trigrams were given one, two, four, or eight 1-sec. visual presentations before retention intervals of 3, 9, 18, and 27 sec. His data are shown in Fig. 6 and require little comment. Obviously, a consonant trigram is re-

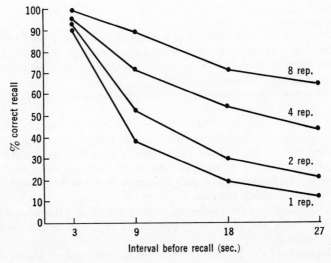

FIG. 6. Percentage frequency of completely correct recall of 3-consonant trigrams as a function of the frequency of 1-sec. presentations of the trigram before beginning the retention interval (Hellyer, 1962).

membered better with repetition even though it is completely and correctly perceived and encoded after only one repetition, as judged by the immediate recall of it. The slopes of the retention curves in our hypothetical family of curves based on the number of chunks in the to-be-remembered unit are, therefore, a joint function of chunks and repetitions. Or perhaps a better theoretical statement of this would be to say that repetition reduces the number of chunks in the to-be-remembered unit. This is why one word and one consonant have the same rate of forgetting.

As for the effect of repetition on just supra-span units, we have no data directly comparable to those of Hellyer for sub-span units, but we have data from a much more severe test of the repetition effect. I refer to the method and data of Hebb's (1961) study in which he disproved to his own satisfaction his own assumption about "activity" traces. In this experiment he presented a fixed set of 24 series of 9-digit numbers. Each of the digits from 1 to 9 was used only once within each to-be-remembered unit. The series was read aloud to S at the rate of about 1 digit/sec., and S was instructed to repeat the digits immediately in exactly the same order. The unusual feature of the experiment was that exactly the same series of digits occurred on every third trial, i.e., the 3rd, 6th, 9th . . . 24th, the others varying in a random fashion.

His results are shown in Fig. 7. Hebb considered the rising curve for

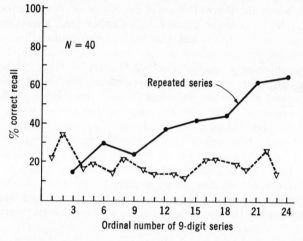

FIG. 7. Percentage frequency of completely correct recall of 9-digit numbers when tested immediately. The "repeated series" was a specific 9-digit sequence that occurred in the 3rd, 6th, 9th . . . 24th position in the series of tests. Other points represent nonrepeated 9-digit numbers (Hebb, 1961).

the repeated 9-digit numbers, when contrasted with the flat curve for the nonrepeated numbers, to be sufficient basis for concluding that some form of structural trace results from a single repetition of an associative sequence of events. Further, he properly considers this to be a demonstration of the cumulative structural effects of repetition under extremely adverse conditions involving large amounts of RI.

Hebb's method in this experiment may well be another important invention in the analysis of human memory. But I was not completely satisfied with his experiment and the reliability of his findings, for reasons that need not be detailed here. As a consequence of these uncertainties, I have repeated and extended Hebb's experiment by giving each of 32 women Ss two practice numbers and then 80 tests for immediate recall of 9-digit numbers. Within these 80 tests there were 4 instances in which a specific 9-digit number occurred 4 times with 2 other numbers intervening between suc-

cessive trials, 4 in which a specific number occurred 4 times with 3 intervening numbers, 4 for 4 trials with 5 intervening numbers and 4 for 4 trials
with 8 intervening numbers. In addition, there were 16 9-digit numbers
that occurred only once. I will not try to describe the interlocking pattern
of events that was used to achieve this design, but the design chosen was
used in both a forward and backward order for different Ss, and the specific
repeated numbers were used equally often under the different spacings of
repetitions. Furthermore, within the entire set of 32 different 9-digit numbers used in this experiment, inter-series similarities were minimized by
insuring that no more than two digits ever occurred twice in the same order.
The numbers were presented visually for 3.7 sec. and S recorded her response by writing on a 3 × 5 in. card which contained 9 blocks. Recall
began .7 sec. after the stimulus slide disappeared, and 8.8 sec. were allowed
for recall.

Unfortunately, my Ss behaved in a somewhat more typical fashion than
did Hebb's, in that they showed substantial nonspecific practice effects.
This complicates the determination of the effects of specific repetition, because later trials on a particular 9-digit number must always be later in
practice than earlier trials, and also because this confounding of specific
and nonspecific practice effects is more serious the greater the interval between repetitions of a specific number. This confounding has been eliminated, at least to my satisfaction, by determining the function that seemed
to be the most appropriate fit to the practice curve based on first occurrences of specific numbers. This function was then used to correct obtained
scores on the 2nd, 3rd, and 4th repetitions of a specific number in a manner and amount appropriate to the expected nonspecific practice effect.

A preferred measure of the effect of repetition in this situation is the
mean number of digits correctly recalled in their proper positions. In Fig. 8
is shown the mean number of digits correctly recalled, as a function of
ordinal position of the first occurrence of a 9-digit number within the experimental session. This merely confirms my statement about practice effects;

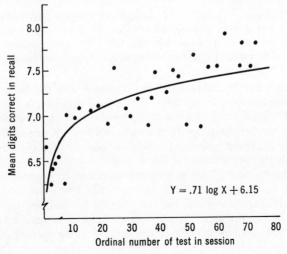

$$Y = .71 \log X + 6.15$$

FIG. 8.   The nonspecific practice effect in the recall of new and different
9-digit numbers in the course of the experiment.

exhibits the equation used for corrections for general practice effects; and permits observation of the large variability of mean performance in this type of experiment.

The principal data from the experiment are shown in Fig. 9. The effect of repetition of a specific 9-digit number is plotted, the parameter being the

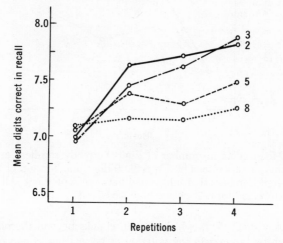

FIG. 9. Mean number of digits correctly recalled, as a function of the number of repetitions of the specific 9-digit number and of the number of other 9-digit numbers that intervened between repetitions. The data points for the first repetition are obtained values; the data points for the second, third, and fourth repetitions reflect corrections for nonspecific practice effects.

number of other different 9-digit numbers that intervened between successive repetitions of the specific number. In these curves the points for first-repetition performance are obtained points, and those for performance on the 2nd, 3rd, and 4th repetitions have been corrected for nonspecific practice effects. In Fig. 10 these last data are expressed as gains in performance over performance on the first occurrence of a number. Comparable data for gains in the frequency with which entire 9-digit numbers were correctly recalled show the same relationships.

These data not only confirm the Hebb data, they also add material substance to an argument for a continuum of immediate, short-term, and long-term memory. Just as a continuum theory would have predicted Hebb's results with two intervening numbers between repetitions of a specific number, it also would predict that the repetition effect would be a decreasing function of the number of intervening numbers because between-repetition retroactive inhibition is being increased. Even so, I am not sure that any theory would have predicted that one would need to place as many as 8 other 9-digit numbers in between repetitions of a specific 9-digit number before the repetition effect would be washed out. Surely, the structural memory trace established by a single occurrence of an event must be extraordinarily persistent.

With respect to our hypothetical family of retention curves based on the number of chunks in the to-be-remembered unit, we can now with some

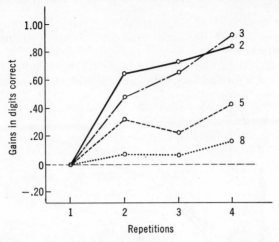

FIG. 10. Mean gains in number of digits correctly recalled, as a function of the number of repetitions of a specific 9-digit number and of the number of other 9-digit numbers that intervened between repetitions. All gain scores have been corrected for nonspecific practice effects.

confidence say that events which contain chunks beyond the normal memory span can be brought to the criterion of perfect immediate recall by reducing the number of chunks through repetition. If this empirical model involving chunks and repetitions to predict short-term forgetting is valid, it should be possible to show that a supra-span 9-chunk unit that is reduced to 7 chunks through repetition, would have the short-term forgetting curve of a 7-chunk unit, and one reduced through repetition to a 3-chunk unit should have a 3-chunk short-term forgetting curve. Even though this prediction is probably much too simple-minded, it now requires no stretch of my imagination to conceive of the "immediate" or short-term memory for single units and the memory for memorized supra-span units, like 12 serial nonsense syllables or 8 paired associates, as belonging on a continuum.

IMPLICATIONS

We may now turn to the implications these data on short-term memory seem to me to have for a theory of memory. I will attempt no finely spun theory, because such is neither my talent nor my interest. Also, I can be brief because, aged Functionalist that I am, I would be the first to admit—even insist—that my inferences are stated with confidence only for the storage and retrieval of verbal material demonstrably encoded by adult human Ss.

The duplexity theory of memory storage must, it seems to me, yield to the evidence favoring a continuum of STM and LTM or else come up with an adequate accounting for the evidence presented here. My preference is for a theoretical strategy that accepts STM and LTM as mediated by a single type of storage mechanism. In such a continuum, frequency of repetition appears to be the important independent variable, "chunking" seems to be the important intervening variable, and the slope of the retention curve is the important dependent variable. I am persuaded of this by the orderly way in which repetition operates on both sub-span units and supra-span units to increase the probability of retrieval in recall, and also by the parallelism between STM and LTM that is revealed as we look at STM with the conceptual tools of the interference theory of forgetting which was developed from data on LTM.

The evidence that implies a continuum of STM and LTM also relates, of course, to some of the other issues about the characteristics of memory storage. While it is perhaps too early to say that the autonomous decay of traces has no part in forgetting, whether short-term or long-term, I see no basis for assuming that such decay has the extreme rapidity sometimes ascribed to it or for assuming that it accounts for a very significant portion of the forgetting that we all suffer continually and in large amounts. On the contrary, the data from both STM and LTM tempt one to the radical hypothesis that every perception, however fleeting and embedded in a stream of perceptions, leaves its permanent "structural" trace in the CNS.

Insofar as I can understand the implications of the consolidation hypothesis about memory storage, I must concur with Hebb's (1961) conclusion that his experiment demonstrates the fixation of a structural trace by a single repetition of an event and without the benefit of autonomous consolidation processes. In fact, I think that our repetition and extension of his experiment establishes that conclusion even more firmly, because it shows that the retrievability of the trace of the first experience of a specific 9-digit number is a decreasing function of the amount of reuse of the elements in the interval between repetitions. Therefore, as far as our present data go, it seems proper to conclude that a consolidation process extending over more than a few seconds is not a necessary condition for the fixation of a structural trace. This does not, of course, deny that consolidation may be a necessary condition in other types of learning or other types of organism, nor does it deny that types of experience (e.g., Kleinsmith and Kaplan, 1963; Walker, 1963) other than the mundane remembering of nonsense strings of letters or words may benefit from such autonomous consolidation processes if they are permitted to occur.

The issue as to whether memory traces are established in an incremental or all-or-none fashion can be refined, but not resolved, on the basis of our observations on short-term memory. In all of the experiments with the Petersons' method, the initial operation was to insure that S encoded, i.e., learned, the to-be-remembered unit in a single 1-sec. presentation of it before the retention interval was introduced. This is "one-trial" learning in a more exact sense than has been true of various attempts to demonstrate the all-or-none principle in associative learning (Postman, 1963). Yet forgetting was rapid and strongly a function of the amount of potential intra-unit interference in the to-be-remembered unit. Also, this unit that was perfectly remembered after one repetition was better remembered after multiple massed repetitions. The proper question in the case of verbal associative learning seems, therefore, to be the characteristics of the trace storage that reflect the effects of repetitions on performance, rather than the question whether such associative connections reach full effective strength in one trial. The question of whether repetitions multiply the number of traces leading to a particular response or produce incremental changes in specific traces seems to me to be subject to direct experimental attack. Perhaps again because of my Functionalist background, I am inclined to believe that future research will show that both the multiplexing of traces and the incremental strengthening of traces results from repetition. Which mode of storage carries the greater burden in facilitating retrieval will depend on the variability of stimulation from repetition to repetition and the appropriateness of the sampling of this prior stimulation at the time of attempted retrieval.

Finally, with respect to the retrieval process, the theory of which is dominated by transfer theory for LTM, it seems that the placing of STM and LTM on a continuum—and the reasons for doing so—forces the interference theory of forgetting to include the prediction of forgetting in STM within its domain. At least, the testing of the theory in that context will extend its importance as a general theory of forgetting, if it survives the tests, and will quickly reveal the discontinuity of STM and LTM, if such is in fact the case.

Whatever may be the outcome of these theoretical and experimental issues in the next few years, of one thing we can be certain at this time. The revival of interest in short-term memory and the new techniques that have been devised for the analysis of short-term memory will enrich and extend our understanding of human memory far beyond what could have been accomplished by the most assiduous exploitation of the techniques of rote memorization of lists of verbal units. In fact, our evidence on STM for near-span and supra-span verbal units suggests that the systematic exploration of the retention of varying sizes of units over short and long time intervals will give new meaning to research employing lists.

REFERENCES

ABELSON, P. H. The need for skepticism. *Science,* 1962, **138**, 75.

AVERBACH, E., AND CORIELL, A. S. Short-term memory in vision. *Bell Syst. Tech. J.,* 1961, **40**, 309–328.

BARNES, J. M., AND UNDERWOOD, B. J. "Fate" of first-list associations in transfer theory. *J. exp. Psychol.,* 1959, **58**, 97–105.

BROADBENT, D. E. A mechanical model for human attention and immediate memory. *Psychol. Rev.,* 1957, **64**, 205–215.

BROADBENT, D. E. *Perception and communication.* New York: Pergamon, 1958.

BROADBENT, D. E. Flow of information within the organism. *J. verb. Learn. verb. Behav.,* 1963, **2**, 34–39.

BROWN, J. Some tests of the decay theory of immediate memory. *Quart. J. exp. Psychol.,* 1958, **10**, 12–21.

CONRAD, R. Accuracy of recall using keyset and telephone dial and the effect of a prefix digit. *J. appl. Psychol.,* 1958, **42**, 285–288.

CONRAD, R., AND HILLE, B. A. The decay theory of immediate memory and paced recall. *Canad. J. Psychol.,* 1958, **12**, 1–6.

DEUTSCH, J. A. Higher nervous function: The physiological bases of memory. *Ann. Rev. Physiol.,* 1962, **24**, 259–286.

DUNCAN, C. P. Controlled fixation of the stimulus-figure in a study of autonomous change in the memory-trace. *Amer. J. Psychol.,* 1960, **73**, 115–120.

EBBINGHAUS, H. *Das Gedächtnis: Untersuchungen zur experimentellen Psychologie.* Leipzig: Duncker & Humbolt, 1885.

ESTES, W. K. Statistical theory of distributional phenomena in learning. *Psychol. Rev.,* 1955, **62,** 369–377.

ESTES, W. K. Learning theory and the new "mental chemistry." *Psychol. Rev.,* 1960, **67,** 207–223.

ESTES, W. K. Learning theory. *Ann. Rev. Psychol.,* 1962, **13,** 107–144.

GERARD, R. W. The material basis of memory. *J. verb. Learn. verb. Behav.,* 1963, **2,** 22–33.

GLICKMAN, S. E. Perseverative neural processes and consolidation of the memory trace. *Psychol. Bull.,* 1961, **58,** 218–233.

GOMULICKI, B. R. The development and present status of the trace theory of memory. *Brit. J. Psychol., Monogr. Suppl.,* 1953, Whole No. 29, 94 pp.

GUTHRIE, E. R. *The psychology of learning.* New York: Harper, 1935.

HEBB, D. O. *The organization of behavior.* New York: Wiley, 1949.

HEBB, D. O. Distinctive features of learning in the higher animal. In J. F. Delafresnaye (Ed.) *Brain mechanisms and learning.* London and New York: Oxford Univ. Press, 1961. Pp. 37–46.

HEBB, D. O., AND FOORD, E. N. Errors of visual recognition and the nature of the trace. *J. exp. Psychol.,* 1945, **35,** 335–348.

HELLYER, S. Supplementary report: Frequency of stimulus presentation and short-term decrement in recall. *J. exp. Psychol.,* 1962, **64,** 650.

HULL, C. L. *Principles of behavior.* New York: Appleton-Century-Crofts, 1943.

JONES, J. E. All-or-none versus incremental learning. *Psychol. Rev.,* 1962, **69,** 156–160.

KEPPEL, G., AND UNDERWOOD, B. J. Proactive inhibition in short-term retention of single items. *J. verb. Learn. verb. Behav.,* 1962, **1,** 153–161.

KLEINSMITH, L. J., AND KAPLAN, S. Paired-associate learning as a function of arousal and interpolated interval. *J. exp. Psychol.,* 1963, **65,** 190–193.

KOFFKA, K. *Principles of gestalt psychology.* New York: Harcourt, Brace, 1935.

LOVIBOND, S. H. A further test of the hypothesis of autonomous memory trace change. *J. exp. Psychol.,* 1958, **55,** 412–415.

McGEOCH, J. A. Forgetting and the law of disuse. *Psychol. Rev.,* 1932, **39,** 352–370.

McGEOCH, J. A., AND IRION, A. L. *The psychology of human learning* (2nd ed.) New York: Longmans, Green, 1952.

MACKWORTH, J. F. The visual image and the memory trace. *Canad. J. Psychol.,* 1962,**16,** 55–59.

MEDNICK, S. A., AND FREEDMAN, J. L. Stimulus generalization. *Psychol. Bull.,* 1960, **57,** 169–200.

MELTON, A. W. Comments on Professor Postman's paper. In C. N. Cofer (Ed.) *Verbal learning and verbal behavior.* New York: McGraw-Hill, 1961. Pp. 179–193.

MELTON, A. W. Comments on Professor Peterson's paper. In C. N. Cofer and B. S. Musgrave (Eds.) *Verbal behavior and learning: Problems and processes.* New York: McGraw-Hill, 1963. Pp. 353–370.

MILLER, G. A. The magical number seven, plus or minus two: Some limits on our capacity for processing information. *Psychol. Rev.,* 1956, **63,** 81–97.

MÜLLER, G. E., AND PILZECKER, A. Experimentelle Beitrage zur Lehre vom Gedachtnis. *Z. Psychol.,* 1900, **1,** 1–300.

MURDOCK, B. B., JR. The retention of individual items. *J. exp. Psychol.,* 1961, **62,** 618–625.

PETERSON, L. R. Immediate memory: Data and theory. In C. N. Cofer

(Ed.) *Verbal learning and behavior: Problems and processes.* New York: McGraw-Hill, 1963.

PETERSON, L. R., AND PETERSON, M. J. Short-term retention of individual verbal items. *J. exp. Psychol.*, 1959, **58**, 193–198.

PETERSON, L. R., PETERSON, M. J., AND MILLER, A. Short-term retention and meaningfulness. *Canad. J. Psychol.*, 1961, **15**, 143–147.

POSTMAN, L. The present status of interference theory. In C. N. Cofer (Ed.) *Verbal learning and verbal behavior.* New York: McGraw-Hill, 1961. Pp. 152–179.

POSTMAN, L. One-trial learning. In C. N. Cofer (Ed.) *Verbal learning and behavior: Problems and processes.* New York: McGraw-Hill, 1963.

POSTMAN, L. Short-term memory and incidental learning. In A. W. Melton (Ed.) *Categories of human learning.* New York: Academic Press, in press.

SHEPARD, R. N., AND TEGHTSOONIAN, M. Retention of information under conditions approaching a steady state. *J. exp. Psychol.*, 1961, **62**, 302–309.

SPENCE, K. W. *Behavior theory and conditioning.* New Haven, Connecticut: Yale Univer. Press, 1955.

SPERLING, G. The information available in brief visual presentations. *Psychol. Monogr.*, 1960, **74**, Whole No. 498.

THOMAS, G. J. Neurophysiology of learning. *Ann. Rev. Psychol.*, 1962, **13**, 71–106.

THORNDIKE, E. L. *Educational psychology: II. The psychology of learning.* New York: Teachers College, Columbia Univer., 1913.

UNDERWOOD, B. J. Interference and forgetting. *Psychol. Rev.*, 1957, **64**, 49–60.

UNDERWOOD, B. J., AND KEPPEL, G. One-trial learning? *J. verb. Learn. verb. Behav.*, 1962, **1**, 1–13.

UNDERWOOD, B. J., AND POSTMAN, L. Extraexperimental sources of interference in forgetting. *Psychol. Rev.*, 1960, **67**, 73–95.

UNDERWOOD, B. J., AND SCHULZ, R. W. *Meaningfulness and verbal learning.* Philadelphia: Lippincott, 1960.

WALKER, E. L. Action decrement and its relation to learning. *Psychol. Rev.*, 1958, **65**, 129–142.

WALKER, E. L. Memory storage as a function of arousal and time. *J. verb. Learn. verb. Behav.*, 1963, **2**, 113–119.

WITMER, L. R. The association-value of three-place consonant syllables. *J. genet. Psychol.*, 1935, **47**, 337–360.

PART FIVE

Physiological Aspects
of Hunger

There is no doubt about the American public's concern with the interrelated topics of hunger, diet, and obesity. It seems that each year is marked by the publication of a new "miracle" diet that will enable people to eat their fill, suffer no hunger pangs, and yet lose a spectacular amount of weight. And each plan has its vogue, is discredited, fades into obscurity, and, the next season, is replaced by another miracle diet. These diets are commercially successful for two reasons: (1) the public wants to believe that weight can be lost without altering eating and activity habits and (2) the scientific study of hunger has proved it to be a complicated and incompletely understood set of phenomena.

For many decades, the study of hunger has been of both psychological and physiological interest. I. P. Pavlov, a key figure in modern psychology, was himself a physiologist. His work on the nature of the digestive juices earned him a Nobel prize in 1904. While studying the nature of salivary secretions, Pavlov observed that his dogs sometimes salivated before food was placed in their mouths; he spent the latter part of his scientific life studying these "psychic" secretions. Just as Pavlov's work was *both* psychological and physiological, so is it difficult to separate neatly into psychological and physiological parts the other basic aspects of hunger. In this section we shall place primary emphasis upon the physiological aspects of hunger.

Most higher animals seem to show definite periods of hunger. Humans verbally report hunger at some times, though not at others. Nonverbal animals also show periodicity in food-seeking behavior, or, if given free access to food, they eat intermittently rather than steadily. The old question of what physiological cues correspond to these hunger behaviors is still not completely answered. In fact, so many different theories of hunger mechanisms have been suggested that we can classify these theories by types. *Local, central,* and *general* theories comprise one popular classification; Rosenzweig[1] states that the Italian physiologist Luciani was the first to use these names in 1906.

Briefly, "local" theories state that a specific noticeable reaction, such as dryness of the throat, signals the animal that it is "time" to eat. "Central" theories postulate that some central nervous system mechanism works as a hunger "thermostat." And "general" theories attribute hunger to pervasive whole-body factors such as tissue depletion or blood sugar level.

The Cannon and Washburn article expounds the theory that hunger is a local phenomenon; it champions the belief that stomach contractions are the particular local hunger signs. After contrasting how well local and central theories of hunger agreed with what was then known about hunger, Cannon and Washburn declare for a local theory. Then they report an ingenious experiment to demonstrate the relationship between stomach movements (physiological) to a verbal report of the sensation of hunger (psychological).

Small children are known for ingesting all sorts of objects the moment their mothers' backs are turned; all of us at one time or another have swallowed such non-nutritive things as pills or capsules. Capitalizing upon this ability to swallow objects, Washburn taught himself to swallow a small balloon attached to an air hose. After it was swallowed, the balloon could be inflated through the hose. Subsequent contractions and expansions of Washburn's stomach would squeeze the balloon, causing air to flow in the tube. The air flow was attached to a recording mechanism, and thus a pictorial record of his stomach activity was established. Then Washburn could report his "subjective" feelings—whenever he "felt" hungry. Cannon and Washburn use the close correspondence between hunger feelings and Washburn's stomach contractions as strong evidence for their point of view.

Cannon was only one of several prominent physiologists who advocated a "stomach contraction" explanation of hunger. However, even Cannon's prestige was not sufficient to override many of the objections to such a theory. One very potent exception was provided by the demonstration that lesions made in certain locations of a rat's brain had marked effects on the rat's eating behavior. Since the lesions had not interfered with stimulation from stomach contractions, it was apparent that central factors (brain lesions) as well as the local factor (stomach contractions) were involved in governing eating and, by inference, hunger. The article by Hetherington and Ranson discusses the effects of lesions in the ventromedial area of the hypothalamus. A lesion is literally a damage or injury; Hetherington and Ranson produced lesions in their animals surgically. The hypothalamus is a region in the floor of the brain composed of many distinct nuclei of fibers; the ventromedial nucleus is one of these.

The lesions produced in the rats had effects not only upon their eating behavior but their activity as well. Hetherington and Ranson show that when food was soft and moist the rats that had been operated upon ate more than the controls (non-operated-upon rats.) When the food was dry and hard, however, the rats with lesions had more nearly normal food intake. There are many factors that influence eating behavior, and one of these, genetic influence, is controlled by the use of litter-mates. Table 1 lists data about 18 rats, separated into four groups, primarily on the basis of age. Each of these groups is composed of a different litter of rat pups. Hetherington and Ranson take advantage of the genetic homogeneity within the litters by using some rats in each litter as experimental ones and their litter-mates as controls. The effect of a lesion on a rat can be determined by comparing the rat's eating and activity to that of its non-operated-upon "twin."

The evidence that central factors are involved in hunger and food intake regulation neither invalidated the stomach contraction findings nor ruled out the possibility of still other mechanisms at work. The selection by Mayer is an excerpt (the first six pages) from a long and comprehensive review of the influences upon obesity. There is a parallel here between psychological and physiological research strategy; just as a psychologist may study abnormal personality in an effort to learn about normal personality, the physiologist may study misregulation of food intake and obesity in an effort to learn about proper regulation and hunger. Mayer begins the main body of his paper by reviewing some previous theories, including the two advanced in the preceding readings, and then goes on to explain his glucostatic hypothesis.

Mayer's article is a technical one; he presents the theory that hunger is triggered by receptors that are sensitive to the difference between the glucose level in arteries and the glucose level in veins. This difference, Δ-glucose, is high soon after eating when arterial blood contains a high amount of glucose. After a while, if no further ingestion has occurred, arterial blood glucose levels recede, the body's stored glucose supply becomes depleted, and the Δ-glucose becomes low. Research results show that eating occurs when Δ-glucose is low, fasting, when it is high. Mayer reports a variety of evidence showing that operations which raise Δ-glucose, such as glucose injections, inhibit eating, while operations that lower it, such as insulin injections, stimulate eating. The glucostatic hypothesis can be classified as a "general" hypothesis since it postulates the theory that general stimuli (blood sugar levels) are some of the ultimate cues to hunger.

It should be apparent that hunger is a complex phenomenon and that probably local, central, *and* general factors are all involved in its regulation. Grossman's paper is an attempt to produce a format for considering joint effects of different mechanisms. Grossman also achieves clarity by the care with which he delimits his terms. As shown in his first figure, he makes several useful distinctions. Our bodily nutrient supplies can vary between depletion and repletion. When depleted, unlearned feeding reflexes are stimulated; when repleted, these feeding reflexes are inhibited. The physiological state of depletion has other effects. It evokes the sensation of hunger and specific food appetites, which in turn lead to learned food-seeking and eating behaviors. Having clearly set up his schema, Grossman can then look at the contribution made by the several hunger theories to each of his states.

The last article in the section is the only one by a psychologist. In it, Stellar has several purposes. He is trying to establish an overall theory of motivation, one appropriate not only for hunger, but for thirst, sleep, sex, and other motive states as well. He also wants to show how this theory relates to behavior. In oversimplified terms, Stellar's theory can be paraphrased as postulating the existence of a cerebral "adding machine" which keeps a summary record of all motivational signals—local, central and general. Not surprisingly, he locates this "totaler" in the hypothalamus as shown in Figure 2. Stellar's notions are intriguing, but speculative, for his paper was published in 1954 and a good deal of the necessary support was not available.

A complete explanation of hunger has still not been developed, but several books provide excellent overviews of the field, going into detail without losing clarity. The article by Rosenzweig, mentioned above, as well as the relevant chapters in books on motivation by Hall,[2] and Cofer and Appley[3] can all be recommended for a more thorough exploration of the topic.

STUDY QUESTIONS

1. What arguments do Cannon and Washburn present for the argument that hunger is local rather than central? What evidence do they present in support of this position?
2. What indices did Hetherington and Ranson employ to demonstrate the effects of hypothalamic lesions? How did the effects of the lesions interact with type of diet and with activity?
3. Restate Mayer's glucostatic hypothesis in your own words. How does the evidence Mayer reports confirm his hypothesis?
4. What is Grossman's evaluation of Mayer's glucostatic theory? Cannon's gastric activity theory? Hetherington and Ranson's hypothalamic control theory?
5. How does Grossman distinguish between physiologic and psychic aspects of hunger? Do different theories of hunger affect the psychic and the physiologic components in the same way?
6. What four classes of control are hypothesized by Stellar to be at work in the hypothalamus?
7. What evidence suggests that control of hunger motivation is similar to that of sex, thirst, or emotion?
8. What sorts of limitations does Stellar explicitly recognize as applicable to his integrative theory?

[2] John F. Hall, *Psychology of Motivation.* (Philadelphia: Lippincott, 1961).

[3] Charles N. Cofer, and M. H. Appley. *Motivation: Theory and Research* (New York: Wiley, 1964).

An Explanation of Hunger[1]

W. B. Cannon and A. L. Washburn

From the Laboratory of Physiology in the Harvard Medical School

Hunger and appetite are so intimately interrelated that a discussion of either requires each to be clearly defined. According to one view the two experiences differ only quantitatively, appetite being a mild stage of hunger.[2] Another view, better supported by observations, is that the two experiences are fundamentally different.[3]

Appetite is related to previous sensations of the taste and smell of food; it has therefore, as Pawlow has shown, important psychic elements. It may exist separate from hunger, as, for example, when we eat delectable dainties merely to please the palate. Sensory associations, delightful or disgusting, determine the appetite for any edible substance, and either memory or present stimulation can thus arouse desire or dislike for food.

Hunger, on the other hand, is a dull ache or gnawing sensation referred to the lower mid-chest region and the epigastrium. It is the organism's first strong demand for nutriment, and, not satisfied, is likely to grow into a highly uncomfortable pang, less definitely localized as it becomes more intense. It may exist separate from appetite, as, for example, when hunger forces the taking of food not only distasteful but even nauseating. Besides the dull ache, however, lassitude and drowsiness may appear, or faintness, or headache, or irritability and restlessness such that continuous effort in ordinary affairs becomes increasingly difficult. That these states differ with individuals—headache in one, faintness in another, for example—indicates that they do not constitute the central fact of hunger, but are more or less inconstant accompaniments, for the present negligible. The dull, pressing sensation is the constant characteristic, the central fact, to be examined in detail.

Of the two theories of hunger— (1) that it is a general sensation with a local reference, and (2) that it has a local peripheral source—the former has

Reprinted from *American Journal of Physiology*, 1912, 29, 441–454.

[1] The indicative evidence of the results here reported was presented to the Boston Society of Medical Sciences, January 17, 1911. See CANNON: The mechanical factors of digestion, London and New York, 1911, p. 204. The full account was presented to the Harvey Society, New York City, December 16, 1911.

[2] BARDIER: Richet's Dictionnaire de physiologie, article "Faim," 1904, vi, p. 1; HOWELL: Text-book of physiology, fourth edition, Philadelphia and London, 1911, p. 285.

[3] See STERNBERG: Zentralblatt für Physiologie, 1909, xxii, p. 653. Similar views were expressed by BAYLE in a thesis presented to the Faculty of Medicine in Paris in 1816.

been more widely accepted. The support for that theory can be shown to be not substantial. The wide acceptance of the theory, however, warrants an examination of it in some detail.

HUNGER NOT A GENERAL SENSATION

Underlying the idea that hunger arises from a general condition of the body is the consideration that, as time passes, food substances disappear from the blood, and consequently the nerve cells, suffering from the shortage of provisions, give rise to the sensation.[4]

In support of this view the increase of hunger as time passes has been pointed out. There is abundant evidence, however, that the period of increase is short, and that during continued fasting hunger wholly disappears after the first few days.[5] On the theory that hunger is a manifestation of bodily need, we must suppose that the body is mysteriously not in need after the third day, and that therefore hunger disappears. The absurdity of such a view is obvious.

Continued hunger soon after eating (when the stomach is full), especially in cases of duodenal fistula,[6] and satisfaction when the escaping chyme is restored to the intestine, have been cited as ruling out the peripheral and thus favoring the central origin of the sensation. As will be seen later, however, other possible peripheral sources of hunger exist besides the stomach. Further consideration of this point will be given in due course.

Because animals eat, sometimes eagerly, when the gastro-intestinal tract is wholly separated from the central nervous system,[7] the conclusion has been drawn that hunger must be a general sensation and not of peripheral origin. But appetite as well as hunger may lead to eating. As Ludwig stated many years ago, even if all afferent nerves were severed, psychic reasons still could be given for the taking of food.[8] Indeed, who accepts dessert because he is hungry? Evidently, since hunger is not required for eating, the fact that an animal eats is no testimony whatever that the animal is hungry, and therefore, after nerves have been severed, is no proof that hunger is of central origin.

Further objections to the theory that hunger is a general sensation lie in the weakness of its main assumption and in its failure to account for certain well-known observations. Thus no evidence exists that the blood has in fact changed when hunger appears. Moreover in fever, when bodily stores are being most rapidly destroyed, and when therefore, according to

4 SCHIFF: Physiologie de la digestion, Florence and Turin, 1867, p. 40.

5 See LUCIANI: Das Hungern, Hamburg and Leipzig, 1890, p. 113; TIGER-STEDT: Nagel's Handbuch der Physiologie, Berlin, 1909, i, p. 376; JOHANSSON, LANDERGREN, SONDÉN, and TIGERSTEDT: Skandinavisches Archiv für Physiologie, 1897, vii, p. 33; CARRINGTON: Vitality, fasting and nutrition, New York, 1908, p. 555; VITERBI: quoted by BARDIER, Loc. cit., p. 7.

6 See BUSCH: Archiv für pathologische Anatomie und Physiologie und für klinische Medicin, 1858, xiv, p. 147.

7 See SCHIFF: Loc. cit., p. 37; also DUCCESCHI: Archivio di fisiologia, 1910, viii, p. 582.

8 LUDWIG: Lehrbuch der Physiologie des Menschen, Leipzig and Heidelberg, 1858, ii, p. 584.

this theory, hunger should be most insistent, the sensation is wholly absent. And the quick abolition of the pangs soon after food is taken, before digestion and absorption can have proceeded far, as well as the quieting effect of swallowing indigestible stuff, such as moss and clay, further weakens the argument that the sensation arises directly from lack of nutriment in the body.

Many have noted that hunger has a sharp onset. If this abrupt arrival of the characteristic ache corresponds to the general bodily state, the change in general bodily state must occur with like suddenness, or have a critical point at which the sensation is instantly precipitated. No evidence exists that either of these conditions occurs in metabolism.

Another peculiarity of hunger which we have noticed is its intermittency. It may come and go several times in the course of a few hours. Furthermore, during a given period, the sensation is not uniform in intensity, but is marked by ups and downs, sometimes changing to alternate presence and absence without alteration of rate. Our observations have been confirmed by psychologists, trained to introspection, who have reported that the sensation has a distinctly intermittent course.[9] In the experience of one of us (C.) the hunger pangs came and went on one occasion as follows:

Came	Went
12–37–20	12–38–30
40–45	41–10
41–45	42–25
43–20	43–35
44–40	45–55
46–15	46–30

and so on, for ten minutes longer. Again in this relation, the intermittent and periodic character of hunger would require, on the central theory, that the bodily supplies be intermittently and periodically insufficient. During one moment absence of hunger would imply abundance of nutriment in the organism, ten seconds later presence of hunger would imply that the stores had been suddenly reduced, ten seconds later still absence of hunger would imply sudden renewal of plenty. Such zigzag shifts of the general bodily state may not be impossible, but, from all that is known of the course of metabolism, they are highly improbable. The periodicity of hunger, therefore, is further evidence against the theory that the sensation has a general basis in the body.

The last objection to this theory is its failure to account for the most common feature of hunger,—the reference of the sensation to the epigastric region. Schiff and others[10] have met this objection by two contentions. First, they have pointed out that hunger is not always referred to the stomach. Schiff interrogated ignorant soldiers regarding the local reference; several indicated the neck or chest, twenty-three the sternum, four were uncertain of any region, and two only designated the stomach. In other words, the stomach region was most rarely mentioned.

The second contention against the importance of local reference is that

[9] We are indebted to Prof. J. W. Baird of Clark University, and his collaborators, for this corroborative testimony.

[10] See Schiff: Loc. cit., p. 31; Bardier: Loc. cit., p. 16.

such evidence is fallacious. Just as the reference of tinglings to fingers which have been removed from the body does not prove that the tinglings originate in those fingers, so the assignment of the ache of hunger to any special region does not demonstrate that the ache arises from that region.

Concerning these arguments we may recall first Schiff's admission that the soldiers he questioned were too few to give conclusive evidence. Further, the testimony of most of them that hunger seemed to originate in the region of the sternum cannot be claimed as unfavorable to a peripheral source of the sensation. The description of feelings which develop from disturbances within the body is almost always indefinite; the testimony is not, therefore, dismissed as worthless. On the contrary, such testimony is used constantly in judging internal disorders.

The force of the contention that reference to the periphery is not proof of the peripheral origin of a sensation depends on the amount of accessory evidence which is available. Thus, if an object is seen coming into contact with a finger, the simultaneous sensation of touch referred to that finger may reasonably be assumed to have resulted from the contact, and not to have been a purely central experience accidentally attributed to an outlying member. Similarly in the case of hunger—all that is needed as support for the peripheral reference of the sensation is proof that conditions occur there, simultaneously with hunger pains, which might reasonably be regarded as giving rise to those pangs. In the fasting stomach may not conditions, in fact, be present which would sustain the theory that hunger has a local peripheral source?

Certain assumptions have been made regarding the state of the fasting stomach, and certain inferences have been drawn from these assumptions which must be considered before the results we have to present will have a proper setting.

OBJECTIONS TO SOME THEORIES THAT HUNGER IS OF LOCAL ORIGIN

Hunger is not due to emptiness of the stomach, for Nicolai found after gastric lavage that the sensation did not appear in some instances for more than three hours.[11] This testimony confirms Beaumont's observation on Alexis St. Martin, that hunger arises some time after the stomach is evacuated.[12]

Hunger is not due to hydrochloric acid secreted into the empty stomach. The gastric wash-water from hungry subjects is neutral or only slightly acid.[13] Furthermore, persons suffering from achylia gastrica declare that they have normal feelings of hunger.

Hunger is not due to turgescence of the gastric glands. This theory, propounded by Beaumont,[14] has commended itself to several recent writers.

[11] NICOLAI: Ueber die Entstehung des Hungergefühls, Inaugural-Dissertation, Berlin, 1892, p. 17.
[12] BEAUMONT: The physiology of digestion, second edition, Burlington, 1847, p. 51.
[13] NICOLAI: Loc. cit., p. 15.
[14] BEAUMONT: Loc. cit., p. 55.

Thus Luciani has accepted it, and by adding the idea that nerves distributed to the mucosa are specially sensitive to deprivation of food, he accounts for the hunger pangs.[15] Also Valenti declared two years ago that the turgescence theory of Beaumont is the only one possessing a semblance of truth.[16] The experimental work reported by these two investigators, however, does not necessarily support the turgescence theory. Luciani severed in fasting dogs the previously exposed and cocainized vagi, and Valenti merely cocainized the nerves; the dogs, eager to eat a few minutes previous to this operation, now ran about as before, but when offered food, licked and smelled it, but did not take it. This total neglect of the food lasted varying periods up to two hours. The vagus nerves seem, indeed, to convey impulses which affect the procedure of eating, but there is no clear evidence that those impulses arise from distention of the gland cells. The turgescence theory would also meet difficulties in an attempt to explain the disappearance of hunger after the swallowing of indigestible material; for such material, not being appetizing, does not cause any secretion of gastric juice.[17] Furthermore, Nicolai found that the sensation could be abolished by simply introducing a stomach tube. The turgescence of the gastric glands would not be reduced by either of these procedures. The turgescence theory, finally, does not explain the quick onset of hunger, or its intermittent and periodic character, for the cells cannot be repeatedly swollen and contracted within periods a few seconds in duration.

HUNGER THE RESULT OF CONTRACTIONS

There remain to be considered, as a possible cause of hunger pangs, contractions of the stomach and other parts of the alimentary canal. This suggestion is not new. Sixty-six years ago Weber declared his belief that "strong contraction of the muscle fibres of the wholly empty stomach, whereby its cavity disappears, makes a part of the sensation which we call hunger."[18] Vierordt drew the same inference twenty-five years later (in 1871);[19] and since then Knapp and also Hertz have declared their adherence to this view. These writers have not brought forward any direct evidence for their conclusion, though Hertz has cited Boldireff's observations on fasting dogs as probably accounting for what he terms "the gastric constituent of the sensation."[20]

The argument commonly used against the contraction theory is that the stomach is not energetically active when empty. Thus Schiff stated "the movements of the empty stomach are rare and much less energetic than during digestion."[21] Luciani expressed his disbelief by asserting that gastric

[15] Luciani: Archivio di fisiologia, 1906, iii, p. 542.
[16] Valenti: Archives italiennes de biologie, 1910, liii, p. 97.
[17] See Pawlow: The work of the digestive glands, London, 1902, p. 70; Hornborg: Skandinavisches Archiv für Physiologie, 1904, xv, p. 248.
[18] Weber: Wagner's Handwörterbuch der Physiologie, 1846, iii², p. 580.
[19] Vierordt: Grundriss der Physiologie, Tübingen, 1871, p. 433.
[20] Knapp: American medicine, 1905, x, p. 358; Hertz: The sensibility of the alimentary canal, London, 1911, p. 37.
[21] Schiff: Loc. cit., p. 33.

movements are much more active during gastric digestion than at other times, and cease almost entirely when the stomach has discharged its contents.[22] And Valenti stated only year before last: "We know very well that gastric movements are exaggerated while digestion is proceeding in the stomach, but when the organ is empty they are more rare and much less pronounced," and therefore they cannot account for hunger.[23]

Contractions of the alimentary canal in fasting animals. Evidence opposed to these suppositions has been in existence for many years. In 1899 Bettmann called attention to the contracted condition of the stomach after several days' fast.[24] In 1902 Wolff reported that after forty-eight hours without food the stomach of the cat may be so small as to look like a slightly enlarged duodenum.[25] The anatomist His has also observed the phenomenon.[26] Seven years ago Boldireff demonstrated that the whole gastrointestinal tract has a periodic activity while not digesting.[27] Each period of activity lasts from twenty to thirty minutes, and is characterized in the stomach by rhythmic contractions 10 to 20 in number. These contractions, Boldireff reports, may be stronger than during digestion, and his published records clearly support this statement. The intervals of repose between periodic recurrences of the contractions last from one and a half to two and a half hours. Especially noteworthy is Boldireff's observation that if fasting is continued for two or three days the groups of contractions appear at gradually longer intervals and last for gradually shorter periods, and thereupon the gastric glands begin continuous secretion, and all movements cease. All these testimonies to increased tone and periodic pulsations definitely prove, contrary to previous statements, that the empty stomach may be the seat of vigorous muscular activities.

Boldireff considered hunger in relation to the activities he described, but solely with the idea that hunger might *provoke* them; and since the activities dwindled in force and frequence as time passed, whereas in his belief they should have become more pronounced, he abandoned the notion of any relation between the phenomena.[28] Did not Boldireff misinterpret his own observations? When he was considering whether hunger might cause the contractions, did he not overlook the possibility that the contractions might cause hunger? A number of experiences have led to the conviction that Boldireff did, indeed, fail to perceive part of the significance of his results. For example, in auscultation of the alimentary canal relatively loud borborygmi have been noted as the hunger pangs were disappearing. Again the sensation can be momentarily abolished a few seconds after swallowing a small accumulation of saliva or a tablespoonful of water. Since the stomach is in high tonus in hunger, this result can be accounted for as due to the momentary inhibition of the tonus by swallowing.[29] Thus also could be explained the disappearance of the ache soon after eating is begun, for repeated swallowing results in continued inhibition.

22 LUCIANI: *Loc. cit.*, p. 542.
23 VALENTI: *Loc. cit.*, p. 97.
24 BETTMANN: Philadelphia monthly medical journal, 1899, 1, p. 133.
25 WOLFF: Dissertation, Giessen, 1902, p. 9.
26 HIS: Archiv für Anatomie, 1903, p. 345.
27 BOLDIREFF: Archives biologiques de St. Petersburg, 1905, xi, p. 1. See also Ergebnisse der Physiologie, 1911, xi, p. 182.
28 BOLDIREFF: *Loc. cit.*, p. 96.
29 CANNON and LIEB: this Journal, 1911, xxix, p. 267.

The concomitance of contractions and hunger in man. Although the evidence above mentioned had led to the conviction that hunger results from contractions of the alimentary canal, direct proof was still lacking. In order to learn whether such proof might be secured, one of us (W.) determined to become accustomed to the presence of a rubber tube in the œsophagus.[30] Almost every day for several weeks W. introduced as far as the stomach a small tube, to the lower end of which was attached a soft-rubber balloon about 8 cm. in diameter. The tube was thus carried about each time for two or three hours. After this preliminary experience the introduction of the tube, and its presence in the gullet and stomach, were not at all disturbing. When a record was to be taken, the balloon, placed just below the cardia, was moderately distended with air, and was connected with a water manometer ending in a cylindrical chamber 3.5 cm. wide. A float recorder resting on the water in the chamber permitted registering any contractions of the fundus of the stomach. On the days of observation W. would abstain from breakfast, or eat sparingly, and without taking any luncheon would appear in the laboratory about two o'clock. The recording apparatus was arranged as above described. In order to avoid the possibility of an artifact, a pneumograph, fastened below the ribs, was made to record the movements of the abdominal wall. Between the records of gastric pressure and abdominal movement one electromagnetic signal marked time in minutes, and another traced a line which could be altered by pressing a key. All these recording arrangements were out of W's sight; he sat with one hand at the key, ready, whenever the sensation of hunger was experienced, to make the current which moved the signal.

When W. stated that he was hungry, powerful contractions of the stomach were invariably being registered. The record of W's introspection of his hunger pangs agreed closely with the record of his gastric contractions. Almost invariably, however, the contraction nearly reached its maximum before the record of the sensation was started (see Fig. 1). This fact may be regarded as evidence that the contraction precedes the sensation, and not *vice versa*, as Boldireff considered it. The contractions were about a half-minute in duration, and the intervals between varied from thirty to ninety seconds, with an average of about one minute. W's augmentations of intragastric pressure ranged between 11 and 13 in twenty minutes; C. had previously counted in himself 11 hunger pangs in the same time (see ten-minute record, p. 169). The rate in each of us, therefore, proved to be approximately the same. This rate is slightly slower than that found in dogs by Boldireff; the difference is perhaps correlated with the slower rhythm of gastric peristalsis in man compared with that in the dog.[31]

Before hunger was experienced by W. the recording apparatus revealed no signs of gastric activity. Sometimes a rather tedious period of waiting had to be endured before contractions occurred, and after they began they continued for a while, then ceased (see Fig. 2). The feeling of hunger, which was reported while the contractions were recurring, disappeared when they stopped. The inability of the subject to control the contractions eliminated

[30] Nicolai (*Loc. cit.*) reported that although the introduction of a stomach tube at first abolished hunger in his subjects, with repeated use the effects became insignificant.

[31] Cannon: The mechanical factors of digestion, London and New York, 1911, p. 54.

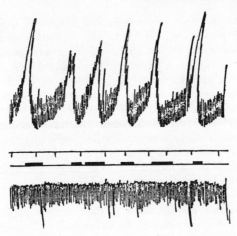

FIG. 1. One half the original size. The top record represents intragastric pressure (the small oscillations due to respiration, the large to contractions of the stomach); the second record is time in minutes (ten minutes); the third record is W's report of hunger pangs; the lowest record is respiration registered by means of a pneumograph about the abdomen.

the possibility of their being artifacts, perhaps induced by suggestion. The close concomitance of the contractions with hunger pangs, therefore, clearly indicates that they are the real source of those pangs.

Boldireff's studies proved that when the empty stomach is manifesting periodic contractions the intestines also are active. Conceivably all parts

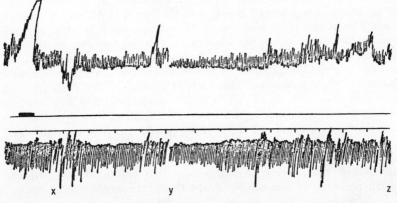

FIG. 2. One half the original size. The same conditions as in Fig. 1 (fifteen minutes). There was a long wait for hunger to disappear. After x, W. reported himself "tired, but not hungry." The record from y to z was the continuance, on a second drum, of x to y.

of the alimentary canal composed of smooth muscle share in these movements. The lower œsophagus in man is provided with smooth muscle. It was possible to determine whether this region in W. was active during hunger.

To the œsophageal tube a thin-rubber finger cot (2 cm. in length) was attached and lowered into the stomach. The little rubber bag was distended

with air, and the tube, pinched to keep the bag inflated, was gently withdrawn until resistance was felt. The air was now released from the bag,
and the tube further withdrawn about 3 cm. The bag was again distended
with air at a manometric pressure of 10 cm. of water. Inspiration now
caused the writing lever, which recorded the pressure changes, to rise; and
a slightly further withdrawal of the tube changed the rise, on inspiration, to
a fall. The former position of the tube, therefore, was above the gastric
cavity and below the diaphragm. In this position the bag, attached to a float
recorder (with chamber 2.3 cm. in diameter) registered the periodic oscillations shown in Fig. 3. Though individually more prolonged than those of
the stomach, these contractions, it will be noted, occur at about the same
rate. It is probable that the periodic activity of the two regions is simultaneous, for otherwise the stomach would force its gaseous content into the
œsophagus with the rise of intragastric pressure.

What causes the contractions to occur has not been determined. From
evidence already given they do not seem to be directly related to bodily
need. Habit no doubt plays an important rôle. For present considerations,
however, it is enough that they do occur, and that they are abolished when
food, which satisfies bodily need, is taken into the stomach. By such indirec-
tion are performed some of the most fundamental of the bodily functions.

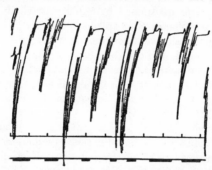

Fig. 3.   One half the original size. The top record represents compression
of a thin-rubber bag in the lower œsophagus. The pressure in the bag
varied between 9 and 13 cm. of water. The cylinder of the recorder was of
smaller diameter than that used in the gastric records. The œsophageal contractions compressed the bag so completely that, at the summits of the
large oscillations, the respirations were not registered. When the oscillations
dropped to the time line, the bag was about half inflated. The middle line
registers time in minutes (ten minutes). The bottom record is W's report of
hunger pangs.

Peculiarities of hunger explained by contractions. If these contractions
are admitted as the cause of hunger, most of the difficulties confronting
other explanations are readily obviated. Thus the occurrence of hunger at
meal-times is most natural, for, as the regularity of defecation indicates, the
alimentary canal has habits. Activity returns at the usual meal-time as the
result of custom. By taking food regularly at a definite hour in the evening
for several days, a new hunger period can be established. Since at these
times the empty stomach, as Boldireff showed, has stronger contractions
than the filled organ, hunger is aroused.

The contractions furthermore explain the sudden onset of hunger and its peculiar periodicity—phenomena which no other explanation of hunger can account for. The quick development of the sensation after taking a cold drink is possibly associated with the well-known power of cold to induce contraction in smooth muscle.

The great intensity of hunger during the first day of starvation, and its gradual disappearance till it vanishes on the third or fourth day, are made quite clear, for Boldireff observed that gastric contractions in his fasting dogs went through precisely such alterations of intensity and were not seen after the third day.

In fever, when bodily material is being most rapidly used, hunger is absent. Its absence is understood from an observation reported four years ago, that infection with systemic involvement is accompanied by a total cessation of all movements of the alimentary canal.[32] Boldireff observed that when his dogs were fatigued the rhythmic contractions failed to appear. Being "too tired to eat" is thereby given a rational explanation.

Another pathological form of the sensation—the inordinate hunger (bulimia) of certain neurotics—is in accord with the well-known disturbances of the tonic innervation of the alimentary canal in such individuals.

Since the lower end of the œsophagus, as well as the stomach, contracts periodically in hunger, the reference of the sensation to the sternum by the ignorant persons questioned by Schiff was wholly natural. The activity of the lower œsophagus also explains why, after the stomach has been removed, or in some cases when the stomach is distended with food, hunger can still be experienced. Conceivably the intestines also originate vague sensations by their contractions. Indeed the final banishment of the modified hunger sensation in the patient with duodenal fistula, described by Busch, may have been due to the lessened activity of the intestines when chyme was injected into them.

The observations recorded in this paper have, as already noted, numerous points of similarity to Boldireff's observations on the periodic activity of the alimentary canal in fasting dogs. Each period of activity, he found, comprised not only widespread contractions of the digestive canal, but also the pouring out of bile, and of pancreatic and intestinal juices rich in ferments. Gastric juice was not secreted at these times; when it was secreted and reached the intestine, the periodic activity ceased.[33] What is the significance of this extensive disturbance? Recently evidence has been presented that gastric peristalsis is dependent on the stretching of gastric muscle when tonically contracted.[34] The evidence that the stomach is in fact strongly contracted in hunger—i.e., in a state of high tone —has been presented above.[35] Thus the very condition which causes hunger and leads to the taking of food is the condition, when the swallowed food stretches the shortened muscles, for immediate starting of gastric peristalsis. In this connection the recent observations of Haudek and Stigler are probably significant. They found that the stomach discharges its contents more

---

[32] CANNON and MURPHY: Journal of the American Medical Association, 1907, xlix, p. 840.

[33] BOLDIREFF: Loc. cit., pp. 108–111.

[34] CANNON: this Journal, 1911, xxix, p. 250.

[35] The "empty" stomach and œsophagus contain gas (see HERTZ: Quarterly journal of medicine, 1910, iii, p. 378; MIKULICZ: Mittheilungen aus dem Grenzgebieten der Medicin und Chirurgie, 1903, xii, p. 596). They would naturally manifest rhythmic contractions on shortening tonically on their content.

rapidly if food is eaten in hunger than if not so eaten.[36] Hunger, in other words, is normally the signal that the stomach is contracted for action; the unpleasantness of hunger leads to eating; eating starts gastric secretion, distends the contracted organ, initiates the movements of gastric digestion, and abolishes the sensation. Meanwhile pancreatic and intestinal juices, as well as bile, have been prepared in the duodenum to receive the oncoming chyme. The periodic activity of the alimentary canal in fasting, therefore, is not solely the source of hunger pangs, but is at the same time an exhibition in the digestive organs of readiness for prompt attack on the food swallowed by the hungry animal.

The Spontaneous Activity and Food Intake

of Rats with Hypothalamic Lesions [1]

A. W. Hetherington and S. W. Ranson

From the Institute of Neurology, Northwestern
University Medical School, Chicago, Illinois

Bailey and Bremer (1921) speak of "apathy" in their two obese dogs which had hypothalamic lesions, and several of Brown's (1923) fat dogs became "sluggish." Smith (1930), evidently referring to certain early postoperative symptoms, stated that rats which had received an injection of chromic acid into the hypophysis, presumably injuring the hypothalamus, like other rats with hypothalamic lesions, displayed periods of quiet interspersed with periods of excitement. Speaking also of rather early postoperative activity, Krieg (1938) mentioned, among other manifestations, an "emotionally hyperactive state," and "depression."

Although these and similar incidental references have been made by various workers to the behavior and activity of animals with damage to the tuber cinereum, apparently with but one exception (Richter, 1930) no one had tried until very recently to compare quantitatively the gross activity spontaneously exhibited by such animals with preoperative or normal values. Richter produced diabetes insipidus in seven rats by stabbing a short narrow blade through the sphenoid bone at a point he judged to be just rostral to the hypophysis. As yet the nature of these hypothalamic lesions, if indeed

---

[36] Haudek and Stigler: Archiv für die gesammte Physiologie, 1910, cxxxiii, p. 159.

Reprinted from American Journal of Physiology, 1942, 136, 609–617.

[1] Aided by a grant from the Committee on Research in Endocrinology of the National Research Council.

such they were, has not been described; but they probably occupied an area in the neighborhood of the median eminence. The result of this procedure was found to be essentially negative. Rats which had run well before the operation continued to do so afterward, and the poor runners remained inactive.

Food intake of these animals, Richter found, was likewise unchanged. Of course, none of the rats observed in these experiments became obese and it may be assumed that they did not bear the sort of hypothalamic lesions attributed by Hetherington and Ranson (1940) with the capacity to cause adiposity.

Other investigators, however, have reported a contrary finding. Keller, Hare and D'Amour (1933) and Keller and Noble (1935) observed enhanced food intake and a tendency to adiposity both in dogs with hypothalamic lesions and in dogs with a variety of pituitary injuries. Ranson, Fisher and Ingram (1938) noticed that one of their monkeys with hypothalamic lesions increased rapidly in weight and displayed marked polyphagia.

Finally in two simultaneous preliminary reports Tepperman, Brobeck and Long (1941) and Hetherington (1941) have added the most recent information on the subject. The former group found that certain rats with hypothalamic lesions became extremely obese and consumed approximately twice as much food as litter-mate controls. Hetherington, on the other hand, observed a group of operated rats which did not eat more than their controls, but which, nevertheless, in some instances did grow fat. The latter's animals were observed, in addition, to engage in a great deal less spontaneous running activity than did the controls.

The following experiments contain an elaboration of the results reported by Hetherington (1941) and a considerable amount of new material which has been added since that time.

METHODS

The present series numbers 18 male rats, 11 operated animals and 7 controls, run in groups of 6. Each group was made up of litter-mates. One control and one operated animal failed to survive the full length of time covered by the experiments and are not included in the results. Hypothalamic lesions were placed in the operated rats by the method described by Hetherington and Ranson (1940).[2]

For study of spontaneous running activity the type of cage, with slight modifications, described by Richter and Wang (1926) was used. The modifications were as follows: The living compartment is considerably smaller on these cages, being 3 inches wide by 5 inches high by 6 inches long. The revolving drum is a little larger, having a diameter of 15 inches. It is balanced in order to enable it to be stopped at any position, and revolves so easily that a weight of less than half a gram at the periphery will cause it to turn.

The cages were not kept in an air-conditioned room; consequently hu-

---

[2] For the Evipal anesthetic used in the operations we are indebted to Dr. J. J. Kuhn of the Winthrop Chemical Co.

midity undoubtedly varied over a considerable range. The temperature of the room, however, was kept within the range between 75° to 78° F. (Animals with hypothalamic lesions generally require a warmer room than normal for maintained good health.) They were subjected to 12 hours of illumination and 12 hours of darkness per day, the lights being controlled by a Tork electric clock.

The food supply was altered from group to group in the following manner: The first group received nothing but Rockland Rat Ration pellets for the first 5 weeks of the experiment. During the final 3 weeks the pellets were ground and moistened with water. The other two groups received a mixture made of 37 per cent ground Rockland rat pellets, 18 per cent ground dry white bread, and 45 per cent raw whole milk by weight. Needless to say, samples of this diet (as well as of the pellets first used) were dried daily to determine their moisture content; and all figures given in the results are dry weights calculated from the dried food residue collected at the end of each 24-hour period.

To determine the influence of activity upon food intake the second two groups were kept part of the time in small cubical living cages (7½ in. on a side), and the remainder of the time in the activity cages. One group spent the first 6 postoperative weeks in the activity cages and the next 4 or 5 weeks in the stationary cages. The process was reversed with the other group, the first 5 weeks being spent in the ordinary living cages and the final 4 weeks in the activity cages.

RESULTS

The lesions found in the hypothalami of the operated rats need not be described in detail at this time. It is sufficient to say that they conformed in a general way with the lesions found in a former series (Hetherington and Ranson, 1940). As before, lesions producing the higher degrees of adiposity in this series lay on both sides in the region of the ventromedial hypothalamic nucleus and its immediate cellular environs. Lesions failing to precipitate the syndrome, or causing it to only a minor degree were rather markedly asymmetrical, not near enough to the base, or for some other reason inadequate.

When the experiment with each group of animals was terminated, the rats were weighed, anesthetized, and their body length (nose-anus) measured. They were not always immediately killed. The data obtained at this time are summarized in the table, which shows age, weight, and body length, and several indices of degree of adiposity which will now be explained.

The formula $W^{1/3}/L$, expressing the ratio of the cube root of the body weight in grams to the body length in centimeters, was borrowed from Lee (1929), who was interested in the expression of metabolic results for white rats. Following Cowgill and Drabkin (1927), who applied the formula to the dog, Lee used this "nutritive correction factor" to indicate the nutritive state observed in an individual animal.

In the table opposite the weight-length ratio of each operated rat is

TABLE 1

TABLE SUMMARIZING THE DATA ON AGE, WEIGHT, AND BODY LENGTH
OF THE RATS AT THE TIME OF THE TERMINATION
OF THE EXPERIMENT

Rat No.	Op. or Con.	Age	Weight	Nose-Anus Length	$W^{1/3}/L$	Degree of Adiposity
		days	*grams*	*cm.*		
Rf-1	C	133	385	24.7	0.294	
Rf-2	O	133	380	23.8	0.304	+
Rf-3	C	136	373	24.3	0.296	
Rf-4	O	133	342	23.1	0.303	?*
Rf-5	O	136	347	20.5	0.342	+++
Rf-6	O	136	325	23.1	0.297	−
Rf-7	O	172	485	23.8	0.330	+++
Rf-8	C	172	413	25.1	0.297	
Rf-9	C	157	371	23.9	0.300	
Rf-10	O	157	473	24.3	0.321	+++
Rf-11	O	157	449	23.4	0.327	++
Rf-12	C	died				
Rf-13	O	153	413	22.9	0.325	+++
Rf-14	O	died				
Rf-15	C	153	323	23.1	0.297	
Rf-16	C	153	335	23.0	0.302	
Rf-17	O	153	349	23.5	0.299	−
Rf-18	O	153	331	22.5	0.307	?

* Indicates presence of adiposity doubted.

placed a symbol, either a minus-sign, or one, two, or three plus-signs, which represents a visual estimate of the degree of an animal's adiposity. This estimate was based on a careful inspection and comparison of the rat with its control, and signifies that the animal was judged either not to be fat, or to be slightly, moderately, or markedly obese. The two classifications of adiposity have not always given results completely consistent with each other, yet they do not in any case fundamentally disagree.

No attempt has been made to divide the weight-length ratios arbitrarily into groups. Inspection of the table will reveal, however, that no control rat exhibits a ratio above 0.302; the average of the ratios of the 6 normal males is 0.298. Determined for a much longer series of normal males used in other experiments the figure is slightly lower—about 0.293—with an upper limit to the range of normal values, as here, at about 0.302. No male which was considered definitely obese has a ratio below 0.304, and the fatter animals have ratios above 0.320.

All data secured from the activity cage experiments and from determinations of food intake are summarized graphically in figures 1 to 4.

The first 6 animals were placed in activity cages at the age of 6 weeks, and 4 of them were operated 2 weeks later. Two of the operated rats in a matter of 4 to 6 weeks showed an unmistakable degree of adiposity, while the other 2 retained an essentially normal appearance. In figure 1 the mean daily food consumption of each rat for any given week is averaged together with the mean daily food consumption of the other fat rat for the same week,

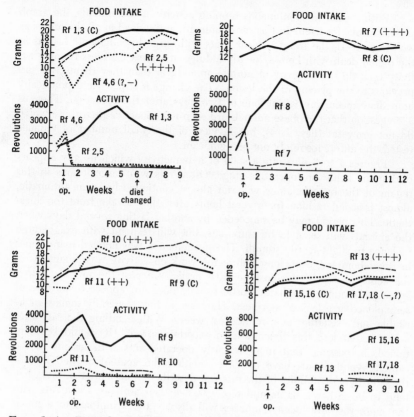

FIGS. 1–4.   Records of food intake and spontaneous activity (running) of obese and nonobese rats with hypothalamic lesions, and of their normal litter-mate controls. In figure 1 the change in diet at the end of the fifth postoperative week should be noticed. In figure 4 note the vertical scale for activity is different from that in the first 3 figures.

and the average of the means is plotted on the graph as a single point. The same procedure is followed with the figures for daily activity, and is applied to the corresponding determinations for the pair of controls and the pair of nonobese operated animals. This has been done purely to reduce for the sake of simplicity and clarity the number of lines on the graph. With particular reference to the upper set of lines in figure 1 the point should be stressed at this time that the paired representation of food intake does not conceal an overlapping of the data of the normal and obese rats. Neither of the fat animals ate as large an amount of food as either of their control litter-mates.

As was mentioned before, the diet of these animals consisted during the first 5 postoperative weeks of whole Rockland rat pellets. On this diet the 2 nonobese rats maintained a considerably lower level of food intake than the others until the final 3 weeks of the experiment, when grinding and moistening of the food pellets (with water) seemed to exert a favorable influence upon their food consumption. The change apparently did not induce the 2 obese and 2 normal animals to alter their eating habits.

With regard to spontaneous running activity of the animals, the graph (fig. 1) speaks for itself. In this set of animals, and indeed in all the others as well (figs. 2–4), the trend is clear. Rats with large hypothalamic lesions in the region dealt with here evidently indulge in a great deal less running activity than do the majority of normal animals, or than they themselves did previous to the placing of the lesions. The change is striking and practically immediate, occurring within one or two days after the operation. There is a suggestion that the obese animals are even more inactive than those which do not grow fat (figs. 1, 4), but in view of the small number of animals tested, the difference might not be significant.

Figures 1 to 3 illustrate a state of hyperactivity which usually appears during the acute postoperative stage. Often rats with large lesions in this region of the hypothalamus will run almost continuously in an automatic, almost frenzied fashion for several hours after they awake from the anesthetic. This period may be succeeded by another lasting several days when the animals will seem to be stuporous, but will respond with exaggerated violence to slight tactile stimuli. The phenomenon was noticed many times in this laboratory, even long before the work on activity was begun. After the acute phases of the postoperative period are past the rats are rather lethargic, though this characteristic usually does not appear to partake of somnolence or a lack of alertness. They are, in fact, generally somewhat irritable and excitable for a number of weeks. With handling the rats after a time often lose this touchiness to a certain extent. (It should be mentioned, in passing, that more recently operated rats with lesions in the caudal hypothalamus have displayed neither the acute hyperactivity nor the later hyperirritability of the rats just described. As a matter of fact, they tend to be rather amiable and more passive than normals. Even rats with the more rostrally located injuries will display the symptoms to a much slighter degree if the lesions in question are small.)

In a preceding section it was explained that the second and third groups of animals were fed a mixture of ground Rockland rat pellets, ground dry white bread, and raw whole milk. Food intake on this diet may now be considered.

Figure 2 shows how one operated rat which was accustomed to eating somewhat more than its control even before placing of the lesions, maintained, or even widened the margin between its food intake and that of its control after operation. After the animals were removed from the activity cages the food intake of the pair became more nearly equal.

In figures 3 and 4 is to be found a much clearer demonstration of the fact that these obese rats with hypothalamic lesions under certain circumstances will consume a good deal more food than do their litter-mate controls.

The final experiment, consisting of a comparison of the food intake of the animals during their sojourn in the activity cages, where it seems likely more exercise is taken by normal rats, with the food intake observed during the period spent in ordinary cages, has been rather inconclusive. In figure 2 there appears to be a slight decline in the food intake of both the normal and the obese rats after removal of the animals from activity cages. There furthermore seems to be a smaller difference between the intakes of the 2 rats, for which the more rapid descent of the curve for the fat animal is responsible. In figure 4 (where again the method of averaged daily means for the pair of controls and the pair of nonobese operated animals is used) is shown a small increase in food intake which occurred when the animals were placed in activity cages.

The rats represented in figure 3, however, reacted at first—apparently somewhat illogically—with a slightly increased food consumption after being transferred from their activity cages. Later these animals, too, decreased intake, and again the margin between the obese and the control rats narrowed because of the more rapid decline in intake by the fat rats. In any case, the changes in food intake which may be associated with the changes in spontaneous activity assumed here are not at all of the same order of magnitude as those which occurred in some of the obese rats, or even in the normal controls during the phase of rapid growth.

DISCUSSION

The phenomenon of adiposity is often regarded as a problem involving as causes either lack of exercise or over-eating, or a combination of the two. Doubtless in many cases these simple and easily understood factors may be an adequate explanation for excessive weight. In many other cases, however, as for instance in hypothyroid obesity, uncontrollable adiposity following pregnancy, and Cushing's syndrome, some more fundamental cause, intimately tied in with pathological physiology must be sought. (For critical analyses of recent theories regarding "exogenous" and "endogenous" obesity, see reviews by Wilder, 1938, and Bauer, 1941.)

Similarly, in the case of the experimental hypothalamic obesity being investigated here, the most obvious explanations, decreased activity and augmented food consumption, were first taken up for examination, with the results that have been cited. It is true that these animals exercise a great deal less than normal rats. Yet animals which have somewhat similar lesions but which do not grow obese also indulge in much less spontaneous activity, though perhaps not as little as fat rats. It is also true that under certain circumstances, as when the food is softer, easier to eat, and possibly more palatable, the obese animals will consume excessively large amounts of it. This observation does not alter the fact, however, that these rats will also grow fat—though in all likelihood more slowly—even when food intake is limited to an amount equal to or even a little smaller than that of normal litter-mates.

When the simultaneous reports of preliminary work by Tepperman, Brobeck and Long (1941) and Hetherington (1941) appeared, the former group (who had done little or no work on activity) emphasized the high food intake of their animals; whereas the latter was more impressed by the tremendously decreased activity of the obese rats. Insistence upon the primary importance of either viewpoint would in all probability represent oversimplification of the problem, and this for at least two reasons.

In the first place, the two factors are complementary in their effect upon body weight. Both would tend to increase it. A very sedentary life, combined with a high caloric intake would seem to be an ideal combination for building up a thick panniculus adiposus.

Secondly, these two factors may be only symptomatic, and not fundamental. It is not difficult to imagine, for example, a condition of hidden cellular semi-starvation caused by a lack of easily utilizable energy-producing material, which would soon tend to force the body either to increase its general food intake, or to cut down its energy expenditure, or both. In this connection, it would be of great interest to determine whether these animals exhibit a preference for any particular class (chemically speaking) of foods.

It should be clearly realized that the apparent reluctance of the bodies of these fat rats to utilize their tremendous stores of fat is only relative and not absolute. Brobeck (1941) has stated that his fat rats can be fasted down to a normal body weight; and it has been noticed many times in this laboratory that a rat can stop eating and lose up to a third or more of its body weight before it recovers its appetite. These animals can, therefore, use fat as a source of energy if necessary, though perhaps at a low level of efficiency. The concept which comes to mind is one much like that expressed by Thomson (1938), who, discussing a somewhat similar matter, speculated upon the varying availability to the cell of different substrates of energy-furnishing material.

Evidence for a more basic disorganization of the physiological economy of these animals is not voluminous, but it is suggestive. To begin with, Hetherington and Weil (1940) showed that there was a pronounced deficit in the total body phosphorus of the obese rats with hypothalamic lesions. Although there was a co-existing calcium deficiency as well, the calcium-phosphorus ratio was irregularly altered in such a way that it was believed other phosphorus containing materials besides bone had suffered. The importance of phosphorus in fat metabolism, particularly fat transport, and as a constituent of numerous physiologically important organic compounds in the body hardly requires elaboration.

In addition, Tepperman, Brobeck and Long found that the basal oxygen consumption of obese rats which had been either fasted for a long time, or pair-fed with their controls was low compared to the normals; while R.Q. determinations in the absorptive state were higher. Daily creatinine excretion was high in their rats, and carbohydrate metabolism in some instances appeared to be affected. Grafe and Grünthal (1929) found lowered B.M.R.'s in obese dogs which were supposed to have hypothalamic lesions.

It is argument along these lines which has suggested the imperative need for further fundamental physiological and biochemical research on rats displaying hypothalamic obesity. The ease with which the syndrome can be produced in the rat, and the wide variety of physiological techniques which can readily be applied to the animal make it an ideal subject for investigation.

SUMMARY

The spontaneous running activity both before and after operation of 10 rats with hypothalamic lesions frequently causing adiposity and of 6 normal litter-mate controls has been investigated. In addition the food intake of all the animals has been measured, in some cases both in activity cages and in ordinary cages.

It has been found that animals having bilateral lesions in the medial hypothalamus in the region in and around the ventromedial hypothalamic nucleus tend to indulge in much less spontaneous running than do the majority of normal controls, or than was exhibited preoperatively.

Food consumption of the obese operated animals may greatly exceed the intake of the normal litter-mate controls or may not exceed it at all, depending upon the nature of the food supplied. A soft palatable diet encourages maximum consumption, and a hard dry pellet diet apparently discourages high intake. Animals probably grow obese more rapidly on the former type of diet. The idea is suggested that the obese animal's efforts to increase food intake and cut down energy expenditure are indicative of a partial inability on the part of its physiological mechanism to metabolize easily all of its available food stores.

REFERENCES

Bailey, P. and F. Bremer. Arch. Int. Med. 28, 773, 1921.

Bauer, J. Arch. Int. Med. 67, 968, 1941.

Brobeck, J. R. Personal communication, 1941.

Brown, C. G. Proc. Soc. Exper. Biol. and Med. 20, 275, 1923.

Cowgill, G. R. and D. L. Drabkin. This Journal 81, 36, 1927.

Grafe, E. and E. Grünthal. Klin. Wchnschr. 8, 1013, 1929.

Hetherington, A. W. This Journal 133, 326, 1941.

Hetherington, A. W. and S. W. Ranson. Anat. Rec. 78, 149, 1940.

Hetherington, A. W. and A. Weil. Endocrinology 26, 723, 1940.

Keller, A.D., W. K. Hare and M. C. D'Amour. Proc. Soc. Exper. Biol. and Med. 30, 772, 1933.

Keller, A. D. and W. Noble. This Journal 113, 79, 1935.

Krieg, W. J. S. Anat. Rec. 70, 48, Suppl. 3, 1938.

Lee, M. O. This Journal 89, 24, 1929.

Ranson, S. W., C. Fisher and W. R. Ingram. Endocrinology 23, 175, 1938.

Richter, C. P. Brain 53, 76, 1930.

Richter, C. P. and G. H. Wang. J. Lab. and Clin. Med. 12, 289, 1926.

Smith, P. E., Am. J. Anat. 45, 205, 1930.

Tepperman, J., J. R. Brobeck and C. N. H. Long. This Journal 133, 468, 1941.

Thomson, D. L. Assn. Research Nerv. and Ment. Dis. Proc. 17, 257, 1938.

Wilder, R. M. Arch. Int. Med. 61, 308, 1938.

Genetic, Traumatic and Environmental

Factors in the Etiology of Obesity [*]

Jean Mayer

From the Department of Nutrition, Harvard School of Public Health, and the Department of Physiology, Harvard Medical School, Boston, Massachusetts

The practical importance of obesity as a medical problem has received increasing attention in recent years. To be sure, clinicians have noted since Hippocrates that obese individuals were often poorer risks than their thin contemporaries. However, as late as the beginning of this century, the three leading causes of death were of infectious origin, tuberculosis, pneumonia, diarrhea and enteritis, with bronchitis and diphtheria also high on the list. The association of obesity with increased risk from degenerative diseases was not emphasized. The pioneer survey of the Connecticut Mutual Life Insurance Company (63) and the studies of Dublin and his associates (76–78, 6) have done much to emphasize the relation between excess weight and increased mortality. The Metropolitan Life Insurance statistics, in particular, show that in their insured population the mortality between ages 20 and 64 is 50 per cent greater among overweight than among normal-weight men and women. The mortality from cardiovascular and renal diseases is increased by more than 50 per cent, that from liver cirrhosis by more than 100 per cent. (By contrast, death rates from cancer are not affected; mortality from tuberculosis, ulcers and suicide, relatively minor causes of death, is actually decreased.) The increase in mortality accompanying obesity justifies, it seems, calling obesity the "Number One Nutrition Problem" and perhaps even the "Number One Public Health Problem" in Western countries at the present time.

The theoretical importance of obesity as a problem in physiologic pathology is hardly less than its practical significance as a problem in clinical medicine and public health. To be sure, the work of Lavoisier, Laplace, Regnault, Liebig, Voit, Rubner, Richet and many other eighteenth and nineteenth century workers gave a firm experimental justification for extending the law of conservation of energy to living organisms. That the first law

Reprinted from *Physiological Review*, 1953, 33, 472–477. (Excerpted from 472–508.)

[*] Work on the subject of obesity done in the author's laboratory and reviewed here was supported by the Nutrition Foundation, Inc., the National Institute of Arthritis and Metabolic Diseases, U.S. Public Health Service, The Milbank Memorial Fund, and others.

applies, in particular, to obese animals and patients has been repeatedly (and it would seem unnecessarily) confirmed in the laboratory and the clinic. No one would deny, therefore, that obesity does betray an imbalance between energy and intake and energy output. This statement, however, casts no light on the problem. It simply defines it in other words. To say that obesity is due to 'overeating' is hardly more illuminating than to equate alcoholism and excessive drinking. The problem is to elucidate the nature of the factors which have disturbed the mechanism of regulation of food intake in such a way that the energy balance is tipped in favor of excessive intake.

It is difficult to discuss abnormal physiology without first describing the normal physiologic processes. In this case, such a description is difficult to make because our knowledge of the normal mechanism of regulation of food intake is, at best, sketchy. In the past few years, a theory based on experimental work using men and animals of various species as subjects has been proposed (168, 170). This 'glucostatic theory,' which seems not to conflict with the known facts on hunger and the regulation of food intake and interprets them, has not yet been independently confirmed. It is summarized here because, irrespective of its intrinsic value, it provides a basis for integration of the findings on obesity into a coherent whole. Once an attempt has been made at describing the normal physiologic process, the definition of the aberration has to be given. In this case, this can be brief as the notion of obesity gives rise to no serious controversy. The relation of obesity to the normal process of aging must, however, be indicated.

The classic epidemiological approach to the study of disease is to discuss etiology in terms of host, agent and environment (107). The etiology of obesity can, similarly, be discussed in terms of hereditary, traumatic and environmental factors. These will be examined in this order. Rather than separate results obtained in man from those obtained on experimental animals, it appears more appropriate to review them under the appropriate etiologic headings. An attempt at a general synthesis will be presented in the concluding section.

I. NORMAL MECHANISM OF REGULATION OF FOOD INTAKE

The regulation of energy intake is fundamental to all homeostatic mechanisms. Yet this basic process has received less attention than many of the other physiologic regulations which it makes possible.

Prior to the beginning of this century, three theories were advanced to account for the phenomenon of hunger. The peripheral origin theories (Haller, Erasmus Darwin, Johannes Muller, Weber) held that the taking of food is the result of the stimulation of either all afferent nerves by some change in the tissues or of a strictly local group of sensory nerves, mainly in the stomach. The central origin theory (Magendie, Tidewald, Milne-Edwards) postulated that a hunger center was sensitive to a starvation state of the blood. The general sensation theories (Roux, Michael Foster) considered that the hunger center of the brain is stimulated not only directly by the hunger state of the blood but also indirectly by afferent impulses from all organs of the body. These older theories have been excellently reviewed by Carlson (58).

After Cannon and Washburn, as well as Carlson, had shown that epigastric sensations of 'hunger pain' coincided with waves of contractions of the empty stomach, Carlson suggested that hypoglycemia, mediated by its effect on the stomach, might be responsible for inducing these hunger sensations. While hunger pangs are found in most individuals, the idea that the sensations elicited by stomach contractions due to hypoglycemia (55) were at the basis of the regulation of food intake was abandoned for the following reasons: it was repeatedly shown, in particular by Sherrington, that total denervation and surgical removal of the stomach did not fundamentally alter the characteristics of food-intake regulation. Adolph (2) showed, by diluting the ration of experimental animals with inert material that differences in the bulk of the diet had only a very transient influence. Scott and his collaborators (220) were unable to correlate spontaneous fluctuations of blood sugar levels with a desire for food. The existence of diabetic hyperphagia and of the phenomenon of hunger diabetes also presented seemingly insurmountable difficulties. Even the increase in spontaneous intake due to insulin-induced hypoglycemia was held by some authors to be of no general significance because of the abnormal, 'unphysiologic,' circumstances in which the organism was placed (136).

The demonstration by Hetherington, Ranson and others (122–124) that destruction of parts of the medioventral nuclei of the hypothalamus leads to obesity, the work of Anand and Brobeck (3) showing that more lateral lesions cause anorexia reopened the problem of the nature of the physiologic mechanism of the regulation of food intake. A 'thermostatic' theory was proposed by Brobeck (37). He summarized his hypothesis as "animals eat to keep warm, and stop eating to prevent hyperthermia." The experimental evidence for this view rested largely on the reduction of food intake which followed short-term exposure to high environmental temperature. Animals, under these conditions, refuse food and lose weight. Brobeck suggested that the refusal of food was due to the fact that rats then call on energy reserves, which are without specific dynamic action, in preference to exogenous food. This theory was unable to explain the mechanism of the hyperphagia due to insulin or diabetes. It appeared to run contrary to the fact that the administration of thyroxine, a hyperthermic agent, increases food intake, while thyroidectomy or thiouracil administration depresses it. Moreover, Kennedy (146) has demonstrated that in acclimatized hypothalamic animals, weight gain is not depressed by high environmental temperature. Mayer and Greenberg (178) have shown that the central temperature of hyperphagic animals is higher than that of non-hyperphagic operated controls or of intact animals. Finally, in intact animals they found that short-term deprivation of food increased the central temperature.

Experimental work using rats, mice, dogs and human subjects culminated in the proposal by Mayer and his associates (168, 173, 170) of a 'glucostatic mechanism' of regulation of food intake. The initial reasoning was as follows: the regulation of food intake proceeds by relatively frequent partaking of food (meals). It appears improbable that hypothalamic centers are sensitive to decrease of the body content in fat or protein: during the short interval between meals, this decrease is proportionally very small. On the other hand, the body stores of carbohydrate are limited. The postprandial liver glycogen content in man is of the order of 75 grams—only 300 calories' worth. In the postabsorptive period, in spite of gluconeogenesis —the synthesizing of glycogen from body proteins—glycogen stores become rapidly depleted. This synthesis of glycogen from proteins and the shifting of metabolic oxidation in non-nervous tissues from glucose to fat (as measured by the lowering of the respiratory quotient) tend to minimize the drop in blood glucose resultant from depletion of liver glycogen stores. Thus, minimum levels, necessary for the survival of the central nervous system, are maintained. Only partaking of food, however, can restore full homeostasis of the central nervous system. It appeared possible, as a working hypothesis, that the central nervous system, dependent exclusively on a continued supply of glucose in blood, should maintain 'glucoreceptors' sensitive to fluctuations of available blood glucose. (That glucoreceptors do in fact exist in the central nervous system has been implicitly recognized by surgeons. A common method for testing the completeness of vagotomies consists in administering insulin and ascertaining that the resultant hypoglycemia fails to elicit or delays gastric secretion of hydrochloric acid. This phenomenon has been analyzed experimentally recently (207). It has been shown specifically that, in the monkey, the anterior hypothalamus was responsible for the immediate hydrochloric secretion after insulin administration). In this 'glucostatic' view, hunger would be integrated among the mechanisms through which the central nervous system insures its homeostasis.

A first (and rather crude) test of this hypothesis was provided by a systematic survey of the effect of administration of various metabolites (173) on the food intakes of groups of normal animals. Increase in levels of reducing sugar in blood was obtained by injections of glucose, fructose or small doses of epinephrine. Decreases were obtained by injections of small graded doses of insulin. Levels below normal fasting values were avoided, so as to stay within physiologic limits. Effects of the injection of substances without influence on blood glucose levels, like sucrose and fat emulsions, were also studied. It was found that temporary increases in blood glucose levels corresponded to decreases in food intake and vice versa, even when the caloric equivalent of injected metabolites was taken into account. Substances without effect on blood glucose did not influence food intake over and beyond caloric value. Although statistically significant, variations in food intake induced by these variations in blood sugar were small because of the efficiency of homeostatic mechanisms concerned with blood glucose levels. To demonstrate more clearly an inhibitory effect of high blood glucose levels on food intake, animals of the 'Houssay' type, in this case alloxan-treated hypophysectomized rats, were injected with glucose. Although these animals do not normally present hyperglycemia, they had been deprived of the mechanisms which insure the rapid removal of injected glucose. Hyperglycemia can thus be conveniently maintained for a much longer period. Two daily glucose injections were found to reduce food intake by half; three such injections, maintaining hyperglycemia around the clock, caused death of these animals from inanition in spite of the presence of food in their cage.

The apparent paradoxes afforded by the hyperphagia of diabetes mellitus, by the phenomenon of hunger diabetes, where a previously fasted individual will continue to eat in spite of blood glucose levels rising abnormally high, by the hyperphagia accompanying tendency to higher glucose levels in the obese, still had to be resolved before it could be concluded that blood glucose levels regulate food intake. It appears that all these conditions may have this in common, namely, that while absolute levels of blood glucose are increased, utilization is decreased. For variations of blood sugar levels to influence hypothalamic glucoreceptors, glucose has to cross the membranes of these cells. This presumably implies phosphorylation through the hexokinase reaction. If phosphorylation is impaired, 'effective sugar levels' will be in fact lower than absolute values as measured.

The concept was tested and put on a quantitative basis in a series of experiments performed on human subjects (168, 170, 240). Because of the inaccessibility of the hypothalamic centers, peripheral arteriovenous differences were determined as an index of rates of glucose utilization. These differences (designated as 'Δ-glucose') were measured in the antecubital region (between finger blood and antecubital vein blood). With one exception, discussed in some detail below, Δ-glucose values were found to correlate closely with the caloric intake of the individual and with hunger feelings.

Diets calorically adequate were associated with Δ-glucose which remained large (168, 240) throughout the day, decreasing only at meal time. By contrast, submaintenance diets were associated with Δ-glucose shrinking rapidly after meals; at the same time hunger returned. When hunger diabetes was present, blood glucose values rose until a difference appeared between arterial and venous levels; only then was hunger assuaged. Generally speaking, there appeared to be a quantitative relationship between food intake and the area represented by the Δ-glucose as a function of time. There was also a quantitative relationship between Δ-glucose values and the incidence of hunger feelings; antecubital arteriovenous differences of more than 15 mg. per cent were never found to be associated with hunger; values staying near zero for any length of time were always found to be associated with hunger.

In uncontrolled diabetes mellitus, a similar picture was obtained; blood sugar values had to be forced up through ingestion of food to levels where arteriovenous differences were introduced for ravenous hunger feelings to be satisfied. Cortisone administration accompanied by increased appetite was shown to cause an elevation of absolute glucose levels but a decrease in Δ-glucose.

The effect of epinephrine deserves special mention as it represents an apparent exception to the general rule. Epinephrine administration caused an immediate increase in blood glucose, it drastically reduced or eliminated any effect of hunger. However, at the same time, it decreased peripheral Δ-glucose to near zero levels. While it may be an over-simplification to ascribe this seeming contradiction to one of the many physiologic effects of epinephrine, it is worth noting that epinephrine introduces a differential between peripheral and central blood flow (227, 228). By the same token, experiments conducted on animals demonstrate that, while it decreases peripheral Δ-glucose values, it increases carotid-jugular glucose differences; thus not only does it produce hyperglycemia, but it increases the proportion of glucose made available by the nervous centers. It has recently been indicated (144) that *in vitro* glucose consumption of hypothalamic tissue is increased within a few minutes after the administration of epinephrine.

Insulin treatment first causes a fall in blood sugar due to increased peripheral utilization of glucose. In a second phase, a compensatory rise takes place which is secondary to decreased utilization of glucose in the periphery (227, 228). Delta-glucose values rapidly decline when the blood sugar falls to or below postabsorbtive levels. The occurrence of increased hunger following insulin administration is therefore easily interpreted if hunger is seen as a direct response to carbohydrate deprivation.

In hyperthyroidism, alimentary hyperglycemia typically occurs and is followed regularly by a postalimentary hypoglycemia. It has been suggested (206) that accelerated metabolism of glucose takes place in the hyperthyroid patient and that the alimentary hyperglycemia may be only a manifestation of starvation diabetes following rapid depletion of carbohydrate stores. It appears that the increased food intake characteristic of hyperthyroidism may thus again be related to metabolic hypoglycemia. It has been shown recently (11) that, in the cold, carbohydrate metabolism is also accelerated and glycogen reserves are decreased. A similar situation is known to prevail in growth.

The possibility that the 'feeding center' in the lateral hypothalamus represents the sensitive area with facilitatory properties in terms of eating mechanisms has been discussed by Brobeck (38). In the glucostatic view proposed here these centers would represent the glucoreceptors. There is an obvious need for a mechanism which would translate available blood glucose into variations in the physiologic state of the glucoreceptors. Such a mechanism is suggested by the observation that a drop in serum inorganic phosphate and in potassium consistently accompanies large Δ-glucose values (240, 158, 153). It is possible that the passage of potassium ions into the glucoreceptor cells along with the glucose phosphate may represent the point at which effective glucose level is translated into an electrical or neural mechanism.

It is recognized that hypothalamic impulses still have to be interpreted, integrated and acted upon by the cerebral cortex; that other afferent impulses (gastric hunger pangs,[1] in particular) also play a role in determining conscious states of hunger; that other psychological and physiological factors may intervene to at least temporarily modify appetite. Conditioned reflexes, in the dog in particular, and habits in man also play an important role. Still, while feelings involving desire for food or satiety are not in any sense quantifiable, they represent a conscious expression of one of the most precise regulatory devices in biology. The glucostatic mechanism seems to provide a basis for such a precise regulation. It may be added that, because of the established decrease by available glucose of the rate of fat (103) and amino acid (255) utilization in non-nervous tissue, and probably of the rate of gluconeogenesis as well (84), the regulation of food intake is easily integrated into the general regulation of metabolism.

Finally, the glucostatic theory has been applied to certain types of alteration of the regulation of energy intake: in particular, hypothalamic obesity (176), the hereditary obese-hyperglycemic syndrome of mice (182) and at least one form of human obesity (24). The demonstration (171) that, in the hereditary obese-hyperglycemic syndrome of mice, the alpha cells of

---

[1] Hunger pangs may be themselves dependent on hypothalamic stimulation (21, 164, 223).

the islets of Langerhans oversecrete a hormone with hyperglycemic, glyco-genolytic and anti-insulin properties opens the possibility that this hormone plays a major role in the regulation of food intake and in the etiology of obesity.

Whether the glucostatic model is eventually retained or not, it must be evident that the physiological mechanism of regulation of food intake is an exceedingly complicated one and, therefore, extremely vulnerable. From the scheme presented above, it can be concluded that any disturbance in carbohydrate metabolism will produce a disturbance of food intake because of its effect on blood sugar. Any disturbance in fat metabolism or in pro-tein metabolism can also be expected to increase or decrease appetite, be-cause of the sparing effect of these metabolites on or of their interaction with carbohydrate metabolism. Increase or decrease of activity beyond the limits of adjustment in terms of carbohydrate utilization, abnormalities of either one of the two centers of the hypothalamus concerned with food in-take or of the thalamic or cortical areas associated with these centers would be also expected to pervert the normal regulatory mechanism.

In higher animals and, more particularly, in man, to the vulnerability associated with the physiological complexity of the mechanism regulating food intake, are added the psychological risks inherent to cerebral integra-tion. Besides habits, such additional factors as abnormal environment, physi-cal characteristics (size, shape, color, odor, presentation) or palatability of the food, the emotional associations it evokes, social stimulations, reactions to mental shock or stress, may all interfere with normal regulation. Such interference, if it is not of short duration or self-limiting, can only end in death in anorexia at one end, or in extreme obesity at the other end. Inter-mediary forms would be emaciation on the deficit side, overweight and moderate obesity on the excess side. In view of the precarious and even-tually lethal character of the deficit type of imbalance, it is to be expected that in areas where the availability of food is not limited by economic con-siderations and where prolonged physical exertion is exceptional, obesity will be found to be the most common symptom of a disordered appetite regulation.

REFERENCES[*]

2. ADOLPH, C. F. *Am. J. Physiol.* 151: 110, 1947.
3. ANAND, B. K. AND J. R. BROBECK. *Yale J. Biol. & Med.* 24: 141, 1951.
6. ANONYMOUS. *Metropolitan Life Insurance Co. Statistical Bulletin.* 1953.
11. BAKER, D. G. AND E. A. SELLERS. *Federation Proc.* 12: 8, 1953.
21. BEATTIE, S. AND A. S. SHECHAN. *Brain* 59: 302, 1936.
24. BEAUDOIN, R., T. B. VAN ITALLIE AND J. MAYER. *J. Clin. Nutrition* 1: 91, 1953.
37. BROBECK, J. R. *Yale J. Biol. & Med.* 20: 545, 1948.
38. BROBECK, J. R. *Proceedings Nutrition Symposium, Harvard School of Public Health.* New York: National Vitamin Foundation, 1953, p. 36.
55. BULATAO, E. AND CARLSON, A. J. *Am. J. Physiol.* 68: 148, 1924.

[*] The article by Mayer is an excerpt from a longer paper. This is an abridged bibliography containing only those of Mayer's references cited in this excerpt.

58. Carlson, A. J. *The Control of Hunger in Health and Diseases,* Chicago: Univ. Chicago Press, 1916.
63. Connecticut Mutual Life Insurance Co., 1912.
76. Dublin, L. I. *Human Biol.* 2: 159, 1930.
77. Dublin, L. I., A. J. Lotka and M. Spiegelman. *Length of Life.* New York: Ronald, 1936.
78. Dublin, L. I., and H. H. Marks. *Metropolitan Life Insurance Co. Statistical Bulletin,* 1935.
84. Engel, F. L. *J. Clin. Endocrinol.* 9: 657, 1949.
103. Geyer, R. P., E. J. Bowie and J. C. Bates. *J. Biol. Chem.* 200: 271, 1953.
107. Gordon, J. E. *Research in Public Health,* 1951 Annual Conference of the Milbank Memorial Fund, New York, 1952.
122. Hetherington, A. W. and S. W. Ranson. *Anat. Rec.* 78: 149, 1940.
123. Hetherington, A. W. and S. W. Ranson. *Am. J. Physiol.* 136: 609, 1942.
124. Hetherington, A. W. and S. W. Ranson. *J. Comp. Neurol.* 76: 475, 1942.
136. Janowitz, H. D. and M. I. Grossman. *J. Mt. Sinai Hosp.* 16: 231, 1949.
144. Keller, M. R., and S. Roberts. *Federation Proc.* 12: 76, 1953.
146. Kennedy, G. C. *Proc. Roy. Soc. London s. B.* 140: 578, 1953.
153. Levine, R., S. D. Loube, and H. F. Weisberg. *Am. J. Physiol.* 195: 107, 1949.
158. McCullagh, D. R. and L. Van Alstine, *Am. J. Clin. Path.* 2: 276, 1932.
164. Masserman, J. H. and E. W. Haertig. *J. Neurophysiol.* 1: 350, 1938.
168. Mayer, J.: *Bull. New England M. Center.* 14: 43, 1952.
170. Mayer, J.: *New England J. Med.* 249: 13, 1953.
171. Mayer, J., S. B. Andrus, and D. J. Silides. *Endocrinology.* In press.
173. Mayer, J. and M. W. Bates. *Am. J. Physiol.* 168: 812, 1952.
176. Mayer, J., M. W. Bates and T. B. Van Itallie. *Metabolism* 1: 340, 1952.
178. Mayer, J. and R. M. Greenberg. *Am. J. Physiol.* 173: 523, 1953.
182. Mayer, J., R. E. Russell, M. W. Bates and M. M. Dickie. *Metabolism* 2: 9, 1953.
206. Peters, J. P., and D. D. Van Slyke. *Quantitative Clinical Chemistry, Vol. 1,* Interpretations, Baltimore: Williams & Wilkins, 1946, p. 328.
207. Porter, R. W., R. L. Longmire and J. D. French. *Federation Proc.* 12: 110, 1953.
220. Scott, W. W., C. C. Scott and A. B. Luckhardt. *Am. J. Physiol.* 123: 243, 1938.
223. Sheehan, D. *Res. Publ., A. Nerv. & Ment. Dis.* 20: 589, 1940.
227. Somogyi, M. *J. Biol. Chem.* 186: 513, 1951.
228. Somogyi, M. *J. Biol. Chem.* 193: 859, 1951.
240. Van Itallie, T. B., R. Beaudoin, and J. Mayer. *J. Clin. Nutrition* 1: 208, 1953.
255. Winzler, R. J. *et al.: J. Biol. Chem.* 199: 485, 1952.

Integration of Current Views on the

Regulation of Hunger and Appetite

Morton I. Grossman

United States Army Medical Nutrition Laboratory, Denver, Colo.

Professor E. F. Adolph (1) has said: "Regulations in organisms are mainte-
nances of relative constancies." What is it that is being "regulated" or
"maintained relatively constant" as regards our subject of hunger and appetite? I submit that it is mainly the body's content of nutrients. Under
special circumstances, regulation of other factors, such as body-heat content
or body-water content, may take precedence but, normally, it is probably
nutrient stores that are being conserved. Although all classes of nutrients
are involved in this regulatory process, for the present discussion we shall
confine our considerations to the energy-yielding nutrients; that is, we shall
be concerned with calorie balance.

The store of energy in the healthy adult animal body remains relatively constant over long periods. It follows that the rates of energy intake
and expenditure are essentially equal. The regulatory process which tends
to keep them equal involves psychic phenomena, hunger, and appetite.
Our interest in these psychic phenomena is from the point of view of how
they are related to this regulatory process.

We are dealing, then, with the psychic adjuncts of a physiological
regulatory mechanism and are at once beset with the problem of whether
these psychic states are an overflow into consciousness of an essentially automatic bodily process or are indispensable in the regulatory mechanism.
In other words, "To what extent are hunger and appetite merely an awareness that the regulatory process is operating, and to what extent do they
participate in the regulation?"

Here, a useful analogy might be drawn between hunger and pain.
Stimuli which damage or threaten damage to tissue evoke pain. These same
stimuli elicit imperative protective reflexes (*e.g.* withdrawal), and these
stimuli continue to occur even when the pathways from the spinal cord to
the brain no longer are intact, thus preventing pain perception (39). Perhaps
a better example comes from respiratory physiology. Here a single word,
dyspnea, refers both to a sensation and to a sign, namely labored breathing.
Obviously, labored breathing can occur in the absence of the sensation of
dyspnea. By analogy, energy deficit evokes feeding reflexes which can per-

Reprinted from *Annals of the New York Academy of Science*, 1955, 63, 76–89.

sist in the absence of the areas of the brain required for sensation and, accordingly, for hunger. Thus, Goltz (10) observed a dog from which both cerebral hemispheres had been completely removed and found that the animal regulated its food intake and maintained normal weight. The anencephalic infant shows essentially normal feeding behavior.

All of this is not to say that the higher brain centers and psychic activity do not participate in the regulation of food intake. Clearly, they do. The extent to which they do increases with ascent of the phylogenetic scale, so that, in man, they assume much importance. The point of view that I wish to convey is that it cannot be gratuitously assumed that intensity of hunger and appetite are always quantitatively correlated with food-taking, either as determinants of the process or as reflections of it. Studies of hunger and appetite must be colligated with studies on food intake and energy balance.

Admittedly, common experience teaches that, in a general way, the intensity of hunger and appetite is correlated with the amount of food eaten. It is unlikely, however, that they are the sole determinants of food-taking behavior. Those physiological regulatory processes in which psychic events participate have an underlying "automatic" mechanism on which the mental components play.

It is usually assumed that the mechanism regulating energy balance involves only the adjustment of intake, output being an independent variable, *i.e.*, that intake is adjusted so as to equal output almost exactly. Adjustments of output do occur, however, and they contribute to the balancing mechanism. Thus, for example, when the body incurs a significant energy deficit, basal metabolic rate falls. To what extent factors of this type may operate within the physiological range of energy imbalance is not known. For the present discussion, however, we shall consider mainly the regulation of intake.

DEFINITIONS

Poinsot, the mathematician, once said: "If anyone asked me to define *time,* I should reply 'Do you know what it is that you speak of?' If he said 'Yes,' I should say 'Very well, let us talk about it.' If he said 'No,' I should answer, 'Very well, let us talk about something else.'" Perhaps it would be wise to heed this example to avoid logomachy. In my own excursions into the literature on the subject of hunger and appetite, however, I have sometimes been so perplexed by the babel of terms that I believe it will be helpful, to me at least, to state as tersely and explicitly as possible what it is I intend to discuss.

Hunger is the complex of sensations evoked by depletion of body nutrient stores.

Appetite has been variously defined as sensation and as desire. For the present discussion, I shall define *appetite* as the desire for food, an affective state.

For lack of a better term, I have selected *fullness* to designate the complex of sensations associated with repletion of body nutrient stores. *Satiety*

is the corresponding affective state in repletion signifying a lack of desire
to eat or, more precisely, a desire not to eat (*vide infra*). It is reasonable to
assume that, between the sensations of hunger and fullness and between
the affective states of appetite and satiety, there must lie a neutral zone in
which the psychic correlatives of energy balance are absent. A corollary of
this view is that fullness and satiety are positive psychic states and do not
represent merely the absence of hunger and appetite.

FIGURE 1 presents a schema interrelating these factors. For the body

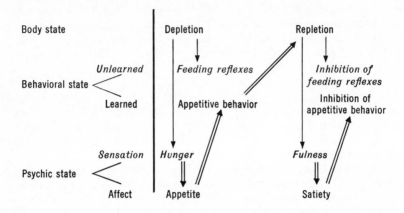

FIG. 1. Schematic representation of relations between behavioral and
psychic states in depletion and repletion. Single lines represent unlearned,
and double lines learned pathways.

states of depletion and repletion, the corresponding behavioral states are
indicated. The behavioral states are divided into learned and unlearned;
the psychic states, into sensation and affect. Before learning has occurred,
as in the infant, depletion calls forth hunger sensations and unlearned feeding reflexes. The latter lead to repletion which, in turn, produces the sensation of fullness. Repetition of this cycle eventually leads to learned behavior
in association with affective responses. Thus, the sensation of hunger evokes
a desire for food, appetite, which, in turn, leads to appetitive behavior,
learned food-seeking and food-taking activities which result in repletion
and the sensation of fullness. When conditioning has become established,
the sensation of fullness is attended by the affective state of satiety which
is reflected in a suppression of appetitive behavior.

AN APPROACH TO INTEGRATION

The eating of food is a motor act performed by voluntary muscles.
Like all voluntary muscles, those concerned with eating are under the control of the central nervous system. Many parts of the central nervous system
participate in this control, but certain areas of the hypothalamus are especially concerned. Brobeck and his co-workers (3) have described two such
hypothalamic areas, both located at the level of the ventromedial nucleus.

Feeding reflexes are facilitated by activity of the more lateral area and are inhibited by activity of the more medial area. In FIGURE 2, a diagram is presented showing some of the theoretically possible relations of these areas and of factors acting on them. This diagram is purely schematic. It is intended to convey the notion that, by considering all of the factors which

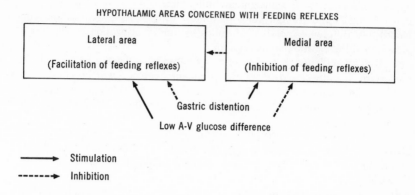

HYPOTHALAMIC AREAS CONCERNED WITH FEEDING REFLEXES

FIG. 2. Schematic representation of possible relations between hypothalamic areas and factors which have been proposed as regulators of their activity.

might alter the activity of areas of the central nervous system concerned with feeding behavior and the interaction of the areas themselves, we may construct a flexible and comprehensive framework on which our ideas concerning regulation of nutrient balance may be arranged and examined. The diagram in FIGURE 2 uses the hypothalamic areas as examples of brain regions controlling feeding. The relations indicated are hypothetical. The factors listed are not known to act on these brain areas. It is also intended to indicate that, theoretically, any one factor could produce its effect by acting on either of the hypothalamic areas, or possibly on both of them. For example, inhibition of feeding reflexes by gastric distention could be accomplished either by stimulation of the medial inhibitory area or by inhibition of the lateral facilitatory area. Studies on ablation of the medial area (32) suggest that factors which normally contribute toward bringing about cessation of eating, such as gastric distention, act mainly through this medial area.

SOME FACTORS WHICH MAY PARTICIPATE IN REGULATION OF FOOD INTAKE

Turning now to a consideration of some of the individual factors which have been proposed as playing a role in regulation of food intake, it must be emphasized (1) that it is unlikely that any one factor plays a predominant role and (2) that a change in one factor may alter the effectiveness of other factors. I have selected for consideration those mechanisms which have recently received the most attention from investigators in this field.

MAYER'S HYPOTHESIS OF THE "GLUCOSTATIC" REGULATION OF FOOD INTAKE

(A) *The hypothesis* (28–30). "Glucoreceptors" in the central nervous system (probably the hypothalamus) are sensitive to the rate at which glucose is being utilized by them. Low utilization rates excite neural activity leading to hunger sensations and food-taking. High utilization rates produce the opposite effect. Arteriovenous glucose differences serve as an index of utilization rate and, for most purposes, peripheral (finger blood—antecubital vein blood) A-V differences serve as an index of rate of utilization by the glucoreceptors in the central nervous system.

(B) *The evidence.* A variety of types of evidence have a bearing on the glucostatic hypothesis. Much of the pertinent evidence will be considered, but it is the opinion of this writer that studies on the relation between glucose utilization rates and food consumption are the most pertinent and crucial.

1. *Blood-glucose levels and gastric-hunger contractions.* Bulatao and Carlson (6) reported that the intravenous infusion of 5 to 10 grams of glucose in the form of 50 per cent glucose solution markedly or completely suppressed gastric contractions in fasting dogs. The inhibition was maximal within a minute or two and then subsided, the normal amplitude and frequency of contractions being restored in less than one hour. Injection of hypertonic saline or lactose was reported not to produce this effect. Although Templeton and Quigley (45) originally reported that they had confirmed this finding, in a later and more extensive study, Quigley and Hallaran (36) concluded that glucose infusion had no effect on fasting gastric motility and that the occasional transient inhibition seen in these studies was attributable to the manipulation incident to intravenous injections. Mulinos (35) came to the same conclusion from an extensive series of investigations involving 87 studies on 11 dogs. Mulinos pointed out that the occasional inhibition which occurred after injection of glucose subsided long before the blood-sugar level returned to the control level. Templeton and Quigley (45) found that the motor activity of the vagally denervated Heidenhain pouch was uninfluenced by intravenous glucose injection. Intragastric or intraduodenal instillation of glucose regularly inhibits contractions of the vagally innervated or vagally denervated stomach, but this effect is mediated by a hormonal mechanism (enterogastrone) from the upper portion of the small intestine, and is not dependent on the occurrence of hyperglycemia (11).

In studies on human subjects, Stunkard and Wolff (44) reported that the intravenous injection of 50 cc. of 50 per cent glucose promptly abolished gastric contractions in normal subjects, but not in subjects with either uncontrolled diabetes mellitus or "hunger diabetes."

In human subjects, Scott *et al.* (37) and, in dogs, Mulinos (35) found no correlation between the occurrence of "hunger periods" of gastric contractions and blood-glucose levels. With the introduction of the concept of glucose-utilization rate as measured by A-V glucose difference, this finding does not contradict the glucostatic hypothesis.

The evidence is thus seen to be contradictory and inconclusive. Since, however, gastric contractions may not be a reliable index of hunger sensations and feeding behavior (as is pointed out elsewhere in this paper), it is best not to place too much weight on this aspect of the glucostatic hypothesis.

2. *Blood-glucose and hunger sensations.* The two studies which have been performed on the effect of intravenous glucose infusions on hunger sensations in human subjects have yielded diametrically opposed results. Janowitz and Ivy (24) reported that hunger sensations were unaltered by intravenous injection of glucose, whereas Stunkard and Wolff (44) state that the subjective experience of hunger was promptly abolished by such treatment. In a recent study in our laboratory (12), the effect of intravenous or intragastric administration of glucose on hunger sensations and appetite was compared with control injections of saline. The test was conducted according to a Latin square design, and neither the test subjects nor the interviewer who recorded the data knew which treatment had been administered. The results, summarized in FIGURE 3, indicate that hyperglycemia produced by

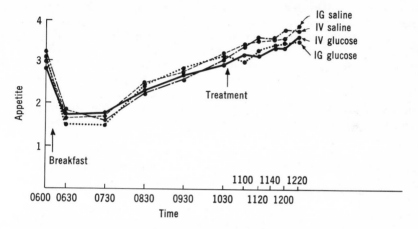

Fig. 3. Twelve normal male subjects received saline and glucose intragastrically and intravenously in random order on four test days. Appetite was scored by interview on a scale of five steps ranging from "no desire to eat" to "intense desire to eat." Each subject ate a fixed breakfast (450 calories) immediately after the first interview of each test.

intravenous or alimentary-glucose administration produced a slight suppression of appetite (not statistically significant), which was very much less than that produced by eating a small breakfast.

Van Itallie *et al.* (46) correlated A-V glucose differences with hunger feelings in five normal and one uncontrolled diabetic subject. They interpreted their findings to support the view that, in general, a satisfactory correlation existed between A-V glucose differences and desire for food. They state that, when this difference was more than 15 mg. per cent, hunger was never reported and that persistent low differences were invariably accompanied by hunger feelings.

3. *Hyperglycemia and food consumption.* A priori, one might assume that the glucostatic hypothesis could be put to a simple and crucial test, namely, a study of the effect in normal animals and human subjects of experimentally induced hyperglycemia (with attendant elevation of "utilization rate" as measured by A-V glucose difference) on the quantity of food eaten. This study would constitute an experimental "counter proof" in the

sense of Bernard (5). Here again, however, the evidence is contradictory and awaits resolution.

Janowitz and Grossman (18) injected 15 cc. of 10 per cent glucose intraperitoneally twice daily in rats and found that the slight depression of food intake that resulted from this treatment was no greater than that which occurred with control injections of saline. In studies on dogs, Janowitz et al. (23) gave large infusions of glucose intravenously (providing as much as 100 per cent of the control voluntary caloric intake) and found that the mean food consumption was unaltered when compared with no treatment or control saline infusions. In these studies, food was offered to the dogs soon after completion of the infusion and was removed after 45 minutes, so that all measurements of food intake after glucose infusion were made at a time when marked hyperglycemia existed. In another study on dogs, Janowitz and Grossman (22) fed 100 cc. of 10 per cent sucrose 20 minutes before the regular daily feeding and found no depression of food consumption. In this study also, the observations were made during the period of hyperglycemia.

Mayer and Bates (31) gave 1 cc. of 37.5 per cent glucose subcutaneously twice daily for 23 days to rats and found approximately 10 per cent decrease in food intake when compared with a control group receiving saline injections. When the control and treated groups did not eat the same amount during the pre-experimental period, a correction was applied to the data compensating for this difference. This experiment is the only study in the literature in which depression of food intake in normal animals has been reported to occur as a result of glucose injections.

Smyth et al. (41) gave infusions of 10 per cent glucose intravenously to two normal subjects three times daily following each meal and found no suppression of voluntary food consumption.

We (12) have recently conducted a study of nine normal male test subjects in which glucose or saline was given intragastrically or intravenously just before a test meal which the subjects could consume *ad libitum*. Two saline controls and two glucose tests were performed on each subject by each route. The dose of glucose was 200 cc. of 10 per cent solution intravenously and 200 cc. of 25 per cent solution intragastrically. The subjects did not know what the test substances were, and they did not know that the purpose of the study was to measure food intake. The control and test treatments were applied in a randomized order by a Latin square design. The results are summarized in TABLE 1. No significant depression of food consumption occurred in association with the glucose treatments, although

TABLE 1

EFFECT OF INTRAVENOUS OR INTRAGASTRIC GLUCOSE ON CONSUMPTION OF TEST MEAL BY HUMAN SUBJECTS

Route	Control		Test	
	Treatment	Calories	Treatment	Calories
Intragastric	200 ml. Saline	1319	200 ml. 25% Dextrose	1260
Intravenous	200 ml. Saline	1333	200 ml. 10% Dextrose	1292

Each value is the mean of 18 tests on 9 subjects.

For the difference between control and test, in both instances $F < 1$, $P > 0.05$, not statistically significant.

these produced marked hyperglycemia and elevation of A-V glucose differences.

4. *The effect of insulin on food intake.* Almost all investigators who have studied the problem have found that insulin increases food consumption (9, 13, 26, 31, 34, 40). At first glance, this would seem to support the glucostatic hypothesis. During the initial phase of the action of insulin, while hypoglycemia is increasing, peripheral A-V glucose differences are elevated (42). During the recovery from hypoglycemia, at which time the hunger symptoms occur, the A-V glucose difference returns toward the fasting level (see FIGURE 4). This return of A-V glucose difference to the fasting level

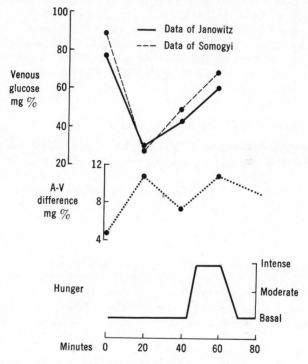

FIG. 4. Venous blood glucose, antecubital A-V glucose difference, and hunger sensations after injection of insulin in human subjects (data of Janowitz and Ivy (24) and Somogyi (42)).

would seem to be an inadequate explanation for the greatly *augmented* hunger sensations which occur at this time. Mayer (46) has recognized that uptake of glucose by the brain, as a whole, is insensitive to the action of insulin (16), but he makes the "pragmatic assumption" that the glucoreceptors in the central nervous system behave as the peripheral tissues do in this regard and not as brain tissue does in general. Even if this gratuitous assumption is granted, it fails to explain the action of insulin on hunger. A more reasonable explanation would appear to lie in the fact that insulin-induced hypoglycemia reduces utilization of glucose by the brain but not by the peripheral tissues (15). The glucoreceptors concerned with hunger would then be considered to behave as does brain tissue generally. Elsewhere (19), we have proposed the concept that hypoglycemia is an emergency mechanism in the regulation of hunger, not operating in the physiological range of blood sugar variations and, in this respect, being analogous to the role of anoxemia in the regulation of respiration.

The assumption that the glucoreceptors in the central nervous system behave as do the peripheral tissues encounters another difficulty in the explanation of the depressing effect of epinephrine on hunger. Epinephrine produces hyperglycemia with decreased peripheral, but not central A-V glucose differences. In this instance, Mayer (29) assumes that the glucoreceptors concerned with hunger behave as does the remainder of the central nervous system.

5. *Comment*. Under controlled experimental conditions, we have found that hyperglycemia with elevated A-V glucose difference did not significantly depress hunger sensations, appetite, or food consumption in normal human subjects. This finding, we believe, constitutes crucial evidence against the glucostatic hypothesis. The possibility remains that a glucostatic mechanism may operate under unusual conditions, but it does not appear to play a major role in normal regulation.

GASTRIC CONTRACTIONS AND THE SENSATION OF HUNGER

The classical studies of Cannon (7) and Carlson (8) established unequivocally that contractions of the empty stomach produce distinctive sensations localized to the epigastrium. Cannon and Carlson chose to define hunger as being this sensation. Carlson (8) expressed the opinion that the other sensations associated with nutrient depletion were secondary to and dependent on the occurrence of gastric contractions, and this suggestion served as the basis for considering the gastric contractions as the central phenomenon of hunger.

If hunger is defined as the complex of sensations associated with nutrient depletion, including but not limited to the epigastric pang produced by contraction of the stomach, then it can be shown that the only element of the hunger complex dependent upon stimuli arising from the stomach is the epigastric pang, and that, in its absence, the remainder of the sensation complex still occurs. Therefore, the assumption that hunger sensations other than the epigastric pang are dependent on the occurrence of gastric contractions would appear to be unwarranted and, *a fortiori*, the designation of the epigastric pang as the essential element in hunger sensation would be dismissed.

Hunger, as a sensation, can be studied only in man. The removal of the entire stomach in man does not abolish hunger sensations (17, 27). Unfortunately, those who have made observations on totally gastrectomized patients have not reported on whether the epigastric pang is abolished, although presumably it would be. We (14) studied the effect of insulin injection on hunger sensations before and after vagotomy or splanchnicotomy in human patients. Neither of these procedures abolished the hunger response to insulin, although both prevented the occurrence of the epigastric pangs in association with insulin-induced hunger. From these studies, we have arrived at the conclusion that the epigastric pang associated with gastric contractions is but one element in the complex of sensations comprising hunger, and that its elimination does not significantly alter the general pattern of hunger sensation.

GASTRIC DISTENSION AND REGULATION OF FOOD INTAKE

A considerable length of time is required for the digestion and assimilation of nutrients after their ingestion. If the quantity of food eaten is to be adjusted to the magnitude of the nutrient deficit, mechanisms must exist for sensing the quantity of nutrients ingested before they undergo metabolism. One such possible mechanism is distention of the stomach by the ingested food, and experiments on this subject have revealed that such distention does, indeed, influence the quantity of food eaten.

In studies designed to evaluate the effect of gastric distention on food intake, it is necessary to take into account the possible role of digestion and absorption of foodstuffs. The use of nutritionally inert materials as distending agents obviates this complication. In studies on dogs, we (38) have used gum arabic, celluflour, and water-filled balloons for this purpose. In dogs weighing 10 to 15 kg., the introduction of 50 to 100 grams of gum arabic into the stomach via gastric fistula, just before offering food, did not significantly decrease food intake. One hundred grams of celluflour, a bulkier material, produced moderate depression of food consumption. Water-filled balloons placed in the stomach and allowed to remain there for several weeks produced sustained depression of food intake. When the amount of water in the balloon occupied a volume equivalent to 75 per cent of the volume of food eaten during the control period, food intake was decreased by about 50 per cent. An inhibitory effect of gastric distention in the duration of sham-feeding in esophagostomized dogs has also been demonstrated (21, 38). Since animals with denervated gastrointestinal tracts show normal regulation of food intake (13), it must be assumed that either the gastric distention mechanism is dispensable or that gastric distention may operate through somatic nerves stimulated by increase in the volume of the abdominal contents.

Within certain definable limits, animals will increase the volume of food eaten to compensate for dilution of food with calorically inert substances (2, 20, 43). The effectiveness of gastric distention as an inhibitor of eating must, therefore, be subject to alteration when other factors regulating food intake change. Here, then, is an instance of dynamic equilibrium between factors regulating food intake.

THE EFFECT OF ENERGY LOAD ON FOOD INTAKE

If the energy content of the body, in the form of stored nutrients, were the primary determinant of further food intake, it would be anticipated that, by increasing body-energy content by parenteral or intragastric feeding, voluntary oral food intake would be correspondingly decreased. When this hypothesis is put to an experimental test (23, 38), it becomes apparent that the body does not make rapid and fine adjustments to induced positive energy loads by decreasing voluntary oral food intake. Only when extra energy intake has persisted for some time does downward adjustment of oral intake begin to occur. For example, we (38) found that, in dogs, the daily intragastric administration of one third of the *ad libitum* control food intake for four weeks did not suppress oral intake and that intragastric administration of one half the control intake for three weeks resulted in a decrease in oral intake to 70 per cent of the control level. A striking finding in these studies was that body weight did not increase, although the combined oral and intragastric intake was considerably in excess of the control *ad libitum* level. For example, dog No. 3, in the study cited above (38), had maintained a constant body weight of 12.2 kg. on an *ad libitum* intake of 950 calories per day. When 325 calories per day were given intragastrically for 28 days, the average daily caloric intake (intragastric plus oral) rose to 1332. Thus total intake was 382 calories per day greater than during the control period, giving a total of 10,702 cumulative extra calories for the 28-day period. Body weight remained constant, although this number of calories would be expected to produce about a 2 kg. weight gain had they been stored as body tissue. This finding suggests either that a change in body composition may be induced by extra calorie intake or that mechanisms may exist for expending calories in excess of requirements for maintenance.

STIMULATION OF HEAD RECEPTORS IN REGULATION OF FOOD INTAKE

If a dog is allowed to eat a portion of its food a short time before food is offered *ad libitum,* the voluntary intake is reduced by an amount approximately equal to the prefeeding (22). If, instead of allowing the dog to eat the portion of food, the food is placed in the stomach just before food is offered *ad libitum,* voluntary intake is suppressed to a lesser extent. If the portion of food be placed in the stomach a number of hours before food is offered, no suppression of oral intake occurs. Conversely, in dogs with esophagostomy (21, 38), sham-feeding, in which the food fails to reach the stomach results in the taking of far greater quantities of food than in intact animals. From these observations, we may hypothesize that stimulation of head receptors by smelling, tasting, chewing, and swallowing, during eating, plays an important role in bringing about satiety and suppression of further eating, but that this factor is relatively ineffective when it is not associated with entry of food into the stomach. Even when an amount of food greater than the quantity which the animal voluntarily eats during a control period is given daily intragastrically, oral intake of significant quantities persists for at least several weeks.

In rats, a comparison has been made of the effect of food introduced by gastric fistula and food eaten normally by mouth. As measured by rate of performing a response (pushing a little panel) (25), consumption of food (4), or by reward value in producing learning (33), oral ingestion was always more effective than intragastric instillation of food, which in turn was more effective than intragastric saline.

Thus, stimulation of head receptors is an important element in the group of factors which normally contribute to satiety.

INTERRELATION OF FACTORS REGULATING FOOD INTAKE

Factors stimulating intake of food. Although energy balance results from regulation of food intake, energy deficit is not the sole stimulus to food ingestion. Repair of the energy deficit by intragastric feeding does not suppress consumption completely. Whether the residual drive to eat when energy balance is positive results from as-yet-unrecognized positive stimuli or simply from absence of inhibitory stimuli remains unknown. One hypothesis worthy of being tested is that there is a drive for oropharyngeal stimulation which can be suppressed but not abolished by repair of energy deficit.

Factors inhibiting intake of food. What causes cessation of eating? The simplest answer to this question is that eating leads to cessation of eating. The ingestion and assimilation of food can be divided, for purpose of analysis, into the following components: (1) *oropharyngeal,* introduction of food into the mouth, chewing and swallowing; (2) *gastrointestinal,* entry of food into the stomach and intestines with subsequent digestion and adsorption; (3) circulation of absorbed nutrients in *blood;* and (4) extraction of nutrients from blood by *tissues* for storage or oxidation. The oropharyngeal component is potent when acting with the gastrointestinal component, weak when acting alone. The gastrointestinal component appears to involve mainly distention. Inert bulk in the stomach is as effective as an equal volume of food in suppressing eating. Of the four components listed, this factor is the only one which has high effectiveness when acting alone. The importance of the blood component has not been clearly established. Of the major nutrients, carbohydrate, as represented by blood glucose, has received the most attention. Hyperglycemia, with rapid uptake of glucose by tissues, does not, when acting alone, produce marked inhibition of eating. The role of the tissue factor can only be presumed. Prolonged overloading of the body with extra calories eventually leads to downward adjustment of voluntary food intake. It has not been demonstrated that this adjustment is associated with extra storage of food energy in tissues. The mechanism of the effect is obscure.

CONCLUDING REMARKS

The aim of this presentation has been heuristic. This is not a comprehensive archive of recent work. It is intended more to pose questions for future investigation than to cull answers from past inquiries. These major points were considered: Hunger and appetite are psychic correlatives of the bodily processes which regulate nutrient balance. They arise from, and participate in, the regulatory processes. Food-taking is a motor act of skeletal muscles, governed by nervous processes like all other voluntary muscles. Specialized hypothalamic areas participating in this control have been discovered. Among the factors which may regulate the activity of these hypothalamic centers and of other brain areas concerned with feeding are oropharyngeal stimulation, gastrointestinal distention, blood levels of nutrients (particularly glucose), and tissue stores of nutrients. For none of these factors is the mechanism of action known.

REFERENCES

1. Adolph, E. F. 1943. *Physiological Regulations.* Cattell Press. Lancaster, Pa.
2. Adolph, E. F. 1947. Urges to eat and drink in rats. *Am. J. Physiol.* **151,** 110.

3. ANAND, B. K. & J. R. BROBECK. 1951. Hypothalamic control of food intake in rats and cats. *Yale J. Biol. and Med.* **24**, 123.

4. BERKUN, M. J., M. L. KESSEN & N. E. MILLER. 1952. Hunger-reducing effects of food by stomach fistula versus food by mouth measured by a consummatory response. *J. Comp. Physiol. Psychol.* **45**, 550.

5. BERNARD, C. 1949. Introduction to the Study of Experimental Medicine. Schuman. New York, N.Y.

6. BULATAO, E. & A. J. CARLSON. 1924. Contributions to the physiology of the stomach. Influence of experimental changes in blood sugar level or gastric hunger contractions. *Am. J. Physiol.* **69**, 107.

7. CANNON, W. B. & A. L. WASHBURN. 1915. An explanation of hunger. *Am. J. Physiol.* **29**, 250.

8. CARLSON, A. J. 1916. The Control of Hunger in Health and Disease. Univ. of Chicago Press. Chicago, Ill.

9. FREYBURG, R. H. 1935. A study of the value of insulin in undernutrition. *Am. J. Med. Sci.* **190**, 28.

10. GOLTZ, 1892. Der Hund ohne Grosshirn. *Arch. ges. Physiol.* **51**, 570.

11. GROSSMAN, M. I. 1950. Gastrointestinal hormones. *Physiol. Revs.* **30**, 33.

12. GROSSMAN, M. I. & L. M. BERNSTEIN. Unpublished studies at the Medical Nutrition Laboratory.

13. GROSSMAN, M. I., G. M. CUMMINS & A. C. IVY. 1947. The effect of insulin on food intake after vagotomy and sympathectomy. *Am. J. Physiol.* **149**, 100.

14. GROSSMAN, M. I. & I. F. STEIN, JR. 1948. Vagotomy and the hunger-producing action of insulin in man. *J. Applied Physiol.* **1**, 263.

15. HIMWICH, H. E. 1951. Brain Metabolism and Cerebral Disorders. Williams & Wilkins. Baltimore, Md.

16. HIMWICH, H. E., K. M. BOWMAN, C. DALY, J. F. FAZWKAS, J. WORTIS & W. GOLDFARB. 1941. Cerebral blood flow and brain metabolism during insulin hypoglycemia. *Am. J. Physiol.* **132**, 640.

17. INGELFINGER, F. J. 1944. Late effects of total and subtotal gastrectomy. *New Engl. J. Med.* **231**, 321.

18. JANOWITZ, H. & M. I. GROSSMAN. 1948. Effect of parenteral administration of glucose and protein hydrolysate on food intake in the rat. *Am. J. Physiol.* **155**, 28.

19. JANOWITZ, H. D. & M. I. GROSSMAN. 1949. Hunger and appetite: some definitions and concepts. *J. Mt. Sinai Hosp. N.Y.* **16**, 231.

20. JANOWITZ, H. D. & M. I. GROSSMAN. 1949. Effect of variations in nutritive density on intake of food of dogs and rats. *Am. J. Physiol.* **158**, 184.

21. JANOWITZ, H. D. & M. I. GROSSMAN. 1949. Some factors affecting the food intake of normal dogs and dogs with esophagostomy and gastric fistula. *Am. J. Physiol.* **159**, 143.

22. JANOWITZ, H. D. & M. I. GROSSMAN. 1951. Effect of prefeeding, alcohol and bitters on food intake of dogs. *Am. J. Physiol.* **164**, 182.

23. JANOWITZ, H. D. & M. I. GROSSMAN. 1949. Effect of intravenously administered glucose on food intake in the dog. *Am. J. Physiol.* **156**, 87.

24. JANOWITZ, H. D. & A. C. IVY. 1949. Role of blood sugar levels in spontaneous and insulin-induced hunger in man. *J. Applied Physiol.* **1**, 643.

25. KOHN, M. 1951. Satiation of hunger from food injected directly into the stomach versus food ingested by mouth. *J. Comp. Physiol. Psychol.* **44**, 412.

26. MCCAY, E. M., J. W. CALLOWAY & R. H. BARNES. 1940. Hyperalimen-

tation in normal animals produced by protamine insulin. *J. Nutrition.* **20,** 59.

27. MacDonald, R. M., F. J. Ingelfinger & H. W. Belding. 1947. Late effects of total gastrectomy in man. *New Engl. J. Med.* **237,** 887.

28. Mayer, J. 1952. The glucostatic theory of regulation of food intake and the problem of obesity. *Bull. New Engl. Med. Cent.* **14,** 43.

29. Mayer, J. 1953. Genetic, traumatic and environmental factors in the etiology of obesity. *Physiol. Revs.* **33,** 472.

30. Mayer, J. 1953. Glucostatic mechanism of regulation of food intake. *New Engl. J. Med.* **249,** 15.

31. Mayer, J. & M. W. Bates. 1952. Blood glucose and food intake in normal and hypophysectomized, alloxan-treated rats. *Am. J. Physiol.* **168,** 812.

32. Miller, N. E., C. J. Bailey & J. A. F. Stevenson. 1950. Decreased "hunger" but increased food intake resulting from hypothalamic lesions. *Science.* **112,** 256.

33. Miller, N. E. & M. L. Kesson. 1952. Reward effects of food via stomach fistula compared with those of food via mouth. *J. Comp. Physiol. Psychol.* **45,** 555.

34. Morgan, C. T. & J. D. Morgan. 1940. Studies in hunger: II. The relation of gastric denervation and dietary sugar to the effect of insulin upon food-intake in the rat. *Genet. Psychol.* **57,** 153.

35. Mulinos, M. G. 1933. The gastric hunger mechanism. IV. The influence of experimental alteration in blood sugar concentration on gastric hunger contractions. *Am. J. Physiol.* **104,** 371.

36. Quigley, J. P. & W. R. Hallaran. 1932. The independence of spontaneous gastrointestinal motility and blood sugar levels. *Am. J. Physiol.* **100,** 102.

37. Scott, W. W., C. C. Scott & A. B. Luckhardt. 1938. Observations on the blood sugar level before, during and after hunger periods in humans. *Am. J. Physiol.* **123,** 243.

38. Share, I., E. Martyniuk & M. I. Grossman. 1952. Effect of prolonged intragastric feeding on oral food intake in dogs. *Am. J. Physiol.* **169,** 229.

39. Sherrington, C. S. 1947. The Integrative Action of the Nervous System. *Cambridge Univ. Press.* Cambridge, England.

40. Short, J. J. 1929. Increasing weight: preliminary report. *J. Lab. Clin. Med.* **14,** 330.

41. Smyth, C. J., A. G. Lasichak & S. Levey. 1947. The effect of orally and intravenously administered amino acid mixtures on voluntary food consumption in normal men. *J. Clin. Invest.* **26,** 439.

42. Somogyi, M. 1949. Studies on arteriovenous differences in blood sugar. III. Effect of insulin administered intravenously in the postabsorptive state. *J. Biol. Chem.* **179,** 217.

43. Strominger, J. L., J. R. Brobeck & R. L. Cort. 1953. Regulation of food intake in normal rats and in rats with hypothalamic hyperphagia. *Yale J. Biol. Med.* **26,** 55.

44. Stunkard, A. J. & H. G. Wolff. 1954. Correlation of arteriovenous glucose differences, gastric hunger contractions and the experience of hunger in man. *Federation Proc.* **13,** 147.

45. Templeton, R. D. & J. P. Quigley. 1930. The action of insulin on the motility of the gastrointestinal tract. II. Action on the Heindenhain pouch. *Am. J. Physiol.* **91,** 467.

46. Van Itallie, T. B., R. Beaudoin & J. Mayer. 1953. Arteriovenous glucose differences, metabolic hypoglycemia and food intake in man. *J. Clin. Nutrition.* **1,** 208.

The Physiology of Motivation

Eliot Stellar

The Johns Hopkins University

In the last twenty years motivation has become a central concept in psychology. Indeed, it is fair to say that today it is one of the basic ingredients of most modern theories of learning, personality, and social behavior. There is one stumbling-block in this noteworthy development, however, for the particular conception of motivation which most psychologists employ is based upon the outmoded model implied by Cannon in his classical statement of the local theories of hunger and thirst (23). Cannon's theories were good in their day, but the new facts available on the physiological basis of motivation demand that we abandon the older conceptualizations and follow new theories, not only in the study of motivation itself, but also in the application of motivational concepts to other areas of psychology.

This argument for a new theory of motivation has been made before by Lashley (42) and Morgan (47). But it is more impelling than ever today because so much of the recent evidence is beginning to fit into the general theoretical framework which these men suggested. Both Lashley and Morgan pointed out that the local factors proposed by Cannon (e.g., stomach contractions or dryness of the throat) are not necessary conditions for the arousal of motivated behavior. Instead, they offered the more inclusive view that a number of sensory, chemical, and neural factors cooperate in a complicated physiological mechanism that regulates motivation. The crux of their theory was described most recently by Morgan as a *central motive state* (*c.m.s.*) built up in the organism by the combined influences of the sensory, humoral, and neural factors. Presumably, the amount of motivated behavior is determined by the level of the *c.m.s.*

Beach (8, 11), in his extensive work on the specific case of sexual motivation, has amply supported the views of Lashley and Morgan. But the important question still remains: Do other kinds of motivated behavior fit the same general theory? As you will see shortly, a review of the literature makes it clear that they do. As a matter of fact, there is enough evidence today to confirm and extend the views of Lashley, Morgan, and Beach and to propose, in some detail, a more complete physiological theory of motivation.

There are a number of ways to present a theoretical physiological mechanism like the one offered here. Perhaps the best approach is to start with an overview and summarize, in a schematic way, the major factors at work in the mechanism. Then we can fill in the details by reviewing the

Reprinted from *Psychological Review*, 1954, 61, 5–22.

literature relevant to the operation of each factor. Some advantage is lost by not taking up the literature according to behavioral topics, that is, different kinds of motivation. But the procedure adopted here lets us focus attention directly on the theory itself and permits us to make some very useful comparisons among the various kinds of motivation. Once the theoretical mechanism and the evidence bearing on it are presented, the final step will be to evaluate the theory and show what experiments must be done to check it and extend it.

THEORETICAL SCHEME

A schematic diagram of the physiological mechanism believed to be in control of motivated behavior is shown in Fig. 1. The basic assumption in this scheme is that *the amount of motivated behavior is a direct function of the amount of activity in certain excitatory centers of the hypothalamus.* The activity of these excitatory centers, in turn, is determined by a large number of factors which can be grouped in four general classes: (*a*) *inhibitory hypothalamic centers* which serve only to depress the activity of the excitatory centers, (*b*) *sensory stimuli* which control hypothalamic activity through the afferent impulses they can set up, (*c*) *the internal environment* which can influence the hypothalamus through its rich vascular supply and the cerebrospinal fluid, and (*d*) *cortical and thalamic centers* which can exert excitatory and inhibitory influences on the hypothalamus.

As can be seen, the present theory holds that the hypothalamus is the seat of Morgan's *c.m.s.* and is the "central nervous mechanism" Lashley claimed was responsible for "drive." Identifying the hypothalamus as the

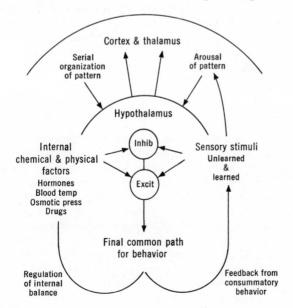

FIG. 1. Scheme of the physiological factors contributing to the control of motivated behavior. (See text.)

main integrating mechanism in motivation makes the experimental problem we face more specific and more concrete than ever before. But it also makes it more complicated, for the physiological control of the hypothalamus is exceedingly complex. The influence of the internal environment on the hypothalamus is changing continuously according to natural physiological cycles, and of course it may often be changed directly by the chemical and physical consequences of consummatory behavior (see Fig. 1). Sensory stimuli may also have varied effects on the hypothalamic mechanism, depending upon their particular pattern, previous stimulation, previous learning, sensory feedback from the consummatory behavior itself, and the influence the internal environment has already exerted on the hypothalamus. Similarly, the influence of the cortex and thalamus will add to the hypothalamic activity already produced by sensory stimuli and the internal environment. Presumably, these cortical and thalamic influences may result directly or indirectly from sensory stimulation, but they may also be controlled partly by the "upward drive" of the hypothalamus itself (43). Then, to complicate the picture even more, there are the inhibitory centers of the hypothalamus which are also controlled by the various internal changes, sensory stimuli, and cortical and thalamic influences. These centers, presumably, depress the activity of the excitatory centers and, therefore, attenuate their output.

Fortunately, this mechanism is not as formidable against experimental attack as it might appear. The basic experimental approach is to isolate the controlling factors in any type of motivation and determine their relative contributions to hypothalamic activity. As you will see, a number of experimental techniques like sensory deprivation, hormone and drug administration, cortical ablation, and the production of subcortical lesions may be used fruitfully to isolate these factors. But that is only half the problem. Obviously, the factors controlling hypothalamic activity and motivation do not operate in isolation. In fact, it is quite clear that their influences interact. Therefore, it becomes an equally important problem to determine the relative contribution of each factor while the others are operating over a wide range of variation.

EXPERIMENTAL EVIDENCE

Before going into the literature bearing on the operation of each of these factors in control of motivated behavior, it will help to raise a few questions that ought to be kept in mind while considering the experimental evidence. Are there different hypothalamic centers controlling each kind of motivation? Does the hypothalamus exert its influence through direct control of the final effector pathways or does it simply have a "priming" effect on effector paths controlled by other parts of the nervous system? Do all these factors operate in the control of each type of motivation or are there cases where sensory stimuli, for example, may not be important or where changes in the internal environment do not contribute? Can the same mechanism describe the control of motivation measured by simple consummatory behavior, preference, and learning? Are the same mechanisms involved in the control of simple, biological motives and complex, learned motives?

Hypothalamic centers. Review of the literature on the role of the hypo-thalamus in motivation brings out three general conclusions. (*a*) Damage to restricted regions of the hypothalamus leads to striking changes in certain kinds of motivated behavior. (*b*) Different parts of the hypothalamus are critical in different kinds of motivation. (*c*) There are both excitatory and inhibitory centers controlling motivation in the hypothalamus; that is, dam-age to the hypothalamus can sometimes lead to an increase in motivation and sometimes a marked decrease.

The evidence bearing on these three points can be summarized briefly. Many experiments have shown that restricted bilateral lesions of the hypo-thalamus will make tremendous changes in basic biological motivations like hunger (16, 22), sleep (49, 50, 53), and sex (6, 18, 20). Less complete evi-dence strongly suggests that the same kinds of hypothalamic integration is also true in the cases of thirst (61), activity (35), and emotions (5, 62). We have only suggestive evidence in the case of specific hungers (59).

It is clear that there is some kind of localization of function within the hypothalamus although it is not always possible to specify precisely the anatomical nuclei subserving these functions. The centers for hunger are in the region of the ventromedial nucleus which lies in the middle third of the ventral hypothalamus, in the tuberal region (16). (See Fig. 2.) Sleep is

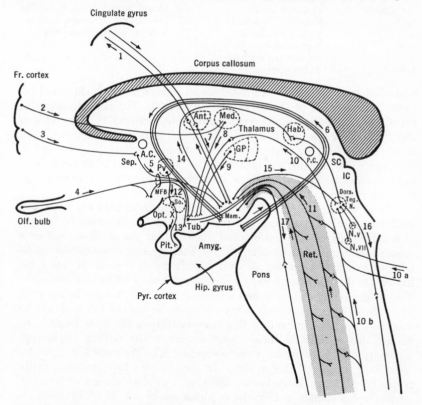

Fig. 2. Schematic drawing of the hypothalamus and its major neural con-nections. Adapted from W. R. Ingram's diagram in Gellhorn (30) and D. B. Lindsley's Figure 9 (43). [See legend, page 212.]

Abbreviations and Description of Pathways

A.C.	Anterior commissure
Amyg.	Amygdala
Ant.	Anterior thalamic nuclei
Cingulate Gyrus	Cortex of cingulate gyrus
Dors. Teg. N.	Dorsal tegmental nucleus
Fr. Cortex	Cortex of frontal lobe
GP	Globus pallidus
Hab.	Habenular nucleus of thalamus
Hip. Gyrus	Hippocampal gyrus
IC	Inferior colliculus
Mam.	Mammillary nuclei
Med.	Dorsal medial thalamic nucleus
MFB	Medial forebrain bundle
N.V	Motor nucleus, Vth nerve
N.VII	Motor nucleus, VIIth nerve
Olf. Bulb	Olfactory bulb
Opt. X	Optic chiasm
P.C.	Posterior commissure
Pit.	Pituitary gland
Pv.	Paraventricular nucleus
Pyr. Cortex	Pyriform cortex
Ret.	Reticular formation
SC	Superior colliculus
Sep.	Septal nuclei
So.	Supraoptic nucleus
Tub.	Tuber cinereum

Afferents to Hypothalamus

1. Corticothalamic fibers
2. Frontothalamic fibers
3. Frontoseptal fibers
4. Olfacto-hypothalamic tract
5. Septo-hypothalamic fibers
6. Fornix
7. Mammillothalamic tract
8. Thalamo-hypothalamic fibers
9. Pallido-hypothalamic fibers
10. Sensory systems ascending to thalamus
    10a. cranial afferents
    10b. somatic and visceral afferents
11. Sensory collaterals to hypothalamus
12. Paraventriculo-supraoptic fibers

Efferents from Hypothalamus

13. Supraoptic hypophyseal tract
14. Mammillohabenular tract
15. Mammillotegmental tract
16. Dorsal longitudinal fasciculus
17. Descending efferents relaying in brain stem and medulla

controlled by centers in the extreme posterior (mammillary bodies) and extreme anterior parts of the hypothalamus (49, 50). The critical region for sexual behavior is in the anterior hypothalamus, between the optic chiasm and the stalk of the pituitary gland (18, 20). The center for activity is not clearly established, but seems to be adjacent with or overlapping the centers for hunger (35). Finally, the centers for emotion are also in the vicinity of the ventromedial nucleus, perhaps somewhat posterior to the hunger centers and overlapping the posterior sleep center (50, 62).

In at least two cases it is clear that there must be both excitatory and inhibitory centers controlling motivated behavior. In the case of hunger, bilateral lesions in the ventromedial nucleus near the midline produce a tremendous amount of overeating (3, 16). Such a center is presumably an inhibitory one since removing it leads directly to an increase in eating behavior. On the other hand, lesions 1½ to 2 millimeters off the midline at the level of the ventromedial nucleus completely eliminate hunger behavior (3, 4). After such lesions animals never eat again, so we can call such centers excitatory centers. Supporting this interpretation is the fact, recently reported, that stimulating these lateral centers in the waking cat through implanted electrodes results in vast overeating (27). The same sort of mechanism turns up in the case of sleep. In the posterior hypothalamus, in the region of the mammillary bodies, there are excitatory centers or "waking" centers which operate to keep the organism awake (49, 50). When they are removed, the animal becomes somnolent and cannot stay awake. In the anterior hypothalamus, around the preoptic nucleus, there is an inhibitory center (49). When that is removed, the animal is constantly wakeful.

So far, only an excitatory center has been found in the case of sexual behavior. Bilateral lesions anterior to the pituitary stalk eliminate all mating behavior (18, 20), but no lesion of the hypothalamus has ever been reported that resulted in an exaggeration of sexual motivation. What little we know about the center for activity near the ventromedial nucleus suggests that it is also an excitatory center since lesions there produce only inactivity and not hyperactivity (35). In the case of emotions, the picture is not yet clear. Lesions near the ventromedial nucleus make cats highly emotional (62), and therefore this center must be inhibitory. But the lateral regions of the posterior hypothalamus seem to be excitatory, for lesions there make animals placid (50). Furthermore, direct stimulation of these posterior regions produces many of the signs of rage reactions (52).

There is some evidence that sheds light on how the excitatory and inhibitory hypothalamic centers may cooperate in the regulation of motivation. In the clear-cut cases of sleep and hunger it appears that the inhibitory centers operate mainly through their effects on the excitatory centers. At least we know that when both centers are removed simultaneously the effect is indistinguishable from what happens when only the excitatory centers are removed (3, 49). So it is convenient for present theoretical purposes to think of the inhibitory center as one of the factors which influences the level of activity of the excitatory center. In fact, to speculate one step further, it is worth suggesting that the inhibitory centers may constitute the primary neural mechanism regulating the satiation of motivation.

Sensory stimuli. What effects do sensory stimuli have upon the hypothalamus and how important are such stimuli in the control of motivation? Some answer to the first part of this question is given by the schematic outline of hypothalamic connections shown in Fig. 2. Clearly the hypothalamus has a rich supply of afferents coming directly or indirectly from all the various sense organs. In fact the diagram is really an understatement of hypothalamic connections because it is an oversimplified and conservative representation. Physiological evidence shows, for example, that there must be connections from the taste receptors via the solitary nucleus of the medulla (36). Also there is evidence of rich connections from the visual system via the lateral geniculate of the thalamus (36). There is no doubt about the fact that the hypothalamus is under very extensive sensory control.

As to the sensory control of motivation, there is excellent reason to believe that the stimuli which can set up impulses in these pathways to the hypothalamus are of particular importance. Perhaps the best example comes from the study of sexual behavior (11). The consensus of a group of studies on different mammals is as follows. Sexual behavior is not dependent upon any single sensory system. Extirpation of any one peripheral sense organ has no appreciable influence on the arousal and execution of sexual behavior. If two sensory avenues are destroyed, however, sexual behavior may be eliminated, especially in the case of the naive animal. With experienced animals, interestingly enough, it may take destruction of three sensory systems. But in neither case does it matter what combination of sensory systems is eliminated. We can conclude, therefore, that it is the sum total of relevant sensory impulses arriving at the central nervous system (hypothalamus) that is important in setting off sexual behavior.

Kleitman's analysis of sleep and wakefulness shows that the same kind of sensory control operates in this case (38). Wakefulness seems to be dependent upon the sum total of sensory impulses arriving at the waking center in the posterior hypothalamus, regardless of the particular sensory systems involved. Direct support of this kind of view is offered by Bremer's (14) physiological data which showed that maintenance of the waking rhythm of the brain is less a matter of any particular sensory input and more a matter of the amount of sensory input.

What we know about hunger and thirst suggests that the amount of motivated behavior in these cases should be a joint function of sensory impulses arising from gastric contractions or dryness of the throat and taste, tactile, and temperature receptors in the mouth. Unfortunately we have no sensory deprivation experiments that are a good test of this point. But all the evidence on the acceptability of foods and fluids of different temperatures, consistencies, and flavoring suggests the joint operation of many stimuli in the control of these types of motivation.

So far, we have mentioned only stimuli which arouse motivation. What stimulus changes could reduce motivation and perhaps lead to satiation? There are three general possibilities: (a) a reduction in excitatory stimuli, (b) interfering or distracting stimuli that elicit competing behavior, and (c) "inhibitory" stimuli. It is easy to find examples of the first two types of stimulus changes and to guess their mechanisms of operation in terms of the present theory. In the case of "inhibitory" stimuli, however, all we have is suggestive evidence. For example, the fact that dogs with esophageal fistulas eat (37) and drink (1, 13) amounts proportional to the severity of deprivation suggests that the stimuli which feed back from consummatory behavior might have a net inhibitory effect on motivation (see Fig. 1). Furthermore, some of the experiments on artificially loading the stomach suggest that a full gut may result in stimuli which inhibit further eating (37) or drinking (2, 13) over and above the possibility that there might be no room left in the stomach or that gastric contractions are reduced.

In summary, we can state the following working hypotheses about the sensory factors which operate in the control of motivation. (a) No one sensory avenue is indispensable in the arousal of motivated behavior. Instead, sensory stimuli have an additive effect on the excitability of the hypothalamus so that it is the sum total of relevant impulses arriving at the excitatory centers of the hypothalamus that determine the amount of motivated behavior. (b) Judging from the resistance of experienced animals to the effects of sensory deprivation in the case of sexual motivation, it seems clear that excitatory influences in the hypothalamus may be exerted by learned as well as unlearned stimuli. (c) There are afferent impulses to the hypothalamus which have a net inhibitory effect on the excitatory centers and thus serve to reduce motivation or produce satiation. The best guess at present is that these "inhibitory" stimuli operate by exerting an excitatory influence on the inhibitory centers of the hypothalamus. Presumably, impulses to inhibitory centers have the same kind of additive properties as impulses to the excitatory centers.

Internal environment. That the internal environment plays an important role in certain kinds of motivated behavior is a well-established fact. Two basic questions must be asked, however, before we can understand much about how the internal environment does its work. What kinds of changes that can occur in the internal environment are the important ones in motivation? How do changes in the internal environment influence the nervous system and, therefore, motivated behavior?

In terms of the present theory, we would expect the internal environment to operate in motivation by changing the excitability of hypothalamic centers. This is a reasonable expectation, for the hypothalamus is the most richly vascularized region of the central nervous system (24). Not only that, but the hypothalamus is also in direct contact with the cerebrospinal fluid in the third ventricle.

The case of sexual behavior again makes an excellent example. Experiments on the spayed, female cat (6, 17) and spayed, female guinea pig (28) have shown that hypothalamic regions must be intact and functioning if injected sex hormones are to arouse estrous behavior. If a section is made through the spinal cord only rudimentary fragments of sexual behavior can be elicited by appropriate stimulation, and injected sex hormones make no contribution to the response. Essentially the same thing is true if the section is made high in the hind brain but excludes the hypothalamus. When the decerebration is just above the hypothalamus, full estrous reactions can be aroused by appropriate stimulation, but only if sex hormones have been administered. It is clear, then, that not only is the hypothalamus the main integrating center for sexual reactions, but it is also most likely the main site of action of the sex hormones. This point is further supported by studies of female guinea pigs with pinpoint lesions of the anterior hypothalamus. These animals fail to show sexual behavior even under the influence of massive doses of sex hormones (19).

A very similar mechanism seems to be involved in the case of motivated behavior dependent upon the organism's defenses against temperature extremes (activity, nesting, hoarding, selection of high-calorie diets). We know, for example, that reactions regulating body temperature in the face of heat and cold are integrated in two separate centers in the hypothalamus (15, 51). Lesions in the anterior hypothalamus destroy the ability to lose heat and, therefore, to survive in high temperatures. Posterior hypothalamic lesions, conversely, result in a loss of heat production mechanisms so that the animal succumbs to cold. Furthermore, artificially raising the temperature of the anterior hypothalamus will quickly induce heat loss, suggesting that normally the temperature of the blood may be important in activating the hypothalamic mechanisms (15, 44). Unfortunately our information stops here. There are no direct physiological studies on the role of these temperature-regulating mechanisms in the control of motivated behavior like activity, hoarding, nesting, or food selection. But it seems clear that the temperature of the blood may be one of the kinds of changes in the internal environment that can affect the hypothalamus, and it may be important in motivated behavior.

Ample evidence demonstrates that there are important changes in the internal environment involved in other kinds of motivated behavior. In hunger it has been shown that chemicals like insulin (32, 33, 48) and d-amphetamine (57) influence the rate of eating. It is clear that these chemicals do not operate primarily through their effects on gastric contractions, but it is only by a process of elimination that we can guess that their sites of action are in the hypothalamus. Supporting this possibility is the evidence that there are chemoreceptors in the hypothalamus which are sensitive to variations in blood sugar and important in the regulation of hunger (45). In the case of specific hungers, much evidence shows that food preference and diet selection depend upon changes in the internal environment produced by such things as pregnancy, dietary deficiencies, or disturbances of endocrine glands (54). Furthermore there are some preliminary experimental data, in the case of salt and sugar appetites, to suggest that there are separate regulatory centers in the hypothalamus which are responsive to changes in salt and sugar balance (59). Finally, in the case of thirst we know that a change in osmotic pressure, resulting from cellular dehydration, is the important internal change leading to drinking behavior (31). We know further that in the hypothalamus there are nerve cells, called "osmoreceptors," which are extremely sensitive to minute changes in osmotic pressure (61). But the direct experiment has not been done to check whether or not it is these nerve cells which are mainly responsible for the control of thirst.[1]

Obviously the experimental evidence on hunger, specific hunger, and thirst is incomplete. But enough of it fits into the scheme of the theoretical mechanism proposed here to suggest the real possibility that the internal changes important in these cases operate largely through their effects on the hypothalamus.

One question still remains. What role does the internal environment play in the mechanism of satiation? About all we have to go on at present is the very striking fact from the case of specific hungers that vastly different amounts of consummatory behavior are needed to bring about satiation for different food substances. In vitamin deficiencies only a few milligrams of substance need be consumed to produce satiation, whereas in caloric deficiencies many grams of carbohydrate, fat, or protein must be ingested. Presumably, it is not the sensory feedback from consummatory behavior that is important in these cases, but rather some inhibitory effects produced by what is consumed (Fig. 1). Within the present theoretical framework, such inhibitory effects could be produced either by depression of excitatory centers of the hypothalamus or by arousal of activity in inhibitory centers. The problem is an important one and it is wide open for study.

It is clear from the foregoing that many types of motivated behavior are dependent upon changes in the internal environment. Several points are worth emphasizing. (a) A variety of kinds of changes in the internal environment can play a role in the regulation of motivation: variation in the concentration of certain chemicals, especially hormones, changes in osmotic pressure, and changes in blood temperature. (b) The best hypothesis at present is that these internal changes operate by contributing to the activity of excitatory hypothalamic centers controlling motivation. (c) An equally important but less well-supported hypothesis is that internal changes, normally produced by consummatory behavior, operate in the production of satiation by depressing excitatory centers or arousing inhibitory centers of the hypothalamus.

Cortical and thalamic centers. Despite the heavy emphasis laid upon

---

[1] In a recent publication, Anderson of Stockholm has shown that injection of small quantities of hypertonic NaCl directly into restricted regions along the midline of the hypothalamus produces immediate and extensive drinking in water-satiated goats. (Anderson, B. The effect of injections of hypertonic NaCl-solutions into different parts of the hypothalamus of goats. *Acta Physiol. Scand.*, 1953, 28, 188–201.)

the hypothalamus in this discussion, it is obvious that it is not the only neural center operating in the control of motivated behavior. In the first place, some of the sensory, motor, and associative functions of the cortex and thalamus are directly important in motivation quite apart from any influence they have on the hypothalamus. Secondly, even though the hypothalamus may be the main integrating center in motivation, it does not operate in isolation. There is much evidence that the hypothalamus is under the direct control of a number of different cortical and thalamic centers (Fig. 2).

The case of emotions offers the best example of how the cortex may operate in motivation. According to the early work of Bard and his co-workers on the production of "sham rage" by decortication, it looked as though the entire cortex might normally play an inhibitory role in emotions (5). More recent work, however, shows that cortical control of emotion is more complicated than this. Bard and Mountcastle (7), for example, have found that removal of certain parts of the old cortex (particularly amygdala and transitional cortex of the midline) produced a tremendous increase in rage reactions in cats. On the other hand, removing only new cortex resulted in extremely placid cats. Results of work with monkeys (40) and some very recent experiments with cats disagree somewhat with these findings in showing that similar old cortex removals lead to placidity rather than ferocity. The disagreement is yet to be resolved, but at least it is clear that different parts of the cortex may play different roles in the control of emotion, certain parts being inhibitory and others excitatory.

In the case of sleep, it appears so far that the cortex and thalamus play excitatory roles, perhaps having the effect of maintaining the activity of the waking center in the posterior hypothalamus. Decortication in dogs, for example, results in an inability to postpone sleep and remain awake for very long, or, as Kleitman puts it, a return to polyphasic sleep and waking rhythms (38, 39). Studies of humans, moreover, show that even restricted lesions of the cortex or thalamus alone can result in an inability to stay awake normally (25, 26). But no inhibitory effects of the cortex in sleep have yet been uncovered.

In sexual behavior it has been found that lesions of the new cortex may interfere directly with the arousal of sexual behavior (9, 11). Large lesions are much more effective than small lesions, as you might expect. Furthermore, cortical damage is much more serious in male animals than in females and is much more important in the sexual behavior of primates than it is in the case of lower mammals. On the other hand, in connection with studies of the cortex in emotions, it has been found that lesions of the amygdala and transitional cortex of the midline can lead to heightened sexuality in cats and monkeys (7, 40). So it looks as though the cortex may exert both excitatory and inhibitory influences in sexual motivation.

Evidence from other types of motivated behavior is only fragmentary, but it fits into the same general picture. In the case of hunger, it has been reported that certain lesions of the frontal lobes will lead to exaggerated eating behavior (41, 55). Hyperactivity may follow similar frontal lobe lesions and is particularly marked after damage to the orbital surface of the frontal lobe (56). The frontal areas may also be involved in what might be called pain avoidance. Clinical studies of man show that lobotomies may be used for the relief of intractable pain (29). The curious thing about these cases is that they still report the same amount of pain after operation but they say that it no longer bothers them. Presumably the frontal cortex normally plays an excitatory role in the motivation to avoid pain.

In all the cases cited so far, the anatomical and physiological evidence available suggests strongly that the main influence of the cortex and thalamus in motivation is mediated by the hypothalamus. But we do not yet have direct proof of this point and need experiments to check it.

Interaction of factors. Up to now, we have treated the various factors that can operate in the control of motivated behavior singly. However, one of the main points of the theory proposed here is that the various factors operate together in the control of motivation. Presumably this interaction of factors occurs in the hypothalamus and takes the form of the "addition" of all excitatory influences and the "subtraction" of all inhibitory influences. Some experimental evidence bears directly on this point.

In the case of sexual behavior, for example, it is clear that excitatory influences of the cortex and hormones are additive. After sexual motivation is eliminated by cortical damage it may be restored by the administration of large doses of sex hormones (10). Since the hypothalamus is the site of action of the sex hormones, it seems likely that it is also the site of interaction of the influences of the hormones and cortex.

In a similar way, it looks as though the contributions of sensory stimulation and sex hormones add in the hypothalamus. Neither hormones nor stimulation alone is sufficient to elicit sexual reactions in most mammals, but the right combination of the two will. Still another example of the addition of excitatory influences is seen in the study of the sexual behavior of the male rabbit. In this case neither destruction of the olfactory bulbs nor decortication will eliminate mating behavior, but a combination of the two operations will (21).

It is very important to know whether excitatory, and perhaps also inhibitory, influences in other kinds of motivation have the same sort of additive properties as in sexual behavior. Indirect evidence suggests they do, but direct experiments of the sort described here are needed to check the possibility.

Most encouraging in this connection is that students of instinctive behavior in inframammalian vertebrates and invertebrates have presented considerable evidence showing that sensory, chemical, and neural influences contribute jointly to the arousal of many kinds of motivated behavior (60). For example, in a number of cases it has been shown that the threshold for arousing behavior by various stimuli is lowered considerably by appropriate changes in the internal environment. In fact, in the extreme case, when internal changes are maximal, the behavior may occur in the absence of any obvious stimulation. Presumably in these cases, as in the examples of mammalian motivation, chemical and neural influences contribute to the arousal of some central response mechanism in an additive way.

The role of learning. It is obvious to every student of mammalian motivation that learning and experience may play extremely important roles in the regulation of motivated behavior. What does this mean in terms of the present physiological theory? Unfortunately, we cannot specify the mechanisms through which learning enters into the control of motivation because we are ignorant of the basic physiology of learning. But we can make some helpful inferences.

The basic hypothesis in the present theoretical framework is that learning contributes to hypothalamic activity along with influences from unlearned afferent impulses, internal changes, and cortical activity. In the case of sexual behavior we know that many animals learn to be aroused sexually by stimuli which were not previously adequate. Further, we know that in such experienced animals it is difficult to reduce sexual motivation by eliminating avenues of sensory stimulation, presumably because the extra excitatory effects produced by learned stimuli contribute to hypothalamic activity along with the impulses from unlearned stimuli. Along the same lines, it is known that sex hormones are relatively unimportant in man and in certain of the subhuman primates that have learned to be aroused by a wide variety of stimuli (12). Again, this may mean that the excitatory effects from the learned stimuli have added enough to the effects of unlearned stimuli to make it possible to dispense with the contribution of the sex hormones in arousing hypothalamic activity.

The evidence available on learning in other types of motivation fits in with this general theoretical picture, but direct physiological experiments have not yet carried us beyond the stage of inference. We know, for example, that vitamin-deficient rats can learn to show motivated behavior in response to certain flavors that have been associated with the vitamin in the past (34, 58). In fact, for a short while they will even pass up food containing the vitamin to eat vitamin-deficient food containing the flavor. Again, it looks as though flavor has become empowered by a process of learning to contribute to the excitability of the neural centers controlling motivation.

LIMITATIONS OF THE THEORY

Like any theoretical approach, the physiological mechanism proposed here has many limitations. Fortunately none of them need be too serious as long as it is recognized that the theory is set up as a general guide for experiments and a framework for further theorizing. Obviously the theory is going to have to be changed and improved many times before it is free of limitations. In this spirit it might be said that the limitations of the theory are not much more than those aspects of motivation which need research the most. But whether we label them limitations or urgent areas of research, they deserve explicit attention.

The concept of "center." Throughout this discussion the terms "neural center" and "hypothalamic center" have been used. "Center" is a useful and convenient term, but it is also a dangerous one, for it may carry with it the implication of strict localization of function within isolated anatomical entities. Actually this implication is not intended, for it is recognized that localization is a relative matter and that no neural mechanism operates in isolation. Furthermore, it is also possible that there may be no discoverable localization of the neural mechanisms governing some types of motivated behavior. The theory simply states at the moment that the best general hypothesis is that some degree of localization of the mechanisms controlling motivation can be found in the hypothalamus.

Execution of motivated behavior. No attempt has been made in this discussion to describe the details of the efferent pathways or effector mechanisms responsible for the execution of motivated behavior. Discussion of the pathways has been omitted because we know very little about them. About all we can do at present is to guess, from anatomical and physiological studies of hypothalamic function, that the hypothalamus exerts some kind of "priming" effect on effector pathways controlled by other parts of the nervous system. Perhaps after the relationship of the hypothalamus to motivated behavior has been more firmly established we can profitably turn to the question of how the hypothalamus does its work.

A second aspect of the execution of motivated behavior has been omitted for the sake of brevity. We all recognize that an animal with certain kinds of cortical lesions, or deprived of certain sensory capacities, may be handicapped in executing motivated behavior quite aside from any effects these operations may have on the arousal of motivation. Fortunately most investigators have been aware of this problem and have taken pains to distinguish these two effects, focusing their attention mainly on the arousal of motivation. Some day, however, this theory should address the question of what neural mechanisms govern the execution of motivated behavior.

General nature of the mechanism. For theoretical purposes it has been assumed that essentially the same mechanism controls all types of motivated behavior. Obviously this is not likely to be the case, nor is it an essential assumption. In some types of motivation only parts of this mechanism may be involved, or factors not included in the present scheme may operate. For example, in some cases the hypothalamus may not be involved at all, or it may turn out that there are no inhibitory centers at work, or that internal chemical factors do not contribute significantly. There is no reason why we should not be prepared for these eventualities. But until specific experimental evidence to the contrary is forthcoming, the general mechanism proposed here still remains as the best working hypothesis for any particular type of biological motivation.

Inadequacy of behavioral measures. To a large degree the present discussion is based upon measures of consummatory behavior. We all know that the various measures of motivation are not always in good agreement, so there is good possibility that what we say about consummatory behavior may not apply to motivation measured by other methods. In fact, Miller, Bailey, and Stevenson (46) have recently shown that whereas rats with hypothalamic lesions overeat in the free-feeding situation, they do not show a high degree of motivation when required to overcome some barrier to obtain food.

Confining the present discussion mainly to consummatory behavior is clearly a weakness. But the logic behind this limited approach is to work out the physiological mechanisms in the simplest case first, and then to see how they must be revised to fit the more complicated cases.

Complex motivation. It can also be argued, of course, that the present theory is confined to the simple, biological motives. Again, it seems eminently advisable to keep the theory relatively narrow in scope until it is developed well enough to permit attack on the more complicated, learned motives.

Comparative approach. No attempt has been made here to make it explicit how the proposed theory applies to organisms representative of different phylogenetic levels. There are many obvious advantages to the comparative approach, but unfortunately, except for the case of sexual motivation, the information we have on different species is too scattered to be useful. Judging from what we have learned from the comparative study of sexual motivation, however, we can expect the various factors governing other types of motivation to contribute somewhat differently in animals at different phylogenetic levels. Certainly learning should be more important in primates than in subprimates, and the contributions of the cortex and thalamus should be greater. Much will be gained if future research in motivation follows the excellent example set in the study of sexual behavior and provides the much needed comparative data.

ADVANTAGES OF THE THEORY

On the assumption that none of these limitations of the theory are critical, it is appropriate to ask: What is gained by proposing an explicit theory of the physiological mechanisms underlying motivated behavior? There are many positive answers to this question, and we can list some of them briefly.

Simplification of the problem. One of the main advantages of the theoretical mechanism proposed here is that it brings together, into one general framework, a number of different kinds of motivation that have been studied separately in the past. Certainly the theory encompasses the basic facts available on sex, hunger, specific hunger, thirst, sleep, and emotion. And it may also be able to handle the facts of pain avoidance, hoarding, nesting, maternal behavior, and other types of so-called instinctive behavior. As you have seen, one of the benefits deriving from this kind of simplification of the problem of motivation is the possibility of speeding up progress by applying what has been learned about physiological mechanisms from the study of one kind of motivation to the study of other kinds of motivation. Not only that, but the assumption that the hypothalamus is central in the control of all types of motivation may make it easier to explain the various types of interaction among motivations that have shown up in many studies of behavior.

Multifactor approach. Another advantage of the present theory is that it gives strong emphasis to the view that motivation is under multifactor control. Single-factor theories, so prevalent since the days of Cannon, can only lead to useless controversies over which factor is the "right" one and must always be guilty of omission in trying to account for the control of motivation. Of course, it must be stressed that the aim of the mulifactor approach is not simply to list the many possible factors operating in motivation, but rather to get down to the concrete experimental task of determining the relevant factors which control motivation and the relative contribution of each.

Satiation of motivation. Unlike most previous theories of motivation, the mechanism proposed here attempts to account for the satiation of motivation as well as its arousal. In terms of the present theory satiation is determined by the reduction of activity in the main excitatory centers of the hypothalamus. More specifically, it looks as though the inhibitory centers of the hypothalamus may constitute a separate "satiation mechanism" which is the most important influence in the reduction of the activity of the excitatory centers. The possibility is an intriguing one, and it can be directly explored by experiment.

Peripheral and central control. In the past the study of motivation has been hampered by the controversy over whether behavior is centrally or peripherally controlled. The controversy is nonsense. The only meaningful experimental problem is to determine how the central and peripheral, or sensory, factors operate together in the control of behavior. It is this problem which the present theory addresses directly, and this is one of its greatest strengths.

Learned and innate control. The present theory avoids another knotty controversy by directly addressing experimental problems. Much time has been lost in psychology, and particularly in the study of motivation, in arguments over whether behavior is primarily innate or instinctive or whether it is primarily learned or acquired. The answer is obviously that it is both, and again the only meaningful experimental problem is to determine the relative contribution of each type of control. As far as the mechanism proposed here is concerned, both innate and learned factors make their contributions to the control of the same hypothalamic centers. There is still much work needed to determine the details of the mechanisms of operation, particularly of the learned factors, but some headway has been made and the problem is clearly set.

Explicit nature of the theory. Finally, a number of advantages derives simply from having an explicit statement of an up-to-date, physiological theory of motivation. In the first place, an explicit theory can serve as a convenient framework within which to organize the physiological facts we already have at our disposal. Second, the systematic organization of the facts sharply points up many of the gaps in our knowledge and suggests direct experiments that should be done in the investigation of motivated behavior. Third, an up-to-date, systematic theory provides a useful and reasonably clear conceptualization of motivation for psychologists working in other areas of research.

SUMMARY AND CONCLUSIONS

A physiological theory of motivated behavior is presented. The basic assumption in this theory is that the amount of motivated behavior is a function of the amount of activity in certain excitatory centers of the hypothalamus. The level of activity of the critical hypothalamic centers, in turn, is governed by the operation of four factors.

1. Inhibitory centers in the hypothalamus directly depress the activity of the excitatory centers and may be responsible for the production of satiation.

2. Sensory stimuli set up afferent impulses which naturally contribute to the excitability of the hypothalamus or come to do so through a process of learning.

3. Changes in the internal environment exert both excitatory and inhibitory effects on the hypothalamus.

4. Cortical and thalamic influences increase and decrease the excitability of hypothalamic centers.

Detailed experimental evidence is brought forward to show how these various factors operate in the management of different kinds of motivated behavior. The over-all scheme is shown diagrammatically in Fig. 1.

Out of consideration of this evidence a number of hypotheses are generated to fill in the gaps in experimental knowledge. All these hypotheses are experimentally testable. The ones of major importance can be given here as a summary of what the theory states and a partial list of the experiments it suggests.

1. There are different centers in the hypothalamus responsible for the control of different kinds of basic motivation.

2. In each case of motivation, there is one main excitatory center and one inhibitory center which operates to depress the activity of the excitatory center.

There is already much experimental evidence supporting these two general hypotheses, but it is not certain that they apply fully to all types of basic biological motivation. The hypotheses should be checked further by determining whether changes in all types of motivation can be produced by local hypothalamic lesions and whether both increases and decreases in motivation can always be produced.

3. The activity of hypothalamic centers is, in part, controlled by the excitatory effects of afferent impulses generated by internal and external stimuli.

4. Different stimuli contribute different relative amounts to hypothalamic activity but no one avenue of sensory stimulation is indispensable.

5. It is the sum total of afferent impulses arriving at the hypothalamus that determines the level of excitability and, therefore, the amount of motivation.

The neuroanatomical and neurophysiological evidence shows that the hypothalamus is richly supplied with afferents coming directly and indirectly from all the sense organs (Fig. 2). The behavioral evidence, furthermore, strongly suggests that motivation is never controlled, in mammals at least, by one sensory system, but rather is the combination of contributions of several sensory systems. Sensory control and sensory deprivation experiments are needed to check this point in the case of most kinds of biological motivation, particularly hunger, thirst, and specific hungers.

6. A variety of kinds of physical and chemical changes in the internal environment influences the excitability of hypothalamic centers and, therefore, contributes to the control of motivation.

The evidence shows that the hypothalamus is the most richly vascularized region of the central nervous system and is most directly under the influence of the cerebrospinal fluid. Furthermore, it is clear that changes in the internal environment produced by temperature of the blood, osmotic pressure, hormones, and a variety of other chemicals are important in motivation and most likely operate through their influence on the hypothalamus. Direct studies are still needed in many cases, however, to show that the particular change that is important in motivation actually does operate through the hypothalamus and vice versa.

7. The cerebral cortex and thalamus are directly important in the temporal and spatial organization of motivated behavior.

8. Different parts of the cortex and thalamus also operate selectively in the control of motivation by exerting excitatory or inhibitory influences on the hypothalamus.

Tests of these hypotheses can be carried out by total decortication, partial cortical ablations, and local thalamic lesions. It should be especially instructive to see what effects cortical and thalamic lesions have after significant changes in motivation have been produced by hypothalamic lesions.

9. Learning contributes along with other factors to the control of motivation, probably through direct influence on the hypothalamus.

10. The relative contribution of learning should increase in animals higher and higher on the phylogenetic scale.

A whole series of experiments is needed here. Particularly, there should be comparisons of naive and experienced animals to determine the relative effects of sensory deprivation, cortical and thalamic damage, and hypothalamic lesions. Presumably animals that have learned to be aroused to motivated behavior by previously inadequate stimuli should require more sensory deprivation but less cortical and thalamic damage than naive animals before motivation is significantly impaired.

11. The various factors controlling motivation combine their influences at the hypothalamus by the addition of all excitatory influences and the subtraction of all inhibitory influences.

Some experiments have already been done in the study of sexual motivation to show that motivation reduced by the elimination of one factor (cortical lesions) can be restored by increasing the contribution of other factors (hormone therapy). Many combinations of this kind of experiment should be carried out with different kinds of motivated behavior.

A number of the limitations and some of the advantages of the present theoretical approach to the physiology of motivation are discussed.

REFERENCES

1. ADOLPH, E. F. The internal environment and behavior. Part III. Water content. *Amer. J. Psychiat.*, 1941, **97**, 1365–1373.

2. ADOLPH, E. F. Thirst and its inhibition in the stomach. *Amer. J. Physiol.*, 1950, **161**, 374–386.

3. ANAND, B. K., & BROBECK, J. R. Hypothalamic control of food intake in rats and cats. *Yale J. Biol. Med.*, 1951, **24**, 123–140.

4. ANAND, B. K., & BROBECK, J. R. Localization of a "feeding center" in the hypothalamus of the rat. *Proc. Soc. exp. Biol. Med.*, 1951, **77**, 323–324.

5. BARD, P. Central nervous mechanisms for emotional behavior patterns in animals. *Res. Publ. Ass. nerv. ment. Dis.*, 1939, **19**, 190–218

6. BARD, P. The hypothalamus and sexual behavior. *Res. Publ. Ass. nerv. ment. Dis.*, 1940, **20**, 551–579.

7. BARD, P., & MOUNTCASTLE, V. B. Some forebrain mechanisms involved in the expression of rage with special reference to the suppression of angry behavior. *Res. Publ. Ass. nerv. ment. Dis.*, 1947, **27**, 362–404.

8. BEACH, F. A. Analysis of factors involved in the arousal, maintenance and manifestation of sexual excitement in male animals. *Psychosom. Med.*, 1942, **4**, 173–198.

9. Beach, F. A. Central nervous mechanisms involved in the reproductive behavior of vertebrates. *Psychol. Bull.*, 1942, **39**, 200–206.

10. Beach, F. A. Relative effect of androgen upon the mating behavior of male rats subjected to forebrain injury or castration. *J. exp. Zool.*, 1944, **97**, 249–295.

11. Beach, F. A. A review of physiological and psychological studies of sexual behavior in mammals. *Physiol. Rev.*, 1947, **27**, 240–307.

12. Beach, F. A. Evolutionary changes in the physiological control of mating behavior in mammals. *Psychol. Rev.*, 1947, **54**, 297–315.

13. Bellows, R. T. Time factors in water drinking in dogs. *Amer. J. Physiol.*, 1939, **125**, 87–97.

14. Bremer, F. Étude oscillographique des activités sensorielles du cortex cérébral. *C. r. Soc. Biol.*, 1937, **124**, 842–846.

15. Brobeck, J. R. Regulation of energy exchange. In J. F. Fulton (Ed.), *A textbook of physiology*. Philadelphia: Saunders, 1950. Pp. 1069–1090.

16. Brobeck, J. R., Tepperman, J., & Long, C. N. H. Experimental hypothalamic hyperphagia in the albino rat. *Yale J. Biol. Med.*, 1943, **15**, 831–853.

17. Bromiley, R. B., & Bard, P. A study of the effect of estrin on the responses to genital stimulation shown by decapitate and decerebrate female cats. *Amer. J. Physiol.*, 1940, **129**, 318–319.

18. Brookhart, J. M., & Dey, F. L. Reduction of sexual behavior in male guinea pigs by hypothalamic lesions. *Amer. J. Physiol.*, 1941, **133**, 551–554.

19. Brookhart, J. M., Dey, F. L., & Ranson, S. W. Failure of ovarian hormones to cause mating reactions in spayed guinea pigs with hypothalamic lesions. *Proc. Soc. exp. Biol. Med.*, 1940, **44**, 61–64.

20. Brookhart, J. M., Dey, F. L., & Ranson, S. W. The abolition of mating behavior by hypothalamic lesions in guinea pigs. *Endocrinology*, 1941, **28**, 561–565.

21. Brooks, C. M. The role of the cerebral cortex and of various sense organs in the excitation and execution of mating activity in the rabbit. *Amer. J. Physiol.*, 1937, **120**, 544–553.

22. Brooks, C. M. Appetite and obesity. *N. Z. med. J.*, 1947, **46**, 243–254.

23. Cannon, W. B. Hunger and thirst. In C. Murchison (Ed.), *A handbook of general experimental psychology*. Worcester, Mass.: Clark Univer. Press, 1934. Pp. 247–263.

24. Craigie, E. H. Measurements of vascularity in some hypothalamic nuclei of the albino rat. *Res. Publ. Ass. nerv. ment. Dis.*, 1940, **20**, 310–319

25. Davison, C., & Demuth, E. L. Disturbances in sleep mechanism: a clinico-pathologic study. I. Lesions at the cortical level. *Arch. Neurol. Psychiat., Chicago*, 1945, **53**, 399–406.

26. Davison, C., & Demuth, E. L. Disturbances in sleep mechanism: a clinico-pathologic study. II. Lesions at the corticodiencephalic level. *Arch. Neurol. Psychiat., Chicago*, 1945, **54**, 241–255.

27. Delgado, J. M. R., & Anand, B. K. Increase of food intake induced by electrical stimulation of the lateral hypothalamus. *Amer. J. Physiol.*, 1953, **172**, 162–168.

28. Dempsey, E. W., & Rioch, D. McK. The localization in the brain stem of the oestrous responses of the female guinea pig. *J. Neurophysiol.*, 1939, **2**, 9–18.

29. Freeman, W., & Watts, J. W. *Psychosurgery*. (2nd Ed.) Springfield, Ill.: Charles C Thomas, 1950.

30. Gellhorn, E. *Autonomic regulations*. New York: Interscience, 1943.

31. Gilman, A. The relation between blood osmotic pressure, fluid distribu-

tion and voluntary water intake. *Amer. J. Physiol.*, 1937, **120**, 323–328.

32. GROSSMAN, M. I., CUMMINS, G. M., & IVY, A. C. The effect of insulin on food intake after vagotomy and sympathectomy. *Amer. J. Physiol.*, 1947, **149**, 100–102.

33. GROSSMAN, M. I., & STEIN, I. F. Vagotomy and the hunger producing action of insulin in man. *J. appl. Physiol.*, 1948, **1**, 263–269.

34. HARRIS, L. J., CLAY, J., HARGREAVES, F. J., & WARD, A. Appetite and choice of diet. The ability of the Vitamin B deficient rat to discriminate between diets containing and lacking the vitamin. *Proc. roy. Soc.*, 1933, **113**, 161–190.

35. HETHERINGTON, A. W., & RANSON, S. W. The spontaneous activity and food intake of rats with hypothalamic lesions. *Amer. J. Physiol.*, 1942, **136**, 609–617.

36. INGRAM, W. R. Nuclear organization and chief connections of the primate hypothalamus. *Res. Publ. Ass. nerv. ment. Dis.*, 1940, **20**, 195–244.

37. JANOWITZ, H. D., & GROSSMAN, M. I. Some factors affecting the food intake of normal dogs and dogs with esophagostomy and gastric fistula. *Amer. J. Physiol.*, 1949, **159**, 143–148.

38. KLEITMAN, N. *Sleep and wakefulness.* Chicago: Univer. of Chicago Press, 1939.

39. KLEITMAN, N., & CAMILLE, N. Studies on the physiology of sleep. VI. Behavior of decorticated dogs. *Amer. J. Physiol.*, 1932, **100**, 474–480.

40. KLÜVER, H., & BUCY, P. C. Preliminary analysis of functions of the temporal lobes in monkeys. *Arch. Neurol. Psychiat., Chicago,* 1939, **42**, 979–1000.

41. LANGWORTHY, O. R., & RICHTER, C. P. Increased spontaneous activity produced by frontal lobe lesions in cats. *Amer. J. Physiol.*, 1939, **126**, 158–161.

42. LASHLEY, K. S. Experimental analysis of instinctive behavior. *Psychol. Rev.*, 1938, **45**, 445–471.

43. LINDSLEY, D. B. Emotion. In S. S. Stevens (Ed.), *Handbook of experimental psychology.* New York: Wiley, 1951. Pp. 473–516.

44. MAGOUN, H. W., HARRISON, F., BROBECK, J. R., & RANSON, S. W. Activation of heat loss mechanisms by local heating of the brain. *J. Neurophysiol.*, 1938, **1**, 101–114.

45. MAYER, J., VITALE, J. J., & BATES, M. W. Mechanism of the regulation of food intake. *Nature, London,* 1951, **167**, 562–563.

46. MILLER, N. E., BAILEY, C. J., & STEVENSON, J. A. F. Decreased 'hunger' but increased food intake resulting from hypothalamic lesions. *Science*, 1950, **112**, 256–259.

47. MORGAN, C. T. *Physiological psychology.* (1st Ed.) New York: McGraw-Hill, 1943.

48. MORGAN, C. T., & MORGAN, J. D. Studies in hunger. 1. The effects of insulin upon the rat's rate of eating. *J. genet. Psychol.*, 1940, **56**, 137–147.

49. NAUTA, W. J. H. Hypothalamic regulation of sleep in rats; an experimental study. *J. Neurophysiol.*, 1946, **9**, 285–316.

50. RANSON, S. W. Somnolence caused by hypothalamic lesions in the monkey. *Arch. Neurol. Psychiat.*, 1939, **41**, 1–23.

51. RANSON, S. W. Regulation of body temperature. *Res. Publ. Ass. nerv. ment. Dis.*, 1940, **20**, 342–399.

52. RANSON, S. W., KABAT, H., & MAGOUN, H. W. Autonomic responses to electrical stimulation of hypothalamus, pre-optic region and septum. *Arch. Neurol. Psychiat., Chicago,* 1935, **33**, 467–477.

53. RANSTRÖM, S. *The hypothalamus and sleep regulation.* Uppsala: Almquist and Wiksells, 1947.

54. RICHTER, C. P. Total self regulatory functions in animals and human beings. *Harvey Lect.*, 1942–43, **38**, 63–103.

55. RICHTER, C. P., & HAWKES, C. D. Increased spontaneous activity and food intake produced in rats by removal of the frontal poles of the brain. *J. Neurol. Psychiat.*, 1939, **2**, 231–242.

56. RUCH, T. C., & SHENKIN, H. A. The relation of area 13 of the orbital surface of the frontal lobe to hyperactivity and hyperphagia in monkeys. *J. Neurophysiol.*, 1943, **6**, 349–360.

57. SANGSTER, W., GROSSMAN, M. I., & IVY, A. C. Effect of d-amphetamine on gastric hunger contractions and food intake in the dog. *Amer. J. Physiol.*, 1948, **153**, 259–263.

58. SCOTT, E. M., & VERNEY, E. L. Self selection of diet. VI. The nature of appetites for B vitamins. *J. Nutrit.*, 1947, **34**, 471–480.

59. SOULAIRAC, A. La physiologie d'un comportement: L'appétit glucidique et sa régulation neuro-endocrinienne chez les rongeurs. *Bull. Biol.*, 1947, **81**, 1–160.

60. TINBERGEN, N. *The study of instinct.* London: Oxford Univer. Press, 1951.

61. VERNEY, E. B. The antidiuretic hormone and the factors which determine its release. *Proc. roy. Soc., London*, 1947, **135**, 24–106.

62. WHEATLEY, M. D. The hypothalamus and affective behavior in cats. *Arch. Neurol. Psychiat.*, 1944, **52**, 296–316.

PART SIX

Visceral Components
of Emotion

The modern psychologist is in somewhat of a dilemma. He thinks, loves, gets angry, becomes happy, and undergoes a wide variety of experiences and feelings which his self-imposed rules of studying only observable behaviors prevent him from analyzing. He does not wish to abandon this behavioristic viewpoint because its scientific utility and philosophic soundness have made such restriction indispensable. If, despite the fact that consciousness, feeling, and thought are in good part out-of-bounds for his research, the psychologist is still interested in these phenomena, he must express his interest during off-duty hours. Then he may become as introspective as he wishes, generating unverifiable hypotheses and drawing conclusions unhampered by probability estimates.

Before psychology settled into its present-day pattern, psychologists expounded in the lecture room and laboratory upon topics now confined to the dining table and drawing room. Wilhelm Wundt, the founder of experimental psychology, devoted a considerable portion of his theory and research efforts to trying to analyze emotions. He sought to determine what their dimensions were. Wundt maintained that, just as any two boxes could be compared in terms of their length, width, and height, any two emotions could be compared in terms of their agreeableness, strain, and excitement. While Wundt, the pre-eminent German psychologist of his day, was analyzing emotion and consciousness into their components, his pre-eminent American counterpart, William James, was talking about emotion and consciousness in a completely different fashion.

James and Wundt had antithetical styles. Wundt was experimental; James, philosophical. Wundt studied limited areas intensively; James ranged broadly over many aspects of human experience. James objected to Wundt's attempts to analyze consciousness. He maintained human consciousness was like a changing, flowing stream, not the series of still pictures postulated by Wundt. James's analysis of emotions also differed from Wundt's; he eschewed the analysis into elements—so characteristic of Wundt—and addressed himself to the problem of how people are able to identify their emotions. How do they know they are angry? Or happy? In general, how do they learn to identify their feeling states? The answer James offered to these questions is contained in the first article in this section. His theory was similar to one published almost simultaneously by the Danish physiologist Länge, and it is usually referred to by the joint reference, the James-Länge theory.

Both James and Länge postulated that an emotion had two components, a physiological one and a cognitive one. In an emotion-producing situation (we suddenly meet a bear while strolling in the woods) we first become physiologically aroused, and our cognition or awareness of this arousal is our emotion. In a nutshell, we are afraid because we tremble, not the reverse. James first published this concept in 1884, Länge in 1885, and many of the physiological questions raised by their formulations were unanswerable at the time. The James-Länge theory did, however, have certain implications. If changes in the viscera and cardiovascular system were the cues or stimuli that identified emotions, then it must follow that when a person reported experiencing emotion A he would have a corresponding set of physiological changes. When he experienced emotion B he must have a discriminably different set of visceral and cardiovascular changes. In addition, he should not report experiencing an emotion unless some visceral change was occurring, nor should a visceral change occur without the concomitant report of an emotion. Data related to these implications of the James-Länge theory could be obtained and evaluated.

Walter B. Cannon, a physiologist at the Harvard Medical School, in the years prior to World War I was engaged in an extensive series of experiments examining the emotion-visceral change connections in great detail. Cannon published his findings in 1915 in a book entitled *Bodily Changes in Pain, Hunger, Fear and Rage*. One of the main findings of the work was the involvement of the sympathetic nervous system with emotion. In 1924, G. Marañon, a Spanish essayist and physician, published the results of an experiment that bore directly upon both the James-Länge theory and Cannon's work. Marañon injected a number of his patients with adrenalin. Adrenalin is a sympathomimetic drug; its action produces effects similar to those produced by sympathetic nervous system discharge. The James-Länge theory would predict that when Marañon's patients became cognizant of the drug's effects, they would report experiencing an emotion. In oversimplified terms, if fear is the recognition of trembling hands, and Marañon's patients noticed that their hands were trembling, they should have been afraid. In point of fact, very few of Marañon's patients reported a "genuine" emotion; instead many said they were experiencing states that could be described as "cold" or "as if" emotions. Marañon felt that his work provided support for the James-Länge emotional hypothesis as well as for Cannon's work on the physiology of the visceral system.

Cannon's own work, buttressed with data from Marañon and other investigators, led him to some grave doubts about the James-Länge theory, and, in 1927, he published an article criticizing that theory[1] and offering an alternative theory of his own. The third reading in this section contains

[1] W. B. Cannon, "The James-Länge Theory of Emotions: A Critical Examination and an Alternative Theory." *American Journal of Psychology*, 1927, XXXIX, 106–124.

Cannon's objections, but it is not his 1927 article. It is a chapter from the 2nd edition of *Bodily Changes in Pain, Hunger, Fear and Rage,* published in 1929. The presentation of his alternative theory is contained in a later chapter of that same edition.

Cannon raised five objections to the James-Länge formulation and documented them with physiological evidence. Cannon's objections were as follows:

1. Animals still demonstrate emotion after their viscera have been surgically separated from the central nervous system.
2. Different emotions are accompanied by the same visceral state.
3. The viscera are insensitive; changes in them are not apt to be noticed.
4. Changes in the viscera are too slow to be the initiating factor in emotions.
5. When the viscera are artificially stimulated, an emotion does not necessarily result.

Cannon's own theory was couched in terms of interactions between the cerebral cortex and the thalamus. It was not received uncritically, for the James-Länge theory had many adherents.[2] Cannon replied to his critics and restated his position.[3] Although Cannon's objections were not effectively rebutted, his attack was not decisive, for a considerable number of psychologists maintained the basic Jamesian position.

The final article in this section is an attempt at a rapprochement between the James-Länge position and the Cannon objections. The procedure used by Schachter and Singer in their study is reminiscent of Marañon: they injected their subjects with adrenalin. They coupled their drug injections with various environmental situations and differing types of information in the test of three hypotheses:

1. A state of physiological arousal is necessary for an emotion.
2. A state of physiological arousal will produce an emotion only if the subject has no simple physical explanation for his arousal.
3. If a subject has a state of "unexplained" arousal, the emotion he experiences will depend upon social and environmental cues.

The Schachter-Singer experiment, plus their supporting studies, provide evidence for the validity of their findings. Yet two points should be borne in mind: Although they posit that physiological arousal is an integral part of an emotion, Schachter and Singer do not, as does James, say it *is* the emotion. For them, it is a necessary but not a sufficient condition. By modifying James, Schachter and Singer are able to avoid three of Cannon's objections, although 1 and 4 above are cogent to their position. The exact relationship of the Schachter-Singer formulation to Cannon's objections is rather detailed; articles by Mandler[4] and Schachter[5] discuss the connections thoroughly.

[2] E. B. Newman, F. T. Perkins, and R. H. Wheeler, "Cannon's Theory of Emotion: A Critique." *Psychological Review,* 1930, 37, 305–326.

[3] W. B. Cannon, "Again the James-Länge and the Thalamic Theories of Emotion." *Psychological Review,* 1931, 38, 281–295.

[4] G. Mandler, "Emotion," in R. Brown *et al., New Directions in Psychology,* (New York: Holt, Rinehart and Winston, 1962).

[5] S. Schachter, "The Interaction of Cognitive and Physiological Determinants of Emotional State," in L. Berkowitz (ed.), *Advances in Experimental Social Psychology,* (New York: Academic Press, 1964).

The articles in this section have dealt with only one aspect of the psychology of emotions, namely, the extent of visceral involvement. There are many other facets of emotion—the involvement of the central nervous system, the learning of appropriate responses, the conditioning of emotion, and the connection of emotion to learning, to name but a few. No one theory or approach could begin to tie together these diverse strands; by concentrating on one particular issue it is possible to see how theories are propounded, criticized, rebutted, and refined. Starting with the James formulation, we led up to the Schachter-Singer article, which caps the series by making two points. First, Schachter and Singer have proposed an alternative theory of emotion, embracing aspects of both of the previous ones discussed; and second, building upon Marañon's technique of adrenalin injections, they have integrated the study of emotion within the constraints of current behaviorally oriented experimental psychology.

STUDY QUESTIONS

1. What type of evidence does James offer in support of his thesis? In what ways is it convincing? In what ways is it unconvincing?
2. What does Marañon mean when he says that patients having a "first degree" reaction have a "cold awareness" of an emotion? How is this relevant to the James-Länge theory?
3. How does each of Cannon's five objections relate to specific aspects of the James-Länge formulation?
4. How does Cannon interpret Marañon's article as a criticism of James? What parts of the Marañon study not mentioned by Cannon would support James?
5. How do Schachter and Singer answer Cannon's statement that the same visceral changes accompany several emotions?
6. How do the Schachter and Singer findings lend support to the James-Länge theory? How do they disagree with it?

What Is Emotion?

William James

The physiologists who, during the past few years, have been so industriously exploring the functions of the brain, have limited their attempts at explanation to its cognitive and volitional performances. Dividing the brain into sensorial and motor centres, they have found their division to be exactly paralleled by the analysis made by empirical psychology, of the perceptive and volitional parts of the mind into their simplest elements. But the *aesthetic* sphere of the mind, its longings, its pleasures and pains, and its

Reprinted from *Mind*, 1884, IX, 188–204.

emotions, have been so ignored in all these researches that one is tempted
to suppose that if either Dr. Ferrier or Dr. Munk were asked for a theory
in brain-terms of the latter mental facts, they might both reply, either that
they had as yet bestowed no thought upon the subject, or that they had
found it so difficult to make distinct hypotheses, that the matter lay for
them among the problems of the future, only to be taken up after the
simpler ones of the present should have been definitively solved.

And yet it is even now certain that of two things concerning the emotions, one must be true. Either separate and special centres, affected to
them alone, are their brain-seat, or else they correspond to processes occurring in the motor and sensory centres, already assigned, or in others
like them, not yet mapped out. If the former be the case we must deny
the current view, and hold the cortex to be something more than the surface of *projection* for every sensitive spot and every muscle in the body.
If the latter be the case, we must ask whether the emotional *process* in the
sensory or motor centre be an altogether peculiar one, or whether it resembles the ordinary perceptive processes of which those centres are already recognised to be the seat. The purpose of the following pages is to
show that the last alternative comes nearest to the truth, and that the
emotional brain-processes not only resemble the ordinary sensorial brain-
processes, but in very truth, are nothing but such processes variously combined. The main result of this will be to simplify our notions of the possible
complications of brain-physiology, and to make us see that we have already
a brain-scheme in our hands whose applications are much wider than its
authors dreamed. But although this seems to be the chief result of the arguments I am to urge, I should say that they were not originally framed for
the sake of any such result. They grew out of fragmentary introspective observations, and it was only when these had already combined into a theory
that the thought of the simplification the theory might bring to cerebral
physiology occurred to me, and made it seem more important than before.

I should say first of all that the only emotions I propose expressly to
consider here are those that have a distinct bodily expression. That there
are feelings of pleasure and displeasure, of interest and excitement, bound
up with mental operations, but having no obvious bodily expression for
their consequence, would, I suppose, be held true by most readers. Certain arrangements of sounds, of lines, of colours, are agreeable, and others
the reverse, without the degree of the feeling being sufficient to quicken
the pulse or breathing, or to prompt to movements of either the body or
the face. Certain sequences of ideas charm us as much as others tire us.
It is a real intellectual delight to get a problem solved, and a real intellectual torment to have to leave it unfinished. The first set of examples, the
sounds, lines, and colours, are either bodily sensations, or the images of
such. The second set seem to depend on processes in the ideational centres
exclusively. Taken together, they appear to prove that there are pleasures
and pains inherent in certain forms of nerve-action as such, wherever that
action occurs. The case of these feelings we will at present leave entirely
aside, and confine our attention to the more complicated cases in which a
wave of bodily disturbance of some kind accompanies the perception of
the interesting sights or sounds, or the passage of the exciting train of
ideas. Surprise, curiosity, rapture, fear, anger, lust, greed, and the like,
become then the names of the mental states with which the person is

possessed. The bodily disturbances are said to be the "manifestation" of these several emotions, their "expression" or "natural language"; and these emotions themselves, being so strongly characterized both from within and without, may be called the *standard* emotions.

Our natural way of thinking about these standard emotions is that the mental perception of some fact excites the mental affection called the emotion, and that this latter state of mind gives rise to the bodily expression. My thesis on the contrary is that *the bodily changes follow directly the* PERCEPTION *of the exciting fact, and that our feeling of same changes as they occur* IS *the emotion.* Common sense says, we lose our fortune, are sorry and weep; we meet a bear, are frightened and run; we are insulted by a rival, are angry and strike. The hypothesis here to be defended says that this order of sequence is incorrect, that the one mental state is not immediately induced by the other, that the bodily manifestations must first be interposed between, and that the more rational statement is that we feel sorry because we cry, angry because we strike, or tremble, because we are sorry, angry, or fearful as the case may be. Without the bodily states following on the perception, the latter would be purely cognitive in form, pale, colourless, destitute of emotional warmth. We might then see the bear, and judge it best to run, receive the insult and deem it right to strike, but we could not actually feel afraid or angry.

Stated in this crude way, the hypothesis is pretty sure to meet with immediate disbelief. And yet neither many nor far-fetched considerations are required to mitigate its paradoxical character, and possibly to produce conviction of its truth.

To begin with, readers of this Journal do not need to be reminded that the nervous system of every living thing is but a bundle of predispositions to react in particular ways upon the contact of particular features of the environment. As surely as the hermit-crab's abdomen presupposes the existence of empty whelk-shells somewhere to be found, so surely do the hound's olfactories imply the existence, on the one hand, of deer's or foxes' feet, and on the other, the tendency to follow up their tracks. The neural machinery is but a hyphen between determinate arrangements of matter outside the body and determinate impulses to inhibition or discharge within its organs. When the hen sees a white oval object on the ground, she cannot leave it; she must keep upon it and return to it, until at last its transformation into a little mass of moving chirping down elicits from her machinery an entirely new set of performances. The love of man for woman, or of the human mother for her babe, our wrath at snakes and our fear of precipices, may all be described similarly, as instances of the way in which peculiarly conformed pieces of the world's furniture will fatally call forth most particular mental and bodily reactions, in advance of, and often in direct opposition to, the verdict of our deliberate reason concerning them. The labours of Darwin and his successors are only just beginning to reveal the universal parasitism of each special creature upon other special relations stamped on its nervous system with it upon the scene.

Every living creature is in fact a sort of lock, whose wards and springs presuppose special forms of key—which keys however are not born attached to the locks, but are sure to be found in the world nearby as life goes on. And the locks are indifferent to any but their own keys. The egg fails to fascinate the hound, the bird does not fear the precipice, the snake waxes not wroth at his kind, the deer cares nothing for the woman or the human babe. Those who wish for a full development of this point of view, should read Schneider's *Der thierische Wille*,—no other book shows how accurately anticipatory are the actions of animals, of the specific features of the environment in which they are to live.

Now among these nervous anticipations are of course to be reckoned the emotions, so far as these may be called forth directly by the perception of certain facts. In advance of all experience of elephants no child can but be frightened if he suddenly find one trumpeting and charging upon him. No woman can see a handsome little naked baby without delight, no man in the wilderness see a human form in the distance without excitement and curiosity. I said I should consider these emotions only so far as they have bodily movements of some sort for their accompaniments. But my first point is to show that their bodily accompaniments are much more far-reaching and complicated than we ordinarily suppose.

In the earlier books on Expression, written mostly from the artistic point of view, the signs of emotion visible from without were the only ones taken account of. Sir Charles Bell's celebrated *Anatomy of Expression* noticed the respiratory changes; and Bain's and Darwin's treatises went more thoroughly still into the study of the visceral factors involved,—changes in the functioning of glands and muscles, and in that of the circulatory apparatus. But not even a Darwin has exhaustively enumerated all the bodily affections characteristic of any one of the standard emotions. More and more, as physiology advances, we begin to discern how almost infinitely numerous and subtle they must be. The researches of Mosso with the plethysmograph have shown that not only the heart, but the entire circulatory system, forms a sort of sounding-board, which every change of our consciousness, however slight, may make reverberate. Hardly a sensation comes to us without sending waves of alternate constriction and dilatation down the arteries of our arms. The blood-vessels of the abdomen act re-paratus. But not even a Darwin has exhaustively enumerated all the bodily the glands of the mouth, throat, and skin, and the liver, are known to be affected gravely in certain severe emotions, and are unquestionably affected transiently when the emotions are of a lighter sort. That the heart-beats and the rhythm of breathing play a leading part in all emotions whatsoever, is a matter too notorious for proof. And what is really equally prominent, but less likely to be admitted until special attention is drawn to the fact, is the continuous co-operation of the voluntary muscles in our emotional states. Even when no change of outward attitude is produced, their inward tension alters to suit each varying mood, and is felt as a difference of tone or of strain. In depression the flexors tend to prevail; in elation or belligerent excitement the extensors take the lead. And the various permutations and combinations of which these organic activities are susceptible, make it abstractly possible that no shade of emotion, however slight, should be without a bodily reverberation as unique, when taken in its totality, as is the mental mood itself.

The immense number of parts modified in each emotion is what makes it so difficult for us to reproduce in cold blood the total and integral expression of any one of them. We may catch the trick with the voluntary muscles, but fail with the skin, glands, heart, and other viscera. Just as an artificially imitated sneeze lacks something of the reality, so the attempt to imitate an emotion in the absence of its normal instigating cause is apt to be rather "hollow."

The next thing to be noticed is this, that every one of the bodily changes, whatsoever it be, is felt, acutely or obscurely, the moment it occurs. If the reader has never paid attention to this matter, he will be both interested and astonished to learn how many different local bodily feelings he can detect in himself as characteristic of his various emotional moods. It would be perhaps too much to expect him to arrest the tide of any strong gust of passion for the sake of any such curious analysis as this; but he can observe more tranquil states, and that may be assumed here to be true of the greater which is shown to be true of the less. Our whole cubic capacity is sensibly alive; and each morsel of it contributes its pulsations of feeling, dim or sharp, pleasant, painful, or dubious, to that sense of personality that every one of us unfailingly carries with him. It is surprising what little items give accent to these complexes of sensibility. When worried by any slight trouble, one may find that the focus of one's bodily consciousness is the contraction, often quite inconsiderable, of the eyes and brows. When momentarily embarrassed, it is something in the pharynx that compels either a swallow, a clearing of the throat, or a slight cough; and so on for as many more instances as might be named. Our concern here being with the general view rather than with the details, I will not linger to discuss these but, assuming the point admitted that every change that occurs must be felt, I will pass on.

I now proceed to urge the vital point of my whole theory, which is this. If we fancy some strong emotion, and they try to abstract from our consciousness of it all the feelings of its characteristic bodily symptoms, we find we have nothing left behind, no "mind-stuff" out of which the emotion can be constituted, and that a cold, a neutral state of intellectual perception is all that remains. It is true, that although most people, when asked, say that their introspection verifies this statement, some persist in saying theirs does not. Many cannot be made to understand the question. When you beg them to imagine away every feeling of laughter and of tendency to laugh from their consciousness of the ludicrousness of an object, and then to tell you what the feeling of its ludicrousness would be like, whether it be anything more than the perception that the object belongs to the class "funny," they persist in replying that the thing proposed is a physical impossibility, and that they always must laugh, if they see a funny object. Of course the task proposed is not the practical one of seeing a ludicrous object and annihilating one's tendency to laugh. It is the purely speculative one of subtracting certain elements of feeling from an emotional state supposed to exist in its fulness, and saying what the residual elements are. I cannot help thinking that all who rightly apprehend this problem will agree with the proposition above laid down. What kind of an emotion of fear would be left, if the feelings neither of quickened heart-beats nor of shallow breathing, neither of trembling lips nor of weakened limbs, neither of goose-flesh nor of visceral stirrings, were present, it is quite impossible to think. Can one fancy the state of rage and picture no ebullition of it in the chest, no flushing of the face, no dilatation of the nostrils, no clenching of the teeth, no impulse to vigorous action, but in their stead limp muscles, calm breathing, and a placid face? The present writer, for one, certainly cannot. The rage is as completely evaporated as the sensation of its so-called manifestations, and the only thing that can possibly be supposed to take its place is some cold-blooded and dispassionate judicial sentence, confined entirely to the intellectual realm, to the effect that a certain person or persons merit chastisement for their sins. In like manner of grief; what would it be without its tears, its sobs, its suffocation of the heart, its pang in the breast-bone? A feelingless cognition that certain circumstances are deplorable, and nothing more. Every passion in turn tells the same story. A purely disembodied human emotion is a nonentity. I do not say that it is a contradiction in the nature of things, or that pure spirits are necessarily condemned to cold intellectual lives; but I say that for us, emotion dissociated from all bodily feeling is inconceivable. The more closely I scrutinise my states, the more persuaded I become, that whatever moods, affections, and passions I have, are in very truth constituted by, and made up of, those bodily changes we ordinarily call their expression or consequence; and the more it seems to me that if I were to become corporeally anaesthetic, I should be excluded from the life of the affections, harsh and tender alike, and drag out an existence of merely cognitive or intellectual form. Such an existence, although it seems to have been the ideal of ancient sages, is too apathetic to be keenly sought after by those born after the revival of the worship of sensibility, a few generations ago.

But if the emotion is nothing but the feeling of the reflex bodily effects of what we call its "object," effects due to the connate adaptation of the nervous system to that object, we seem immediately faced by this objection: most of the objects of civilised men's emotions are things to which it would be preposterous to suppose their nervous systems connately adapted. Most occasions of shame and many insults are purely conventional, and vary with the social environment. The same is true of many matters of dread and of desire, and of many occasions of melancholy and regret. In these cases, at least, it would seem that the ideas of shame, desire, regret, &c., must first have been attached by education and association to these conventional objects before the bodily changes could possibly be awakened. And if in these cases the bodily changes follow the ideas, instead of giving rise to them, why not then in all cases?

To discuss thoroughly this objection would carry us deep into the study of purely intellectual Aesthetics. A few words must here suffice. We will say nothing of the argument's failure to distinguish between the idea of an emotion and the emotion itself. We will only recall the well-known evolutionary principle that when a certain power has once been fixed in an animal by virtue of its utility in presence of certain features of the environment, it may turn out to be useful in presence of other features of the environment that had originally nothing to do with either producing or preserving it. A nervous tendency to discharge being once there, all sorts of unforeseen things may pull the trigger and let loose the effects. That among these things should be conventionalities of man's contriving is a matter of no psychological consequence whatever. The most important part of my environment is my fellow-man. The consciousness of his attitude towards me is the perception that normally unlocks most of my shames and indignations and fears. The extraordinary sensitiveness of this consciousness is shown by the bodily modifications wrought in us by the awareness that our fellow-man is noticing us at all. No one can walk across the platform at a public meeting with just the same muscular innervation he uses to walk across his room at home. No one can give a message to such a meeting without organic excitement. "Stage-fright" is only the extreme degree of that wholly irrational personal self-consciousness which every one gets in some measure, as soon as he feels the eyes of a number of strangers fixed upon him, even though he be inwardly convinced that their feeling towards him is of no practical account. This being so, it is not surprising that the additional persuasion that my fellow-man's attitude means either well or ill for me, should awaken stronger emotions still. In primitive societies "Well" may mean handing me a piece of beef, and "Ill" may mean aiming a blow at my skull. In our "cultured age," "Ill" may mean cutting me in the street, and "Well," giving me an honorary degree. What the action itself may be is quite insignificant, so long as I can perceive in it intent or *animus*. That is the emotion-arousing perception; and may give rise to as strong bodily convulsions in me, a civilised man experiencing the treatment of an artificial society, as in any savage prisoner of war, learning whether his captors are about to eat him or to make him a member of their tribe.

But now, this objection disposed of, there arises a more general doubt. Is there any evidence, it may be asked, for the assumption that particular perceptions do produce widespread bodily effects by a sort of immediate physical influence, antecedent to the arousal of an emotion or emotional idea? The only possible reply is, that there is most assuredly such evidence. In listening to poetry, drama, or heroic narrative, we are often surprised at the cutaneous shiver which like a sudden wave flows over us, and at the heart-swelling and the lachrymal effusion that unexpectedly catch us at intervals. In listening to music, the same is even more strikingly true. If we abruptly see a dark moving form in the woods, our heart stops beating, and we catch our breath instantly and before any articulate idea of danger can arise. If our friend goes near to the edge of a precipice, we get the well-known feeling of "all-overishness," and we shrink back, although we positively know him to be safe, and have no distinct imagination of his fall. The writer well remembers his astonishment, when a boy of seven or eight, at fainting when he saw a horse bled. The blood was in a bucket, with a stick in it, and, if memory does not deceive him, he stirred it round and saw it drip from the stick with no feeling save that of childish curiosity. Suddenly the world grew black before his eyes, his ears began to buzz, and he knew no more. He had never heard of the sight of blood producing faintness or sickness, and he had so little repugnance to it, and so little apprehension of any other sort of danger from it, that even at that tender age, as he well remembers, he could not help wondering how the mere physical presence of a pailful of crimson fluid could occasion in him such formidable bodily effects.

Imagine two steel knife-blades with their keen edges crossing each other at right angles, and moving to and fro. Our whole nervous organisation is "on-edge" at the thought; and yet what emotion can be there except the unpleasant nervous feeling itself, or the dread that more of it may come? The entire fund and capital of the emotion here is the senseless bodily effect the blades immediately arouse. This case is typical of a class: where an ideal emotion seems to precede the bodily symptoms, it is often nothing but a representation of the symptoms themselves. One who has already fainted at the sight of blood may witness the preparations for a surgical operation with uncontrollable heart-sinking and anxiety. He anticipates certain feelings, and the anticipation precipitates their arrival. I am told of a case of morbid terror, of which the subject confessed that what possessed her seemed, more than anything, to be the fear of fear itself. In the various forms of what Professor Bain calls "tender emotion," although the appropriate object must usually be directly contemplated before the emotion can be aroused, yet sometimes thinking of the symptoms of the emotion itself may have the same effect. In sentimental natures, the thought of "yearning" will produce real "yearning." And, not to speak of coarser examples, a mother's imagination of the caresses she bestows on her child may arouse a spasm of parental longing.

In such cases as these, we see plainly how the emotion both begins and ends with what we call its effects or manifestations. It has no mental status except as either the presented feelings, or the idea, of the manifestations; which latter thus constitute its entire material, its sum and substance, and its stock-in-trade. And these cases ought to make us see how in all cases the feeling of the manifestations may play a much deeper part in the constitution of the emotion than we are wont to suppose.

If our theory be true, a necessary corollary of it ought to be that any voluntary arousal of the so-called manifestations of a special emotion ought to give us the emotion itself. Of course in the majority of emotions, this test is inapplicable; for many of the manifestations are in organs over which we have no volitional control. Still, within the limits in which it can be verified, experience fully corroborates this test. Everyone knows how panic is increased by flight, and how the giving way to the symptoms of grief or anger increases those passions themselves. Each fit of sobbing makes the sorrow more acute, and calls forth another fit stronger still, until at last repose only ensues with lassitude and with the apparent exhaustion of the machinery. In rage, it is notorious how we "work ourselves up" to a climax by repeated outbreaks of expression. Refuse to express a passion, and it dies. Count ten before venting your anger, and its occasion seems ridiculous. Whistling to keep up courage is no mere figure of speech. On the other hand, sit all day in a moping posture, sigh, and reply to everything with a dismal voice, and your melancholy lingers. There is no more valuable precept in moral education than this, as all who have experience know; if we wish to conquer undesirable emotional tendencies in ourselves, we must assiduously, and in the first instance cold-bloodedly, go through the outward motions of those contrary dispositions we prefer to cultivate. The reward of persistency will infallibly come, in the fading out of the sullenness or depression, and the advent of real cheerfulness and kindliness in their stead. Smooth the brow, brighten the eye, contract the dorsal rather than the ventral aspect of the frame, and speak in a major key, pass the genial compliment, and your heart must be frigid indeed if it does not gradually thaw!

The only exceptions to this are apparent, not real. The great emotional expressiveness and mobility of certain persons often lead us to say "They would feel more if they talked less." And in another class of persons, the explosive energy with which passion manifests itself on critical occasions, seems correlated with the way in which they bottle it up during the intervals. But these are only eccentric types of character, and within each type the law of the last paragraph prevails. The sentimentalist is so constructed that "gushing" is his or her normal mode of expression. Putting a stopper on the "gush" will only to a limited extent cause more "real" activities to take its place; in the main it will simply produce listlessness. On the other hand the ponderous and bilious "slumbering volcano," let him repress the expression of his passions as he will, will find them expire if they get no vent at all; whilst if the rare occasions multiply which he deems worthy of their outbreak, he will find them grow in intensity as life proceeds.

I feel persuaded there is no real exception to the law. The formidable effects of suppressed tears might be mentioned, and the calming results of speaking out your mind when angry and having done with it. But these are also but specious wanderings from the rule. Every perception must lead to some nervous result. If this be the normal emotional expression, it soon expends itself, and in the natural course of things a calm succeeds. But if the normal issue be blocked from any cause, the currents may under certain circumstances invade other tracts, and there work different and worse effects. Thus vengeful brooding may replace a burst of indignation; a dry heat may consume the frame of one who fain would weep, or he may, as Dante says, turn to stone within; and then tears or a storming-fit may bring a grateful relief. When we teach children to repress their emotions, it is not that they may feel more, quite the reverse. It is that they may think more; for to a certain extent whatever nerve-currents are diverted from the regions below, must swell the activity of the thought-tracts of the brain.

The last great argument in favour of the priority of the bodily symptoms to the felt emotion, is the ease with which we formulate by its means pathological cases and normal cases under a common scheme. In every asylum we find examples of absolutely unmotivated fear, anger, melancholy, or conceit; and others of an equally unmotived apathy which persists in spite of the best of outward reasons why it should give way. In the former cases we must suppose the nervous machinery to be so "labile" in some one emotional direction, that almost every stimulus, however inappropriate, will cause it to upset in that way, and as a consequence to engender the particular complex of feelings of which the psychic body of the emotion consists. Thus, to take one special instance, if inability to draw deep breath, fluttering of the heart, and that peculiar epigastric change felt as "precordial anxiety," with an irresistible tendency to take a somewhat crouching attitude and to sit still, and with perhaps other visceral processes not now known, all spontaneously occur together in a certain person; his feeling of their combination is the emotion of dread, and he is the victim of what is known as morbid fear. A friend who has had occasional attacks of this most distressing of all maladies, tells me that in his case the whole drama seems to centre about the region of the heart and respiratory apparatus, that his main effort during the attacks is to get control of his inspirations and to slow his heart, and that the moment he attains to breathing deeply and to holding himself erect, the dread, *ipso facto*, seems to depart.

If our hypothesis be true, it makes us realise more deeply than ever how much our mental life is knit up with our corporeal frame, in the strictest sense of the term. Rapture, love, ambition, indignation, and pride, considered as feelings, are fruits of the same soil with the grossest bodily sensations of pleasure and of pain. But it was said at the outset that this would be affirmed only of what we then agreed to call the *standard* emotions; and that those inward sensibilities that appeared devoid at first sight of bodily results should be left out of our account. We had better, before closing, say a word or two about these latter feelings.

They are, the reader will remember, the moral, intellectual, and aesthetic feelings. Concords of sounds, of colours, of lines, logical consistencies, teleological fitnesses, affect us with a pleasure that seems ingrained in the very form of the representation itself, and to borrow nothing from any reverberation surging up from the parts below the brain. The Herbartian psychologists have tried to distinguish feelings due to the form in which ideas may be arranged. A geometrical demonstration may be as "pretty," and an act of justice as "neat" as a drawing or a tune, although the prettiness and neatness seem here to be a pure matter of sensation, and there to have nothing to do with sensation. We have then, or some of us seem to have, genuinely cerebral forms of pleasure and displeasure, apparently not agreeing in their mode of production with the so-called *standard* emotions we have been analysing. And it is certain that readers whom our reasons have hitherto failed to convince, will now start up at this admission, and consider that by it we give up our whole case. Since musical perceptions, since logical ideas, can immediately arouse a form of emotional feeling, they will say, is it not more natural to suppose that in the case of the so-called *standard* emotions, prompted by the presence of objects or the experience of events the emotional feeling is equally immediate, and the bodily expression something that comes later and is added on?

But a sober scrutiny of the cases of pure cerebral emotion gives little force to this assimilation. Unless in them there actually be coupled with the intellectual feeling a bodily reverberation of some kind, unless we actually laugh at the neatness of the mechanical device, thrill at the justice of the act, or tingle at the perfection of the musical form, our mental condition is more allied to a judgment of right than to anything else. And such a judgment is rather to be classed among awareness of truth: it is a cognitive act. But as a matter of fact the intellectual feeling hardly ever does exist thus unaccompanied. The bodily sounding-board is at work, as careful introspection will show, far more than we usually suppose. Still, where long familiarity with a certain class of effects has blunted emotional sensibility thereto as much as it has sharpened the taste and judgment, we do get the intellectual emotion, if such it can be called, pure and undefiled. And the dryness of it, the paleness, the absence of all glow, as it may exist in a thoroughly expert critic's mind, not only shows us what an altogether different thing it is from the *standard* emotions we considered first, but makes us suspect that almost the entire difference lies in the fact that the bodily sounding-board, vibrating in the one case is in the other mute. "Not so very bad" is, in a person of consummate taste, apt to be the highest limit of approving expression. *Rien ne me choque* is said to have been Chopin's superlative of praise of new music. A sentimental layman would feel, and ought to feel, horrified, on being admitted into such a critic's mind, to see how cold, how thin, how void of human significance, are the motives for favour or disfavour that there prevail. The capacity to make a nice spot on the wall will outweigh a picture's whole content; a foolish trick of words will preserve a poem; an utterly meaningless fitness of sequence in one musical composition set at naught any amount of "expressiveness" in another.

I remember seeing an English couple sit for more than an hour on a piercing February day in the Academy at Venice before the celebrated "Assumption" by Titian; and when I, after being chased from room to room by the cold, concluded to get into the sunshine as fast as possible and let the pictures go, but before leaving drew reverently near to them to learn with what superior forms of susceptibility they might be endowed, all I overheard was the woman's voice murmuring: "What a deprecatory expression her face wears! What self-abnegation! How unworthy she feels of the honour she is receiving!" Their honest hearts had been kept warm all the time by a glow of spurious sentiment that would have fairly made old Titian sick. Mr. Ruskin somewhere makes the (for him) terrible admission that re-religious people as a rule care little for pictures, and that when they do care for them they generally prefer the worst ones to the best. Yes! in every art, in every science, there is the keen perception of certain relations being right or not, and there is the emotional flush and thrill consequent there-upon. And these are two things, not one. In the former of them it is that experts and masters are at home. The latter accompaniments are bodily commotions that they may hardly feel, but that may be experienced in their fulness by Cretins and Philistines in whom the critical judgment is at its lowest ebb. The "marvels" of Science, about which so much edifying popular literature is written, are apt to be "caviare" to the men in the laboratories. Cognition and emotion are parted even in this last retreat,—who shall say that their antagonism may not just be the one phase of the world-old struggle in which it seems pretty certain that neither party will definitively drive the other off the field.

To return now to our starting-point, the physiology of the brain. If we suppose its cortex to contain centres for the perception of changes in each special sense-organ, in each portion of the skin, in each muscle, each joint, and each viscus, and to contain absolutely nothing else, we still have a scheme perfectly capable of representing the process of the emotions. An object falls on a sense-organ and is apperceived by the appropriate cortical centre; or else the latter, excited in some other way, gives rise to an idea of the same object. Quick as a flash, the reflex currents pass down through their pre-ordained channels, alter the condition of muscle, skin and viscus; and these alterations, apperceived like the original object, in as many specific portions of the cortex, combine with it in consciousness and transform it from an object-simply-apprehended into an object-emotionally-felt. No new principles have to be invoked, nothing is postulated beyond the ordinary reflex circuit, and the topical centres admitted in one shape or another by all to exist.

It must be confessed that a crucial test of the truth of the hypothesis is quite as hard to obtain as its decisive refutation. A case of complete internal and external corporeal anesthesia, without motor alteration or alteration of intelligence except emotional apathy, would afford, if not a crucial test, at least a strong presumption, in favour of the truth of the view we have set forth; whilst the persistence of strong emotional feeling in such a case would completely overthrow our case. Hysterical anaesthesias seem never to be complete enough to cover the ground. Complete anesthesias from organic disease, on the other hand, are excessively rare. In the famous

case of Remigius Leims, no mention is made by the reporters of his emotional condition, a circumstance which by itself affords no presumption that
it was normal, since as a rule nothing ever is noticed without a pre-existing
question in the mind. Dr. George Winter has recently described a case
somewhat similar, and in reply to a question, kindly writes to me as follows:

The case has been for a year and a half entirely removed from my
observation. But so far as I am able to state, the man has characterised by a
certain mental inertia and indolence. He was tranquil, and had on the whole
the temperament of a phlegmatic. He was not irritable, not quarrelsome,
went quietly about his farm-work, and left the care of his business and
house-keeping to other people. In short, he gave one the impression of a
placid countryman, who has no interests beyond his work.

Dr. Winter adds that in studying the case he paid no particular attention to the man's psychic condition, as this seemed *nebensachlich* to his
main purpose. I should add that the form of my question to Dr. Winter
could give him no clue as to the kind of answer I expected.

Of course, this case proves nothing, but it is to be hoped that asylum-
physicians and nervous specialists may begin methodically to study the
relation between anaesthesia and emotional apathy. If the hypothesis here
suggested is ever to be definitively confirmed or disproved it seems as if it
must be by them, for they alone have the data in their hands.

A Contribution to the Study of the Action

of Adrenalin on the Emotions[*]

G. Marañon

General Hospital, Madrid

The physiological effects of adrenalin on man. Recently many authors have
studied the action of adrenalin on the human organism. Studied from either
a strictly physiological point of view, or with the idea of obtaining reactions
which would be useful for some differential diagnosis, or with therapeutic
objectives, adrenalin has been so often used under all types of administration that at the present time almost all doctors have had a great deal of
experience with this drug. In 1920 (1) we were able to describe a new series

Reprinted from the *Revue Francaise D'Endocrinologie*, 1924, 2, 301–325.

[*]This article was originally published as *Contribution a l'etude de l'action
emotive de l'adrenaline.* The translation was made by Marjorie Schacter and Bibb
Latané.

of effects of adrenalin on man, effects whose existence we had already noted a few years before, (2) and which we called "emotional reaction." These effects, since they occur in as high a realm as the affective, have seemed to us from the beginning of great interest for the pathologist, and even the psychologist.

During the last two years we have carefully studied this reaction among a large number of subjects, most of whom were patients, and we succeeded in gathering data essential to the understanding of this reaction, which we will summarize in this present work.

In our previous study (1) we listed the known effects of adrenalin on the human organism and we will repeat this list here in more precision. Here are the characteristic effects:

A. *Local effects.* An area of skin around the injection (entracutaneous or intradermic) becomes pale and takes the shape of a spot of variable dimensions (approximately the size of a fifty-cent piece) having clear contour and deep indentation. This pale, almost entirely white, spot appears after some time, surrounded by a reddish line which separates it from the normal skin. Sometimes, as Ascoli and Fagiouli (3) have indicated, when the injection is intradermic the center of the white spot is bluish. Finally, the whole spot is covered with horripilation or goose pimples, due to the contraction of the arrector muscles.

B. *Circulatory effects.* During the minutes that follow the injection, the blood pressure increases, usually by 5 to 30 mm but sometimes much more, for a period of time varying with the dose and the temperamental and pathological condition of the subject, etc. Sometimes hypertension does not occur, and there can even be a clear decrease of the blood pressure if the injected dose is very small.

The number of pulsations increases (generally 10 to 30 pulsations per minute) and this increase is followed by a more or less noticeable decrease according to the intensity of the hypertension.

Some cases involve the occurrence of a noticeable arrhythmia, sometimes accompanied by a more or less disagreeable subjective sensation. When the cardiac contraction is very intense, one can by auscultation hear a very clear systolic murmur. This finding, which was not mentioned by the authors, is, according to my observations, rather frequent. The vasomotors contract and the subject becomes visibly pale. Sometimes a phase of vaso-dilation follows the original vaso-constriction, and then the face becomes red.

C. *Respiratory effects.* Polypnea, or panting, is almost always present but is often not noticed if one does not count or graphically register the number of breaths. Sometimes, the opposite occurs; breathing becomes slow, deep, and labored, with a subjective sensation of dyspnea. These effects, which according to Wearn and Sturgis are very variable, are extremely constant in our experience. (4)

D. *Motor effects.* The most interesting of these is a tremor, sometimes only in the hands, but at other times spreading to the legs and to the whole body. Occasionally, the shaking becomes so intense that not only is the subject's whole body agitated, but also the chair on which he sits or the bed on which he lies. If the subject already has a tremor (hyperthyroidism, Parkinson's disease, alcoholism, lead poisoning, etc.) it is enormously increased. Delavierre (15) indicates that the trembling produced by the primary emotions is localized most often on the right side of the body; we have observed the same thing for the adrenal tremor.

A shivering, produced by the contraction of the spinal muscles, is almost always present, as is mydriasis, or abnormal pupillary dilation.

E. *Secretory effects.* These effects are less frequent and less constant than those already mentioned. Some authors have noted an increase in salivary secretion and perspiration, especially palmar. However, according to my observations, perspiration is rare, and not only is increased salivation unusual, we more often noticed a dryness of the mouth which the patients spontaneously and often complained of. This discrepancy is probably due to individual differences in glandular innervation, differences which, as Gottlieb (6) points out, were noticed by the anatomists and only became known as a result of the study of poisons affecting the autonomous system. Indeed, several years ago when we observed the types of reaction to Pilocarpine, Atropine, and adrenalin among a large number of subjects (7), we made the hypothesis that differences in the effects of such drugs upon the various organs were probably due to individual differences in the amount of sympathetic or autonomous innervation each organ was receiving.

In many cases the lachrymal secretion is excited by adrenalin, resulting in a more or less abundant production of tears (usually weak).

Finally, renal secretion is often excited, the injected subject emitting somewhat more urine than usual. More remarkable even than this polyuria is an urgent sensation to urinate even when no excessive amount of urine is present. This phenomenon, as we pointed out in our first article (1) is due to bladder contraction, and is not necessarily related to secretory effects.

F. *Metabolic effects.* The injection of adrenalin causes a physiological action of the carbohydrates, which is manifested in hyperglycemia and sometimes glycosuria.

Hyperglycemia was positive in all 31 cases we examined for it. With the adrenalin dosage used in our study, glycosuria is, in our opinion, relatively rare. Bloch (8) found it positive in 36% of his cases but only when the patient took 150 gr of glucose before the injection.

Recently Veil and Resert observed that in many normal subjects, an injection of adrenalin results in an increased urinary acidity and even the appearance of acetone. Among diabetics, pre-existing urinary acidity and acetonuria increased. At the present time we are studying, with Carrasco and Solar, the action of adrenalin on basal metabolism.

G. *Subjective effects.* Most authors do not pay much attention to the frequency, intensity, or meaning of the subjective phenomena in the injected subjects. Gostsch (10) mentions only a certain nervousness of which some injected subjects complained. Most American authors, Peabody, Sturgis, Tompkins, and Wearn (11), Sturgis and Wearn (4), mention this same fact and add to it sensations of asthenia, palpitations, dizziness, etc., which sometimes accompany the nervousness. Some investigators like Bloch (8) go so far as to state that these subjective disturbances are "relatively rare." Escudero is more explicit (12); according to him, "injections of adrenalin are accompanied by general phenomena such as tremor of the hands and body, palpitations, nervousness, discomfort, fear," etc.

We have already indicated the existence and the importance of these subjective phenomena in our first article (2) and in subsequent publications (13, 14, 15). Indeed, one of the most interesting consequences of an injection of adrenalin in man is, in our opinion, the appearance of a subjective syndrome characterized by circulatory phenomena (praecordal or epigastric palpitation, feeling of redness), thoracic phenomena (sensation of a constriction in the throat), motor phenomena (feeling of internal tremor, awareness of tremor in the limbs, shivering), digestive phenomena (salivation or dryness of the throat, nausea), and nervous phenomena (sensation of nervousness, discomfort, asthenia).

Finally, in certain cases, *a clearly emotional sensation occurs which we will describe in detail:*

The emotional reaction. Some time after the injection (rarely less than 15 minutes, but sometimes much longer), some subjects experience an emotional phenomenon which can take two forms: either as a *subjective perception, "en froid," of somatic disturbance leading to an unidentifiable emotional sensation,* or as an *entire, involuntary emotion having the same somatic elements as in the previous case but also a psychological, affective involvement.*

The first type of reaction is the most frequent. The subject is aware of the post-injection phenomena: a tremor, both internally and of the limbs, a praecordial oppression, shivering of the spine, coldness of the hands, dryness of the mouth, heart palpitations, and tears. Since these phenomena coincide with the complete framework of the autonomic symptomatology of emotion (autonomic emotion), the subject's awareness of them results in the feeling of "being moved," without, however, the psychological element of emotion. Thus, the injected subject expresses his psychological reaction, either after questioning or spontaneously, in sentences like those which follow, taken from our clinical records and quoted because they are more expressive than any other description.

"I feel as if I were afraid," "as if I were awaiting a great happiness," "an internal spasm," "as if I were moved," "as though I were going to cry not knowing why," "as if I were very frightened, however, I am calm," "as though someone were going to do something to me."

One sees clearly in these examples that the subject makes a clear-cut distinction between the perception of the peripheral phenomenon of autonomic emotion and the strictly psychological emotion, allowing a calm awareness of the autonomic syndrome without real emotion. We shall insist later on the importance of this phenomenon for the experimental study of the emotional state.

We should like to point out before going further, that in the only work in which there is even the most incidental reference to the post-adrenal emotional reaction, the female patient uses sentences identical to those of our patients. This was a woman injected with one milligram of adrenalin by Cawadias (16) in an investigation of the tonus of the sympathetic nervous system. After a few minutes, a complex symptomatology occurred and the patient, who had been put in jail during a period of political unrest, said; "I feel as I did the day they put me in jail."

The second type of reaction may be called the *second degree reaction.* The injected subject not only perceives the autonomic somatic manifestations of emotion, but he also, gradually or suddenly, feels his mind invaded by an emotional flux. The "psychological emotion" is superimposed upon the "autonomic emotion," and is apprehended as a complete affective state, usually of the anxiety type, with abundant tears, sobs, and sighs. Frequently, a "psychological motif" for the depression appears. The man or woman under observation recalls absent or dead loved ones or other sad events in life. At other times, such a motif does not appear, and the subject states that he is crying and sad and depressed, but that "he doesn't know why."

This *second degree* reaction to adrenalin is certainly less frequent than the first and appears in some cases spontaneously. To produce it in other cases one must suggest a memory with strong affective force but not so strong as to produce an emotion in the normal state. For example, in several cases we spoke to our patients before the injection of their sick children or dead parents and they responded calmly to this topic. The same topic presented later, during the adrenal commotion, was sufficient to trigger emotion. This adrenal commotion places the subject in a situation of "affective imminence" similar to that of patients suffering from cerebral softening, and like them, the emotion springs up sometimes without any intellectual reason (which may or may not be added later). At other times it is the intellectual reason which provokes the emotional reaction.

Pathological states in which the reaction is found and its frequency. As we have already stated, the adrenal emotional reaction does not occur in all the injected subjects but only in a certain number of them. We cannot give the percentage, for statistics have no value in this case since the experimental results depend upon a multitude of circumstances inherent in the previous state of the subjects and upon the injected dosage which can not be subject to the rigor of numbers. It is thus impossible to deduce any conclusions from the datum that among 210 injected subjects, 62 (29%) gave positive reactions. These cases were mostly among patients suffering from disorders of the autonomic nervous system or from disorders of the internal secretion glands.

Most of our positive cases were observed among hyperthyroid patients. Undoubtedly the habitual emotional instability among these patients constitutes an important predisposing factor. The proof is that *the negative reaction can be converted into a positive reaction by previously treating the subject with thyroidine:* as one can see in the following examples:

Case XXI. A boy of 19 suffering from Reklinghausen's disease, with an endemic thyroid deficiency. An injection of 1 milligram of adrenalin caused: a) the appearance of a white spot with little horripilation; b) no change in pulse, respiratory rhythm or arterial pressure but slight paleness; c) no subjective sensation and complete absence of emotion. Consequently, the reaction was clearly negative.

For one month, the patient ingested 60 drops of thyroidine per day. A new adrenalin injection caused: a) intense dermic reaction which reached its maximum at the end of eight minutes and which lasted for 45 minutes; b) an increase in the pulse from 100 to 132 per minute, an increase from 16 to 21 breaths per minute, and an increase in the maximum arterial pressure from 9 to 9.6; c) subjective sensations of tremor, and "something which comes up from the guts as when one is awaiting a great happiness." That is to say, the reaction was clearly positive.

Case XI. A 25-year-old woman with progressive tendency to obesity. An injection of three-quarters of a milligram of adrenalin resulted in: a) a cutaneous reaction of medium intensity; b) an increase in the pulse rate (72 to 78) and of the respiratory rate (15–17), and no change in the blood pressure which was constant at 13 maximum and 7 minimum, slight shaking of the hands and eyelids; c) a slight sensation of tremor without any emotion at all. Summary: negative reaction.

For three months she was given a weight-reducing treatment, to which she added on her own initiative a considerable quantity of thyroidine. When we saw her again, she showed the typical clinical hyperthyroid syndrome (loss of weight, tachycardia, tremor, palpitations, fears, etc.). An injection of three-quarters of a milligram of adrenalin under these new circumstances produced: a) an intense and immediate cutaneous reaction; b) an increase in the pulse rate from 100–110 after four minutes, then a lessening to 88 at the end of six minutes, 72 at the end of 20 minutes, and finally a return to the normal rate. The number of breaths increased in the first five minutes from 16 to 19 per minute, and after 10 minutes it diminished to 14 and 12 per minute with deep and labored sighing. Arterial blood pressure increased from 13 maximum, eight minimum to 17 maximum, nine minimum at the end of 10 minutes, remaining that high for more than 20 minutes; paleness, large increase of tremor, systolic breath; c) a sensation of strong tremor, undefinable uneasiness and anxiety, "as though she were very moved." Summary: very positive reaction.

However, if the dose of thyroidine is small, the reaction does not change. Example:

Case CI. A forty-two-year-old woman. Typical myxedema. Injection of three-quarters of a milligram of adrenalin resulted in: a) very attenuated local reaction; b) very slight circulatory, respiratory, motor reaction; c) no emotional reaction.

For four days she took six tablets of 0.5 gr. of thyroidine per day. After a new injection of three-quarters of a milligram of adrenalin, both local and general reactions were even less evident than before. No emotion.

It should be noted that this "reactivation" effect has also been described by Ascoli and Fagiouli (3), Wearn and Sturgis (4), Bloch (8), and Escudero (12).

In ten cases of myxedema which we checked, the reactions were absolutely negative, a fact which runs counter to the data on the influence of thyroid activity on the success of the emotional reaction. Among these ten cases, two were especially interesting, for notwithstanding a habitual emotionality, the adrenal reaction was negative. This data suggests several hypotheses and notions which we cannot describe here.

One of these cases (Case LII) was a 35-year-old man with acute Basedow's disease and intense emotionality. A sympathectomy and a thyroidectomy so complete as to give him a very accentuated post-operative myxedema syndrome did not reduce the high emotionality of his hyperthyroid phase; he cried for no reason and spoke of committing suicide because he couldn't stand his pusillanimity, which incapacitated him for military life. Despite all of this, the injection of a milligram of adrenalin, which produced a moderate positive cutaneous reaction and general positive reactions, did not result in any emotional syndrome at all.[*]

Another case (Case LXI) was that of a 50-year-old woman with typical intense myxedema, high emotionality, and perhaps premature arterial sclerosis as shown by hypertension (19–10). The injection of a milligram of adrenalin produced a slight cutaneous reaction, some hardly perceptible circulatory and respiratory changes, a slight sensation of tremor and asthenia, and no emotional effect.

Another patient who had exhibited signs of myxedema in her youth, now cured, but suffering from an intense neurosis which appeared with the onset of menopause, no longer had any emotional reaction.

It seems that the hyperfunction of the thyroid doubtlessly increases the likelihood of the appearance of the post-adrenal emotional phenomena, and that consequently the hypofunction of the thyroid should weaken or pre-

[*] This case has just been studied by Bonilla and Blanco (17).

vent them. However, there are many cases of typical hyperthyroidism where the emotional reaction is negative, and some cases of non-hyperthyroidism where the reaction is positive. This is why one cannot, as Goetsch (10) wants, assign a diagnostic value in this sense to the activity of the thyroid. This applies both to the local reaction and the general phenomena according to the work of Wearn and Sturgis (4), their collaborators (11), Escudero (12), and Bloch (8), as well as our own (1, etc.).

In what other pathological states, in addition to hyperthyroidism, can the emotional reaction be observed? According to our experience, *it is often positive in the transitory psychopathic conditions with high affective instability which often occur in women at the time of menopause.* (17 positive reactions in 33 cases.) As we have shown elsewhere, hyperthyroidism plays an important role in such cases of involutional melancholia so that they could have been considered in the preceding section. However, in some women a careful clinical examination and a basal metabolism revealed no true hyperthyroidism. Thus it would seem that the sensitivity of the emotional reaction is not always tied to the thyroid factor, but may be related to other pathological conditions peculiar to menopause. Ovarian deficiency, contrary to expectation, is not one of these conditions, for in seven cases of *juvenile ovarian deficiency* (outside of the menopause) *the reaction was always negative,* even in two cases where due to a hyperthyroid reaction in one and a clear hysteria in the other, one could expect, *a priori,* a positive reaction.

In cases of affective instability at the menopause, there is often an instability of arterial blood pressure, with a tendency to hypertension. Many authors, including ourselves, suppose that this circulatory condition may stem from a suprarenal hyperfunction. This supposition is confirmed by the clinical study of the menopause and by experimental and anatomicopathological data (13). Theoretically, it is understandable that adrenalin should be more efficacious among individuals with an exaggerated suprarenal function than among those with a normal or hyponormal suprarenal function. In our group of cases, however, there were five patients with a chronic and serious suprarenal deficiency (Addison's disease) who should, according to the above, show very slight reactions. Not only was this not the case, but all the post-adrenal reactions were intensely positive, including, naturally, the emotional ones. The following is an example of this:

Case XLI. A twenty-one year old girl with a typical case of Addison's disease. Injection of half a milligram of adrenalin produced: a) a rapid and intense local reaction; b) an increase in the pulse rate from 104 to 116 per minute at the end of twelve minutes, an increase in respiratory rate from 20 to 26 per minute with the breathing becoming more labored and deep, an increase in arterial blood pressure from 13 maximum 8 minimum to 16 maximum 8 minimum at the end of 15 minutes, paleness, strong tremor of the hands, need to urinate; c) a feeling of "internal tremor as if she were afraid." We spoke to her of her sister who had been dead for two years, and whose sickness and death had been calmly described to us before the injection. After the injection, the mere evocation of this memory produced an intense anxiety attack with abundant tears and deep sobs lasting for four minutes.

The frequency of the positive reaction in convalescing cases of serious infectious diseases concurs with this result. Bloch (8), Escudero (12), and others have also pointed out the intensity of general and cutaneous reactions among this class of patients. One might suppose, in some cases at least, that there would be a lowering of the suprarenal function, more or less exhausted by the fight against the infection. For one of our thyroid fever convalescents, whom we diagnosed as showing a typical syndrome of post-infectious suprarenal deficiency (a diagnosis we rarely make), the injection of half a milligram of adrenalin, which we expected to be followed by mild effects, produced in him such an intense local, general, and affective perturbation that on several occasions we thought he would die. This paradoxical result could be explained by assuming that the exhausted suprarenal system is more unstable, by the very fact of its exhaustion, than a normal system. In the same way, as we have observed rather frequently, hypothyroid patients react more strongly than individuals with a normal thyroid function to small doses. But perhaps this interpretation is too far-fetched.

Another interesting group of cases are those with a *neurosis of the affective type without clinical endocrinous disorders.* In twelve cases of this type that we examined, seven showed a clearly positive reaction.

Sierra, in an interesting study (18) which we will discuss later, states that he has frequently found a positive emotional reaction among *primary melancholics, manic depressives* (especially during the depressive period), and some *dementia praecox* of the catatonic type.

It seems that the post-adrenal emotional reaction appears principally in cases where *the emotional index of the subject is high,* without respect to the relationship that this high emotional index might have with certain functional endocrinous states.

Indeed, abstracting from clinical diagnoses, the fact is that in most of our positive cases the previous emotional index was abnormally high.

The following fact reinforces the preceding argument: with normal subjects the reaction is always negative as our results show, *but if a sufficiently intense state of emotional excitation is induced in a normal individual, the reaction can become positive.* We were able to verify this fact by injecting subjects who were normal from the neuroendocrine point of view, but who were in a high state of emotional excitation in the minutes immediately preceding an operation. Dentists' experience in this sort of situation is especially significant.

Dentists and surgeons frequently use novocaine or cocaine, which are related to adrenalin, as an anesthetic in some operations. When patients come to the operation very excited by pain, insomnia, or fear, the use of the anesthetic frequently results in "tachycardia, paleness of the flesh, goose flesh, shivering, worry, feeling of anxiety, tears, etc." (19). Despite the serious appearance of their exaggerated symptomatology, these manifestations almost always end rapidly.

One can assert that these events, which used to be attributed to various causes, are only simple emotional post-adrenal reactions. My previous statement to this effect (13) was verified later by various authors, Valderrama, Chornet (quoted by Landette), Landette (19). According to the latter, very minimal doses of adrenalin, much smaller than those that we used, were sufficient to induce the appearance of emotional effects in those patients who became very excited over a minor operation. In summary: *post-adrenal emotion appears more readily among subjects with a high emotional index. It seems that this index is related in many cases, although not always, to hyperthyroidism, and that it can be induced artificially by previous treatment with a sufficient amount of thyroid substance.*

The influence of sex and of age. According to Sierra, the emotional reaction occurs with greater frequency among women (33%) than among men (10%). Our statistics are valueless in this context because of the nature of our case material. We treated a much larger number of women than men (170 women and 40 men); of our 62 positive reactions, however, 41 were from women (66%), and 21 from men (33%).

For age also we can not give exact numbers because the relationship of the effect to age is hidden by the pathological state of the patient. In general it seems that the most intense emotional reactions occur among subjects in the 40's.

These two findings concur with the general fact that the emotional state is more unstable in the feminine than in the masculine sex, and at the critical age of 40 to 50 than during other periods.

The relationship between the emotional reaction and other post-adrenal phenomena. In several places in the text we have established comparisons between the intensity of the emotional reaction and the other general or local phenomena which are induced by the injection of adrenalin into the human organism. We must now add that *this relationship is not always absolutely parallel.* In many cases one observes an intense local and general reaction but only a mild emotional reaction if any. On the other hand, a very strong emotional reaction may be accompanied in some individuals by moderate local and general reactions (never negative). For example:

Case III. A 25-year-old woman with typical Basedow's disease, but with a slow gain in weight rather than a loss. Basal metabolism = +15%. An injection of three-quarters of a milligram of adrenalin produced: a) a typical intense local reaction; b) a greatly heightened Basedow tremor, an increase in pulse from 88 to 108 per minute by the end of 12 minutes, arrhythmia, palpitations and sensations of carotid and epigastric pulsations, paleness, an increase in arterial blood pressure from 14 maximum—7 minimum to 16.5 maximum—8 minimum at the end of 14 minutes; c) no emotional reaction.

That is to say there was an intense local and general reaction but no local reaction. By contrast, in the following case, the emotional reaction is very intense while the other post-adrenal phenomena are mild:

Case XVI. A 39-year-old woman who had had an affective neurosis since the death of a daughter two years previous. No signs of hyperthyroidism. An injection of three-quarters of a milligram of adrenalin produced in her: a) a hardly perceptible local reaction; b) mildly marked general reactions; an increase in blood pressure from 14 maximum—9 minimum to 15 maximum—9 minimum (the pulse rate increased from 88 to 94; no change in breathing until the emotional period, slight tremor of the hands); c) intense anxiety reaction, spontaneous recall of dead daughter (of whom she had previously talked calmly), and an instantaneous deep sorrow with abundant tears and sobs, etc.

We have observed this dissociation between the local and the general phenomena, that is to say, between the goose pimples and the circulatory and glandular disturbances. It has often seemed to us that there is some kind of opposition between the local and the general phenomena, for we have observed very small changes in blood pressure and tremor when there has been a very precocious horripilation and vice versa. It would seem that adrenalin exhausts its effectiveness in producing some phenomena and remains inactive for the others.

We note, however, that of all the measures taken in our study, those which show the greatest correlation are arterial blood pressure and the emotional reaction. In general, the clearest emotional reactions take place among individuals whose blood pressures rose from 10–20 mm and even more, and the weakest or negative reactions are found in subjects whose blood pressure underwent little or no increase or were even hypotensive, which was not rare.

The following table, in which 23 of our cases with characteristic blood pressure variation are tabulated, is in this sense very relevant.

CASES	Maximum variation of arterial blood pressure after the injection[1]	Emotional reaction		
II	+50 mm	+	+	+
X	+40	−		
XII	+30	+	+	+
XXII	+30	+		
XXIX	+20	+	+	+
XXXIX	+20		+	+
XL	+20		+	+
XLII	+20		−	
XLIX	+14		−	
LVIII	+10	+	+	+
LXXIII	+10		+	+
LXXXV	+10		+	
XC	+10		+	
XCVII	+10		+	
CII	+10		+	
CV	+ 0.5		−	
XXI	+ 0.5		−	
CXIX	0		−	
CXXI	0		+	
CXXII	−10		+	
CXXIX	−15		−	
CXXX	−20		−	

[1] We only give the maximum blood pressure since the minimum varies very little after an adrenalin injection.

The course of the reaction. There is a great deal of variation in the course of the emotional reaction. We have already said that the reaction usually appears about fifteen minutes after the injection. Sometimes, however, it is very rapid and occurs at the end of 8 or 10 minutes. At other times it is very slow, sometimes appearing when the other post-adrenal manifestations are declining or even when one has begun to consider the task finished, as has happened to us several times and is mentioned by other authors (Torre Bianco). This probably depends upon the rapidity with which the drug is absorbed. When the injection is very superficial and the absorption is very slow, the local reaction is intense and the general phenomena (including the emotional) are moderate. When the injection is somewhat deeper, by contrast, the absorption is more rapid and consequently, the local reaction is less marked and the general phenomena (circulatory and emotional) are more accentuated. It would be interesting to determine the effects of the various modes whether intradermic, subcutaneous, intramuscular, intravenous or intrarecta, of introduction upon the post-adrenal phenomena. Hoskins (20) has recently studied the intrarectal case and found that since the drug is rapidly conducted to the system of the Vena Cava, this method can give, with the greatest of precision, a spontaneous secretion of the suprarenal glands.

The duration of the emotional phenomena is always very short, generally never lasting longer than two or three minutes.

Dosage. The doses we used to induce the reaction were either ½, ¾, or 1 milligram of adrenalin in a solution of 1 to 1000. It is evident that this is an arbitrary dose, but we do not believe that it would be prudent to inject more than 1 milligram in an adult. Even this dose would be excessive for predisposed individuals (with hyperthyroidism, menopause, convalescence). Consequently we frequently use a dose of ½ or ¾ of a milligram. For these reasons we were not able to investigate the interesting question of whether a negative reaction produced by a certain dose could become a positive reaction if the dose were increased. We tend to believe, *a priori,* that such is not the case, for among some predisposed subjects reactions occur with doses of ½ milligram and even much less, according to Landette (19).

Mechanisms of the post-adrenal emotional phenomena. The mechanisms of the post-adrenal emotional reaction are clearly understandable in terms of recent points of view in the physiology of emotion. Injected adrenalin causes a diffuse excitation of the sympathetic part of the autonomic nervous system. The visceral phenomena occasioned by this sympathetic therapeutic excitation are, in many cases, the same that take place during spontaneous emotion. The subject, in perceiving them, interprets them as being an emotion, either cold without the participation of his mind in the affective process as in the case of the first degree reaction, or as a complete and authentic emotion as in the case of the second degree reaction. These considerations need several explanations.

The correspondence of the post-adrenal autonomic phenomena and of the autonomic phenomena of emotion is obvious. It is sufficient to review the description which we made of the induced phenomena at the beginning to demonstrate that they are but a repetition of the visceral disturbances of spontaneous emotion. We have demonstrated that these disturbances are common to any emotion regardless of its position in the hierarchy (15). This identity will be still more evident if we compare the list of the "emotional manifestations" made by any psychologist—for example that of Achille-Delmas and Boll (21)—with the list of our post-adrenal phenomena.

The correspondence is so complete that the items in our series which are not also in the psychologists' were overlooked by them, for they are real emotional phenomena.

The virtual identity of two types of phenomena makes it easy to understand that when a subject is aware of the post-adrenal syndrome, he will report it spontaneously in terms of the visceral complex of emotion, keeping, however, his own affective equilibrium.

Functional manifestations according to D.B.	Post-adrenal visceral phenomena
cries, complaints, moaning	sighs
sighs	sobs
sobs	polypnea (panting)
tremor	tremor
shivering	shivering
startles	nausea
nausea	visceral spasms
spasms of the esophagus and pharynx	vesical spasms
intestinal and vesical spasms	tears
tears	salivation
salivation	sweat
sweat	polyuria
polyuria	blushing
diarrhea	paleness
blushing	palpitations
paleness	tachycardia
palpitations	hypertension
	hyperglycemia
	glycosuria

The disassociation between the autonomic and the psychic elements of emotion is of great importance in understanding the affective mechanism. We cannot enter at this point into psychological reports, but we can, however, note that the 'cold' awareness of emotional phenomena which takes place in the first degree reaction definitely demolishes the point of view of James and Lange. Their theory, though fruitful, makes the psychological emotion a consequence of the perception by the brain of the autonomic peripheral phenomena which are characteristic of an affective state. We had among our subjects many individuals who were fully aware of the peripheral symptoms and who described them in admirably exact terms, but who, however, *were not moved.*

It is true that there was another group of individuals (second degree reaction) among whom the psychological emotions appeared following the perception of the peripheral disturbances. These cases support the James-Lange hypothesis, and would be an absolute experimental confirmation if it were not for the fact that the first degree reaction is much more common. The second degree reaction not only occurs less often, but also only when the emotional predisposition of the subject is extreme. This inverse 'centripetal' mechanism can then be considered the exception, and not the rule as James and Lange propose. The habitual mechanism is 'centrifugal' in nature; the peripheral or autonomic emotion adds itself to the central, psychological emotion.

The possibility of producing the peripheral emotion by the inverse or centripetal path using adrenalin only confirms commonly observed facts utilized by the partisans of peripheral theories of emotion. For example, Baudin (23) uses the following arguments: 1) the simulation of autonomic emotion can induce the corresponding psychological emotion, 2) to control an emotion, one controls its autonomic effects as in conquering fear by singing and walking with head held high, 3) the exhaustion of the peripheral reaction exhausts in its turn the psychological emotion; anger is calmed by motor excitation, sadness by tears and isolation.

We repeat, however, that these cases are examples *of an exceptional mechanism,* as opposed to the one of normal emotion.

It is clear that there is some truth in the James-Lange hypothesis, and so it (aside from its virtue in having brought the problem of emotion from the realm of psychology to that of physiology) has been very fecund. In fact, the individual *is not conscious of being moved* until he *is conscious of the autonomic emotion.* Our post-adrenal reaction greatly aids in isolating this phenomenon and putting it into perspective. The consciousness of the autonomic emotion is but the final phase of a process which first takes place from the center to the periphery. We can, in summary, schematize the physiological processes of emotion in the following way: 1) initial psychological element (sensation, idea, memory); 2) production of the autonomic or peripheral emotion; 3) consciousness of the peripheral emotion by the brain; 4) authentic emotion when the consciousness of the autonomic emotion is superimposed on the primary psychological element.

If we first create the autonomic emotional phenomena, whether voluntarily as in the case of actors or clinically through the use of adrenalin, the brain is aware of them but does not emote because there is no liaison with the psychological element. This is the case of the first degree reaction. If the subject, however, is abnormally emotional, we can provoke the appearance of the psychological element by recalling, for example, a sad memory, or it may appear unaided through the centripetal action of the autonomic emotion. The emotion is complete once the liaison between the autonomic and the psychological is established.

The facts that we have presented give rise to many other theoretical considerations, but I believe at least that the preceding schema can be accepted as correct. The use of the experimental method by laboratories of experimental psychology, as already done by Sierra, can bring about fertile conclusions.

The biological significance of the emotional reaction. We wish to add a few words upon another question which relates to our study: the physiological significance of the emotional reaction. We will not try to discuss this point in detail for this would drag us into the question of the importance of glandular reactions in the mechanism of normal emotion and even into the one of the importance of adrenalin in physiology and in the pathology of higher organisms. The studies of Gley and his students have put the latter question into sharper focus.

We will restate the position which we have taken many times in the past few years when we have become involved in endocrinological controversies. It seems to us that to consider the specific effects produced in an organism by the injection of the extracts of internal secretion glands as simple pharmacological results is the most elementary biological abstraction.* If the ovarian extract congests the matrix and is conducive to the production of the menstrual flow, what else can one think but that this organ has physiologically elaborated a product to regulate the catamenial function? If the adrenalin found in the suprarenal capsules acts in such a con-

---

* See the remarkable work of Tournade and his collaborators recently summarized in this journal (24).

stant and specific way upon the circulation, why not think that these glands habitually produce adrenalin and thereby contribute to the equilibrium of the circulatory mechanism? And if this very adrenalin, injected in sometimes even very small doses, starts off the typical, complete autonomic phenomena of emotion, why not think that a sudden secretion of adrenalin, as the one we get with an injection, contributes to the production of peripheral affective symptoms which are both diffuse and definite?

We will not cite the other experimental results favoring this theory. Cannon's (25) support of this theory is far more cogent than are the arguments of its opponents. But we will call attention to the fact that *no other drug used by pharmacologists or physiologists possesses the emotional virtue of adrenalin*. Other chemical substances are certainly capable of producing various affective states, as, for example, chioral chlorogorm, quinine, hydrogen peroxide, alcohol, etc. There are two fundamental differences between their effects and those of adrenalin: 1) as Sierra (18) has observed, these other drugs only influence the affective sphere when administered in toxic doses, incompatible with the physiological equilibrium of the organism; 2) in all of these cases, the emotion stems from a primitive excitation of the nervous centers; that is to say, all of the functions of the nervous centers, affective as well as ideational, are stimulated. The emotional excitation, however, is not isolated.

Whatever the physiological significance of the emotional post-adrenal phenomena, our aim in this work was only to clarify the conditions under which they occur and to emphasize their importance for the experimental study of the affective life.

BIBLIOGRAPHY

1. Marañon. La reaccion emotiva a la adrenalina. *La Medicina Ibera.* XII, Agosto, 1920.
2. Marañon. Observaciones sobre la accion de la adrenalina en el hombre. *Boletin de la Sociedad Espanola De Biologia.* Junio, 1920.
3. Ascoli E. Fagiouli. Saggi farmacodinamici sottoepidermici. *Reale Accademia dei Lincei.* XXVIII. Jiug. 1919.
4. Wearn and Sturgis. Studies on epinephrin. *Archives of Internal Medicine.* XLII. Sept., 1919.
5. Delavierre. Les Reactions emotives. *These de Paris.* 1920.
6. H. H. Meyer and Gottlieb. *Die experimentelle Pharmakologia.* 14E Auf. 1920.
7. Marañon. El sistema nervioso de la vida vegetativa en Clinica. *Revizta Clinica de Madrid.* 1910.
8. Bloch. Epreuve de Goetsch. *These de Paris.* 1921.
9. Veil und Reisert. Ueber die probatorische Adrenalinwirkung beim Diabetiker. *Deutch. Arch. fur klin. Med.* 139 Bd. 1922.
10. Goetsch. Newer Methods in the Diagnosis of Thyroid Disorders. *Pathological and Clinical New York State.* S.M. July, 1918.
11. Peabody, Sturgis, Tompkins, and Wearn. Epinephrin hypersensitiveness and its relation to hyperthyroidism. *Amer. Jour. of the Medical Sciences.* CLBI, August, 1921.
12. Escudero. La prueba e la adrenalina en el diagnostico del hipertiroidismo. *Revista de la Asocianacion Medica Argentina.* N. 193–194. 1921.
13. Marañon. La Edad Critica, 2 adit, Madrid, 1925.

14. MARAÑON. La diabstes Insipida, Madrid. 1920.
15. MARAÑON. Introduccion al estudio de la teoria Neuro-humoral de la Emocion. Valencia, 1921.
16. PAWADIAS. La fievre d'origine sympathique. *Annales de Medecine,* 1920.
17. BONILLA and BLANCO. A case of post-operative mixedema. *Endocrinology.* March, 1924.
18. SIERRA, (A.M.). Estudio psicopathologico referente a la emocion experimental. *Semana Medica.* (Buenos-Ayres), No. 34, 1921.
19. LANDETE. Accidentes y Complicaciones de la anestesia local. *La Odontologia.* XXX. Julio, 1921.
20. HOSKINS, (R.G.). The reaction to epinephrin administered by rectum. *The Journ. of Pharmocaology and Experim. Therapeutis.* XVII. Oct., 1921.
21. ARCHILLE-DELMAS et M. BOLL. La Personnalite humaine. Son Analyse. *Bibliotheque de Philosophie.* Paris, 1922.
22. MARAÑON. Breve ansayo sobre la edad y la emocion. *Archivos de Medicina Cirugia, y Espe cialidades de Madrid.* Avril, 1921.
23. BAUDIN, (E). Psychologie, 2 edit. Paris, 1921.
24. TOURNADE. L'hyperadrenalinemie par excitation du nerf splanchinique. *Revue franc. d'Endocrinologie,* 1924, No. 3.
25. CANNON. Bodily Changes in Pain, Hunger, Fear and Rage. New York and London, 1915.

A Critical Examination of the James-Lange

Theory of Emotions

W. B. Cannon

The famous theory of emotions associated with the names of James and Lange was propounded by them independently. James first presented his view in 1884, Lange's monograph appeared in Danish in 1885. The cardinal points in their respective ideas of the nature of emotions are so well known that for purposes of comment only brief references need be made to them. James' theory may be summarized, in nearly his own terms, as follows (1). An object stimulates one or more sense organs; afferent impulses pass to the cortex and the object is perceived; thereupon currents run down to muscles and viscera and alter them in complex ways; afferent impulses from these disturbed organs course back to the cortex and when there perceived transform the "object-simply-apprehended" to the "object-emotionally-felt." In other words, "the feeling of the bodily changes as they occur is the emotion—the common sensational, associational and motor elements explain all." The main evidence cited for the theory is that we are aware of the tensions, throbs, flushes, pangs, suffocations—we feel them, indeed, the moment they occur—and that if we should take away from the picture of a fancied emotion these bodily symptoms, nothing would be left.

Reprinted from *Bodily Changes in Pain, Hunger, Fear and Rage* (2nd ed.) (New York: Appleton, 1929) Chapter XVIII, 346–359.

According to Lange (1) stimulation of the vasomotor center is "the root of the causes of the affections, however else they may be constituted." "We owe all the emotional side of our mental life," he wrote, "our joys and sorrows, our happy and unhappy hours, to our vasomotor system. If the impressions which fall upon our senses did not possess the power of stimulating it, we would wander through life unsympathetic and passionless, all impressions of the outer world would only enrich our experience, increase our knowledge, but would arouse neither joy nor anger, would give us neither care nor fear." Since we are unable to differentiate subjectively between feelings of a central and peripheral origin, subjective evidence is unreliable. But because wine, certain mushrooms, hashish, opium, a cold shower, and other agencies cause physiological effects which are accompanied by altered states of feeling, and because abstraction of the bodily manifestations from a frightened individual leaves nothing of his fear, the emotion is only a perception of changes in the body. It is clear that Lange had the same conception as James, but elaborated it on a much narrower basis—on changes in the circulatory system alone.

The backflow of impulses from the periphery, on which James relied to account for the richness and variety of emotional feeling, was assumed to arise from all parts of the organism, for the muscles and skin as well as the viscera. To the latter, however, he inclined to attribute the major rôle—on "the visceral and organic part of the expression," he wrote, "it is probable that the chief part of the felt emotion depends." We may distinguish, therefore, his two sources of the afferent stream. We shall now consider critically the visceral source. In connection therewith we shall comment on Lange's idea that the vasomotor center holds the explanation of emotional experience.

TOTAL SEPARATION OF THE VISCERA FROM THE CENTRAL NERVOUS SYSTEM DOES NOT ALTER EMOTIONAL BEHAVIOR

Sherrington (2) transected the spinal cord and the vagus nerves of dogs so as to destroy any connection of the brain with the heart, the lungs, the stomach and the bowels, the spleen, the liver and other abdominal organs —indeed, to isolate all the structures in which formerly feelings were supposed to reside. Recently Lewis and Britton and I (3) have succeeded in keeping cats in a healthy state for many months after removal of the entire sympathetic division of the autonomic system, the division which operates in great excitement. Thus all vascular reactions controlled by the vasomotor center were abolished; secretion from the adrenal medulla could no longer be evoked; the action of the stomach and intestines could not be inhibited, the hairs could not be erected, and the liver could not be called upon to liberate sugar into the blood stream. These extensively disturbing operations had little if any affect on the emotional responses of the animals. In one of Sherrington's dogs, having a "markedly emotional temperament," the surgical reduction of the sensory field caused no obvious change in her emotional behavior; "her anger, her joy, her disgust, and when provocation arose, her fear, remained as evident as ever." And in the sympathectomized cats all superficial signs of rage were manifested in the presence of a barking dog—hissing, growling, retraction of the ears, showing of the teeth, lifting of the paw to strike—*except* erection of the hairs. Both sets of animals behaved with full emotional expression in all the organs still connected with the brain; the only failure was in organs disconnected. The absence of reverberation from the viscera did not alter in any respect the appropriate emotional display; its only abbreviation was surgical.

As Sherrington has remarked, with reference to his head-and-shoulder dogs, it is difficult to think that the perception initiating the wrathful expression should bring in sequel angry conduct and yet have been impotent to produce "angry feeling."

At this point interpretations differ. Angell (4) has argued that Sherrington's experiments afford no evidence that visceral sensation plays no part in the emotional psychosis, and further that they do not prove that the psychic state, "emotion," precedes its "expression." And Perry (5) has declared that whether, in the absence of sensations from the organs surgically isolated, the emotion is *felt* remains quite undecided.

It must be admitted, of course, that we have no real basis for either affirming or denying the presence of "felt emotion" in these reduced animals. We have a basis, however, for judging their relation to the James-Lange theory. James attributed the chief part of the felt emotion to sensations from the viscera—Lange attributed it wholly to sensations from the circulatory system. Both affirmed that if these organic sensations are removed *imaginatively* from an emotional experience nothing is left. Sherrington and the Harvard group varied this procedure by removing the sensations *surgically*. In their animals all visceral disturbances through sympathetic channels—the channels for nervous discharge in great excitement—were abolished. The possibility of return impulses by these channels, and in Sherrington's animals by vagus channels as well, were likewise abolished. According to James's statement of the theory the felt emotion should have very largely disappeared, and according to Lange's statement it should have wholly disappeared (without stimulation of our vasomotor system, it will be recalled, impressions of the outer world "would arouse neither joy nor anger, would give us neither care nor fear"). The animals *acted*, however, insofar as nervous connections permitted, with no lessening of the intensity of emotional display. In other words, operations which, in terms of the theory, largely or completely destroy emotional feeling, nevertheless leave the animals behaving as angrily, as joyfully, as fearfully as ever.

THE SAME VISCERAL CHANGES OCCUR IN VERY DIFFERENT EMOTIONAL STATES AND IN NONEMOTIONAL STATES

The preganglionic fibers of the sympathetic division of the autonomic system are so related to the outlying neurones, as we have seen, that the resulting innervation of smooth muscles and glands throughout the body is not particular but diffuse. At the same time with the diffuse emission of sympathetic impulses adrenin is poured into the blood. Since it is thereby generally distributed to all parts and has the same effects as the sympathetic impulses wherever it acts, the humoral and the neural agents coöperate in producing diffuse effects. In consequence of these arrangements the sympathetic system goes into action as a unit—there may be minor variations as, for example, the presence or absence of sweating, but in the main features integration is characteristic.

The visceral changes wrought by sympathetic stimulation may be listed as follows: acceleration of the heart, contraction of arterioles, dilation of bronchioles, increase of blood sugar, inhibition of activity of the digestive glands, inhibition of gastro-intestinal peristalsis, sweating, discharge of adrenin, widening of the pupils and erection of hairs. These changes are seen in great excitement under any circumstances. They occur in such readily distinguishable emotional states as fear and rage. Fever (6) and also exposure to cold (7) are known to induce most of the changes—certainly a faster heart rate, vasoconstriction, increased blood sugar, discharge of adrenin and erection of the hairs. Asphyxia at the stimulating stage evokes all the changes enumerated above, with the possible exception of sweating. A too great reduction of blood sugar by insulin provokes the "hypoglycemic reaction"—characterized by pallor, rapid heart, dilated pupils, discharge of adrenin, increase of blood sugar and profuse sweating (8).

In this group of conditions which bring about in the viscera changes which are typical of sympathetic discharge are such intense and distinct emotions as fear and rage, such relatively mild affective states as those attending chilliness, hypoglycemia and difficult respiration, and such a markedly different experience as that attending the onset of fever. The responses in the viscera seem too uniform to offer a satisfactory means of distinguishing emotions which are very different in subjective quality. Furthermore, if the emotions were due to afferent impulses from the viscera, we should expect not only that fear and rage would feel alike but that chilliness, hypoglycemia, asphyxia, and fever should feel like them. Such is not the case.

In commenting on this criticism of the James-Lange theory Angell (4) admits that there may be a considerable matrix of substantially identical visceral excitement for some emotions, but urges that the differential features may be found in the extra-visceral disturbances, particularly in the differences of tone in skeletal muscles. Perry (5) likewise falls back on the conformation of the proprioceptive patterns, on the "motor set" of the expression, to provide the distinctive elements of the various affective states. The possible contribution of skeletal muscles to the genesis of the felt emotion will be considered later. At present the fact may be emphasized that Lange derived no part of the emotional psychosis from that source; and James attributed to it a minor rôle—the chief part of the felt emotion depended on the visceral and organic part of the expression.

THE VISCERA ARE RELATIVELY INSENSITIVE STRUCTURES

There is a common belief that the more deeply the body is penetrated the more sensitive does it become. Such is not the fact. Whereas in a spinal nerve trunk the sensory nerve fibers are probably always more numerous than the motor, in the nerves distributed to the viscera the afferent (sensory) fibers may be only one-tenth as numerous as the efferent (9). We are unaware of the contractions and relaxations of the stomach and intestines during digestion, of the rubbing of the stomach against the diaphragm, of the squeezing motions of the spleen, of the processes in the liver—only after long search have we learned what is occurring in these organs. Surgeons have found that the alimentary tract can be cut, torn, crushed or burned in operations on the unanesthetized human subject without evoking any feeling of discomfort. We can feel the thumping of the heart because it presses against the chest wall, we can also feel the throbbing of blood vessels because they pass through tissues well supplied with sensory nerves, and we may have abdominal pains but apparently because there are pulls on the parietal peritoneum (10). Normally the visceral processes are extraordinarily undemonstrative. And even when the most marked changes are induced in them, as when adrenalin acts, the results, as we shall see, are sensations mainly attributable to effects on the cardiovascular system.

VISCERAL CHANGES ARE TOO SLOW TO BE A SOURCE OF EMOTIONAL FEELING

The viscera are composed of smooth muscle and glands—except the heart, which is modified striate muscle. The motions of the body with which we are familiar results from quick-acting striate muscle, having a true latent period of less than 0.001 second. Notions of the speed of bodily processes acquired by observing the action of skeletal muscle we should not apply to other structures. Smooth muscle and glands respond with relative sluggishness. Although Stewart (11) found that the latent period of smooth muscle of the cat was about 0.25 second, Sertoli (12) observed that it lasted for 0.85 second in the dog and 0.8 second in the horse. Langley (13) reported a latent period of 2 to 4 seconds on stimulating the *chorda tympani* nerve supply to the submaxillary salivary gland; and Pavlov (14) a latent period of about 6 *minutes* on stimulating the vagus, the secretory nerve of the gastric glands. Again, Wells and Forbes (15) noted that the latent period of the psychogalvanic reflex (in man), which appears to be a phenomenon due to sweat glands, was about 3 seconds.

In contrast to these long delays before peripheral action in visceral structures barely starts are the observations of Wells (16); he found that the latent period of affective reactions to pictures of men and women ended not uncommonly within 0.8 second. More recent studies with odors as stimuli have yielded a similar figure (personal communication). According to the James-Lange theory, however, these affective reactions result from reverberations from the viscera. But how is that possible? To the long latent periods of smooth muscles and glands, cited above, there must be added the time required for the nerve impulses to pass from the brain to the periphery and thence back to the brain again. It is clear that the organic changes could not occur soon enough to be the occasion for the appearance of affective states, certainly not the affective states studied by Wells.

ARTIFICIAL INDUCTION OF THE VISCERAL CHANGES TYPICAL OF STRONG EMOTIONS DOES NOT PRODUCE THEM

That adrenin acts in the body so as to mimic the action of sympathetic nerve impulses has repeatedly been mentioned. When injected directly into the blood stream or under the skin it induces dilation of the bronchioles, constriction of blood vessels, liberation of sugar from the liver, stoppage of gastro-intestinal functions, and other changes such as are characteristic of intense emotions. If the emotions are the consequence of the visceral changes we should reasonably expect them, in accordance with the postulates of the James-Lange theory, to follow these changes in all cases. Incidental observations on students who received injections of adrenalin sufficiently large to produce general bodily effects have brought out the fact that no specific emotion was experienced by them—a few who had been in athletic competitions testified to feeling "on edge," "keyed up," just as before a race (17). In a careful study of the effects of adrenin on a large number of normal and abnormal persons Marañon (18) has reported that the subjective experiences included sensations of precardial or epigastric palpitation, of diffuse arterial throbbing, of oppression in the chest and tightness in the throat, of trembling, of chilliness, of dryness of the mouth, of nervousness, malaise and weakness. Associated with these sensations there was *in certain cases* an indefinite affective state coldly appreciated, and without real emotion. The subjects remarked, "I feel as if afraid," "as if awaiting a great joy," "as if moved," "as if I were going to weep without knowing why," "as if I had a great fright yet am calm," "as if they are about to do something to me." In other words, as Marañon remarks, a clear distinction is drawn "between the perception of the peripheral phenomena of vegetative emotion (i.e., the bodily changes) and the psychical emotion proper, which does not exist and which permits the subjects to report on the vegetative syndrome with serenity, without true feeling." In a smaller number of the affected cases a real emotion developed, usually that of sorrow, with tears, sobs and sighings. This occurs, however, "only when the emotional predisposition of the patient is very marked," notably in hyperthyroid cases. In some instances Marañon found that this state supervened only when the adrenin was injected after a talk with the patients concerning their sick children or their dead parents. In short, only when an emotional mood already exists does adrenalin have a supporting effect.

From the evidence adduced by Marañon we may conclude that adrenin induces in human beings typical bodily changes which are reported as sensations, that in some cases these sensations are reminiscent of previous emotional experiences but do not renew or revive those experiences, that in exceptional cases of preparatory emotional sensitization the bodily changes may tip the scales towards a true affective disturbance. These last cases are exceptional, however, and are not the usual phenomena as James and Lange supposed. In normal conditions the bodily changes, though well marked, do not provoke emotion.

The numerous events occurring in the viscera in consequence of great excitement, as detailed in earlier chapters, have been interpreted as supporting the James-Lange theory (19). From the evidence just presented it should be clear that that interpretation is unwarranted. Since visceral processes are fortunately not a considerable source of sensation, since even extreme disturbances in them yield no noteworthy emotional experience, we can further understand now why these disturbances cannot serve as a means for discriminating between such pronounced emotions as fear and rage, why chilliness, asphyxia, hyperglycemia and fever, though attended by these disturbances, are not attended by emotion, and also why total exclusion of visceral factors from emotional expression makes no difference in emotional behavior. It is because the returns from the thoracic and abdominal "sounding-board," to use James's word, are very faint indeed, that they play such a minor rôle in the affective complex. The processes going on in the thoracic and abdominal organs in consequence of sympathetic activity are truly remarkable and various; their value to the organism, however, is not to add richness and flavor to experience, but rather to adapt the internal economy so that in spite of shifts of outer circumstance the even tenor of the inner life will not be profoundly disturbed.

REFERENCES

1. JAMES and LANGE, The Emotions (Baltimore, 1922).
2. SHERRINGTON, Proceedings of the Royal Society of London, lxvi (1900), p. 397.
3. CANNON, LEWIS and BRITTON, Boston Medical and Surgical Journal, cxcvii (1927), p. 514.
4. ANGELL, The Psychological Review, xxiii (1916), p. 259.
5. PERRY, General Theory of Value (New York, 1926), p. 298.
6. CANNON and PEREIRA, Proceedings of the National Academy of Sciences, x (1924), p. 247.
7. CANNON, QUERIDO, BRITTON and BRIGHT, American Journal of Physiology, lxxix (1927), p. 466.
8. CANNON, McIVER and BLISS, ibid., lxix (1924), p. 46.
9. LANGLEY and ANDERSON, Journal of Physiology, xvii (1894), p. 185.
10. LENNANDER, et al., Journal of the American Medical Association, xlix (1907), p. 836; see also p. 1015.
11. STEWART, American Journal of Physiology, iv (1900), p. 192.
12. SERTOLI, Archives Italiennes de Biologie, iii (1883), p. 86.
13. LANGLEY, Journal of Physiology, x (1889), p. 300.
14. PAVLOV and SCHUMOWA-SIMANOWSKAJA, Archiv für Physiologie (1895), p. 66.
15. WELLS and FORBES, Archives of Psychology, ii (1911), p. 8.
16. WELLS, Journal of Experimental Psychology, viii (1925), p. 64.
17. PEABODY, STURGIS, TOMPKINS and WEARN, The American Journal of the Medical Sciences, clxi (1921), p. 508; also personal communication from J. T. WEARN.
18. MARAÑON, Revue Française d'Endocrinologie, ii (1924), p. 301.
19. HUMPHREY, The Story of Man's Mind (Boston, 1923), p. 211.

Cognitive, Social, and Physiological Determinants of Emotional State [1]

Stanley Schachter and Jerome E. Singer

Columbia University   Pennsylvania State University

The problem of which cues, internal or external, permit a person to label and identify his own emotional state has been with us since the days that James (1890) first tendered his doctrine that "the bodily changes follow directly the perception of the exciting fact, and that our feeling of the same changes as they occur *is* the emotion" (p. 449). Since we are aware of a variety of feeling and emotion states, it should follow from James' proposition that the various emotions will be accompanied by a variety of differentiable bodily states. Following James' pronouncement, a formidable number of studies were undertaken in search of the physiological differentiators of the emotions. The results, in these early days, were almost uniformly negative. All of the emotional states experimentally manipulated were characterized by a general pattern of excitation of the sympathetic nervous system but there appeared to be no clear-cut physiological discriminators of the various emotions. This pattern of results was so consistent from experiment to experiment that Cannon (1929) offered, as one of the crucial criticisms of the James-Lange theory, the fact that "the same visceral changes occur in very different emotional states and in non-emotional states" (p. 351).

More recent work, however, has given some indication that there may be differentiators. Ax (1953) and Schachter (1957) studied fear and anger. On a large number of indices both of these states were characterized by a similarly high level of autonomic activation but on several indices they did differ in the degree of activation. Wolf and Wolff (1947) studied a subject with a gastric fistula and were able to distinguish two patterns in the

Reprinted from *Psychological Review*, 1962, 69, 379–399.

---

[1] This experiment is part of a program of research on cognitive and physiological determinants of emotional state which is being conducted at the Department of Social Psychology at Columbia University under PHS Research Grant M-2584 from the National Institute of Mental Health, United States Public Health Service. This experiment was conducted at the Laboratory for Research in Social Relations at the University of Minnesota.

The authors wish to thank Jean Carlin and Ruth Hase, the physicians in the study, and Bibb Latané and Leonard Weller who were the paid participants.

physiological responses of the stomach wall. It should be noted, though, that for many months they studied their subject during and following a great variety of moods and emotions and were able to distinguish only two patterns.

Whether or not there are physiological distinctions among the various emotional states must be considered an open question. Recent work might be taken to indicate that such differences are at best rather subtle and that the variety of emotion, mood, and feeling states are by no means matched by an equal variety of visceral patterns.

This rather ambiguous situation has led Ruckmick (1936), Hunt, Cole, and Reis (1958), Schachter (1959) and others to suggest that cognitive factors may be major determinants of emotional states. Granted a general pattern of sympathetic excitation as characteristic of emotional states, granted that there may be some differences in pattern from state to state, it is suggested that one labels, interprets, and identifies this stirred-up state in terms of the characteristics of the precipitating situation and one's apperceptive mass. This suggests, then, that an emotional state may be considered a function of a state of physiological arousal[2] and of a cognition appropriate to this state of arousal. The cognition, in a sense, exerts a steering function. Cognitions arising from the immediate situation as interpreted by past experience provide the framework within which one understands and labels his feelings. It is the cognition which determines whether the state of physiological arousal will be labeled as "anger," "joy," "fear," or whatever.

In order to examine the implications of this formulation let us consider the fashion in which these two elements, a state of physiological arousal and cognitive factors, would interact in a variety of situations. In most emotion inducing situations, of course, the two factors are completely interrelated. Imagine a man walking alone down a dark alley, a figure with a gun suddenly appears. The perception-cognition "figure with a gun" in some fashion initiates a state of physiological arousal; this state of arousal is interpreted in terms of knowledge about dark alleys and guns and the state of arousal is labeled "fear." Similarly a student who unexpectedly learns that he has made Phi Beta Kappa may experience a state of arousal which he will label "joy."

Let us now consider circumstances in which these two elements, the physiological and the cognitive, are, to some extent, independent. First, is the state of physiological arousal alone sufficient to induce an emotion? Best evidence indicates that it is not. Marañon[3] (1924), in a fascinating study, (which was replicated by Cantril & Hunt, 1932, and Landis & Hunt, 1932) injected 210 of his patients with the sympathomimetic agent adrenalin and then simply asked them to introspect. Seventy-one percent of his subjects simply reported their physical symptoms with no emotional overtones; 29% of the subjects responded in an apparently emotional fashion. Of these the

[2] Though our experiments are concerned exclusively with the physiological changes produced by the injection of adrenalin, which appear to be primarily the result of sympathetic excitation, the term physiological arousal is used in preference to the more specific "excitation of the sympathetic nervous system" because there are indications, to be discussed later, that this formulation is applicable to a variety of bodily states.

[3] Translated copies of Marañon's (1924) paper may be obtained by writing to the senior author.

great majority described their feelings in a fashion that Marañon labeled "cold" or "as if" emotions, that is, they made statements such as "I feel *as if* I were afraid" or "*as if* I were awaiting a great happiness." This is a sort of emotional "déjà vu" experience; these subjects are neither happy nor afraid, they feel "as if" they were. Finally a very few cases apparently reported a genuine emotional experience. However, in order to produce this reaction in most of these few cases, Marañon (1924) points out:

> One must suggest a memory with strong affective force but not so strong as to produce an emotion in the normal state. For example, in several cases we spoke to our patients before the injection of their sick children or dead parents and they responded calmly to this topic. The same topic presented later, during the adrenal commotion, was sufficient to trigger emotion. This adrenal commotion places the subject in a situation of 'affective imminence' (pp. 307–308).

Apparently, then, to produce a genuinely emotional reaction to adrenalin, Marañon was forced to provide such subjects with an appropriate cognition.

Though Marañon (1924) is not explicit on his procedure, it is clear that his subjects knew that they were receiving an injection and in all likelihood knew that they were receiving adrenalin and probably had some order of familiarity with its effects. In short, though they underwent the pattern of sympathetic discharge common to strong emotional states, at the same time they had a completely appropriate cognition or explanation as to why they felt this way. This, we would suggest, is the reason so few of Marañon's subjects reported any emotional experience.

Consider now a person in a state of physiological arousal for which no immediately explanatory or appropriate cognitions are available. Such a state could result were one covertly to inject a subject with adrenalin or, unknown to him, feed the subject a sympathomimetic drug such as ephedrine. Under such conditions a subject would be aware of palpitations, tremor, face flushing, and most of the battery of symptoms associated with a discharge of the sympathetic nervous system. In contrast to Marañon's (1924) subjects he would, at the same time, be utterly unaware of why he felt this way. What would be the consequence of such a state?

Schachter (1959) has suggested that precisely such a state would lead to the arousal of "evaluative needs" (Festinger, 1954), that is, pressures would act on an individual in such a state to understand and label his bodily feelings. His bodily state grossly resembles the condition in which it has been at times of emotional excitement. How would he label his present feelings? It is suggested, of course, that he will label his feelings in terms of his knowledge of the immediate situation.[4] Should he at the time be with a beautiful woman he might decide that he was wildly in love or sexually excited. Should he be at a gay party, he might, by comparing himself to others, decide that he was extremely happy and euphoric. Should he be arguing with his wife, he might explode in fury and hatred. Or, should the situation be completely inappropriate he could decide that he was excited about something that had recently happened to him or,

---

[4] This suggestion is not new for several psychologists have suggested that situational factors should be considered the chief differentiators of the emotions. Hunt, Cole, and Reis (1958) probably make this point most explicitly in their study distinguishing among fear, anger, and sorrow in terms of situational characteristics.

simply, that he was sick. In any case, it is our basic assumption that emotional states are a function of the interaction of such cognitive factors with a state of physiological arousal.

This line of thought, then, leads to the following propositions:

1. Given a state of physiological arousal for which an individual has no immediate explanation, he will "label" this state and describe his feelings in terms of the cognitions available to him. To the extent that cognitive factors are potent determiners of emotional states, it could be anticipated that precisely the same state of physiological arousal could be labeled "joy" or "fury" or "jealousy" or any of a great diversity of emotional labels depending on the cognitive aspects of the situation.

2. Given a state of physiological arousal for which an individual has a completely appropriate explanation (e.g., "I feel this way because I have just received an injection of adrenalin") no evaluative needs will arise and the individual is unlikely to label his feelings in terms of the alternative cognitions available.

Finally, consider a condition in which emotion inducing cognitions are present but there is no state of physiological arousal. For example, an individual might be completely aware that he is in great danger but for some reason (drug or surgical) remain in a state of physiological quiescence. Does he experience the emotion "fear"? Our formulation of emotion as a joint function of a state of physiological arousal and an appropriate cognition, would, of course, suggest that he does not, which leads to our final proposition.

3. Given the same cognitive circumstances, the individual will react emotionally or describe his feelings as emotions only to the extent that he experiences a state of physiological arousal.[5]

PROCEDURE

The experimental test of these propositions requires (a) the experimental manipulation of a state of physiological arousal, (b) the manipulation of the extent to which the subject has an appropriate or proper explanation of his bodily state, and (c) the creation of situations from which explanatory cognitions may be derived.

In order to satisfy the first two experimental requirements, the experiment was cast in the framework of a study of the effects of vitamin supplements on vision. As soon as a subject arrived, he was taken to a private room and told by the experimenter:

> In this experiment we would like to make various tests of your vision. We are particularly interested in how certain vitamin compounds and vitamin supplements affect the visual skills. In particular, we want to find out how the vitamin compound called 'Suproxin' affects your vision.

[5] In his critique of the James-Lange theory of emotion, Cannon (1929) also makes the point that sympathectomized animals and patients do seem to manifest emotional behavior. This criticism is, of course, as applicable to the above proposition as it was to the James-Lange formulation. We shall discuss the issues involved in later papers.

What we would like to do, then, if we can get your permission, is to give you a small injection of Suproxin. The injection itself is mild and harmless; however, since some people do object to being injected we don't want to talk you into anything. Would you mind receiving a Suproxin injection?

If the subject agrees to the injection (and all but 1 of 185 subjects did) the experimenter continues with instructions we shall describe shortly, then leaves the room. In a few minutes a physician enters the room, briefly repeats the experimenter's instructions, takes the subject's pulse and then injects him with Suproxin.

Depending upon condition, the subject receives one of two forms of Suproxin—epinephrine or a placebo.

Epinephrine or adrenalin is a sympathomimetic drug whose effects, with minor exceptions, are almost a perfect mimicry of a discharge of the sympathetic nervous system. Shortly after injection systolic blood pressure increases markedly, heart rate increases somewhat, cutaneous blood flow decreases, while muscle and cerebral blood flow increase, blood sugar and lactic acid concentration increase, and respiration rate increases slightly. As far as the subject is concerned the major subjective symptoms are palpitation, tremor, and sometimes a feeling of flushing and accelerated breathing. With a subcutaneous injection (in the dosage administered to our subjects), such effects usually begin within 3–5 minutes of injection and last anywhere from 10 minutes to an hour. For most subjects these effects are dissipated within 15–20 minutes after injection.

Subjects receiving epinephrine received a subcutaneous injection of ½ cubic centimeter of a 1 : 1000 solution of Winthrop Laboratory's Suprarenin, a saline solution of epinephrine bitartrate.

Subjects in the placebo condition received a subcutaneous injection of ½ cubic centimeter of saline solution. This is, of course, completely neutral material with no side effects at all.

MANIPULATING AN APPROPRIATE EXPLANATION

By "appropriate" we refer to the extent to which the subject has an authoritative, unequivocal explanation of his bodily condition. Thus, a subject who had been informed by the physician that as a direct consequence of the injection he would feel palpitations, tremor, etc. would be considered to have a completely appropriate explanation. A subject who had been informed only that the injection would have no side effects would have no appropriate explanation of his state. This dimension of appropriateness was manipulated in three experimental conditions which shall be called: Epinephrine Informed (Epi Inf), Epinephrine Ignorant (Epi Ign), and Epinephrine Misinformed (Epi Mis).

Immediately after the subject had agreed to the injection and before the physician entered the room, the experimenter's spiel in each of these conditions went as follows:

Epinephrine Informed. I should also tell you that some of our subjects have experienced side effects from the Suproxin. These side effects are transitory, that is, they will only last for about 15 or 20 minutes. What will probably happen is that your hand will start to shake, your heart will start to pound, and your face may get warm and flushed. Again these are side effects lasting about 15 or 20 minutes.

While the physician was giving the injection, she told the subject that the injection was mild and harmless and repeated this description of the symptoms that the subject could expect as a consequence of the shot. In this condition, then, subjects have a completely appropriate explanation of their bodily state. They know precisely what they will feel and why.

Epinephrine Ignorant. In this condition, when the subject agreed to the injection, the experimenter said nothing more relevant to side effects and simply left the room. While the physician was giving the injection, she told the subject that the injection was mild and harmless and would have no side effects. In this condition, then, the subject has no experimentally provided explanation for his bodily state.

Epinephrine Misinformed. I should also tell you that some of our subjects have experienced side effects from the Suproxin. These side effects are transitory, that is, they will only last for about 15 or 20 minutes. What will probably happen is that your feet will feel numb, you will have an itching sensation over parts of your body, and you may get a slight headache. Again these are side effects lasting 15 or 20 minutes.

And again, the physician repeated these symptoms while injecting the subject.

None of these symptoms, of course, are consequences of an injection of epinephrine and, in effect, these instructions provide the subject with a completely inappropriate explanation of his bodily feelings. This condition was introduced as a control condition of sorts. It seemed possible that the description of side effects in the Epi Inf condition might turn the subject introspective, self-examining, possibly slightly troubled. Differences on the dependent variable between the Epi Inf and Epi Ign conditions might, then, be due to such factors rather than to differences in appropriateness. The false symptoms in the Epi Mis condition should similarly turn the subject introspective, etc., but the instructions in this condition do not provide an appropriaite explanation of the subject's state.

Subjects in all of the above conditions were injected with epinephrine. Finally, there was a placebo condition in which subjects, who were injected with saline solution, were given precisely the same treatment as subjects in the Epi Ign condition.

PRODUCING AN EMOTION INDUCING COGNITION

Our initial hypothesis has suggested that given a state of physiological arousal for which the individual has no adequate explanation, cognitive factors can lead the individual to describe his feelings with any of a diversity of emotional labels. In order to test this hypothesis, it was decided to manipulate emotional states which can be considered quite different— euphoria and anger.

There are, of course, many ways to induce such states. In our own program of research, we have concentrated on social determinants of emotional states and have been able to demonstrate in other studies that people do evaluate their own feelings by comparing themselves with others around them (Schachter 1959; Wrightsman 1960). In this experiment we have attempted again to manipulate emotional state by social means. In one set of conditions, the subject is placed together with a stooge who has been trained to act euphorically. In a second set of conditions the subject is with a stooge trained to act in an angry fashion.

EUPHORIA

Immediately[6] after the subject had been injected, the physician left the room and the experimenter returned with a stooge whom he introduced as another subject, then said:

> Both of you have had the Suproxin shot and you'll both be taking the same tests of vision. What I ask you to do now is just wait for 20 minutes. The reason for this is simply that we have to allow 20 minutes for the Suproxin to get from the injection site into the bloodstream. At the end of 20 minutes when we are certain that most of the Suproxin has been absorbed into the bloodstream, we'll begin the tests of vision.

The room in which this was said had been deliberately put into a state of mild disarray. As he was leaving, the experimenter apologetically added:

> The only other thing I should do is to apologize for the condition of the room. I just didn't have time to clean it up. So, if you need any scratch paper or rubber bands or pencils, help yourself. I'll be back in 20 minutes to begin the vision tests.

As soon as the experimenter had left, the stooge introduced himself again, made a series of standard icebreaker comments, and then launched his routine. For observation purposes, the stooge's act was broken into a series of standard units, demarcated by a change in activity or a standard comment. In sequence, the units of the stooge's routine were the following:

1. Stooge reaches for a piece of paper and starts doodling saying, "They said we could use this for scratch, didn't they?" He doodles a fish for some 30 seconds, then says:

2. "This scrap paper isn't even much good for doodling" and crumples paper and attempts to throw it into wastebasket in far corner of the room. He misses but this leads him into a "basketball game." He crumples up other sheets of paper, shoots a few baskets, says "Two points" occasionally. He gets up and does a jump shot saying, "The old jump shot is really on today."

3. If the subject has not joined in, the stooge throws a paper basketball to the subject saying, "Here, you try it."

4. Stooge continues his game saying, "The trouble with paper basketballs is that you don't really have any control."

5. Stooge continues basketball, then gives it up saying, "This is one of my good days. I feel like a kid again. I think I'll make a plane." He makes a paper airplane saying, "I guess I'll make one of the longer ones."

6. Stooge flies plane. Gets up and retrieves plane. Flies again, etc.

7. Stooge throws plane at subject.

8. Stooge, flying plane, says, "Even when I was a kid, I was never much good at this."

9. Stooge tears off part of plane saying, "Maybe this plane can't fly but at least it's good for something." He wads up paper and making a slingshot of a rubber band begins to shoot the paper.

---

[6] It was, of course, imperative that the sequence with the stooge begin before the subject felt his first symptoms for otherwise the subject would be virtually forced to interpret his feelings in terms of events preceding the stooge's entrance. Pretests had indicated that, for most subjects, epinephrine-caused symptoms began within 3–5 minutes after injection. A deliberate attempt was made then to bring in the stooge within 1 minute after the subject's injection.

10. Shooting, the stooge says, "They [paper ammunition] really go better if you make them long. They don't work right if you wad them up."

11. While shooting, stooge notices a sloppy pile of manila folders on a table. He builds a tower of these folders, then goes to the opposite end of the room to shoot at the tower.

12. He misses several times, then hits and cheers as the tower falls. He goes over to pick up the folders.

13. While picking up, he notices, behind a portable blackboard, a pair of hula hoops which have been covered with black tape with a few wires sticking out of the tape. He reaches for these, taking one for himself and putting the other aside but within reaching distance of the subject. The stooge tries the hula hoop, saying, "This isn't as easy as it looks."

14. Stooge twirls hoop wildly on arm, saying, "Hey, look at this—this is great."

15. Stooge replaces the hula hoop and sits down with his feet on the table. Shortly thereafter the experimenter returns to the room.

This routine was completely standard, though its pace, of course, varied depending upon the subject's reaction, the extent to which he entered into this bedlam and the extent to which he initiated activities of his own. The only variations from this standard routine were those forced by the subject. Should the subject originate some nonsense of his own and request the stooge to join in, he would do so. And, he would, of course, respond to any comments initiated by the subject.

Subjects in each of the three "appropriateness" conditions and in the placebo condition were submitted to this setup. The stooge, of course, never knew in which condition any particular subject fell.

ANGER

Immediately after the injection, the experimenter brought a stooge into the subject's room, introduced the two and after explaining the necessity for a 20 minute delay for "the Suproxin to get from the injection site into the bloodstream" he continued, "We would like you to use these 20 minutes to answer these questionnaires." Then handing out the questionnaires, he concludes with, "I'll be back in 20 minutes to pick up the questionnaires and begin the tests of vision."

Before looking at the questionnaire, the stooge says to the subject,

I really wanted to come for an experiment today, but I think it's unfair for them to give you shots. At least, they should have told us about the shots when they called us; you hate to refuse, once you're here already.

The questionnaires, five pages long, start off innocently requesting face sheet information and then grow increasingly personal and insulting. The stooge, sitting directly opposite the subject, paces his own answers so that at all times subject and stooge are working on the same question. At regular points in the questionnaire, the stooge makes a series of standardized comments about the questions. His comments start off innocently enough, grow increasingly querulous, and finally he ends up in a rage. In sequence, he makes the following comments.

1. Before answering any items, he leafs quickly through the questionnaire saying, "Boy, this is a long one."

2. Question 7 on the questionnaire requests, "List the foods that you

would eat in a typical day." The stooge comments, "Oh for Pete's sake, what did I have for breakfast this morning?"

3. Question 9 asks, "Do you ever hear bells? _____. How often? _____." The stooge remarks, "Look at Question 9. How ridiculous can you get? I hear bells every time I change classes."

4. Question 13 requests, "List the childhood diseases you have had and the age at which you had them" to which the stooge remarks, "I get annoyed at this childhood disease question. I can't remember what childhood diseases I had, and especially at what age. Can you?"

5. Question 17 asks "What is your father's average annual income?" and the stooge says, "This really irritates me. It's none of their business what my father makes. I'm leaving that blank."

6. Question 25 presents a long series of items such as "Does not bathe or wash regularly," "Seems to need psychiatric care," etc. and requests the respondent to write down for which member of his immediate family each item seems most applicable. The question specifically prohibits the answer "None" and each item must be answered. The stooge says, "I'll be damned if I'll fill out Number 25. 'Does not bathe or wash regularly'—that's a real insult." He then angrily crosses out the entire item.

7. Question 28 reads:

"How many times each week do you have sexual intercourse?" 0–1 _____ 2–3 _____ 4–6 _____ 7 and over _____. The stooge bites out, "The hell with it! I don't have to tell them all this."

8. The stooge sits sullenly for a few moments then he rips up his questionnaire, crumples the pieces and hurls them to the floor, saying, "I'm not wasting any more time. I'm getting my books and leaving" and he stamps out of the room.

9. The questionnaire continues for eight more questions ending with: "With how many men (other than your father) has your mother had extramarital relationships?"

4 and under _____: 5–9 _____: 10 and over _____.

Subjects in the Epi Ign, Epi Inf and Placebo conditions were run through this "anger" inducing sequence. The stooge, again, did not know to which condition the subject had been assigned.

In summary, this is a seven condition experiment which, for two different emotional states, allows us (a) to evaluate the effects of "appropriateness" on emotional inducibility and (b) to begin to evaluate the effects of sympathetic activation on emotional inducibility. In schematic form the conditions are the following:

EUPHORIA	ANGER
Epi Inf	Epi Inf
Epi Ign	Epi Ign
Epi Mis	Placebo
Placebo	

The Epi Mis condition was not run in the Anger sequence. This was originally conceived as a control condition and it was felt that its inclusion in the Euphoria conditions alone would suffice as a means of evaluating the possible artifactual effect of the Epi Inf instructions.

MEASUREMENT

Two types of measures of emotional state were obtained. Standardized observation through a one-way mirror was the technique used to assess the subject's behavior. To what extent did he act euphoric or angry? Such behavior can be considered in a way as a "semiprivate" index of mood for as far as the subject was concerned, his emotional behavior could be known only to the other person in the room—presumably another student. The second type of measure was self-report in which, on a variety of scales, the subject indicated his mood of the moment. Such measures can be considered "public" indices of mood for they would, of course, be available to the experimenter and his associates.

OBSERVATION

Euphoria. For each of the first 14 units of the stooge's standardized routine an observer kept a running chronicle of what the subject did and said. For each unit the observer coded the subject's behavior in one or more of the following categories:

Category 1: Joins in activity. If the subject entered into the stooge's activities, e.g., if he made or flew airplanes, threw paper basketballs, hula hooped, etc., his behavior was coded in this category.

Category 2: Initiates new activity. A subject was so coded if he gave indications of creative euphoria, that is, if on his own, he initiated behavior outside of the stooge's routine. Instances of such behavior would be the subject who threw open the window and, laughing, hurled paper basketballs at passersby; or, the subject who jumped on a table and spun one hula hoop on his leg and the other on his neck.

Categories 3 and 4: Ignores or watches stooge. Subjects who paid flatly no attention to the stooge or who, with or without comment, simply watched the stooge without joining in his activity were coded in these categories.

For any particular unit of behavior, the subject's behavior was coded in one or more of these categories. To test reliability of coding two observers independently coded two experimental sessions. The observers agreed completely on the coding of 88% of the units.

Anger. For each of the units of stooge behavior, an observer recorded the subject's responses and coded them according to the following category scheme:

Category 1: Agrees. In response to the stooge the subject makes a comment indicating that he agrees with the stooge's standardized comment or that he, too, is irked by a particular item on the questionnaire. For example, a subject who responded to the stooge's comment on the "father's income" question by saying, "I don't like that kind of personal question either" would be so coded (scored +2).

Category 2: Disagrees. In response to the stooge's comment, the subject makes a comment which indicates that he disagrees with the stooge's meaning or mood; e.g., in response to the stooge's comment on the "father's income" question, such a subject might say, "Take it easy, they probably have a good reason for wanting the information" (scored −2).

Category 3: Neutral. A noncommittal or irrelevant response to the stooge's remark (scored 0).

Category 4: Initiates agreement or disagreement. With no instigation by the stooge, a subject, so coded, would have volunteered a remark indicating that he felt the same way or, alternatively, quite differently than the stooge. Examples would be "Boy I hate this kind of thing" or "I'm enjoying this" (scored +2 or −2).

Category 5: Watches. The subject makes no verbal response to the stooge's comment but simply looks directly at him (scored 0).

Category 6: Ignores. The subject makes no verbal response to the stooge's comment nor does he look at him; the subject, paying no attention at all to the stooge, simply works at his own questionnaire (scored −1).

A subject was scored in one or more of these categories for each unit of stooge behavior. To test reliability, two observers independently coded three experimental sessions. In order to get a behavioral index of anger, observation protocol was scored according to the values presented in parentheses after each of the above definitions of categories. In a unit-by-unit comparison, the two observers agreed completely on the scoring of 71% of the units jointly observed. The scores of the two observers differed by a value of 1 or less for 88% of the units coded and in not a single case did the two observers differ in the direction of their scoring of a unit.

SELF REPORT OF MOOD AND PHYSICAL CONDITION

When the subject's session with the stooge was completed, the experimenter returned to the room, took pulses and said:

Before we proceed with the vision tests, there is one other kind of information which we must have. We have found, as you can probably imagine, that there are many thing beside Suproxin that affect how well you see in our tests. How hungry you are, how tired you are, and even the mood you're in at the time—whether you feel happy or irritated at the time of testing will affect how well you see. To understand the data we collect on you, then, we must be able to figure out which effects are due to causes such as these and which are caused by Suproxin.

The only way we can get such information about your physical and emotional state is to have you tell us. I'll hand out these questionnaires and ask you to answer them as accurately as possible. Obviously, our data on the vision tests will only be as accurate as your description of your mental and physical state.

In keeping with this spiel, the questionnaire that the experimenter passed out contained a number of mock questions about hunger, fatigue, etc., as well as questions of more immediate relevance to the experiment. To measure mood or emotional state the following two were the crucial questions:

1. How irritated, angry or annoyed would you say you feel at present?

I don't feel at all irritated or angry (0)	I feel a little irritated and angry (1)	I feel quite irritated and angry (2)	I feel very irritated and angry (3)	I feel extremely irritated and angry (4)

2. How good or happy would you say you feel at present?

I don't feel at all happy or good (0)	I feel a little happy and good (1)	I feel quite happy and good (2)	I feel very happy and good (3)	I feel extremely happy and good (4)

To measure the physical effects of epinephrine and determine whether or not the injection had been successful in producing the necessary bodily state, the following questions were asked:

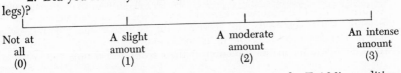

1. Have you experienced any palpitation (consciousness of your own heart beat)?

| Not at all (0) | A slight amount (1) | A moderate amount (2) | An intense amount (3) |

2. Did you feel any tremor (involuntary shaking of the hands, arms or legs)?

| Not at all (0) | A slight amount (1) | A moderate amount (2) | An intense amount (3) |

To measure possible effects of the instructions in the Epi Mis condition, the following questions were asked:

1. Did you feel any numbness in your feet?
2. Did you feel any itching sensation?
3. Did you experience any feeling of headache?

To all three of these questions was attached a four-point scale running from "Not at all" to "An intense amount."

In addition to these scales, the subjects were asked to answer two open-end questions on other physical or emotional sensations they may have experienced during the experimental session. A final measure of bodily state was pulse rate which was taken by the physician or the experimenter at two times—immediately before the injection and immediately after the session with the stooge.

When the subjects had completed these questionnaires, the experimenter announced that the experiment was over, explained the deception and its necessity in detail, answered any questions, and swore the subjects to secrecy. Finally, the subjects answered a brief questionnaire about their experiences, if any, with adrenalin and their previous knowledge or suspicion of the experimental setup. There was no indication that any of the subjects had known about the experiment beforehand but 11 subjects were so extremely suspicious of some crucial feature of the experiment that their data were automatically discarded.

SUBJECTS

The subjects were all male, college students taking classes in introductory psychology at the University of Minnesota. Some 90% of the students in these classes volunteer for a subject pool for which they receive two extra points on their final exam for every hour that they serve as experimental subjects. For this study the records of all potential subjects were cleared with the Student Health Service in order to insure that no harmful effects would result from the injections.

EVALUATION OF THE EXPERIMENTAL DESIGN

The ideal test of our propositions would require circumstances which our experiment is far from realizing. First, the proposition that: "A state of physiological arousal for which an individual has no immediate explanation will lead him to label this state in terms of the cognitions available to him" obviously requires conditions under which the subject does not and cannot have a proper explanation of his bodily state. Though we toyed with such fantasies as ventilating the experimental room with vaporized adrenalin, reality forced us to rely on the disguised injection of Suproxin—a technique which was far from ideal for no matter what the experimenter told them, some subjects would inevitably attribute their feelings to the injection. To the extent that subjects did so, differences between the several appropriateness conditions should be attenuated.

Second, the proposition that: "Given the same cognitive circumstances the individual will react emotionally only to the extent that he experiences a state of physiological arousal" requires for its ideal test the manipulation of states of physiological arousal and of physiological quiescence. Though there is no question that epinephrine effectively produces a state of arousal, there is also no question that a placebo does not prevent physiological arousal. To the extent that the experimental situation effectively produces sympathetic stimulation in placebo subjects, the proposition is difficult to test, for such a factor would attenuate differences between epinephrine and placebo subjects.

Both of these factors, then, can be expected to interfere with the test of our several propositions. In presenting the results of this study, we shall first present condition by condition results and then evaluate the effect of these two factors on experimental differences.

RESULTS

EFFECTS OF THE INJECTIONS ON BODILY STATE

Let us examine first the success of the injections at producing the bodily state required to examine the propositions at test. Does the injection of epinephrine produce symptoms of sympathetic discharge as compared with the placebo injection? Relevant data are presented in Table 1 where it can be immediately seen that on all items subjects who were in epinephrine conditions show considerably more evidence of sympathetic activation than do subjects in placebo conditions. In all epinephrine conditions pulse rate increases significantly when compared with the decrease characteristic of the placebo conditions. On the scales it is clear that epinephrine subjects experience considerably more palpitation and tremor than do placebo subjects. In all possible comparisons on these symptoms, the

TABLE 1

THE EFFECTS OF THE INJECTIONS ON BODILY STATE

Condition	N	Pulse		Self-rating of				
		Pre	Post	Palpitation	Tremor	Numbness	Itching	Headache
Euphoria								
Epi Inf	27	85.7	88.6	1.20	1.43	0	0.16	0.32
Epi Ign	26	84.6	85.6	1.83	1.76	0.15	0	0.55
Epi Mis	26	82.9	86.0	1.27	2.00	0.06	0.08	0.23
Placebo	26	80.4	77.1	0.29	0.21	0.09	0	0.27
Anger								
Epi Inf	23	85.9	92.4	1.26	1.41	0.17	0	0.11
Epi Ign	23	85.0	96.8	1.44	1.78	0	0.06	0.21
Placebo	23	84.5	79.6	0.59	0.24	0.14	0.06	0.06

mean scores of subjects in any of the epinephrine conditions are greater than the corresponding scores in the placebo conditions at better than the .001 level of significance. Examination of the absolute values of these scores makes it quite clear that subjects in epinephrine conditions were, indeed, in a state of physiological arousal, while most subjects in placebo conditions were in a relative state of physiological quiescence.

The epinephrine injection, of course, did not work with equal effectiveness for all subjects; indeed for a few subjects it did not work at all. Such subjects reported almost no palpitation or tremor, showed no increase in pulse and described no other relevant physical symptoms. Since for such subjects the necessary experimental conditions were not established, they were automatically excluded from the data and all further tabular presentations will not include such subjects. Table 1, however, does include the data of these subjects. There were four such subjects in euphoria conditions and one of them in anger conditions.

In order to evaluate further data on Epi Mis subjects it is necessary to note the results of the "numbness," "itching," and "headache" scales also presented in Table 1. Clearly the subjects in the Epi Mis condition do not differ on these scales from subjects in any of the other experimental conditions.

EFFECTS OF THE MANIPULATIONS ON EMOTIONAL STATE

Euphoria: Self-report. The effects of the several manipulations on emotional state in the euphoria conditions are presented in Table 2. The scores recorded in this table are derived, for each subject, by subtracting the value of the point he checks on the irritation scale from the value of the point he checks on the happiness scale. Thus, if a subject were to check the point "I feel a little irritated and angry" on the irritation scale and the point "I feel very happy and good" on the happiness scale, his score would be +2. The higher the positive value, the happier and better the subject reports himself as feeling. Though we employ an index for expositional simplicity, it should be noted that the two components of the index each yield results completely consistent with those obtained by use of this index.

Let us examine first the effects of the appropriateness instructions. Comparison of the scores for the Epi Mis and Epi Inf conditions makes it immediately clear that the experimental differences are not due to artifacts resulting from the informed instructions. In both conditions the subject was warned to expect a variety of symptoms as a consequence of the injection. In the Epi Mis condition, where the symptoms were inappropriate to the subject's bodily state the self-report score is almost twice that in the Epi Inf condition where the symptoms were completely appropriate to the subject's bodily state. It is reasonable, then, to attribute differences between informed subjects and those in other conditions to differences in manipulated appropriateness rather than to artifacts such as introspectiveness or self-examination.

It is clear that, consistent with expectations, subjects were more susceptible to the stooge's mood and consequently more euphoric when they had no explanation of their own bodily states than when they did. The means of both the Epi Ign and Epi Mis conditions are considerably greater than the mean of the Epi Inf condition.

TABLE 2

SELF-REPORT OF EMOTIONAL STATE IN THE EUPHORIA CONDITIONS

Condition	N	Self-Report scales	Comparison	p^a
Epi Inf	25	0.98	Epi Inf vs. Epi Mis	<.01
Epi Ign	25	1.78	Epi Inf vs. Epi Ign	.02
Epi Mis	26	1.90	Placebo vs. Epi Mis,	ns
Placebo	26	1.61	Ign, or Inf	

[a] All p values reported throughout paper are two-tailed.

It is of interest to note that Epi Mis subjects are somewhat more euphoric than are Epi Ign subjects. This pattern repeats itself in other data shortly to be presented. We would attribute this difference to differences in the appropriateness dimension. Though, as in the Epi Ign condition, a subject is not provided with an explanation of his bodily state, it is, of course, possible that he will provide one for himself which is not derived from his interaction with the stooge. Most reasonably he could decide for himself that he feels this way because of the injection. To the extent that he does so he should be less susceptible to the stooge. It seems probable that he would be less likely to hit on such an explanation in the Epi Mis condition than in the Epi Ign condition for in the Epi Mis condition both the experimenter and the doctor have told him that the effects of the injection would be quite different from what he actually feels. The effect of such instructions is probably to make it more difficult for the subject himself to hit on the alternative explanation described above. There is some evidence to support this analysis. In open-end questions in which subjects described their own mood and state, 28% of the subjects in the Epi Ign condition made some connection between the injection and their bodily state compared with the 16% of subjects in the Epi Mis condition who did so. It could be considered, then, that these three conditions fall along a dimension of appropriateness, with the Epi Inf condition at one extreme and the Epi Mis condition at the other.

Comparing the placebo to the epinephrine conditions, we note a pattern which will repeat itself throughout the data. Placebo subjects are less euphoric than either Epi Mis or Epi Ign subjects but somewhat more euphoric than Epi Inf subjects. These differences are not, however, statistically significant. We shall consider the epinephrine-placebo comparisons in detail in a later section of this paper following the presentation of additional relevant data. For the moment, it is clear that, by self-report manipulating appropriateness has had a very strong effect on euphoria.

Behavior. Let us next examine the extent to which the subject's behavior was affected by the experimental manipulations. To the extent that his mood has been affected, one should expect that the subject will join in the stooge's whirl of manic activity and initiate similar activities of his own. The relevant data are presented in Table 3. The column labeled "Activity index" presents summary figures on the extent to which the subject joined in the stooge's activity. This is a weighted index which reflects both the nature of the activities in which the subject engaged and the amount of

TABLE 3

BEHAVIORAL INDICATIONS OF EMOTIONAL STATE
IN THE EUPHORIA CONDITIONS

Condition	N	Activity index	Mean number of acts initiated
Epi Inf	25	12.72	.20
Epi Ign	25	18.28	.56
Epi Mis	25	22.56	.84
Placebo	26	16.00	.54

p value

Comparison	Activity index	Initiates[a]
Epi Inf vs. Epi Mis	.05	.03
Epi Inf vs. Epi Ign	ns	.08
Plac vs. Epi Mis, Ign, or Inf	ns	ns

[a] Tested by X^2 comparison of the proportion of subjects
in each condition initiating new acts.

time he was active. The index was devised by assigning the following
weights to the subject's activities: 5—hula hooping; 4—shooting with slingshot; 3—paper airplanes; 2—paper basketballs; 1—doodling; 0—does nothing.
Pretest scaling on 15 college students ordered these activities with respect
to the degree of euphoria they represented. Arbitrary weights were assigned
so that the wilder the activity, the heavier the weight. These weights are
multiplied by an estimate of the amount of time the subject spent in each
activity and the summed products make up the activity index for each subject. This index may be considered a measure of behavioral euphoria. It
should be noted that the same between-condition relationships hold for the
two components of this index as for the index itself.

The column labeled "Mean number of acts initiated" presents the data
on the extent to which the subject deviates from the stooge's routine and
initiates euphoric activities of his own.

On both behavioral indices, we find precisely the same pattern of relationships as those obtained with self-reports. Epi Mis subjects behave
somewhat more euphorically than do Epi Ign subjects who in turn behave
more euphorically than do Epi Inf subjects. On all measures, then, there
is consistent evidence that a subject will take over the stooge's euphoric
mood to the extent that he has no other explanation of his bodily state.

Again it should be noted that on these behavioral indices, Epi Ign and
Epi Mis subjects are somewhat more euphoric than placebo subjects but
not significantly so.

Anger: Self-report. Before presenting data for the anger conditions, one
point must be made about the anger manipulation. In the situation devised,
anger, if manifested, is most likely to be directed at the experimenter and
his annoyingly personal questionnaire. As we subsequently discovered, this
was rather unfortunate, for the subjects, who had volunteered for the experi-

ment for extra points on their final exam, simply refused to endanger these points by publicly blowing up, admitting their irritation to the experimenter's face or spoiling the questionnaire. Though as the reader will see, the subjects were quite willing to manifest anger when they were alone with the stooge, they hesitated to do so on material (self-ratings of mood and questionnaire) that the experimenter might see and only after the purposes of the experiment had been revealed were many of these subjects willing to admit to the experimenter that they had been irked or irritated.

This experimentally unfortunate situation pretty much forces us to rely on the behavioral indices derived from observation of the subject's presumably private interaction with the stooge. We do, however, present data on the self-report scales in Table 4. These figures are derived in the same

TABLE 4

SELF-REPORT OF EMOTIONAL STATE IN THE ANGER CONDITIONS

Condition	N	Self-Report scales	Comparison	p
Epi Inf	22	1.91	Epi Inf vs. Epi Ign	.08
Epi Ign	23	1.39	Placebo vs. Epi Ign or Inf	ns
Placebo	23	1.63		

way as the figures presented in Table 2 for the euphoria conditions, that is, the value checked on the irritation scale is subtracted from the value checked on the happiness scale. Though, for the reasons stated above, the absolute magnitude of these figures (all positive) is relatively meaningless, we can, of course, compare condition means within the set of anger conditions. With the happiness-irritation index employed, we should, of course, anticipate precisely the reverse results from those obtained in the euphoria conditions; that is, the Epi Inf subjects in the anger conditions should again be less susceptible to the stooge's mood and should, therefore, describe themselves as in a somewhat happier frame of mind than subjects in the Epi Ign condition. This is the case; the Epi Inf subjects average 1.91 on the self-report scales while the Epi Ign subjects average 1.39.

Evaluating the effects of the injections, we note again that, as anticipated, Epi Ign subjects are somewhat less happy than Placebo subjects but, once more, this is not a significant difference.

Behavior. The subject's responses to the stooge, during the period when both were filling out their questionnaires, were systematically coded to provide a behavioral index of anger. The coding scheme and the numerical values attached to each of the categories have been described in the methodology section. To arrive at an "Anger index" the numerical value assigned to a subject's responses to the stooge is summed together for the several units of stooge behavior. In the coding scheme used, a positive value to this index indicates that the subject agrees with the stooge's comment and is growing angry. A negative value indicates that the subject either disagrees with the stooge or ignores him.

The relevant data are presented in Table 5. For this analysis, the stooge's routine has been divided into two phases—the first two units of his behavior (the "long" questionnaire and "What did I have for breakfast?")

are considered essentially neutral revealing nothing of the stooge's mood; all of the following units are considered "angry" units for they begin with an irritated remark about the "bells" question and end with the stooge's fury as he rips up his questionnaire and stomps out of the room. For the neutral units, agreement or disagreement with the stooge's remarks is, of course, meaningless as an index of mood and we should anticipate no difference between conditions. As can be seen in Table 5, this is the case.

TABLE 5

BEHAVIORAL INDICATIONS OF EMOTIONAL STATE IN THE ANGER CONDITIONS

Condition	N	Neutral units	Anger units
Epi Inf	22	+0.07	−0.18
Epi Ign	23	+0.30	+2.28
Placebo	22[a]	−0.09	+0.79

Comparison for anger units	p
Epi Inf vs. Epi Ign	$< .01$
Epi Ign vs. Placebo	$< .05$
Placebo vs. Epi Inf	ns

[a] For one subject in this condition the sound system went dead and the observer could not, of course, code his reactions.

For the angry units, we must, of course, anticipate that subjects in the Epi Ign condition will be angrier than subjects in the Epi Inf condition. This is indeed the case. The Anger index for the Epi Ign condition is positive and large, indicating that these subjects have become angry, while in the Epi Inf condition the Anger index is slightly negative in value indicating that these subjects have failed to catch the stooge's mood at all. It seems clear that providing the subject with an appropriate explanation of his bodily state greatly reduces his tendency to interpret his state in terms of the cognitions provided by the stooge's angry behavior.

Finally, on this behavioral index, it can be seen that subjects in the Epi Ign condition are significantly angrier than subjects in the Placebo condition. Behaviorally, at least, the injection of epinephrine appears to have led subjects to an angrier state than comparable subjects who received placebo shots.

CONFORMATION OF DATA TO THEORETICAL EXPECTATIONS

Now that the basic data of this study have been presented, let us examine closely the extent to which they conform to theoretical expectations. If our hypotheses are correct and if this experimental design provided a perfect test for these hypotheses, it should be anticipated that in the euphoria conditions the degree of experimentally produced euphoria should vary in the following fashion:

$$\text{Epi Mis} \geqq \text{Epi Ign} > \text{Epi Inf} = \text{Placebo}$$

And in the anger conditions, anger should conform to the following pattern:

$$\text{Epi Ign} > \text{Epi Inf} = \text{Placebo}$$

In both sets of conditions, it is the case that emotional level in the Epi Mis and Epi Ign conditions is considerably greater than that achieved in the corresponding Epi Inf conditions. The results for the Placebo condition, however, are ambiguous for consistently the Placebo subjects fall between the Epi Ign and the Epi Inf subjects. This is a particularly troubling pattern for it makes it impossible to evaluate unequivocally the effects of the state of physiological arousal and indeed raises serious questions about our entire theoretical structure. Though the emotional level is consistently greater in the Epi Mis and Epi Ign conditions than in the Placebo condition, this difference is significant at acceptable probability levels only in the anger conditions.

In order to explore the problem further, let us examine the experimental factors identified earlier, which might have acted to restrain the emotional level in the Epi Ign and Epi Mis conditions. As was pointed out earlier, the ideal test of our first two hypotheses requires an experimental setup in which the subject has flatly no way of evaluating his state of physiological arousal other than by means of the experimentally provided cognitions. Had it been possible to physiologically produce a state of sympathetic activation by means other than injection, one could have approached this experimental ideal more closely than in the present setup. As it stands, however, there is always a reasonable alternative cognition available to the aroused subject—he feels the way he does because of the injection. To the extent that the subject seizes on such an explanation of his bodily state, we should expect that he will be uninfluenced by the stooge. Evidence presented in Table 6 for the anger condition and in Table 7 for the euphoria conditions indicates that this is, indeed, the case.

As mentioned earlier, some of the Epi Ign and Epi Mis subjects in their answers to the open-end questions clearly attributed their physical state to the injection, e.g., "the shot gave me the shivers." In Tables 6 and 7 such

TABLE 6

THE EFFECTS OF ATTRIBUTING BODILY STATE TO THE INJECTION
ON ANGER IN THE ANGER EPI IGN CONDITION

	N	Anger index
Self-informed subjects	3	−1.67
Others	20	+2.88
Self-informed versus Others		$p = .05$

subjects are labeled "Self-informed." In Table 6 it can be seen that the self-informed subjects are considerably less angry than are the remaining subjects; indeed, they are not angry at all. With these self-informed subjects eliminated the difference between the Epi Ign and the Placebo conditions is significant at the .01 level of significance.

Precisely the same pattern is evident in Table 7 for the euphoria conditions. In both the Epi Mis and the Epi Ign conditions, the self-informed subjects have considerably lower activity indices than do the remaining subjects. Eliminating self-informed subjects, comparison of both of these conditions with the Placebo condition yields a difference significant at the .03 level of significance. It should be noted, too, that the self-informed subjects have much the same score on the activity index as do the experimental Epi Inf subjects (Table 3).

It would appear, then, that the experimental procedure of injecting the subjects, by providing an alternative cognition, has, to some extent, obscured the effects of epinephrine. When account is taken of this artifact, the evidence is good that the state of physiological arousal is a necessary component of an emotional experience for when self-informed subjects are removed, epinephrine subjects give consistent indications of greater emotionality than do placebo subjects.

Let us examine next the fact that consistently the emotional level, both reported and behavioral, in Placebo conditions is greater than that in the Epi Inf conditions. Theoretically, of course, it should be expected that the two conditions will be equally low, for by assuming that emotional state is a joint function of a state of physiological arousal and of the appropriateness of a cognition we are, in effect, assuming a multiplicative function, so that if either component is at zero, emotional level is at zero. As noted earlier this expectation should hold if we can be sure that there is no sympathetic activation in the Placebo conditions. This asumption, of course, is completely unrealistic for the injection of placebo does not prevent sympathetic activation. The experimental situations were fairly dramatic and certainly some of the placebo subjects gave indications of physiological arousal. If our general line of reasoning is correct, it should be anticipated that the emotional level of subjects who give indications of sympathetic activity will be greater than that of subjects who do not. The relevant evidence is presented in Tables 8 and 9.

TABLE 7

THE EFFECTS OF ATTRIBUTING BODILY STATE TO THE INJECTION ON EUPHORIA IN THE EUPHORIA EPI IGN AND EPI MIS CONDITIONS

Epi Ign		
	N	Activity index
Self-informed subjects	8	11.63
Others	17	21.14
Self-informed versus Others		$p = .05$
Epi Mis		
	N	Activity index
Self-informed subjects	5	12.40
Others	20	25.10
Self-informed versus Others		$p = .10$

TABLE 8

SYMPATHETIC ACTIVATION AND EUPHORIA IN THE
EUPHORIA PLACEBO CONDITION

Subject whose:	N	Activity index
Pulse decreased	14	10.67
Pulse increased or remained same	12	23.17
Pulse decreasers versus pulse increasers or same		$p = .02$

As an index of sympathetic activation we shall use the most direct and unequivocal measure available—change in pulse rate. It can be seen in Table 1 that the predominant pattern in the Placebo condition is a decrease in pulse rate. We shall assume, therefore, that those subjects whose pulse increases or remains the same give indications of sympathetic activity while those subjects whose pulse decreases do not. In Table 8, for the euphoria condition, it is immediately clear that subjects who give indications of sympathetic activity are considerably more euphoric than are subjects who show no sympathetic activity. This relationship is, of course, confounded by the fact that euphoric subjects are considerably more active than non-euphoric subjects—a factor which independent of mood could elevate pulse rate. However, no such factor operates in the anger condition where angry subjects are neither more active nor talkative than calm subjects. It can be seen in Table 9 that Placebo subjects who show signs of sympathetic ac-

TABLE 9

SYMPATHETIC ACTIVATION AND ANGER IN ANGER
PLACEBO CONDITION

Subjects whose:	N[a]	Anger index
Pulse decreased	13	+0.15
Pulse increased or remained same	8	+1.69
Pulse decreasers versus pulse increasers or same		$p = .01$

[a] N reduced by two cases owing to failure of sound system in one case and experimenter's failure to take pulse in another.

tivation give indications of considerably more anger than do subjects who show no such signs. Conforming to expectations, sympathetic activation accompanies an increase in emotional level.

It should be noted, too, that the emotional levels of subjects showing no signs of sympathetic activity are quite comparable to the emotional level of subjects in the parallel Epi Inf conditions (see Tables 3 and 5). The similarity of these sets of scores and their uniformly low level of indicated emotionality would certainly make it appear that both factors are essential to an emotional state. When either the level of sympathetic arousal is low or a completely appropriate cognition is available, the level of emotionality is low.

DISCUSSION

Let us summarize the major findings of this experiment and examine the extent to which they support the propositions offered in the introduction of this paper. It has been suggested, first, that given a state of physiological arousal for which an individual has no explanation, he will label this state in terms of the cognitions available to him. This implies, of course, that by manipulating the cognitions of an individual in such a state we can manipulate his feelings in diverse directions. Experimental results support this proposition for following the injection of epinephrine, those subjects who had no explanation for the bodily state thus produced, gave behavioral and self-report indications that they had been readily manipulable into the disparate feeling states of euphoria and anger.

From this first proposition, it must follow that given a state of physiological arousal for which the individual has a completely satisfactory explanation, he will not label this state in terms of the alternative cognitions available. Experimental evidence strongly supports this expectation. In those conditions in which subjects were injected with epinephrine and told precisely what they would feel and why, they proved relatively immune to any effects of the manipulated cognitions. In the anger condition, such subjects did not report or show anger; in the euphoria condition, such subjects reported themselves as far less happy than subjects with an identical bodily state but no adequate knowledge of why they felt the way they did.

Finally, it has been suggested that given constant cognitive circumstances, an individual will react emotionally only to the extent that he experiences a state of physiological arousal. Without taking account of experimental artifacts, the evidence in support of this proposition is consistent but tentative. When the effects of "self-informing" tendencies in epinephrine subjects and of "self-arousing" tendencies in placebo subjects are partialed out, the evidence strongly supports the proposition.

The pattern of data, then, falls neatly in line with theoretical expectations. However, the fact that we were forced, to some extent, to rely on internal analyses in order to partial out the effects of experimental artifacts inevitably makes our conclusions somewhat tentative. In order to further test these propositions on the interaction of cognitive and physiological determinants of emotional state, a series of additional experiments, published elsewhere, was designed to rule out or overcome the operation of these artifacts. In the first of these, Schachter and Wheeler (1962) extended the range of manipulated sympathetic activation by employing three experimental groups—epinephrine, placebo, and a group injected with the sympatholytic agent, chlorpromazine. Laughter at a slapstick movie was the dependent variable and the evidence is good that amusement is a direct function of manipulated sympathetic activation.

In order to make the epinephrine-placebo comparison under conditions which would rule out the operation of any self-informing tendency, two experiments were conducted on rats. In one of these Singer (1961) demonstrated that under fear inducing conditions, manipulated by the simultaneous presentation of a loud bell, a buzzer, and a bright flashing light, rats injected with epinephrine were considerably more frightened than rats injected with a placebo. Epinephrine-injected rats defecated, urinated, and trembled more than did placebo-injected rats. In nonfear control conditions, there were no differences between epinephrine and placebo groups, neither group giving any indication of fear. In another study, Latané and Schachter (1962) demonstrated that rats injected with epinephrine were notably more capable of avoidance learning than were rats injected with a placebo. Using a modified Miller-Mowrer shuttlebox, these investigators found that during an experimental period involving 200 massed trials, 15 rats injected with epinephrine avoided shock an average of 101.2 trials while 15 placebo-injected rats averaged only 37.3 avoidances.

Taken together, this body of studies does give strong support to the propositions which generated these experimental tests. Given a state of sympathetic activation, for which no immediately appropriate explanation is available, human subjects can be readily manipulated into states of euphoria, anger, and amusement. Varying the intensity of sympathetic activation serves to vary the intensity of a variety of emotional states in both rats and human subjects.

Let us examine the implications of these findings and of this line of thought for problems in the general area of the physiology of the emotions. We have noted in the introduction that the numerous studies on physiological differentiators of emotional states have, viewed en masse, yielded quite inconclusive results. Most, though not all, of these studies have indicated no differences among the various emotional states. Since as human beings, rather than as scientists, we have no difficulty identifying, labeling, and distinguishing among our feelings, the results of these studies have long seemed rather puzzling and paradoxical. Perhaps because of this, there has been a persistent tendency to discount such results as due to ignorance or methodological inadequacy and to pay far more attention to the very few studies which demonstrate *some* sort of physiological differences among emotional states than to the very many studies which indicate no differences at all. It is conceivable, however, that these results should be taken at face value and that emotional states may, indeed, be generally characterized by a high level of sympathetic activation with few if any physiological distinguishers among the many emotional states. If this is correct, the findings of the present study may help to resolve the problem. Obviously this study does *not* rule out the possibility of physiological differences among the emotional states. It is the case, however, that given precisely the same state of epinephrine-induced sympathetic activation, we have, by means of cognitive manipulations, been able to produce in our subjects the very disparate states of euphoria and anger. It may indeed be the case that cognitive factors are major determiners of the emotional labels we apply to a common state of sympathetic arousal.

Let us ask next whether our results are specific to the state of sympathetic activation or if they are generalizable to other states of physiological arousal. It is clear that from our experiments proper, it is impossible to answer the question for our studies have been concerned largely with the effects of an epinephrine created state of sympathetic arousal. We would suggest, however, that our conclusions are generalizable to almost any pronounced internal state for which no appropriate explanation is available. This suggestion receives some support from the experiences of Nowlis and Nowlis (1956) in their program of research on the effects of drugs on mood. In their work the Nowlises typically administer a drug to groups of four subjects who are physically in one another's presence and free to interact. The Nowlises describe some of their results with these groups as follows:

At first we used the same drug for all 4 men. In those sessions seconal, when compared with placebo, increased the checking of such words as expansive, forceful, courageous, daring, elated, and impulsive. In our first statistical analysis we were confronted with the stubborn fact that when the same drug is given to all 4 men in a group, the N that has to be entered into the analysis is 1, not 4. This increases the cost of an already expensive experiment by a considerable factor, but it cannot be denied that the effects of these drugs may be and often are quite contagious. Our first attempted solution was to run tests on groups in which each man had a different drug during the same session, such as 1 on seconal, 1 on benzedrine, 1 on dramamine, and 1 on placebo. What does seconal do? Cooped up with, say, the egotistical benzedrine partner, the withdrawn, indifferent dramamine partner, and the slightly bored lactose man, the second subject reports that he is distractible, dizzy, drifting, glum, defiant, languid, sluggish, discouraged, dull, gloomy, lazy, and slow! This is not the report of mood that we got when all 4 men were on seconal. It thus appears that the moods of the partners do definitely influence the effect of seconal (p. 350).

It is not completely clear from this description whether this "contagion" of mood is more marked in drug than in placebo groups, but should this be the case, these results would certainly support the suggestion that our findings are generalizable to internal states other than that produced by an injection of epinephrine.

Finally, let us consider the implications of our formulation and data for alternative conceptualizations of emotion. Perhaps the most popular current conception of emotion is in terms of "activation theory" in the sense employed by Lindsley (1951) and Woodworth and Schlosberg (1958). As we understand this theory, it suggests that emotional states should be considered as at one end of a continuum of activation which is defined in terms of degree of autonomic arousal and of electroencephalographic measures of activation. The results of the experiment described in this paper do, of course, suggest that such a formulation is not completely adequate. It is possible to have very high degrees of activation without a subject either appearing to be or describing himself as "emotional." Cognitive factors appear to be indispensable elements in any formulation of emotion.

SUMMARY

It is suggested that emotional states may be considered a function of a state of physiological arousal and of a cognition appropriate to this state of arousal. From this follows these propositions:

1. Given a state of physiological arousal for which an individual has no immediate explanation, he will label this state and describe his feelings in terms of the cognitions available to him. To the extent that cognitive fac-

tors are potent determiners of emotional states, it should be anticipated that precisely the same state of physiological arousal could be labeled "joy" or "fury" or "jealousy" or any of a great diversity of emotional labels depending on the cognitive aspects of the situation.

2. Given a state of physiological arousal for which an individual has a completely appropriate explanation, no evaluative needs will arise and the individual is unlikely to label his feelings in terms of the alternative cognitions available.

3. Given the same cognitive circumstances, the individual will react emotionally or describe his feelings as emotions only to the extent that he experiences a state of physiological arousal.

An experiment is described which, together with the results of other studies, supports these propositions.

REFERENCES

Ax, A. F. Physiological differentiation of emotional states. *Psychosom. Med.*, 1953, **15**, 433–442.

Cannon, W. B. *Bodily changes in pain, hunger, fear and rage.* (2nd ed.) New York: Appleton, 1929.

Cantril, H., & Hunt, W. A. Emotional effects produced by the injection of adrenalin. *Amer. J. Psychol.*, 1932, **44**, 300–307.

Festinger, L. A theory of social comparison processes. *Hum. Relat.*, 1954, **7**, 114–140.

Hunt, J. McV., Cole, M. W., & Reis, E. E. Situational cues distinguishing anger, fear, and sorrow. *Amer. J. Psychol.*, 1958, **71**, 136–151.

James, W. *The principles of psychology.* New York: Holt, 1890.

Landis, C., & Hunt, W. A. Adrenalin and emotion. *Psychol. Rev.*, 1932, **39**, 467–485.

Latané, B., & Schachter, S. Adrenalin and avoidance learning. *J. Comp. physiol. Psychol.*, 1962, **65**, 369–372.

Lindsley, D. B. Emotion. In S. S. Stevens (Ed.), *Handbook of experimental psychology.* New York: Wiley, 1951. Pp. 473–516.

Marañon, G. Contribution à l'étude de l'action émotive de l'adrénaline. *Rev. Francaise Endocrinol.*, 1924, **2**, 301–325.

Nowlis, V., & Nowlis, H. H. The description and analysis of mood. *Ann. N. Y. Acad. Sci.*, 1956, **65**, 345–355.

Ruckmick, C. A. The psychology of feeling and emotion. New York: McGraw-Hill, 1936.

Schachter, J. Pain, fear, and anger in hypertensives and normotensives: A psychophysiologic study. *Psychosom. Med.*, 1957, **19**, 17–29.

Schachter, S. *The psychology of affiliation.* Stanford, Calif.: Stanford Univer. Press, 1959.

Schachter, S., & Wheeler, L. Epinephrine, chlorpromazine, and amusement. *J. abnorm. soc. Psychol.*, 1962, **65**, 121–128.

Singer, J. E. The effects of epinephrine, chlorpromazine and dibenzyline upon the fright responses of rats under stress and non-stress conditions. Unpublished doctoral dissertation, University of Minnesota, 1961.

Wolf, S., & Wolff, H. G. *Human gastric function.* New York: Oxford Univer. Press, 1947.

Woodworth, R. S., & Schlosberg, H. *Experimental psychology.* New York: Holt, 1958.

Wrightsman, L. S. Effects of waiting with others on changes in level of felt anxiety. *J. abnorm. soc. Psychol.*, 1960, **61**, 216–222.

PART SEVEN

The Development of

Conservation

The studies in this section of the book stem from the theories of just one remarkable man—Jean Piaget. Until recently most American psychologists knew about him only vaguely. They did know that he was Swiss and that he had investigated such unfamiliar and unexplored topics as animism, egocentric speech, moral justice, and conservation, and that he had done all this in unusual and nonexperimental "conversations" with children. Very few of his books had been translated into English, and those that had contained difficult syntax and many neologisms which made them obscure to the American psychologic public.

But suddenly Piaget has been "discovered," as indicated by Flavell's[1] introduction to his full-scale review and critique of him. Here the author points out that originally he had intended to devote only one or two chapters of a graduate text on theories in child development to Jean Piaget. But his study of Piaget led him to modify his plans so that, six years later, his published book had as sole topic the psychology of Piaget. There are other measures of Piaget's present stature. J. McV. Hunt[2] devoted about one half of his epochal reanalysis of the concept of intelligence to a discussion of Piaget's contributions. And a casual frequency count of articles in contemporary journals which refer to or test Piaget's concepts supports Roger Brown's[3] assertion that: "After Freud, it is Jean Piaget, I think, who has made the greatest contribution to modern psychology." (Page 197.)

Piaget has been concerned with understanding the development of intellectual operations. Thus he has dealt with such topics as the acquisition of concepts, language, and intelligence. Like Freud, he has emphasized the continuity of development from infancy through adulthood and has

[1] John H. Flavell, *The Developmental Psychology of Jean Piaget* (Princeton, New Jersey: Van Nostrand, 1963).

[2] J. McV. Hunt, *Intelligence and Experience* (New York: The Ronald Press Company, 1961).

[3] Roger Brown, *Social Psychology* (New York: The Free Press, 1965).

perceived therein an inexorable progress through a series of definable stages. For Piaget, the four main stages are the sensorimotor (0–18 months), the preoperational (18 months–7 years), the concretely operational (7–11 years), and the formally operational (11 plus). Again as in Freud's system, these stages are not discrete, nor are the age limits rigid and universal. The order is assumed to be universal, but the rate at which individual children progress through them may vary.

As we said earlier, Piaget's writing is not simple, nor are translations of it readily available. And even when an original article does appear in English, as in the *Scientific American*,[4] a thorough understanding of it will depend upon the reader's prior knowledge of the Piaget system.

The concept of conservation serves as a convenient peg on which to hang a discussion of both Piaget's theory and studies of the theory. Piaget points out that children below the concretely operational stage are not able to "conserve"; for example, they are not able to realize that the volume of a substance remains constant no matter what the shape of its container. This concept of the invariance of a substance requires the process of reversibility, which is the intellectual operation of conceptually returning to the previous condition and thus frees the subject from his dependence upon perception. Thus a child who has seen a substance divided into several parts can "visualize" (or conceptualize) the substance again as the whole only if he is intellectually capable of "reversibility." Hence one can speak of a conservation of weight, volume, number, etc.

A typical example will illustrate this. A child is presented with two identical glasses filled to the same level with a liquid, and the child agrees that both hold the same amount. Now, with the child watching, the liquid from one glass is poured into a much taller, thinner glass, and the child is asked which glass has more. Many adults, even those familiar with children, are surprised when the child is unable to conserve—to perform the mental process of reversibility—and when he replies that the taller glass has more.

This is intriguing and raises many questions. Is this typical of children of a certain age? Does it relate to past experience? Can you teach a younger child to understand this? Is it an artifact of the way you perform the experiment or of the way you phrase the questions? Several psychologists have asked the same questions. Some of the earliest research tackled the easier question—age norms. Piaget suggested that the ability to conserve appears at about the age of seven. Curious (even incredulous) investigators checked this with larger numbers of subjects and in other cultures (for example, see Lovell[5]), and found that the ages and stages conform closely to Piaget's conclusions.

More sophisticated research, however, sought answers to the question of *how* this transition from nonconservation to conservation occurred and whether it could be experimentally manipulated. A classic study, the first one in this set, is reported by Wohlwill and Lowe. They restricted their study to the conservation of number. Their objective was to "teach" a child that the number of objects remained constant even though the arrangement of

[4] Jean Piaget, "How Children Form Mathematical Concepts," *Scientific American*, 1953, 189 (5), 74–79.

[5] K. Lovell, *The Growth of Mathematical and Scientific Concepts in Children* (University of London Press, 1961).

the objects varied. They reasoned that this might be facilitated by specific kinds of training, such as:

1. *Direct reinforcement of conservation.* In this, the subjects were given 18 trials in which they were made to give the correct (conservation) response, which was then reinforced.
2. *Experience with addition and subtraction.* The thought here was that if the child saw that adding to or subtracting from the number of objects changed that number, he might then conserve when nothing was added or subtracted.
3. *Differentiation of cues.* They reasoned that a child might fail to conserve because he was attending to an irrelevant cue—in this case the length of a line made up by the objects instead of the number of objects in the line. In this case the subjects were directed to count the objects each time.
4. They also included a control group which had the same number of trials as each of the experimental groups, but each time the controls responded to the same stimulus (the same number of objects in a line of a fixed length).

Subjects were tested before and after training on both performance and verbal measures of conservation. Comparisons of the gains made by the respective groups would indicate whether conservation could be induced and if so, what aspects governed the ability to conserve.

The results were not encouraging. You can sense some of this by footnote 4 of the article in which the investigators report a subsequent attempt to test these differences. Reasoning that they might have been on the right track but provided too little training, they increased the training trials from 18 to 24. The results were similarly negative.

The second article in this section is not an experimental study. It is, rather, a discussion of the Wohlwill and Lowe study. Zimiles asks the question: "To what was the child responding in the Wohlwill and Lowe task?" He points out that number conservation is a complex concept and that the child possesses many definitions of quantity. Before he can count, he has to depend upon such cues as length and density; as he learns to count, these tend to be correlated, and only gradually does he learn to differentiate between these two bases. Zimiles contends that this transition is a developmental phenomenon and requires a more prolonged period than Wohlwill and Lowe provided in their study.

The third article, Feigenbaum's, explores some other aspects of testing conservation. He suspected that conservation might be related to intelligence as well as chronological age. That is, might not a bright 6-year-old conserve better than a dull one of the same age? If so, it would indicate that the mental processes involved in conservation did not depend solely upon maturation, but related to the mental operations tapped by intelligence tests. He also raised a question about the unidimensionality of conservation. If a child can conserve when tested with one number of objects (e.g., 14 beads and one range of size of containers), is this ability a general one that would be manifest with a larger number (28 beads) or a different range in the sizes of the containers?

Wallach and Sprott begin with the assumption that some kind of experience accounts for the increment in conservation with age, and ask what this experience might be. They review the results of studies such as are presented here, in which investigators have tried to teach conservation. They found only one that was successful (see the discussion of Smedslund's studies below). They center their attention on the concept of reversibility, and set up an experimental situation in which children have an opportunity to see that, even though objects were rearranged, equality was maintained. A control group did not have this experience. Both groups were given a pre- and post-test, and a second post-test two or three weeks later. All tests used both checkers and dolls to measure conservation, and the second post-test also used bowls and spoons.

Wallach and Sprott report that "the training procedure had a striking effect on conservation." Their discussion helps us understand both the effect and the puzzling finding of others (Wohlwill and Lowe, for example) that the control groups improved in conservation. Their point is that reversibility is a necessary but not sufficient factor in conservation. That is, a child who is incapable of reversibility cannot conserve; however, if he has achieved reversibility, he may not evidence conservation in some situations.

Again, the set which the subject has plays a role in his performance. A "reversible" child may attend to other cues such as the length of a line of objects and ignore reversibility. If the reversibility set is activated, however, either by the testing for conservation or by sensitization procedures, he may then utilize it and demonstrate conservation. It is noteworthy that this study did not attempt to teach reversibility as such, and it still leaves open the question of how this is attained by the child. It is also interesting that Wohlwill and Lowe attempted to experimentally induce counting in their study of conservation. In this study, however, it constituted a contaminating variable. Therefore, Wallach and Sprott tried to eliminate its effects, by both deliberately avoiding the induction of a counting set and excluding its effect in the analysis of their results.

The final report in this group differs from the others in several ways. Instead of engaging in an experimental study, Uzgiris looks primarily at age differences. Second, she deals with conservation in several areas (substance, weight, and volume) rather than one, and investigates each with a variety of situational materials. Her findings confirm the belief that conservation is not a unidimensional concept which one has or has not attained, but that it may be evidenced at one age in one aspect or situation independently of the others.

Early in this introduction we tried to indicate that the work of Piaget is monumental and complex. We have selected only five papers on just one aspect of his work—conservation. This is by no means the total of studies, even in this area. Several of the papers referred to the work of Smedslund (whose work since 1960 has appeared primarily in the *Scandinavian Journal of Psychology*). Through a long series of studies, Smedslund has systematically explored the acquisition of conservation. In many of these he has attempted to induce conservation. In one striking study,[6] he compared two groups in a test of *extinction of conservation*. One group was composed of children who demonstrated conservation on a pre-test; the

[6] J. Smedslund, "The acquisition of conservation of substance and weight in children. III. Extinction of conservation of weight acquired "normally" and by means of empirical controls on a balance." *Scandinavian Journal of Psychology*, 1961, 2, 85–87.

other (the experimental group) was composed of those who did not show conservation on the pre-test, but who did on a post-test after an experimental period in which conservation responses were reinforced. Then, in the testing sessions, Smedslund "gimmicked" the trials by surreptitiously changing the amount of material. The crucial test was how the subjects reacted to this. The control group (those who had "naturally" acquired conservation) treated these as mistakes or tricks, and persevered in their belief in conservation; those who had "experimentally acquired" conservation reverted to nonconservation explanations.

This result, plus the general conclusion about the difficulty of inducing conservation in young children, provides rather convincing support for the early and less than rigorously derived conclusions of Piaget. They have provided some information about the process Piaget has described. The increasing amount of research in this and related areas, however, suggests that the next decade may bring more insights into what experiences are important for this intellectual development, and how they may be controlled and manipulated to increase the child's ability to comprehend and deal with his environment.

STUDY QUESTIONS

1. Wohlwill and Lowe test three different alternative explanations of how the child acquires conservation. Recapitulate the three and indicate how the training given the groups relates to them.
2. Zimiles provides a note on the findings of Wohlwill and Lowe. Indicate how you might test his notion empirically.
3. Feigenbaum uses measures of "correspondence" and "conservation." How are they different, and how does their use add to his investigation?
4. Wallach and Sprott distinguish between "reversibility" and "conservation." How do they differ? What is the relationship between them?
5. Suppose Wohlwill and Lowe had been successful in inducing number conservation in children. What are the implications of the Uzgiris finding for the transfer of this induced number conservation to conservation of weight and volume?

Experimental Analysis of the Development of the Conservation of Number[1]

Joachim F. Wohlwill* and Roland C. Lowe

Clark University

In Piaget's theory of intellectual development (8), a central role is assigned to the child's conceptualization of the principle of "conservation," i.e., his realization of the principle that a particular dimension of an object may remain invariant under changes in other, irrelevant aspects of the situation. For instance, children who lack conservation will assert that the relative weight of two objects has changed when the shape of one of them is altered or that numerical equality between two collections of objects no longer holds following a change in the length over which they extend. This phenomenon, which has been demonstrated for a variety of other dimensions, including those of volume, area and length, represents, according to Piaget, a manifestation of the immature level of functioning of the child's mental processes and of their failure to conform to the operational structures of logical thought.

Although Piaget has described some of the precursors of this notion of conservation in children who have not yet attained this level, little is known thus far about the specific ways in which the transition from lack of conservation to the presence of conservation takes place. It is apparent, however, that an adequate explanation of this problem ultimately requires a clearer understanding of the psychological processes at work in this transition phase.

One approach to this goal is to expose children presumed to be slightly below the age of onset of conservation to selected, systematically manipulated learning experiences, designed to call into play different factors believed to be important in the development of conservation. Any differential changes in the children's tendency to give conservation responses should then reflect the role played by the particular factors manipulated: At the same time, a more detailed examination of the interrelationship among different tasks involving conversation and closely related concepts should likewise extend our understanding of the nature of this problem.

Reprinted from *Child Development*, 1962, 33, 153–167.

[1] This investigation was supported by a research grant to the senior author from the National Science Foundation (G-8608). Nelson Butters assisted in the collection of data.

* Department of Psychology, Clark University, Worcester 10, Massachusetts.

The domain of number lends itself particularly well to the investigation of the development of conservation, for several reasons. First of all, recent empirical work (3, 4, 12) has given strong support to the notion that the attainment of the level of conservation marks a clearly defined stage in the formation of the number concept. Secondly, in this domain the problem of conservation can be readily related to development in other aspects of the number concept (e.g., counting, arithmetical skills, etc.), rather than constituting the somewhat isolated, *sui generis* problem which conservation appears to represent for such dimensions as weight or volume. Thirdly, and most important, the number dimension occupies a unique position in regard to the question of conservation, insofar as the number of elements contained in a particular collection is exactly identifiable by the corresponding integer; by the same token, the *fact* of conservation—i.e., that the number of a collection remains invariant under changes in the spatial arrangement of its elements—is readily verifiable, through the operation of counting. This feature creates an opportunity for assessing the role of symbolic, mediational processes, as well as of reinforcement, in the development of conservation.

This very uniqueness of the number dimension represents of course a potential limitation, as regards the applicability of the results to the problem of conservation in general. It is of considerable interest, therefore, that a rather similar investigation of the acquisition of the conservation of weight has simultaneously been carried out by Smedslund (10); its results will thus provide us with a valuable basis for comparison, as we will note in the discussion section.

THREE ALTERNATIVE THEORETICAL VIEWS OF NUMBER CONSERVATION

If one looks closely at the problem confronting the child in the conservation situation, several different interpretations of the acquisition of this principle suggest themselves. We may label these alternatives the reinforcement hypothesis, the differentiation hypothesis, and the inference hypothesis.

The *reinforcement hypothesis* would propose that, as a child obtains increasing experience in counting numerical collections of different types and in different arrangements, he gradually learns that alterations in the perceptual dimensions of a set do not change its number, i.e., that the same number is obtained from counting the set after as before such a change. Accordingly, systematic reinforced practice in counting rows of elements prior and subsequent to changes in the length of the rows should promote conservation.

The *differentiation* hypothesis would interpret lack of conservation in the young child as a response to an irrelevant but highly visible cue (length) which typically shows substantial correlation with that of number. The child thus has to learn to differentiate the dimension of number from this irrelevant cue. Repeated experience designed to neutralize the cue of length, and thus to weaken the association between it and the dimension of number in the child's thinking, should be expected, then, to facilitate conservation responses.

The *inference* hypothesis, finally, is based in part on Piaget's own analysis of the role of learning in the development of logical operations (9). Piaget maintains that experiential factors can only become effective, in this realm of development, to the extent that it builds on the child's previously developed structures of thought, as through the activation of a reasoning process prior to, but logically related to the one to be developed. In the case of conservation, one possible implication might be that by dint of cumulative exposure to the effects of adding an element to a collection, or subtracting one from it, the child may be led to *infer* conservation as the result of a change involving neither addition nor subtraction. This implication is supported, incidentally, by the explanations frequently voiced by children who admit conservation, e.g., "it's still the same, because you haven't taken any away."

Prior work by the senior author also bears on this last alternative. First, in the course of a sequential analysis of the development of the number concept (12), it was found that success on tasks involving simple addition and subtraction not only regularly preceded success on a task embodying the principle of conservation, but appeared, in a certain number of subjects, to lead to the emergence of conservation responses. In a subsequent pilot study (11), it was found, furthermore, that subjects given a limited set of trials involving addition and subtraction subsequently made more conservation responses than subjects given equivalent training on conservation, though the difference did not reach significance.

The results of this pilot study suggested the possibility of a more extended investigation of the development of the conservation of number, by bringing to bear each of the above-mentioned theoretical interpretations in the context of a small-scale learning experiment and determining the effectiveness of the various conditions of learning in bringing about conservation, both in a limited and a generalized sense. This is the main aim of the study to be reported, a subsidiary purpose being to provide information regarding the cross-situational generality of number conservation and its relationship to other types of number skills.

METHOD

The experiment was conducted in two sessions over two successive days (except for two Ss, for whom the interval between sessions was two and six days, respectively). The general design called for (a) a predominantly verbal

TABLE 1

DESIGN OF THE STUDY

Order	First Day	Order	Second Day
1.	Diagnostic Questions	1.	Training Series (trials 10 to 18)
2.	Verbal Conservation Pretest	2.	Nonverbal Conservation Posttest
3.	Pretraining in Number Matching	3.	Verbal Conservation Posttest
4.	Nonverbal Conservation Pretest		
5.	Training Series (trials 1 to 9)		

pretest, partly of a diagnostic character, to reveal S's ability to deal with number concepts, and partly dealing specifically with conservation; (b) a "nonverbal" test of conservation given in the form of a series of multiple-choice trials; (c) a training series on tasks presumed to be related to number conservation; and finally (d) a repetition of both the nonverbal and verbal tests of conservation to provide a measure of learning or change with respect to the understanding of this notion. This design is summarized in Table 1.

PROCEDURE

DIAGNOSTIC QUESTIONS

1. *Number Production.* S was shown a pile of red poker chips and was told, "Give me six of them."

2. *Number Equivalence.* E laid out a row of seven red chips. S was told, "Put down just as many of your chips over here (indicating an imaginary row paralleling E's row), as I have here."

3. *Number vs. Length.* E laid out a row of six blue chips extending beyond the limits of his own row of seven red chips (S's row being longer than E's). S was asked, "Who has more chips, you or I?" If he answered that he had more, but without having counted the chips, he was asked, "How do you know?"

These three questions concerned, respectively, the child's ability to (a) reproduce a particular cardinal number, (b) establish a relationship of numerical equivalence between two collections, and (c) respond to the dimension of number independent of irrelevant perceptual cues (e.g., length).

VERBAL CONSERVATION PRETEST

4. Two rows of seven chips each, one blue and the other red, were placed parallel to each other so that both rows were of the same length, and the chips in one row were directly opposite those in the other. S was asked, "Who has more chips, you or I?" This question, hereafter referred to as Q, was repeated for all the items in this part.

5a. E then extended the red row in both directions to a length about twice that of the blue row. (Q)

5b. The red row was subdivided into two rows of four and three chips placed parallel to S's blue row. (Q)

5c. The red chips were placed in a vertical pile in front of the blue row. (Q)

5d. The red chips were inserted into an opaque tube. (Q)

Question 4 served chiefly a preparatory function, i.e., to set up the following questions of conservation. Question 5a represented the main criterion of number conservation, while 5b to 5d indicate the generalizability of conservation. Accordingly, questions 5a to 5d were cumulative: if a S did not assert equality at any point, the remaining questions were omitted.

6. Questions 4 and 5a were repeated with 12 chips in each row instead of seven.

The suggestive nature of the questions (Q) used above ("Who has more chips, you or I?") requires comment. It should be noted that its initial use (in question 4) is in a situation where perceptual cues mitigate against the child's following the suggestion of inequality implicit in the question: the matched rows of chips afford a strong cue for direct perception of equivalence.[2] Second, the suggestion applied both in the pre- and the posttests and thus may be presumed to have played a constant role on both occasions.

PRETRAINING IN NUMBER MATCHING

The apparatus used here, shown in Figure 1, consisted of an upright panel containing three windows which had the numerals 6, 7, 8 inscribed on them from left to right. The Ss were told they were going to play a game, in which they would find a chip hidden behind one of the windows, and that the object of the game was to get as many chips as they could. For the pretraining phase, the procedure consisted in presenting singly a series of six 5 by 5 in. cards showing six, seven, or eight colored stars arranged in simple configurations. On each trial a colored chip was hidden behind the corresponding window. S was informed that the number of stars on the card would tell him behind which window the chip was hidden and urged

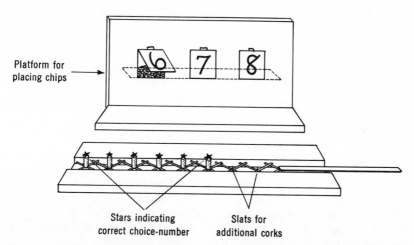

Fig. 1—Apparatus for nonverbal conservation and training trials, showing device for presenting variable-length rows of sample numbers and display-board for choice numbers.

[2] All but 14 of the Ss did in fact resist E's suggestion, usually through some such answer as "we both do" or "you and me." The 14 Ss who failed to do so were made to count the two rows, whereupon the question was again put to them. If S persisted in following the suggestion of inequality, E confronted them with the results of their counting and, if necessary, told him outright "So we both have the same, don't we?" This procedure was necessary in order to proceed to the following part, where S's prior knowledge of the equivalence of the two rows had to be presupposed.

to count the stars. When S opened the correct window, he was instructed to remove the chip and place it onto a board at his side. He was told to fill up the board with chips; if he found "a lot" of them, he would on the following day receive a toy. The purpose of this series was to create a set in the child to respond to number, as well as to familiarize Ss with the specific numbers shown. A correction procedure was used which involved having Ss correct any mistakes made in counting the stars and guiding S to the correct window when, as occasionally happened, a S counted correctly but made an incorrect choice.

NONVERBAL CONSERVATION PRETEST

This series consisted of three two-phase trials. Ss were presented with a row of colored stars, either six, seven, or eight in number, mounted on a set of corks which rested on a series of connected scissors-like slats. This apparatus, depicted in Figure 1, permitted lengthening or shortening the row while preserving the straight-line arrangement. E told S that he was to count the stars in order to find the chip behind the correct window. Following S's initial response, he was made to return the chip to E, who replaced it behind the same window, and then, depending on the trial, either extended or shortened the row of stars. S was allowed to count only on the first phase; he thus had to find the correct window on the second phase on the basis of the knowledge gained in the first and in the face of the perceptual changes in the row of stars.

TRAINING

There were four conditions of training: Reinforced Practice, Addition and Subtraction, Dissociation, and Control. The three experimental conditions were designed to relate, respectively, to the reinforcement, inference, and differentiation hypotheses presented in the introduction. Each training series consisted of 18 trials, broken up into two sets of nine which were administered on successive days. The apparatus used was the same as in the conservation pretest trials.

a. *Reinforced Practice* (RP). The procedure here was the same as for the preceding conservation trials, with this modification: if S made an incorrect response on the second phase of the trial, he was told to count the stars, so as to find out which window he should have chosen. E then exposed the chip behind that window but did not allow S to remove the chip.

b. *Addition and Subtraction* (A&S). These trials were similar to the conservation trials, except that on two-thirds of the trials, following the S's initial response after counting, E either added or subtracted a star at the end of the row before changing its length. The remaining third of the series consisted of straight conservation trials which were interspersed with the A&S trials.

c. *Dissociation* (Diss.). Unlike the above, these were single-phase trials, with the length of the row varying from one trial to the next over a range of four times the smallest length. S was urged to count the stars and open the corresponding window; if correct, he received the chip. Over the series of trials each number of stars appeared equally often at each of the different settings of length.

d. *Control.* This series of trials consisted likewise of single-phase trials as in the Dissociation condition, but the length of the row remained fixed throughout at its minimum spread.

POSTTESTS

The *nonverbal* conservation posttest, consisting of three conservation trials as in the pretest, followed immediately upon the completion of the training trials. (For Ss in groups Diss. and Control, E prefaced these trials with a remark to the effect that they would again have to find the chips twice in a row, the second time without counting.) Any S responding correctly on the last trial of this posttest was asked: "How did you know where to look for the chip that time?"

The *verbal* conservation posttest, consisting of a repetition of questions 4 through 6 as given in the pretest, concluded the experimental session.

At the end of the second session, each child was shown a variety of dime-store toys from which he picked one to take back with him as his "prize." Altogether, each of the sessions lasted about 20 to 25 minutes per child. The children's level of attention and motivation appeared to have remained high throughout these sessions, the "game" aspect of the situation apparently having proved effective in capturing their interest. This was reflected in their universal eagerness to return to it when called for the second session.

SUBJECTS

Subjects for this study were 72 kindergarten children, 35 boys and 37 girls, with a mean CA of 5 years, 10 months. (This age level was selected as one at which most children would still show lack of number conservation, while yet being old enough to be able potentially to profit from the learning experience; in other words, an interaction between learning and developmental level is presumed.) There were 18 Ss in each condition of training, Ss being assigned to their group according to a predetermined order. The four subgroups were closely matched as to their mean CA. (The range of the means was one month.)

The children were enrolled in the kindergarten classes of three public schools in Worcester, Massachusetts, located in predominantly lower-middle-class neighborhoods. They thus had been and were being exposed to a variety of activities in the area of number skills, consisting mainly of counting, number-matching, and identifying simple numerals.[3]

[3] The authors are greatly indebted to the principals and teachers of the Freeland, Columbus Park and Woodland Elementary Schools in Worcester, Massachusetts, for their splendid cooperation in providing subjects and facilities for this investigation. We also wish to acknowledge the assistance of the Worcester Country Day School in connection with a pilot study from which this investigation evolved.

RESULTS

The presentation of the results of the experiment is divided into three sections: the verbal pretest, including the diagnostic and verbal conservation questions; the learning of nonverbal conservation; and the transfer of training to the verbal posttest.

VERBAL PRETEST

Considering first the diagnostic questions, only one of the 72 Ss failed question 1, while four failed question 2. On question 3, however, only 20 Ss gave a correct response (i.e., based on counting the chips either before or in justification of their judgments). These results show that the Ss had adequate facility in counting and dealing with numbers symbolically in simple situations, such as producing a required number of elements and in matching two groups for number. Their success on these two tasks, however, contrasted sharply with their performance on question 3 where the task required the abstraction of number as independent from certain irrelevant perceptual cues. It should be noted that, since this question followed question 2 without a break, some Ss may have seen E take a chip from his row in setting up question 3. Thus, some of the correct responses may have been facilitated by this circumstance. In fact, nine Ss explicitly based their answers on this cue. (Control over this factor in a subsequent study did indeed result in lowering still further the number of Ss succeeding on this question, so as to equate it in difficulty with the conservation question, 5a.)

On the verbal conservation items, only nine of the 72 Ss answered correctly on question 5a. A breakdown of the incorrect responses shows that 41 Ss responded to the length of the rows, while 22 responded to the density of the elements. This tendency to regard the longer row as more numerous was also found on question 3 of the diagnostic questions.

As for the generality of the Ss' concept of number conservation, of the nine Ss who succeeded on question 5a, six extended their conservation to 5b, five to 5c, and four to 5d. On question 6, on the other hand, involving conservation for 12 elements, seven of these Ss showed conservation, in addition to one who had not responded correctly on question 5a. Thus, when conditions were qualitatively different, generalization was somewhat lower than it was when the new situation differed only in a quantitative way.

NONVERBAL CONSERVATION LEARNING

Table 2 summarizes the performance of each group on the verbal and nonverbal tests of conservation, before and after the learning series.

An analysis of variance revealed no significant differences among training groups with respect to learning of nonverbal conservation ($F = 1.73$; $p > .05$ for 3 and 68 df). However, the mean over-all difference scores differed significantly from 0 ($t = 3.95$; $p < .01$), showing that for the total group as a whole conservation did increase from pre- to posttest.

TABLE 2

PERFORMANCE ON CONSERVATION BEFORE AND AFTER TRAINING

Condition of Training	Verbal Conservation*			Nonverbal Conservation†		
	Pre-test	Post-test	Net Change	Pre-test	Post-test	Change Net
A&S	1	3	+2	1.05	1.77	+.72
RP	2	3	+1	1.22	1.50	+.28
Diss.	4	2	−2	1.05	1.16	+.11
Control	2	4	+2	1.44	1.96	+.52

* Number of Ss giving correct responses on question 5a.
† Mean correct responses out of three trials.

A comparison between the responses of the A&S and RP groups on the conservation trials of their respective training series shows that the former Ss were correct on 48 per cent of their trials, while the latter were correct on 47 per cent. It will be recalled that only six conservation trials were given in the A&S series, while the RP series consisted wholly of 18 conservation trials for which, in addition, a correction procedure was used. Hence, direct training on conservation was no more effective than the more intermittent practice afforded on the A&S trials.

It was also found that the A&S group had greater success on the A&S trials than on the straight conservation trials: for the former, 59 per cent of the responses were correct, as compared to the 48 per cent for the conservation trials. This finding, which is consistent with the results of previous research (12), represents of course a prerequisite for the use of the A&S trials as a training experience.

The training trials under the control and dissociation condition, which involved only rote counting, were quite easy for these Ss: a near perfect performance was the norm.

TRANSFER OF TRAINING TO VERBAL POSTTEST

With respect to verbal conservation, there were very few changes in any group. The number of Ss showing conservation of number on the pretest was nine, while 12 Ss showed it on the posttest. Two Ss changed to conservation from the A&S group, two from the Control group, and one from the RP group. Two Ss, in the Diss. group, who had shown conservation on the pretest, failed to do so on the posttest (cf. Table 2).

It is interesting to note that, whereas on the pretest of verbal conservation only four of the nine Ss having conservation showed perfect extension of this concept on items 5b through 5d, on the posttest nine of the 12 Ss showing conservation did show this extension, the remaining three Ss belonging to the group of five who had not shown conservation on the pretest. This seems to indicate the unstable nature of the Ss' conservation, as acquired in this situation.

Of the 12 Ss showing conservation on question 5a of the posttest, 11 again showed conservation for 12 elements (question 6).

DISCUSSION

In this section we will consider some of the more specific implications of the results for the nonverbal conservation learning and for the transfer to the verbal test, leaving until a later section certain more general conclusions suggested by this investigation.

Nonverbal conservation learning. As regards the "learning" of conservation within the limited context of the training trials, a significant amount of improvement from pre- to posttest did take place for the group as a whole, but the lack of significant differential effects due to the conditions of training and the fact that the Control group gained more than either the Reinforced Practice or the Dissociation groups clearly prevents us from attributing beneficial effects to any specific learning condition.

The failure of the RP group to outperform the others nevertheless deserves comment. It had actually been anticipated that this group, which received essentially one continuous series of conservation trials, would as a result of this extended practice show the greatest amount of learning from pre- to posttest, although such learning might not necessarily transfer to the verbal posttest. The contrary results bear out the ineffectiveness of continued reinforced practice in bringing about conservation responses, even of a purely empirical sort (i.e., "pick the window where the chip was before"), which the above-mentioned pilot study (11) had already hinted at in a much shorter training series. Whether a still more extended series than that used in the present study might have yielded a greater amount of learning remains an open question, of course.

The greatest amount of improvement from the pre- to the posttest trials, on the other hand, took place in the A&S group, exposed to 12 addition and subtraction trials, set off against six conservation trials; these results are thus at least consistent with the possible role of a process of inference (i.e., conservation as the end-product of changes involving neither addition nor subtraction) to which the previous studies (11, 12) had pointed.[4]

Finally, as regards the virtual absence of learning in the Dissociation group, it might be suggested, in retrospect, that the very act of counting the stars interfered with directing the child's attention to the cue of length, which the condition was designed to neutralize. If so, no improvement on the conservation trials, based on explicit disregard of the biasing cue of length, would result.

Transfer to verbal conservation questions. Perhaps the major finding of the study is that none of the above procedures proved in any way effective in leading to an understanding of the principle of number conservation, such as the verbal posttest demanded. For instance, over the four training

---

[4] It is worth noting that in a subsequent study, modeled closely after the present one, training with addition and subtraction again resulted in the greatest amount of improvement in (nonverbal) conservation, though the superiority over the control group still failed to be significant. In other respects, too, this study, in which the learning series was increased to 24 trials and the pre- and posttests of conservation to six trials each, yielded results which were closely comparable to those reported here.

groups combined, a total of 10 Ss shifted from zero or one conservation responses on the nonverbal pretest to three on the posttest, yet these shifts did not bring with them a single change to conservation on the verbal posttest.

In explanation for this failure of the nonverbal conservation learning to transfer to the verbal posttest, one might suggest that the nonverbal learning situation favored the development of an essentially empirical rule, i.e., "the correct number remains the same as before after E shortens or lengthens the row," or simply "look for the chip behind the window where the chip was just previously." If this were the case, little if any transfer to the very different situation confronting the child in the verbal conservation questions would be expected. The verbalizations elicited from those Ss who made a correct response on the last posttest conservation trial lend some support to this argument: many of the Ss actually gave no meaningful explanation for their choice at all (e.g., "I just knew," or "I thought hard about the stars"), while most of the rest responded in such terms as "It was there before."

Interestingly enough, Smedslund (10), on the basis of his work on the learning of the conservation of weight, similarly argues for the very limited, nonconceptual nature of such learning. In his study Ss were exposed to an extended series of judgments of the relative weight of two masses of plasticine, before and after one of these was deformed in shape; each judgment was reinforced by weighing the two objects on a balance. While Ss did learn to anticipate correctly the conservation of weight of the deformed object, the author feels that this learning was mainly that of an empirical fact, rather than of a logical principle, as shown both in the kind of explanations offered by the children, and in the lack of transfer of the learning to problems embodying logically equivalent principles (e.g., transitivity relationships).[5] Parenthetically, it is worth noting that in Smedslund's study a training procedure embodying addition and subtraction of matter, in a manner somewhat analogous to that of our A&S condition, yielded nearly as much learning as continued practice on conservation problems.

There remains, however, an alternative interpretation of our results. It is based on a major difference between the nonverbal and verbal tests of conservation, which might itself have accounted for the lack of transfer observed: while the nonverbal test involved a match between a given collection of elements and the corresponding, symbolically indicated number, the verbal test entailed rather the equivalence of the numerosity of two

---

[5] Perhaps more convincing evidence on this point comes from an ingenious "extinction" procedure which Smedslund (personal communication) has most recently utilized. This consisted in confronting Ss with apparent nonconservation, the weight of the deformed object being altered by surreptitiously adding or removing a small amount of plasticine. Under these circumstances Ss who had acquired conservation through their learning experience readily acceded to the lack of conservation which they seemed to be witnessing, i.e., abandoned their recently "learned" conservation. In contrast, Ss who had developed conservation spontaneously tended to invent explanations in order to reconcile this apparent contradiction, such as "we must have lost something on the floor."

Since the preparation of this paper portions of Smedslund's work (including the material of the personal communication referred to in the previous paragraph) have appeared in print (10). (Additional papers in this series, to be published in the same journal, are in press as of this writing.)

collections of elements. Thus, it is conceivable that the children did in fact learn, in their nonverbal training, that the *absolute* number of elements remained unchanged, without transferring this principle to the *relative* number of elements in two collections, in the verbal test. Implausible as this possibility may seem to a sophisticated adult, it is borne out by the total inefficacy of asking the children to count the two collections after a non-conservation response on the verbal posttest: of 23 Ss who were asked to do so, 19 persevered in their nonconservation responses when the question was repeated, immediately after ascertaining that there were seven chips in each row. Most recently, furthermore, Greco (5) has obtained clear evidence that children may show conservation in the first or absolute sense, without showing it in the second or relative sense.

Finally, the use of nonverbal methods in the investigation of children's thinking deserves brief comment. While the ineffectiveness of the nonverbal training procedures in our study may seem to cast doubt on the fruitfulness of such methods, they have been used to good advantage in several other recent studies (2, 12); moreover, the pitfalls of the verbal interrogation approach, at least as used by Piaget, have been persuasively analyzed (1, pp. 536f; 2).[6] Perhaps the central point is that it is incumbent on those applying nonverbal methods to determine, by varied and appropriate transfer tests, the breadth and depth of the child's understanding of the principles or concepts in question—a point which appears of special relevance to the application of automatic teaching methods to instruction in this and similar areas.

CONCLUSIONS

Although the predominantly negative outcome of this investigation does not allow us to give any definitive answer to the question posed at the outset, concerning the mechanisms involved in the child's acquisition of the concept of the conservation of number, a few general conclusions regarding this problem may be permissible.

First, the strong tendency of the children in this investigation to respond on the basis of differences in length in making numerical comparisons between two collections, even without the element of perceptual *change* introduced in the conservation situation (cf. question 3), lends some weight to the interpretation of lack of conservation as a failure to differentiate number from irrelevant perceptual cues, pointing to an aspect of the problem which appears to have received insufficient attention in Piaget's theoretical account of conservation.

Second, the consistent tendency across several studies for the A&S

---

[6] Relevant in this connection is a study most recently reported by Yost, Siegel, and McMichael (13), demonstrating considerable positive transfer from a nonverbal presentation of a probability-relationship problem to the corresponding verbal version of this problem as used by Piaget. These authors likewise found that by their nonverbal procedures the problem could be dealt with successfully at a much earlier age than Piaget had found, thus confirming the similar findings of Braine (2).

conditions to yield the most improvement in nonverbal conservation suggests that a process of inference may be operative in the development of number-conservation, even if this inference may be too limited in scope to lead to a generalized understanding of the principle. In view of the fact that children typically receive considerable experience in simple addition and subtraction in the very time period in which conservation generally appears (i.e., in late kindergarten and early first grade), this factor merits further attention.

Third, our investigation highlights the considerable gap separating the ability to *enumerate* collections by counting from a true understanding of the number concept, as it is reflected in the principle of conservation. In this respect the present results are entirely in agreement with those obtained in previous work on the development of the number concept (3, 12). Furthermore, even repeated identification of a collection with a particular number symbol, independent of length, appears to be relatively ineffective in bringing about conservation, thus raising the question of the adequacy of a mediation-theory approach to this particular aspect of concept formation.

In a more positive vein, two suggestions for future attacks on this problem might be offered. The first is to construct a set of learning experiences which would not only be more extended but, more important, cover a wider variety of situations (i.e., stimulus materials, configurations, specific numbers involved, etc.). This would be in line with Harlow's (6) emphasis on *generalized* experience as a prerequisite for the learning of broad concepts and principles in primates as well as in man. It is plausible to suppose, in fact, that it is precisely such generalized experience—in the classroom, at play, and in other everyday activities of children of this age level—which represents the basis for the seemingly spontaneous appearance of conservation in the child.

The second suggestion is to undertake a thorough, intensive analysis of the ontogenesis of conservation in a selected number of children followed longitudinally. Special attention might be paid to the types of explanations given by the child at various stages, as well as to the stability and generalizability of conservation responses once they appear. Inhelder and Noelting, at the University of Geneva, have in fact already launched such a longitudinal project, with preliminary results that appear promising (cf. 7).

SUMMARY

This study represents an attempt to determine more specifically the nature of the processes at work in the development of the notion of the conservation of number (invariance of number under changes in length or configuration of a collection), as studied by Piaget. The investigation was in the form of a nonverbal matching-from-sample type learning experiment, preceded and followed by verbal questions to measure the child's understanding of the conservation principle. There were four conditions of training, involving respectively the role of reinforced practice on conservation, of dissociation of biasing perceptual cues, and of inferential mechanisms based on the recognition of the effects of addition and subtraction of elements; a control group was also included. Subjects were 72 kindergarten-age children.

The results indicate an over-all increase in nonverbal conservation responses from a pre- to a posttest, within the limited context of the learning task, but they show no significant differences attributable to the conditions of training. Transfer of conservation learning to the verbal posttest was negligible under all conditions, indicating that whatever learning may have taken place was of a rather restricted type, representing perhaps more the formation of an empirical rule than the understanding of a general principle.

These results, together with additional findings pertaining to the relationship of certain number skills to conservation, are discussed in terms of their implications for the problem of the development of conservation.

REFERENCES

1. BERKO, J., & BROWN, R. *Psycholinguistic research methods.* In P. H. Mussen (Ed), *Handbook of research methods in child development.* Wiley, 1960. Pp. 517–557.

2. BRAINE, M. D. S. The ontogeny of certain logical operations: Piaget's formulation examined by nonverbal methods. *Psychol. Monogr.,* 1959, **73**, No. 4 (Whole No. 475).

3. DODWELL, P. C. Children's understanding of number and related concepts. *Canad. J. Psychol.,* 1960, **14**, 191–203.

4. ELKIND, D. The development of quantitative thinking: a systematic replication of Piaget's studies. *J. genet. Psychol.,* 1961, **98**, 37–46.

5. GRECO, P. Quotité et quantité. In J. Piaget (Ed.), *Structures numériques élémentaires.* Paris: Presses Univer. France, in press. (Etudes d'épistémologie génétique, XIII).

6. HARLOW, H. F. Thinking. In H. Helson (Ed.), *Theoretical foundations of psychology.* Van Nostrand, 1951. Pp. 452–505.

7. INHELDER, B., & NOELTING, G. Le passage d'un stade au suivant dans le développement des fonctions cognitives. *Proc. 15th Int. Congr. Psychol.,* Brussels 1957, 435–438.

8. PIAGET, J. *The psychology of intelligence.* London: Routledge & Paul, 1950.

9. PIAGET, J. Apprentissage et connaissance. In J. Piaget (Ed.), *La logique des apprentissages.* Paris: Presses Univer. France, 1959. Pp. 159–188. (Etudes d'épistémologie génétique, X).

10. SMEDSLUND, J. The acquisition of conservation of substance and weight in children. *J. Scan. Psychol.,* 1961, **2**, 71–87.

11. WOHLWILL, J. F. Un essai d'apprentissage dans le domaine de la conservation du nombre. In J. Piaget (Ed.), *L'apprentissage des structures logiques.* Paris: Presses Univer. France, 1959. Pp. 125–135. (Etudes d'épistémologie génétique, IX).

12. WOHLWILL, J. F. A study of the development of the number concept by scalogram analysis. *J. genet. Psychol.,* 1960, **97**, 345–377.

13. YOST, P. A., SIEGEL, A. E., & MCMICHAEL, J. E. Nonverbal probability judgments by young children. Paper read at Soc. Res. Child Develpm., Univer. Park, Pa., March, 1961.

A Note on Piaget's Concept of Conservation

Herbert Zimiles[*][1]

Bank Street College of Education

In his discourse on the development of the number concept Piaget (1) gives central emphasis to the concept of conservation as an essential principle that forms the basis for a framework of numerical reasoning. He describes conservation as developing in three stages: an initial stage in which perceptual factors exclusively determine the judgment of quantity, an intermediate stage of transition when perceptual as well as conservation considerations influence the judgment, and finally a last stage of complete conservation. These stages are, according to Piaget, one manifestation of a general trend from a preceptual-intuitive to an operational orientation, which characterizes the development of conceptual thinking.

Some of the most thoughtful experimental analyses of Piaget's theoretical speculations regarding the development of number concept have been recently conducted by Wohlwill (3, 4). In an attempt to gain some further understanding of the factors that contribute to the development of the principle of conservation, Wohlwill and Lowe (4) report a study in which they evaluated the relative contribution of three forms of specific training on the development of conservational thinking. The three experimental conditions of training were: (a) Reinforced Practice—S determined the number of objects immediately before and immediately after their spatial arrangement (in terms of their spread in a horizontal line) had been changed; (b) Addition and Subtraction—S was trained in observing the effects of addition or subtraction of one object from a larger aggregate on the determination of the number of such objects after their spatial arrangement had been changed; and (c) Dissociation—S received practice in counting an aggregate of objects under varying spatial arrangements. All the experimental conditions as well as the Control Condition, wherein S was given practice in counting the row of varying number of objects always presented in the same spatial arrangement, were found to have significant effects on a nonverbal measure of conservation, but virtually no demonstrable effect on verbal tests of the same characteristic. Moreover, although

Reprinted from *Child Development*, 1963, 34, 691–695. © Society for Research in Child Development, Inc., 1963.

[*] Research Division, Bank Street College of Education, 216 West 14th Street, New York 11.

[1] The author is grateful to Barabar Biber and Martin Kohn for their critical reading of the manuscript.

no reliable differences in effectiveness were found among the four training procedures employed, the greatest changes were observed in the Control and Addition and Subtraction conditions, those least concerned with providing explicit training in conservational thinking. It is the primary purpose of this note to help account for such perplexing results and, in so doing, to emphasize an aspect of number concept development which tends to be neglected.

Although Wohlwill suggests that the role of lack of differentiation between numerical and perceptual estimates of quantity may have been insufficiently considered, he himself helps to obscure this issue by repeatedly describing the tendency to judge quantity on the basis of greater length or density as a response to "irrelevant perceptual cues." It must not be overlooked that the concept of quantity exists for the child prior to the concept of conservation. The earliest ideas about quantity are nonconservational and are based exclusively on perceptual cues of length, density, height, weight, and so forth. These dimensions constitute the definition, insofar as there is a definition, of quantity for the preschool child. Such perceptual cues may be misleading in the experiments by Piaget and Wohlwill in the same sense that the trapezoidal rooms were misleading in the Ames experiments, but in both instances such perceptual cues have great relevance.

Accordingly, it would seem more accurate to describe the development of the concept of quantity as something that gradually changes in the direction of greater clarity and precision. The preschool child possesses not one, but a great many definitions of quantity. His concept of quantity is somewhat amorphous and ambiguous. He does not demand the level of clarity, internal consistency, and logical rigor that the analytic adult mind does.

With the advent of counting, cardination, and ordination, the child adds to his concept of quantity. He now employs counting as well as perceptual estimates of magnitude to make quantitative evaluations. Just as before when quantitative evaluations based on length and density tended to correlate with each other, so now evaluations based on perceptual cues and on counting also tend to agree with each, but also, as before, not perfectly. As he gains facility with the counting schema, he begins to rely more and more on such methods for quantitative evaluations since they provide more precision, differentiation, and information and because they are universally employed and easily communicated. His need for precision and accuracy has increased as he has begun to master complexity, and his exposure to numbers has in turn introduced him to levels of precision never before encountered. The new criteria of precision introduced by the use of number systems facilitate the evaluation of the efficiency of alternate methods of quantitative estimation and consequently lead to their abandonment insofar as they contradict quantitative numerical evaluations.

But these prior methods of quantification do not totally disappear, rather their influence wanes. Restaurants still use thick glasses with high bases so that the capacity of their glasses will be overestimated; packagers of food and other produce are continually exploring methods of creating the impression of great quantity; many people still feel that two dollars in change is either more, or less, money than two bills. Such factors continue to operate in the adult and may be regarded as a manifestation of the wish-fulfilling function of perception. It may be appropriate to consider them as irrelevant in the case of the adult, but it is important to remember that they constitute the definition of quantity for the child.

Let us return to Piaget's developmental stages. Children who respond at the nonconservational level have a less stable, less differentiated, pre-numerical concept of quantity. It is a multidimensional concept; it encompasses whatever perceptual magnitudes are involved in a particular situation. It is therefore most probable that these children will respond to the word "more" in terms of whatever dimension is suggested by the E. Since children do not possess a fixed, specific concept of quantity, they will interpret E's manipulation of specific perceptual dimensions as an indication of the particular concept of quantity required by the task.

The child in the intermediate stage is one who employs a rudimentary command of numbers together with various perceptual criteria in his evaluation of quantity. He has not yet had sufficient experience with number systems to reduce the role of perceptual factors in quantity estimation. The third and final stage, that of complete conservation, appears when there has been sufficient opportunity to master cardination and to compare counting with alternative perceptual methods of quantification.

These considerations help to explain some of Wohlwill's findings, for example, the difference between the verbal and nonverbal test results. The verbal test presents a situation in which one of two rows of objects, previously indicated as equal, undergoes a spatial, but not a numerical rearrangement. For the child who possesses many concepts of "more," the tendency of the E to manipulate a specific aspect of quantity (i.e., length) is likely to be decisive in determining the dimension of quantity to which the child will respond. At no time in the verbal test is a specific request made for a numerical rather than a spatial response. This is in sharp contrast with the nonverbal test procedure where S's response to the altered spatial arrangement must be made in terms of numerical symbols rather than ambiguous language. According to the interpretation presented here, the necessity to respond in terms of number serves as a set to use numerical rather than spatial criteria, hence the superiority of nonverbal as opposed to verbal test performance in both the pre- and postsessions.

In this regard, Wohlwill reports that, when 23 Ss were asked to count the two collections after having given nonconservational responses in the verbal post test, 19 repeated their nonconservational response when the question was asked of them again. These results demonstrate that at least four Ss could adopt the numerical set when it was suggested to them. With respect to the remaining 19, it remains possible that the suggestion implied by the counting was not explicit enough for them to abandon their spatial set. If this is true, it is dramatic evidence of how disconnected these two different concepts of quantity are in the minds of some of these children.

The same explanation may account for the substantial differences found between the pre- and post-nonverbal tests. All four training periods entailed counting activity involving the objects appearing on the nonverbal test of conservation. This interpolated experience facilitated the adoption of a number set during the posttest sessions and thereby improved performance.

The reasons for the differential effect of certain training conditions, i.e., the slightly greater gains achieved by the Control and Addition and Subtraction conditions, may be attributed to the same factor. The Control condition was the only one of the four training periods in which no spatial rearrangement of the test objects took place. The numerical, rather than the perceptual, cue was manipulated. In the Addition and Substraction condition the length of the row was varied, but this was probably obscured by the novelty of adding or subtracting an object on two thirds of the trials, once again supporting a numerical rather than a spatial orientation. On the other hand, the Dissociation condition generated the most conflict between the spatial and numerical attitudes. S was required to count rows of varying length, thereby observing that the length and number of a row were completely unrelated, but was never given any indication as to which dimension of quantity was favored by E. Since on the test trials it was the length variable that was manipulated, it is to be expected that S would be more inclined to turn to the spatial orientation. In a similar manner, but to a lesser degree, the Reinforced Practice training period also gave prominence to the variation of length, this time under a circumstance when the number was unchanged. Consequently, both the Dissociation and Reinforced Practice conditions tended to inhibit the adoption of a number set.

These speculations are reinforced by the findings of an earlier study by Wohlwill (3). As part of a scalogram analysis of number concept development, Wohlwill investigated the level of conservational thinking by having S count a group of buttons and then estimate their number after the aggregate had been scrambled so that the buttons were closer together. The preponderance of nonconservational responses regarded the more dense group as being more numerous. These results are in contrast with Wohlwill and Lowe's findings in which the longer of two rows rather than the shorter or more dense array was usually considered to be greater. These trends of response would appear to be contradictory. They have in common, however, the fact that in both cases S considered the aggregate manipulated by E as larger. The decisive cue in both instances appears to be the change introduced by E.

According to the present analysis of the development of conservation of quantity, it is not to be expected that short training periods of the type employed by Wohlwill and Lowe will be effective in changing the child's approach to conservation. The move from the first to the second stage of conservational thinking requires the assimilation of counting and other number skills, abilities which cannot be cultivated in a short training period. The transition from the second to the third stage where there is a more exclusive reliance on numerical reasoning in the attitude toward conservation is also not likely to develop within a short period of time. For it requires a gradual familiarization and incorporation of the mechanics and implications of numerical reasoning. Whatever changes do occur during an experimental procedure most probably will result from S's changing interpretation of those criteria of "more" that E would like him to employ. Although the growth of concepts of quantity may undergo dramatic spurts, quantitative reasoning is seen as unfolding in the manner suggested by Werner (2) for all forms of cognition, from the diffuse to the articulated, from the indefinite to the definite, from the labile to the stabile. The introduction and mastery of specific symbol systems represent landmarks in this transition, and from the viewpoint of the logical structure of mathematics the acquisition of complete conservation marks an important point in development, but it is the essential continuity of the developmental process which must not be overlooked.

REFERENCES

1. PIAGET, J. *The child's conception of number.* Humanities Press, 1952.
2. WERNER, H. *Comparative psychology of mental development.* (Rev. Ed.) International Universities Press, 1957.
3. WOHLWILL, J. F. A study of the development of the number concept by scalogram analysis. *J. genet. Psychol.,* 1960, **97**, 345–377.
4. WOHLWILL, J. F., & LOWE, R. C. Experimental analysis of the development of the conservation of number. *Child Develpm.,* 1962, **33**, 153–167.

Task Complexity and IQ as Variables

in Piaget's Problem of Conservation[1]

Kenneth D. Feigenbaum[*]

Wayne State University

In Piaget's genetic epistemological theory one dimension of cognitive development is reflected in how the child utilizes the principle of conservation of discontinuous quantities (8).

As used by Piaget, understanding of the principle of "conservation" involves understanding that the number or quantitative aspect of an aggregate is considered to be independent of the spatial arrangements of the items or the material in the aggregate, e.g., if beads are moved from one container to another of smaller dimensions, the number of beads remains constant even though there "looks to be" a larger amount in the smaller container.

In order to study mastery of the "conservation" principle, Piaget presented children 4 to 7 years of age with two glasses of equal size and a number of beads. He put one bead into one glass while the child put one into the other, or he allowed the child to put one bead into one glass with one hand while putting another bead into the other glass with the other hand. Piaget then asked questions such as "Which glass has more beads?"

Reprinted from *Child Development,* 1963, 34, 423–432. © Society for Research in Child Development, Inc., 1963.

[1] This study was part of a doctoral dissertation submitted to the Committee on Human Development, University of Chicago. The author wishes to express his gratitude to Helen L. Koch for her generous advice.

[*] Monteith College, Wayne State University, Detroit 2, Michigan.

to ascertain if the child "understood" one-to-one correspondence. He then poured the contents from a given container into another of smaller dimensions and asked the child whether there were more, fewer, or the same number of beads in the smaller one. If the child understood that there were still the same number of beads in the smaller glass, Piaget concluded that the child understood the principle of conservation of discontinuous quantities.

Piaget contends that "mastery" of the conservation concept occurs in three definite stages. In stage I, "Absence of Conservation," the quantity of an aggregate tends to be estimated on the basis of aspects of the perceptual situation that are irrelevant to the number of items. The number of items is judged to change as their spatial distribution changes. According to Piaget, the child in the first stage of reasoning is egocentric and judges on the basis of global properties or centers upon one aspect of a problem at a time. In stage II, "Beginning of Construction of Permanent Set," there is a vacillating belief that alteration of the spatial arrangement of items does not alter their number or quantity. The child begins to show awareness of the principles of reversibility, identity, and compensated relations, principles which are necessary for the understanding of conservation. In stage III, "Conservation and Quantifying Coordination," the child understands the concept of conservation. His cognitive field has become a coherent organized whole from which he can abstract.

Piaget indicates that each of the stages constitutes a new way of thinking about the problem. The stages are derived from the logical operations available to the child, which in turn determine the method he employs in the solving of the problem. A dominant mode of operation prevails during any particular age span. Furthermore, without reference to a general measure of abstract ability such as mental age, Piaget suggests that analysis of the operations employed by a child can account for his success or failure with a given set of problems involving the conservation principle.

Unfortunately Piaget limits his study and discussion of conservation to one type or level of complexity of problem. He states that, for the greater part of childhood, logical operations are not independent of their concrete content. However, nowhere in his discussion of the development of the conservation principle does he consider the following relationships: (a) the difficulty of the problem and the child's propensity for solution; (b) the effect of practice with one set of problems on changing performance in others; or (c) the relation between ability to generalize a solution to a new problem involving the conservation principle and the similarity between the two problems. Let us assume that the subject has only partially assimilated[2] conservation; that is, he cannot generalize the principle in all contexts. It is reasonable that such variables as familiarity of stimuli, past training, and "reinforcement" would play some role in determining the child's ability to cope with the principle involved in the problems presented.

The conceptual difficulties of Piaget's approach are partially based upon his reportorial techniques. As in many of his studies, Piaget fails to give an accurate report of his procedures (5). Nowhere does he tell his reader

---

[2] Assimilation as defined by Piaget (9) is the action of the organism on surrounding objects, insofar as this action depends on previous behavior involving the same or similar objects.

exactly what he said to all his subjects, how many children he employed in the sample, how many succeeded or failed to comprehend the conservation principle at each level, or what the IQs of the subjects were. Nor does he give any idea as to the standard of the materials used (i.e., how many beads were employed, their sizes, the dimensions of the glasses used). These variables are relevant if they influence the empirical data upon which Piaget's theory is based. It has been shown by at least one experimenter (3) that intelligence is a factor in number concept attainment. Furthermore, if success varies with the complexity of the task, Piaget's logical stages would be dependent upon the particular conditions and materials involved in the experiment. To be able to generalize, he would have to incorporate his learning principles of assimilation and accommodation into his discussion of conservation.

The purpose of this experiment was to test whether Piaget's explanation emphasizing logical operations occurring in an invariable age-stage system is sufficient to account for success or failure in understanding the principle of conservation.

HYPOTHESES

1. The levels of thinking involved in the development of conservation of discontinuous quantities are not solely the product of age.

2. The level of success that subjects achieve on tests of correspondence and conservation is related to IQ, as measured by the Stanford-Binet Test. This hypothesis is based on the assumptions that the acquisition of the concepts of correspondence and conservation involves the ability to abstract and that there is a correlation between this ability and IQ.

3. (a) The greater the number of beads used, the more difficult the attainment of conservation and correspondence tends to become.[3] (b) There is a relation between differential size of the containers employed and the solution of the conservation problem. The greater the container size differential, the more difficult the attainment of the solution.[4]

METHOD

PROCEDURE

PRELIMINARY TESTING

Since the E was interested in the relation between the child's IQ and his understanding of the principle of conservation, each of the Ss participating in the study was given a Stanford-Binet Test (Short Form L).

Correspondence Test I. In order to ascertain the child's understanding of the principle of one-to-one correspondence, the following procedure was employed. Each S was presented with 28 white beads all of the same dimen-

---

[3] This relation need not be considered linear.
[4] This relation need not be considered linear.

sions and was instructed to drop one bead into a glass, G-1 (1⅜ in. circumference) and one bead into a second glass of different dimensions (1 in. circumference). After S put all of the 14 bead pairs into the two glasses, he was asked: "Which glass has more beads in it, or do the two glasses both have the same number of beads?" "Can you tell me why?"

After the above procedures, the Ss were placed into three experimental subgroups. The treatments applied to each subgroup consisted exactly of the same sequence of tests, the materials employed being different for each treatment (relative size of containers, number of beads). The description of the tests is given under treatment I.

TREATMENT I

Correspondence Test II. The Ss in treatment group I were presented with 28 beads all of same dimensions. They were instructed to drop simultaneously one bead into one glass and another bead into a second glass of the same dimensions. After putting all of the beads into the two glasses, S was asked the following questions: "What glass has more beads in it, or do the two glasses both have the same number of beads?" "Can you tell me why?"

Correspondence Test with prompting. If the Ss failed Correspondence Test II by indicating that they thought that one glass contained more beads than the other, they were asked to count the number of beads in the glasses. If after counting they still could not state that there were the same number of beads in the two glasses, the beads were removed from the glasses. They were then placed into the glasses by the E. After each pair of beads was placed into the glasses, the question of Correspondence Test II was asked, "Now are there still the same number of beads in both glasses?" This procedure was continued until all of the beads were placed into the glasses.

Conservation Test I. E took the beads that the S had put into one of the glasses of equal size and poured them into a glass of smaller dimensions, causing the level of the beads in the smaller glass to appear higher than the level in the other glass. The Ss were then asked the following questions: "Which glass has more beads in it or do the two glasses both have the same number of beads?" "Can you tell me why?" The Ss were considered to have solved the problem referred to as Conservation Test I if their answers were not "guesswork" or based upon perceptual equivalence ("They're the same because they look the same"), but rather by reference to the operation of provoked correspondence ("Because I put them in one by one") or conservation of set ("Because we poured them all out").

Tests for understanding of "more" and "bigger." Following the tests for Correspondence II and Conservation I, the Ss were presented a form board consisting of one large triangle and one smaller triangle, one large circle and a smaller circle, one large square and a smaller square, one large triangle and two smaller triangles, one large circle and two smaller circles, and one large square and two smaller squares. Each set of these geometric figures was arranged horizontally on a single line, and the area of the larger figure was always greater than the sum of the areas of the smaller ones. The Ss were also questioned to see if they could differentiate the concept "more" (number) from "bigger" (size), in order to test the notion that the development of the understanding of mathematical concepts may proceed concurrently with the development of the understanding of the conservation principle.

Conservation Test II and Correspondence Test III. In order to determine if the experience on the form board had any positive transfer, the Ss were retested on correspondence (this is referred to as Correspondence Test III) and conservation (this is referred to as Conservation Test II), using the original materials.

TREATMENT II

In order to assess if any relation exists between the number of beads employed and solution of the tests of correspondence and conservation, a second group of 21 Ss matched approximately as to IQ, age, and social class with the Ss in treatment group I were given the same set of tests as those employed in treatment group I with one exception. In the tasks labeled Conservation Tests I and II and Correspondence Tests II and III the number of beads employed was one half the number of beads employed in treatment.

TREATMENT III

In order to test the hypothesis that the greater the size differential of the containers the more difficult would the tests of correspondence and conservation become, 15 Ss approximating in IQ, age, and social class the Ss in treatment groups I and II were given the same set of tests as those in the treatment group I with the following exceptions: (a) the number of beads employed in Correspondence Test II and III and Conservation Tests I and II was one half of those used in treatment group I. (b) In the test labeled Conservation I and II the size differential of the glasses was smaller so as to produce less perceptual distortion than in the case of either treatments I or II.

MODE ANALYSIS

An area of inquiry relating age to understanding of the conservation principle involved an analysis of the modes employed by the children in their attempt at solution of the correspondence and conservation problems. Modes refer to categories of responses deduced from the S's responses to the question "Why?" posed after the Test of Correspondence and Conservation. The reasons offered by the Ss were classified as follows: (a) perceptual (looks bigger); (b) conservation of set ("We poured them all out"); (c) reference to provoked correspondence ("We put them in two-by-two").[5]

Due to the fact that the investigator did not have complete protocols for all his subjects, a subpopulation of 66 Ss (those for whom remarks were complete) furnished the data for this analysis. The mean age of the sample was 65.5 months and the mean IQ was 119.8.

---

[5] The latter two modes imply some understanding of what Piaget calls the operations of reversibility, identity, and compensated relation.

The *E* and an assistant listened to the transcripts and attempted to characterize the reasons the children gave in accounting for their answers in Conservation Tests I and II.

POPULATION

The sample for this study consisted of 90 Ss drawn from nursery and elementary schools. As in Piaget's study, their ages ranged between 4 and 7 years.

The sample consisted of bright normals (*see* Table 1), and there were no significant differences between the sexes with respect to age and IQ.

TABLE 1

DEMOGRAPHIC CHARACTERISTICS OF THE SUBJECTS IN VARIOUS
TREATMENT GROUPS

	Number of Subjects			Age in Months		IQ	
	Total	Male	Fe-male	Mean	SD	Mean	SD
Treatment Group I	54	34	20	65.4	11.4	119.3	14.7
Treatment Group II	21	10	11	67.7	10.2	121.1	14.2
Treatment Group III	15	8	7	65.3	9.3	117.0	16.0
Total	90	52	38				

RESULTS AND DISCUSSION

AGE AND THE MASTERY OF THE PRINCIPLES OF CORRESPONDENCE AND CONSERVATION

It was anticipated that the age variable would account for only part of the variance of the ability or method used to solve the problems of correspondence and conservation. This investigation supports this view.

As Piaget suggests, however, there was a strong positive relation between age and success in understanding the conservation principle (Table 2).

TABLE 2

PERCENTAGE OF SUBJECTS AT DIFFERENT AGE LEVELS WHO SUCCEEDED
WITH THE TESTS OF CORRESPONDENCE AND CONSERVATION

	Age in Months			
	45–54	55–64	65–74	75–87
Correspondence Test I	7	21	32	71
Correspondence Test II	14	31	67	100
Correspondence Test III	45	61	80	100
Conservation Test I	0	47	56	91
Conservation Test II	16	49	73	91

An age-numerical ability relation was computed employing chi squares or Fisher exact tests of the difference between Ss below the median age of the group (designated as younger [45 to 64 months]) and those above the median (65 to 87 months). There was a significant difference between the performance of the two age groups for all groups tested ($p < .01$). In contrast with Piaget's report, which describes stages defined by definite age barriers, inspection of the results indicated that the frequency of success in solving the problems gradually increased with age. Furthermore, in the youngest age group (45 to 54 months) (Table 2) there were some subjects who could solve most of the problems. These findings are not congruent with Piaget's thesis that the child cannot comprehend the conservation principle until the age of approximately 65 months.

TABLE 3

PERCENTAGE OF SUBJECTS AT DIFFERENT AGE LEVELS EMPLOYING THE VARIOUS MODES OF SOLUTION

Mode	Age in Months			
	45–54	55–64	65–74	75–87
Conservation of Set	0	10	50	77
Provoked Correspondence	14	13	14	9
Perceptual	72	63	27	7
Counts	14	14	9	7

MODE ANALYSES (TABLE 3)

Eight different modes were discriminated in the analysis: two major ones, into which a majority of the responses fell, and six minor ones. The rater agreement on the individual protocols was 86.2 per cent.

1. *Perceptual.* A group of 22 Ss employed this category. The mean age of this subgroup was 59 months and the mean IQ was 118. An analysis of variance indicated that Ss who used the perceptual mode differed significantly ($F = 14.73$; $p < .01$) in age from the children who employed the other modes. The Ss who employed the perceptual mode were the youngest subjects in the sample. This suggests that the perceptual "stage," as Piaget indicates, tends to be first in the developmental sequence of "modes of operation."

2. *Conservation of set.* There were 22 Ss who employed this mode of reasoning. The mean age of this subgroup was 77 months and the mean IQ was 125. An analysis of variance comparing the age of this subgroup with the rest of the sample produced a significant difference ($F = 44.1$; $p < .01$). The mean age of this subgroup was higher than that of the subgroups employing other modes. The result indicated that conservation of set was the most employed by the older children in the sample and constituted the most advanced of the developmental states explored.

3. *Provoked correspondence.* There were four Ss who employed this mode. Their mean age was 61 months and the mean IQ was 120. The N was too small for any meaningful statistical analysis.

4. *Marginal group.* There were 13 Ss who used combinations of the

above three modes, employing one mode on Conservation Test I and another one on Conservation Test II. This group of Ss constituted a marginal group advancing from one mode of thought to another.

5. *Counts.* When Piaget analyzed the children's approaches to the problem he presented, he did not mention that any of his Ss attempted to use the counting method. Among the Ss of the present study, however, when asked, "Are there the same number of beads in the two glasses?" etc., some proceeded to count the beads in the glass. The mean age was 67.7 months. This group is older than the group of Ss who used the perceptual mode ($p < .01$).

In summary, Piaget is generally correct in stating that perception tends to overrule one-to-one correspondence in the earliest stages of development of the conservation principle. But this mode of response is not confined to children of a particular age period. As can be seen from Table 3, a mode may be dominant during a particular age period, but it may also be employed by children over the entire age continuum encompassed by this sample. In addition, there were a number of cases in which the Ss employed more than one method in their attempt to fathom the conservation principle. It appears that any claim for rigid stages of development needs qualification.

IQ AND FREQUENCY OF SUCCESS

The second hypothesis states that a positive relation exists between IQ, as measured by the Stanford-Binet, and ability to solve the problems concerning correspondence and conservation. From Table 4, one can discern

TABLE 4

RESULTS OF χ^2 TESTS OF DIFFERENCES IN TESTS OF CORRESPONDENCE
AND CONSERVATION BETWEEN BRIGHTER AND DULLER
SUBJECTS (OVER AND UNDER AN IQ OF 119)

Test	χ^2	p
Correspondence I	7.05	.01
Correspondence II	3.76	.05–.10
Conservation I	4.49	.05
Conservation II	5.02	.05
Correspondence III	2.75	.10

a positive relation between IQ and success in the tasks labeled Correspondence Tests I and II and Conservation Tests I and II. In the case of Correspondence Test III, the incidence of success among children above the median in IQ was not significantly greater than the incidence among children with IQ below 119. In a number of cases the performance of younger subjects with higher IQs was also superior to that of older children with the lower IQs. These findings are in agreement with Dodwell (3). It is apparent that age does not account completely for differences in levels of success with the "conservation problems." One might suggest that there is an interplay between general intelligence and possession or propensity for assimilation of the logical operations involved in the comprehension of the conservation principle.

PROBLEM DIFFICULTY AND THE COMPLEXITY VARIABLES

RELATION BETWEEN NUMBER OF BEADS EMPLOYED AND SUCCESS ON THE TASKS

The performance differences for groups equated as to IQ, age, and ability in the performance of the task of Correspondence Test I were assessed with regard to the number of beads employed in the problem (treatment I, 28 beads; treatment II, 14 beads).[6] In the case of Conservation Test I, no significant difference was noted ($\chi^2 = 1$). However, in the case of Correspondence Test II, the difference was significant at the 5 per cent level ($\chi^2 = 4.4$). Inspection of the data indicated that success by the younger children accounted for the difference. In addition, evidence from the protocols suggested that some Ss solved the relevant problems with 2, 3, or 4 pairs of beads, but failed when the number was increased. The evidence gives tentative support to a view that the complexity of the stimuli presented affected Ss' frequency of success in case of incomplete assimilation of the principle of one-to-one correspondence and to a view that the crucial discrimination for young children regarding enumeration or logical derivatives of a number sort occurs in the first few numbers of the system (6).

EFFECT OF PERCEPTUAL DISTORTION ON FACILITY WITH THE TASKS

In order to determine the effect of degree of similarity of the containers on the child's ability to resist the influence of irrelevant characteristics of the perceptual field in his thinking about conservation, the results of treatment III were compared with those of treatment II. These two treatments were the same except for the size of containers. Chi square tests revealed no significant differences between treatments II and III in the cases of Conservation Tests I and II or Correspondence Test III. In the case of Correspondence Test II there was a significant difference between the performance of the two treatment groups. Since Correspondence Test II, however, did not involve different size containers, the data cannot be looked upon as proof for hypothesis 3b.

[6] The use of 14 beads rather than two or three or four beads, etc., was dictated by two factors. First, in a pretest it was found that some of the Ss who failed the problems with 14 pairs of beads could solve it with seven pairs. Second, under Piaget's definition of the conservation problem, an ability to resist the suggestion created by the perceptual distortion of the aggregates in the containers, the employment of two, three, or four beads, etc., could not produce the perceptual distortion required. It is quite probable, however, as McLaughlin (6) has indicated, that the crucial difference in the Ss' performance might be in their ability to discriminate between one and more than one, two and more than two, and three and more than three, rather than between 14 and 28. By using Piaget's definition of conservation, one therefore in effect limits the possibility of a more adequate test of the hypothesis, suggesting that reducing the number of beads would increase success with the conservation test.

DISCUSSION

The study has been fruitful in indicating overlapping stages of development in the acquisition of the conservation principle and a positive relation between IQ and knowledge of the concept of conservation. However, the inconclusive results of the study regarding the role of complexity lead to the suggestion that further testing is necessary in order to unravel the relation among the irrelevant perceptual stimuli, the number of beads employed, and the logical processes used by children and the relation between understanding one-to-one correspondence and conservation. Another type of approach to the study of the development of the concept of conservation is indicated. A test of understanding of conservation which is independent of that of correspondence is needed. It would be reasonable to take as evidence for some understanding of conservation the ability to see number constancy when aggregates are simply moved from one area to another. The investigator could then test for understanding of one-to-one correspondence by varying the degree of the irrelevant perceptual stimuli, while under independent conditions varying the number and kinds of aggregates employed to test the subject's possession of a conception of the simplest form of conservation.

SUMMARY

The present investigation was part of an evaluation of Piaget's study of the child's development of the concept of conservation of discontinuous quantities. The sample consisted of 90 children, 4 to 7 years of age, drawn from nursery and elementary schools in Chicago and Greater Detroit. The evidence indicated that "stages of development" in the acquisition of the conservation concept were not defined by definite age barriers, but rather descriptive general trends. The data also indicated that the children's grasp of the conservation concept tended to vary with their IQ and with the nature of the concrete experimental operations.

REFERENCES

1. DENNIS, W. Animistic thinking among college and university students. *Sci. Mon.*, 1953, **76**, 247–249.
2. DEUTSCHE, J. M. *The development of children's concepts of causal relations.* Univer. of Minnesota Press, 1937.
3. DODWELL, P. C. Children's understanding of number and related concepts. *Canad. J. Psychol.*, 1960, **14**, 191–205.
4. ESTES, B. W. Some mathematical and logical concepts in children. *J. genet. Psychol.*, 1956, **88**, 219–222.
5. HUANG, I. Children's conceptions of physical causality: a critical summary. *J. genet. Psychol.*, 1943, **63**, 71–121.

6. McLAUGHLIN, K. A study of number ability in children of ages three to six. Unpublished doctoral dissertation, Univer. of Chicago, 1932.
7. NASS, M. L. The effect of three variables on children's concepts of physical causality. *J. abnorm. soc. Psychol.*, 1956, **53**, 191–196.
8. PIAGET, J. Child's conception of number. Routledge, Kegan Paul, 1950.
9. PIAGET, J. *The psychology of intelligence*. Harcourt, Brace, 1950.

Inducing Number Conservation in Children [1]

Lise Wallach* and Richard L. Sprott

University of North Carolina

Number conservation was induced in first-grade children by giving them experience with the reversibility of rearrangements which they regarded as implying changes in number. The effects transferred to new sets of objects, and conservation was still maintained several weeks later, despite a suggestion to the contrary by the experimenter. If two sets of objects are initially clearly matched, their continued equality despite changes in arrangement seems to be recognized when it is realized that they could be matched again. Such recognition of reversibility may account for the normal development of number conservation, and also of some other conservations such as amount.

This paper is concerned with the problem of the attainment of conservation. Piaget and others in the Geneva tradition have shown that young children do not recognize that amount of matter, number of objects, and other properties remain unchanged with variations of form and arrangement. For example, a child below the age of about 6 or 7 will say that the amount of clay changes when a ball of clay is flattened into a pancake, and that the number of objects changes when a row of objects is spread further apart. The literature on conservation has been extensively reviewed by Flavell (2) and by Wallach (15).

How is conservation acquired? What leads a somewhat older child to say that the amount of matter and the number of objects remain the same under such transformations? It is clear that experience of some kind is involved, but it is not easy to specify just what this experience is. Current learning theories would suggest as the most likely possibilities that conservation is learned from direct observation or social reinforcement. However, not only are there theoretical difficulties in attempting to explain conservation

Reprinted from *Child Development*, 1964, 35, 1057–1071. © Society for Research in Child Development, Inc., 1964.

[1] The authors wish to express their gratitude to Dr. Jan Smedslund, Dr. Joachim F. Wohlwill, and Dr. Herbert Zimiles for their helpful comments on the manuscript.

* Department of Psychology, University of North Carolina, Chapel Hill.

through either of these possibilities, but experimental efforts to induce conservation through them (9, 10, 17) have not proved successful.

Several other factors have been proposed as responsible for conservation but have also failed to induce it when experimentally manipulated. Practice in addition and subtraction, and experience designed to indicate the unreliability of the cues the children were using (e.g., length for the number of objects in a row) have not led to greater increases in conservation than control procedures (9, 11, 17). On only one experiment (13) has training produced a significant increase in conservation relative to a control procedure. The training in this experiment was designed to give practice in situations involving conflict between expectations based on addition and subtraction and expectations based on changes of form, but the procedure was so complex that it is not really clear what aspect of it was responsible for the effect.

There is another possible factor on which the attainment of conservation might crucially depend, which has often been stressed by Piaget (5, 6), but has not yet been investigated—reversibility. An adult, or older child, knows that changes in form or arrangement are reversible, i.e., that whenever such a change occurs, the initial situation can be brought about again by an inverse change. For example, if a ball of clay is turned into a pancake, it can be turned back into a ball of the same size again. If a row of objects is spread farther apart, they can be placed closer together again, and the row will have the same length it did previously. The recognition that changes in form or arrangement are reversible may play a critical role in the realization that they do not imply changes in amount or number. Smedslund (8) has argued against this view, on the grounds that many children already know that it is possible to return to the initial situation, prior to attaining conservation.[2] There are several reasons, however, which will be discussed below, that suggest that conservation may nonetheless result from experience with reversibility, and the present experiment was designed to see whether this is the case.

An attempt was made to induce conservation of number by showing children the reversibility of rearrangements which they, prior to conservation, regarded as implying changes in number. The first step, following Piaget's work with correspondence between complementary objects (6), consisted of the child's placing a set of dolls in a set of beds, one doll to each bed. The dolls were then taken out and placed closer together than the beds. A child who did not yet recognize conservation would now maintain that there were no longer the same number of dolls as beds, even though just previously when the dolls were in the beds, he had asserted their equality. The reversibility of rearrangements of the dolls was demonstrated to the child by showing him that, so long as nothing was taken away or added, the dolls would fit exactly in the beds again. The experiment thus attempted to induce conservation of number in children by making them realize that rearranged objects which fit together before rearrangement can be made to fit together again.

---

[2] That children frequently show reversibility and not conservation is also discussed by Lovell and Ogilvie (4), but what they mean by reversibility is awareness, after a change in form, of what the previous situation was, rather than awareness of the possibility of return to that situation, as we do.

METHOD

SUBJECTS

The subjects were 66 children in three first-grade classes of a predominantly middle-class public school in a small university town. They ranged in age from 6 years, 5 months, to 7 years, 8 months, with a mean of 6 years, 11 months.

PRETEST

The child was seated at a table with two adults, one (E) working directly with him, and the other recording everything the child said and did.

Checkers. Five 3 by 5 inch cards were laid out in a straight line on the table, and five red checkers were placed in a small pile in front of the cards. The subject was asked to put one checker on each card. The experimenter then asked, "Are there more checkers than cards?" If S said there were not, E went on, "Are there more cards than checkers?" If S again said there were not, E continued, "Are there the same number of checkers as cards?"

Counting was discouraged if it occurred here or at any other time during the experiment, which it seldom did. The child was always carefully observed, and notation was made of any possible indications of counting, including appropriate eye movements, mention of any number names, etc.

If S said there were more checkers or cards, as eight Ss did, he was given a simple kind of number training, in which he was asked to compare rows of equally spaced red and black checkers. Then the checkers were placed on the cards again and the above questions were repeated. Those Ss who, after the number training, still said the number of checkers was different from the number of cards, were classified in a separate category, called Unequal When Paired (see below), and asked no further questions.

If, either without or after number training, the child said there were neither more cards nor more checkers but an equal number of each, E said, "Now watch what I do." One by one E then took each checker off its card and placed it in a row directly in front of and parallel to the cards, but slightly closer together, so that at the end there was one card without a checker in front of it (Figure 1). Then E asked, "Now are there the same

Fig. 1

number of checkers as cards?" If S said there were not, E asked, "Which are more?"

Dolls. The checkers and cards were then put away, and six dolls and six beds were put on the table. The subject was asked to put a doll in each bed. After he had done so, E placed the beds in a straight line, and asked, "Are there the same number of dolls as beds?"

If S said there were not the same number at this point, he was also placed in the Unequal When Paired category and asked no further questions. If he said there were the same number, E again said, "Now watch," took each doll out of its bed, and placed the dolls in a row in front of the beds but closer together, so that one bed had no doll in front of it. The experimenter then asked, "Now are there the same number of dolls as beds?" Again, if S said there were not, E asked, "Which are more?" Now, if S said there were the same number, E asked, "How do you tell?"

CLASSIFICATION OF SUBJECTS

On the basis of their answers to the pretest questions, the Ss were classified into four categories: Unequal When Paired, Conservation, Partial Conservation, and Nonconservation. The Nonconservation Ss are those of greatest concern, since half of them constitute the Experimental group, with whom an attempt was made to induce conservation, and the other half the Control group. The categories were defined as follows:

Unequal When Paired. Subjects who, even after number training, said there were not the same number of checkers as cards, or dolls as beds, when either of these were fit together in coordinate pairs.

Conservation. Subjects who said there were the same number of checkers as cards, and dolls as beds, not only when these sets were placed in coordinate pairs, but when they were taken apart again and one set was put closer together.

Partial Conservation. Subjects who said there were the same number of checkers as cards, and dolls as beds, when they were paired; and also, *either* with checkers and cards *or* with dolls and beds, when they were taken apart, but not with both.

Nonconservation. Subjects who said there were the same number of checkers as cards, and dolls as beds, when they were paired; but who said there were a different number both of checkers and cards, and of dolls and beds when they were taken apart.

The subjects were run in alphabetical order within each class, and the Nonconservation Ss were divided into the Experimental and Control group by alternate assignment.

TRAINING PROCEDURE

The experiment ended with the pretest for Ss in the Unequal When Paired, Conservation, and Partial Conservation categories. For the two groups of Ss in the Nonconservation category the procedure continued as follows:

Experimental group. After the Experimental Ss said there were a different number of dolls than beds, and which were more, when the dolls were closer together than the beds, they were asked, "Do you think we can put a doll in every bed now? Will there be any beds left over? Any dolls left over?" After answering, S was asked to try putting a doll in each bed.

This was the first of a series of situations which were presented, S being asked in each case to predict whether the dolls could fit exactly in the beds again and then to try it. Number was never mentioned during this training procedure. Each situation began with all the dolls in the beds, one doll to each bed. The dolls were then always taken out and placed closer together or farther apart in a row in front of the beds, so that there was a bed without out a doll or a doll without a bed. In half of the situations either a doll or a bed was then removed or added in such a way that the two rows became the same length. When an item was removed, it was placed at the other end of the table and S was told it could not be used; items which were added were taken, with some emphasis, out of a box E had at her side. The situations were as follows:

1. Dolls closer together.
2. Dolls closer together, bed removed.
3. Dolls farther apart.
4. Dolls farther apart, bed added.
5. Dolls closer together.
6. Dolls closer together, doll added.
7. Dolls farther apart.
8. Dolls farther apart, doll removed.

Each situation was repeated till S made the correct prediction and confirmed it. As many situations were presented as were necessary to reach a criterion of correct prediction on the first trial of four situations in succession. Eight situations turned out to be all that were needed, as all Ss reached criterion within this number.

Control group. After the Control Ss said there were a different number of dolls than beds, and which were more, when the dolls were closer together than the beds, a simple children's checker game called "fox and geese" was played, which took approximately the same length of time as the training procedure for the Experimental Ss.

FIRST POSTTEST

After the Experimental Ss had predicted fit correctly on the first trial in four situations in succession, and after the Control Ss had completed their game, most of the pretest was repeated.

Dolls. The six dolls were again placed in the six beds, and thereafter taken out by E and put closer together as before. The experimenter then said, to the Experimental Ss, "Now I'll ask you something else again. Are there the same number of dolls as beds?" Exactly the same wording was used with the Control Ss except for omission of the word "else." If S answered that the dolls and beds were the same number, E asked, "How do you tell?"

Checkers. The dolls and beds were then put away, and S was again asked to put the five checkers on the five cards. The experimenter then took the checkers off, placing them closer together as before, and asked, "Are there the same number of checkers as cards?" Whether S said there were the same or a different number, he was then always asked, "How do you tell?"

SECOND POSTTEST

Between 14 and 23 days after the pretest, training procedure, and first posttest, the second posttest was administered. The first objects used here were different ones from those used earlier—bowls and spoons; after these, the checkers and cards, and then the dolls and beds, were used again.

In each case the procedure followed the same familiar pattern: The bowls (cards, beds) were lined up in a row, the spoons (checkers, dolls) were placed in a pile in front of them, and S was requested to put one spoon (checker, doll) in each bowl (card, bed). The experimenter then asked, "Are there the same number of spoons (etc.) as bowls (etc.)?" Then E took the smaller items from the larger and placed the former in a row in front of and parallel to the latter, but closer together, so that one larger object did not have a smaller in front of it. The experimenter then asked, "Now are there the same number of spoons (etc.) as bowls (etc.)?"

Nonconservation suggestion. At the end of the second posttest, if S said there were the same number of dolls as beds, E now pointed to the bed without a doll before it and said, "But look—here is a bed without a doll in front of it. Aren't there more beds?"

RESULTS

PRETEST

Number and age of children in each category. As shown in Table 1, most of the subjects fell into either the Conservation or the Nonconservation category, dividing themselves almost equally between these two. There are no significant differences in age between any of the categories, or between the Experimental and the Control groups.

The lack of difference in the ages of the Conservation and the Nonconservation subjects deserves a word of comment, since typically conservation is found with greater frequency among older children. This result is probably due to the present sample's being drawn from a single grade in school. Age is thus relatively homogeneous, and a few of the oldest children

TABLE 1

NUMBER AND AGE OF CHILDREN IN EACH CATEGORY

Category	N	Mean Age*	Age Range*
Conservation	28	6-11	6-6 to 7-6
Nonconservation total	30	6-11	6-5 to 7-8
Experimental	15	7-0	6-6 to 7-8
Control	15	6-11	6-5 to 7-5
Partial conservation	4	6-6	6-5 to 6-9
Unequal when paired	4	7-0	6-8 to 7-5
Grand total	66	6-11	6-5 to 7-8

* In years and months.

—repeating the same grade over again—may be among the least intelligent; further, school experience here does not increase with age, as it does in a broader sample.

Nonconservation answers. The majority of the subjects who gave non-conservation answers said there were more of those items which were spread further apart. Of the 30 Nonconservation subjects, 25 said that there were both more beds than dolls, and more cards than checkers ($z = 3.47, p < .001$ by the binomial test).[3] The remaining five all said there were more checkers than cards, and two of them said there were more dolls than beds.

FIRST POSTTEST

Experimental vs. Control group on conservation. The results indicate that the training procedure has a striking effect on conservation. On the first posttest when the dolls were placed closer than the beds, and the checkers closer than the cards, all 15 of the Control subjects again asserted that there was a difference both in the number of dolls and beds, and in the number of checkers and cards. Of the 15 Experimental subjects, 14 now maintained that the number of dolls was the same as the number of beds ($p = .0000002$ by the Fisher exact probability test). Further, 13 of the 15 showed transfer to the checkers situation, asserting that the number of checkers was the same as the number of cards ($p = .000002$). Every Experimental subject recognized equality in at least one of the two situations.

Justification of conservation answers. The Experimental subjects who said that there were an equal number of dolls and beds, and of checkers and cards, were frequently able to justify these answers, showing no significant difference in understanding of conservation from the Conservation subjects.

Responses to the question "How do you tell?" were judged to indicate understanding of conservation when they referred to one of the following facts:

1. The objects fit together or were the same number before.
2. The objects could be fit back together again.
3. Nothing was added or taken away; the objects were only rearranged.
4. One set was closer together than the other set, or an object in one set was between two in the other.

Judgments were made independently by the two experimenters, with agreement on all but three of the 55 responses given by the Experimental and the Conservation subjects. The three disagreements were resolved by discussion.

Of the 28 Conservation subjects, 18 gave responses judged as showing understanding of conservation upon being asked how they told the number of dolls was the same as the number of beds. The Experimental subjects had been asked "How do you tell?" both after the dolls and beds, and after the checkers and cards. Six of the 14 asserting equality between the dolls and beds gave answers indicating understanding of conservation here; 8 of the 13 who said the numbers of checkers and cards were equal gave such answers after the checkers and cards. Neither of these proportions is significantly different from that of the Conservation subjects.

[3] All probability values are for two-tailed tests.

Ability to predict fit. The training thus clearly had a strong effect. What was responsible for this effect, however, was not simply that the training provided the subjects with a knowledge of reversibility. Many of the subjects already knew that rearrangements were reversible prior to training, as was shown by the fact that 8 of the 15 Experimental subjects made correct predictions of fit on every training trial. Yet these subjects were also led to conservation by the training: 7 of the 8 recognized equality between the dolls and beds in the first posttest, and the eighth recognized it between the checkers and cards. The implications of this finding will be further discussed below.

SECOND POSTTEST

Experimental vs. Control group on conservation. The effect of training had not diminished by the second posttest. All the subjects behaved consistently in the three different situations here: if equality was maintained when any one set of objects was placed closer together than its corresponding set, then equality was also maintained when the other sets were placed closer than their corresponding sets. Of the 15 Experimental subjects, 13 maintained equality in the three situations; only two said the numbers were not equal. On the other hand, only one Control subject out of 15 asserted equality, while 14 asserted inequality. The difference between the Experimental and Control subjects is significant with $p = .00002$ by the Fisher exact probability test.

Effect of nonconservation suggestion. Eleven of the 13 Experimental subjects who had said the numbers were equal on the second posttest continued to maintain this when the suggestion to the contrary was given ($p = .02$ by the binomial test). Of the two subjects who did follow the suggestion, one seemed particularly shy and anxious to please; the other said the experimenter must have added another bed, and upon being assured that this was not the case, changed her mind again and asserted equality. The one Control subject who had said the numbers were equal also followed the suggestion.

DISCUSSION

The results clearly indicate that the training procedure was effective in inducing conservation, and thus support the hypothesis that conservation may be acquired by experience with reversibility.

CAN THE RESULTS BE ACCOUNTED FOR BY DIRECT OBSERVATION OR SOCIAL REINFORCEMENT?

As mentioned earlier, current learning theories would tend to suggest direct observation or social reinforcement as responsible for conservation. Can these factors account for the results of the present experiment? The subjects might have observed that the number of objects in each set was still the same by counting; or possibly the experimenters unintentionally provided social reinforcement. That either of these is responsible for the Experimental subjects' high frequency of equality judgments in the posttests, however, seems extremely unlikely for the reasons now to be considered.

Counting. Counting, particularly in children the age of the subjects in this experiment, is fairly readily recognizable. Although, of course, there need not be overt verbalization of the numbers "one, two, three," etc., certain kinds of movements of the eyes are almost inevitable, even should (for which there was little reason here) the subject wish to avoid them. The subject was under the constant surveillance of the E who was working directly with him—as well as of the other E when not writing—and any possible indication of counting, of whatever kind, was carefully noted.

There are two different ways in which counting might have led to the results. One is that the subjects might have counted during training, and observed that number remained the same when the objects were only rearranged and nothing was added or removed. However, only three of the 15 Experimental subjects gave any indication of counting during training, and none of them ever counted after as well as before a rearrangement.

The other possibility is that the judgments of equality in the posttests themselves were based on counting, thus actually having nothing to do with conservation. Of the 15 Experimental subjects, five may have counted at some time during the posttests (one of whom is also one of those who may have counted during training). To all but two of these five the interpretation that equality was recognized through counting cannot be applied. Thus, one was the single Experimental subject who did not assert equality between the dolls and beds in the first posttest; he said the number of dolls and beds was different, and counted only after being asked how he told this. Another of the five counted the cards as they were put out, and the checkers as he put them on the cards. This subject cannot have recognized equality through counting instead of conservation either, for he did not count again when the checkers were taken off and put closer together. A third subject did start counting when the dolls were taken out and put closer together, but was stopped before he got very far. The fourth and fifth subjects are the only ones who recognized equality where this might have been due to counting and not conservation, and one of these recognized equality only in the first posttest, and not the second. There is, then, very little support for either interpretation in terms of counting.

It may seem surprising that counting was not more frequently used to answer the question whether two sets of objects were the same number. However, there is much evidence that counting is frequently a rather rote procedure for young children, which carries very little meaning. Particularly striking evidence for this was obtained in a study by Wohlwill and Lowe (17). These investigators asked 23 kindergarten children who maintained that the number of chips in two equal rows was different when one row was arranged differently from the other, to count the chips in each row. Nineteen of the 23 continued to assert that there was a different number in the two rows immediately after counting seven chips in each.

Social reinforcement. Observation of sameness of number by counting, then, does not appear to be capable of explaining the frequent recognition of equality by the Experimental subjects after the training procedure. If the increase in their judgments of equality cannot be accounted for by increased observation of equality, can it be explained by social reinforcement of such judgments?

The difficulty with this alternative is that during the entire training procedure differentiating the Experimental group from the Control, the subjects were only asked to make predictions as to whether the two sets of objects would fit together again, and never to make any statements regarding number. Thus there was no opportunity for judgments of equality to be reinforced, quite apart from the attempts of the experimenters to avoid giving reinforcement at all. It cannot be argued that the predictions of fit were equivalent to judgments of equality, since, as discussed above, many subjects were able to correctly predict that the dolls would fit back in the beds immediately after stating that the number of dolls and beds were not equal.

Neither direct observation of equality, nor social reinforcement of equality judgments, then, seems capable of explaining the results of this experiment.

INTERPRETATION IN TERMS OF REVERSIBILITY

The role reversibility may play. The inadequacy of direct observation and social reinforcement in explaining the effectiveness of the training procedure lends further support to a reversibility interpretation. Let us now examine more closely the role reversibility may play.

When the dolls are in the beds, or the checkers are on the cards, the subjects recognize the equality of their number by the fact of their fitting together. Fitting vs. not fitting appears to function as a defining attribute for equality. But when the dolls are taken out and put closer together, or the checkers are rearranged after being taken off the cards, this defining attribute is removed. In the absence of counting no continuing criterion of equality remains. How, therefore, can judgments of equality still be made?

Adults and older children tend to take the continuation of equality for granted. Obvious as it may seem, however, one cannot establish logically that the numbers continue to be equal. (Attempting to derive it from statements such as "Quantity does not change if nothing is added or taken away" would, of course, be tantamount to assuming what one was trying to prove.) Continued equality is assumed, we believe, as a result of the knowledge that if the defining attribute were brought back (if the dolls and beds, or the checkers and cards, were put back together), then the criterion of equality (fitting, nothing being left over) would be observable again. More generally, our hypothesis is that *a property will be regarded as conserved under an operation which removes a defining attribute of that property, if the inverse operation is expected to lead to the attribute's reappearance at the same value.*[4]

---

[4] The conservation of equality is not, of course, logically deducible from the fact that the objects will fit back together again. It is, however, efficient and economical to regard a property as unchanging upon an operation's removing a defining attribute, if the inverse operation will lead to the attribute's reappearance at the same value. One can in this way "keep tabs," as it were, on the possibilities. Conservation may thus belong to the same category as other examples of economical cognition (3).

The experimental training in reversibility was, of course, specifically designed to lead to the expectation that if one tried to put the dolls and beds, or the checkers and cards, back together, one would find that they would again fit exactly, just as before. It is the development of this expectation in the children, we submit, which accounts for their conservation responses in the posttests. They act as if they could still see the fitting together, once they come to expect that when fitting or not fitting becomes observable again, it will be the former rather than the latter which is observed.

Indeed, we believe that the recognition of reversibility, as here described, is the only interpretation of the development of conservation in the current literature which provides a tenable explanation of the results of this experiment. Direct observation and social reinforcement have already been shown to be inadequate. The other interpretations which have been proposed are conflict (12, 13), set (18), reduction of immediate stimulus dependence (6, 16), differentiation (5, 11, 16, 17), recognition of compensation (6, 7), and inference from change with addition and subtraction (8, 9, 10, 13, 14, 17). None of these provides a basis for explaining the striking difference between the results of the present experiment and previous ones. It will be recalled that in only one previous study (13) had an increase in conservation been found among experimental subjects which was significantly greater than that found among control subjects. Even in that study, improvement in conservation was found only in 12 out of a total of 30 subjects who were given training, as against improvement in all 15 trained subjects in the present experiment.

Further—although this is not, strictly, a critique of these interpretations when applied only to the present experiment—it may be noted that conflict, set, reduction of immediate stimulus dependence, and differentiation do not really provide alternative explanations of the general phenomenon of conservation. These interpretations all assume that there already is a tendency towards conservation, rather than explaining such a tendency— they are thus insufficient to account fully for conservation by themselves. The most they could possibly do is to account for given increases in conservation responses in situations where a prior tendency towards conservation may be assumed—and even this, of course, would be possible only where there were no other problems such as the differences in results between our experiment and previous ones.

The last two interpretations do not assume a prior tendency towards conservation, but there are additional difficulties with these as well. It seems highly improbable that conservation results from the recognition of compensation for changes in one dimension (length) by changes in another (density), since one is never able to observe directly that a given change in one exactly compensates for a given change in the other. Recognition of such compensation thus would appear to result from conservation rather than to be its cause. As to the last interpretation, the absence of change without addition or subtraction does not follow from the presence of change with them. The length of a row of objects, for example, as well as number, changes when an object is added or taken away, but length is not therefore assumed to stay constant if nothing is added or removed.

Our proposal that a property is regarded as conserved under an operation removing a defining attribute, when the inverse operation is expected to lead to the attribute's reappearance at the same value, thus seems to be the only interpretation adequate to explain the results of this experiment.

The subjects who already recognized reversibility. If conservation results from the recognition of reversibility, as here proposed, however, then how is the fact to be explained that many of the nonconservation subjects already knew that rearrangements were reversible? As mentioned above, the observation that reversibility could be known without conservation was, in fact, used by Smedslund (8) to argue against the possibility that conservation results from reversibility's recognition. Further, training in reversibility can hardly be expected to bring about knowledge of reversibility in subjects who already have such knowledge, and it will be recalled that the training procedure induced conservation in these subjects as well as the others.

However, the possibility of a return to the original situation probably has not occurred, prior to their being asked, to those subjects who are able to answer correctly when asked about reversibility, but who have denied conservation. To think of this possibility, after all, involves going well beyond the immediate stimuli, and children seem to be particularly likely to respond to immediate stimuli rather than to possible inferences from them, even when they are quite capable of the inferences (1). But conservation is probably caused by actually thinking of the inverse operation, and realizing that it would bring about again the situation implying equality, and not by the mere ability to answer correctly, if asked, that it would do so.

The difference between such actual thinking and the mere (dispositional) ability thus explains how conservation can result from the recognition of reversibility, although reversibility may be "known" (in the dispositional sense) without conservation. It also explains how even nonconservation subjects who have such knowledge may be led to conservation by experience with reversibility, for although this experience will not provide them with new information, it will tend to induce them to think of the possibility of reversal without being prompted.

The training in reversibility given in this experiment, then, probably contributed to conservation both by providing subjects who did not already have it with the information that rearrangements are reversible, and by inducing subjects to think of reversal's possibility.

CONCLUSION

The present experiment supports the hypothesis that a property is regarded as conserved under an operation removing a defining attribute, when it is expected that the inverse operation will lead to the attribute's reappearance at the same value. Experiences with such consequences—experiences with reversibility, in our sense of the term—thus may be what leads to the development of number conservation, not only in the present experiment, but in normal life.

Similarly, other conservations, such as that of amount, may also be acquired through experience with reversibility. Thus, for example, the realization that the amount of liquid does not change when it is poured from one container into another may result from experience with the fact that if the liquid is poured back into the original container again, it will always fill it to just the same degree it did initially.[5]

The attainment of conservation in previous experiments—when it has occurred—may also have been due to subjects' coming to think of the possibility of reversal. Experience with reversibility was of course never provided in these experiments, but experience was given which could be expected to lead subjects who already knew about reversibility from normal life to take it into consideration. Thus, Smedslund's procedure involving practice in conflict situations referred to above (the only procedure heretofore found to result in an increase in conservation greater than that in control groups) involved changing the form of some material before the subject in a variety of ways. This could well have served to focus the subject's attention away from the immediate perceptual situation and towards possible ways in which the material could be transformed, and if he already knew that the changes in form were reversible, he would be likely to think of the possibility of returning the material to its original shape and size. The effect of training here would of course be expected to be weaker than in the present experiment, where not only transformation but reversibility itself was experienced and, as already discussed, this was indeed the case.

The unexpected increase in conservation among control as well as experimental subjects in other previous experiments may also be due to the subjects having been encouraged to think about the possibility of reversal. Some experience with transformations is, of necessity, provided by testing for conservation itself, and hence any extensive testing may be expected to increase attention to possible transformations. Again, only a relatively small effect would be expected, and only relatively few subjects have been led to conservation in these experiments.

Reversibility thus appears capable of explaining not only the results of the present experiment, but also those of previous studies, as well as the normal development of conservation of number and amount.

REFERENCES

1. BALDWIN, A. L. *Behavior and development in childhood.* Dryden, 1955.
2. FLAVELL, J. H. *The developmental psychology of Jean Piaget.* Van Nostrand, 1963.
3. HOCHBERG, J. E. Effects of the Gestalt revolution: the Cornell symposium on perception. *Psychol. Rev.*, 1957, **64**, 73–84.
4. LOVELL, K., & OGILVIE, E. A study of the conservation of substance in

---

[5] It may be noted that there are certain cases of amount conservation—such as conservation of the amount of sugar when it is dissolved in water—in which reversibility cannot have been experienced, because the inverse of the operation removing the defining attributes cannot be performed. Nonetheless, in these cases as well as the others it is believed that the inverse operation *would* lead to the attributes' reappearance at the same value, if it *could* be performed. Although this belief—and, hence, conservation—cannot be due here to experience with reversibility in the very situations at issue, it may be based on such experience in other, similar situations. For example, the belief that the dissolved sugar would again make up a piece of the same size and shape as before if it could be put back together again probably results from experiences with other objects which had been broken up into several pieces and then were put back together again.

the junior school child. *Brit. J. Educ. Psychol.*, 1960, **30**, 109–118.

5. PIAGET, J., & INHELDER, B. *Le développement des quantités chez l'enfant.* Paris: Delachaux and Niestlé, 1941.

6. PIAGET, J. *The child's conception of number.* Humanities, 1952.

7. PIAGET, J. Equilibration and the development of logical structures. In Tanner, J. M., & Inhelder, B. (Eds.), *Discussions on child development, Vol. IV:* The proceedings of the fourth meeting of the World Health Organization Study Group on the Psychobiological Development of the Child. International Universities Press, 1960. Pp. 98–105.

8. SMEDSLUND, J. The acquisition of conservation of substance and weight in children: I. Introduction. *Scand. J. Psychol.*, 1961, **2**, 11–20.

9. SMEDSLUND, J. The acquisition of conservation of substance and weight in children: II. External reinforcement of conservation of weight and of the operations of addition and subtraction. *Scand. J. Psychol.*, 1961, **2**, 71–84.

10. SMEDSLUND, J. The acquisition of conservation of substance and weight in children: III. Extinction of conservation of weight acquired "normally" and by means of empirical controls on a balance. *Scand. J. Psychol.*, 1961, **2**, 85–87.

11. SMEDSLUND, J. The acquisition of conservation of substance and weight in children: IV. Attempt at extinction of the visual components of the weight concept. *Scand. J. Psychol.*, 1961, **2**, 153–155.

12. SMEDSLUND, J. The acquisition of conservation of substance and weight in children: V. Practice in conflict situations without external reinforcement. *Scand. J. Psychol.*, 1961, **2**, 156–160.

13. SMEDSLUND, J. The acquisition of conservation of substance and weight in children: VI. Practice on continuous vs. discontinuous material in problem situations without external reinforcement. *Scand. J. Psychol.*, 1961, **2**, 203–210.

14. SMEDSLUND, J. The acquisition of conservation of substance and weight in children: VII. Conservation of discontinuous quantity and the operations of adding and taking away. *Scand. J. Psychol.*, 1962, **3**, 69–77.

15. WALLACH, M. A. Research on children's thinking. In Stevenson, H. W. (Ed.), Child psychology. *Yearb. nat. Soc. Stud. Educ.*, 1963, **62**, (I). Pp. 236–276.

16. WOHLWILL, J. F. From perception to inference: a dimension of cognitive development. In Kessen, W., & Kuhlman, C. (Eds.), Thought in the young child. *Child Develpm. Monogr.*, 1962, **27**, No. 2 (Serial No. 83). Pp. 87–107.

17. WOHLWILL, J. F., & LOWE, R. C. Experimental analysis of the development of the conservation of number. *Child Develpm.*, 1962, **33**, 153–167.

18. ZIMILES, H. A note on Piaget's concept of conservation. *Child Develpm.*, 1963, **34**, 691–695.

Situational Generality of Conservation[1]

Ina C. Uzgiris[*]

University of Illinois

The influence of situational variables (materials used to test for the attainment of conservation) on the sequential development of the conservation of substance, weight, and volume as proposed by Jean Piaget was studied in 120 grade school children. A scalogram analysis indicated that conservation of the three quantities is achieved in the above sequence on each of the materials. In an analysis of variance, the effects of the type of quantity, age, material, and the interaction of age and quantity were found to be significant. Although variation across materials was present, inversions in the conservation sequence were rare. The finding that variation across materials is greater at some age levels than others suggested that a relation between situational variables and conservation behavior may be most evident during the formation of a conservation schema.

A marked awakening of interest has recently occurred in the work of Jean Piaget on the intellectual development of children, particularly in the studies performed after 1930 (17, 18, 24, 19, 22, 23, 10). Good summaries of this work are available elsewhere (1, 3, 7).

At around the age of 7, Piaget finds reasoning becoming operational in that it attains the characteristics of logical and mathematical operations. Although this early operational reasoning is still limited to concrete situations, it nevertheless depends on the availability of invariant concepts or conservations. The most general of these concepts are the ideas of number, space, time, substance, weight, volume, etc. Prior to attaining operational reasoning, children evaluate such quantities by relying almost exclusively on their perceptual appearances. Procedures like measuring, weighing, and enumerating are not used, because children under about 7 years of age are not convinced that length, weight, and number remain invariant through every rearrangement of an object. The study of the development of logical thinking, therefore, must study the attainment of such invariant concepts and the child's coming to recognize them as self-evident.

The attainment of conservation of substance, of weight, and of volume

---

Reprinted from *Child Development*, 1964, 35, 831–841. © Society for Research in Child Development, Inc., 1964.

[1] This paper is based on a dissertation done under the direction of Prof. J. McV. Hunt and submitted to the University of Illinois in partial fulfillment of the requirements for the Ph.D. degree.

[*] Department of Psychology, University of Illinois, Urbana.

at around the ages of 7, 9, and 12, respectively, was first described in a study by Piaget and Inhelder (20), and the sequence was verified on a group of mentally retarded children by Inhelder (9). Furthermore, Piaget and Inhelder (21) have proposed that this sequence follows the law of logical implication, i.e., that the conservation of weight always implies the conservation of substance, and the conservation of volume always implies the conservation of both weight and substance. Other investigators have generally confirmed Piaget's findings (4, 5, 6, 12, 13, 14, 25).

Piaget used the now classical technique of two plasticine balls to test for the achievement of conservation. Since other investigators were concerned with either replicating the gradual achievement of the invariance of these concepts, the ages at which they are achieved, or with showing the crucial role of particular logical operations, they have also used the two plasticine balls. However, several studies (2, 4, 8, 12, 13, 15) have mentioned, mostly parenthetically, that some children who demonstrated conservation of a particular concept with the plasticine balls did not show conservation of the same concept when confronted with a different material, or vice versa.

If each of these levels of conceptual invariance is based on a particular development of logical operations and these operations are organized in a hierarchical sequence, then the type of material used to test for the attainment of the levels of invariance should not affect the sequence of their attainment, although there might be some variation in the time of attainment of a particular concept in the sequence with different types of materials.

The purpose of the present study was to investigate systematically the effect of varying the materials used to test for the conservation of substance, weight, and volume on the observed sequential attainment of these concepts.

METHOD

In lieu of a longitudinal study of the sequential attainment of the conservation of substance, weight, and volume with several materials, the technique of scalogram analysis was adopted for cross-sectional data. Although this technique has been most frequently applied in the field of attitude measurement, Wohlwill (28) has used it to study the development of the concept of number and has discussed at length the assumptions underlying the use of this technique for such a purpose. A somewhat modified version of Guttman's original technique of scalogram analysis, Jackson's Plus Percent Ratio (PPR), discussed by White and Saltz (27) was chosen in this study.

SUBJECTS

A total of 120 subjects comprised the sample. All the Ss were students at a parochial school in Champaign, Illinois. Since this school is the only one of its kind within the town, it draws students from various socioeconomic groups, and its student body may be considered fairly typical of the town's student population.

The sample of Ss consisted of 20 children from each of the first through sixth grades, 10 boys and 10 girls from each grade. The classroom teachers selected which students would participate in the study, having been asked to pick neither the brightest nor their "problem" cases.

MATERIALS

The following four materials were used in this study:

1. Plasticine balls, each 2 in. in diameter, of a greenish color.
2. Metal nuts, ½ in. across and ½ in. high, to serve as metal cubes.
3. Wire coils, 1¼ in. in diameter, 3 coils high, made of multi-stranded, twisted wire.
4. Straight pieces of red, plastic-insulated wire, each 6 in. long and ⅟₁₆ in. in diameter.

Two glass jars and metal-cutting shears were also used in the course of the study.

PROCEDURE

In general, the procedure was very similar to that used by Piaget and Inhelder (20). Ss were tested individually, in a conference room of the school. They were seated across a table from the experimenter, and all materials to be used in the study were visible on the table. The experiment was introduced by E in the following manner:

When people make a judgment, when they say that two things are alike, or that two things are different, they usually have a reason in mind. It seems that these reasons change as people grow up. I am trying to learn more about this. Therefore, I am going to show you different things and ask you questions about them, and then ask you "why" each time, because I want to know *your* reasons for what you say. OK?

The materials were presented one at a time, in a counterbalanced order, so that each material appeared in the same position an equal number of times in each grade. For any one material, questions regarding the conservation of substance were always asked first, then those regarding the conservation of weight and, finally, those of volume. S was always presented with two identical objects made of a given material and was asked if he thought they were alike in terms of the quantity being considered. S was urged to make the objects alike or to pick out two others that were alike if he did not think that the ones presented to him were. Once S was convinced that the two test objects were identical, one of them was deformed into a different shape and S was asked if he thought they were still identical in terms of the quantity considered. To ascertain the conservation of volume, one of the test objects was placed in a glass jar half-filled with water, S observed the water level rise, and was then questioned about the amount of water that the other object would displace if immersed in an identical jar equally filled with water, which was also present.

Three deformations were performed on each material, which were repeated for substance, weight, and volume. The deformations were as follows:

Plasticine balls. Of the two identical balls, one was (a) rolled into a sausage; (b) further elongated into a long cylinder; (c) torn into three pieces.

Metal nuts. Of two buildings, each containing 18 nuts arranged 3 by 2 by 3, one was (a) changed into a 3 by 3 by 2 structure; (b) formed into a column with 3 nuts as a base, 6 nuts high; (c) broken up into three separate piles, each with 3 nuts as a base, 2 nuts high.

Wire coils. Of two identical coils of wire, one was (a) slightly stretched; (b) stretched farther into an almost straight piece; (c) about ⅓ of the strands were separated to form two pieces of wire.

Plastic wire. Of two straight pieces, one was (a) tied with a simple knot; (b) tied with a second knot and twisted to almost a round shape; (c) straightened and cut into three separate pieces.

A standard set of questions was used. S was required to give a reason for each response and, sometimes, an additional question was asked to clarify these reasons. The following questions were asked to test for the conservation of substance on the plasticine balls:

1. Is there as much clay in this ball as in this one?
2. Is there as much clay in the ball as in the sausage? Why?
3. Is there as much clay in the ball as in the sausage now? Why?
4. Is there as much clay in the ball as over here? Why?

The questions were appropriately modified for each type of quantity and each material. E did not proceed further until the first question was answered affirmatively. All responses made by S were recorded by E, verbatim as far as possible.

METHOD OF ANALYSIS

In analyzing the responses and deciding whether a particular S was conserving the quantity under consideration, each response following each deformation was evaluated separately, together with the reason for it.

Since the questions were somewhat repetitious, it was conceivable that Ss could carry over response sets from one quantity to another, so that the quality of the reasons became crucial. Few problems arose in classifying the responses for substance and weight, since whenever S stated that the original and the deformed objects were alike in terms of substance or weight, he usually gave an adequate and acceptable reason. However, for volume, quite a number of Ss maintained that the two objects (the original and the deformed) would make the water rise the same amount, but gave either obviously unacceptable or questionable justifications. Reasons like "because it could be made the same shape as before" or "it just looks like it would" were considered unacceptable, while statements like "there is the same amount in both" or "they both weigh the same" were considered questionable, since they did not deal directly with volume or the three-dimensionality of the two objects. Consequently, those who claimed that the original and the deformed object would raise the water the same amount and gave a questionable explanation were generally asked whether the two objects took up the same amount of space. If they answered this in the affirmative, they were classified as conservers, but if they denied that the two objects took up the same amount of space, their affirmative response to the first question was discounted.

RESULTS

A specific set of criteria was used to rate the responses of all Ss. Responses of a sample of 24 Ss, four from each grade, were rated independently by two raters. The percentage agreement between the two sets of ratings for the conservation of substance was 99 per cent, for the conservation of weight 97 per cent, and for the conservation of volume 94 per cent.

The differences between the mean scores of boys and those of girls on the four materials at each age level were nonsignificant. Thus, the scores of boys and girls were grouped together in all subsequent analyses.

The effect of the order in which the different materials were administered was also investigated. A compounded score across all three quantities for the two materials administered first and for the two materials administered last was computed for each S. The difference between the means of such scores for each grade level and for the sample as a whole was found to be nonsignificant.

Numerical scores were computed by awarding 1 point for each conservation response on each type of quantity for each material. This means that the distribution of scores was quite curtailed, since a S's score could range only from 0 to 3 for any quantity on a given material, from 0 to 9 on any given material, and from 0 to 12 on any given quantity.

TABLE 1

SCALABILITY OF RESPONSES FOR SUBSTANCE, WEIGHT, AND VOLUME

Material	Jackson's Plus Per Cent Ratio (PPR)
Plasticine balls	.98
Metal cubes	.98
Wire coils	.98
Plastic wire	.98
Total	.99

SCALOGRAM ANALYSIS

For the scalogram analysis, the ratings on the three separate questions ascertaining the conservation of a quantity on any given material were collapsed into a single judgment of either conservation or nonconservation. Only those who obtained a score of 3 on any one quantity on a given material were classified as conservers.

Insofar as the scalogram analysis is a valid index of the sequential attainment of conservation of the three quantities by individual Ss, it may be concluded that the conservation of substance, of weight, and of volume is clearly attained in the order postulated by Piaget, since Jackson has suggested a PPR of .70 as the cutoff point for scalability. In fact, out of 120 Ss, only 8 gave a nonscale pattern on some one of the materials used. It seems that chance factors such as the wandering of a child's attention, fatigue, and the like can easily account for these few exceptions, especially since no single S gave a nonscale pattern on more than one material.

Furthermore, the responses scaled for each of the materials separately, so it may be said that conservation of the three quantities develops in the same sequence with various types of materials as well.

AGE AT ACHIEVING CONSERVATION

Increased conservation with age is an indirect method of assessing the sequential development of conservation. If the various patterns delineated by the scalogram analysis are compared in terms of the mean age of Ss giving each pattern, it can be seen that age increases with the attainment of conservation of the three quantities (see Table 2).

TABLE 2

MEAN AGE OF SUBJECTS SHOWING VARIOUS SCALE PATTERNS
(+ indicates presence of conservation)

Scale Pattern			
Substance	Weight	Volume	Mean Age
−	−	−	7 years, 9 months
+	−	−	9 years, 3 months
+	+	−	10 years, 0 months
+	+	+	10 years, 7 months

CONSISTENCY OF RESPONSES ACROSS MATERIALS

One way of looking at the consistency of responses across materials is to compare the percentage of Ss conserving substance, weight, and volume at the various grade levels from one material to another. Table 3 shows that there is considerable variation in the percentage of Ss who conserve any given quantity across materials, especially at certain grade levels. Some Ss

TABLE 3

PERCENTAGE CONSERVING SUBSTANCE (s), WEIGHT (w), AND VOLUME (v)
ON DIFFERENT MATERIALS

Grade	Mean Age*	Plasticine Balls			Metal Cubes			Wire Coils			Plastic Wire		
		S	W	V	S	W	V	S	W	V	S	W	V
1st	6–11	30	20	0	40	20	0	35	10	5	35	0	0
2nd	7–10	70	35	10	70	55	0	55	35	15	45	35	5
3rd	8–11	90	65	20	95	80	5	90	60	10	90	60	10
4th	10– 0	90	65	15	100	70	20	85	55	5	85	65	10
5th	10–11	85	75	15	95	80	30	90	70	25	95	70	10
6th	12– 2	90	85	20	100	80	30	95	80	20	95	80	25

* Age in years and months.

must change their position in the conservation sequence across materials to give the variation.

A correlational analysis was performed to evaluate further the extent to which individual Ss varied their responses across materials. The scores of Ss at each grade level on one material (summed for all three quantities) were correlated with their scores on all other materials.

Table 4 shows that although none of the correlations are perfect, they indicate considerable consistency. It is also notable that the consistency of

TABLE 4

CORRELATION OF CONSERVATION RESPONSES ACROSS MATERIALS

	1st Grade	2nd Grade	3rd Grade	4th Grade	5th Grade	6th Grade	Total
Plasticine Balls *with*							
Metal Cubes	.80	.56	.76	.47	.31	.51	.72
Wire Coils	.81	.84	.84	.58	.48	.33	.75
Plastic Wire	.82	.74	.72	.65	.45	.34	.75
Metal Cubes *with*							
Wire Coils	.78	.60	.74	.58	.46	.82	.75
Plastic Wire	.88	.37	.84	.73	.60	.72	.78
Wire Coils *with*							
Plastic Wire	.82	.77	.73	.62	.77	.91	.83
Average *r*	.82	.67	.77	.61	.53	.66	.76

responses across materials is greater at some ages than at others. The correlations are high, for instance, at grade 1 when almost no Ss conserve any of the three quantities and at grade 3 when about 90 per cent conserve substance. At grade 6 the correlations tend to be high again when 80 per cent of Ss are conserving weight and practically all are conserving substance. In between these times, when conservation is being achieved, the mean correlation across materials decreases considerably.

Furthermore, a comparison of the percentage of Ss giving only one or two conservation responses for substance, weight, and volume at the various

TABLE 5

PERCENTAGE GIVING ONE OR TWO CONSERVATION RESPONSES FOR
SUBSTANCE (s), WEIGHT (w), AND VOLUME (v) ON
DIFFERENT MATERIALS

	Percentage Conserving on											
	Plasticine Balls			Metal Cubes			Wire Coils			Plastic Wire		
Grade	S	W	V	S	W	V	S	W	V	S	W	V
1st	5	10	10	20	10	0	10	5	0	10	20	5
2nd	5	10	0	5	5	0	20	15	0	30	20	0
3rd	5	25	0	10	15	0	5	20	0	0	20	0
4th	10	25	5	0	20	5	10	20	0	10	25	0
5th	5	15	0	5	10	10	5	5	0	5	25	5
6th	5	0	5	0	20	5	5	10	5	5	10	5

grade levels across different materials indicates a greater preponderance of such responses when the respective conservation schemata are being formed (see Table 5). Thus, such limited conservation responses for substance are most prevalent in grades 1 and 2, for weight in grades 3 and 4, and for volume in grade 6.

ANALYSIS OF VARIANCE

The data were cast in a type VI analysis of variance design described by Lindquist (11). The analysis was undertaken with full awareness that the present data do not quite meet all the assumptions. The sample was not selected randomly and the distribution of scores was quite curtailed, but it has been demonstrated that failure to meet the assumptions does not completely invalidate the procedure (11, pp. 78–86).

The analysis of variance indicates that the attainment of conservation varies with age, with the type of material used for testing, and with the type of quantity (substance, weight, or volume). It also shows a significant interaction between age and type of quantity conserved, which was expected on the basis of the sequential development of conservation of the three quantities.

TABLE 6

ANALYSIS OF VARIANCE SUMMARY

Source	Sum of Squares	df	Mean Square	Error Term	F
Between subjects	947.383	119			
Age (grade level)	377.279	5	75.456	(b)	5.080**
Error (b)	570.104	114	5.001		
Within subjects	2041.750	1320			
Material	12.325	3	4.107	$(w)^1$	6.984**
Quantity	1039.406	2	519.703	$(w)^2$	305.889**
Material × Quantity	4.394	6	.732	$(w)^3$	1.710*ns*
Material × Age	5.246	15	.349	$(w)^1$	.593*ns*
Quantity × Age	78.711	10	7.871	$(w)^2$	4.632**
Material × Quantity × Age	20.122	30	.670	$(w)^3$	1.565*
Error (w)	881.546	1254			
Error $(w)^1$	201.512	342			
Error $(w)^2$	387.383	228			
Error $(w)^3$	292.651	684			

* $p < .05$.
** $p < .01$.

DISCUSSION

In general, the results of the present study support Piaget's theory of sequential intellectual development and, particularly, the sequential attainment of conservation of substance, weight, and volume in the above order by each individual.

The ages at which about half the Ss of this sample conserved substance and weight are reasonably consistent with those suggested by Piaget and other investigators. In contrast, only 20 per cent of the sixth graders (average age, 12–2) were found to conserve volume. This is at variance with Piaget's findings, with those of Lovell and Ogilvie (14), and of Lunzer (16); but it corresponds rather nicely with the findings of Elkind (6), who reported that only 27 per cent of his sample of children between 11 and 12 years of age conserved volume. It may be that this difference in the age at which children come to conserve volume reflects the effect of certain experiential factors, but it also may reflect a difference in testing procedure. Most other studies (20, 14, 16) asked their Ss to compare how far an object in each of two shapes would cause water to rise in a jar. This may be tapping the conceptualization of volume at a level more concrete (less abstract) than that used here and by Elkind (5). In the latter cases, the Ss were asked to indicate which shape would occupy the greater space, by verbalizing this either as an explanation for the rise in water level or in reply to a direct question. It is interesting to note that Lovell and Ogilvie (14) report that only 19 per cent of their Ss who conserved volume, according to their criteria, stated spontaneously, as a reason for equal rise in water level for objects of different shape, the fact that the two objects "take up the same room." Subtle differences in procedure may have appreciable effects on age results and should be carefully investigated.

Furthermore, the conservation of substance, weight, and volume seems to be attained in the same sequence with any material. However, this does not imply a perfect coordination of steps in the conservation sequence across different materials in any one individual. Both the analysis of variance and the correlational analysis lead to the conclusion that an individual's position on the conservation sequence is not constant across materials. The variation does not seem to be systematic, in that there was no single material on which all Ss were either accelerated or lagging behind. It seems more a matter of individual differences, although the discrepancies generally were not large.

Individual past experience may well underlie situational differences and account for the observed inconsistency across the various materials. Although Piaget does not focus on the effects of specific environmental variables on development, he does not deny their importance, as has been sometimes suggested (29), since he describes the schemata as evolving and differentiating in contact with the environment. Encounters with the environment are thought to be desirable and necessary, except that the internal satisfaction of recognition or the confirmation of an expectation is substituted for external reward. It may well be that when a schema is developing, specific contacts with the environment will lead it to accommodate more in certain areas than in others, producing situational specificity in terms of specific past experiences of the individual. But after a certain number or a certain variety of encounters, a schema may develop independence and start to be applied universally. This leads to the expectation that schemata would be in a greater state of flux while developing, showing situational specificity, but once they consolidate, the situational variability would be expected to disappear. The waxing and waning of consistency, to be noted in Table 4, fits such a view.

Another approach to the understanding of the observed situational variability is to look for broader classes of variables that would subsume groups of different materials. Piaget has classified materials into continuous and discontinuous ones. Smedslund (26) has observed that the conservation of substance is first achieved with discontinuous materials and only later with the continuous. The present study seems to bear this out. Metal cubes would qualify as the only discontinuous material and it appears that a greater percentage of Ss attained conservation of each of the three quantities on this material. There might well be other salient classifications of materials that would merit investigation and would lead to a better understanding of the observed situational variation.

REFERENCES

1. ANTHONY, J. Symposium on the contribution of current theories to understanding of child development. IV. The system makers: Piaget and Freud. *Brit. J. med. Psychol.*, 1957, **30**, 255–269.
2. BEARD, R. M. An investigation of concept formation among infant school children. Unpublished doctoral dissertation, London Univer., 1957.
3. BERLYNE, D. E. Recent developments in Piaget's work. *Brit. J. educ. Psychol.*, 1957, **27**, 1–12.
4. CARPENTER, T. E. A pilot study for a qualitative investigation of Jean Piaget's original work on concept formation. *Educ. Rev.*, 1955, **7**, 142–149.
5. ELKIND, D. Children's discovery of the conservation of mass, weight, and volume: Piaget's replication study II. *J. genet. Psychol.*, 1961, **98**, 219–227.
6. ELKIND, D. Quantity conceptions in junior and senior high school students. *Child Develpm.*, 1961, **32**, 551–560.
7. HUNT, J. McV. *Intelligence and experience.* Ronald, 1961.
8. HYDE, D. M. An investigation of Piaget's theories of the development of the concept of number. Unpublished doctoral dissertation, London Univer., 1959.
9. INHELDER, B. *Le diagnostic du raisonnement chez les débiles mentaux.* Neuchâtel: Delachaux et Niestlé, 1944.
10. INHELDER, B., & PIAGET, J. (1955).* *The growth of logical thinking from childhood to adolescence.* Basic Books, 1958.
11. LINDQUIST, E. F. *Design and analysis of experiments in psychology and education.* Houghton Mifflin, 1956.
12. LOVELL, K., & OGILVIE, E. A study of the conservation of substance in the junior school child. *Brit. J. educ. Psychol.*, 1960, **30**, 109–118
13. LOVELL, K., & OGILVIE, E. A study of the conservation of weight in the junior school child. *Brit. J. educ. Psychol.*, 1961, **31**, 138–144.
14. LOVELL, K., & OGILVIE, E. The growth of the concept of volume in junior school children. *J. child Psychol. Psychiat.*, 1961, **2**, 118–126.
15. LUNZER, E. A. A pilot study for a quantitative investigation of Jean Piaget's original work on concept formation. *Educ. Rev.*, 1956, **8**, 193–200.
16. LUNZER, E. A. Some points of Piagetian theory in the light of experimental criticism. *J. child Psychol. Psychiat.*, 1960, **1**, 191–202.
17. PIAGET, J. (1936).* *The origins of intelligence in children.* Int. Univer. Press, 1952.
18. PIAGET, J. (1937).* *The construction of reality in the child.* Basic Books, 1954.

19. PIAGET, J. (1945).* *Play, dreams, and imitation in childhood.* Norton, 1951.
20. PIAGET, J., & INHELDER, B. *Le développement des quantités chez l'enfant.* Neuchâtel et Paris: Delachaux et Niestlé, 1941.
21. PIAGET, J., & INHELDER, B. Diagnosis of mental operations and theory of intelligence. *Amer. J. ment. Defic.,* 1947, 51, 401–406.
22. PIAGET, J., & INHELDER, B. (1948).* *The child's conception of space.* London: Routledge & Kegan Paul, 1956.
23. PIAGET, J., INHELDER, B., & SZEMINSKA, A. (1948).* *The child's conception of geometry.* Basic Books, 1960.
24. PIAGET, J., & SZEMINSKA, A. (1941).* *The child's conception of number.* Humanities Press, 1952.
25. SMEDSLUND, J. The acquisition of conservation of substance and weight in children. II. External reinforcement of conservation of weight and of the operations of addition and subtraction. *Scand. J. Psychol.,* 1961, 2, 71–84.
26. SMEDSLUND, J. The acquisition of conservation of substance and weight in children. VI. Practice on continuous vs. discontinuous material in problem situations without external reinforcement. *Scand. J. Psychol.,* 1961, 2, 203–210.
27. WHITE, B. W., & SALTZ, E. Measurement of reproducibility. *Psychol. Bull.,* 1957, 54, 81–99.
28. WOHLWILL, J. F. A study of the development of the number concept by scalogram analysis. *J. genet. Psychol.,* 1960, 97, 345–377.
29. WOHLWILL, J. F. From perception to inference: a dimension of cognitive development. In W. Kessen & C. Kuhlman (Eds.), Thought in the young child. *Monogr. Soc. Res. Child Develpm.,* 1962, 27, No. 2 (Serial No. 83). Pp. 87–107.

* This is the date of original publication in French. The date given at the end of each citation is that of the translation available to the author.

PART EIGHT

The Constancy of

Intelligence

In 1964 the New York City School Board banned the use of intelligence testing and its results in their schools; Dr. Allison Davis of the University of Chicago has lectured that intelligence tests should be abandoned, since they do more harm than good; in almost any year a number of books and articles in popular magazines attack the widespread use of intelligence and achievement tests. The layman is tempted to ask whether psychologists have perpetrated a fraud upon the American public.

The fact that intelligence testing has been controversial from its early days is attested to by a survey of the professional literature as far back as the first decade of this century. The specific questions and allegations have varied some, but in general people have asked: What is intelligence? Can it be measured? Is it a relatively stable commodity? What, if anything, can influence it?

The latter two concerns are illustrated in this section. Binet worked with the brilliantly simple idea that if one could find a number of tasks that the *average* child of a given age—6, for example—could perform, this might be used to determine whether any child of 6 was average, retarded, or accelerated. Since these tasks could be discovered for each age, it would be possible to determine how many years a child was retarded or accelerated by taking the difference between his mental age (the age level of the tasks he was able to master) and his chronological age. Thus Binet provided the basis for a quantitative evaluation of the intellectual level at which a person was operating, replacing the gross, subjective opinions often based solely on talking with the parents of a child.

Inevitably, however, people were interested in more than an assessment of current functioning: could not a prediction of future performance be made from this mental age?

Lewis Terman, working at Stanford to adapt Binet's tests to American children (thus the name Stanford-Binet) utilized a suggestion of Stern's and introduced the IQ. This is a simple ratio of mental age to chronological age; its significance lies in its being a measure of *rate* of intellectual development, rather than the *level* of current intellectual functioning measured by the mental age. This assumes that a 10-year-old whose MA is 15, and whose IQ is therefore 150, grows 1½ years mentally for each chronological year. If it is assumed that this rate is constant—that is, that the child grows 1½ mental years each chronological year—the MA at any age is thus 1½ times the chronological age. If your child has an MA of 4 when he is 6, you thus predict that when he is 15 he will be functioning at the same intellectual level as the average 10-year-old. This kind of prediction requires both an adequate measure of intelligence and a constant rate of intellectual development. Psychologists were concerned about the validity of both assumptions and attempted to get relevant data.

An obvious technique is to compare the scores of children tested two or more times with the same test. Ideally, they would get the same IQ each time. The Rugg and Colloton article is one of many such early investigations. They concluded that, although their subjects did not get the same scores, the differences could be accounted for by the reliability of the test. That is, the differences in scores were not indicative of real differences in the level of performance of the children, but were due to imperfections in the test. These imperfections are analogous to a bathroom scale giving a slightly different reading when a given weight is weighed several times. The more nearly these readings coincide, the greater the reliability. Since the Stanford-Binet test was not perfectly reliable, some variability in repeated test scores is expected. If the differences are no greater than those predicted from the reliability of the tests, evidence is provided for the "constancy of the IQ."

The data of Stenquist raise several other questions, however. Rugg and Colloton, in reviewing these data, find that they show greater differences than those of other studies. They suggest that this may have been caused by inexperienced testers (which is thus seen to be another factor influencing the measured IQ). Stenquist argues against this being a factor in his data, but points to another potential source of IQ change. Intelligence tests actually measure what a child has learned, and assume that all those tested have had an opportunity to learn. With this common background, those who are bright will do better than those who are not as bright. If, however, a child had a different background, he may not have had the opportunity to learn, so that his lower score reflects this deprivation rather than a lesser ability. Stenquist points out that many of his subjects were foreign born, and their increase in IQ on the second examination may well reflect this previous inopportunity to learn, rather than a change in intellectual capacity. An intelligence test in English is manifestly more difficult for a child who is just beginning to learn English than for a child of comparable ability who has grown up with English. Much of the current misuse of IQ's reflects this same disregard of environmental deprivation.

Stenquist also raises another concern echoed in the current literature. Even if most of the subjects have a change in IQ of only 5 points or so, some of them have changes of 20 or more points, just as a function of probability in the test reliability. If these exceptions were tested only once, their ability could be grossly misjudged, and decisions based on this might seriously influence the child's future. Thus Stenquist presages today's concern about using an IQ as a definitive measure.

Another long-standing controversy about intelligence developed gradually and reached a kind of "showdown" in the *National Society for the Study of Education Thirty-ninth Yearbook,* published in 1940. The controversy is exemplified by the yearbook's subtitle, *Intelligence: Its Nature and Nurture.*[1] From the beginning, some saw intelligence as an ability to learn, judge, and adapt, which one inherits in some quantity. This intellectual capacity, manifesting itself in the various intellectual activities, was a genetic "given," and could not be influenced by environmental variability. In this case, of course, the IQ would be constant.

Not everyone subscribed to this view, and those who didn't looked for situations in which changes in IQ could be related to specific environmental conditions. A group of investigators at the University of Iowa interested themselves in the effects of adoption or foster placement, and of nursery school attendance. The third selection in this section, by Beth Wellman, is illustrative of the reports of these studies. She refers to some early findings of the Skodak and Skeels studies indicating that children from low-IQ parents show substantially higher IQ's when adopted by or foster-placed in "good" homes. She also reports that Iowa workers found significant increases in IQ in children who attended nursery school, concluding that IQ can be changed. Wellman proceeds to analyze factors that affect this change. Her view is that the change in IQ is not just the result of learning a few more answers to items on the test, but is due to a real difference in the level of intellectual functioning. This is accomplished by providing a stimulating environment that encourages independence in thinking and intellectual curiosity. A modern counterpart to this is the work on creativity and the "divergent intelligence" of Guilford.[2]

Such reports as Wellman's met instant skepticism and rejoinder. Professor McNemar, then at Stanford, was one who saw many flaws in their argument. His 1940 article in the *Psychological Bulletin*[3] was a detailed, devastating attack. While it is much too long and detailed for the present readings, the selection by Simpson illustrates one aspect of McNemar's critique. In it, Simpson refers not to the report of Wellman included here, but to a similar one dealing with the same basic data. He is concerned about the fact that the reader will accept the conclusions at face value when a careful consideration of the methods by which the data were collected and analyzed would make these conclusions not as readily acceptable. By now, you must realize that close concern with the way evidence is gathered is also the guiding concern of this book of readings. Simpson is interested primarily in statistics. He points out that Wellman bases her conclusions on a small percentage of the initial group, on the assumption that this smaller group is typical of the larger one, while he assumes that it is, in reality, a biased group.

[1] *National Society for the Study of Education Thirty-ninth Yearbook. Intelligence: Its Nature and Nurture* (Bloomington, Illinois: Public School Publishing Company, 1940).

[2] Joy P. Guilford, "Three Faces of Intellect," *American Psychologist,* 1959, 14, 469–79.

[3] Quinn McNemar, "A critical examination of the University of Iowa studies of environmental influences upon the IQ," *Psychological Bulletin,* 1940, 37, 63–92.

A point-by-point refutation of McNemar's charges is presented by Wellman, Skeels, and Skodak,[4] but again this is too detailed for inclusion here. A more general statement is presented by Dr. Stoddard, who was at Iowa during this period and later became the president of the University of Illinois. His reasoned review of the literature was one of many such which forced people to assume, with him, that "heredity, constitution, and environment make for IQ inconstancy." Thus the question, "Is intelligence determined by heredity or environment?" abated.

Dr. Stoddard's analysis of the claim that nursery school attendance had no effect upon intelligence provides still another illustration of the necessity for a reader to look carefully at the data, rather than to readily accept the conclusions of an investigator. Incomplete data can also lead one astray, and Stoddard unwittingly illustrates this in his discussion of IQ's in the early years. He argues that, although IQ's derived in the first 6 months of life give a poor prediction of later mental development, the IQ's derived from testing children 2 years old and older are both highly reliable and based on items similar to those used in testing adults. Thus he implies that one can adequately predict adult IQ's from testing 2-year-olds. Later studies, such as Honzik, Macfarlane, and Allen's,[5] in which correlation of IQ's at age 1¾ and age 18 is +.07 and that of age 2 and age 18 is only +.31, have led most people to consider the age of 6 or so (the correlation of IQ at ages 6 and 18 is +.61) as a more satisfactory basis for predicting adult IQ's.

It is interesting to compare Stoddard's final point with recent concern about intelligence testing. Both the action of the New York City schools (in banning the use of tests) and legislation in New York State compelling schools to make psychological test data available to parents relate to the misuse and misinterpretation of scores by those who do not understand the subtleties and qualifications of such scores.

By the early 1940's there was an increasing amount of longitudinal data, that is, scores from the same children tested over a period of many years. These data confirmed the belief that the IQ did indeed vary considerably, and led Bayley,[6] among others, to conclude that these changes could not be accounted for on the basis of test characteristics (including reliability) or environmental shifts alone. She became convinced that mental development itself varied from time to time. Just as a child experiences spurts and plateaus in his physical growth, his rate of intellectual growth is also irregular, and varies in this pattern from child to child.

The last two selections are more contemporary and reflect current concerns. Recently, Professor J. McV. Hunt,[7] of the University of Illinois, has provided a stimulating re-analysis of our concepts of intelligence. He deals

[4] Beth L. Wellman, Harold M. Skeels, and Marie Skodak, "Review of McNemar's Critical Examination of Iowa Studies," *Psychological Bulletin*, 1940, 37, 93–111.

[5] M. P. Honzik, J. W. Macfarlane, and L. Allen, "The Stability of Mental Test Performance Between Two and Eighteen Years," *Journal of Experimental Education*, 1948, 17, 309–324.

[6] Nancy Bayley, "Consistency and Variability in the Growth in IQ from Birth to Eighteen Years," *Journal of Genetic Psychology*, 1949, 75, 165–196.

[7] J. McVickers Hunt, *Intelligence and Experience* (New York: Ronald Press Company, 1961).

with the intellectual processes and relates them to early development, concluding:

. . . it is no longer unreasonable to consider that it might be feasible to discover ways to govern the encounters that children have with their environments, especially during the early years of their development, to achieve a substantially faster rate of intellectual development. . . .[8]

The staff of the Fels Research Institute, in Yellow Springs, Ohio, has been gathering longitudinal data for several decades. From the studies of these data we have selected two dealing with the early experiences. In the first, the authors hypothesize that certain personality characteristics would "facilitate the acquisition of skills that are measured by the intelligence tests." In the second, the IQ's of children were studied in relationship to the mothers' behavior.

STUDY QUESTIONS

1. Rugg and Colloton argue that IQ remains constant because of small test-retest differences. How would you evaluate their arguments if 10 days elapsed between successive tests? 10 years?
2. On what basis does Stenquist maintain that small test-retest differences do not necessarily mean constant IQ?
3. In what ways, according to Wellman, did the preschool or the orphanage experiences modify the children's IQ's?
4. The major inadequacy of Wellman's position pointed to by Simpson is directed at Table 2 (reprinted from an article by Wellman not included in this collection). Summarize the gist of his complaints and assess their reasonableness.
5. Recapitulate Stoddard's defense of the Iowa studies for the issues of:
   (a) Universality of the nursery school findings.
   (b) Effect of home residence.
   (c) Validity of testing at an early age.
6. In what ways do Kagan, Sontag, Baker, and Nelson relate their concepts of curiosity, achievement, and aggression to IQ change? Do their results support their hypotheses?
7. In the Moss and Kagan study, how do they account for the fact that maternal acceleration correlates with IQ's for boys but not for girls? How do they explain (in the second study) a correlation for 3-year-old boys but not for 6-year-old boys?

[8] *Ibid.*, p. 363.

Constancy of the Stanford-Binet I.Q.
as Shown by Retests

Harold Rugg and Cecile Colloton

The Lincoln School of Teachers' College

If the Stanford-Binet Intelligence Test is taken two or more times by the same pupils, how closely will the I.Q.'s agree?

At least six reports are now available* from which the answer to this question can be formulated: (a) Terman (see Bibliography, No. 1); (b) Cuneo and Terman (2); (c) Garrison (3); (d) Poull (4); (e) Wallin (5) (d and e appear in this issue of the *Journal of Educational Psychology*); (f) Fermon (6); (g) Stenquist (7).

This article will summarize and interpret the evidence reported by these workers and add evidence secured in the educational psychology laboratory of the Lincoln School of Teachers College, 1920–1921. The data of the six investigations are summarized in Tables I and II. We have incorporated our own data in these tables on bases, so far as possible, which are comparable with those of other studies. The Binet testing in the Lincoln School was done as follows: Of the 137 retests, Mr. Rugg gave 73 initial tests and Miss Anne Brown 64 tests in the winter and spring of 1920. Miss Colloton gave 45 initial tests in 1920–1921 and 121 retests. Mr. Rugg gave 16 retests. Our individual average differences are as follows:

		Number of Retests
Mr. Rugg with himself	5.5**	16
Miss Colloton with Mr. Rugg	4.9**	59
Miss Colloton with Miss Brown	4.5	62

Constancy of the I.Q. can be expressed in three ways: (1) by the average difference between the initial and successive tests; (2) by the limits of

Reprinted from *Journal of Educational Psychology*, 1921, 12, 315–322.

* As shown by a search of the following magazines for the years 1915, 1916, 1917, 1918, 1919, 1920, 1921: JOURNAL OF EDUCATIONAL PSYCHOLOGY; *Journal of Educational Research; Journal Experimental Psychology; School and Society; Training School Bulletin; Psychological Clinic; Psychological Review*, and *Psychological Index*. We will appreciate information from any reader who knows of other published or unpublished studies of Stanford-Binet Retests.

** These average differences become 4.9 and 4.4 respectively if cases are omitted in which the pupils' mental ability was not completely explored at the initial test. This was caused by a rigorous following of directions.

TABLE I

SUMMARY OF INVESTIGATIONS ON RETESTS WITH THE STANFORD-BINET

			Number of children			
Investigator	Date	Total	3-5-11 Yrs.	6-8-11 Yrs.	9-11-11 Yrs.	12 + Yrs.
Terman	1918	4315	99	139	134	63
Cuneo and Terman	1918	77	70	7	0	0
*Garrison	1921	62	0	12	49	1
Poull	1921	126	(4–28 Yrs.)			
Wallin	1921	Scale 1908 61				
		1911 61				
		Stanford 19				
		1911 + Stan. 120				
		1908 + Stan. 120				
Rugg-Colloton	1921	137	0	51	50	36
Fermon (unpublished)	1920	233**		233		
Stenquist (unpublished)	1920	274**	28	198	48	0

the middle 50 per cent of the differences; (3) by the coefficient of correlation between the successive tests. Table I presents these facts for the seven studies. In these studies 1,487 retests are reported. All studies are recent— five, the work of the past year.

The present answer to the question concerning constancy of I.Q. The findings of Fermon and Stenquist are sharply distinguished from those of all other workers. Terman, Terman and Cuneo, Garrison, Poull, Wallin and the

Interval	Central Tendency of Change Between 1st + 2nd Test	Limits of Middle 50%		Average Difference	Coefficient of Correlation
Less than 1 Yr.–86 1 Yr. to 3 Yrs.–138 3 to 5 Yrs.–85 More than 5 Yrs.–127	+ 1.76	+5.7	−3.3	4.5 (P.E.)	.93
2 Days–2.5 5–7 Mos.–21 20–24 Mos.–31	Median Change = 6	+8	−3		.95 .942 .052
3 Yrs				4.66	
6 Mos.-3 Yrs.	Average Change = 1.28	+4.8	−3.3	4.6	
	Avg. Imp. 6.6 Avg. Reduct. 7.5			6.6	
	4.3 7.8			6.2	
	8.1 5.1			6.1	
				10.2	
				14.1	
10 Mos. to 1 Yr. 4 Mos.	Median Difference = 1.6	+5.6	−2.3	4.7	.84
7 Mos. to 4 Yrs.		+15	0	6 Yrs. = 10.8 7 Yrs. = 9.6 7.5 (P.E.)	
Less than 1 Yr.–32 1 Yr.-3 Yrs.–24	Med. Gains 9.5 Med. Losses 5.9				72

* First Test–Goddard Revision.
  Second Test–Stanford Revision.
** 274 cases reported by Stenquist include the 233 reported by Fermon. Miss Fermon did her testing with pupils in a New York City east side school.

present writers report average differences in I.Q. between first and second tests of approximately 5 points I.Q. The investigations by Terman, Garrison and Poull, together with ours, represent 760 children. The average difference for these studies is closely 4.5 points I.Q. This means that the chances are approximately 20 to 1 that the I.Q. of a pupil reported from a single test (as measured in the Stanford-Binet with the care represented by these studies) is within 13 points of his true I.Q.

Middle fifty per cent. For all studies *the positive differences are nearly twice as large as the negative differences.* Even so, the studies show that *typical positive differences are less than 6 points. Typical negative differences are approximately 3 points.* This means that the chances are one in two that an I.Q. from a single test will increase as much as 6 points or decrease as much as 3; that the chances are 1 in 5 that it will increase as much as 12, or decrease as much as 6; that the chances are 1 in 20 that it will increase as much as 18 or decrease as much as 9.

A significant fact therefore: much confidence can be put on a single I.Q. if the examination is made by experienced and well-trained examiners who use rigorously the standardized procedure for giving the test. In a range of intelligence for large bodies of public school children of, say, 50 points (from 80 to 130 I.Q.) it is very helpful to be able to predict intelligence with as much precision as is implied by these figures. Furthermore, the giving of a retest in all doubtful cases will increase the stated degree of reliability by about 40 per cent. That is, for two tests the P.E. becomes approximately 3 points.

Thus, the recent studies, except those of Stenquist and Fermon, closely confirm Terman in his earlier statements.

We have studied the details of the reports by Fermon and Stenquist. The latter are careful to state that the examiners who did the testing were carefully trained and had tested at least 20 pupils under critical supervision. The comparison of their findings with those of the other studies throws great doubt on the validity of the examining which was done by these workers. We are convinced that the great differences in I.Q. must have been caused primarily by non-uniform scoring of responses by those who gave the tests. Stenquist says, however, "it seems certain that the differing I.Q.'s obtained from the successive tests cannot be accounted for by the personal equation of examiners. They are probably due, on the one hand, to actual differences in the child from time to time, and on the other hand to the fallibility of the crude instruments with which we are measuring a most complex thing." (He is careful to state that his criticism is of the Binet scale and the I.Q. as *absolute measures of intelligence.*)

Study the charts presented as Table II. These present a very interesting and important comparison of the detailed distribution of differences in I.Q. The extreme differences in retest are important as well as the central tendencies. It is significant that four different groups of investigators, working independently, obtain differences in retest of more than 10 points in less than one-sixth of the cases. In our own work no difference was greater than $+17$ or -15; 12% were more than 10. In Terman's 67 out of 435, or 15%, were greater than 10 points. Of our 137 retests 23 were greater than 8. *Eight of these can be definitely explained by the fact that the first test did not completely explore the pupil's mental ability. This raises an important point of technique,—that of not carrying the testing far enough to* completely explore the pupil's general mental ability.

Only 6% of Garrison's cases showed differences greater than 10.

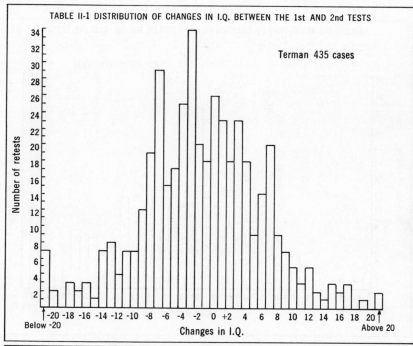

TABLE II-1 DISTRIBUTION OF CHANGES IN I.Q. BETWEEN THE 1st AND 2nd TESTS

Terman 435 cases

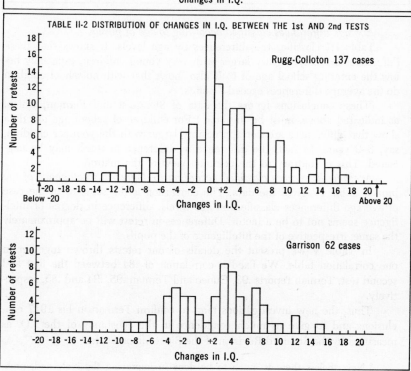

TABLE II-2 DISTRIBUTION OF CHANGES IN I.Q. BETWEEN THE 1st AND 2nd TESTS

Rugg-Colloton 137 cases

Garrison 62 cases

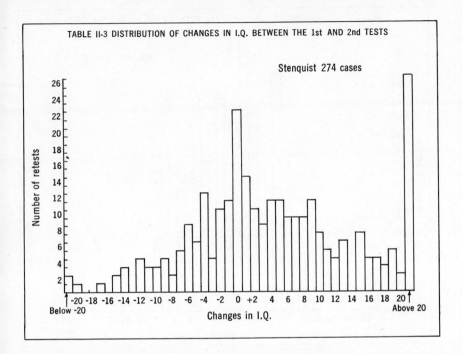

TABLE II-3 DISTRIBUTION OF CHANGES IN I.Q. BETWEEN THE 1st AND 2nd TESTS

Average differences classified according to age of pupils.

Table III classifies the differences by age levels. It shows that these differences are only slightly larger with very young children, especially below the entering school age of 6. It also shows that with no school children do the average differences exceed 7 points.

(These conclusions ignore the data of Stenquist and Fermon, which, as indicated above, must be unsound.) For children of school age our data show that differences are *not* appreciably larger with the younger children, say, 6–9 years. In fact, the difference in difference in retest may be neglected. This is contrary to the common view of the matter.

Average differences classified according to degree of intelligence of the pupils. Table IV gives the data. The conclusion is the same as in the case of average differences classified on age levels: difference in degree of intelligence seems not to be a factor. Differences in retest will be approximately the same, irrespective of the intelligence of the pupils.

In Table V we present the details of our retests thrown together in one correlation table. We fixed a correlation of .84 between the first and second test. Terman reports .93, Cuneo and Terman .95, .94 and .85, respectively.

Thus, the new investigations tend to confirm Terman in his 1917 conclusions and to give us much confidence in the constancy of the I.Q. as measured by the Stanford Revision of the Binet-Simon Scale.*

* Nevertheless there is much to be done in improving the scale and, probably, in making new individual scales. We will present definite criticisms of the scale at a later time.

TABLE III

COMPARISON OF AVERAGE DIFFERENCES BETWEEN 1ST AND 2ND TESTS, CLASSIFIED ACCORDING TO AGE LEVELS

Investigator	3 yrs.— 5 yrs. 11 mo.	Average Difference	6 yrs.— 8 yrs. 11 mo.	Average Difference	9 yrs.— 11 yrs. 11 mo.	Average Difference	12 yrs. and over	Average Difference
Terman	99	6.9	139	6.0	134	5.3	63	6.3
Garrison	0	—	12	3.6	49	4.7	1	—
Stenquist	28	13.5	198	7.7	48	6.9	0	—
Rugg—Colloton	0	—	51	4.5	50	5.5	36	3.7

TABLE IV

COMPARISON OF AVERAGE DIFFERENCES BETWEEN 1ST AND 2ND TESTS,
CLASSIFIED ACCORDING TO DEGREE OF INTELLIGENCE

Investigator	Bright Above 110 I.Q.	Average Difference	Average 90–109 I.Q.	Average Difference	Dull Below 90 I.Q.	Average Difference
Terman	183	5.8	147	6.2	104	5.8
Garrison	26	5.6	31	4.0	5	9.2
Stenquist	118	8.4	101	8.0	55	8.2
Rugg–Colloton	97	4.6	39	4.7	1	—

TABLE V

AGREEMENT BETWEEN 1ST AND 2ND TEST RUGG-COLLOTON
137 CASES CORRELATION R — .84

I.Q. at 2nd test

I.Q. at 1st test	80	85	90	95	100	105	110	115	120	125	130	135	140	145	150	155	160	165
165																		
160																		
155													1	1	1			
150														1	1			
145															1			
140												4	3	1				
135								1		1	4							
130										1	1	3	1	1				
125							1	1	1	7	1	1	1					
120							3	2	3	3	1	1						
115							3	16	5	2								
110						2	7	5	2	3								
105					2	3	3	2	2									
100				4	3	3												
95			2	2	1	1												
90		2	1															
85			1															
80																1	3	7

BIBLIOGRAPHY

1. TERMAN, LEWIS, M., *The Intelligence of School Children.* Chapter IX, p. 135.
2. CUNEO, IRENE AND TERMAN, L. M. *Stanford-Binet Tests of 112 Kindergarten Children and 77 repeated tests,* Pedagogical Seminary, 1918, 25, 414–428.
3. GARRISON, S. C., *Fluctuation of Intelligence Quotient.* School and Society, June, 1921.
4. POULL, LOUISE E., *Constancy of I.Q. in Mental Defectives According to the Stanford Revision of Binet Tests.* Journal Educational Psychology, September, 1921.
5. WALLIN, J. E. WALLACE, *The Results of Retests by Means of the Binet Scale.* Journal Educational Psychology, September, 1921.
6. FERMON, MARCELLA L., *Validity of I.Q. as Established by Retests.* M. A. Thesis, Columbia University, May, 1920.
7. STENQUIST, JOHN L., *Unreliability of Individual and Group Intelligence Tests in Grades 1, 2, and 3.* (Unpublished: includes data of Fermon, 6.)

Constancy of the Stanford-Binet IQ

as Shown by Retests

John L. Stenquist

Bureau of Reference, Research and Statistics Board of Education, New York City

In the September 1921 issue of this Journal appeared a summary of six reports[1] on the above topic including a study reported to have been made by the writer, and another by Miss Fermon. While mention was made of the fact in a footnote, it should be made clearer that the same cases are involved in both reports but the data were treated in a somewhat different way in each case. In this article the "conclusions ignore the data of Stenquist and Fermon which—must be unsound," in view of the contradictory results reported by the other workers. We are anxious to be the first to express our gratification, at the higher constancy found by other investigators. In fact, it was precisely because of the disappointingly low constancy found by us that the complete report has been withheld from publication in the

Reprinted from *Journal of Educational Psychology,* 1922, 13, 54–56.

[1] Rugg, Harold and Colloton, Cecile: Constancy of the Stanford-Binet as Shown by Retests. *Journal of Educational Psychology,* September, 1921, pp. 315–322.

hope that, other, and more encouraging ones would appear. We yield to none in our insistence upon the importance of proper standards of qualification for mental testers, but we do not feel there is necessarily final ground for admitting the unsoundness of our data. Frankly, however, *we hope they are unsound.* We fully agree that the other reports do strongly tend to cast doubt upon the validity of our results, and naturally the five reports summarized in the article referred to are therefore of particular interest to us. Our tests were given by four persons, and errors made by any of these may of course be responsible. Their training and experience was as follows:

One, a Smith College graduate and graduate student at New York University, has acted as examiner for the Public Education Association for several years, giving hundreds of Binet tests, and hence her proficiency was unquestioned.

The second examiner is a Vassar graduate where she had substantial psychological training. At least 20 Binet tests were given there by her under close supervision. Following this she had the experience of testing between 50 and 60 cases in a psychological clinic in New York City. After this she gave approximately 40 Binet tests in a survey by the Department of Ungraded Classes in New York City. All this experience plus a thorough psychological training should make her more proficient than many examiners.

The third examiner is also a Vassar graduate, where she had had 3 years of work in various branches of psychology, and at the time the present study was conducted she was taking a graduate course in psychology at Columbia University. In connection with the course in applied psychology at Vassar College she had given about 25 Binet tests, during a period of 9 months. The first of these tests were given in the presence of the instructor and the results in the remainder were checked by the instructor, in so far as that is possible.

The fourth examiner, also a graduate student, had given at least 200 tests prior to this experiment and had had thorough college and clinical training.

Whether or not our examiners were competent can only be inferred. That our larger differences may be due to the foreign character of the population tested seems most likely, however, as in our group the language factor was a serious one. If a pupil who lives in a home where English is not spoken is tested at the beginning of school, say at age 6 to 7—and then retested after a period of 6 months to 18 months in school where the English language is acquired, it is reasonable to suppose that this knowledge of English will improve his score appreciably—as much as the improvement shown in our retests.

Thus while on the whole we too would prefer to assume that in some way the technique of our examiners differed sufficiently to explain the differences, rather than to destroy our confidence in the fairly high average constancy of the Stanford-Binet test, the language-difficulty factor alone seems adequate to explain our higher retest scores. Even with the assumption that the Stenquist-Fermon data are unsound, however, there still remain some troublesome points in the matter of the constancy of an IQ. Leaving our data entirely out of consideration for the moment we may still note the wide range—from −20 IQ to over 20 IQ in the Terman data, from −15 IQ to 17 IQ in the Rugg-Colloton data, and from −14 IQ to 15 IQ in the cases of Garrison. Does this not mean, that when we cite the case of a pupil tested within say, 6 months to 18 months, *the IQ assigned to him may be wrong by as much as* 20 *or more points?* To be sure it is chiefly a question of *how often* this will occur, but the disturbing fact is that this can and does occur at all. Even if we limit it to the large error of, say, 'not more than 15 points wrong,' it still occurs too frequently for comfort. The percentages of cases which differed 15 points or over as shown in the article referred to are:

For Terman's data: in 29 out of 435, or in about 7 per cent of the cases.

For the Rugg-Colloton data: In 6 out of 137, or in about 4 per cent of the cases.

For Garrison's data: In 1 out of 62, or in about 2 per cent of the cases.

In our data this percentage rises to 11 per cent, which in the light of the other data seems too high. But whether it is 2 or 7 or 11 children in a hundred, in whose cases we make this huge blunder, it is serious. Assuming adequate proficiency of all testers the imperfect reliability of our scales of course also contributes to the unreliability of our constancy figures. That the Intelligence Quotient is very closely constant for each child seems doubtful in view of these wide ranges, and the relatively high reliability of Binet test, no matter what may be the case "on the average." In the Stenquist-Fermon data if we eliminate the 26 children who differed by 20 or more, the distribution is not markedly different from that of Terman's data. It is these 26 cases[1] that look the most questionable. We shall await with much interest the findings of other workers.

Guiding Mental Development

Beth L. Wellman

University of Iowa

The viewpoint that education is a guiding process permits us to look at all of the experiences of the child both inside and outside the schoolroom. It permits us to realize that education begins long before the child enters school. The importance of the infancy period for setting the tone of mental development has been dramatically emphasized in recent studies of foster children by Skeels (5) and Skodak (7). These two workers studied children born into underprivileged homes whose parentage was such as is commonly

---

Reprinted from *Childhood Education*, 1939, 15, 108–112.

---

[1] Are these 26 cases those having language difficulties? This should be ascertained. H.O.R.

considered to be inferior stock. The parents were unquestionably of the lowest orders in socio-economic status and economic self-sufficiency, and many were undesirables from the standpoint of such social criteria as crime, morality, and mental disease. Yet infants and very young children from such parentage when placed in good foster homes showed excellent mental development, testing at the preschool ages superior in intelligence. Furthermore, these children are giving every evidence of maintaining a superior status over a period of several years. These foster homes have demonstrated the influence of guidance of mental development in the earliest years.

Studies of children at the preschool ages have amply demonstrated the potency of nursery school attendance in improving children's IQ's between the ages of two and six years. The children who are enrolled in the preschool laboratories of the Iowa Child Welfare Research Station are a superior group. They come from excellent homes. The mean IQ of an entering group in any one year is about 115. Yet in spite of a superior initial status, there is a mean gain in six months' time of approximately six to eight IQ points. There are further gains in the second year of preschool, but no gains during the summer when not in preschool. Children of similar initial ability and similar home backgrounds who never attend preschool do not show gains.

EFFECTS OF UNFAVORABLE ENVIRONMENT

It is possible to make conditions so bad that there will be large decreases in IQ at the preschool ages. We (6) have recently studied a group of children in an orphanage under a regime where the concept of need of guidance for adequate development was, for practical purposes, nonexistent. The children under school age were herded together in a "cottage" under the supervision of an untrained matron who was assigned, among other duties, the responsibility for mending the clothes of thirty to thirty-five children. The children were bathed and dressed by older orphanage girls assigned to the task without reference to their desires. Play equipment was not provided. The children were well taken care of physically and under excellent medical supervision. In two years' time a group of twenty-six children who averaged 90 in IQ (average intelligence) dropped 16 points. On the final test their mean IQ was thus 74, or only slightly above feeble-mindedness.

Two case illustrations of children who were average in intelligence and became feeble-minded will show how great can be the effects of lack of guidance. Child No. 1 tested 98 (average) at 18 months of age. At 25 months he tested 93, at 28 months 83 (dull-normal), at 31 months 80, at 40 months 61 (feeble-minded), and at 52 months again 61. Child No. 2 tested 103 at 18 months, 72 (borderline) at 27 months, 63 (feeble-minded) at 38 months, and 60 at 50 months. These two children lost 37 and 43 points in IQ in less than three years' time. They are now residents of an institution for the feeble-minded. Changes such as these are not accidents. There was nothing physically wrong with these children, but there was something decidedly wrong with their environment. Motor achievements, social competence, and language ability, particularly vocabulary, all likewise showed the effects of the unfavorable environment.

We would not be so positive that these decreases were due to environment were it not for the fact that a modern preschool building was erected on the orphanage grounds, where half of the children of preschool age were privileged to spend several hours a day under the guidance of trained teachers. During the hours when not attending preschool, these children lived the same lives in the same cottages as the group just described. They were initially of the same intelligence. The children who attended preschool did not lose in IQ.

The non-preschool orphanage children illustrate how mental development suffers when children are deprived of the guidance usually provided by parents in family life. They were bereft of the varied intellectual and emotional experiences associated with family life. Whole areas of learning were cut off from their experiences because of institutional life. They had no opportunity to learn about household equipment or the mechanics of home living—areas particularly important to the very young child. They had no extensions of environment either through themselves moving beyond the confines of the institution or through experiences brought in from outside by visitors. No one read stories to them, explained picture books, or sought to help them build up an adequate vocabulary.

CHANGES IN IQ DUE TO PRESCHOOL ATTENDANCE

Good nursery schools enrich the intellectual experiences even of children fortunately situated in regard to family life. In our preschool laboratories we have noted that the amount of gain in IQ is related to initial level. Children below the very superior level gain, the average group gaining more than the superior. Usually we do not find gains at the highest levels. This led to a study by McCandless (4) of six very superior four-year-old children who were given an especially enriched curriculum. They worked on special projects for about an hour a day for several months. Otherwise they experienced the usual preschool regime for their group. These six children ranged in IQ from 125 to 165 at the beginning of the year. Their progress was compared with that of six other four-year-old children of equal initial ability who were enrolled in the same preschool group. At the end of the year it was found that the experimental group stood slightly higher than the control group intellectually.

A companion study by Carr (1) of the social and emotional changes of the two groups indicated that the differences in changes, although slight, were in favor of the experimental group. The social and emotional measures used included social participation, leadership, ascendant behavior, popularity, behavior problem tendencies, nervous habits, and ratings on selected social behavior items. There was thus no indication that such a program was harmful to the children.

In the experimental group observations were taken of the activities of the children in the midst of carrying out the projects. The projects included a trip to a farm and consequent building and equipping of a miniature farm, a visit to various downtown stores, and the construction of individual flower shops and similar activities, interspersed with stories and expeditions of other sorts. An attempt was made to answer all questions fully and to make suggestions leading to higher levels of thinking, but at the same time to leave the children free to pursue their own ends. Within the small experimental group a positive correlation was found between changes in intelligence and percentage of constructive behavior (here defined as including the following behavior: initiates activity, asks constructive questions, applies or originates concepts, predicts the outcome of an activity, uses number concepts). A negative correlation was obtained between changes in intelligence and negative behavior (here defined as asks for help, makes wrong answer, shows destructive behavior). Thus within this small group differences in the activities of the children during the time they were engaged in the project were reflected in different amounts of gain in intelligence. For the twelve experimental and control children a negative correlation was obtained between changes in Binet IQ and changes in behavior problem tendencies, indicating that the children who gained most in IQ made the most favorable changes in behavior problems.

One of the most interesting pairs of children in the study was a pair of twins, presumably identical. The difference in growth of these two children was the largest obtained for any of the six pairs. On Stanford-Binet tests in the fall the twins were equal, each testing 128 IQ. On the California Test of Mental Maturity each tested 145 IQ in the fall. On the Minnesota Preschool Scale the experimental twin tested 120 and the control twin 130. In the spring the experimental twin clearly excelled the control twin in all measures. Her Stanford-Binet was 143 (a gain of 15 points) while the control's Stanford-Binet was 125. On the California test, the experimental twin received an IQ of 153 and the control 147. On the Minnesota scale the experimental twin tested 132 and the control twin 123.

Studies of the later development of preschool children indicate that the increases in IQ due to preschool attendance are permanent. Comparisons of the college entrance examination percentiles and of scores on an intelligence test in high school have shown that children who attended preschool made higher scores on these later measures than other children who did not attend preschool (10). The two groups were matched on initial IQ and attended the same elementary schools.

LATER CHANGES IN IQ

Not all increases in IQ come at the preschool ages, however. Differences in intellectual growth have been found in different elementary school systems. Some school environments are more intellectually stimulating than others. We have found that preschool children who attend certain elementary schools continue to increase in IQ, while other preschool children attending other elementary schools do not make further gains after leaving

preschool (9). These differences have been found in Stanford-Binet IQ, and
have been verified recently in a study by Haslam (3) of changes from the
Merrill-Palmer performance tests at the pre-school ages to the Arthur performance scale about five years later.

Another study by Starkweather (8) has shown that children gain more
in Stanford-Binet in a five-year period in some schools than in other schools.
Three school systems were compared. Two of the school systems had kindergarten or first grade groups of very superior ability, the mean IQ of entering
groups being about 120. In the one school, children initially below 115 IQ
showed an excess of gains over losses in the five-year period, and children
initially above 115 IQ showed an excess of losses over gains. We can thus
speak of the "mental stimulation value" of this school as being about 115.
In the other school the mental stimulation value was about 125, about 10
points higher. In the third school there was an average population, the
mean IQ of entering groups being around 95. The mental stimulation value
of this school was about 100 IQ, or 15 points below the one school and 25
points below the other. Children of the same initial ability showed quite
different patterns of growth in the three school systems.

From these and other studies, particularly one by Crissey (2) on insti-

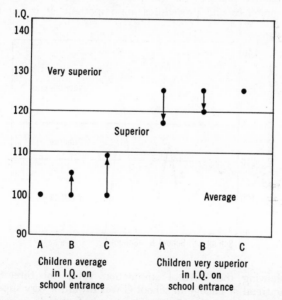

Diagram showing changes in IQ over a five-year period of children in
three elementary schools. Children in school A who were average in intelligence on school entrance did not change, but children of average intelligence in school C gained considerably. Children in school A initially very
superior lost considerably in IQ, while very superior children in school C
did not change.

tutional children, we have come to believe that group mental level of the
children is an important factor in the change in IQ of a particular child.
A child of 110 IQ in a group whose mean IQ is 120 will gain more than
a child of 110 IQ in a group whose mean IQ is 100. Group mental level is

by no means the only factor, however. We feel that differences in educational procedures and practices play an important part, too.

The extent of upward change that may take place is truly remarkable. We have examples of children entering preschool with average intelligence who, under especially favorable circumstances, have later tested at the "genius" levels (10). For example, Child No. 1 tested 98 at 3 years of age, 109 at 4 years, 126 at 5 years, 125 at 7 years, 153 at 10 years. In seven years' time he changed 55 points in IQ. On an intelligence test at 15 years of age he made a score corresponding to the top 1 percent and when he entered college he was in the top 10 percent on the college entrance examination. Child No. 2 tested 124 at 3 years of age, 135 at 4 years, 146 at 5 years, 160 at 9 years, 165 at 10 years, and 154 at 12 years. She also was in the top 1 percent on an intelligence test at 15 years of age.

FACTORS THAT CHANGE IQ

What makes children increase in IQ? We have indicated above that the child's relative place in his group is a factor and that differences in educational practices and procedures are important. It is our experience

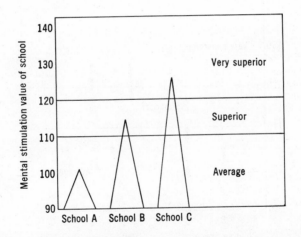

Diagram showing the "mental stimulation value" of three elementary schools. The trend of change in school C was toward a very superior status, all groups moving toward 125 IQ. The trend of change in school A was toward average ability, all groups moving toward 100 IQ.

that children gain mentally through mental exercise. By this is not meant drill. The best type of mental growth is not accomplished by putting the child through paces like a race horse, or by practicing something over and over like the scales on the piano. It is accomplished in part by providing the child with the opportunity for a life rich in experiences. This is enhanced by what is sometimes called extensions of environment and requires teacher and parent to be thinking constantly ahead of the children. Intellectual development flourishes in an atmosphere which encourages independence of thinking and intellectual curiosity. Fortunate is the child who is never disillusioned from the attitude that learning is fun and that it reaps its own rewards.

There is no really satisfactory substitute for association with other children of high ability. Children set goals for themselves in terms of what other children can do. Complacency about one's own achievements is not conducive to further intellectual efforts. Freedom from personality difficulties, such as jealousy, lack of self-confidence, and shyness, leaves the child freer to make the most of experiences that are offered. An alert teacher can do much to help a child overcome such difficulties, thus putting him in a position to profit more by an enriched curriculum.

REFERENCES

1. CARR, VIRGINIA THURSTON: *The Social and Emotional Changes in a Group of Children of High Intelligence During a Program of Increased Educational Stimulation.* State University of Iowa, Unpublished Master's thesis, 1938. Pp. 70.

2. CRISSEY, ORLO L.: *Mental Development as Related to Institutional Residence and Educational Achievement.* University of Iowa Studies, Studies in Child Welfare, 1937, 13, No. 1, pp. 81.

3. HASLAM, PHYLLIS: *The Prediction of Ability on the Arthur Point Performance Scale from the Merrill-Palmer Scale.* State University of Iowa, Unpublished Master's thesis, 1938. Pp. 102.

4. McCANDLESS, BOYD ROWDEN: *The Effect of Enriched Educational Experiences Upon the Growth of Intelligence of Very Superior Preschool Children.* State University of Iowa, Unpublished Master's thesis, 1938. Pp. 127.

5. SKEELS, HAROLD M.: "Mental Development of Children in Foster Homes." *Journal of Consulting Psychology,* 1938, 2:33–43.

6. SKEELS, HAROLD M.; UPDEGRAFF, RUTH; WELLMAN, BETH L., AND WILLIAMS, HAROLD M.: *A Study of Environmental Stimulation: An Orphanage Preschool Project.* University of Iowa Studies, Studies in Child Welfare, 1938, 15, No. 4. (In press.)

7. SKODAK, MARIE PAULA: *Children in Foster Homes: A Study of Some Factors Related to Mental Development.* State University of Iowa, Unpublished Ph.D. Dissertation, 1938. Pp. 240.

8. STARKWEATHER, ELIZABETH K.: *IQ Changes Over a Long Interval in Relation to Sex and Group Mental Level.* State University of Iowa, Unpublished Master's thesis, 1938. Pp. 79.

9. WELLMAN, BETH L.: "Growth in Intelligence Under Differing School Environments." *Journal of Experimental Education,* 1934–1935, 3:59–83.

10. WELLMAN, BETH L.: "Mental Growth from Preschool to College." *Journal of Experimental Education,* 1937–1938, 6:127–138.

The Wandering IQ: Fact or

Statistical Illusion?

Benjamin R. Simpson

Western Reserve University

From the University Schools of the University of Iowa during the past few years have come a series of articles describing the results of investigations in child development which have attracted wide popular attention. According to the claims summarized in a recent issue of *Childhood Education* (November, 1938), little is left to be desired in the way of child development if only the child is so fortunate as to be able to attend the University Schools of the University of Iowa, Preschool Laboratories, Elementary Schools or High Schools, but particularly at the preschool stage. Following is a partial list of the startling findings stated to be demonstrated by investigations carried on over a period of years, and reported in the scientific journals:

Studies of children at the preschool ages have amply demonstrated the potency of nursery school attendance in improving children's IQ's between the ages of two and six years. "The extent of upward change that may take place is truly remarkable. We have examples of children entering preschool with average intelligence who, under especially favorable circumstances have later tested at 'genius levels.'"

The most impressive gains in intellectual ability are made by children of average or inferior ability. Those of initially highest ability hold their superiority but make little or no gain. The gains are made only while in attendance at the University Schools. During the summer vacation they do not gain, etc.

Such findings as these are startling in their educational and social significance. If true, the secret of such transformation should be made known and acted upon throughout the country. But if the claims made are the result of erroneous statistical interpretation, they ought to be rectified without delay.

Analysis of the validity of these impressive claims calls for critical examination of one or more of the foundation studies upon which they are based. Not all the claims can be examined here, but those interested in a more detailed, documented analysis may be interested in consulting an article appearing under the name of the present writer in *The Journal of Psy-*

Reprinted from *School and Society*, 1939, 50, 20–23.

chology,[1] entitled "The Wandering IQ: Is it Time for It to Settle Down?" In the following analysis attention will be largely confined to consideration of the basic article by Dr. Wellman to be found in the *Journal of Genetic Psychology*,[2] entitled "Some New Bases for the Interpretation of the IQ."

The obvious straightforward method of indicating the course of mental development of children under given conditions is to give the results of the measurements of the *same individual child* on a general intelligence test year after year at periodic intervals while he continues his development under the influence of a given environment—preschool, elementary or high school. This is what has been done in other studies of mental development, notably in the Harvard Growth Study and in the California Studies of the development of gifted children. Yet for some unspecified reason Dr. Wellman fails to present her data in this straightforward fashion. The children considered in the study entered the University Schools, including the Preschool Laboratories, at all ages from 2 up to 14, and these children at the preschool ages were given mental tests twice a year and at longer intervals

TABLE 1

NUMBER OF CHILDREN ON REPEATED TESTS

Age (years)	2	3	4	5	6	7	8	9	10	11	12	13	14	All
1st test	93	172	150	176	180	95	72	69	77	67	71	50	61	1,333
2nd–3rd test		112	181	162	137	107	71	53	54	60	40	30	20	1,027
4th–7th test			39	98	79	35	43	52	53	42	55	46	32	574

while in attendance at the elementary or high school. But one who will take the pains to examine the article referred to above will find that the data are presented in a most confusing way.

Table 1 gives the number of children who took *their first* test at age 2, age 3, age 4, etc., up to age 14, including 1,333 children in all. Obviously it can not be the same child who took his *first* test at age 2, and again at age 3, 10 or any later age. Yet the assumption is that the average mental ability should be the same for the children who enter at age 2 as for the different children who enter at any later age up to 14, provided the mental measuring stick is accurate. Finding a drop of 22 points in IQ from the five-year-old group to the fourteen-year-old group, this drop is attributed to faulty standardization of the Stanford-Binet test, whereas it is obvious that the drop may be accounted for by the fact that different groups of children are measured at each successive age.

This alleged defect of the Stanford-Binet test—the test universally acknowledged to be by far the best for accurate measurement during these ages—is made the basis for a transmutation of IQ measurements into terms of percentile scores. This has the effect of magnifying gains by those at the level of average ability (IQ 90–109), by the proportion of 180 to 1, in relation to gains made by those of the genius level (IQ 140 and above).

In the second table, appearing below as Table 2, the figures are given

[1] 7: 351–367, 1939.
[2] 41: 116–126, 1932.

showing the number of children on repeated tests, for children classified into IQ levels on the basis of their first test. Thus, as in Terman's classification, children of IQ 90–109 are classed as average, those of IQ 110–119 as superior, etc. But there are marked discrepancies between the numbers of the children as given in Table 2, and those given in Table 1. For example the number of children taking the first test according to Table 1 is 1,333, whereas in Table 2 this number is reduced to 647 by a new grouping the reason for which does not appear. Even this total of 647 is in doubt, for the figures in this column add up to 624 instead of to 647.

Table 1 indicates that the total number taking at least 3 tests was 1,027, while Table 2 gives the total number as 395 (365 if correctly added).

TABLE 2

NUMBER OF CHILDREN ON REPEATED TESTS FOR CHILDREN CLASSIFIED
INTO IQ LEVELS ON FIRST TEST

Test	1	2	3	4	5	6	7
Below average	41	41	20	11	7	..	..
Average	246	246	135	87	57	37	11
Superior	155	155	96	77	47	30	11
Very superior	148	148	88	61	43	25	11
Genius	34	34	26	16	14	6	..
All	647	647	395	259	174	105	37

The number completing 7 tests according to Table 1 was 574. According to Table 2 it was 37 (33 if correctly added).

Such shifting of groups and gross errors in simple calculation are not likely to inspire confidence in the final conclusions. But much more confusing is the fact that when one checks up the numbers stated in Table 1 with the graph purporting to represent these numbers, it is found that there is hardly a semblance of correspondence between them. This baffling puzzle is not to be solved unless one happens to hit upon the note of correction appearing in a later issue of the same journal stating that Figure 1 as it appeared in the article was "upside down."

It would be instructive to know how many persons have read the article in question without noticing that the first figure was upside down or other glaring errors and inconsistencies. If a large percentage of readers have done so it surely indicates a marked tendency on the part of busy people to accept uncritically the conclusions stated by investigators whose work is believed to be authentic. Thus fallacious conclusions become quoted and requoted.

It is illuminating to examine critically one of the most crucial statements made in the whole article. It is stated that: "By the time the average group has had seven tests, at least two-thirds *of the group* are classified as superior and very superior." (Italics mine.) Interpreted in connection with the context and with Table 2, this is apparently intended to convey the impression that at least two thirds of this group of 246 who started as average in their first test, are classified as superior and very superior by their seventh test. But by the seventh test only 33 of the original 246 remained. Of these 33, 11 were now classed as average, and 11 (one third of the 33) were classed as superior, and 11 (one third of the 33) as very superior.

In the first place it is naïvely assumed that the 33 who took the seventh test are representative of the 246 who took the first test. In the second place in accordance with this interpretation, all the 155 who started as superior, all the 148 who started as very superior, all the 34 who started as geniuses and all the 41 who started as below average, had been eliminated. Is it reasonable to assume that all the 33 finalists originated in the average group, and that all other groups become eliminated? Is that environment ideal which eliminates all levels of ability except the average?

It seems hardly possible that this interpretation of the expression "at least two-thirds *of the group*" can be made to fit the facts as given in Table 2. Apparently then, the expression "By the time the average group has had seven tests, at least two-thirds *of the group* are classified as superior and very superior" in reality means that by the time *the average group* of 246 has had seven tests, at least two thirds of *the whole group* of 647 (or rather of the mere handful of 33 remaining) are classed as superior and very superior. One almost suspects an intention to be ambiguous or cleverly obscure.

But if the latter meaning is the one intended, surely it gives no evidence in the way of improvement in mental level brought about by the influence of the Iowa University Schools. Is it to be innocently assumed that the 33 finalists must be representative of the 647 who started, and that all the rise as indicated by the difference between the average IQ's of the initial and final groups is to be attributed to the stimulating environment supplied during continued attendance at the University Schools? Surely in this day and age there is no excuse for this cardinal sin of statistical procedure—gross neglect of the factor of selection as the numbers are reduced from 647 (if not 1,333) to 33 (or possibly 37). The whole of the rise of 14 points in IQ average may easily be accounted for on the principle of the survival of the fittest as the personnel of the groups measured changed in the drastic reduction of their numbers from 647 to 33.

One might in passing inquire into the perplexing finding that, while the gain in ability is said to result from the mental exercise involved in learning, it is the children of average or of inferior ability who gain greatly by their learning, which is relatively small in amount and mediocre in quality, whereas the children of genius level fail to gain by their learning which is by comparison vastly greater in amount and far superior in quality.

As for the "truly remarkable" upward change of mental performance in the case of two individuals from that of the average level to that of the genius, that is something which is likely to be found in any fairly large group in an occasional child. But such a change is as likely to be downward as upward, and it happens in such cases without any known or intended change in the environment one way or the other.

One will search in vain for any new psychological or educational principle in accordance with which the supposed increases in mental ability are secured. Emphasis is placed upon the principle that ability is stimulated "when learning is fun." But this principle is surely as old as Froebel's kindergarten.

Mental functioning is being improved at all levels of ability and at all ages though not to any miraculous degree. But this improvement is not brought about by disregarding individual differences, but by a gain in precision in identifying the nature and amount of such inherent differences, and by adjustment to them.

Intellectual Development of the Child: An

Answer to the Critics of the Iowa Studies[*]

George D. Stoddard

Iowa Child Welfare Research Station, State University of Iowa

This paper on the intellectual development of children is elliptic in form, revolving as it does about two foci, one in certain Iowa research materials, and the other in some issues arising from the thirty-ninth Yearbook of the National Society for the Study of Education.[1] Since you have all read the Yearbook, or perhaps know somebody who did, it will be difficult to say anything new. Rather I shall outline some differences of approach and interpretation in the hope that you will be encouraged to refer to the original sources.

After reading materials published on the question of intelligence and nursery education over the past ten years, I am amazed at such statements as these:

1. Wellman was the first research worker to report gains on the part of children attending preschool.
2. Except at Iowa, studies fail to show IQ gains.

Actually, as far back as 1925, H. T. Woolley reported that 43 children at the Merrill-Palmer School gained an average of 14 points with one year's attendance, while 33 comparable children on the waiting list lost 2 points over the same period.[2]

Even before the 1940 Yearbook was published, an interesting preview was offered:

Reprinted from *School and Society*, 1940, 51, 529–536.

[*] Address before the National Society of College Teachers of Education, Joint Conference on Teacher Education in the United States, St. Louis, February 27, 1940.

[1] "Intelligence: Its Nature and Nurture." *39th Yearbook*, NSSE. Bloomington, Ill., Public School Publishing Co., 1940.
[2] Helen T. Woolley, *School and Society*, 1925, 21, 476–482.

Eight of the nine [child development centers] show no effect whatever upon child intelligence as a result of nursery school experience.[3]

Since this is the kind of simple, straightforward statement that is likely to be cited in the years to come, it may be helpful to spend a few minutes in its analysis. Perhaps this exercise in logic will provide a clew for uncovering one source of controversy.

With the manuscripts of the 1940 Yearbook now available to all, I should like to make this statement: Seven of the ten research centers reporting demonstrate that children attending preschool do tend to gain in IQ, while in the reports of three research centers the average IQ gain is not given. This leaves the score seven plus and three unknown.

Also, if I were to recast the data, not in terms of the number of institutions, but in terms of the number of children involved, it is quickly seen that the Iowa samplings respectively for one year of attendance, two years of attendance and three years of attendance are much greater than those for all the other institutions combined. In fact a sampling of 13 children for the three-year nursery school attendance group at the University of Minnesota is based on a thirteen-year study, an average of exactly one child per year!

If you find all this annoying, I suggest a look at the evidence. It is set forth in Table I.

It will be seen that no institution reported a *loss* on the retesting of children attending the preschools from a period of six months to three years. In some cases the gain was substantial; in others it was not statistically significant.

Why then do some experimenters, as well as commentators, say that nothing had taken place in the mental lives of these children? The answer lies in the way control groups are utilized. When it was found that a control group of children of preschool age, matched on such criteria as chronological age, mental age and socioeconomic status of the parents, made gains not significantly different from those of the children attending preschools, the whole factor of gain was canceled out. The unwary reader of summaries, conclusions and critiques is left with the thought that children did not gain in the nursery schools, rather than the thought that most nursery-school groups gained, but some of them not more than non-attending equally bright children of families socially selected.

The general picture is one of gain. How can one explain this? There are two possible explanations. The first is that there exists a constant error in the standardization of the tests at these ages. Such an error would have to run through the 1916 Stanford Revision, the Kuhlmann Revision, the Minnesota preschool tests, the Merrill-Palmer tests and the 1937 Stanford Revision. If such an error existed, very likely it would have been found long ago, and appropriate adjustments made in the latest revisions. There is another alternate; namely, some nursery schools and comparable homes, of the high quality found when careful matching is done with nursery-school children, are really exerting a favorable effect upon mental development. In some cases such a group of homes may do about as well as the nursery school; in other situations, the nursery school is able to maintain

[3] Florence T. Goodenough, *Educational Method*, 1939, 19, 73–79, p. 78.

TABLE I

Institution	One year (or less)		Two years		Three years	
	Average IQ gain	No. cases	Average IQ gain	No. cases	Average IQ gain	No. cases
University of Minnesota	4.6	84	6.2	51	5.8	13
Rhode Island College of Education	1.8	54	..	..	3.7	19
Western Reserve University	2.6	26	..	..	..	..
Utah State Agricultural College	3.3	30	14.2	29	..	..
University of California	(not given)		..	..		
University of Michigan	(not given)					
University of Cincinnati	(not given)					
Winnetka Public Schools	5.5	103				
Merrill-Palmer School	6.6	652	10.4	228	10.5	67
University of Iowa						

a superiority. (In Iowa City, for example, the nursery-school children made their gains from fall to spring, that is, while attending the nursery school.)

There is no mysterious advantage accruing to the nursery school as such. In homes that can provide their children with good play and reading facilities, with good opportunities for exploration, companionship and language, stimulation should equal that in the nursery school.

It is clear that most psychologists over the past twenty years have been brought up on a diet of IQ constancy. Many persons think that this doctrine goes straight back to Binet, but this is not the case. Probably most of the recent pronouncements on IQ constancy stem from a paragraph of Burks's in the 1928 Yearbook of the National Society for the Study of Education. To quote:

> The maximal contribution of the best home environment to intelligence is apparently about 20 IQ points, or less, and almost surely lies between 10 and 30 points. Conversely, the least cultured, least stimulating kind of American home environment may depress the IQ as much as 20 IQ points. But situations as extreme as either of these probably occur only once or twice in a thousand times in American communities.[4]

Of course from the very day that Burks made these statements, reports small and large, weak and strong, began to appear in the literature, indicating a definite counter trend. For example, a doctoral thesis by John Munroe at the University of Chicago, also published in 1928, reached these conclusions:

> (1) The individual intelligence quotient is highly inconstant over long periods of time. (2) Environment modifies intelligence and the intelligence quotient which measures it. (3) There are increasing, decreasing and constant IQ's on all levels of IQ except the very lowest, where decreases in IQ seem to be general. Changes of from twenty to forty points in IQ over eight years are quite common. (4) Within reasonable limits of error the IQ's are valid measures of intelligence at the time they are secured. However, environment must be taken into consideration, if the IQ's are to be used for purposes of prediction over long periods of time. (5) Environment is highly important in its effect on the intelligence of developing children. Environmental conditions which produce real increases of from thirty to forty points in IQ are common in favorable homes. Conditions which produce borderline dullness in children are common in poorer homes. (6) Developing intelligence must be highly stimulated at all times and on all levels if it is to reach the highest levels possible.[5]

Up-to-date materials on IQ inconstancy will be found in various portions of the 1940 Yearbook. The most extensive of these are reported by Robert L. Thorndike who gives IQ's on retests after an interval of at least 2½ years for over 1,100 children in three New York City private schools (Ethical Culture, Horace Mann and Lincoln). These highly selected children, with an average IQ of 118, stayed in their home and school environments throughout the testing interval. They did not meet the conditions for wide IQ changes in relation to radical shifts upward from impoverishment or

[4] Barbara Stoddard Burks, 27th Yearbook, NSSE, 219–316, p. 309.

[5] John Munroe, "Inconstancy of the Intelligence Quotient and the Influence of Environment upon Intelligence." University of Chicago Abstract of Theses, Humanistic Series, 1928–29, 7, 133–136, p. 137.

downward from enrichment. Yet we find that the larger increases in IQ run as is given in Table II. Large-size losses are somewhat less, as is shown in Table III. On the whole, instead of a shift of 20 or more IQ points "once or twice in a thousand times," we find it occurring in 16 per cent of the cases.

TABLE II

Points IQ increase	Number of children
50	2
45	3
40	7
35	11
30	15
25	45
20	60

Certainly these data should prepare the open mind for a calm consideration of even greater changes, when cultural conditions are allowed to vary widely.

TABLE III

Points IQ loss	Number of children
45	1
40	1
35	6
30	4
25	8
20	21

It is strange that persons have ever expected IQ's to remain constant or to be unrelated to the nature of environmental effects. It may be recalled that in the work of Crissey[6] the effect of long-time residence in an institution was a general lowering of the IQ's and similar mental deterioration has been brought out vividly in other studies of cultural impoverishment. Studies on canal-boat children, on families in remote or impoverished regions, on Negroes living in the South have been consistent. We know that young children as they grow up in such circumstances tend to lose in IQ. Sherman,[7] for example, showed that among the hollow folk in Virginia there may be a shift from IQ averages in the 90's to averages in the 60's and 70's over a ten-year range.

[6] Orlo L. Crissey, "Mental Development as Related to Institutional Residence and Educational Achievement." University of Iowa Studies in Child Welfare, 1937, 13, No. 1, p. 81.
[7] Mandel Sherman and Thomas R. Henry, "Hollow Folk," pp. viii, 215. New York: Crowell, c. 1933.

Reporting in the Yearbook on extensive materials at the Institute of Child Welfare of the University of California, based on the California preschool scale for the preschool years and the new Stanford Revision for ages six to eight years, Honzik states:

None of the children of the most poorly educated parents ever made an above-average record, but rather consistently scored below the group average. . . . A high school education was the least amount of schooling for any parent whose child showed marked gains in score.

In explanation, Honzik suggests not only a multiplicity of environmental factors but also "intrinsic differences in rates of mental growth and maturation." In short, these California materials led directly to the conclusion that all three factors in child development, heredity, constitution and environment, make for IQ inconstancy.

My own feeling is that all the laborious work, all the confusion and bitterness engendered by IQ defenders in the past few years, will have been worth the cost if we can place on the record, once and for all, that, intelligence being what it is, and mental testing being what it is, *there is no guarantee whatsoever that a child's IQ will remain constant through life.*

In the 1940 Yearbook, Skeels reports consistent findings for children residing in underprivileged homes: for samplings of all ages, a difference of three-years' stay in an impoverished home leads to a significant difference in IQ. The longer the residence in such a home, the lower the average IQ. But when such children are removed from their inferior homes to an institution, they make slight gains; when the children are placed in foster homes, the gains are marked.

In this Yearbook Skeels also brings up to date his important studies of the development of illegitimate children placed shortly after birth for adoption in good foster homes. The total sampling now includes 306 children, and the results are directly comparable to those reported for a smaller number of cases by Skeels[8] and Skodak.[9] It will be recalled that the average IQ of the mothers was 88 while that of the fathers was probably similar, inasmuch as 80 per cent of all true fathers are found in the lowest three occupational classes. (Case histories are now being made of the fathers available for study. For the 11 cases completed, the average IQ is 85.) The children were taken from their mothers at birth or shortly afterward and placed in good homes according to standard qualitative criteria. The average age of placement was 2.7 months and all the children were placed before the age of 6 months. After a lapse of time averaging 2 years, the children were measured by the Kuhlmann Revision of the Binet tests. The mean IQ was 116. Sixty-five per cent of the group had IQ's of 110 or above and 41 per cent, IQ's of 120 or above. There were no children under IQ 80. Later on, at an average age of 4 years and 4 months, Skodak tested the sampling, reporting a mean IQ of 112. All these figures have been published. We now have Stanford-Binet IQ's for the children of this study who have reached 6 years of age. The mean IQ is 111.

The subsequent mental development of children whose mothers were

[8] Harold M. Skeels, *Journal of Consulting Psychology*, 1938, 2, 33–43.
[9] Marie Skodak, "Children in Foster Homes: A Study of Mental Development," p. 155. University of Iowa *Studies in Child Welfare*, 1939, 16, No. 1.

definitely feeble-minded is only slightly below that of the group as a whole and well above the average of an unselected population.

The inference is clear that these parents of "poor stock," with an extraordinary incidence of feeble-mindedness, incompetence, institutionalization and all-round impoverishment, have produced, on the average, bright offspring through the dramatic circumstance of relinquishing their children in early infancy for adoption by selected foster parents.

There has been furious criticism of this study, and there will be more to come. The Yearbook indicates clearly the source and nature of the criticism, and a detailed bicameral account appears in the February, 1940, number of *Psychological Bulletin*. In the meantime, the data are piling up. Every child is accounted for and every statistical procedure has been checked. The conclusions remain unchanged.

Much ado has been made over what was considered the impossible educational attainment of the parents of Skeels's foster children. It will be recalled that, even though the average IQ of the mothers was 88, the mothers had reported to the case worker that they had completed ten grades of school, on the average. Since many of these mothers were over-age for their grade on leaving school, it can be inferred that they were the inferior members of their classes. In any case, at these grade levels there is but slight selection of students in terms of mental ability. This tendency toward non-selection arises out of three factors: (1) compulsory attendance laws, (2) a social pressure that attaches an inferior status to children who drop out early, and (3) the promotion of children who have not mastered academic subjects, with permission to substitute manual and mechanical achievements.

There is not time here to cite comparative statistics, but a report by Mitchell based on the records in a Pennsylvania high school illustrates the tendency.[10] The Terman and Otis tests of intelligence had been given for an eleven-year period to all entering high-school freshmen, 1,146 in number. The median IQ was 99. The median for those who dropped out of high school before graduating was 91. However, very little of this selective factor occurred within the first two years of high school, that is, within the ninth and tenth grades; for it is shown that the dull pupil had 95 per cent as much chance of being found in ninth or tenth grade as the average or the bright. Mitchell's distribution of intelligence quotients indicates that a substantial number of beginning high-school students fall in the low 80's, and that IQ's run down to 69.

Perhaps the chief mystery of the Skeels-Skodak study is this: why have not these results been found elsewhere? The answer to this question is now clear. Placement centers the country over have failed to analyze the results of their own services. Good social-agency procedure has emphasized such factors as own mother care (thus indicating an underprivileged environment for the child) or selective boarding-home placement (thus assuring a measure of class distinction). Scarcely any situations have met the criteria of the Skeels study; namely, (1) that the children be placed under six months of age, not in institutions or boarding homes, but in superior foster homes for adoption, (2) that there be a substantial sampling of such

[10] Claude Mitchell, *Journal of Educational Research*, 1934–35, 28, 577–581.

children measured over a period of two or more years, and (3) that selection as between true home and foster home be low or absent.

In the 1940 Yearbook one of the points in the Skeels's discoveries, namely, that children living with inferior parents would deteriorate, has been corroborated by Speer, of Springfield, Illinois. Speer had available 68 feeble-minded mothers, all but one of whom had been committed to an institution for the mentally defective. Their IQ's ranged from 38 to 64 with a mean of 49. All social criteria were consistent with the diagnoses of mental deficiency. The fathers of the children were largely unemployed or in unskilled labor. The children studied were now in boarding homes. A control group, also in boarding homes, consisted of 57 children of normal mothers. The paired tabulations given in Table IV indicate a strong contrast between children who resided with feeble-minded mothers and those who resided with normal mothers. Since *all* children were declared dependent when the mother died or deserted, there is no selection among these children.

TABLE IV

EFFECTS OF RESIDENCE IN OWN HOME

Years in own home	Feeble-minded mothers		Normal mothers	
	Number of cases	Children's median IQ	Number of cases	Children's median IQ
0– 2	12	100	9	97
3– 5	19	84	9	97
6– 8	12	75	18	92
9–11	9	72	14	95
12–15	16	53	7	82

Speer states further that not one of the children of feeble-minded mothers taken out of his own home before the third birthday had an IQ below 90; and no child of a feeble-minded mother placed after the twelfth birthday achieved an IQ above 70.

In reviewing such data, one must be careful not to jump to the conclusion that a good foster home assures an average or bright child. This of course is not true. The IQ's for Skeels's sampling ranged from 80 to 160. There are wide individual differences in the abilities of children; with this concept we have no quarrel. But that these differences can be predicted from the measured or estimated abilities of parents is another matter.

In the 1940 Yearbook you will find the following statement:

The instability of IQ, found by Wellman and other investigators in Iowa, is no doubt closely connected with the fact that their results rest upon the validity of initial tests made when the children were under forty-eight months of age. The weight of expert opinion, however, is preponderantly that inferior deviates can not be reliably classified as such until the age of five or six years—with the exception of those extreme degrees of deviation later to be classified as idiocy or imbecility, and even these extreme degrees may sometimes be mistakenly classified by tests made in the early pre-school years. . . . At and after school age, however, mental inferiority be-comes highly predictable on the basis of intelligence tests now available.

But Terman and Merrill,[11] like Gesell, do not hold to this. The former state the following:

The difference between one-year and two-year intelligence is far greater than that which separates the average fifteen-year-old from the average sixteen-year-old. The former difference is so large that it is obvious to any one, the latter so small that it is barely detectable by the most elaborate mental tests.

Now it is true that throughout the first six months, the simple tests available give a poor prediction of later mental development. Also, below the age of twelve months it is difficult to get test items that are character-istically Binet. But by the age of two, children are measured by test items available throughout their whole mental life, and only slightly less reliably at preschool than at school ages.

Thus in a recent study of the new Stanford-Binet, conducted at the Harriet Johnson Nursery School in New York City, Black arrives at the following conclusions:

The new Stanford-Binet is highly stable and reliable for a preschool test. Even over a period of change, such as entry into nursery school, it shows a high correlation on retests (.80) and when this factor of changing status is eliminated by giving the first test *after* nursery-school experience, the correlation rises to .94, which compares favorably with reliabilities in school-age children. . . . The new Stanford-Binet in this study shows the same tendency to reflect such environmental changes as nursery-school attendance, as Wellman found for the Kuhlmann-Binet and the old Stanford-Binet. Test results on both the new Stanford-Binet and the Merrill-Palmer show a decided increase with experience in nursery school.[12]

All this is to be expected. Among the tests in the new Stanford Revision which appear in ages 2, 3 or 4, we find the identification of objects by name and by use, vocabulary tests, form-board problems and the repetition of digits, together with tests of comprehension, analogies and the performing of three commissions. When we reach the higher flights of mental matura-tion, as expressed in the Form L tests for superior adults, what do we find? Among other things, a vocabulary test, the repetition of digits and the un-derstanding of analogies. It is true that a few tests now appear to which the preschool child is not subjected. For example, the superior adult is asked to perform again the Binet paper-cutting test in which the examiner says, "Watch carefully what I do. See, I fold the paper this way. Then I fold it this way, and then this way. Now I will cut out a piece right here." Those of you who have been through it, either as a trained examiner or a superior adult, will recall that at this point the person being tested must make a little drawing to show where the holes will appear when the paper is un-folded.

[11] Lewis M. Terman and Maud A. Merrill, "Measuring Intelligence; A Guide to the Administration of the New Revised Stanford-Binet Tests of Intelligence," p. 25. New York: Houghton Mifflin Co., 1937.

[12] Ira Simonton Black, *Child Development*, 1939, 10, pp. 163, 162.

It is easy to indulge in a little playfulness at the expense of test items, but I am trying to show that there is no essential change in the ideology of Binet testing, as we go up the scale from age two to age eighteen.

One of the common complaints in connection with the Iowa researches on child plasticity is that false hopes will be raised, that parents and teachers will now feel that all dull or feeble-minded children can be made mentally whole. You may be sure that we are sensitive to this situation; but in fairness I should add that we are also sensitive to its reverse; namely, to the predicament of vast numbers of children who would make a better mental showing if provided decent home, school or institutional conditions.

The difficulty lies in applying a general principle to an individual case. We have never prescribed any cure-all, and in every Iowa study you will find differentials of child growth. It is painfully clear that some children do not improve, and that other children, under apparently excellent environmental conditions, may continue to deteriorate. For example, to quote from a talk of mine recently published in the *California Journal of Secondary Education:*

Obviously there are many children who, by reason of factors hereditary, constitutional or environmental, are so caught in feeble-mindedness as never to emerge.

That the more popular articles do not offer undue encouragement is clear from letters that we receive. For instance, a mother wrote us only last week: "The report of your recent survey on mental development of children appearing in a popular journal has discouraged me completely, for you dismiss the cause of birth-injured children by stating that the damage done was irreparable." Actually this article stated: "Certain bodily malformations, birth injuries and infectious diseases may cause damages to the nervous system that no environment can repair or overcome." Whether or not her child falls in this category is of course something for the local physician and psychologist to determine.

In closing I should like to indulge in a frank opinion of possible interest to college teachers of education. It is that mental testing as a standard procedure in schools should be allowed to decline. Testing for intelligence is like using a fever thermometer—a good practice for the nurse or clinician, but a perplexity for the individual parent or teacher. It may be better, on the whole, to turn to measures of special abilities, relying for insight as to general ability on cumulative records of scholastic achievement. This plan would avoid the bad error of labeling a child as permanently dull, average or bright. Mental tests would be reserved for research and clinical purposes. With such safeguards, they could be properly interpreted and utilized.

In short, we should be careful not to let the persuasion of test makers and test publishers determine educational policy. They have done their work conscientiously, but only the educators themselves are in a position, at all times and from every angle, to consider the welfare of the child.

Personality and IQ Change[1]

*Jerome Kagan, Lester W. Sontag, Charles T. Baker,
and Virginia L. Nelson*

The Fels Research Institute, Antioch College

Research on mental development during the last twenty years has indicated that a child's IQ score does not necessarily remain constant with age (2, 3, 4, 10). Several reports (9, 10, 12) suggest that changes in environmental conditions can depress or raise IQ level and it is sometimes implied that these changes may be explained by recourse to personality variables. The purpose of this paper is to demonstrate that changes in IQ during childhood are correlated with certain personality predispositions as inferred from projective test data. The personality variables under study include (a) need for achievement, (b) competitive strivings, (c) curiosity about nature, and (d) passivity.

Performance on an IQ test is assumed to be a function of at least two major variables; the variety of skills and abilities the person brings to the test situation and his motivation to perform well on the test (2, 6). Since the IQ scores of some children change markedly during the school years, it seems plausible to assume that those children who show marked increases in IQ have a very strong motivation to acquire or develop the various intellectual skills tapped by an IQ test and to perform well in a testing situation. It is suggested that need for achievement, competitive strivings, and curiosity about nature motivate the acquisition and improvement of cognitive abilities and by so doing facilitate increases in tested IQ.

The social environment often awards praise and recognition for intellectual accomplishment, and school age children with a high need for achievement might seek to gratify this need through intellectual activity. Thus it was predicted that children showing marked increases in IQ would produce more achievement imagery on the TAT than those with minimal gains in IQ.

Secondly, the school environment emphasizes competitive intellectual activity, and children with strong competitive needs would be highly motivated to acquire the intellectual skills which result in successful competition

Reprinted from *Journal of Abnormal and Social Psychology*, 1958, 56, 261–266.

[1] This investigation was supported in part by a research grant (PHS M 1260) from the National Institute of Mental Health of the National Institutes of Health, United States Public Health Service. The writers wish to thank Dr. Seymour B. Sarason for his critical reading of the manuscript.

with one's classmates. Thus it was predicted that children showing IQ gains would show more competitive strivings than children displaying minimal gains in IQ. In choosing an index of competitive strivings, besides the related measure of TAT achievement fantasy, it was decided to use aggressive content on the Rorschach. The bases for this choice rested on the assumptions that (*a*) incidence of aggressive imagery reflected degree of aggressive motivation and (*b*) competition was a socially accepted form of aggressive behavior. For in competition, as in aggression, the child desires to defeat another individual and assert his superiority over him. The population of children in this study is predominantly middle class and apt to place strong inhibitions on direct, overt expression of aggression. Therefore, there would be a tendency for the individual with high aggressive motivation to seek socially accepted channels for aggressive expression such as competitive activity with peers. Thus it was predicted that children showing IQ gain would report more Rorschach aggressive content than those with minimal gain because of their greater competitive predisposition.

A third motive that might facilitate a child's acquisition of knowledge and skills in dealing with the environment could be curiosity about nature. Interest in birth, death, sexual anatomy, and other processes of nature is a frequent phenomenon in young children. It is suggested that the more intense this curiosity the greater the motivation to acquire the habits which would gratify this motive. Since reading, questioning, and manipulating the environment are effective behavioral methods of gratifying one's curiosity, it might be expected that the highly curious child would be more likely to develop these skills and therefore apt to gain in IQ score. The TAT measure used to evaluate curiosity was presence of themes of interest in nature and its phenomena. For the Rorschach, it was hypothesized that concern with the body might reflect, in part, heightened interest in natural processes, and it was suggested that anatomy content might be more frequent for children who showed marked IQ gains than for those with minimal increases in IQ. It is recognized that many clinical psychologists regard anatomy content in adults as indicative of psychopathology. This study is concerned with the correlates of IQ gain rather than psychopathology, and it is not implied that children who show increases in IQ are completely free of conflict. Secondly, it was felt that the determinants of anatomy content for children might be different from those which produce this content in adults.

A final prediction dealt with the predisposition to behavioral passivity. The children who show IQ gains have been characterized as having high need achievement, competitive strivings, and curiosity about the environment. This constellation of motives implies that when these children are confronted with a problem, they would have a tendency to attack and attempt to solve the problem rather than withdraw from the situation or seek help. On this basis, it was predicted that children who showed IQ gains would be less likely than those with minimal IQ increases to characterize their TAT heroes as passive in attitude or behavior.

The Fels Research Institute is uniquely equipped to test these ideas about IQ change since it has continuous longitudinal information on the development of a sample of normal children. These data include intelligence and projective tests, observations of the children, and reports on the parent-child interaction. In a recent study, Sontag, Baker, and Nelson (11) related personality information on a sample of children with changes in IQ and found that those children who showed marked increases in IQ were rated as more competitive, more likely to display self-initiated behavior and less passive than those who showed decreases in IQ. The TAT and Rorschach protocols were not utilized in making these personality ratings, and the results from this study served as a major stimulus for the present investigation.

METHOD

A sample of 140 Fels subjects (Ss), 70 of each sex, were chosen for study because a fairly complete record of test information was available on them. From ages 2½ to 6, the Stanford-Binet intelligence test (1916 or 1937 revision) was administered to most Ss twice yearly, on their birthdays and six months after their birthdays. From ages 6 to 12, most Ss received alternately Form L or Form M of the 1937 revision annually on or near each S's birthday. All of the tests were administered by one of the authors (VLN). The mean IQ of the Fels population is near 120, with standard deviation varying from 14 to 20 IQ points.

In order to obtain groups of Ss who showed the most change in IQ score from ages 6 to 10, a smoothed longitudinal plot of each S's IQ was prepared by averaging the mean of three consecutive test scores around each age. This procedure is explained in detail in other reports (1, 10, 11). This technique tends to eliminate erratic variations in IQ and hopefully furnishes a more valid measure of IQ changes. Then each S's smoothed IQ at age 6 was subtracted from his smoothed IQ at age 10, and this distribution of differences, positive if S gained in IQ and negative if S lost in IQ, was divided into quartiles. This report deals with the projective test information on those Ss in the two extreme groups; those who increased and those who decreased the most in IQ score. These will be called Group A, the IQ ascenders, and Group B, the IQ descenders, respectively. There was no significant difference between the mean IQ of the two extreme quartiles at age six, the means being 119 and 116 for Groups A and D respectively. The average amount of increase in IQ for Group A was larger (plus 17 points) than the corresponding decrease for the members of Group D (minus 5 points) and while 46 per cent of Group D lost five or more points, every child in Group A gained 10 or more points during the years 6 through 10. The mean IQ of the entire sample of 140 tends to increase slightly from ages 6 to 10, probably as a result of practice effects with the same test. Since every S in Group D showed a decrease in IQ, it might be inferred that the members of Group D did not benefit from practice and familiarity with the test, and it is probably more accurate to view Group D Ss in this light rather than as Ss who showed marked decreases in IQ score.

The projective tests used in the analysis were the Rorschach and selected TAT pictures. Two factors governed the choice of the TAT cards which were analyzed. Because the protocols were gathered over a period of years, there was not complete comparability for all Ss for the number of cards administered. Secondly, the specific hypotheses of the study dictated the cards chosen for analysis and Cards 1, 3 BM, 3 GF, 5, 6 BM, 12 F, 14, and 17 BM were selected for analysis. The age at which the TAT protocols were administered ranged from 8–9 to 14–6 with median at 11–6 and 80 per cent of the protocols obtained between the ages of 11 and 12. The age at which the Rorschachs were administered ranged from 6–5 to 13–6 with median at 10–5 and 63 per cent of the sample having had the test between ages 10 and 11. Since the Rorschach and TAT were administered by different examiners there was no comparability with respect to inquiry or probing. Thus, the analysis of both the Rorschach and TAT was restricted to the S's spontaneous verbalization to the stimulus before any questions or inquiry were conducted by the examiner. The protocols were scored for the following fantasy categories.

1. *Need achievement on the TAT.* Achievement imagery on the TAT was scored according to the definition of McClelland et al. (8); and themes involving a reference to competition with a standard of excellence were scored achievement imagery.

2. *Rorschach aggression.* The definition of aggressive content on the Rorschach included (*a*) people, animals, or creatures engaged in physical or verbal aggression, e.g., fighting or quarreling, (*b*) explosive objects or explosions, e.g., volcanoes, bombs exploding, fireworks, and (*c*) objects or animal parts normally regarded as instruments of aggression, e.g., spears, rifles, clubs, guns, knives, horns, and claws.

3. *Intellectual curiosity about nature.* For the TAT, curiosity was defined in terms of themes in which someone is interested in the processes or phenomena of nature. Curiosity on the Rorschach was restricted to anatomy or X-ray responses of internal organs or boney parts, e.g., stomach, backbone, ribs.

4. *Passivity.* Because of the limited amount of thematic material in the spontaneous performance, themes of passivity were limited to stories in which the central figure was described as sleepy, tired, or resting.

The fantasy categories were independently scored by the senior author and an assistant without knowledge of the S's IQ scores.[2] Reliability was very high because of the limited amount of content scored for each response and the objectivity of the definitions. Percentage of agreement for the three TAT categories was 95 per cent and for the two Rorschach categories 99 per cent.

RESULTS

Although there was a total of 70 Ss in the two extreme quartiles, not all of the Ss had Rorschach or TAT data for the age range under study. Table 1 shows the distribution of Ss, by sex and direction of IQ change, for the TAT and Rorschach analyses. Because there are approximately twice as many boys as there are girls in Group A, all comparisons were first made separately by sex and results were only combined if the direction of the result for both boys and girls in the same IQ group was in the predicted direction.

1. *Need achievement.* All achievement themes, save one, occurred to Cards 1 and 17 BM. The typical achievement story to Card 1 concerned a boy who wanted to master the violin and/or become a famous violinist, while the typical achievement theme to 17 BM involved competitive activity with regard to rope climbing. Table 2 shows the percentage of Ss in

[2] The writers wish to thank Mary Schnurer for her assistance in assessing the reliability of the scoring.

each group reporting achievement imagery plots to Cards 1, 17 BM, and to both pictures.

For both Cards 1 and 17 BM, more male and female Ss in Group A report achievement imagery than the boys or girls of Group D. For Card 1,

TABLE 1

DISTRIBUTION OF Ss BY SEX AND DIRECTION OF IQ
CHANGE USED IN THE ANALYSIS OF THE
TAT AND RORSCHACH

Group	TAT		Rorschach	
	Boys	Girls	Boys	Girls
Group A	22	11	22	10
Group D	10	20	9	18
Both groups	32	31	31	28

TABLE 2

PERCENTAGE OF Ss REPORTING ACHIEVEMENT
IMAGERY TO CARDS 1 AND 17 BM

TAT Card	Group A			Group D		
	Boys	Girls	Boys and Girls	Boys	Girls	Boys and Girls
Card 1	36.4	50.0	40.6	27.3	15.0	19.4
Card 17 BM	36.4	30.0	34.4	0.0	15.0	9.7
Cards 1 and 17 BM	22.7	10.0	18.8	0.0	0.0	0.0

the difference between Group A and Group D girls is reliable at the .03 level; the difference for boys is in the predicted direction but not significant. For Card 17 BM, the difference between Group A and Group D boys is significant ($P = .03$) and in the predicted direction for girls. All P values are for one tail and were evaluated using the exact method suggested by Fisher (5). When the sexes were pooled, comparisons between Groups A and D were significant not only for Cards 1 and 17 BM separately but also for the number of Ss telling achievement imagery to both Cards 1 and 17 BM ($P < .10$, .03, and .01 respectively). Thus, the Ss who showed increases in IQ were more prone to structure Cards 1 and 17 BM in terms of achievement oriented behavior than the Ss in Group D.

2. *Aggressive content on Rorschach.* There was no significant difference between Groups A and D or between boys and girls with respect to the mean number of responses per protocol, and the mean for the entire sample was 27 responses. There was no difference between Group A and Group D girls with respect to percentage of each group reporting one or more aggressive responses per protocol (30.0 per cent for Group A versus 33.0 per cent for Group D). However, the difference between Group A and D boys approached significance with 59.1 per cent of the former and 22.2

per cent of the latter reporting one or more aggressive images ($P = .07$). Thus, the prediction of a correlation between IQ increase and aggressive imagery held only for the boys. Because of the tentativeness of this result and the more speculative nature of the hypothesis relating competitive striving and aggressive content, an attempt was made to validate this finding by analyzing a later Rorschach protocol for the boys in Groups A and D. Not all of the boys had Rorschachs administered to them at a later age, and only 15 Ss in Group A and five in Group D were available for analysis. The median ages at the time of administration were 13–8 and 15–0 for Groups A and D respectively, and there was no significant difference in the lengths of the protocols of the two groups. The results were in the same direction for 86.7 per cent of Group A, and 20.0 per cent of Group D reported one or more aggressive images, and this difference is highly significant ($P = .01$).

3. *Intellectual curiosity.* The only TAT card eliciting curiosity plots was Card 14, and the typical theme described a person gazing at or interested in the stars or the heavens. Table 3 shows the percentage of each group telling such themes to Card 14.

Both the boys and girls in Group A told more themes of interest in the stars or heavens than the males and females in Group D ($P = .14$, $P = .10$, respectively) and combining of the sexes yielded a highly significant difference between Groups A and D ($P < .01$).

4. *Anatomy and X-ray responses on the Rorschach.* There was no

TABLE 3

PERCENTAGES OF Ss REPORTING THEMES OF CURIOSITY
TO CARD 14

Sex	Group A	Group D
Boys	40.9	18.2
Girls	30.0	5.0
Boys and girls	37.5	9.7

TABLE 4

PERCENTAGES OF Ss REPORTING THEMES OF PASSIVITY
TO CARD 3 BM

Sex	Group A	Group D
Boys	9.1	27.3
Girls	10.0	45.0
Boys and girls	9.4	38.7

difference between Group A and Group D girls reporting one or more anatomy responses (30.0 per cent versus 38.9 per cent for Groups A and D respectively). For the boys, 31.8 per cent of Group A and 0.0 per cent of Group D reported anatomy or X-ray imagery, a difference that approached significance ($P = .06$). This finding was also validated on the same sample of 20 boys that was used to check the differences in aggressive content. The results were in the same direction with 60.0 per cent of Group A and 20.0 per cent of Group D reporting anatomy content $(P = .15)$.

5. *Passivity.* Card 3 BM accounted for most of the passivity themes and the groups were compared with respect to the incidence of stories to Card 3 BM in which the central figure was sleepy, tired, or resting. Table 4 shows the percentage of each group telling such themes. Both the boys and girls in Group D showed more passivity themes than the boys and girls in Group A. Although only the difference for the girls was significant $(P = .06)$, when the sexes were pooled the difference was highly reliable $(P < .03)$.

Cards 3 GF, 5, 6 BM, and 12 F did not furnish data relevant to the hypotheses under test and these results are not summarized.

DISCUSSION

In the main, the hypotheses about the differences between Groups A and D have been verified. Boy and girl ascenders produced more TAT achievement imagery and curiosity about nature than Group D children and male ascenders displayed more aggressive content on the Rorschach than the boys in Group D. The higher incidence of aggressive imagery for the boys who gained in IQ was interpreted as reflecting stronger competitive motivation. Finally, the Ss in Group D were presumed to have a more passive orientation since they were more likely to perceive the ambiguous figure on Card 3 BM as sleeping or tired. The relation between Rorschach anatomy content and IQ gain was the most tentative finding.

The results are interpreted as indicating that high motivation to achieve, competitive strivings, and curiosity about nature may motivate the acquisition of intellectual skills and knowledge which, in turn, facilitates increases in tested IQ. If one accepts the generally assumed notion that boys are more competitive and achievement oriented than girls, the fact that there were twice as many boys in Group A as there were girls supports the present interpretation. A recent study using the Edwards Personal Preference Schedule found that high school boys obtained higher need achievement scores than high school girls (7).

These results are not interpreted as indicating that strong achievement, competitive, and curiosity motives are the only variables involved in producing gains in IQ. The Ss in this study are all average or above in IQ and there is not adequate sampling of children with lower IQ levels. One would not expect Ss with low IQs or language handicaps to suddenly show an interest in reading despite achievement needs or intellectual curiosity. The child who spends increased time reading because of a heightened interest in natural processes must have already learned the basic reading skills so that this behavior is not a difficult or unlikely choice for him.

Similarly, needs for achievement and successful competition should only motivate attempts at improvement of intellectual abilities in a social milieu where praise, recognition, and superior status are awarded for such accomplishment. That is, achievement-oriented children from homes in which intellectual activity was praised would probably be more likely to master intellectual skills than achievement-oriented children from homes in which such accomplishment was not rewarded. In a cultural environment where athletic ability, fighting prowess, or sucess with the opposite sex was highly valued, one might expect the child to choose these behavioral channels to gratify his achievement and competitive needs. The parents in the Fels population are predominantly middle class and tend to place importance on intellectual accomplishment. A large majority of the parents have attended college, and since enrollment in the Fels program is voluntary it might be inferred that only parents who valued knowledge and scientific pursuits would be predisposed to become part of the research population. Thus, the children under study tend to come from homes which value intellectual ability.

Study of the educational attainment of the parents of the Ss in Groups A and D revealed no significant difference between the groups with respect to the percentage of families in which both parents attended college (57.1 per cent for Group A versus 42.9 per cent for Group D; $P > .30$). Although there is a slight difference favoring the educational level of Group A families, the difference was not dramatic. There may be important differences between Groups A and D with respect to the differential encouragement of intellectual achievement, but measurement of these differences would probably require variables more refined than educational level of the parents. However, even though parental emphasis on intellectual activity may increase the child's desire to improve his cognitive skills, the child's predisposition to adopt or rebel against parental values should selectively influence his motivation to strive for intellectual accomplishment. Thus, the type of relation between parent and child may be an important factor in this process.

Finally, there is the possibility that genetic and/or constitutional variables may play a role in facilitating marked IQ changes. There is considerable data indicating that genetic factors influence general IQ level but less evidence relevant to the role of these variables in producing childhood increases in IQ score. For most of the children in our population, IQs tend to level off during the ages 6–10 and most of the marked changes in level occur during the preschool years. However, the exact relationship between genetic variables and IQ change has yet to be determined. The phenomenon of IQ increase during the school years is admittedly complex and it is not implied that the child's motives are the major factor. However, it is suggested that personality needs may influence this process. Perhaps the most accurate generalization is that for middle-class children with average or above IQ levels, strong achievement, competitive, and curiosity needs may facilitate IQ gains by motivating the child to master intellectual skills.

A final implication of these findings is that they add indirect evidence for the usefulness of the Rorschach and TAT as research instruments. Validation of a predicted relationship between TAT achievement imagery and IQ gain increases one's confidence in the hypothesis that TAT plots can serve as an index of achievement-oriented tendencies. The results of the Rorschach analysis suggest that aggressive content may be an index of an individual's aggressive predispositions but not necessarily a measure of his tendency to express direct, physical aggression. Although Sontag, Baker, and Nelson (11), using behavioral observations, rated the boys in Group A as more competitive than those in Group D, there was no difference between these groups with respect to intensity or incidence of direct verbal or physical aggression or destruction of property. We have assumed that competition is a socially approved form of aggressive behavior and the higher incidence of aggressive content for Group A boys was presumed to be a result of their more intense competitive strivings. Some clinicians who use projective tests are too prone to focus on predictive statements about direct, physical aggression when confronted with a protocol containing aggressive content. One is apt to overlook the fact that the individual may have alternative behavioral channels for expression of aggressive motives.

SUMMARY

For a group of 140 boys and girls in the Fels Research population on whom continuous Binet IQ data were available, a distribution of IQ change was obtained by subtracting each S's smoothed IQ at age 6 from his smoothed IQ at age 10. This distribution of differences was divided into quartiles, and the Rorschach and TAT protocols of the upper (maximum increase in IQ), and lower (maximum decrease in IQ) quartiles were analyzed and compared. The results showed that in comparing the Ss who showed IQ increases with those showing IQ decreases, the former had, on the TAT, significantly more (a) achievement imagery on Cards 1 and 17 BM and (b) themes of curiosity about nature on Card 14, and significantly fewer themes of passivity on Card 3 BM. For the boys only, more of the Ss who increased in IQ had anatomy responses and aggressive imagery on the Rorschach. The results were interpreted as indicating that high need achievement, competitive striving, and curiosity about nature are correlated with gains in IQ score because they may facilitate the acquisition of skills that are measured by the intelligence test.

REFERENCES

1. BAKER, C. T., SONTAG, L. W., & NELSON, VIRGINIA L. Specific ability in IQ change. *J. consult. Psychol.*, 1955, **19**, 307–310.
2. BAYLEY, NANCY. Mental growth in young children. *Yearb. Nat. Soc. Stud. Educ.*, 1940, **39**, (II), 11–47.
3. BAYLEY, NANCY. Consistency and variability in the growth in IQ from birth to eighteen years. *J. genet. Psychol.*, 1949, **75**, 165–196.
4. BRADWAY, KATHERINE. IQ constancy on the Revised Stanford-Binet from the preschool to the junior high school level. *J. genet. Psychol.*, 1944, **65**, 197–217.
5. FISHER, R. A. *Statistical methods for research workers.* (5th ed.) Edinburgh: Oliver & Boyd, 1934.
6. HAGGARD, E. A., DAVIS, A., & HAVIGHURST, R. J. Some factors which influence performance of children on intelligence tests. *Amer. Psychol.*, 1948, **3**, 265–266.
7. KLETT, C. J. Performance of high school students on the Edwards Personal Preference Schedule. *J. consult. Psychol.*, 1957, **21**, 68–72.

8. McCLELLAND, D. C., ATKINSON, J. W., CLARK, R. A., & LOWELL, E. L. *The achievement motive.* New York: Appleton-Century-Crofts, 1953.

9. RICHARDS, T. W. Mental test performance as a reflection of the child's current life situation: A methodological study. *Child Develpm.*, 1951, **22**, 221–233.

10. SONTAG, L. W., BAKER, C. T., & NELSON, VIRGINIA L. Personality as a determinant of performance. *Amer. J. Orthopsychiat.*, 1955, **25**, 555–562.

11. SONTAG, L. W., BAKER, C. T., & NELSON, VIRGINIA L. Mental growth and personality development. *Monogr. Soc. Res. Child Develpm.*, in press.

12. WELLMAN, BETH L., & McCANDLESS, B. R. Factors associated with Binet IQ changes of preschool children. *Psychol. Monogr.*, 1946, **60**, No. 2 (Whole No. 278).

Maternal Influences on Early IQ Scores[1]

Howard A. Moss and Jerome Kagan

Fels Research Institute, Yellow Springs, Ohio

In recent years considerable effort has been exerted toward evaluating the factors determining the development of intellectual abilities (2, 3, 5, 9, 10). Many of these efforts were concerned with either the degree to which intelligence was a reflection of environmental experiences or the unfolding of hereditary potential. The present status of this literature is essentially equivocal. The current consensus among psychologists is that hereditary and environmental variables interact in determining intellectual abilities. However, recognition that both of these variables contribute to intelligence test performance does not provide us with information about the developmental processes that influence the acquisition of intellectual abilities.

A number of recent studies have investigated the relationships among more specific variables that seem functionally related to intelligence test performance. Sontag, Baker, and Nelson (11), in a recent monograph, reported a positive relationship between a child's aggressive and competitive behavior and increases in IQ during the years six through ten. Kagan, Sontag, Nelson, and Baker (7) found that IQ increase was positively correlated with the frequency of TAT achievement stories. These two studies at-

Reprinted from *Psychological Reports*, 1958, 4, 655–661. © Southern Universities Press, 1958.

[1] This research was supported, in part, by Grant M-1260 from the National Institute of Mental Health, United States Public Health Service. The authors wish to acknowledge the assistance of Thomas McElvein and Eliot Stadler in the analysis of the data. Parts of this report were presented at the 1958 annual convention of the American Psychological Association.

tempted to relate the individual's motive states to his intellectual performance. The purpose of the present investigation was to add a new dimension
to this recent body of research. Specifically, this study was concerned with
the influence of early maternal encouragement of intellectual development
on the child's IQ score. The major hypothesis was that maternal concern
with a child's early achievement and development would be positively related to the child's intelligence test performance. This hypothesis was
investigated initially with a pilot sample (Study A) and was repeated with
a larger, independent sample (Study B).

STUDY A

METHOD

The following information was available on a sample of 19 boys and 25
girls from the Fels population which is a predominantly middle-class group
residing in southwestern Ohio. The reader is referred to a recent report (11)
for a detailed description of the Fels sample.

IQ scores.—A series of Stanford-Binet intelligence tests were administered to these Ss at 6-mo. intervals from Ages 2½ to 6 and annually from
6 to 11 yr. of age. Forms L and M of the test were administered alternately
and all tests were administered by the same psychologist. In order to reduce
chance errors of testing, the average IQ score for Ages 2½, 3, and 3½ was
computed to arrive at a smoothed IQ score for Age 3. Similarly, a smoothed
IQ for Age 6 was computed by averaging the IQ scores obtained at Ages
5½, 6, and 7. Details of this procedure are described in a recent report (11).
The smoothed IQ scores for Ages 3 and 6 were used for this analysis.

Maternal acceleration.—Each child was given a single score on a 7-point
rating scale measuring the mother's concern with her child's growth,
achievement, and development for the first three years of life (maternal acceleration).

The variable of maternal concern with achievement focused on the
mother's acceleratory behavior toward her child and was defined in an
unpublished manual prepared by the authors as follows:

> This variable assesses the degree to which the mother shows concern
> over her child's cognitive and motor development and tends to place ex-
> cessive expectations on his achievements. It reflects the degree to which the
> mother "pushes" the child's development beyond his abilities and her con-
> cern with his general achievement level. Major sources of data include (a)
> concern over the age when the child talks, walks, rolls over, etc., the mother
> questions the Fels visitor and doctors constantly; (b) showing off of the
> child's skills and abilities to the Fels visitor and others; (c) maternal dis-
> satisfaction with the child's development; (d) maternal encouragement of the
> child to achieve in various areas.

Each child was given a single score for this variable. This score was
based on study of an average of six narrative reports written by a psychologist after observing the mother-child interaction in the home during the first

three years of the child's life. The inter-rater reliability of this score was .80. The ratings on maternal acceleration for the first three years of life were then correlated (product-moment correlations) with the smoothed IQ scores at Ages 3 and 6 for boys and girls separately.

RESULTS

Table 1 shows the correlations between the ratings of maternal acceleration and the boys' and girls' IQ scores for Ages 3 and 6. The results reveal that maternal acceleration only facilitates the Age 3 IQ for boys. There is no statistical support for any positive relationship between maternal acceleration and boys' IQ at Age 6 or for girls' IQ at either age. Because of the

TABLE 1
CORRELATES OF MATERNAL ACCELERATION WITH CHILD'S IQ

	Boys			Girls		
	N	Age 3	Age 6	N	Age 3	Age 6
Maternal acceleration	19	.42*	.27	25	−.07	.01

* $p > .05$ for two tails

provocative nature of this result, the relationship between maternal acceleration and child's IQ was re-examined on a larger, independent sample of Fels Ss.

STUDY B

METHOD

The following information was available for a sample of 59 boys and 40 girls [comparable to the sample used for Study A (11)]: (a) Stanford-Binet Intelligence Test scores; (b) a series of ratings for each child for the first three years of life on the Fels Parent Behavior Rating Scale which measures maternal acceleration; (c) the mother's Otis IQ score; and (d) the educational level attained by the mother.

Stanford-Binet IQ scores.—As in Study A, continuous IQ scores were available for this sample and the smoothed IQs for Ages 3 and 6 years were computed. In this study all the smoothed IQs were normalized using McCall's T-score technique (6).

Fels Parent Behavior Rating Scale for maternal acceleration (PBR 3.3).— For this second sample, the measure of maternal acceleration was based on ratings from the standardized Fels scale (1) which deals with this aspect of the mother's behavior. The Fels scale defines this variable in the following manner:

Rate the parent's striving to increase the rate at which the child's behavior is maturing. Does the parent deliberately train the child in various mental and motor skills which are not yet essential; or is the child left to "grow naturally;" or even shielded from accelerational influences?

This variable is restricted to purposeful teaching and training. It includes mental, motor, social, language and personal skills. Disregard the effectiveness of the training. Consider the energy the parent exerts in striving to accelerate the child's behavior development (1, p. 67).

Although the definition of maternal acceleration in the Fels rating scale is phrased somewhat differently from the definition used in Study A, there is sufficient overlap in the behavior under surveillance for us to assume comparability of the two measures.

Each child had several ratings (in standard scores) distributed over the first three years of life and all ratings were averaged for each child in order to arrive at a single score for this variable.

Maternal IQ and education.—An IQ score based on Form A of the Otis was available for each mother. The level of maternal education was estimated by assigning each mother a score of 1 through 6 on the following scale: 1, Eighth grade or less; 2, Part High school; 3, High school graduate; 4, Part college; 5, College graduate; and 6, Post graduate training. The distributions for maternal IQ scores and education levels were normalized by McCall's T-score technique. The mean educational level of the mothers in this sample was 3.9 (part college).

The average Parent Behavior Rating on maternal acceleration for the Age period 0 to 3 was then correlated with the boys' and girls' smoothed IQ scores at Ages 3 and 6. In addition, the variance contributed by maternal IQ was partialled out in arriving at the correlation relating maternal acceleration to child's IQ scores.

In order to observe how some of the more traditional correlates of the child's IQ compared with maternal acceleration, the children's IQs were also correlated with mother's attained educational level and her own IQ. In addition, intercorrelations among the three maternal variables, acceleration, education, and IQ, were computed.

RESULTS

Table 2 shows the product-moment correlations between the child's IQ (boys and girls separately for Ages 3 and 6) and each of the maternal variables (acceleration, education, and IQ). The correlations involving maternal

TABLE 2

MATERNAL CORRELATES OF CHILD'S IQ

Maternal variable	Boys			Girls		
	N	Age 3	Age 6	N	Age 3	Age 6
Acceleration	59	.41*	.08	40	.16	.09
Education	59	.32*	.43*	40	.64*	.57*
IQ (Otis)	59	.37*	.42*	40	.59*	.40*

* $p < .01$ for two tails

acceleration and child's IQ are partial correlations in which the variance due to maternal IQ is statistically controlled.

For Study B, maternal acceleration correlated .41 and .08 with boys' smoothed IQ scores at ages 3 and 6. The correlation of .41 is statistically significant ($p < .01$, two tails) and cross-validates the positive relationship obtained in Study A. This relationship gains increased psychological significance since it was computed with mother's IQ partialled out. For Study B, as for Study A, none of the other correlates of maternal acceleration with child's IQ approached statistical significance. The replication of this finding on two independent samples contributes considerably to the validity of this relationship.

The product-moment correlations between the child's IQ and maternal IQ and educational level are also given in Table 2. These correlations are consistent with previous results described in the psychological literature (2, 3, 9). Maternal education, acceleration, and IQ all correlate to about the same magnitude with boys' IQ at Age 3. However, maternal IQ and education, unlike acceleration, continue to relate to a significant degree with boys' IQ at Age 6 and girls' IQ at both age levels. Maternal education was more highly correlated with girls' IQ than it was with boys' IQ at both age levels. The difference between these two correlations at Age 3 is statistically significant ($p < .05$, two tails).[2]

TABLE 3

INTERCORRELATIONS AMONG MATERNAL VARIABLES

	Maternal IQ		Maternal education	
	Boys	Girls	Boys	Girls
Maternal acceleration	.28*	.21	.27*	.27
Maternal IQ	—	—	.65**	.70**

* $p < .05$ for two tails
** $p < .01$ for two tails

Table 3 shows the intercorrelations among the maternal variables used in Study B. Evidence that maternal acceleration is not strictly a function of maternal IQ or educational level is provided by the relatively low intercorrelations between either of these two variables and maternal acceleration.[3]

[2] The procedure for determining the significance of the difference between product-moment correlations is described by Edwards (4, p. 132). The formula is:

$$Z = (Z_1' - Z_2') - Z'/\sigma_{z1'-z2'}$$

where the Z' values are conversion values based on r and appear in Table VII in Edwards.

[3] The correlation between maternal acceleration and boys' IQ at Age 3 was .46 prior to the partialling out of maternal IQ. Since maternal acceleration seems relatively independent of the mother's IQ, it was felt thaat both of these variables might contribute in an additive manner to the child's intelligence test performance. A multiple correlation relating the mothers' IQ and acceleration rating on the Fels scale with the boys' IQ at Age 3 yielded a multiple R of .53 ($p < .01$).

DISCUSSION

In summary, the findings indicate that maternal acceleration facilitates the preschool (Age 3) intelligence test performance for boys, but not for girls. Both studies failed to find any relationship between maternal acceleration and children's IQs at Age 6. The fact that maternal acceleration only predicts boys' IQ at Age 3 and not at Age 6 may explain, in part, the frequently reported low correlations between the child's preschool IQ and those obtained at later ages. It is possible that the mother's encouragement of the child's developmental skills may temporarily facilitate her son's achievement on the early intelligence test items.[4]

Although the correlations between maternal IQ and education are quite high, these two variables have relatively low correlations with maternal acceleration for both sexes. This suggests that the mother's early concern with her child's achievement may be quite independent of her intellectual skills and educational background. Therefore, early maternal acceleration and the mother's intellectual status might be regarded as two relatively independent variables, both contributing in different ways to the child's intellectual test performance.

The sex differences obtained are not readily explicable from any current theoretical position. However, a line of speculative reasoning is suggested to explain the sex differences in response to maternal acceleration.

The authors have additional data which suggest that one group of variables predicts boys' IQ scores while a quite different pattern of variables predicts girls' IQ scores. Each group of variables is suggestive of a cohesive pattern of interaction between the mother and the child. The patterns differ depending on the sex of the child. To illustrate, dependency, poor motor coordination, maternal protectiveness, low maternal hostility, maternal preference over other sibs, and maternal acceleration are all positively correlated with IQ scores for the boys. This cluster of variables suggests that when a close, symbiotic relationship exists between mother and son (based on the boys' helplessness and the mothers' nurturance), the mother's efficacy as a reinforcing agent of developmental skills is maximized. For the girls we found that good motor coordination, high imitative behavior of mother, and low maternal restrictiveness positively correlated with girls' IQ scores at Age 3. This suggests that when the female child is given sufficient latitude (both in terms of being non-restricted either by the mother and/or by her own physical limitations) she is able to exhibit greater developmental progress as measured by the Stanford-Binet.

Most of these results were obtained with relatively small Ns (approximately 24 Ss for each sex) and must be regarded as tentative in nature. The only other results which were replicated with a larger sample (that used in Study B) were the relationships between maternal restrictiveness and IQ

[4] Inspection of the Stanford-Binet scale at Age 2½ suggests that four of the six items at this age level are composed of skills that accelerating mothers usually emphasize in their early training of the child. These items all involve language acquisition, e.g., identification of objects by use, identification of body parts, naming objects, and picture vocabulary.

scores. For this larger sample a product-moment correlation of $-.41$ ($p < .01$, two tails) was obtained between girls' Age 3 IQ scores and ratings on maternal restrictiveness. The comparable correlation for boys was only $-.16$ (non-significant).

Additional evidence suggests that maternal acceleration is related to maternal hostility for girls but not boys. It is also hypothesized, on the basis of minimal data, that mothers may be more restrictive of daughters than sons. This greater restriction of girls and the fact that maternal acceleration may be communicated to them in a hostile context may tend to nullify or inhibit some of the expected effects of maternal acceleration on girls' IQ at Age 3.

Our findings to date indicate that the correlation of any one variable with IQ can best be understood by viewing this correlation as part of an intricate network of relationships. Further research is in progress at the Fels Institute to determine the composition of clusters of behavior so that we can better understand the inter-personal interactions and intra-personal processes that influence intellectual development. This type of analysis may help to explain the fact that different variables have differential effects on boys' and girls' IQ scores.

SUMMARY

This paper presented the findings of two separate studies concerned with the maternal correlates of children's early IQs. Initially, a sample of 19 boys and 25 girls were selected on whom ratings of maternal concern with achievement (based on observations of the mother-child interactions in the home) and the Stanford-Binet IQ scores were available. The product-moment correlation between the ratings of maternal concern with achievement and the child's IQ at Ages 3 and 6 yielded coefficients of .42 ($p > .05$) and .27 for boys, and $-.07$ and .01 for girls. These relationships were re-examined on a larger independent sample consisting of 59 boys and 40 girls. In this second study, the rating of maternal concern with the child's achievement was obtained from the Fels Parent Behavior Rating scale. For the second sample, maternal IQ and attained educational levels were also available. Product-moment correlations were then obtained between the child's IQ (boys and girls separately) at Ages 3 and 6 and each of the three maternal variables (acceleration, education, and IQ). The results of this study paralleled those of the first. The correlations between maternal acceleration and child's IQ at Ages 3 and 6 (with maternal IQ held constant) was .41 ($p < .01$) and .08 for boys, and .16 and .09 for girls. The cross-validation was regarded as supporting the hypothesis that early maternal concern with achievement facilitates boys' early intelligence test performance.

REFERENCES

1. BALDWIN, A. L., KALHORN, J., & BREESE, F. H. Patterns of parent behavior. Psychol. Monogr., 1945, 58, No. 3 (Whole No. 268).

2. BURKS, B. S. The relative influence of nature and nurture upon mental development: a comparative study of foster parent-foster child resemblance and true parent-true child resemblance. *Yearb. nat. Soc. Stud. Educ.*, 1928, **27**, Part 1.

3. CONRAD, H. S., & JONES, H. E. A second study of familial resemblances in intelligence: environmental and genetic implications of parent-child and sibling correlations in the total sample. *Yearb. nat. Soc. Stud. Educ.*, 1940, 39, Part 2.

4. EDWARDS, A. L. *Experimental design in psychological research.* New York: Rinehart, 1950.

5. EELS, K., DAVIS, A., *et al. Intelligence and cultural differences: a study of cultural learning and problem solving.* Chicago: Univer. of Chicago Press, 1951.

6. JOHNSON, P. O. *Statistical methods in research.* New York: Prentice Hall, 1949.

7. KAGAN, J., SONTAG, L. W., BAKER, C. T., & NELSON, V. L. Personality and IQ change. *J. abnorm. soc. Psychol.*, 1958, **56**, 261–266.

8. KAGAN, J., & MOSS, H. A. Parental correlates of child's IQ and height: a cross-validation of the Berkeley Growth Study results. *Child Develpm.*, in press.

9. LEAHY, A. M. Nature-nurture and intelligence. *Genet. Psychol. Monogr.*, 1935, **17**, 235–308.

10. SKEELS, H. M. Some Iowa studies of the mental growth of children in relation to differentials of environment: a summary. *Yearb. nat. Soc. Stud. Educ.*, 1940, **39**, Part II.

11. SONTAG, L. W., BAKER, C. T., & NELSON, V. L. Mental growth and personality development: a longitudinal study. *Monogr. Soc. Res. Child Develpm.*, 1958, **23**, No. 68.

PART NINE

Clinical and Actuarial

Prediction

A book of readings in psychology will, of necessity, consist of research reports, for most of the articles written by psychologists discuss research findings and implications. But even though it may be their most publicized activity, not all psychologists engage in research, and few of those who do conduct studies are full-time researchers. Other psychological activities, such as teaching and clinical practice, occupy central roles in the professional duties of psychologists. And just as there are divergent viewpoints in research, clinical practice also has its issues. Points of view are expressed, sides are taken, and the issues are more often joined than resolved. But discussion and debate can have effects other than resolution of differences: they can bring problems into focus, and clarify the understanding of the clinical and therapeutic process.

In this section's initial article, Sarbin points out that clinical psychologists do more than just administer tests and engage in psychotherapy. Their practice requires them to make innumerable predictions: they predict, in effect, that the patient will not commit suicide; that he will react favorably to one kind of treatment, unfavorably to another; that he will benefit from therapy, etc. Since these predictions must be made, and since clinicians make them, Sarbin's concern is the *basis* on which they're made. Two procedures are considered: the clinical and the actuarial.

The actuarial procedure can be illustrated by the familiar insurance company method of determining premium rates. Automobile insurance rates, for example, reflect the insuring company's estimate of the likelihood that a driver will have an accident. The rates are not based on the characteristics unique to the driver. They are based, rather, on such factors as age, sex, marital status, or type of driver education course. A clerk, or, more likely, a computer, using a preset formula, cranks in the data on the driver's class membership (for example, he belongs to the class of men who are married) and mechanically (more accurately, actuarially) determines his premium. This formula depends upon previous information about the frequency of accidents occurring for drivers in these classes. If teenagers have had a disproportionately large number of accidents, the prediction is that a teenager is more likely than an older person to have an accident and thus pays a higher premium. Although some of the variables in the formula, such as age, are numerically precise, others, such as the quality of the driver's training course, need not be. As long as some characteristic of the course can be quantified—the driver took it or he didn't—the course can be used as a predictor in an actuarial formula.

To continue with the same illustration, insurance companies might use the clinical method. In this case, the company (or the agent) would, in essence, do a case study of the individual, and base the rate (prediction of the likelihood of an accident) on his personal characteristics rather than his class membership. An agent might, for example, interview an applicant, conclude that he was absent-minded, and set a high rate for him on the assumption that he was highly likely to have an accident. Or he might think that another applicant was highly moral (and so would obey traffic regulations), ultracautious, and very concerned about the beauty of his new car; he predicts that this one is unlikely to have an accident, and so sets the rate low for him.

Sarbin, in the first of his two articles, presents this dilemma of the clinician: should he base the predictions he must make about his client on actuarial or clinical grounds? He points out that the resolution to this problem also has important consequences both for the training of clinicians and for the kind of questions to be answered by clinical research. He also anticipates the argument that a clinician, operating under actuarial prediction procedures, surrenders one of his major functions to a clerk. He asserts, however, that the significant job for the clinician is that of formulating hypotheses. These hypotheses, arising from both theory and the clinician's firsthand experiences with actual behavior, then become the focus of research, and those which are verified return as components in the prediction formulas.

Sarbin's article stimulated the writing of many articles and books on the clinical versus actuarial prediction problem, since it penetrated to the core of clinical training, practice, and research.

Persuasive as they were, Sarbin's arguments did not sweep the field. The Chein article is an example of the rebuttal and alternatives presented for the clinical prediction case. The major argument presented by the defenders of clinical prediction is that actuarial methods can be no more accurate than their base rates. For example, a college guidance counselor may know from past records that 80 percent of the male freshmen with certain IQ scores and high-school records will not complete their first year of college. If he has to make individual judgments about each freshman in that category, the best actuarial prediction will be that each will drop out. The actuarial counselor will be right on the average of 8 out of 10 times, but he will be wrong 20 percent of the time. The sophisticated statistical techniques of multiple regression, factor scoring, patterning, or Bayesian formulas may reduce the error, but they cannot eliminate it completely. The clinicians argue that their skills in readjusting and tailoring predictions for each case will result in fewer errors of prediction in the long run.

Chein also takes issue with Sarbin's treatment of intuition. He implies that there are individual differences in this facility, some being more gifted than others. The more gifted ones can make better predictions than actuarial methods now permit, given the inadequate information now available. Although this implies a distinction between intuition (or "understanding") and scientific "knowledge," Chein argues that the intuitive psychologist should strive to explain how this process operates.

By now, many of you have probably suggested a compromise between these two polar positions. Why not use both methods, or why not use the actuarial method to get a general estimate, and then modify this by what you know of the individual client? Meehl deals with these questions in the last reading in this group. He points out that in hinging a prediction on some special factor in a client's case, the clinician presumably has had some experience with this factor, which leads him to conclude that a person with X is not likely to do Y. In effect, the clinician's experience has provided him with the type of information that could be incorporated into an actuarial prediction. (Sarbin, who also dealt with this point, suggested that factor X, if it has any real relationship to Y, ought then to be brought into the prediction equation. If it does not, it contributes nothing to the prediction.) Meehl then reviews (as he had done in a previous monograph[1]) the experimental literature of comparisons between actuarial and clinical predictions. Although he exhibits a commendable reserve about some of the studies, he finds little support for the claim that the clinical method produces more accurate predictions.

Professor Meehl is a clinician; he was speaking to clinicians at a session of the American Psychological Association. Thus, in a forthright attempt to influence clinical psychology he exhorts his colleagues to do two things:

1. Employ more rigor in their research so that predictions can be more accurately made and so that comparisons of methods of prediction can be made more precise.
2. Use their heads (that is, use the clinical method) instead of the formula, whenever it is obvious that the formula is inappropriate. (Meehl's last sentence, of course, provides for a stringent criterion for overriding the actuary.)

The issue treated in this section, like virtually all important ones in psychology and in all disciplines, is never settled with one article. New evidence becomes available; there are always new visions and revisions. Holt's study[2] is an example of a redefined clinical statement made partially in reply to Meehl's resolution. An excellent historical discussion of the topic has been presented by Gough[3]: he presents a detailed description of both the theories and methods under contention.

STUDY QUESTIONS

1. How does Sarbin relate the question of prediction to diagnosis? To treatment?
2. How does Sarbin define what we have called clinical prediction? What are his comments on these several possible definitions?

[1] Paul E. Meehl, *Clinical Versus Statistical Prediction* (Minneapolis: University of Minnesota Press, 1954).

[2] Robert R. Holt, "Clinical and Statistical Prediction: a Reformulation and Some New Data," *Journal of Abnormal and Social Psychology*, 1958, 56, 1–12.

[3] Harrison Gough, "Clinical Versus Statistical Prediction in Psychology," in Leo Postman, (ed.) *Psychology in the Making* (New York: Alfred A. Knopf, 1962).

3. What are Sarbin's two concepts of probability? How do they apply to prediction about a single case?
4. How does Sarbin (in his second article) relate the problem of measurement errors to that of prediction?
5. Why does Chein feel that every prediction about a single case is, in fact, an unverifiable hypothesis?
6. If a clinician said, "It is probably true that my patient will do X," how would Chein interpret that statement?
7. How does Meehl feel that the clinician validly functions as an hypothesis-maker in research? In prediction?
8. What are the situations in which clinical prediction, according to Meehl, is a reasonable method of prediction?
9. Does Meehl regard the clinician who wishes to override an actuary as wrong in principle? How does Meehl suggest that the clinician's plea of "special cases" be verified?

Clinical Psychology—Art or Science[*][†]

Theodore R. Sarbin

University of Chicago

This paper questions the oft-repeated statement that clinical psychology is an art by examining the main functions of clinical psychologists, i.e., diagnosis and treatment. In examining the concept of diagnosis, evidence is presented which supports the notion that a diagnostic statement has meaning only when it has a referent in the future—when it provides a prediction. A prediction (probability-statement) is determined empirically and may be stated in terms of a regression equation or in terms of a crude generalization from clinical experience. Treatment likewise is determined by tacit or expressed predictions of behavior under alternative conditions. The various conceptions of art as applied to clinical psychology are examined and the conclusion is drawn that clinical psychology is a scientific as opposed to an artistic or intuitive enterprise.

The problem under discussion is in need of clarification for at least two reasons. First, the manner in which we provide training for the growing number of clinicians will depend largely upon our conception of clinical psychology as art or science. If our analysis shows it to be an art, then we are faced with the admittedly difficult task of training people in various forms of art. Second, the increasing interest in clinical research creates prob-

Reprinted from *Psychometrika*, 1941, 6, 391–400.

[*] Paper read at the 49th annual meeting of the American Psychological Association at Evanston, Illinois, September 3–6, 1941.

[†] This analysis may be applied with little modification to the fields of social work, psychiatry, vocational guidance, and related professions.

lems around the art-or-science question. Research based on artistic conceptions may have to be interpreted differently from research based on scientific conceptions. Incidental to the discussion of this theme, we shall attempt briefly to clarify the concepts of diagnosis and treatment.

That we are dealing with a real and not an imaginary problem may be inferred from a casual perusal of the writings of prominent clinical psychologists. Louttit (7) and Westburgh (17), for example, have expressed themselves categorically on this point with the declaration that the practice of clinical psychology is an art. They imply that the clinician, by virtue of some artistic gift, adds something to the objective measures obtained by scientific means.

Perhaps the most insistent question in this inquiry has to do with the definition of the field of clinical psychology. The activities of those who profess to be clinical psychologists are so diverse, so heterogeneous, that we cannot be content with an answer to the simple question: "what do clinical psychologists do?" As a matter of fact, psychologists disagree among themselves as to the delimitation of the field. Louttit (7) has shown that there are at least four conceptions of clinical psychology. The interpretation most acceptable to this writer (and to many of his colleagues) may be stated as follows: clinical psychology consists of those activities necessary for the diagnosis and treatment of individuals who require assistance in the solution of their social psychological problems. Diagnosis and treatment, according to this definition, are the chief functions of clinical psychologists. Parenthetically, it should be added that in most clinics the psychologist serves only a diagnostic function, the therapeutic function being delegated to psychiatrists, teachers, or social workers. For the present we shall be concerned only with the concept of diagnosis, delaying analysis of the treatment phase until later.

Our task now is to determine whether diagnosing is artistic or scientific. Before we can do this, we must clarify the referent for which the term "diagnosis" stands. A search of the literature reveals that diagnosis has two principal meanings. The first takes the form of a literary description of an individual from a sampling of his present and past behaviors. Such descriptions are to be found in historical research, in literary efforts, and in places where mere description of an individual or event is the aim of the writer.

A second meaning of diagnosis likewise is that of description of an individual, *but with a future referent*. Here the main purpose is to provide a statement of prophecy from a statement of status; that is to say, to uncover the events of the past which will serve as predictive indices for the future. The clinical psychologist, like the physician, is interested in the past only as it reveals vectors into the future. An example from a case history will clarify the distinction. The results of examination and history-taking reveal that Jack Smith, age 10, is in the fourth grade but that his reading skills are equivalent to those of the average second-grade pupil. The case notes might state the diagnosis as follows: Diagnosis—two year retardation in reading achievement. If this sentence carried no more meaning than that of the present state of the individual with regard to his reactions to printed words, it would be a literary description. But the clinician implies something more—he implies that this current behavior will lead to certain kinds of behavior in the future. More specifically, the diagnosis of reading disability in Jack Smith means that unless something is done about it, Jack will become an academic failure, perhaps engage in anti-social forms of conduct, and do many of the other things which are associated with academic failure. This clinical diagnosis has a referent in the future. As such it is a prediction. The clinician makes this tacit prediction: if nothing is done to remedy the reading disability, the boy will probably fail in school.

As used in the applied sciences of medicine and psychology the term *diagnosis* usually implies *prognosis*—not only the description of the disease but also the course that it will take, not only a statement of the social psychological conflict but also the behavior of the individual in the future. The interest in prediction differentiates the applied scientist from the literary artist. Without a system of knowledge of the course of the particular disease in similar cases, the physician cannot make a predictive diagnosis: all he can do is describe the symptoms, i.e., make a literary diagnosis. The psychologist faced with a problem child is likewise thwarted by the absence of knowledge; if he has never had experiences with similar symptom-complexes he can do no more than write a literary description of the child.

Rogers (13) recognizes this need for diagnoses which have referents in the future when he writes: "The fact-finding and classifying aspects of diagnosis have their place, but in dealing with the individual child there must be a diagnosis which goes deeper, discovers the meaning of the various elements, and points the way toward treatment."

This discussion leads to the conclusion that diagnosis, in order to be meaningful, must have a referent in the future. A clinician's diagnosis is static, i.e., purely descriptive of past events without implications for the future, when it has no function in terms of treatment. His diagnosis is meaningful and dynamic when it provides a probability-statement of future behavior under alternative conditions.

All this means that whenever a clinical psychologist formulates a meaningful diagnosis, he expresses or implies a prediction. The next step in our examination probes briefly into the nature of psychological prediction. Psychological writers, among them Gordon Allport (1), Brown (4), Williamson (18), and Viteles (16), have postulated two forms of prediction: the statistical or actuarial method, and the clinical or case study method. To this point, the mathematician Reichenbach (11) has clearly demonstrated (1) that all meaningful predictions are probability-statements, and (2) that the postulation of two forms of prediction calls for two interpretations of probability. In another paper (15), the author has applied Reichenbach's treatment of this problem to clinical and statistical prediction in psychology. The conclusions in that paper point out that only one interpretation of probability, the frequency interpretation, is necessary in making clinical or statistical predictions of behavior. Predictions may be made on the basis of a regression equation, such as $X_0 = b_1X_1 + b_2X_2 + C$, or on the basis of crude generalizations from previous cases. An example of the latter would be: if a clinician's experience has shown an association of antecedents X, Y, and Z, with consequent "neurosis" in 80 out of 100 cases, the diagnosis of a case where X, Y, and Z were present could be meaningfully stated as "potential neurosis."

In dealing with a series of individuals who present similar antecedents, the psychologist predicts for any single individual on the basis of relative frequency of occurrence in the past. If the psychologist happens to be interested in studying only one individual, then he will make his predictions by ordering to a class similar behavior-segments of that individual and formulating a probability-statement in the same way—namely, on the basis of the relative frequency of occurrence. (The term *teleonomic* has been used by F. Allport (2) to designate the prediction of behavior for an individual on the basis of a series of observations of that individual.)

It is submitted, then, that a diagnosis, to be meaningful, must be predictive, and that predictions are the result of statistical generalizations. Since prediction is considered the hallmark of science, we may safely conclude that diagnosis is a scientific enterprise. This conclusion will immediately draw fire from clinicians of all schools of psychological thought. They will maintain stoutly that statistical generalizations destroy vital and dynamic elements gathered in the case study. We might answer that these so called dynamic elements, though interesting from a literary point of view, are scientifically meaningless unless they have predictive value. If these factors cannot be shown to have some observed association with the criterion, they are utterly useless.

Among sociologists, the problem of the relative merits of the case study and statistical generalization has been a subject of prolonged discussion. Lundberg's remarks may profitably be quoted here:

". . . case studies become significant scientifically only when they are *classified* or *summarized* in some way so that the uniformities in large numbers begin to stand out and group themselves into general patterns or types. It is in this process of summarization, without which a large number of case studies are practically useless for scientific purposes, that the statistical method, in cruder or more refined form, is not only useful but absolutely necessary." (8)

The present author agrees with Lundberg in that useful diagnoses always proceed from generalizations, whether based on a rigorous statistical method or upon a crude empirical method which has been variously named intuition, insight, *verstehen*, etc. When a clinician is put to the test to defend a diagnosis, he may resort to the statement that it was "the general feel of things" in the interview that influenced him. By pushing him back, however, it is possible usually to discover the empirical basis for the diagnosis. That these inferences are informal and not made with the benefit of Hollerith cards and Monroe calculators is beside the point. They are drawn from the clinician's cumulative experience. If they are not, then the diagnostic function must be relegated to individuals with some sort of magical power. "Thus the only possible question as to the relative value of the case (or clinical) method resolves itself into a question as to whether the classification of, and generalization from, the data shall be carried out by the informal, qualitative, and subjective method . . . or the systematic, quantitative, and objective procedure of the statistical method." (8).

At this point the critic will hold up his hand and bid us go no further: All that you say is true, he tells us, if you accept the postulate that clinical psychology is a science. But (and I quote from Westburgh's text) "Clinical psychology is an art—not a science. The clinical psychologist uses those scientific findings and techniques which are applicable to his clinical problems. . . . Then even while he is developing such a complete personality study, he engages upon the *genuinely artistic task* of helping the patient to solve his own problem." (17) (italics added).

This expression, genuinely artistic task—without further definition—

leads us into a morass. The possible meanings for the words art and artistic as used here are: (a) skill in the use of tools; (b) individual explorations into the unknown; (c) possession of a unique talent or gift; (d) so-called intuitive operations.

(a) If art means the skillful use of tools, then we must ask, whence come these skills? It is unnecessary to elaborate on the point that skills are acquired from experience with tools. For example, if a clinician can make ingenious predictions of social adjustment from the perusal of certain psychological tests, he would be demonstrating his skill. Such predictions are obviously made against a background of previous experience with psychological tests and social behavior. With this conception, the writer has no quarrel. It does not postulate a super-empirical method of understanding. It is not therefore, a material departure from the proposition that clinical psychology is scientific in that predictions are made on the basis of empirical data.

(b) If art means individual explorations into the unknown, we have no way of checking on the validity of predictions formulated in the name of art. If a clinician should make a diagnosis and prescribe treatment for a case that was unique, idiosyncratic, in every conceivable way, he would be venturing into the unknown. He would be guessing. This would be an expression of personal taste. If the clinician had no experiential background, no knowledge of similar cases, then he would be making a truly individual prediction. Unless such a single prediction is ordered to a class of events, it cannot be verified and is, therefore, meaningless.

(c) If, in this context, art means the possession of a gift or talent for "making friends and influencing people," then we can look for little progress in the field of clinical psychology. If clinical psychology is an art because some clinicians possess unique traits, and if complex human problems can be solved only by these specially-gifted people, then we must agree with Rogers and "admit that we can never deal in any large way with the multitude of ills which we group together as conduct problems, since the talents of the artist can be little conveyed to his fellows." (13). Recognition of this problem is also given in one of the most provocative books to be published recently on personnel administration. Roethlisberger and Dickson make this generalization on the basis of the outcome of a thorough-going research program in personnel administration:

"The skill (of diagnosing human situations) should be 'explicit' because the implicit or intuitive skills in handling human problems which successful administrators . . . possess are not capable of being communicated and transmitted. They are the peculiar property of the person who exercises them; they leave when the executive leaves the organization. An 'explicit' skill, on the other hand, is capable of being refined and taught and communicated to others." (9)

In this connection, it should be pointed out that the so-called art of interviewing, long considered an implicit or intuitive skill, has recently been studied, refined, and communicated to others. Porter (10) and Bordin and Sarbin (3) have studies in progress which show how these so-called artistic skills may be taught and learned.

(d) If art means some super-empirical method of understanding, then we must surrender our ideas about communicating techniques and procedures in clinical psychology. If we depart from the method of logical inference, i.e., the scientific method, then we must perforce adopt some so-called intuitive approach. Not inductive, not based on logical inference, the intuitive method of understanding is described by Klein as follows:

". . . (it is) the task of fathoming human motives or appreciating the entire gamut of human desires . . . (it) requires a knowledge of human nature. It represents the type of understanding indispensable for the development of psychology as a social science or as a Geisteswissenschaft." (6).

The traditional methods of science, he points out, have a place in psychology, but the intuitive approach, characterized by the quotation above, is to reap the harvest in psychology. One question that is raised but not answered is this: how does one acquire this "knowledge of human nature" which is so indispensable to the social scientist? Windelband suggests that it cannot be acquired:

"The psychology which the historian uses is a very different thing (from scientific psychology). It is the psychology of daily life: the practical psychology of the poet and the great statesman—the psychology that cannot be taught and learned, but is the gift of intuitive intelligence, and in its highest form a genius for judging contemporary life and posterity. This sort of psychology is an art and not a science." (19).

Other writers have pointed out that these so-called intuitions, if they are valid at all, are the products of experience. They are inferences which are not recognized as such. Those who still cling to the theory that intuitive predictions of behavior are more accurate must show two things: first, that intuitive predictions are not formulated from empirically-observed data; and second, that such "intuitions" are more accurate than predictions made from statistical generalizations. The research that has been reported to date suggests that intuitive, artistic predictions are not more accurate than those based on statistical and scientific concepts. Sarbin (14) has submitted evidence which shows that predictions of a complex social psychological activity—academic achievement—made by experienced clinicians are not more accurate than those made from a regression equation. The clinicians had available numerous psychological test scores, personal data sheets, the notes of another interviewer, and whatever data they could gather in the face-to-face interview. The regression equation was one in which two measurement variables were used to predict the criterion. In Wittman's studies (20, 21), a prognostic rating scale of 30 items was found to be more accurate in predicting the behavior of psychotic patients than the use of "intuitive" psychiatric generalizations. These reports are cited in evidence of the greater accuracy of predictions made on the basis of scientific concepts.

At this point we may briefly look into the other major aspect of clinical psychology—treatment. Are therapeutic efforts artistic or scientific in nature? If we accept the postulate stated earlier, that prediction is the hallmark of science, then we need but apply the same logic here. Upon what logical basis does a clinician prescribe treatment? He first makes a number of implicit predictions of this kind: "If treatment A is used in this-and-this problem there is a higher probability of improvement than if treatment B or C is used." These predictions may be, and usually are, based on clinical experience. Prediction of probable outcome of alternative conditions, whether implied or stated overtly, is always the first step. Unfortunately, few critical studies have been made which would give us prediction tables for various types of treatment of social psychological problems. As an example of the type of study which can be used to predict efficacy of treatment, we can refer to one in the field of neuro-psychiatry. Dub and Lurie (5) report the beneficial effects of benzedrine on depressive patients in 75% of their cases. If these findings are verified, the psychiatrist, when faced with a patient presenting the depressive syndrome, will prescribe treatment on the basis of statistics for treated and cured cases. In so doing, of course, he will be making an implicit prediction: the chances are $n - m/n$ or ¾ that this treatment will result in a change of behavior of psychiatric significance. Until studies of this general type have been made for various clinical syndromes, psychologists will continue to rely on subjective and crude generalizations based on clinical experience.

A critic may rise to this occasion and declare that statistics have not been developed adequately to deal with clinical material. This is fallacious. That many kinds of clinical data are crude and not adapted to refined treatment is obvious. It is needless to emphasize that at this point in clinical research refined statistical analyses are usually unnecessary. Parker (9) has suggested that the Chi-square test be applied to statistics of treated and cured cases where pharmacological preparations have been used. This same procedure is well-adapted to many of the problems of clinical research and should be considered by those interested in evaluating clinical procedures. Analysis of variance may also be utilized for certain problems. Once the hypothesis is formulated and the data collected, the appropriate statistical tool will not be difficult to discover.

Because of efforts at condensation, I may have left the impression that investigations not immediately adapted to statistical treatment are not of value. This is not so. It is true that any scientific investigation must deal with precise relations. But before the period of mathematical precision, there must first be a period of crude observation and hypothesizing. The history of science shows many instances where scientists had to learn how to enumerate the objects of their inquiries or to discover what sort of measurement it was most profitable to make.

I believe the psychological clinic has been overlooked as a starting place for research investigations in social psychology. That the clinical psychologist is in a most enviable position for formulating hypotheses soon becomes apparent to anyone. Every case abounds in hypotheses which arise out of the clinician's interbehaving with concrete human beings in social psychological situations. By submitting these hypotheses to test, the clinician may make important contributions not only to applied science, but to theoretical science as well. At the same time that he discovers a relationship between antecedent and consequent which is clinically useful, he makes a contribution to social psychological theory.

To summarize: on the basis of a logical analysis of the two chief functions of clinical psychologists—diagnosis and treatment—it is submitted that clinical psychology is a scientific enterprise. Prediction, the *sine qua non* of science, is closely bound up with the concepts of diagnosis and treatment. Predictions are made from empirically-observed events. To observe and deal with these events it is unnecessary to postulate artistic and intuitive concepts. It is submitted that the traditional method of science, logical inference, provides a pattern for clinical psychology as it does for the rest of the scientific world.

REFERENCES

1. ALLPORT, GORDON W. The psychologist's frame of reference. *Psychol. Bull.*, 1940, **37**, 1–28.
2. ALLPORT, F. H. Teleonomic description in the study of personality. *Character and Personality*, 1937, **5**, 202–214.
3. BORDIN, EDWARD S. and SARBIN, THEODORE R. Studies in interviewing (in preparation).
4. BROWN, J. F. Psychology and the social order. New York: McGraw-Hill, 1936.
5. DUB, L. A. and LURIE, L. S. Use of benzedrine in the depressed phase of the psychotic state. *Ohio State Medical Journal*, 1939, **35**, 39–45.
6. KLEIN, D. B. Scientific understanding in psychology. *Psychol. Rev.*, 1932, **32**, 552–569.
7. LOUTTIT, C. M. The nature of clinical psychology. *Psychol. Bull.* 1939, **36**, 361–389.
8. LUNDBERG, GEORGE. Social research, New York: Longmans Green, 1929.
9. PARKER, M. M. A method for evaluating the experimental use of drugs in psychopathology. *J. abnor. soc. Psychol.*, 1939, **34**, 465–480.
10. PORTER, T. H., JR. The development and evaluation of a measure of counseling interview procedure. *Psychol. Bull.*, 1941, **38**, 524–525.
11. REICHENBACH, H. Experience and Prediction. Chicago: Univ. of Chicago Press, 1938.
12. ROETHLISBERGER, F. J. and DICKSON, W. J. *Management and the worker.* Cambridge: Harv. Univ. Press, 1939.
13. ROGERS, CARL R. The clinical treatment of the problem child. Boston: Houghton-Mifflin, 1939.
14. SARBIN, THEODORE R. The relative accuracy of clinical and statistical predictions of academic achievement. Paper read at the 1941 meetings of the Midwestern Psychological Association, Athens, Ohio (soon to be published).
15. SARBIN, THEODORE R. The logic of prediction in psychology (adapted from Ph.D. thesis on file in the library of the Ohio State University) (soon to be published).
16. VITELES, M. S. The clinical viewpoint in vocational psychology. *J. appl. Psychol.*, 1925, **9**, 131–138.
17. WESTBURGH, EDWARD M. Introduction to clinical psychology. Philadelphia: P. Blakiston's Sons, 1937.
18. WILLIAMSON, E. G. How to counsel students. New York: McGraw-Hill, 1939.
19. WINDELBAND, W. An introduction to philosophy. London: T. Fisher Unwin, 1921.
20. WITTMAN, MARY PHYLLIS. A scale for measuring prognosis in schizophrenic patients. *Elgin Papers*, 1941, **4**, 20–33.
21. WITTMAN, MARY PHYLLIS. Evaluation of prognosis in the functional psychoses. *Psychol. Bull.*, 1941, **38**, 535–536.

The Logic of Prediction in Psychology

Theodore R. Sarbin

Northwestern University

I. INTRODUCTION

To an increasing extent psychologists and other social scientists have become concerned with problems associated with the prediction of behavior. This is evidenced by a number of papers recently published which have dealt with the problem of actuarial versus individual approaches to prediction (14, 30, 32, 36, 37, 42, 46, 53). Several studies have attempted prediction of marital adjustment (11, 47). The Social Science Research Council recently published an extensive monograph which reviewed the literature on the prediction of personal adjustment and pointed the way to some needed research (18). Since this topic has important methodological implications for the psychological and social sciences, it would be appropriate at this time to essay a logical analysis of the concept of prediction.

Probably the most insistent problem has to do with the relative accuracy of clinical or case study predictions versus actuarial or statistical predictions. G. W. Allport, in his brilliant attacks on the actuarial method, sets the problem:

Suppose we set out to discover the chances of John Brown to make good on parole, and use for the purpose an index of prediction based upon parole violations and parole successes of men with similar histories. We find that 72% of the men with John's antecedents make good, and many of us conclude that John, therefore, has a 72% chance of making good. There is an obvious error here. The fact that 72% of the men having the same antecedent record as John will make good is merely an actuarial statement. It tells us nothing about John. If we knew John sufficiently well, we might say not that he had a 72% chance of making good, but that he, as an individual was almost certain to succeed or else to fail. Indeed, if we believe in determinism at all, his chances are either zero or else 100; he is bound to succeed or else to violate because the germs of his future are already contained in his attitudes, in the meaning to him of his antecedent life, and in the specific psychological environment that molds him. Even admitting the possibility of unforeseeable accidents, as scientific determinists we ought to strive for a prediction more accurate than the senseless 72% that is derived from a table of norms based on the antecedents of paroled men en masse. Or again, if seven in ten Americans go to the movies each week, it does not

Reprinted from *Psychological Review*, 1944, 51, 210–228.

follow that I have seven in ten chances of attending. Only a knowledge of my attitudes, interests, and environmental situation will tell you my chances, and bring your prediction from a 70% actuarial statement to a 100% certain individual prediction (3, pp. 16–17).

Using different terminology, Brown (9) considers two kinds of prediction, a statistical causal analysis and a dynamic causal analysis. Viteles asserts that two kinds of predictions can be made when he writes: ". . . the statistical point of view must be supplemented by the clinical point of view" (49, p. 134). Bingham and Moore (5) likewise point out the presence of two kinds of prediction: statistical prediction based on regression equations derived from groups, and clinical prediction based upon statistical prediction but refined and modified by including the consideration of factors not treated in the regression equation. Burgess and Cottrell hold a similar point of view. In common with other writers in the social sciences they maintain that because statistical methods deal with averages and probabilities that dynamic combinations of behavior are excluded. The statistical prediction is considered to be quite limited in its applicability whereas the prediction made from the case study is more valid (11).

These citations are presented merely to reflect the current trends in systematic and applied psychology with regard to the concept of prediction. From these representative excerpts two propositions emerge for further consideration:

(1) A statistical notion, probability, is involved in the prediction of behavior.
(2) Two kinds of prediction are made in psychology—the statistical and the clinical.[1]

II. PROBABILITY LOGIC IN RELATION TO PREDICTION

The essential notion of probability is understood by nearly everybody and is used in everyday life in all sorts of situations. The popular expressions "I think so," "presumably," "I don't think so," etc., are the ways in which the man-in-the-street uses the concept. But if we stay close to this mythical man-in-the-street we are likely to be led astray. If the same proposition is presented to him and two of his neighbors, he might hold that the proposition was certain to be true, one of his neighbors might declare the proposition to be probable, while the other might express no judgment at all. This might lead us to the erroneous conclusion that the notion of probability is a matter of individual differences. But the probability of the proposition being true is not a matter of personal opinion. It is a matter of logical demonstration.

. . . The proposition is either proved or not proved, and . . . such differences of opinion are the result of not understanding the proof. . . . On a given set of data p we say that a proposition q has in relation to these data

[1] The term 'clinical' is used here to express the meaning generic to such terms as 'individual,' 'dynamic causal analysis,' 'case study approach,' etc.

one and only one probability. If any person assigns a different probability, he is simply wrong. . . . Personal differences in assigning probabilities in everyday life are not due to any ambiguity in the notion of probability itself, but to mental differences between individuals, to the differences in the data available to them, and to differences in the amount of care taken to evaluate the probability (22, p. 10).

Scientists are somewhat more rigorous in their use of the concept of probability than is the man in the street. Instead of using an expression such as "I think so" the scientist considers probability as expressing "a relation between a proposition and a set of data. When the data imply that the proposition is true, the probability is said to amount to certainty; when they imply that it is false, the probability becomes impossibility. All intermediate degrees of probability can arise" (22, p. 9). Pushing one step beyond, we come to a mathematical formulation. If n trials have been made, and if, in these n trials, the event has occurred m times and has failed to occur $(n - m)$ times, then the relative frequency of occurrence is m/n and the relative frequency of failure is $(n - m)/n$. The probability may be said to be "the limit to which the relative frequencies tend when the number of members in the field of statistical measurement approaches infinity" (50, p. 266).[2]

The concept of probability which hereinafter is referred to as the frequency concept (based on the notion of relative frequency), is rather clearly defined and its mathematics are fairly well-known. No one will question that this frequency concept is at the bottom of the notion of probability used in making statistical predictions.

In order to consider the other form of prediction variously called 'individual prediction,' 'dynamic causal analysis' and 'clinical' prediction, it seems necessary to treat of a second concept of probability. This vague concept does not present itself in a mathematical form. The quotations above taken from Allport, Brown, and others indicate that the frequency interpretation is not appropriate in making predictions of an individual's behavior. Instead of referring to future behavior as 72 chances in 100 of success the clinician would use non-numerical terms, such as 'presumably,' 'probably,' 'more than likely,' etc. This concept cannot be submitted to experimental test. Reichenbach (34) refers to this as the logical concept of probability in contra-distinction to the frequency concept. For clarity we shall refer to it as the non-frequency concept of probability.

Except for a brief controversy between Viteles (49) and Freyd (15) about 18 years ago, psychological theorists and practitioners have considered the problem not at all or as already solved. At that time, Viteles maintained that a statistical clerk could compute for any applicant the statistical probability of success on the job, but that a trained psychologist had to consider other factors which were not included in the regression equation, and ". . . an adequate diagnosis involves interpretation by a trained psychologist based on the observation of performance and a con-

---

[2] It is beyond the scope of this paper to describe or evaluate the various mathematical formulae used in prediction. These are treated in current textbooks. For an up-to-date treatment the reader is referred to the statistical appendices in Horst, Wallin, and Guttman (18), to Hotelling's critique (20), and to Guttman's rejoinder (20).

sideration of related data" (49, p. 134). Freyd countered with a consistently logical argument from which the following is representative:

> This (clinical point of view) appears very much as if it were a case of changing horses in the middle of the stream. The psychologist starts out to measure the abilities required for a job. When he has evaluated statistically a series of tests he states that the tests are inadequate for the purpose and that the applicants can be selected properly only by a supplementary judgment of their performance which the psychologist alone by virtue of his special training is competent to give (15, p. 352).

The clinical method as here characterized is the basis upon which vocational, educational and personnel guidance is administered. First batteries of tests are given, then the clinicians, by supplementary judgments, formulate diagnoses and prognoses.

Freyd states further:

> The writer is not in disagreement with the clinical point of view if it means that social, personal history and economic information should receive the same consideration as psychological abilities. These very important facts have been unaccountably neglected by research workers in spite of the fact that in many instances of their use, notably with life insurance salesmen, they have proved to be important. When they are studied, they should be evaluated in the same statistical way as the tests (15, p. 355).

The problem may now be narrowed down to this statement: if the viewpoint expressed by Freyd is correct—that we can apply the frequency interpretation to the non-frequency statement—then it would appear that these superficially different concepts are actually *identical;* if the viewpoint expressed by Viteles is correct, then these concepts are *disparate.* The present author is concerned with this problem because the presence of both interpretations of probability runs counter to the principles of empiricism which demand that predictions be verified. But verification cannot take place without repetition. The frequency of occurrence, then, is seen as a *sine qua non* for prediction. But what of the single case? If an event occurs but once, how can the frequency interpretation of probability be considered? It is to this question that we turn next.

III. THE SINGLE CASE

Lewin, for one, is opposed to the notion that the frequency of occurrence has any particular significance for the single case.

> The accidents of historical processes are not overcome by excluding the changing situations from systematic consideration, but only by taking the fullest account of the individual nature of the concrete case. *It depends upon keeping in mind that general validity of the law and concreteness of the individual case are not antitheses, and that reference to the totality of the concrete whole situation must take the place of reference to the largest possible historical collection of frequent repetitions.* This means methodologically that the importance of a case, and its validity as proof, cannot be evaluated by the frequency of its occurrence . . . (28, pp. 41–2).

With the same insistence upon the individual case is the point of view adopted by Williamson: "Most of our statistical studies are based upon the [fact] . . . that only rarely do we discover an individual whose working conditions even approximate the general conditions of the original investigation. For this reason, the clinical counselor must be extremely careful in applying the results of such studies . . . to predictions for particular individuals. He must modify the *general* prediction in terms of relevant data known about a particular individual" (51, p. 107). The problem before us now is to determine whether we can meet the objection that the single case cannot be dealt with adequately unless we have the two conceptions of probability.

To the clinician the single case represents an individual with a complex of behavior characteristics which is like no other individual's. The clinician studies this individual, then makes a prediction of the future behavior in terms of probabilities. For example: "Student X has one chance in six of meeting the standards of competition in the University." In keeping with the principles of empiricism, it is necessary to verify the statement of probability. But this is impossible if we deal with only one case. If our student does not meet the standards, we cannot say that our prediction was correct; we cannot tell whether the correct probability-statement should have been $\frac{1}{3}$, $\frac{1}{4}$, $\frac{1}{10}$ or 1/infinity. If we accept as one of the canons of science the verification of predictions, we must deny the single-case interpretation. Up to this point our analysis does not enable us to treat the single event in terms of the frequency interpretation of probability. We have only demonstrated that the clinical or single-case prediction is not subject to verification.

Verification of the probability-statement is possible as soon as the event can be repeated. In other words, as soon as the single case *becomes a member of a class*, the relative frequency of occurrence can be determined and verification of the prediction obtained. The frequency interpretation asserts that the occurrence is not an isolated, individual event, but that it is a member of a class of similar events. The problem now is the construction of the class to which the single case may be ordered.

If the probability statement is to have meaning, the event in question must be considered in the light of similar events. If the clinician can find no similar individuals or events—if the case and the problem are so unique— then he has no experience from which to make a prediction. As soon as he compares the concrete case in front of him with other cases from his clinical experience or from his statistical tables, then he orders the case to a class. According to Reichenbach:

The origin of the single-case interpretation is to be found in the fact that for many cases the construction of the class is not so obviously determined as in the case of the die, or in the fact that ordinary language suppresses a reference to a class, and speaks incorrectly of a single event where a class of events should be considered. If we keep this postulate clearly in mind, we find that the way toward the construction of the corresponding class is indicated in the origin and use of probability statements. Why do we ascribe, say a high probability to the statement that Napoleon had an attack of illness during the battle of Leipsig, and a smaller probability to the statement that Caspar Hauser was the son of a prince? It is because chronicles of different types report these statements: one type is reliable because its statements, in frequent attempts at control, were confirmed; the other is not reliable because attempts at control frequently lead to the refutation of the statement. The transition to the type of chronicle indicates the class of the frequency interpretation; the probability occurring in the statements about Napoleon's disease, or Caspar Hauser's descent, is to be interpreted as concerning a certain class of historical reports and finds it[s] statistical interpretation in the frequency of confirmations encountered within this class . . . (34, pp. 307–8).

This method of verifying historical events is certainly applicable to the other cultural phenomena. Psychologists who maintain that a prognosis is based on data from a single case with no reference to other cases, fail to recognize the frame of reference into which they have fitted their generalizations or else they engage in non-scientific guesswork. Incidentally, the single-case method of interpretation of natural and social phenomena is not new—it has a long history. Primitive peoples utilized single cases to support their beliefs and dogmas. The allegory, the myth, the fable, and so on, are examples of the single-case used to illustrate or prove propositions. The methodological fallacy, both for the psychologist and the aborigine, is that prediction from the single case takes place without some sort of counting operation. The common-sense inferences from the single case are usually performed with the benefit of informal, subjective statistical comparisons (4).

The operations of those who reject the statistical method of prediction and substitute for it a 'dynamic' clinical or individual prediction, may be described in one of two ways: Either they are making statistical predictions in an informal, subjective, and uncontrolled way, or else they are performing purely verbal manipulations which are unverifiable and akin to magic. Forty years ago Jastrow warned the general public against this practice.

This tendency to insist that the laws of science shall be precisely and in detail applicable to individual experiences possessing a personal interest for us, has wrought much havoc; it has contributed to superstition, fostered pseudo-science and encouraged charlatanism. To antagonize this tendency it is necessary to insist upon the statistical nature of the inquiry . . . (21, pp. 84–5).

The problem can be further clarified by an investigation of the behavioral situations in which we utilize predictions. Why do we make predictions about future events for which we can never have certain knowledge? No one will deny that predictions are practical guides to conduct. Reichenbach puts it this way: ". . . *the meaning of probability statements is to be determined in such a way that our behavior in utilizing them for action can be justified*" (34, p. 309).

We could follow the behavior of any individual through a typical day to see the role that predictions play in his planning. He mails a letter because there is a high probability that it will arrive at its destination. He waits for a trolley car because there is a high probability that a car will arrive within the next half-hour. He does not plan a picnic in November because there is a high probability that the weather will not be suitable, and so on *ad infinitum*. Every action falls within a series of actions. If each action is

planned in the light of the most probable event occurring, then we are
bound to have a large number of successes. If, on the other hand, we do
not plan our actions with the idea in mind of the most probable event, then
there would be a marked diminution in the number of successes.[3]

To bring into sharper focus the last point, an illustration follows which
shows that clinical data which are not submitted to a probability analysis
apparently do not improve the accuracy of prediction of academic success.
Suppose the clinician is faced with a student who wants to know his
chances of succeeding in the University. The usual data, high school marks
and college aptitude test scores, provide us with a probability statement
that correctly predicts success or failure in seven out of ten cases. But the
clinician has more data available than the scores that go into the regression
equation. First, this student works 30 hours a week in a restaurant; second,
he is in love with a girl back home; third, he does not make a good impression in the interview. On the basis of these three additional observations,
the clinician modifies the prediction so that he now tells the student his
chances of success are poor, i.e., "Your chances of success are 1 in 10."

His prediction is presumably based on the fact that students in the
past who worked 30 hours a week did poorer work than was expected, that
love-sick boys did not achieve up to standard, and that students who did
not impress him favorably in the interview usually did not succeed. But all
available evidence (16) shows that these three variables, when partialled
out from the two measurement variables, add nothing to prediction of
academic success. If they did, that is to say, if they were associated with
successful achievement or failure, then prediction tables could be devised
so that the 'clinical' prediction would be unnecessary. If the clinician holds
that these three variables apply *only* in this case and not necessarily to
others, the burden of proof lies with him. He cannot verify his prediction.
If the boy succeeds in school, upsetting the prediction, then the clinician
might offer weakly that this case was the one in ten. But if a single case,
where are the other nine? If the boy fulfills the prediction, we do not know
whether the three designated events had any influence upon achievement,
or whether other factors were responsible. The prediction can be verified
only by ordering the event to a class and then counting the number of successes. It matters not whether the class is intra-individual—determined from
events occurring in the individual's reaction biography, or determined from
events occurring in a population of individuals.

In the foregoing paragraphs I have followed Reichenbach in attempting to demonstrate that for scientific prediction the two concepts of probability are essentially the same and that the frequency interpretation stands
unassailed. In fine, both concepts rely upon ordering to a class of events,
any particular event for which we wish to make a probability statement or
prediction. The class may be defined as events of a similar nature which
occur for groups of people, or events of a similar nature which occur at
different times to the same individual. "We need not introduce a 'single-

[3] Bridgman makes some pithy comments in regard to the application of the
mathematical solutions in individual events. ". . . people seem unwilling to recognize that probability roughly measures their confidence in their plans for future
action, but they seem to demand something sharper. Everyone recognizes that if
he has to devise unique plans for the future he is a fool if he does not base his
plans on the 'most probable' eventuality" (7, p. 99).

case meaning' of the probability statement; a 'class meaning' is sufficient because it suffices to justify the application of probability statements to actions concerned with single events" (34, p. 312).

IV. CONCEPT OF THE CLASS

The concept of the class needs further clarification. As usually interpreted, and as used in the preceding section, the class means a grouping of events. Suppose, however, we were interested in an individual who was in a class by himself. Suppose he were a Harvard professor and we wanted to predict whether he would attend the movies on any particular day. In the absence of information on our professor we would make a prediction on the basis of the movie-going habits of college professors rather than people-in-general. The class, then, becomes the group of college professors. But in our supposition we are ignorant of the habits of this group. Therefore, we study the movie-going habits of our professor over a period of time independent of others. The class now consists of events—'attendance at movies.' Our study might reveal that the professor attends the local theaters on the average of once a month. Therefore, for any single day we would make the prediction that the chances are $^{29}\!/_{30}$ for non-attendance. The most probable event is that he will not attend on any particular day. We will have the greatest number of successes if we predict that he will not go on any given day. Over the period of a year, we may be wrong 12 times; but we shall be correct 353 times. From this illustration it would appear that actuarial predictions are appropriate for individuals as well as for groups.[4]

V. CLINICAL AND STATISTICAL METHODS OF PREDICTION COMPARED

The statistical method of prediction is essentially the same for all types of criteria. Whether predicting the performance of an individual operating a welding-torch, the efficiency of a certain drug in combatting a disease process, success in college, or adjustment in marriage, the same general methodology prevails. Predictions are made on the basis of empirical observations.

The steps in the method may be summarized as follows: (1) An explicit statement of the criterion to be predicated is formulated. (2) Variables or attributes presumably associated with the attainment of the criterion are estimated. These may be psychometric scores, items from a reactional biography, physiological signs, or social facts such as marital status, urban or rural residence, etc. (3) These variables or attributes are correlated with

---

[4] The 'teleonomic' conception of studying personality considers predictions made for one individual on the basis of multiple observations of a single case. See F. H. Allport (1).

the criterion variable. The most simple case is illustrated below with a four-fold surface.[5] (4) Wider ranges of measurement for criterion and predictor variables call for more complicated procedures. The underlying no-

N = 1200	Percent improved after hospitalization	Percent unimproved after hospitalization
Presence of shut-in personality in childhood	12	88
Absence of shut-in personality in childhood	59	41

tion, however, is the same. (5) Weights are assigned according to observed differences. (In the illustration above, a weight of 47 is assigned to the presence of the item in future cases, 0 to absence of item.) (6) Where there are multiple predictors, the multiple regression equation can be used to determine the contribution of each variable to the total prediction score. (7) The probability-value of the prediction made from the regression education is available prior to the forecast. (8) Finally, from the equation, or from tables or nomograms derived from such equations, predictions for a new set of individuals are made with known margin of error.

The clinical method offers a sharp contrast to this rather uninspired, mechanical method. Although both methods call for a prior statement of the criterion or predictand, the clinical or intuitive worker is not bound to any systematic methodology in arriving at his forecasts. He may begin with the same data that are put into the regression equations, or may actually use such equations. But, if he wishes, he can disregard, modify, or magnify any measurement on the basis of his previous experience or clinical intuitions. He may have a kind of informal statistical method (of which he may be unaware [36]) but he is not bound by any rigorous mathematical procedures. His methods are the very essence of flexibility and he is free to apply whatever meaning (predictive-value) he chooses to data about an individual. Further, and this is considered of utmost importance by the protagonists of the non-statistical method, the clinician usually has much more information at hand about any one person than can be conveniently used statistically.

Let us examine this last proposition that clinicians usually have more data available than go into the regression equation. The obvious and plausible assumption is that the more data, the more accurate the prediction. In prediction of psychological criteria, the clinician will use ratings, paper-and-pencil tests, health reports, school histories, inventories, projective personality tests, and interview-data. Although the clinician does not have a regression equation in front of him, he may treat the data as though he had. In so doing, he is using an informal, implicit, statistical method. There is nothing super-empirical about it. In the clinical situation, the clinician's implicit regression equation may have 15 or 20 or 50 variables. The clinician may apply the same weights systematically to all cases, or he may apply the weights differentially in each individual case. The clinician, in

[5] Data from Sarbin and Wittman (37).

other words, makes judgments on the basis of a large number of facts taken from different sources. Because predictions are usually made in a relatively brief period of time, it is impossible for the clinician to perform all the mathematical operations necessary. Thorndike, writing in 1918, analyzes what happens when a so-called intuitive judgment is made.

The competent impressionistic judge of men does respond to these interrelations of the facts and sums up in his estimate a consideration of each in the light of the others. If there are ten traits involved, say ten entries on an application blank, he may be said to determine his prophecy by at least $10 + 9 + 8 + 7 + 6 + 5 + 4 + 3 + 2 + 1$ quantities, since he responds to each trait in relation to all the others. There is a prevalent myth that the expert judge of men succeeds by some mystery of divination. Of course, this is nonsense. He succeeds because he makes smaller errors in the facts or in the way he weights them (48, pp. 75–76).

Elsewhere (36) the author has given a free-association account of a typical clinical prediction. Space limitations prohibit its reproduction here. Suffice it to say that the introspective account indicates that clinical predictions are made on the basis of (1) deductions from known and tested generalizations (informal or implicit statistical predictions); (2) deductions from plausible but untested hypotheses; (3) deductions from false generalizations; and (4) so-called intuitions.

With regard to the first item above (1) it is apparent to anyone that deductions from tested generalizations can be accomplished with greater precision and efficiency by using prediction tables or equations. In regard to (2), deductions from untested hypotheses, a clinician may find himself embarrassed when the superficial plausibility of his hypothesis is exploded by empirical or experimental studies (36).[6] As to (3), it is needless to mention that clinical predictions are not made more acceptable by the use of deductions from false generalizations. (Parenthetically, these are more common than most clinicians realize.) The point where the clinical method seems to be different is in (4), the use of so-called intuitive data which have not and cannot be subjected to the same scientific tests as those which are amenable to empirical observations.

The shift in American psychology in recent years toward concepts variously named *Verstehen,* intuition, sympathetic understanding and insight has caused us to stop and question whether this method of comprehending data will replace the more conventional form or will be a supplement to the logical type of understanding that we have traditionally used.

In order for us better to understand what is meant by the intuitive method in psychology as opposed to the empirical method, we must consider the differentiae between the natural sciences, and the cultural sciences. Natural sciences are said to be nomothetic, that is to say, they seek laws, causality, etc. Cultural sciences, on the other hand, seek uniqueness, individuality, they are idiographic. So far the differentiae do not lead to any schism in psychology. Uniqueness or individuality can be studied with the same empirical methods as behavior common to groups (2).

The differentiae lie elsewhere, namely in the conception of psychology as a science. Klüver has remarked "Whether there is one scientific psychology or whether there are two kinds of psychology, whether there is a

[6] Also see p. 34 f. of this article.

necessary antagonism between 'causal' and 'understanding' psychology, or whether they supplement each other—these and kindred questions have not been answered with finality" (27, p. 455). A brief acquaintance with the writings of those who profess to follow the psychology of understanding will immediately raise the question: Is this kind of psychology a science?

In this connection, Klein has written a paper describing the nomothetic and idiographic concepts. He points out that there are four ways of understanding things: (1) a structural continuity type, (2) a functional type, (3) a logical or implicative type, and (4) an empathetic type. The first is illustrated as that which uses mechanical models. The second deals with concepts, such as those of physics and chemistry, *e.g.*, gravitation. The third is the method common to all science—the inductive method. The fourth method of understanding, empathy, is

The task of fathoming human motives or appreciating the entire gamut of human desires. To understand the football player struggling for a touchdown, the philologist tracking down an obscure root, . . . requires neither mechanical models, a knowledge of functional relationships, nor expert mastery of local implications. But it does require a knowledge of human nature. It represents the type of understanding indispensable for the development of psychology as a social science or as a Geisteswissenschaft (26, p. 565).

The first three methods, he goes on to say, have a place in psychology, but the idiographic method, characterized by the above quotation, will lead to the most fruitful generalizations. One question that is not answered is this: how does one acquire "a knowledge of human nature"? Windelband has an answer:

The psychology which the historian uses is a very different thing [from scientific psychology]. It is the psychology of daily life: the practical psychology of the poet, and the great statesman—the psychology that cannot be taught and learned, but is a gift of intuitive intelligence, and in its highest form a genius for judging contemporary life and posterity. This sort of psychology is an art, not a science (52, p. 280).

The writer has no space to repeat the logical argument presented in another paper (40) which rejected artistic, intuitive methods in psychological practice and research. Talking about such super-empirical vagaries as the 'gift of intuitive intelligence' is little short of autistic conduct. To posit, as G. W. Allport does, "a structuring activity of the mind" (2, p. 547) seems gratuitous to any sophisticated psychological system.[7]

R. B. Cattell (13) also offers a logical argument to show the illusory nature of the intuitive approach when applied to psychological formulations.

[7] Sophisticated, that is, as of 1943. Sophistication in scientific constructs calls for formulations that embrace the present orientation in science. Kantor points to five trends which illustrate this newer approach: (1) relativity theory, (2) quantum mechanics, (3) the indeterminacy principle, (4) "the Kant-Bridgman discrimination against meaningless questions, the consequence of which is that only such problems are considered valid as can be solved by observation and experiment—in short, complete operations of the scientist. To these must be added (5) an equally cogent consideration—namely, scientific success is a definite function of the freedom from conventional bias with which the scientist approaches his field of operation" (25, p. 175).

The intuitionist desires to know another personality directly, by empathy instead of in an objective fashion. . . . Because the mind of another human being is more akin to his own than is the mind of an insect, he is misled into believing that he can apprehend it directly. . . . It is the especial danger of psychology that the psychologist is encouraged to use intuition because by reason of the partial similarity of minds, it yields an attractive proportion of correct guesses in predicting the thoughts, feelings, and behavior of others. But even in practice its use leads in the end to errors more impressive than its successes. . . . Every intuitive judgment made in a psychological clinic is a . . . stereotype distortion of a unique mind. Intuition has an indispensable place in research, as a scaffolding under the shadow of which objective investigations may be built up; but propounded as an independent method of arriving at psychological knowledge, it would seem to be a pure illusion (13, p. 130–131).

The previous paragraphs may appear to contain an obvious bias against intuitive methods of personality study. The intuitionists—who usually get along so well without empirical data—by this time must be clamoring for evidence. All these polemics, they may assert, mean nothing in the absence of evidence which would disprove the hypothesis that predictions based on intuitions are more accurate than predictions made from the less exciting equations of the actuarial method. Therefore, we turn to the available evidence.

VI. EMPIRICAL STUDIES

The empirical studies that have been reported to date seem to favor the actuarial method. They are briefly reviewed below.

(1) Wittman (53, 54) has offered evidence on prognosis in schizophrenia. Predictions of outcome of hospitalization were made by the psychiatric staff on the basis of anamnesis, mental examination, physical examination, conference with patient, and discussion of the case in a diagnostic staff conference. These clinical predictions were made on an intuitive, i.e., non-statistical basis. Statistical predictions were made with the aid of a 30-item rating scale which assigned weights of items appearing in the anamnesis or mental examination.[8] Her results showed the unmistakable superiority of the scale over the staff judgments. Table 1 shows these differences.[9]

(2) A continuation of this study was carried on by Sarbin and Wittman (37). In the former study, the scale items were arbitrarily though systematically weighted according to the author's experience with thousands of dementia precox patients. This system of weighting allowed for a certain degree of subjectivity and incommunicability. In the continuation study, therefore, the weights were derived empirically. The scale was reduced to 22 items. On a new sample of 200 patients, the comparisons were similar to those of Table 1.

---

[8] The reader will note that case study material is possible of quantification and statistical treatment in the same manner as other kinds of data, such as I.Q.'s. The terms 'statistical' and 'psychometric' are not synonymous.

[9] Adapted from Wittman (53).

TABLE 1

PERCENTAGE OF CORRECT PREDICTIONS OF THE RESULT OF
HOSPITALIZATION WITH PROGNOSIS SCALE AND WITH
MEDICAL STAFF PROGNOSTIC JUDGMENTS

	Prognosis Scale	Medical Staff
Remission N = 56	90	52
Much Improved N = 66	86	41
Improved N = 51	75	36
Slight Improvement N = 31	46	34
Unimproved N = 139	85	49

(3) A third study was reported by the present writer in which clinical predictions of academic achievement were compared with predictions made from regression equations. The clinical predictions were presumably made on the basis of the multifarious data available to the clinician. These included numerous tests of aptitude, achievement, personality and interest; a personal record form; the written observations of a preliminary interviewer; and whatever information the clinician could gather in the face-to-face interview. The results are reported in Table 2.[10] The comparisons seem

TABLE 2

COMPARISON OF CLINICAL AND STATISTICAL PREDICTIONS
OF ACADEMIC SUCCESS AND FAILURE

Achievement	Clinical Predictions	
	Success	Failure
Success	75	35
Failure	13	39
	Statistical Predictions	
Success	75	26
Failure	13	48
$\chi^2 = 5.63; P < .02$		

to favor the statistical method of prediction. From this study we can say with some assurance that the prediction of academic success or failure can be done simpler and with greater accuracy by the statistical method.

(4) Burgess (21) cites a study by Scheidt (42) on the prediction of parole violation. The evidence in the prediction of this criterion seems to corroborate the other empirical studies. The mechanical predictions were superior to those made by the prison physician.

[10] Data from Sarbin (36, 38); statistical treatment according to Snedecor (41).

The preceding argument together with the empirical studies just cited would seem to throw considerable doubt on the validity of non-inferential intuitive modes of predicting conduct.[11]

VII. PREDICTION AND THE APPROXIMATE CHARACTER OF KNOWLEDGE

The view expressed by some writers that predictions must be stated as one or zero likewise needs examination. G. W. Allport, for one, declares that a thorough knowledge of one's interests, attitudes, and environmental situation will raise an actuarial prediction of 70 per cent (in his illustration) to '100 per cent certain individual prediction' (3, p. 17). The case study (2) is suggested to point the way to this scientific El Dorado.

Illustrative of this same view is Brown's statement, to which a reference has been made previously. He asserts that 'dynamical causal analyses' express predictions in terms of *exact* amounts (9). The implications of those who speak for the superiority of the clinical method as opposed to the more approximate statistical method force us to think in terms of probability statements of one or zero. The same notion obtrudes from this statement by Burgess and Cottrell:

. . . while statistical prediction may be valid for averages and for stated probabilities that results will fall within certain defined limits, *it can only be approximate.*

Implied in the above-noted limitations is the fact that present statistical methods deal with averages and probabilities and not with specific dynamic combinations of factors . . . (11, p. 33) (italics mine).

In the absence of objective data on larger numbers of cases, these authors then go on to place their faith in 'case studies' for the important configurations of dynamic factors (11, p. 340). From these statements, the reader of their monograph infers that the case study method yields predictions which are based upon 'specific, dynamic combinations of factors' and which are not approximate, but exact.

The point which is missed, probably because it is taken for granted, is that the results of all measurement are only approximate. Psychologists, in using tests and measures of the traditional sort, expect only approximate results. Usually however, this expectation is based on the assumption that the results are approximate only because the test or measure is a psychological one, not a physical one. But all measurement, regardless of the object to be measured or the scientific label attached to the individual who is taking the measurement, is approximate. To quote Bridgman:

That such is true [the approximation of measurement] is evident after the most superficial examination of any measuring process; any statement

---

[11] Polansky's study (31) has sometimes been cited as evidence that clinical methods produce better predictions than statistical. This is an error in that it has been assumed that statistical predictions are always made from psychometric data. Polansky showed that for his three cases, predictions made from data presented in 'structural analysis' forms were more accurate than predictions made from other forms of analysis—including psychometric. The problem of intuitive, clinical prediction versus actuarial was not actually considered by Polansky.

about numerical relations between measured quantities must always be subject to the qualification that the relation is valid only within limits. Furthermore, all experience seems to be of this character; we never have perfectly clean-cut knowledge of anything, but all our experience is surrounded by a twilight zone, a penumbra of uncertainty, into which we have not yet penetrated. This penumbra is as truly an unexplored region as any other region beyond experiment, such as the region of high velocities, for example, and we must hold no preconceived notions as to what will be found within that region. The penumbra is to be penetrated by improving the accuracy of measurement . . . (8, pp. 32–34).

It is not my intention to belittle the contributions that have been made and that will be made by the case study approach; I merely want to caution against the prevailing tendency to think of this method as the only salient against the approximations we are forced to make because of the very nature of measurement. This caution is reflected in the discussion of a more predictable criterion of academic achievement by Sarbin and Bordin (39). They have accepted this axiom and question whether predictive coefficient even of .95 will ever be attained. A reference to Heisenberg's principle of indeterminacy, which has proven so fruitful in modern physics, supports their conclusion that correlation coefficients between psychological measurements will never attain a point where predictions of one or zero can be made.

A critic may suggest that the experiments of physical theorists cannot be applied to the problem of measurement and prediction in psychology. He may even warn us against reproducing the errors of an earlier psychology which uncritically adopted the concepts of the physical sciences and which tragically turned out to be sterile. Heisenberg's indeterminacy principle, however, is a general statement for all science. It is based upon the experiments in modern physics in which attempts were made to measure the simultaneous positions and velocities of electrons. In general, it was discovered that when an attempt is made to measure velocity, the position is disturbed; when the position is measured, the velocity is disturbed. That we have analogous and even similar situations in psychological measurement will be revealed below. At this point it would be informative to quote Heisenberg's introduction to his discussion of the indeterminacy relationship.

Particularly characteristic . . . is the interaction between observer and object; in classical physical theories it has always been assumed either that this interaction is negligibly small, or else that its effects can be eliminated from the result from calculations based on 'control' experiments. This assumption is not permissible in atomic physics; the interaction between observer and object causes uncontrollable and large changes in the system being observed, because of the discontinuous characteristic of atomic processes. The immediate consequence of this circumstance is that in general every experiment performed to determine some numerical quantity renders the knowledge of others illusory, since the uncontrollable perturbation of the observed system alters the values of previously determined quantities. If this perturbation is followed in its quantitative details, it appears that in many cases it is impossible to obtain an exact determination of the simultaneous values of two variables, but rather that there is a lower limit to the accuracy with which they can be known (17, p. 3).

The indeterminacy relationship is admirably suited to psychological measurement. Every attempt at measurement introduces changes in the event which precludes our obtaining an exact representation of that event. The interaction between observer and object is as much a reality in psychology as in physics. Any prediction made from obtained measurements must therefore allow for a margin of error—the prediction must be stated as an approximation rather than as an exact value. This holds for macroscopic science as well as for atomic physics. Three illustrations of this principle of indeterminacy as applied to psychological measurement are here presented:

A. Taking an experiment at the psycho-physiological level, suppose we wish to determine blood pressure while the individual is being presented a list of stimulus words. The very act of applying the cuff of the sphygmomanometer introduces changes in the blood pressure which are not and cannot be measured. Other changes in the event are brought about by the measurement process—these 'uncontrollable perturbations' belonging more particularly to the whole psychological field than to the initial act of applying the cuff. The presence of the observer will alter some of the characteristics of the field. The unfamiliarity of the subject with the laboratory situation likewise may result in changes in the blood pressure which are not controllable. The sphygmomanometer reading must therefore be regarded as an approximation.

B. Suppose we wish to assist a student to discover whether or not he should become an engineer. He makes a verbal statement, "I want to become an engineer." We begin to make measurements. In this case we use paper-and-pencil tests. Suppose we use, among other measurement devices, a placement test in mathematics. When the student subsequently reports for an interview, his verbal statement has been changed to "I want to become a business man." The act of taking a measurement of mathematics achievement served to change the verbally expressed interest statement. The changes to the organism being measured by paper-and-pencil tests are usually not as obvious as in this illustration. Experience with hundreds of students who have been subjected to psychological tests of all kinds has convinced the writer that such changes do occur. Of course, these perturbations may not have great significance in terms of planning for future actions. The proposition is submitted, however, that the act of taking a measurement —even with a paper-and-pencil test—introduces certain alterations in the psychological field which precludes our making an exact measurement.

C. Obtaining measurements by means of an instrument such as a sphygmomanometer or of a test such as a placement examination in mathematics show certain resemblances to the situation in the physical experiment described by Heisenberg. Application to the psychological interview is less obvious. The interview is not designed to take measurements as we ordinarily think of them. The interviewer usually determines the presence or absence of certain characteristics in the reactional biography of the interviewee. In some cases he applies values to degrees of presence or absence of traits. That is to say, he makes ratings. The gathering of information by the interview method is an analogue to the taking of measurements in other disciplines. The interviewer, or perhaps the total interview situation, is to be regarded as the measuring rod. In either case the data that are elicited from the interviewee are conditioned by the total field of which he is but a part. When the clinician enters into the total psychological field of a patient, he cannot avoid a train of consequences which may work to the advantage as well as to the disadvantage of the patient (45). Such known mechanisms as the identification of the clinician with, say, a domineering parent; the kind of question asked; the strangeness of the social psychological situation; these and many other factors influence the accuracy of obtaining information in the interview.

The foregoing illustrations are intended to support *a fortiori* the proposition that predictions of 1 or zero cannot be obtained because of the approximate character of measurement, and further, that no form of measurement, be it the measurement of intelligence by tests or of certain 'intangible' factors by the clinical interview, can be stated with certitude. As Bridgman has stated: "It is a consequence of the approximate character of all measurement that no empirical science can make exact statements" (8, p. 34).

The writer will not quarrel with a critic who replies that it is too premature in the development of our science to invoke the Heisenberg indeterminacy principle. Certainly the elimination of errors in observing, recording, and interpreting human conduct would greatly increase our predictive powers. So would the abolition of the autistic search for old demons in new garments, for instincts with new names, etc. (23). This discussion is offered principally to show the untenability of such statements as "Indeed, if we believe in determinism at all, his chances are either zero or else 100 . . ." (3, p. 17) rather than to pass off our imperfect predictions behind the cloak of the Heisenberg principle of indeterminacy. The scientist must evermore strive to penetrate the penumbra of uncertainty surrounding every conclusion. Boring's remarks are apposite here:

> With the Heisenberg principle itself one cannot quarrel: When we must be ignorant, we must be ignorant. Let us not encourage ourselves, however, into any patient acceptance of any ignorance that can be dispelled. The use of statistical indeterminacy in most macroscopic science is an unnecessary and premature denial of the effectiveness of determinism (6, p. 301).

In line with this discussion, we might point out that some social scientists deny that predictive generalizations can be made at all. They hold that psychological, social, and cultural events are so unique and so complex that predictions from generalization of observations are beyond the realm of possibility. In short, as Kimball Young (55) has contended, the future is *indeterminate* for personal or social events in contradistinction to natural events which recur and are therefore predictable.

Sorokin and Berger (44) also make this point. After showing that individuals can predict accurately four-fifths of their activities for the next 24 hours, they go on to theorize on the possibility of predicting social events. They maintain that most predictions of social events are little more than guesses and should not be paraded as science. The difficulty here is that social scientists have not succeeded in formulating their problems so that apparently unique events may be ordered to a class. These writers are too pessimistic. Lundberg is more optimistic for the future of social science.

> The apparent unpredictability of group behavior . . . is due to our present limited knowledge of the nature of stimuli and responses operative in such groups. Some of the simpler chemical reactions were considered unpredictable some centuries ago for the same reason. Painstaking observations and classification of these reactions under given conditions, however, yielded our present chemical laws. The same method has already yielded us some power of generalization and prediction of group behavior. There is every reason to believe that we can vastly extend this power (29, p. 22).

Advances in modern scientific methodology may suggest ways of treating their complex data so that predictions—utilizable for action—may be stated. The shibboleth of *complexity* of subject matter so often stands in the way of scientific progress in the social and psychological sciences. Despairing social scientists look longingly at the greener pastures of the physical sciences where events are considered to be less complex. In this connection, the statement of Sir Ernest Rutherford, President of the British Association for the Advancement of Science (in 1923) is enlightening:

When we consider the extraordinary complexity of the electronic system, we may be surprised that it has been possible to find any order in the apparent medley of motions.[12]

VIII. INTERPRETING CLINICAL HYPOTHESES IN TERMS OF PROBABILITY

The statistical method of prediction, it is submitted, is fundamental to diagnosis and to the prescription or choice of treatment in clinical psychology and psychiatry. The discussion so far takes from the clinician many of his functions and assigns them to the psychologist in the laboratory. One major aspect remains—one that is seldom recognized by practicing clinicians —namely, *the formulation of hypotheses*. The present author maintains that this is the most significant function that the clinician can perform. Every case abounds in hypotheses, many tested, many waiting upon the research psychologist for testing. No other area of psychology is so fertile in the production of hypotheses. Every time the clinician has a 'hunch' he formulates an hypothesis. In the absence of crucial experiments these hypotheses are often treated as 'laws.' If predictions from the hypothesis are verified, then the hypothesis may be stated as a principle.[13]

This series of events is idealistic, to be sure. In practice, many of our hypotheses are left untested. The clinician many times is forced by the demand for action to utilize the untested hypothesis as though it were tenable upon evidence. For example, many student personnel workers have counseled students from the hypothesis that agreement of a student's educational-vocational choice with ratings on the Strong Vocational Interest Blank contributes to academic achievement. The hypothesis is plausible. Segel and Brintle (43), however, have demonstrated that this instrument, as conventionally used, adds practically nothing to the prediction of academic success. Another hypothesis frequently transformed into principle relates in universal manner academic achievement and outside work. Reader and Newman (33) have shown that the hypothesis is untenable.

This treatment of hypothesis as verified principle is an example of what has been referred to in another paper as one of the meanings of clinical

[12] In Buckley (10) quoted by Lundberg (29, p. 10 n.).
[13] In a more formal sense, the clinician is interbehaving with phenomena. This is one of the steps in Brown's exposition of the hypothetico-deductive method. He minimizes, however, the importance of the behavior which leads to the 'hunches.' See J. F. Brown (9) for an exposition of the hypothetico-deductive method. For a critique of this methodology, see J. R. Kantor (24).

psychology as *art*, viz., 'individual explorations into the unknown' (40).

In his chapter 'The Art of Diagnosing' Williamson (51) not only condones but encourages using hypotheses as yet unverified by research.

Some personnel workers assert that diagnosing must be scientific, that the research or experimental approach is the only valid one. While personnel research is necessary for effective analysis, yet diagnosing is not scientific. Although the counselor must use facts, principles and generalizations derived from experimentation, he must also use hunches (insights, reduced clues, intuitions) and hypotheses unverified as yet by personnel research. Moreover, while indebted to statisticians for valid generalizations derived from analyses of groups, the counselor must be constantly alert in inferring whether these generalizations are *validly applicable* to the particular student being counseled. If such a student does not possess characteristics similar to the group from which the generalization was derived, then it would be a distortion of logic, as well as of science, to diagnose this student on the basis of the group generalization (51, p. 105).

This statement is based on a sort of rational belief and is at variance with empirical findings cited above and with the fundamental propositions reiterated before, viz., in the absence of knowledge of the predictive powers of single-appearing data, the probability based on *observed* relative frequencies is taken as the most accurate prediction.

We must return for a moment to the theory of probability for an understanding of this use of hypothesis as fact. The probability of occurrence of an event is expressed as the limit to which the relative frequencies tend when the number of members in the field of statistical measurement approaches infinity. It was agreed that the scores or class to which we ordered our data might appear too general, too heterogeneous, to formulate a meaningful probability-statement for the single case. To this point Von Wright has written:

. . . if there are special circumstances which make the rational degree of belief in an event (q) to differ from the limiting frequency of the event in such series (p), it is because *if* there were a probability series, defined by these special circumstances, then the limiting-frequency of the event in question in this series would be that value q. And this hypothetical statement is just what makes the degree of belief q in the event, under these special circumstances *rational* (50, p. 283).

When a clinician predicts behavior on the basis of a plausible but untested hypothesis (one in which he has a 'rational degree of belief') he unwittingly postulates a class or series of which the event in question is a member. Else how would he be able to attach a value to the event? The writer has read case records in which one clinician regarded the influence of 30 hours per week of outside work on the academic achievement of a high aptitude student as deleterious, while another clinician regarded the same event as beneficial because it was a sign of strong motivation.

The inference must not be drawn that clinicians should cease making hypotheses. The recognition of this hypothesizing function is a step in the direction of making clinical psychology more scientific and less artistic (35). The clinician's hypotheses may contribute significantly not only to applied psychology, but also to theoretical science. His hypotheses arise out of interbehaving with concrete human beings in specific social psychological situations. The lack of significant progress in many branches of psychology might be remedied by placing theoretical psychologists in close touch with significant human problems which come to light in the clinical situation.

A brief digression might clarify the meaning of the last statement. The clinical psychologist too often preoccupies himself with phenotypic descriptions. That is to say, his daily contacts with patients, clients, or counselees are expressed in 'protocol language,' in 'statements belonging to the primitive protocol' (12). The theoretical psychologist, on the other hand, tends to concern himself primarily with genotypic descriptions. He is interested more in the general laws of nature, in the statements of general propositions from which singular propositions can be derived.

Greater cooperation between the clinical and the theoretical psychologists will result in more meaningful research and theory. The designs for experiment based on clinical hypotheses may lack the simplicity and perhaps the rigor of the animal laboratory, but the results will be more meaningful as guides to human action if we accept the principle behind the statement of Hogben that "the real credentials of a science lie in its capacity to yield information which is a guide to practical conduct" (19, p. 189).

IX. SUMMARY

The prevailing conceptions with regard to prediction of behavior have been outlined. There seem to be two schools of thought as to the nature of prediction—so-called intuitive methods and inferential methods. The postulation of two forms of prediction necessitated the further postulation of two interpretations of probability. Empirical data and logical argument have been submitted in evidence of the fact that the two interpretations of probability are essentially one, namely, the frequency interpretation. All meaningful prediction is based on informal or formal statistical (inferential) manipulations.

An inference drawn from the writings of those who hold that predictions are based on other than statistical data is this: Statistical predictions are only approximative—clinical or case-study predictions are exact. In order to refute this statement, certain propositions were offered, among them applications of the Heisenberg indeterminacy principle which illustrated the scientific principle that all knowledge is approximate.

The use of unverified hypotheses by trained clinical workers is considered unwarranted. This does not mean that clinicians should cease hypothesizing. Hypotheses are the essential ingredients for building up not only diagnostic and treatment procedures, but important psychological theory as well. Every case contains many hypotheses. These the clinician should turn over to laboratory and field workers to test, or he should turn experimenter himself and set out to see if predictions made from his hypotheses can be verified. When the clinician uses an untested hypothesis as fact, he wittingly or unwittingly places a probability value upon it. The accuracy of this value can never be known unless subjected to test.

BIBLIOGRAPHY

1. ALLPORT, F. H. Telonomic description in the study of personality. *Character & Pers.*, 1937, **5**, 202–214.
2. ALLPORT, G. W. *Personality: a psychological interpretation.* New York: Henry Holt, 1937.
3. ———. The psychologist's frame of reference. *Psychol. Bull.*, 1940, **37**, 1–28.
4. BERNARD, L. L. The development of methods in sociology. *Monist*, 1928, **38**, 292–320.
5. BINGHAM, W. V., & MOORE, B. V. *How to interview.* New York: Harper & Bros. (rev. ed.), 1934.
6. BORING, E. G. Statistical frequencies as dynamic equilibria. *Psychol. Rev.*, 1941, **48**, 279–301.
7. BRIDGMAN, P. W. *The intelligent individual and society.* New York: Macmillan, 1938.
8. ———. *The logic of modern physics.* New York: Macmillan, 1927.
9. BROWN, J. F. *Psychology and the social order.* New York: McGraw-Hill, 1937.
10. BUCKLEY, H. *A short history of physics.* London: Methuen, 1927.
11. BURGESS, E. W., & COTTRELL, L. S., JR. *Predicting success or failure of marriage.* New York: Prentice-Hall, 1939.
12. CARNAP, R. *The unity of science.* London: Kegan Paul, Trench, Trubner, 1934.
13. CATTELL, R. B. Measurement versus intuition in applied psychology. *Character & Pers.*, 1937–38, **6**, 114–131.
14. COTTRELL, L. S., JR. The case study method in prediction. *Sociometry*, 1941, **4**, 358–370.
15. FREYD, M. The statistical viewpoint in vocational selection. *J. appl. Psychol.*, 1925, **9**, 349–356.
16. HARRIS, D. Factors affecting college grades: a review of the literature, 1930–37. *Psychol. Bull.*, 1940, **37**, 125–166.
17. HEISENBERG, W. *The physical principles of the quantum theory.* Chicago: University of Chicago Press, 1930.
18. HORST, P., WALLIN, P., GUTTMAN, L., *et al. The prediction of personal adjustment.* New York: Social Science Research Council, 1941.
19. HOGBEN, L. *Dangerous thoughts.* New York: Norton, 1940.
20. HOTELLING, H., SOROKIN, P. A., GUTTMAN, L., & BURGESS, E. W. The predictions of personal adjustment: a symposium. *Amer. J. Sociol.*, 1942, **48**, 61–86.
21. JASTROW, J. *Fact and fable in psychology.* Boston: Houghton-Mifflin, 1900.
22. JEFFREYS, H. *Scientific inference.* Cambridge: University Press, 1937.
23. KANTOR, J. R. Toward a scientific analysis of motivation. *Psychol. Rec.*, 1942, **5**, 225–275.
24. ———. Current trends in psychological theory. *Psychol. Bull.*, 1941, **38**, 29–65.
25. ———. Preface to interbehavioral psychology. *Psychol. Rec.*, 1942, **5**, 173–193.
26. KLEIN, D. B. Scientific understanding in psychology. PSYCHOL. REV., 1932, **32**, 552–569.
27. KLÜVER, H. Contemporary German psychology as a "natural science." In *An historical introduction to modern psychology* (G. Murphy, Ed.). New York: Harcourt, Brace, 1929.

28. LEWIN, K. *A dynamic theory of personality.* New York: McGraw-Hill, 1935.

29. LUNDBERG, G. A. *Social research.* New York: Longmans, Green, 1942.

30. ——. Case studies vs. statistical methods—an issue based on misunderstanding. *Sociometry,* 1941, **4**, 379–383.

31. POLANSKY, N. A. How shall a life history be written? *Character & Pers.,* 1940–41, **9**, 188–207.

32. QUEEN, S. A. Social prediction—development and problems. *Sociometry,* 1941, **4**, 371–373.

33. REEDER, C. W., & NEWMAN, S. C. The relationship of employment to scholarship. *Educ. Res. Bull., Ohio State Univ.,* 1939, **18**, 203–214.

34. REICHENBACH, H. *Experience and prediction.* Chicago: University of Chicago Press, 1938.

35. ROGERS, C. R. *The clinical treatment of the problem child.* Boston, Houghton-Mifflin, 1939.

36. SARBIN, T. R. *The relative accuracy of clinical and statistical predictions of academic success.* Columbus: Ohio State University Library 1941 (Ph.D. thesis).

37. ——, & WITTMAN, M. P. Further research on the Elgin prognostic rating scale in schizophrenia (in preparation).

38. ——. A contribution to the study of actuarial and individual methods of prediction. *Amer. J. Sociol.,* 1942, **48**, 593–602.

39. ——, & BORDIN, E. S. New criteria for old. *Educ. & Psychol. Meas.,* 1941, **1**, 173–186.

40. ——. Clinical psychology—art or science. *Psychometrica,* 1941, **6**, 391–400.

41. SNEDECOR, G. W. *Statistical methods.* Ames, Iowa: Collegiate Press, 1937.

42. SCHEIDT, R. *Ein Beitrug zum Problem der rückfall Prognose.* Munich: Munchener Zeitung, Verlag, 1936.

43. SEGEL, D., & BRINTLE, S. L. The relation of occupational interest scores as measured by the Strong interest blank to achievement test results, etc. *Educ. Res.,* 1934, **27**, 442–445.

44. SOROKIN, P. A., & BERGER, C. Q. *Time-budgets of human behavior.* Cambridge: Harvard University Press, 1939.

45. STEVENSON, G. S., & SMITH, G. *Child guidance clinics.* New York: Commonwealth Fund, 1934.

46. STOUFFER, S. A. Notes on the case study and the unique case. *Sociometry,* 1941, **4**, 349–357.

47. TERMAN, L. M. *Psychological factors in marital happiness.* New York: McGraw-Hill, 1938.

48. THORNDIKE, E. L. Fundamental theorems in judging men. *J. appl. Psychol.,* 1918, **2**, 67–76.

49. VITELES, M. S. The clinical viewpoint in vocational psychology. *J. appl. Psychol.,* 1925, **9**, 131–138.

50. VON WRIGHT, G. H. On probability. *Mind,* 1940, **49**, 265–283.

51. WILLIAMSON, E. G. *How to counsel students.* New York: McGraw-Hill, 1939.

52. WINDELBAND, W. *An introduction to philosophy.* London: T. Fisher Unwin, 1921.

53. WITTMAN, M. P. A scale for measuring prognosis in schizophrenic patients. *Elgin Papers,* 1941, **4**, 20–33.

54. ——. Evaluation of prognosis in functional psychosis. *Psychol. Bull.,* 1941, **38**, 535–536.

55. YOUNG, K. Method, generalization, prediction in sociology. *Publ. Amer. Sociol. Soc.,* 1933, **27**, 23–34.

The Logic of Prediction: Some Observations

on Dr. Sarbin's Exposition

Isidor Chein

College of the City of New York

In a recent issue of the PSYCHOLOGICAL REVIEW, Dr. Sarbin (3) contrasts two points of view, one statistical and the other dynamic-causal or, as Sarbin prefers to refer to it, 'clinical.' Sarbin presents the case for the statistical point of view, but it may help to clarify the issue to present the case for the 'clinical'[1] point of view in terms of Sarbin's analysis.

Ostensibly, Sarbin is concerned with the logic of prediction. Actually, he is concerned with two conceptions of science as is indicated by his references to Brown's (1) contrast of statistical causal analysis and dynamic causal analysis and Lewin's (2) argument that the individual case may be understood in terms of general law. In other words, the issues involved are broader than the question of prediction and may be fully understood only in the broader context of the nature of science.

In choosing prediction as the central issue Dr. Sarbin has picked his battleground with the 'clinician,' but this is not the ground on which the latter would stake his major claims. The 'clinician' is not primarily concerned with *prediction*, but with *control*. He is not content with anticipating what will happen if he does nothing, and that is only one of his minor problems; he wants to know what will happen in view of what he does or in view of his recommendations being followed.

In view of the subordination of prediction to control, it follows that Sarbin's statistics of empirically determined frequencies would be insufficient for the 'clinician's' purposes. Thus, on Sarbin's basis, one can predict that there will always be wars, for wars have been as regular a past occurrence as the inclement weather of November. That there always have been

Reprinted from *Psychological Review*, 1945, 52, 175–179.

[1] In following Sarbin's usage I am well aware that the group name 'clinical' includes a rather heterogeneous membership. Neither Sarbin's remarks nor mine apply to all members of the group. Also, many psychologists who are actually engaged in clinical practice come closer to Sarbin's point of view than to the viewpoint he calls 'clinical.' Similarly, when I speak of 'statistician' I realize that the viewpoint involved need not be subscribed to by all nor even by most actual statisticians. 'Clinician' and 'statistician' are thus two straw men. Yet, I believe that the apposition of their viewpoints may contribute to clearer psychological thinking.

wars is, for the 'clinician,' beside the point; he wants to know how to *stop* war.

Sarbin may well contend that the statistical approach does also serve as a guide to conduct. Thus, it is possible to correlate war against other variables than mere time and, thereby, to tease out the *significant* correlates of war and to use the results of this analysis to do something about war. But the fact remains that what is involved here is the prediction of something which has *never yet happened* (permanent peace) and that something more is required than a set of prediction tables.

It is precisely here that one can find the central issue between the 'clinician' and the 'statistician.' The former does not object to the use of statistics, but sees in statistics only one *tool* in his major methodological objective of conceptually or actually manipulating circumstances to arrive at an understanding of the conditions of events. The 'statistician,' on the other hand, sees in his prediction tables and formulae the last word in scientific endeavor. The 'statistician' is looking for statistical generalizations, the 'clinician' for conditional principles. The 'statistician' is case-centered, the 'clinician,' despite superficial impression to the contrary, is condition-centered.

Sarbin may, at this point, protest that I have convicted myself of the very sin which he finds at the core of the clinical approach, the scientific sin of making, or even worse, seeking unverifiable predictions. How can one possibly verify a prediction of *permanent* peace?

The issue here is akin to that involved in connection with the prediction of the single case. That, too, is to Sarbin unverifiable. Sarbin is, of course, correct in affirming that science demands verification, but he shows here a curious distortion of perspective as to whether it is more important to verify the individual prediction or the principle on which the prediction is based.

Sarbin argues that a prediction concerning a single case cannot be verified unless the case can be ordered to some statistical class. Thereby he misses the point that a prediction of a single case can, in point of fact, be verified, by implication, through a verification of the predicting principle. No psychologist will claim that a prediction can be made on the basis of data from a single case without reference to anything else. Sarbin contends that this reference has to be to other cases or else that the prognosticator is engaged in non-scientific guesswork. The reference, however, is to conditional principles arrived at from the study of other cases, to be sure, but study directed, not at the discovery of empirical frequency tabulations, but at the manipulation of circumstances to elucidate the determining conditions.

Sarbin misses the further point that while on the basis of the frequency interpretation of probability which he is advocating, the individual predictions may be verified, the predictive principle cannot be. The principle underlying the statistical approach is that because something has happened so many times in the past, it will happen so many times in the future. That this principle is verified by the verification of the predictions is a *non sequitur*, because as soon as the predictions are verified they belong to the data of the past and we are left again with an unverified principle. Every prediction made on this basis is thus itself a *non-sequitur* and the fact that the predictions ever do come true is left by the 'statisticians' in the realm of miracles.

This may be clarified by a consideration of one of Sarbin's examples. A person, Sarbin points out, quite rightly does not plan picnics in November, presumably because of the probability of inclement weather. This 'rightness' is for Sarbin not accompanied by logic; it is merely an empirical fact that November weather is not suitable for picnics. In point of fact the person in question has logic on his side as well as a knowledge of past occurrence. His logical justification is found in the principle of sufficient reason, namely that there does not seem to be any reason to expect that the weather for the coming November will be any different than it was in past Novembers. The appeal to the principle of sufficient reason is a justifiable appeal to ignorance, but the clinician's endeavors are directed in large measure to reduce the need for this kind of appeal to ignorance. Of more direct relevance is the fact that whereas the sole rational justification the 'statistician' has for making predictions on the basis of past occurrences lies in the principle of sufficient reason, the principle itself presupposes another principle which is diametrically opposed to the philosophy of the 'statistician,' namely, that these *are* sufficient reasons (*i.e.*, conditions) for events. The 'statistician' resolutely turns his attention away from these conditions and the 'clinician' just as resolutely pursues them. But who is it that is content with mere guesswork, Dr. Sarbin or the 'clinicians'?

That Sarbin does not comprehend the 'clinical' approach may well be demonstrated from his illustrations. Thus, he describes a situation where, in addition to the usual data for predicting scholastic success, the clinician may have for a given student the additional data that the student (1) has 30 hours outside work per week, (2) that he is in love, and (3) that he makes a poor impression in the interview. To Sarbin these are, at best, merely three additional variables for which prediction tables can be constructed. He doesn't seem to comprehend that for the clinician these are not simply *quantitative* variables. The clinician is not concerned with how many lovesick students succeed or fail. What he wants to know is whether the lovesickness will affect this student's diligence and, if so, how.[2]

Sarbin's failure to comprehend the 'clinical' approach is more fundamentally revealed in his assertion, to which he seems to attach considerable importance, that in several instances it has been found that 'statistical' predictions were superior to 'clinical' predictions. It is not necessary to examine the adequacy of these findings as representative of the general situation today to see that Sarbin again misses the point. Suppose that the statistical prediction procedure were better developed than it is today and that the 'clinician' had to start from scratch (*i.e.*, that his predictions at present *never* came true). The 'clinician' would still feel justified in following his approach; he would still want to discover the kind of things he knows today and, having attained it, he would still want to pursue this kind of knowledge further.

But, Sarbin contends, knowledge is only approximate and therefore it seems that all knowledge must be statistical or, in other words, that the clinician can hope for nothing better than the statistical approach can give

---

[2] Of course, the 'clinician' may be well aware that a measure of the student's past diligence is already contained in the usual data for predicting scholastic success. He is not content, however, merely to *assume* that there is no special reason why this degree of diligence should not continue. The additional 'clinical' data he is seeking is precisely to gather information with regard to this point.

him. There is a confusion here which can be clarified as follows: One can make two kinds of statements, one a statement of fact, the other a statement of probability. Either kind of statement may be true or false. In view of various uncertainties pertaining to knowledge, neither kind of statement may ever be held to be absolutely beyond question. That is to say, at best, we may only say, "This is probably a true statement of fact." As contradictions of this statement appear, we substitute a new improved statement which we now say is probably a true statement of fact. The point I am now making is that the same holds true of statements of probability. They are never absolutely beyond question and the best we can hope for is to improve them by successive approximations. The choice that confronts us is between probably true statements of fact and probably true statements of probability. The approximate nature of knowledge has nothing whatever to do with the issue between the 'clinician' and the 'statistician.' The former is concerned with arriving at statements concerned with conditional facts, the latter at statements of probability.

Some clarification is needed of the phrase 'probably true,' because it bears on one of Sarbin's misunderstandings of the 'clinician.' 'Probably true,' means that to the best of our knowledge this is true and that we have no reason to suppose it false. It is an expression of confidence, not a statement of statistical probability. Sarbin, referring to the 'clinician's' concept of probability (3, p. 212), says, "This vague concept does not present itself in a mathematical form. . . . Instead of referring to future behavior as 72 chances in 100 of success the clinician would use non-numerical terms, such as 'presumably,' 'probably,' 'more than likely,' etc." And, he adds, "This concept cannot be submitted to experimental test." Sarbin fails to understand that these are not statements about the statistical probabilities of events and do not require statistical verification. They roughly express the speaker's degree of confidence that what follows is true. They may be expanded into statements about the speaker's caution, his knowledge of the determining conditions and of the specific conditions which characterize that case, his ability to think of alternative hypotheses, and so on. Even such statements as "The chances are 90 in a 100 that so and so will happen" may often be seen, from the context, to be expressions of confidence rather than statements about probability.

At several points Sarbin seems to attack the 'clinician' on less than rational grounds. Thus, he interposes in his discussion of the problem of the single case some remarks on the antiquity of the single case method, to wit (3, p. 214), that "Primitive peoples utilized single cases to support their beliefs and dogmas." Since the issue concerns the *prediction* of the single case and not *proof* on the basis of a single case, and since these remarks are no contribution in themselves, they can only serve the function of drawing a red herring across the issue and of allying the 'clinicians,' by emotional innuendo, with the primitives.

Similarly, although I do not know with which 'clinicians' Sarbin is familiar, the tone of his remark (3, p. 218) that "a clinician[3] may find himself embarrassed when the superficial plausibility of his hypothesis is exploded by emipirical or experimental studies" needlessly reflects on the scientific integrity of the clinician. There is no more basis for a clinician's

[3] Sarbin is here using 'clinician' in the narrower sense.

being embarrassed by being proven wrong than for a similar reaction of any scientist under similar circumstances. Like any good scientist the 'clinician' would welcome the 'explosion' and make suitable amendments in his prediction procedure. Errors may be the stepping stones to more secure knowledge.

When, in this connection, Sarbin attacks the clinician for restoring to "deductions from plausible but untested hypotheses . . . and . . . so-called intuitions" (3, p. 218),[4] he fails to understand the clinician's situation. In other words, pending the 'explosion,' should the clinician use his sense to the best of his ability or should he suspend judgment and wait for prediction tables or verification of his hypotheses? By the time he or someone else has constructed the tables, or provided the verification of principles, the patient may already be dead. No one will deny, least of all the clinician, that it is desirable to test hypotheses. It does not follow that what the 'statistician' accepts as a satisfactory test will *ipso facto* be accepted as disproof of his hypothesis. In this connection, too, it may be added that, while it is correct to attack any attempt to separate psychology from natural science or any attempt to place intuition and 'understanding' above verification, this attack should not be perverted into an attack on intuition itself. Intuition above verification leads to intellectual anarchy. At the same time, those of us who are less intuitively gifted may well afford to adopt some humility in the presence of those who have proven to be more gifted. There is a dual responsibility here: on the part of the intuitive psychologist, to strive to articulate his intuitive processes; on the part of the non-intuitive psychologist to clarify his intellectual difficulties in comprehension. The intuitive psychologist, however, is not likely to meet his obligations if he is greeted from the first with hostility or attack.

In conclusion I would like to add that, when Sarbin calls for greater cooperation between the clinical and the theoretical psychologists, such cooperation is not likely without greater mutual understanding. Such understanding, I am sorry to say, Sarbin does not seem to give.

REFERENCES

1. BROWN, J. F. *Psychology and the social order.* New York: McGraw-Hill, 1937.
2. LEWIN, K. *A dynamic theory of personality.* New York: McGraw-Hill, 1935.
3. SARBIN, T. R. The logic of prediction in psychology. PSYCHOL. REV., 1944, **51**, 210–228.

[4] Dr. Sarbin, himself, apparently does not hesitate to resort to unverified and unverifiable assertions. Thus, in discussing the application of Heisenberg's principle to psychology, Sarbin writes (3, p. 222), "The very act of applying the cuff of the sphygmomanometer introduces changes in the blood pressure which are not and cannot be measured." To me, this is a very reasonable assumption, but on Dr. Sarbin's grounds it must be severely condemned. If they are not and cannot be measured, how does Dr. Sarbin know about them?

When Shall We Use Our Heads

Instead of the Formula?

Paul E. Meehl[1]

University of Minnesota

My title question, "When should we use our heads instead of the formula?" is not rhetorical. I am sincerely asking what I see as an important question. I find the two extreme answers to this question, namely, "Always" and "Never," equally unacceptable. But to formulate a satisfactory answer upon the present evidence seems extraordinarily difficult.

I put the question in the practical clinical context. This is where Sarbin put it in his pioneering study 14 years ago, and this is where it belongs. Some critics of my book (5) have repudiated the whole question by saying that, always and necessarily, we use *both* our heads and the formula. No, we do not. In research, we use both; the best clinical research involves a shuttling back and forth between clever, creative speculation and subsequent statistical testing of empirical derivations therefrom. So far as I am aware, nobody has ever denied this. Even the arch-actuary George Lundberg approved of the clinician as hypothesis-maker. In research one cannot design experiments or concoct theories without using his head, and he cannot test them rigorously without using a formula. This is so obvious that I am surprised to find that people will waste time in discussing it. The clinical-statistical issue can hardly be stated so as to make sense in the research context, and I should have thought it clear that a meaningful issue can be raised only in the context of daily clinical activity.

In the clinical context, on the other hand, the question is sensible and of great practical importance. Here we have the working clinician or administrator, faced with the necessity to make a decision at *this* moment in time, regarding *this* particular patient. He knows that his evidence is inadequate. He can think of several research projects which, *had* they been done already, would be helpful to him in deciding the present case. If he is research-oriented he may even make a note of these research ideas and later

Reprinted from *Journal of Counseling Psychology*, 1957, 4, 268–273.

[1] Presented at the 1956 Convention of the American Psychological Association, Chicago. This will also appear in a forthcoming book: Herbert Feigl, Michael Scriven, and Grover Maxwell (Eds.), *Concepts, Theories, and the Mind-Body Problem*, Vol. II of Minnesota Studies in the Philosophy of Science. Minneapolis, Minnesota: University of Minnesota Press, 1958.

carry them out or persuade someone else to do so. But none of that helps him *now*. He is in a sort of Kierkegaardian existential predicament, because he has to act. As Joe Zubin kept repeating when I last tangled with him on this subject, "Every clinical decision is a *Willensakt*." And so it is; but the question remains, how do we make our *Willensakts* as rational as possible upon limited information? *What clinician X knows today* and *what he could find out by research in ten years* are two very different things.

The question, "When shall we use our heads instead of the formula?" presupposes that we are about to make a clinical decision at a given point in time, and must base it upon what is known to us at that moment. In that context, the question makes perfectly good sense. It is silly to answer it by saying amicably, "We use both methods, they go hand in hand." If the formula and your head invariably yield the same predictions about individuals, you should quit using the more costly one because it is not adding anything. If they don't always yield the same prediction—and they clearly don't, as a matter of empirical fact—then you obviously can't "use both," because you cannot predict in opposite ways for the same case. If one says then, "Well, by 'using both,' I mean that we follow the formula except on special occasions," the problem becomes how to identify the proper sub-set of occasions. And this of course amounts to the very question I am putting. For example, does the formula tell us "Here, use your heads," or do we rely on our heads to tell us this, thus countermanding the formula?

THE PRAGMATIC DECISION PROBLEM STATED

Most decisions in current practice do not pose this problem because no formula exists. Sometimes there is no formula because the prediction problem is too open-ended, as in dream analysis; sometimes the very categorizing of the raw observations involves Gestalted stimulus equivalences for which the laws are unknown, and hence cannot be mathematically formulated (although the clinician himself exemplifies these laws and can therefore "utilize" them); in still other cases there is no formula because nobody has bothered to make one. In any of these three circumstances, we use our heads because there isn't anything else to use. This presumably will be true of many special prediction situations for years to come. The logical analysis of the first two situations—open-endedness and unknown psychological laws—is a fascinating subject in its own right, especially in relation to psychotherapy. But since our original question implies that a formula does exist, we will say no more about that subject here.

Suppose then that we have a prediction equation (or an actuarial table) which has been satisfactorily cross-validated. Let us say that it predicts with some accuracy which patients will respond well to intensive outpatient therapy in our VA clinic. We are forced to make such predictions because our staff-patient ratio physically precludes offering intensive treatment to all cases; also we know that a minority, such as certain latent schizophrenias, react adversely and even dangerously. The equation uses both psychometric and non-psychometric data. It may include what the Cornell workers called

"Stop" items—items given such a huge weight that when present they override any combination of the remaining factors. It may be highly patterned, taking account of verified interaction effects.

So here is veteran Jones, whose case is under consideration at therapy staff. The equation takes such facts as his Rorschach $F+$, his Multiphasic code, his divorce, his age, his 40 per cent service-connection, and grinds out a probability of .75 of "good response to therapy." (The logicians and theoretical statisticians are still arguing over the precise meaning of this number as applied to Jones. But we are safe in saying, "If you accept patients from this population who have this score, you will be right 3 times in 4.") Here is Jones. We want to do what is best for him. We don't *know for sure*, and we can't, by any method, actuarial or otherwise. We act on the probabilities, as everyone does who chooses a career, takes a wife, bets on a horse, or brings a lawsuit. (If you object, as some of the more cloudheaded clinikers do, to acting on "mere probabilities," you will have to shut up shop, because probabilities are all you'll ever get.)

But now the social worker tells us that Jones, age 40, said at intake that his mother sent him in. The psychology trainee describes blocking and a bad $F-$ on Rorschach VII; the psychiatrist adds his comments, and pretty soon we are concluding that Jones has a very severe problem with mother-figures. Since our only available therapist is Frau Dr. Schleswig-Holstein, who would traumatize anybody even without a mother-problem, we begin to vacillate. The formula gives us odds of 3 to 1 on Jones; these further facts, not in the equation, raise doubts in our minds. What shall we do?

IMPORTANCE OF 'SPECIAL CASES'

In my little book on this subject, I gave an example which makes it too easy (5, p. 24). If a sociologist were predicting whether Professor X would go to the movies on a certain night, he might have an equation involving age, academic specialty, and introversion score. The equation might yield a probability of .90 that Professor X goes to the movie tonight. But if the family doctor announced that Professor X had just broken his leg, no sensible sociologist would stick with the equation. Why didn't the factor of "broken leg" appear in the formula? Because broken legs are very rare, and in the sociologist's entire sample of 500 criterion cases plus 250 cross-validating cases, he did not come upon a single instance of it. He uses the broken leg datum confidently, because "broken leg" is a subclass of a larger class we may crudely denote as "relatively immobilizing illness or injury," and movie-attending is a subclass of a larger class of "actions requiring moderate mobility." There is a universally recognized "subjective experience table" which cuts across sociological and theatrical categories, and the probabilities are so close to zero that not even a sociologist feels an urge to tabulate them! (That this is the correct analysis of matters can be easily seen if we ask what our sociologist would do if he were in a strange culture and had seen *even a few* legs in casts at the movies?)

I suppose only the most anal of actuaries would be reluctant to abandon the equation in the broken leg case, on the ground that we were unable to cite actual statistical support for the generalization: "People with broken legs don't attend movies." But clinicians should beware of overdoing the broken lag analogy. There are at least four aspects of the broken leg case which are very different from the usual "psycho-dynamic" reversal of an actuarial prediction. First, a broken leg is a pretty objective fact, determinable with high accuracy, if you care to take the trouble; secondly, its correlation with relative immobilization is near-perfect, based on a huge N, and attested by all sane men regardless of race, creed, color, or what school granted them the doctorate; thirdly, interaction effects are conspicuously lacking—the immobilization phenomenon cuts neatly across the other categories under study; fourthly, the prediction is mediated without use of any doubtful theory, being either purely taxonomic or based upon such low-level theory as can be provided by skeletal mechanics and common sense. The same cannot be said of such an inference as "Patient Jones has an unconscious problem with mother-figures, and male patients with such problems will not react well in intensive therapy with Frau Dr. Schleswig-Holstein."

THEORETICAL DERIVATION OF NOVEL PATTERNS

When the physicists exploded the first atomic bomb, they had predicted a novel occurrence by theoretical methods. No actuarial table, based upon thousands of combinations of chemicals, would have led to this prediction. But these kinds of theoretical derivations in the developed sciences involve combining rigorously formulated theories with exact knowledge of the state of the particular system, neither of which we have in clinical psychology. Yet we must do justice to the basic *logical* claim of our clinician. I want to stress that he is not in the untenable position of denying the actuarial data. He freely admits that 75 per cent of patients having Jones' formula score are good bets for therapy. But he says that Jones belongs to the other 25 per cent, and therefore thinks we can avoid one of our formula's mis-predictions by countermanding the formula in this case. There is nothing intrinsically wrong with this suggestion. Perhaps the clinician *can* identify a subclass of patients within the class having Jones' actuarial attributes, for which the success rate is less than .5. This would be perfectly compatible with the over-all actuarial data, provided the clinician doesn't claim it too often.

At this point the actuary, a straightforward fellow, proposes that we tabulate the new signs mentioned in staff conference as indicating this subclass before proceeding further. Here we again reduce our clinician to a hypothesis-suggestor, and seem to put the current prediction problem back on an actuarial basis. But wait. Are we really prepared to detail someone to do such "case-oriented" research every time a clinical prediction is made? Actually it is impossible. It would require a superfile of punch-cards of colossal N to be available in each clinic, and several major staff doing nothing but running case-oriented minor studies while clinical conferences went into recess pending the outcomes.

However, this is a "practical" objection. Suppose we circumvent it somehow, so that when a sign or pattern is used clinically to support a counter-actuarial prediction, we can proceed immediately to subject the sign to actuarial test on our clinic files. There are serious difficulties even so. Unless the several staff who produced these records had in mind all of the signs that anybody subsequently brings up, we have no assurance that they were looked for or noted. Anyone who has done file research knows the frustration of having no basis for deciding when the lack of mention of a symptom indicates its absence. But even ignoring this factor, what if we find only 3 cases in the files who show the pattern? *Any split* among these 3 cases as to therapy outcome is statistically compatible with a wide range of parameter values. We can neither confirm nor refute, at any respectable confidence level, our clinician's claim that this pattern brings the success-probability from .75 to some value under .5 (he doesn't say how far under).

Here the statistician throws up his hands in despair. What, he asks, can you do with a clinician who wants to countermand a known probability of .75 by claiming a subclass probability which we cannot estimate reliably? And, of course, one wonders how many thousands of patients the clinician has seen, to have accumulated a larger sample of the rare configuration. He also is subject to sampling errors, isn't he?

NON-FREQUENTIST PROBABILITY AND RATIONAL ACTION

This brings us to the crux of the matter. Does the clinician need to have seen *any* cases of "mother-sent-me-in" and Card VII blockage who were treated by female therapists? Here we run into a philosophical issue about the nature of probability. Many logicians (including notably Carnap, Kneale, Sellars, and most of the British school) reject the view (widely held among applied statisticians) that *probability* is always *frequency*. Carnap speaks of "inductive probability," by which he means the logical support given to a hypothesis by evidence. We use this kind of probability constantly, both in science and in daily life. No one knows how to compute it exactly, except for very simple worlds described by artificial languages. Even so, we cannot get along without it. So our clinician believes that he has inductive evidence from many different sources, on different populations, partly actuarial, partly experimental, partly anecdotal, that there is such a psychological structure as a "mother-surrogate problem." He adduces indirect evidence for the construct validity (1) of Rorschach Card VII reactions. I am not here considering the actual scientific merits of such claims in the clinical field, on which dispute still continues. But I think it important for us to understand the methodological character of the clinician's rebuttal. If Carnap and some of his follow-logicians are right, the idea that *relative frequency* and *probability* are synonymous is a philosophical mistake.

Of course there is an implicit future reference to frequency even in this kind of inductive argument. Carnap identifies inductive probability with the betting odds which a reasonable man should accept. I take this to mean that if the clinician decided repeatedly on the basis of what he thought were high inductive probabilities, and we found him to be wrong most of the time, then he was presumably making erroneous estimates of his inductive probabilities. The claim of a high inductive probability implies an expectation of being right; in the long run, he who (correctly) bets odds of 7:3 will be able to point to a hit-rate of 70 per cent. But this *future* reference to success-frequency is not the same as the *present evidence for* a hypothesis. This seems a difficult point for people to see. As a member of a jury, you might be willing to bet 9 to 1 odds on the prisoner's guilt, and this might be rational of you; yet no calculation of frequencies constituted your inductive support in the present instance. The class of hypotheses where you have assigned an inductive probability of .9 should "pan out" 90 per cent of the time. But the assignment of that inductive probability to each hypothesis need not itself have been done by frequency methods. If we run a long series on Sherlock Holmes, and find that 95 per cent of his "reconstructions" of crimes turn out to be valid, our confidence in his guesses is good *in part just because they are his.* Yet do we wish to maintain that a rational man, ignorant of these statistics, could form no "probable opinion" about a *particular* Holmesian hypothesis based on the evidence available? I cannot think anyone wants to maintain this.

The philosophical recognition of a nonfrequency inductive probability does not help much to solve our practical problem. No one has quantified this kind of probability (which is one reason why Fisher rejected it as useless for scientific purposes). Many logicians doubt that it can be quantified, even in principle. What then are we to say? The clinician thinks he has "high" (How high? Who knows?) inductive support for his particular theory about Jones. He thinks it is so high that we are rationally justified in assigning Jones to the 25 per cent class permitted by the formula. The actuary doubts this, and the data do not allow a sufficiently sensitive statistical test. Whom do we follow?

MONITORING THE CLINICIAN

Well, the actuary is not quite done yet. He has been surreptitiously spying upon the clinician for, lo, these many years. The mean old scoundrel has kept a record of the clinician's predictions. What does he find, when he treats the clinician as an empty decision-maker, ignoring the inductive logic going on inside him? Let me bring you up to date on the empirical evidence. As of today, there are 27 empirical studies in the literature which make some meaningful comparison between the predictive success of the clinician and the statistician. The predictive domains include: success in academic or military training, recidivism and parole violation, recovery from psychosis, (concurrent) personality description, and outcome of psychotherapy. Of these 27 studies, 17 show a definite superiority for the statistical method; 10 show the methods to be of about equal efficiency; none of them show the clinician predicting better. I have reservations about some of these studies; I do not believe they are optimally designed to exhibit the clinician at his best; but I submit that it is high time that those who are so sure that the "right kind of study" will exhibit the clinician's prowess, should *do* this right kind of study and back up their claim with evidence. Furthermore, *a good deal of routine clinical prediction is going on all over the country in which the data available, and the intensity of clinical contact, are not materially different from that in the published comparisons.* It is highly probable that current predictive methods are costly to taxpayers and harmful to the welfare of patients.

Lacking quantification of inductive probability, we have no choice but to examine the clinician's success-rate. One would hope that the rule-of-thumb assessment of inductive probability is not utterly unreliable. The indicated research step is therefore obvious: We persuade the clinician to state the odds, or somehow rate his "confidence," in his day-by-day decisions. Even if he tends over-all to be wrong when countermanding the actuary, he may still tend to be systematically right for a high-confidence sub-set of his predictions. Once having proved this, we could thereafter countermand the formula in cases where the clinician expresses high confidence in his head. It is likely that studies in a great diversity of domains will be required before useful generalizations can be made.

In the meantime, we are all continuing to make predictions. I think it is safe to say, on the present evidence, that we are not as good as we thought we were. The development of powerful actuarial methods could today proceed more rapidly than ever before. Both theoretical and empirical considerations suggest that we would be well advised to concentrate effort on improving our actuarial techniques rather than on the calibration of each clinician for each of a large number of different prediction problems. How should we meanwhile be making our decisions? Shall we use our heads, or shall we follow the formula? Mostly we will use our heads, because there just isn't any formula, but suppose we have a formula, and a case comes along in which it disagrees with our heads? Shall we then use our heads? I would say, yes—provided the psychological situation is as clear as a broken leg; otherwise, very, *very* seldom.

REFERENCES

1. Cronbach, L. J. & Meehl, P. E. Construct validity in psychological tests. *Psychol. Bull.*, 1955, 52, 281–302.
2. Humphreys, L. G., McArthur, C. C., Meehl, P. E., Sanford, N., & Zubin, J. Clinical versus actuarial prediction. *Proceedings of the 1955 Invitational Conference on Testing Problems*, pp. 91–141.
3. McArthur, C. C. Analyzing the clinical process. *J. counsel. Psychol.*, 1954, 1, 203–207.
4. McArthur, C. C., Meehl, P. E., & Tiedeman, D. V. Symposium on clinical and statistical prediction. *J. counsel. Psychol.*, 1956, 3, 163–173.
5. Meehl, P. E. *Clinical versus statistical prediction: a theoretical analysis and a review of the evidence.* Minneapolis: Univer. of Minn. Press, 1954.
6. Meehl, P. E. Comment on Analyzing the Clinical process. *J. counsel. Psychol.*, 1954, 1, 207–208.
7. Meehl, P. E. Wanted—a good cookbook. *Amer. Psychologist*, 1956, 11, 263–272.
8. Meehl, P. E. & Rosen, A. Antecedent probability and the efficiency of psychometric signs, patterns, or cutting scores. *Psychol. Bull.*, 1955, 52, 194–216.

PART TEN

Operant Conditioning

in Therapy

Clinical psychologists constitute the largest single group within the American Psychological Association. While most of them are occupied principally as psychotherapists, this in no way separates them from the necessities and practice of research. Most of them face the daily despair of being less effective than possible. Indeed, Eysenck[1] widely trumpeted the conclusion that disturbed people who went untreated fared in general about as well as those who were given psychotherapy.

Although it is pointless to feed the false dichotomy of "pure" and "applied" research, the typical clinician looks to research on psychotherapy with more than the mountain climber's classic response to the question of why he climbed the mountain. This research, interesting enough in its own right, could provide improved treatment for the estimated one in ten who may expect to be institutionalized for some psychological disturbance during his lifetime.

As might be expected, clinical researchers have investigated an imposing array of variables: personality characteristics, age, sex, social status, and intelligence of both therapists and patients; length and kind of training, experience of the therapists, etc. Although there have been a few significant findings, no one overriding variable or factor has emerged to change the course of clinical practice or to change the nature of the therapeutic process.

Krasner, in the first article, reviews this unhappy state. He points out that research conducted in the "field" setting of actual therapy (as opposed to a controlled laboratory setting) carries with it a host of complications that make it even more difficult to isolate the really important operating variables. In this setting, it is not too surprising that no startling differences are discovered in gross comparisons of "schools" of psychotherapy, as, for example, the client-centered approach of Carl Rogers versus the traditional

[1] H. J. Eysenck, "The Effects of Psychotherapy: An Evaluation." *Journal of Consulting Psychology*, 1952, 16, 319–324.

Freudian psychoanalytic therapy. Krasner's postulates, disarming in their simplicity, state that research should emphasize three aspects:

1. It should look to learning theory for a cogent model of how the patient "learns" in therapy.
2. It should try to isolate, under controlled, experimental conditions, "the dimensions of the therapeutic situation and determine what the lawful relationships are between the therapist's behavior as the independent variable and the patient's behavior as the dependent variable."
3. The one factor common to all psychotherapy is that the patient talks in the presence of another person who listens, pays attention, and shows some interest. In the parlance of learning theory, these therapist behaviors are reinforcements: the modification of behavior through reinforcement lies at the heart of learning.

Krasner's position strikes some psychotherapists as being akin to Jonathan Swift's "modest proposal" (in order to alleviate the starvation in Ireland, Swift satirically suggested that the starving eat babies, thus providing nourishment and reducing the population at one fell swoop). To see why they might make this analogy, it is important to look first at contemporary research in another area.

Krasner's pronouncement came at about the time that Greenspoon[2] published a celebrated paper. In this (and in a flood of papers evoked by Greenspoon's article) it was reported that an experimenter could influence a subject's verbal behavior by selective reinforcement. For example, suppose the experimenter decided to increase the number (or proportion) of adverbs the subject used while speaking with him, or increase the personal references, or increase his verbalizations about the experimenter, etc. The essential aspect is that each time the subject emitted an expression of the response class selected to be reinforced, the experimenter provided some form of "social reinforcement," i.e., he acted interested, smiled, nodded, or said "uh huh" or "good." Not only did the data show that the reinforced class of responses increased over a base rate (before reinforcement was provided), but they were shown to decrease when reinforcement was no longer provided and rise again in a period of reinforcement. But even more astounding was the report that the subjects were unaware of what had happened. At the conclusion of the session, the subjects usually were asked questions to tap whether they had noticed anything unusual, or whether they thought the experimenter was trying to do anything to them. Only a few subjects reported an awareness of any pattern of responses on the part of the experimenter, and only a small fraction of these verbalized a knowledge of the correct relationship.

The phenomenon is probably neither mysterious nor insidious. Thousands of young women (or men) probably have selectively reinforced certain kinds of behavior of their dates without the special knowledge gained from a course in psychology. Many demure young ladies have adopted the strategy of smiling sweetly whenever their swains talk about their sports prowess. (However, this may be different from the therapist's calculated use of selective reinforcement to alter the patient's behavior unobtrusively.)

[2] J. Greenspoon, "The Reinforcing Effect of Two Spoken Sounds on the Frequency of Two Responses." *American Journal of Psychology*, 1955, 68, 409–416.

This sounds like *1984, Brave New World,* and far-out science fiction in which a group (psychotherapists) consciously manipulates the behavior of others. It reminds some uneasy psychologists of the plight of the atomic physicist—should he develop tools and techniques that could be used for immoral or unethical purposes? A basic tenet held by nearly all psychotherapists is that while it is ethical to help a person view himself and his problems more realistically and to consider alternatives for appropriate choices, the therapist should refrain from making judgments or manipulating behavior. Krasner has suggested that manipulation rather than clarification is the effective component of therapy.

This professional dilemma is graphically illustrated in the confrontation[3] between two eminent psychologists: Carl Rogers, the proponent of client-centered therapy (the essential feature of which is the "nondirectiveness of the therapist leaving the direction of the discourse up to the patient") and B. F. Skinner, a nonclinical psychologist whose very name epitomizes operant control of a subject. (Operant control chambers for animals are known as Skinner Boxes, and Skinner has authored a novel, *Walden Two,*[4] in which Utopia is achieved by society-wide use of operant conditioning.) Skinner strongly favors direct therapist activity; Rogers does not.

Many therapists weren't (and aren't) sure that they, or for that matter anyone, should have this power to control the behavior of others. Many were willing, even anxious, to emulate the ostrich in the hope that this phenomenon would disappear. Or, more realistically, they hoped, with some basis, that later research would fail to support the early suggestions that social reinforcement procedures could be applied to therapy. At any rate, here we find Krasner, a psychotherapist, urging his co-workers to use these very techniques. Later he enlarges on this, and speaks favorably of "The Therapist as a Social Reinforcement Machine"[5] who deliberately manipulates the behavior of the patient.

Not only do such papers, with their use of words like "machine" and "manipulation," cause uneasiness, they also raise questions. One, raised by Dr. Shlein[6] in a discussion following Krasner's paper, was this: "If a therapist is a reinforcement machine, is the reinforcement machine a therapist?" He is not raising the question of technological unemployment; Dr. Shlein is asking whether therapy isn't more than a system of selective social reinforcement. A prior question, however, is whether Krasner's basic proposition is valid. Is the client's behavior in the therapy session really under the control of the therapist's reinforcement?

So now we return to the text to see whether Krasner can build a case for the argument introduced in his first paper (the first in this set). In addition to his other propositions, Krasner suggests a solution to a perpetual

---

[3] B. F. Skinner and C. R. Rogers, "Some Issues Concerning the Control of Human Behavior: A Symposium." *Science,* 1956, 124, 1057–1066.

[4] B. F. Skinner, *Walden Two* (New York: Macmillan, 1948).

[5] L. Krasner, "The Therapist as a Social Reinforcement Machine," in H. H. Strupp and L. Luborsky (eds.), *Research in Psychotherapy,* Volume II (Washington: American Psychological Association, 1962), 61–94.

[6] J. M. Shlein, "Toward What Level of Abstraction in Criteria?" in H. H. Strupp and L. Luborsky (eds.), *Research in Psychotherapy,* Volume II (Washington: American Psychological Association, 1962), 142–154.

embarrassment in research on psychotherapy—what to use as the dependent variable. In medicine, survival itself is a gross measure; temperature, blood composition, respiration, and other quantifiable aspects are available to evaluate treatment. But how do you measure effectiveness in psychotherapy? Measures of "adjustment" are scarce and hardly survive a penetrating glance. And after all what kind of experiment can be evaluated in the absence of an adequate measure of change? To Krasner, it appears that the social reinforcement model neatly provides both the experimental condition and the dependent variable. Thus he concludes that one should do a frequency count of whatever class of verbal responses one chooses to manipulate.

The result of this conclusion is the second paper in this group. Krasner works here with a laboratory approximation of therapy in which he asks two "patients" to make up stories. The data confirm his hypothesis, since the "experimenter" (not therapist) does produce differences in the frequency of references to "all nouns and pronouns referring to the mother figure in the S's story." This is interesting, but, with a sample size of two, it can hardly be considered conclusive.

The next article, by Buss and Durkee, again centers upon the technique itself (rather than testing it in therapy). A therapist often has to help a patient deal with his hostile impulses and feelings. However, the verbalization of this content typically induces anxiety in the patient, which acts to inhibit further verbalization. Since therapy is primarily a verbal interaction, it follows that the therapist has use for a technique that could increase this class of response. Thus it is not surprising that Buss and Durkee investigated the effect of verbal conditioning upon the verbalization of hostile material. They found evidence for this, such as significant increases in frequency of the reinforced response on successive blocks of trials. They also investigated sex differences and differences between hostile and neutral words, but these are of less concern to us in this particular context.

J. M. Rogers' paper employs a more sophisticated design. Using students from an introductory psychology course, a quasi-therapy situation, and the familiar use of social reinforcement to alter verbalizations (self-references), Rogers adds the embellishments of a second experimental group, a control group, and pre- and post-test measures of personality.

Having decided on self-reference verbalizations as the conditioning target, Rogers aims his subject toward this in "pre-therapy" sessions by using two tests that required responses of this kind. In each of his six individual "therapy" interviews, the subject was asked to talk about himself. In the first such session, the interviewer provided no reinforcement; in the subsequent five he reinforced positive self-references in one experimental group, negative ones in another group, and none in the control group. Comparisons were made of changes from the base rate (interview 1) to conditioned rate (interviews 2 through 6) in positive, negative and ambiguous self-references, and non-self-references, and differences in all these among the three groups. Table 1 in the article presents the mean scores for all these categories and explicates the basic comparisons.

Rogers found that negative self-references increased in the reinforced group and showed no change in the group receiving no reinforcement. As

Rogers says, this is straightforward. Less straightforward are the data on positive self-references. They show no increase in the group in which they are reinforced; on the other hand, they decrease in the two groups in which they are not reinforced. Since these differences are significant, one can assert that conditioning has had an effect. In this situation, at least, the subjects made fewer and fewer positive self-references when these were not reinforced (extinction occurred) while reinforcement prevented this process in the experimental group. If this can be generalized, the continued egotistical performance of life's bores attests to their having received reinforcement for this behavior, even though this strains credulity.

Rogers digs further by checking the relationship between conditioning and changes (pre- to post-test scores) in anxiety and emotional adjustment. One short sentence repeats the sad refrain, "No significant changes were found." But hope dies slowly, and he writes ". . . with a longer period of conditioning . . . adjustment scores may be significantly increased."

The next paper, by Rickard, Dignam, and Horner, edges us closer to the arena—therapy itself. We have dealt in the previous papers with story-telling, multiple-choice word selection, and free-interview in a laboratory setting. The technique is here applied to a real patient in real therapy. The advance is modest; it is one real patient. The investment is less modest; there were some 60 sessions of about 45 minutes each (the report leaves this quantification somewhat unclear). The experimenters attempted to reinforce rational speech in the verbalizations of a patient. In the early stages, he produced about two minutes of rational speech during a 45-minute session in which he maintained a steady flow of speech! Although their evidence, at face value, supports Krasner's position, it is not unequivocally encouraging. The report points out that these effects were specific to situational cues and had markedly little resistance to extinction.

The last paper in this section still doesn't directly attack the crucial question: "Does social reinforcement work in therapy?" Instead, the authors had psychiatric patients tell stories about pictures. Emotional words were reinforced in one group by the conventional social reinforcers, in another group by an impersonal "click" of a counter, and, in the control group, not at all. The investigators introduced an interesting variation in this study, however. They didn't bother with the changes in emission of emotional words. Apparently confident that their independent variable (selective reinforcement of verbal behavior) would function adequately, they provided no check on this measure. Their dependent variable was the amount of change (pre- to post-test measures) in ratings made of the behavior of these subjects in group therapy sessions by personnel unaware of the subjects' treatment conditions. This time they obtained positive results. Ratings of the socially reinforced group changed significantly, while the others did not.

This is one cycle in research in psychotherapy. Krasner proposed in 1955 that therapists should investigate the one factor common to all psychotherapy, social reinforcement by the therapists. By now, it is clear that this can affect the verbal behavior of the patient within the therapeutic setting. The crucial concern is whether this can be generalized to the patient's "real" life. The last article gives a glimpse of the path this research may take in the future.

STUDY QUESTIONS

1. In Krasner's first article he indicates that therapy is more than "the application of behavioral cues to reinforce. . . ." Why then does he ask that investigations in psychotherapy study the relationship of these behavioral cues to changes in the patient?

2. In his second paper, Krasner provides reinforcement only in alternate blocks of 5 sessions. What are the implications of proceeding this way instead of reinforcing only during the first (or last) series of 5 sessions?

3. The analysis of the Buss and Durkee data on the frequency with which the reinforced word was used in a sentence included both the height and the shape of the curves. How do these provide different data?

4. Assume that you believe that the procedure employed by J. M. Rogers would produce changes in the self-concept of the subjects. How would you rationalize the failure of his study to support this?

5. Rickard, Dignam, and Horner used a schedule of partial reinforcement. What considerations argued for this, rather than continuous reinforcement?

6. Ullmann, Krasner, and Collins had an observer rate the group therapy behavior of their subjects. Defend or critique the use of these ratings as a dependent variable.

The Use of Generalized Reinforcers

in Psychotherapy Research[1]

Leonard Krasner

Veterans Administration Hospital, Lexington, Kentucky

The purpose of this paper is to suggest a theoretical framework into which a program of systematic investigation in the area of psychotherapy can be fitted. It does not intend to give a specific research design, but rather to raise some broad problems which have to be considered before any basic progress can be made in understanding the therapeutic situation.

Reprinted from *Psychological Reports*, 1955, 1, 19–25.

[1] From the Veterans Administration Hospital, Lexington, Kentucky. Part of this paper was read at the 1954 meetings of the American Psychological Association. The author wishes to express his appreciation to Dr. Charles B. Ferster for his stimulation of the ideas presented in this paper.

Despite the ever-increasing number of studies designed to give us information about the processes and results of psychotherapy, there have been few systematic studies reported of attempts to work with human beings to determine what might be the basic variables of the therapeutic situation, nor have there been attempts to manipulate relevant variables in order to determine any degree of relationship between these variables. Although the behavior of the organisms involved in this particular situation has often been "explained," it has rarely been experimented with.

Few attempts have been made to isolate any aspects of psychotherapy in a controlled laboratory setting, mainly on the basis of the argument that psychotherapy is such an intricate, complex, subtle relationship that it would be impossible to reproduce it in any rigid experimental situation. To do so, it is argued, would destroy the essence of the therapeutic situation. But until such attempts are made to determine what the relevant variables and parameters are, we cannot even be certain what we are talking about when we refer to "psychotherapy."

In pointing out the very real problems of the complexities of psychotherapy we are apt to become lost in the proverbial forest and be unable to see the trees of which it is composed. Miller (5) has commented that "it is to be expected that the first efforts at an objective, quantitative approach to any intricate matter like the evaluation of process and outcome of various forms of therapy would necessarily seem oversimplified and naive. Relevant variables must be discovered and isolated, methods for measuring them must be devised."

Since a certain process, usually termed "psychotherapy" by its practitioners, takes place under such a great variety of circumstances, then either there is a common element in all these situations, or all are not entitled to be given the same title. Hunt (4), defining psychotherapy broadly, calls it "a helping method which involves one person, a professional, consciously using his speech and gestures to develop a social relationship aimed at providing a corrective experience with another person, his client." It need not be pointed out that among "professionals" there is a very great variety of techniques, approaches, and theories used to develop this "corrective" type of relationship or experience. Of the formal type of psychotherapy with which psychologists are concerned, we find in the literature that all approaches, techniques, and so-called "schools" report improvements in a certain number of cases. From the reported evidence and the few attempts at evaluation of it (1), there does not appear to be much difference in the percentage of reported cures from approach to approach. That the basic variables of psychotherapy, whatever they may be, are not limited in operation to any one approach is further attested to by the factor-analytic studies of Fiedler (2, 3), who found that there was significantly greater agreement among "expert" therapists of different schools, both in what they considered to be the ideal therapeutic relationship and in their actual therapeutic practice, than between expert and novice of the same school. Thus the type of therapeutic relationship which one establishes seems to be a function of one's length of experience in therapy rather than of one's basic theoretical viewpoint.

From the above it might be hypothesized that, since widely diversified techniques seem to be effective to some extent in changing behavior, there should be a common or general factor in all these techniques. Furthermore, it would seem that effective techniques in psychotherapy are learned by the therapist as he becomes more experienced in the practice of therapy. The therapist learns what behavior on his own part is most effective with particular types of patients and behaves accordingly.

Put in terms which would permit a behavioral analysis, the problem is to isolate the dimensions of the therapeutic situation and determine what the lawful relationships are between the therapist's behavior as the independent variable and the patient's behavior as the dependent variable. Seen in this light, the problem of analyzing the therapeutic situation becomes one of analyzing the relationship of two people in terms of their specific behavior. No matter how psychotherapy is defined or just what approach is used, there is general agreement that something called a "relationship" between two people is involved. What we are suggesting is that future experimenters interested in the problems of psychotherapy focus their efforts at understanding this "relationship" by studying the effects of certain behavior of the therapist which might reinforce certain responses of the patient. It is thus to reinforcement theory that the experimenting clinician can turn, in order to find a conceptual frame of reference within which he can work. This does not mean that other theoretical conceptualizations might not prove as useful. However, the experimental orientation suggested here fits most comfortably into the general tenets of a reinforcement theory. This is of course not to imply, for example, that every time the therapist behaves in a certain way, by speech or actions, the patient will respond to this stimulus in the same predictable manner. Rather it becomes a question of the probability of the patient's emitting a certain class of behavior in the light of the type of reinforcement this behavior has received previously in the therapeutic situation and prior to that, in life situations. What aspect of the therapist's behavior can be isolated and used as a stimulus in the control of the patient's behavior? In essence, the question is what are the basic irreducible elements of an interpersonal situation which must exist in order to term the situation a psychotherapeutic one?

What does the behavior of the therapist consist of? First of all, we must start with the fact that the therapist is physically present with the patient. In all psychotherapies, the therapist, if only by his presence in the same room, indicates that he is interested in the patient, and pays attention to the behavior of the patient. It sounds like the simplest and most axiomatic thing to say about psychotherapy, but it would seem reasonable to assume that the factor of the therapist listening, paying attention, showing some interest, is a basic and indispensable variable of the therapeutic situation. The therapist focuses more attention on those aspects of the patient's verbal emissions which his particular orientation calls for, but in any case he displays a generalized form of behavior cues which we may label as "attention." These behavior cues may consist of looking at the patient's face, smiling, writing, nodding of the head, picking up or putting down a pen, saying "mm hum," or, most common of all, using overt speech. It would certainly seem that these cues have some effect on the patient's behavior, more specifically his rate of verbalizing and the types of material he verbalizes. It is possible that "warmth," "understanding," and "acceptance," which terms are often used to describe the therapist's behavior, can be analyzed into behavioral cues which indicate a more intense type of attention.

We might speculate why these behavioral cues should serve as a means of reinforcing the behavior of another individual. Skinner (10) classifies attention as a generalized reinforcer, in addition to approval, affection, and tokens such as money. These arise when behavior is reinforced by other people. The attention of other people is reinforcing, Skinner further points out, because it is a necessary condition or prelude to receiving other more specific reinforcements from them. In general, only people who are attending to us reinforce our behavior. Such reinforcement is of an intermittent nature and is less dependent upon the momentary condition or on deprivation of the organism. We are continually making use of attention to shape or manipulate the behavior of others. "It is difficult to define, observe, and measure attention within the framework of a natural science" (10). Skinner points out that attention is not a thing but merely an aspect of behavior. The actual physical dimensions may be difficult to identify, but there is no reason for denying that they exist. Further, and this is an important consideration for psychotherapy, Skinner points out that generalized reinforcers are eventually effective even though the primary reinforcement upon which they are ultimately based is not received. In other words, the therapist does not have to supply the food or sex demands of the patient in order for his attention-indicating behavior to be effective in reinforcing certain aspects of the patient's behavior.

Thus it would seem that the behavioral cues indicating attention on the part of the therapist are one of the most, if not the most, important of the variables in the therapeutic situation. In analyzing the therapy process these behavioral cues seem to offer us the best stimuli with which to start experimentation with humans. These cues could serve as the independent variable in any systematic experimental program.

There is one element in the patient's behavior which could readily serve as the dependent variable, namely his verbalizations. There is agreement among adherents to all schools of therapy that one important aspect of the patient's behavior which the therapist works with is that of verbalization; Shaffer and Lazarus (7) go so far as to say that "the techniques of getting the patient to talk and to continue to talk must be the real core of the treatment." These verbalizations would seem to serve several functions. As both Shaw (8) and Shoben (9) point out in their applications of learning theory to psychotherapy, one means of extinguishing previously repressed behavior, and all the anxiety it evokes, is to have it verbalized (symbolically produced) and followed by no disapproval. But, before the patient can find out that his speech is not going to be disapproved or punished, he must actually verbalize and see for himself that no negative reinforcement follows.

The first problem of the therapist, once the patient has taken the initial step of coming to see him, is to use whatever techniques he has available to get the patient to feel sufficiently at ease to talk freely. This in itself is often very difficult, especially with non-college people, who are often unable to verbalize spontaneously. A secondary problem is for the therapist to use his techniques to guide the patient's verbalizations into certain areas which he feels will eventually be more beneficial to the patient. He does this by a variety of reinforcing techniques such as suggestion, interpretation, questioning, or other ways of indicating that he is interested in or paying particular attention to certain aspects of the patient's verbalizations. Thus, since verbalization is of such importance in therapy, and since it is a segment of general behavior which is measurable, it would seem to be the logical dependent variable with which to start an experimental approach to the problem of psychotherapy.

The problem of the values or goals of psychotherapy is certainly one that must be considered in any attempted experimentation in this area. Although the goals may vary, and sometimes widely, from approach to approach, all techniques try to achieve some change. If the patient were satisfied with his present behavior, he would not be seeking help in changing it. Thus to start with, leaving out any question of long-time goals, we would postulate that some change, reported or overt, in behavior is desired. We also leave out for the present any value judgments as to the desirability or the direction of change.

Thus we have the independent variable—the behavior cues of the therapist—and the dependent variable—the verbal behavior of the patient. Indices of change in the dependent variable could consist of quantitative changes in a particular class of verbal behavior, e.g., words of feeling tone, or self-reference, or changes in amount of time devoted to a particular class of behavior, such as family, or sex references. These measurements could take place within any one session or over a number of sessions. Determining in advance what class of verbalizations he wished to reinforce, the therapist could start with one piece of behavior, a nod of the head, for example, and proceed to use this behavior in a systematic way to follow (reinforce) the patient's desired verbalizations. Other relationships, such as the effect of different schedules of reinforcement or different behavior cues, could also be worked out. Control groups would of course have to be used.

At this point certain very basic objections to this type of approach on the part of clinicians can be anticipated. As anyone who has done extensive therapy realizes, one cannot divorce the overt behavior of the therapist from the feelings behind it. A patient is quick to realize when the therapist nods his head and is not really listening or interested, or when the therapist smiles but is insincere in his attitude toward the patient. We assume that there may be a vast difference in a nod of the head from one therapist to the next. In analyzing the therapeutic situation as above are you not losing the quality of the situation itself?

The writer well realizes the possible validity of such objections. It is not envisioned that psychotherapy will consist of the application of behavioral cues to reinforce as a formal, mechanical device to be put on or off like a water tap. Nor do we seek to encourage those who hope to be able to learn the techniques of psychotherapy as one learns recipes from a cookbook. But it is felt that there are certain lawful relationships between the behaviors of two people which are basic to any other things which may occur in psychotherapy, and these relationships have yet to be discovered. In analyzing the psychotherapeutic relationship in these terms it is not in any way implied that this is all that takes place during therapy. Anyone who has undertaken a therapeutic relationship could validly protest that this type of analysis misses many of the subtle complexities of therapy. However, science has not as yet given us a real understanding of just what "psychotherapy" is, or how it works, when it does. Experimentation along the lines proposed here would be a starting point for exploring certain aspects of psychotherapy under more rigorously controlled conditions than the usual therapy situation allows.

What might we expect from such an investigation? First of all we could determine if there is a lawful relationship between these two variables. If such a relationship exists, is it the same for all types of patients, for all diagnostic groups, for all therapists? Are the learning and extinction curves the same for such different groups? We might hypothesize, for example, either that neurotics need fewer attention cues to act as a reinforcement since they probably have a history of greater deprivation, or that they need more such cues to overcome the effects of previous punishment accompanying attention. It would seem reasonable to assume that in very seriously disturbed patients attention has been extinguished as a reinforcer, since it has usually preceded punishment in the life history of the patient. We might find that attention is not enough with more severely disturbed psychotics, and instead of generalized reinforcers we can use only primary ones related to a physical deprivation. Peters (6) used fudge candy as reinforcers with psychotics who had first been deprived of sugar.

Other questions about this behavioral relationship can be posed. Does it hold at all stages of therapy? Is there a hierarchy of behavioral cues with respect to degree of effectiveness? But even more important than its answers to specific problems, many of which will suggest themselves as experimentation proceeds, is the fact that this approach gives us a means of attacking experimentally the problem of psychotherapy "from the ground up."

It is certainly to be doubted, for example, that the effects of psychotherapy are due merely to a continuum of attention-indicating behavioral cues on the part of the therapist. That is, in the early stages of such experimentation it may be found that the therapist adds behavior cues upon behavior cues. In addition to merely looking at the patient, he smiles, nods his head and says "mm hum." Perhaps the rate of responding of the patient increases in a lawful relationship as the cues are added. However, the addition of such behavioral cues must reach a point of diminishing returns and possibly some variable other than "attention" cues takes over. This would be crucial in understanding the therapeutic process. However, it would be studied only after the effects of the more basic and elementary techniques had been determined.

Once these general relationships had been established, the whole problem of individual differences, the individual personality variables of both patient and therapist, could then be explored. There is the primary need to find out if certain lawful relationships exist in the therapeutic situation at the gross level before more subtle complex analysis of behavior is made. It is felt that the basic processes of psychotherapy, indeed of the relationship between any two humans, will not be fully known, until a systematic program as outlined above can be undertaken by groups of psychologists working with many individuals, both those emotionally disturbed and those in psychological "good health."

SUMMARY

To achieve understanding and control of psychotherapy, we must experiment to determine the effective variables and their functional interrelationships in the psychotherapeutic situation. It is proposed that a start be made by studying the relationship between behavioral cues indicating attention on the part of the therapist (independent variable) and changes in language behavior on the part of the patient (dependent variable). The objections of oversimplification and artificiality are rejected on the basis of practical and scientific necessity.

REFERENCES

1. Eysenck, H. J. The effects of psychotherapy: an evaluation. *J. consult. Psychol.*, 1952, **16**, 319–324.
2. Fiedler, F. A comparison of therapeutic relationships in psychoanalytic, non-directive and Adlerian therapy. *J. consult. Psychol.*, 1950, **14**, 436–445.
3. Fiedler, F. Factor analyses of psychoanalytic, non-directive, and Adlerian therapeutic relationships. *J. consult. Psychol.*, 1951, **15**, 32–38.
4. Hunt, J. McV. Toward an integrated program of research on psychotherapy. *J. consult. Psychol.*, 1952, **16**, 237–246.
5. Miller, J. Objective methods of evaluating process and outcome in psychotherapy. *Amer. J. Psychiat.*, 1951, **108**, 258–263.
6. Peters, H. N. An experimental evaluation of learning vs. therapy in schizophrenia. *Amer. Psychologist*, 1952, **7**, 354 (abstract).
7. Shaffer, G. W., & Lazarus, R. S. *Fundamental concepts in clinical psychology.* New York: McGraw-Hill, 1952.
8. Shaw, F. S. Some postulates concerning psychotherapy. *J. consult. Psychol.*, 1948, **12**, 426–432.
9. Shoben, E. J., Jr. Psychotherapy as a problem in learning theory. *Psychol. Bull.*, 1949, **46**, 366–392.
10. Skinner, B. F. *Science and human behavior.* New York: Macmillan, 1953.

A Technique for Investigating the Relationship

Between the Behavior Cues of the Examiner

and the Verbal Behavior of the Patient[1,2]

Leonard Krasner

Veterans Administration Hospital, Palo Alto, California

In a previous paper, the writer suggested that techniques of conditioning verbal behavior be used in a program of systematic investigation into the process of psychotherapy and offered a rationale for such a procedure (2). It was proposed that such a program be initiated by studying the relationship between behavioral cues indicating "attention" on the part of the examiner (independent variable) and changes in specified verbal behavior on the part of the patient (dependent variable). The purpose of this paper is to present an experimental technique that can be utilized in such an approach and its results with two patients.

A technique was devised to create an interpersonal situation which would have as many of the characteristics of the psychotherapeutic situation as possible. Further consideration was to control variables of experimenter's behavior and to quantify the subject's verbal behavior. It was hypothesized that systematic changes in the experimenter's behavior would result in specifiable changes in the subject's verbal behavior.

METHOD

Subjects. Two male, white, veterans, 30 years of age, with high school education, and diagnosed as schizophrenic reactions in remission, were asked to participate in a study to determine how people "tell stories."

Reprinted from *Journal of Consulting Psychology*, 1958, 22, 364–366.

1 From the Veterans Administration Hospital, Palo Alto, California. Research was conducted at the Veterans Administration Hospital, Lexington, Kentucky.
2 A paper based on this study was presented at the 1957 American Psychological Association meetings.

457

Procedure. The equipment consisted of a standard timer, placed on the desk so that both S and E could see it, and a tape recorder. Prior to the first session, S was given the following instructions: "I want you to make up a story with at least four characters in it, a mother, a father, a child, and an animal. It can be any kind of a story. I want you to tell me the story for ten minutes. I'll start the timer now, and it will ring when the ten minutes have passed. All right, go ahead." Prior to each of the following 24 sessions, the same instructions were repeated with one change. Instead of "I'll start the timer now, and it will ring when ten minutes have passed," E said, "You can either continue your story from the last session or start a new one."

Each S participated in 25 ten-minute sessions, which were divided into five blocks of five sessions each. During the first block of five 10-minute sessions (nonreinforcement), E avoided looking at the S. E either looked down at the blank pad in front of him or looked out of the nearby window. During the second block of five sessions (reinforcement), E responded with a combination of behavior cues after each time the S made reference to the class of verbal behavior "mother." E's combined behavior cue during the reinforcement condition consisted of looking at S, nodding his head, smiling, and emitting an "mmm-hmm" sound. The class of verbal behavior "mother"

TABLE 1

NUMBER OF "MOTHER," "FATHER," AND TOTAL "REFERENCES" (NOUNS AND PRONOUNS), AND PERCENTAGES OF "MOTHER" TO "MOTHER AND FATHER" AND TO TOTAL "REFERENCES" FOR SUCCESSIVE BLOCKS OF FIVE TEN-MINUTE SESSIONS

Subject and 10-minute sessions	Condition	Number references "Mother"	"Father"	Total	Per cent references "Mother"/ "Mother and Father"	"Mother"/ Total
Subject I
1–5	nonreinf.	161	201	1306	45	12
6–10	reinf.	272	138	1315	66	21
11–15	nonreinf.	255	235	1212	52	21
16–20	reinf.	313	245	1222	56	26
21–25	nonreinf.	190	227	1197	46	16
Subject II
1–5	nonreinf.	68	48	384	59	18
6–10	reinf.	90	51	319	64	28
11–15	nonreinf.	18	109	261	14	7
16–20	reinf.	129	114	519	53	25
21–25	nonreinf.	100	153	552	40	18

was defined as "all nouns and pronouns referring to the mother figure in the S's story."

In the third and fifth block of five sessions the nonreinforcement condition, as in the first block of five sessions, was repeated. The fourth block of five sessions repeated the reinforcement condition of the second block of five sessions.

After completion of the 25th session, the Ss were interviewed to determine their degree of awareness of the conditioning procedure. This interview consisted of a dozen questions such as, "What do you think was the purpose of these sessions," "Did you notice any changes in the stories as you went on," "Do you think that my sitting here in any way influenced your stories?"

RESULTS

The total number of "references" made by S to each of the major characters in the stories—"mother," "father," "child," and "animal"—were summarized for each individual session. To be scored as a "reference," the verbalization had to be a noun or pronoun referring to one of the four major characters. The ratios of "mother references" to "mother–father references" and to total "references" were computed for each of the 25 sessions.

These two ratios were divided into those verbalizations emitted under reinforcement conditions and those verbalizations emitted under nonreinforcement conditions. The Mann-Whitney U test (5, pp. 116–126) for the significance of differences of "references" under the conditions of reinforcement and nonreinforcement for these two ratios was computed for both subjects. All four of the ratios were in the predicted direction, and three of the four, both ratios of S_I, and the "Mother"/total ratio for S_{II}, were significant beyond the .05 level.

An examination of these two sets of ratios for successive blocks of five sessions indicates that the ratios of the reinforced class of behavior increased under reinforcement conditions and decreased under nonreinforcement, increased again during the succeeding reinforcement series, and decreased again during the final block of nonreinforcement sessions. These systematic variations were also true of the absolute number of "references" as well as the percentages. Table 1 presents both percentages and numbers of "references" for successive blocks of five 10-minute sessions.

DISCUSSION

This technique of verbal conditioning enables the testing of hypotheses concerning what happens to various classes of verbal behavior under selected experimental conditions. The hypothesis in the present study that the reinforced class of verbalization varies systematically with the application of E's behavior cues was confirmed with two patients. It is of interest to note what happened to the other categories of verbal behavior which appeared in the stories, i.e., "father," "child," "animal." All three of these categories varied sharply from session to session, but in no systematic manner.

In a review of "verbal conditioning" studies with their implications for psychotherapy (3), the writer divided the techniques of conditioning verbal behavior into four general categories of experimental situations: saying plural nouns; completing sentences; "storytelling" and interview situations; and testlike situations. The technique used here falls in the "storytelling" category and is similar to the techniques reported in studies by Ball (1) and Mock (4).

SUMMARY

A storytelling technique was used to study the relationship between examiner behavior cues and patient's verbal behavior. The results indicate that changes in a preselected class of verbal behavior varied as a function of the systematic application of behavior cues by the examiner. It is concluded that this experimental procedure permits the systematic isolation and study of important variables of the interpersonal process basic to psychotherapy.

REFERENCES

1. BALL, R. S. Reinforcement conditioning of verbal behavior by verbal and non-verbal stimuli in a situation resembling a clinical interview. Unpublished doctoral dissertation, Indiana Univer., 1952.
2. KRASNER, L. The use of generalized reinforcers in psychotherapy research. *Psychol. Rep.*, 1955, 1, 19–25.
3. KRASNER, L. Studies of the conditioning of verbal behavior. *Psychol. Bull.*, 1958, 55, 148–170.
4. MOCK, J. F. The influence of verbal and behavioral cues of a listener on the verbal productions of the speaker. Unpublished doctoral dissertation, Univer. of Kentucky, 1957.
5. SIEGEL, S. *Nonparametric statistics for the behavioral sciences.* New York: McGraw-Hill, 1956.

Conditioning of Hostile Verbalizations in a

Situation Resembling a Clinical Interview[1]

Arnold H. Buss and Ann Durkee

University of Pittsburgh   Purdue University

A recurrent obstacle in interviewing and psychotherapy is the verbal inhibition of clients. Topics that are associated with anxiety are avoided or discussed only with the greatest reluctance. Since little progress can be expected unless problems are brought up and discussed, verbal inhibition is clearly an important area for clinical research.

The research may take two forms. First, verbatim interviews could be examined to determine the psychologist's techniques of facilitating verbalization, and then the success of the techniques might be measured. The second form involves setting up a laboratory analogue of the interview situation and investigating the effect of the experimenter's (E's) verbal behavior on the subject's (S's) verbalizations. The present study is of the second kind.

It was felt that while the situation should resemble a clinical interview as closely as possible, discrete trials should be employed for better control of reinforcement by the E. Therefore the task of making up sentences was used. The task was first used by Taffel (2), who had a series of 3 x 5 cards, each containing a verb and six pronouns. The S was instructed to make up a sentence using the verb and one of the six pronouns. After an initial period of free responding, the S was reinforced for every sentence containing the pronoun "I" or "We." Taffel compared this procedure to a therapist's reinforcing a client's talking about himself.

Self-reference content is not usually associated with anxiety, whereas anxiety often accompanies verbalization of hostile content. Often clients are able to talk about their hostile impulses only after their strong inhibitions are removed or weakened. Such inhibition may also be expected in a nonclinical population because it is part of general cultural training to suppress and punish hostility.

The present study seeks to investigate the verbal conditioning of hostile and neutral material. Since inhibition is expected to retard verbalization of hostile content, the learning of hostile material should be slower than the

Reprinted from *Journal of Consulting Psychology*, 1958, 22, 415–418.

[1] The writers are indebted to Herbert Gerjuoy, George Wischner, and Melvin Manis for their helpful suggestions.

learning of neutral material. Also, since men are allowed a greater variety and intensity of hostile response in our culture, men should learn hostile material faster than women.

METHOD

STIMULI

Two considerations dictated the initial choice of words. First, the grammatical form should be constant, and therefore only verbs in the past tense were used. Second, slang and pedantry should be avoided, and only relatively familiar verbs were selected.

In compiling a list of hostile words a wide range of intensity was noted, e.g., *stabbed, tortured* vs. *criticized, resented.* It was decided to have two degrees of hostility, mild and intense. A compilation of hostile and neutral words was submitted to six judges,[2] who sorted them into neutral, mildly hostile, and intensely hostile groups. The criterion of acceptance of a word was agreement by five of the six judges.

Next, the Thorndike-Lorge word count (3) was used to match the frequencies of the three types of verbs.[3] Finally, the matched words were placed on 3 x 5 white index cards. There were 30 such cards, each with a neutral, a mildly hostile, and an intensely hostile verb. Since a pilot study revealed that 50 or 60 trials would be required for learning to occur, the number of cards had to be doubled. This was accomplished by using each of the words twice. The second time a word was used, it was accompanied on the card by different words than had accompanied it the first time. For example, *tortured* appeared on a card with *argued* and *invented* the first time and with *flattered* and *rebelled* the second time. The order of placement of the verbs on the cards and the order of presentation of cards were randomized for the series of 60 trials.

EXPERIMENTAL DESIGN

There were two groups of Ss and 60 trials. During Trials 1–10, the Ss made up sentences but received no reinforcement. This free responding period established the frequency of response for each type of word prior to conditioning. During Trials 11–60, one group of Ss was reinforced for using neutral verbs, and the other group was reinforced for using intensely hostile words. There was no group that was reinforced for using mildly hostile words; in this exploratory research the writers felt that any differences in learning should be maximized by using the extreme of hostility. Therefore, of the hostile verbs, only the intensely hostile ones were reinforced, and hereafter the term *hostile verbs* will refer only to intensely hostile verbs.

[2] The writers wish to thank Idel Bruckman, Mary Oltean, Jerry Wiggins, and Marvin Zuckerman for serving as judges. The writers served as the fifth and sixth judges.

[3] Words were grouped into three categories: 0–24, 25–50, and above 50 times per million according to the Thorndike-Lorge count. Thus the three kinds of verbs were matched on the basis of the frequency *range* in which they fell.

PROCEDURE

Each S was instructed to make up a sentence using one of the three verbs on each card. During Trials 1–10 the E said nothing. During Trials 11–60 the E said Right after the correct verb was used and Wrong after an incorrect verb was used.

SUBJECTS

The Ss were 80 college students, 40 men and 40 women. Within each sex, Ss were assigned randomly to either the neutral reinforced group or the hostile reinforced group, and each group had 20 men and 20 women.

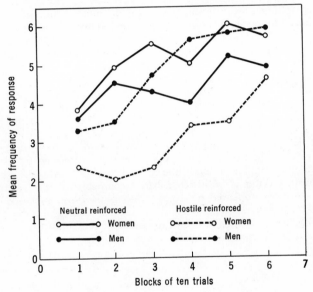

FIGURE 1.   Acquisition curves of men and women reinforced for hostile and neutral words.

RESULTS

The 60-trial series was divided into six blocks of ten trials each. The measure of learning is the frequency of occurrence of *the response class that was reinforced.* For the Neutral group the frequency of neutral words per block of ten trials is the measure, and for the Hostile group the frequency of hostile words per block of ten trials is the measure. The learning curves for the two groups and for both sexes are plotted in Fig. 1. Inspection of these curves reveals clear-cut differences in the *height* of the curves. Also the *rate* of learning hostile words (the shape of the curves) appears to be slightly faster than the rate of learning neutral words.

The significance of these trends was tested by a Lindquist Type III analysis of variance (1). This analysis of variance is summarized in Table 1. In this table the main effects for Words, the main effects for Sex, and the Words × Sex interaction reflect differences in the *height* of the curves. Differences in the shape of the curves (rate of learning) are reflected in the Words × Trials and Sex × Trials interactions.

The significant F ratios for Words and for Words × Sex indicate that there are significant differences in the height of the four curves. Since there

TABLE 1

ANALYSIS OF VARIANCE OF HOSTILE AND NEUTRAL RESPONSES
OF MEN AND WOMEN FOR BLOCKS OF 10 TRIALS

Source	df	Mean square	F
Words	1	93.64	5.05*
Sex	1	30.00	1.62
Words × Sex	1	200.21	10.79**
Error (between)	76	18.55	
Trials	5	49.45	15.46**
Trials × Words	5	11.47	3.58**
Trials × Sex	5	.66	.21
Trials × Sex × Words	5	4.70	1.47
Error (within)	380	3.20	
Total	479		

* $p < .05$.
** $p < .01$.

was a significant Words × Sex interaction, four comparisons were made: men's neutral vs. men's hostile; women's neutral vs. women's hostile; men's neutral vs. women's neutral; and men's hostile vs. women's hostile. Two of the four comparisons yielded significant differences. The women's hostile curve was (*a*) significantly lower than the women's neutral curve ($t + 3.19$, $p < .001$ for 76 *df*) and (*b*) significantly lower than the men's hostile curve ($t = 2.63$, $p < .02$ for 380 *df*).

The significant F ratio for trials indicates that conditioning did occur (significant increases in frequency of response on successive blocks of trials). The significant Words × Trials interaction suggests that the shape of the neutral curves was significantly different from the shape of the hostile curves. Evidently the rate of learning hostile words is significantly faster than the rate of learning neutral words.

The first 10 trials constituted the free responding period, during which the E said nothing after all of the Ss' responses. Since all Ss were treated alike during this period, the data from each group may be pooled.

On each trial the S could respond with a neutral, a mildly hostile, or an intensely hostile word. In order to simplify the chi square test of difference in frequency of response, the neutral and mildly hostile words were pooled.

It was now possible to test the significance of sex differences in frequency of response of intensely hostile vs. neutral and mildly hostile words during the first ten trials.

For the 10-trial period there were 11 possible combinations of frequencies: 10 neutral-mildly hostile, 0 intensely hostile; 9 neutral-mildly hostile, 1 intensely hostile; . . . 0 neutral-mildly hostile, 10 intensely hostile. These combinations for men and women constituted a contingency table which yielded a chi square of 21.2, which is significant at the .01 level of confidence. Thus the women gave significantly fewer intensely hostile and significantly more neutral-mildly hostile responses than the men during the free responding period.

DISCUSSION

It was predicted that neutral material would be learned at a faster rate than hostile material. The results proved otherwise, with hostile words being conditioned faster than neutral words. A variable that was not discussed previously may have contributed to these findings: size of response class. The hostile verbs were sampled from a population of a few hundred hostile verbs, but the population of neutral verbs is many thousands. Learning of a large class of responses is expected to be slower than learning of a small class. Hence neutral verbs were conditioned at a slower rate than hostile verbs, despite the inhibition associated with the latter.

It was also predicted that women would manifest slower learning of hostile verbalizations than men. This prediction was not borne out. Rather, the greater inhibition present in women was revealed in the absolute number of hostile verbs used. Both in free responding and acquisition, women produced significantly fewer intensely hostile verbs than men. The intensely hostile verbs referred mainly to physical violence, e.g., *lynched, mauled, smashed, stabbed, strangled,* and *tortured.* The actions represented by these words are severely punished in our culture; they are occasionally allowed by men but never by women. This difference in cultural training would seem to account for the sex difference in frequency of hostile response.

However, the inhibition that depressed frequency of response did not prevent the women from conditioning. While their frequency of hostile response was initially low, it increased with successive acquisition trials. If this finding is confirmed with clinical populations, it would prove encouraging, for it suggests that initial inhibition of response can be overcome by reinforcement. In the investigation of this and other clinical issues the present analogue to a clinical interview would seem to be promising.

SUMMARY

The task of making up sentences was conceptualized as a laboratory analogue of a clinical interview. There were two groups of college students, each group consisting of 20 men and 20 women. One group was reinforced for intensely hostile verbalizations and the other group for neutral verbalizations.

It was found that intensely hostile verbalizations were conditioned faster than neutral verbalizations. This was attributed to the larger size and the diffuseness of the neutral class in comparison to the intensely hostile response class. Women produced significantly fewer intensely hostile responses than men, which was held to be consistent with sex differences in cultural training. Initial inhibition of response did not prevent conditioning from occurring in women. It was suggested that both the findings and the technique have clinical implications.

REFERENCES

1. LINDQUIST, E. F. *Design and analysis of experiments in psychology and education*. Boston: Houghton Mifflin, 1953.
2. TAFFEL, C. Anxiety and the conditioning of behavior. *J. abnorm. soc. Psychol.*, 1955, **51**, 496–501.
3. THORNDIKE, E. L., & LORGE, I. *The teacher's word book of 30,000 words*. New York: Teachers Coll., Columbia Univer., 1944.

Operant Conditioning in a

Quasi-Therapy Setting[1]

J. Maurice Rogers

Stanford University

Recent studies of verbal conditioning, although not designed as investigations of the process of psychotherapy, have important implications for the understanding of interactions between the therapist and the patient. Conducted along the lines of Skinner's operant conditioning paradigm with rats and stimulated by Greenspoon's pioneering study (1955), subsequent experimenters have amply demonstrated that human verbal behavior can be operantly conditioned, that such conditioning can be accomplished without awareness, that a large variety of verbal behaviors may constitute Skinnerian "responses" and an equally large variety of environmental events serve

Reprinted from *Journal of Abnormal and Social Psychology*, 1960, 60, 247–252.

[1] This report is based on the author's dissertation for the degree of doctor of philosophy, completed at Stanford University June 1958 under a committee consisting of Albert Bandura (Chairman), C. Leland Winder, and Paul R. Farnsworth, whose counsel is gratefully acknowledged.

as "reinforcing stimuli," and that typical conditioning phenomena (positive and negative reinforcement, discrimination, extinction, etc.) analogous to that found in animal experimentation can be produced.

Psychotherapists, whatever their theoretical affiliation, agree that psychotherapy implies effort directed toward the production of personality changes and is successful to the extent that specified changes occur. Although changes have been claimed in a variety of classes of behavior, such as anxiety, aggression, and dependency, the bulk of such claims have been unsupported by objective data. Among the more systematic studies are those of Rogers (1951) and his associates (Rogers & Dymond, 1954), who have repeatedly shown that an important change that occurs with psychotherapy is modification of the patient's self-concept. Raimy (1948), who was the first to demonstrate a decrease in negative and an increase in positive self-references in successful therapy, construed this as evidence of a reorganization of the self, and this view has since been strongly advanced by the Rogerian school. Reinforcement theory, however, makes tenable an alternative explanation—that the reported changes in self-reference verbalizations are elicited via unintentional selective reinforcement by the Rogerian therapist.

Research in operant conditioning of verbal behavior is gradually approaching the natural clinical setting of psychotherapy itself. In order for experimental findings to have maximal relevance for both the process and outcome of psychotherapy, it is essential that conditioning investigations be conducted in situations paralleling as closely as possible those of psychotherapy itself, yet retaining the controls and rigor essential to objective scientific study. Under such conditions, research findings will be more directly applicable to psychotherapy as it is characteristically conducted without the necessity of translating them into other terms and another frame of reference with the consequent hazard of overextrapolation. Manipulation of actual therapy itself, however, is limited by the clinician's ethical responsibility toward the patient, which compels him to exercise restraint in introducing conditions which conceivably might produce adverse effects in the patient. It was with these considerations in mind that the present experiment was designed and carried out. The hypotheses tested were, that an interviewer can produce changes in a subject's self-reference verbalizations by consistently reinforcing a particular class of such statements with simple stimuli, and that such reinforcements can alter a subject's concept of himself, as measured by personality tests.

METHOD

The experiment consisted of setting up a quasi-therapy situation involving a series of free-interviews with individual Ss in which all self-reference verbalizations were reinforced by the interviewer with a simultaneous "Mm-hm" and nod of the head. Each S was told that the interviewer was making a study to learn how people think and feel about themselves and was asked to describe spontaneously his personality characteristics and traits without questions or comments from the interviewer. Every interview was tape recorded so that content analyses could subsequently be done directly from the tapes.

Ss were 36 male students drawn from the introductory psychology course at Stanford University. They were randomly assigned to two experimental groups and a control group—Group A, reinforced for *positive* self-references; Group B, reinforced for *negative* self-references; and Group C, not reinforced at all. A total of 216 ten-minute "therapy" interviews (6 per S) were tape recorded, and a detailed content analysis of all self-references was made to ascertain if any relationship existed between self-references[2] and reinforcements.

A battery of four personality tests was administered prior and subsequent to the therapy to see if changes would occur, and whether such changes would be related to self-reference changes in therapy. Two of these tests, Adjective Self-Descriptions and Sentence Completions, were designed by the experimenter to induce the appropriate "set" for the ensuing therapy interviews by eliciting self-referent ideation. The other two tests were utilized to provide measures of personality change. These tests were the 50-item form of the Taylor Scale of Manifest Anxiety (Taylor, 1953) and the Q Sort Emotional Adjustment Test. The latter is a universe of 100 self-reference statements developed by Haigh and Butler and converted by Dymond into an adjustment test (Rogers & Dymond, 1954, p. 76).

Finally, a structured interview, likewise tape recorded, was conducted to ascertain Ss' awareness of the conditioning and their reaction to the total experiment. All Ss were individually tested and interviewed, four 1-hr. sessions being conducted with each S.

In scoring all the self-reference categories in the interviews and in the Sentence Completion Test, reliabilities were established by correlating ratings of two independent judges. Product moment reliability coefficients ranged from .83 to .95. In scoring self-references in the Adjective Self-Description Test, coding was done by three independent judges, the code assigned each item being based on majority agreement of the judges. Agreement was high, there being unanimity on almost three-fourths of the items.

RESULTS

EFFECT OF REINFORCEMENT ON SELF-REFERENCES IN THERAPY

Table 1 shows the mean therapy interview scores for the three groups. The response classes signify positive, negative, and ambiguous self-references, other or non-self-references, and total number of responses. Interview 1 represents S's operant level since the interviewer was silent throughout that interview. Interviews 2 through 6 were *conditioned* interviews for the experimental Ss in Group A and Group B, but were *unconditioned* for the control Ss in Group C.

---

[2] "Self-reference" was operationally defined as a verbal response by S which describes him in some way, tells something about him, or refers to some affect he experiences. A self-reference may be positive (favorable), negative (unfavorable), or ambiguous (neither). The unit to be coded was termed a "response" and was defined basically as a grammatical sentence. This was a synthesis of "Sentence-Unit" and "Thought-Unit" scoring (Dollard & Mowrer, 1947), on which they achieved high rater reliability.

TABLE 1

MEAN THERAPY INTERVIEW SCORES FOR THE THREE GROUPS

Response Class	P%	N%	A%	O%	Total
Experimental Group A					
Interview 1	27.31	33.77	27.07	11.77	47.92
Interviews 2–6	30.47	23.29	22.78	23.70	53.20
Change	3.16	−10.49	−4.29	11.93	5.28
Experimental Group B					
Interview 1	31.53	27.22	34.21	7.04	61.17
Interviews 2–6	22.01	37.47	27.19	13.33	61.15
Change	−9.52	10.25	−7.02	6.30	−.02
Control Group C					
Interview 1	33.17	33.07	25.37	8.40	54.00
Interviews 2–6	18.93	29.67	29.86	21.53	54.75
Change	−14.23	−3.39	4.49	13.14	.75

TABLE 2

t VALUES OF DIFFERENCES BETWEEN THERAPY
INTERVIEW CHANGE SCORES

Response Class	P%	N%	A%	O%	Total Number of Responses
Group A vs. Group C	3.27[a]	1.86	1.76	.30	1.18
Group B vs. Group C	.81	3.40**	2.50*	1.71	.23
Group A vs. Group B	3.45[a]	5.24[b]	.55	1.44	1.31

     * Significant beyond the .05 level.
     ** Significant beyond the .01 level.
     [a] Significant beyond the .005 level.
     [b] Significant beyond the .0005 level.

TABLE 3

t VALUES OF DIFFERENCES BETWEEN OPERANT
AND CONDITIONED RESPONSES

Response Class	P%	N%
Group A	1.02	1.60
Group B	2.90**	1.78*
Group C	2.99**	.59

     * Significant beyond the .05 level.
     ** Significant beyond the .01 level.

In Table 2 the changes in each group are compared with those in the other groups and the significances of those comparisons determined by means of the t test.

In Table 3 the operant response level (Interview 1) is compared with the conditioned response level (Interviews 2 through 6) in each group and the significance of the change determined by the t test.

When the data are examined regarding the outcome of reinforcing *negative* self-references, a straightforward conditioning effect is found. From Table 3, it is seen that Group B, reinforced for negative self-references, showed a significant increase in that response class, while Groups A and C showed no significant change in that response. Table 2 shows that the change from operant to conditioned level in Group B was significantly different from the change in Groups A and C.

When the data are scrutinized for *positive* self-references, the picture is more complex. As shown in Table 3, Group A (reinforced for positive self-references) did not increase in that response class, and Groups B and C each showed a significant decrease in the response. From Table 2, however, it is seen that the change from operant to conditioned level in Group A is significantly different from the change in Groups B and C. It is clear, therefore, that the significance of the differences between the changes in the three groups is attributable to the decline in both Group B's and Group C's positive self-references rather than to the increase in Group A's positive self-references. Without reinforcement, positive self-references may tend to extinguish, whereas, with reinforcement, their extinction is arrested. The prediction that the interviewer's reinforcement of the S's positive self-references would increase their frequency is thus only obliquely confirmed.

RELATIONSHIP OF CONDITIONABILITY TO INITIAL LEVEL OF ANXIETY AND EMOTIONAL ADJUSTMENT

It was predicted that conditionability (i.e., the readiness with which the S responded to reinforcement) is positively correlated with initial level of anxiety and negatively correlated with initial emotional adjustment. In other words, anxiety and poor emotional adjustment should facilitate the conditioning process. Rank difference correlation coefficients were computed between the Taylor Anxiety Score and conditionability, and between the Q Sort Adjustment Score and conditionability. The data did not support the hypothesis—no significant relationship was found between conditionability and anxiety, or between conditionability and emotional adjustment for either experimental group.

EFFECT OF THERAPY CONDITIONING ON PERSONALITY TESTS

Reduction in anxiety and improvement in emotional adjustment as a result of the conditioning in therapy was predicted. Accordingly, pre- and posttherapy scores were compared on the Taylor Scale and on the Q Sort Adjustment Test. No significant changes were found. It was noted, nonetheless, that on the Q Sort both experimental groups showed improved adjustment, the change in each group, however, not being significantly different from that in the control group. This suggests that with a longer period of conditioning—i.e., more or lengthier interviews—adjustment scores may be significantly increased.

To determine whether the conditioning of self-references *within* therapy would generalize to self-references *outside* of therapy, pre- and posttherapy scores were compared on the Adjective Self Description Test and on the Sentence Completion Test. Again, no significant changes were found.

Thus, it may be concluded from the data that the effect of the reinforcing stimuli was confined to the interview itself.

CONSISTENCY OF PERSONALITY IN INTERVIEW AND TESTS

By correlating the S's responses to the four psychological tests with his *unconditioned* responses in quasi therapy, i.e., in Interview 1, it was possible to measure the consistency of personality. As would be anticipated, the data shows considerable, though by no means complete, personality consistency. The well adjusted person, it was found, has less manifest anxiety and refers to himself in more favorable terms in the free-interview, as well as in adjectives and in sentence completions, than the less well-adjusted person. Similarly, the person who refers to himself most unfavorably in the free-interview talks least. These, of course, are hardly revelations, being common clinical observations by psychotherapists. It may be somewhat comforting to clinicians, however, to have objective confirmation of some of their views.

EXPERIMENTAL SS' AWARENESS OF THE CONDITIONING

"Awareness" was operationally defined as an explicit statement by S that the interviewer responded with "Mm-hm" or with a nod whenever S made a positive (or negative) self-reference. From the recordings of the structured interviews, it was determined that not a single S was aware of the head-nod conditioning; no one even mentioned it. Since Ss in the main tended to avoid looking at the interviewer during the therapy interviews, this is not surprising. As for the "Mm-hm" conditioning, only 2 of the 24 experimental Ss met the operational criterion for awareness, although 23 of them reported that they had noticed the "Mm-hm." Most of the latter interpreted the sound as a positive, rewarding response, signifying one or more of the following: a sign of encouragement or approval from the interviewer; an indication that the interviewer was listening, interested in, in agreement with or understanding of what S was talking about; or a sign that S was "on the right track" in talking about his personality characteristics rather than about extraneous matters. In short, while denying more categorical influence by the interviewer and failing to connect the "Mm-hm" with the specific verbal response class which it followed, they described the "Mm-hm" as a kind of generalized reinforcer which, by encouraging or reassuring them, helped them to continue talking or to remain on the over-all topic of their personality.

A few Ss interpreted "Mm-hm" idiosyncratically: one thought it meant different things at different times—that the interviewer agreed with him, wanted him to speed up, or wanted him to change the topic. Another thought that it sometimes was meant as agreement and encouragement to continue with the topic, sometimes as a sign that he should drop the topic, and sometimes "to distract me." A third felt that it occurred "in disconnected places." A fourth held that it was intended "to get me off balance and upset my thinking . . . you were trying to see if I was easily disturbed."

Some Ss insisted that they were entirely uninfluenced by the interviewer's "Mm-hm." One, affirming that the "Mm-hms" had had no effect on him, asserted, "I was just talking what I felt. I didn't care whether you agreed with me or not." Another declared, "I think if you had walked out of the room and given me the mike and stop-watch and asked me to talk for ten minutes about myself, I would have said exactly the same thing."

The single S who did not report that he had even noticed the "Mm-hms" declared that the interviewer was paying no attention at all to what he was saying but was focusing solely on his bodily manifestations of emotional tension.

It will be remembered that in the therapy interviews with the control group, the experimenter made no response whatsoever to S's verbalizations except the generalized response of attention. The twelve subjects in this group unanimously asserted that the experimenter had in no way influenced their verbalizations.

In their reaction to the experimenter, however, they fell into two subgroups: those who reported that they pretty much ignored his presence, and those who reported that they were sensitive to his presence. The latter felt the experimenter was observing them closely either to detect signs of "nervousness" or "to analyze" what they were saying. The former tended to describe themselves as so absorbed by their self-verbalizations that they rapidly became oblivious to the presence of the experimenter.

DISCUSSION

The major finding of this experiment, that S's verbalizations are influenced by an interviewer's reinforcements, is consistent with the evidence already accumulating in human operant conditioning investigations. This finding has considerable relevance for psychotherapy since changes in patient verbalizations are characteristically adduced as proof of personality change via psychotherapy. The various schools of psychotherapy generally attribute such changes primarily to monadic, intrapsychic events in the patient; ignoring, denying, or minimizing the immediate influence of the therapist. Even when they do acknowledge it, they typically fail to specify how the therapist is instrumental in determining the nature of the material elicited from the patient or the directions in which the patient changes. Since both positive and negative self-references were shown to be modifiable by interviewer reinforcement, one may ask if such changes signify, for example, changes in the Self, as the Rogerians assert, or if they are correlated with more general changes in the patient's motivational and attitudinal characteristics? Can one expect changes in behavior, verbal or otherwise, outside therapy to be correlated with verbal changes in therapy?

The present experiment suggests that the influence of minimal reinforcements, such as "Mm-hm," is restricted to the interview itself, for there were no correlative alterations of non-interview self-references or of personality test scores. Thus, as Winder (1957) put it, "One line of thought would consider psychotherapy as a complex and not always efficient conditioning process in which the patient learns to talk differently and little else." The present data may be construed as supporting such a generalization. On the other hand, psychotherapists could argue that personality modification results only from intensive and prolonged therapy and is not to be expected from a few short interviews.

The finding that conditioning took place without awareness (all Ss were unaware of the head-nod conditioning and all but two were unaware of the "Mm-hm" conditioning) confirms what most verbal conditioning studies have previously found. It thus appears that changes in verbal behavior can be produced without S knowing that his behavior has been manipulated.

Since the data did not show a relationship between conditionability and initial level of either anxiety or emotional adjustment, no light is cast on the question of what personality variables in S facilitate or impede verbal conditioning. The results regarding anxiety conflict with those of Taffel (1955), whose data confirmed the thesis that anxiety connotes heightened responsiveness to stimuli. He found a positive relationship between manifest anxiety and conditionability. The fact that his Ss were hospitalized psychiatric patients while the present ones were "normals" may account for this discrepancy. Presumably, his Ss had higher anxiety, and the mean level of anxiety here may not have been of sufficient magnitude to exercise a discriminatory effect on conditionability.

As Krasner stated (1955, p. 21), "It sounds like the simplest and most axiomatic thing to say about psychotherapy, but it would seem reasonable to assume that the factor of the therapist listening, paying attention, showing some interest, is a basic and indispensable variable of the therapeutic situation." From the experimenter's experience with the control group, however, where he sat silently, making no response throughout the therapy, and where the majority of the Ss reported themselves so absorbed in their own verbalizations that they became oblivious of his presence, he is tempted to challenge this axiom. Certainly, it would be worth investigating whether or not Ss could verbalize as productively in the absence of an "interviewer" and whether the character of such verbalizations would differ systematically from those made with an interviewer present.

An equally heretical notion is that a form of psychotherapy might be devised which did not require the "therapist" to acquire clinical knowledge and training but merely to learn how to administer simple reinforcements (like "Mm-hm") to specified classes of verbal response! If subsequent investigations were to disclose a significant relationship between conditioning of particular classes of verbal response in the interview and desirable changes in personality test scores, it might well be that a simple verbal conditioning technique could be advantageously employed for circumscribed therapeutic purposes.

It may be argued that the quasi therapy was more quasi than therapy and that, therefore, the findings have little but analogic meaning for psychotherapy. Certainly, the situation was not structured to S as therapy, but rather as a laboratory experiment in personality. The Ss themselves had not, ostensibly, sought therapy. On the other hand, the task for the S was almost identical with that in psychotherapy; to talk about his characteristics and traits and how he felt about them. Moreover, the behavior of the interviewer —listening attentively, nodding his head, saying "Mm-hm" at times, or saying nothing—was characteristic behavior for all therapists at least some of the time. Furthermore, the experiment did what other verbal conditioning experiments have not done, that is, dealt with areas of conflict (negative self-references), which is genuinely relevant to psychotherapy.

The demonstration that experiments in operant conditioning can be performed in therapy-like situations suggests the extension of such experimentation to actual psychotherapy. Tentative beginnings in this direction have been made with psychotics (Lindsley & Skinner, 1954; King, Merrell, Lovinger & Denny, 1957). It seems proven that at least some aspects of the complex phenomena represented by psychotherapy are amenable to behavioral analysis and experimental manipulation. Further investigations utilizing operant conditioning designs are indicated since such experimental designs appear to have heuristic value.

SUMMARY

The purpose of this experiment was to test the hypotheses that an interviewer can produce changes in a S's self-reference verbalizations by applying simple reinforcements, and that such reinforcements can alter a S's concept of himself.

The experiment consisted of setting up a quasi-therapy situation by conducting a series of free interviews with individual Ss in which operant self-reference verbalizations were reinforced with a simultaneous "Mm-hm" and head-nod. All interviews were tape recorded. A battery of four personality tests, two designed to induce "set" and two chosen as measures of anxiety and emotional adjustment, was administered prior and subsequent to the therapy. Finally, a structured interview, likewise tape recorded, was conducted to ascertain the S's awareness of the conditioning.

Ss were 36 male university students in an introductory psychology course, randomly assigned to two experimental groups (one conditioned for positive and the other for negative self-references) and to a control group (not conditioned). A total of 216 ten-minute therapy interviews (6 per S) were recorded and a detailed content analysis of self-references made. Scoring reliabilities were established by correlating ratings of independent judges. The results were as follows:

1. Operant conditioning of verbal behavior in a quasi-therapy situation was demonstrated by establishing, beyond the .01 level, that negative self-references could be increased by interpolating simple reinforcing stimuli and that such conditioning could be accomplished without the S's awareness. It was further shown, beyond the .01 level, that whereas positive self-references without reinforcement tended to extinguish themselves in quasi-therapy, with reinforcement their extinction could be arrested, this too without the S's awareness.

2. Conditionability was not related to initial level of either anxiety or emotional adjustment.

3. Successful conditioning of self-references in therapy did not modify self-references outside of therapy or alter scores on tests of anxiety or emotional adjustment, indicating that the effect of the reinforcing stimuli was confined to therapy itself.

4. Consistency of personality was shown by Ss' unconditioned responses in therapy and in psychological tests.

REFERENCES

DOLLARD, J., & MOWRER, O. H. A method of measuring tension in written documents. *J. abnorm. soc. Psychol.*, 1947, **42**, 3–32.

GREENSPOON, J. The reinforcing effect of two spoken sounds on the frequency of two responses. *Amer. J. Psychol.*, 1955, **68**, 409–416.

KING, G. F., MERRELL, D. W., LOVINGER, E., & DENNY, M. R. Operant motor behavior in acute schizophrenics. *J. Pers.*, 1957, **25**, 317–26.

KRASNER, L. The use of generalized reinforcers in psychotherapy research. *Psychol. Rep.*, 1955, **1**, 19–25.

LINDSLEY, O. R., & SKINNER, B. F. A method for the experimental analysis of the behavior of psychotic patients. *Amer. Psychologist*, 1954, **9**, 419–420. (Abstract)

RAIMY, V. C. Self-reference in counseling interviews. *J. consult. Psychol.*, 1948, **12**, 153–163.

ROGERS, C. R. *Client-centered therapy.* New York: Houghton Mifflin, 1951.

ROGERS, C. R., & DYMOND, ROSALIND (Eds.) *Psychotherapy and personality change.* Chicago: Univer. of Chicago Press, 1954.

TAFFEL, C. Anxiety and the conditioning of verbal behavior. *J. abnorm. soc. Psychol.*, 1955, **51**, 496–501.

TAYLOR, J. A. A personality scale of manifest anxiety. *J. abnorm. soc. Psychol.*, 1953, **48**, 285–290.

WINDER, C. L. Psychotherapy. *Annu. Rev. Psychol.*, 1957, **8**, 309–330.

Verbal Manipulation in a

Psychotherapeutic Relationship[1]

Henry C. Rickard, Patrick J. Dignam[2] and Robert F. Horner

Veterans Administration Hospital, Tuscaloosa, Alabama

PROBLEM

Numerous verbal conditioning studies have been reported in the literature and excellent reviews of the area are available (2, 3). The writers have been unable to locate, however, a single study reporting verbal conditioning in an actual therapeutic treatment case. This paper reports the manipulation of verbal behavior in a 60 year old male who has been hospitalized continuously for over twenty years. The patient was verbose, expressing

Reprinted from *Journal of Clinical Psychology*, 1960, 16, 364–367.

[1] Appreciation is extended to Dr. M. Dinoff and Dr. E. O. Timmons for critical readings of the manuscript.

[2] Now at Florida State Hospital, Hollywood, Florida.

freely delusions of grandeur and persecution. It was decided that rational speech would be designated as the dependent variable to be increased while the verbalization of delusions would be ignored or mildly punished. In other words, a direct attempt was made to reduce a specific class of deviant verbal behavior; no attempt was made to cope with underlying attitudes, dynamics, or feelings.

PROCEDURE

Three different Es worked with the S in the experiments to be described. In Experiment I the patient was seen for 35 sessions each of which was 45 minutes in duration. Sixteen of the sessions were tape recorded and later timed by E 1 for minutes of rational speech. The delusional systems in the S were easily identified.[3] E 1 turned away from the S, gazed at the floor, looked out the window, etc., while the S's speech was delusional. This procedure was operationally defined as mild "punishment." E 1 reinforced all rational verbalizations at a rate of from six to ten reinforcements per minute. Reinforcement was grossly defined as a smile, nod, exclamation expressing interest, etc. Since resistance to extinction of the response class "rational verbalization" was desired, an attempt was made to place the response under a lower partial reinforcement schedule during the last 5 sessions. Reinforcement was cut in frequency from approximately 8 per minute to less than 1 per minute.

In Experiment II the same S was used and, again, rational verbalization was the class of behavior to be reinforced. At this point a second experimenter (E 2) saw the patient once a week for approximately 6 additional months and followed the same conditioning procedure used in Experiment I. No attempt was made to record the data during this period. After 6 months, delusional material was still prominent in the patient's verbalizations, but contrary to earlier sessions it seemed evident that the delusional stream could be turned on and off by experimental manipulation. To test this hypothesis the patient was subjected to alternating 10 minute periods of "minimal reinforcement" and "maximal reinforcement." The former consisted of E 2 aperiodically directing his gaze toward the patient (who always maintained a steady flow of speech) at the rate of three times per minute, smiling, and saying "um-hum." This "minimal reinforcement" was administered regardless of what the patient might be saying at the time and was designed to maintain rapport and keep the patient from becoming too uncomfortable. During "maximal" reinforcement, delusional verbalizations by the S were interrupted; the experimenter encouraged the expression of non-delusional material of known valence to the S. E 2 saw the S for four 30 minute sessions over a period of two weeks, during which the S was exposed to alternating periods of "minimal" and "maximal" reinforcement.

---

[3] Examples of delusional speech were as follows: "I have a fractured head and a broken nose because of spinal pressure." "Stars have metal bottoms and exert a magnetic pressure on the earth."

After the fourth session *E* 3 was introduced to the *S* and the above procedure replicated.

RESULTS

In Experiment I the patient initially gave approximately two minutes of rational speech per 45 minute session. By the 21st session this had jumped to approximately 25 minutes of rational speech. The mean number of minutes of rational speech for the 21st through the 31st sessions was 30 minutes with a range from 8 to 44 minutes. It should be noted that during the period of time that Experiment I was being carried out, ward personnel were instructed to essentially ignore the patient when he was delusional on the ward, but to elicit and reinforce rational speech through questions, smiles, etc. It was hoped that this procedure, which was very similar to that followed by *E* 1, would promote maximal generalization from psychotherapy to the ward environment. Generalization from the ward treatment back to the psychotherapy sessions is an equally tenable hypothesis. At the beginning of the 31st session the *S* was put on a lowered schedule of reinforcement. For the remaining 5 sessions a sharp, progressive decrement in amount of rational speech resulted; an average of only 7 minutes of rational speech occurred during the last two 45 minute sessions. The rapid drop in

TABLE 1

MINUTES OF RATIONAL SPEECH EMITTED DURING ALTERNATING
10-MINUTE PERIODS OF MINIMAL AND MAXIMAL REINFORCEMENT

10-Minute Periods		*E* 2	*E* 3
1st Session	1	1*	1*
	2	9	8
	3	8*	1*
2nd Session	1	9	10*
	2	5*	10
	3	9	5*
3rd Session	1	9*	10
	2	10	5*
	3	9*	10
4th Session	1	10	8*
	2	10*	10
	3	10	9*

* Represents minimal reinforcement periods.

rational speech when a lower partial reinforcement schedule was attempted, the fluctuating nature of the dependent variable, and the fact that a full session of rational material was never achieved, demonstrates the tremendous resistance to the extinction of the delusional verbalizations.

The results of Experiment II are presented in Table 1. It is obvious that, initially, rational material was expressed at a very low level to the new experimenter (E 2), during periods of minimal reinforcement. Apparent also, is the fact that E 2 very quickly elicited a high percentage of rational speech during the maximal reinforcement period. The acquisition of rational verbalizations during periods of minimal reinforcement was less rapid. Table 1 also shows the second phase of Experiment II in which another experimenter (E 3) participated. It is apparent that both phases of Experiment II show similar trends. There is a suggestion that the dependent variable was expressed at a lower level to E 3 as compared to E 2 during the minimal reinforcement period.

DISCUSSION

The results of Experiment I strongly suggest that in a structured psychotherapeutic relationship a selected class of verbal behavior can be modified through reinforcement techniques. It is further indicated, however, that this modification may be quite tenuous, existing only under a high frequency of reinforcement. Attempts to place the dependent variable on a lower frequency of reinforcement and thus build a habit which would show substantial resistance to extinction (1) resulted in rational verbalizations dropping to a very low level.

At the time Experiment II was initiated it had become a simple matter to manipulate the dependent variable through elicitation and reinforcement. It was then demonstrated that the patient could be conditioned to increasing amounts of rational speech during reinforcement periods over a series of alternating periods of minimal and maximal reinforcement. The fact that the S tended to talk more rationally to E 2 than to E 3 can be viewed in different ways. Perhaps E 2 possessed more reinforcement value since he had previously seen the patient in a therapeutic relationship. On the other hand, it might simply be that E 2 could more easily initiate topics which would lead to rational speech since he had greater knowledge of the patient. The S's responses to both Es in Experiment II clearly show a progressive increment in the amount of rational speech for the 10 minute periods. In addition, learning in the maximal reinforcement periods apparently generalized to the minimal reinforcement periods. It should be noted that when E 3 began working with the S the dependent variable dropped 90 per cent. Apparently the learned habit of rational responding to E 2 was disrupted by the radical "cue change" of a new experimenter.

A high level of rational speech was obtained in this patient through elicitation and reinforcement techniques. It is apparent, however, that the newly established behavior showed little resistance to extinction in either experiment. This is not too surprising since the incompatible habit, verbalization of delusional material, had been reinforced over a long period of time and under a wide range of stimulus conditions. Various other attempts could be made to build in the desired verbal behavior. For example, a series of experimenters could repeat the procedure followed by E 2 and E 3 in the expectation that generalization of the rational verbalizations to the stimulus class "other people" would eventually be enhanced.

SUMMARY

Rational verbalizations in a neuropsychiatric patient were chosen at the class of behavior to reinforce while an effort was made not to reinforce the incompatible class, delusional material. E 1 conditioned the dependent variable, rational speech, to a high level of occurrence under a high frequency of reinforcement, but the conditioned response dropped sharply when an attempt was made to lower the frequency of reinforcement. E 2 exposed the same S to alternating ten minute periods of "minimal" and "maximal" reinforcement and demonstrated conditioning of the same dependent variable. E 3 replicated the procedure which E 2 had followed and obtained similar results.

REFERENCES

1. JENKINS, W. O. and STANLEY, J. C. Partial reinforcement: a review and critique. *Psychol. Bull.*, 1950, **27**, 193–234.
2. KRASNER, L. Studies of the conditioning of verbal behavior. *Psychol. Bull.*, 1958, **55**, 148–170.
3. SALZINGER, K. Experimental manipulation of verbal behavior: a review. *J. gen. Psychol.*, 1959, **61**, 65–94.

Modification of Behavior Through Verbal

Conditioning: Effects in Group Therapy[1]

Leonard P. Ullmann, Leonard Krasner, and Beverly J. Collins

Veterans Administration Hospital, Palo Alto, California

A recent conference on research in psychotherapy (Rubinstein & Parloff, 1959) pointed up the difficulties of validating the effectiveness of psychotherapy by the current methods of assessing change in behavior. The number of relevant variables in the therapy situation is such that even random assignment of cases to treatment or no treatment groups (Fairweather,

Reprinted from *Journal of Abnormal and Social Psychology*, 1961, 62, 128–132.

[1] From the Psychology Research Laboratory, Veterans Administration Hospital, Palo Alto, California. This investigation was supported in part by Research Grant M-2458, National Institute of Mental Health, United States Public Health Service.

Simon, Gebhard, Weingarten, Holland, Sanders, Stone, & Reahl, 1960; Rogers & Dymond, 1954) does not guarantee that differences obtained may be reasonably associated with the form of *treatment* as distinct from either the *practitioner* or the unique interaction among the variables in the situation. Rather than attempting to assess the value of the total therapy situation, it seems more efficient first to isolate the behaviors of the therapist and the patient which are characteristic of the psychotherapy situation. Then these characteristic behaviors may be systematically manipulated in order to test hypotheses about the psychotherapeutic process. Among these hypotheses are: (*a*) that one person can influence the behavior of another in a predictable direction; (*b*) that this change has a desirable effect on behavior in a second, criterion situation; and (*c*) that as far as possible, the changed behavior in the criterion situation is associated with a specific aspect of the already circumscribed behavior of the experimenter.

The first point, that one person can influence another person's verbal behavior in a specifiable manner, may be accepted as reasonably well established by the studies of operant verbal conditioning reviewed by Krasner (1958) and Salzinger (1959). It is primarily to the second point, the change of subjects' behavior in a situation other than the experimental one, that this article is addressed. Relevant studies in which behavior has been manipulated in one situation and the effect of this manipulation has been measured in a second may be roughly categorized into three types: motor operant conditioning, verbal operant conditioning, and "psychotherapy."

Motor operant conditioning techniques as a means of deliberate "therapeutic" manipulation of patient behavior has been employed in a series of recent investigations (King, Merrell, Lovinger, & Denny, 1957; Lindsley & Skinner, 1954; Peters, 1952; Peters & Jenkins, 1954; Tilton, 1957). In these studies, motor operant conditioning was purposefully used as a therapeutic technique to bring patients into more active contact with reality.

In the verbal conditioning literature, reports on generalization effects are infrequent. The usual procedure has been to present a series of test-like tasks prior to and immediately following a verbal conditioning session, and then to ascertain changes in these tests. For example, Williams (1959) used as his pre- and post-measures an "interpersonal check-list" and the Osgood Semantic Differential Scale. In one of his experimental groups, "feeling statements" were reinforced; in a second experimental group, "nonfeeling statements" were reinforced. The experimental situation itself was presented to the subjects as "psychotherapy." Although use of the reinforced verbal classes was increased during the experimental sessions, there were no significant differences between groups on the pre- and posttest measures. Using a similar design, Rogers (1960) also reported significant effects of conditioning but failure to obtain generalization as measured by a battery of four personality tests. However, Sarason (1957) did report significant generalization effects as measured by a "free word naming" situation before and after a verbal conditioning situation.

The "psychotherapy" studies generally involve the use of a series of psychological measures before and after a stated "treatment" period (Rogers & Dymond, 1954). Some studies (Grossman, 1952; Keet, 1948) make use of a specified number of experimental sessions to test the effectiveness of a given therapeutic technique. There have been several discussions (Berg, 1952; Leary & Harvey, 1956; Miller, 1954) of the rationale of the use of such tests as projective techniques, rating scales, and Q sorts as measures of therapeutic effectiveness. Using a different criterion and one closer to the present study, Brown (1957), working with "chronic ward patients," used as his dependent measure responsiveness to an avoidance conditioning situation (paired tone and light stimuli alternately reinforced by a painful faradic shock). After the pre-experimental measures, half the patients were subjected to various psychotherapeutic manipulations, principally group therapy. The group that had received therapy was significantly more responsive to conditioning after therapy than before, whereas the control (no therapy) group showed no significant increase after the same period of time.

Where Brown used responsiveness to conditioning as a dependent variable, the present study used verbal operant conditioning sessions as the independent variable and ratings of behavior in group therapy as the dependent variable. The purpose of this design was the attempt to test two hypotheses basic to psychotherapy: that interpersonal interaction can lead to change in a desirable manner in a second, nonexperimental situation, and that the observed change may be associated with a specific aspect of the experimenter's behavior.

METHOD

Three groups, each consisting of 10 male "continued treatment" patients at a VA neuropsychiatric hospital, served as subjects. At the start of the experiment the median age of the subjects was 35 (range: 21–47), the median education was 12 years (range: 7–16 years), and the median length of current hospitalization was 5 months (range: 1–133 months). On admission, 28 of the subjects had been diagnosed as schizophrenic reaction, one had been diagnosed as manic depressive, and one as depressive reaction. Each group was given the same experimental task, the experimenter's response being varied. All subjects were rated by group therapists before and after the experimental sessions.

Experimental task. Subjects were seen for two sessions per week for 2 weeks. The situation was structured to the patient as "a study into how people make up stories about pictures shown to them." In each session, the patients were shown four pictures and asked to make up stories to last for 5 minutes each. If responses lagged, the usual TAT instructions and encouragement were used by the experimenter. The picture stimuli used were line drawings of situations common to the experiences of patients in hospitals and were scenes such as buying a tie, mowing a lawn, fishing, buying a movie ticket, ordering a meal in a restaurant. The situations were selected to be commonplace and not emotionally arousing in themselves. This procedure minimized differential "card-pull" (Gurel & Ullmann, 1958; Ullmann, 1957a) and reduced the possibility that emotionally toned stimuli would alter verbal production in a schizophrenic sample (Ullmann, 1958). The use of less direct stimuli is in line with Krasner and Ullmann's (1958) suggestion that minimal cues (e.g., "mmm-hmm") about which the schizophrenic subject is less aware may be less threatening and therefore more effective in increasing and guiding his verbal behavior than overt examiner responses (e.g., "good-bad," "right-wrong," "true-false") which the schizophrenic may perceive as evaluative of his behavior.

Experimental groups. Each subject was assigned, in the manner described below, to one of three conditions. Once in a condition, the same examiner behavior was maintained throughout the four story-telling sessions, each of which involved four stories. That is, the pattern of examiner reinforcement started on the first trial of the first session. In the first condition, the *positive-personal* reinforcement group, the examiner responded to the verbal class to be reinforced by a head nod and the approving sound "mmmhmm." In the second group, the *impersonal-unstructured* reinforcement group, the examiner responded by pushing a button attached to an electric counter which emitted a loud click. The dial of the counter faced the patient, and he saw an increase in the number on the dial. At the end of each story, the counter was reset to zero. Questions about the meaning of the counter were answered with the phrase that it was one of the experimental measures. In the third group, the *no reinforcement* group, the experimenter made no responses to the stories told by the subjects.

Verbal class reinforced. The verbal class reinforced was "emotional words" as defined by Ullmann and McFarland (1957). There were two reasons for the selection of this group of words. The first was the relevance of such words to group therapy ratings. Ullmann (1957b) found that ability to express feeling resulting from social premises presented in a projective test was significantly correlated with group therapy scale ratings. Similarly, Ullmann and McFarland (1957) found that the number of emotional words used in response to TAT cards was highly correlated with the group therapy ratings. In terms of relevance, then, emotional words represent the sort of material that is produced in therapy and is of particular interest to psychotherapists. An increase in the use of emotional words in the experimental situation may be therapeutic in itself, or the practice of these words during experimental sessions may lead to an increase in their use in the group therapy situation. If either or both of these possibilities were the case, it could be hypothesized that an improvement in group therapy ratings would result.

A second reason for the use of emotional words was the high rater reliability previously obtained in the use of this class of verbal behavior. In the original work with TAT protocols (Ullmann & McFarland, 1957), rater reliability was .92. Using a single "hearing" of 16 nonreinforced 4-minute tapes of college students, three raters (including the examiner in this study) obtained a coefficient of concordance significant beyond the .001 level (Weiss, Krasner, & Ullmann, 1960).

Dependent criterion measure. The dependent measure used was the Palo Alto Group Therapy Scale (GTS) (Finney, 1954). The GTS is an 88-item scale, checked by therapists for the patient's behavior during the most recent four therapy sessions. Finney (1954) reported that for 18 groups in a neuropsychiatric hospital a median rank order correlation of .84 was obtained between scale scores and global rankings of patients by group leaders. In the same study, a rank order correlation of .80 was obtained between the average ratings by 10 ward personnel of adequacy of interpersonal relationships throughout the hospital and the patients' GTS scores.

In the present study, five group therapists[2] on two wards completed GTS forms about their patients. The therapists knew that a number of conditions were involved in the experiment but not to which one the specific patient would be assigned. One of the authors scored the ratings and then assigned patients to the three experimental groups. A restriction on absolute randomness of patient assignment was that the means and standard devia-

[2] The authors wish to express their thanks to George Fairweather, Ben Finney, Ralph Forsyth, Sidney Gelfand, and Donald Lim for making the criterion ratings.

tions of the preratings for the three groups were kept as equal as possible. Another of the authors (BJC) was the examiner in all cases and did not know the subjects' GTS scores. Immediately after the last experimental session, the group therapist rerated the patient.[3] In all cases, the same therapist made both the pre- and post-GTS ratings.

RESULTS

The major results of the experiment are presented in Table 1. The means and standard deviations of the pre-experimental groups were not significantly different. The average gain $(\bar{x}_1 - \bar{x}_2)$ for the positive-personal reinforcement group was 5.70 GTS points; for the impersonal-unstructured

TABLE 1

MEANS AND STANDARD DEVIATIONS OF GROUP THERAPY RATINGS BEFORE AND AFTER STORY-TELLING UNDER THREE DIFFERENT REINFORCEMENT CONDITIONS

Type of Reinforcement	N	Pre-experimental		Post-experimental		r_{12}	$\bar{x}_1 - \bar{x}_2$	t
		$\bar{x}_1$	σ_1	$\bar{x}_2$	σ_2			
positive-personal	10	58.2	20.6	63.9	25.5	.94	5.70	1.83
impersonal-unstructured	10	56.8	18.4	57.8	21.1	.91	1.00	0.43
no reinforcement	10	61.0	20.0	61.5	21.1	.89	0.50	0.15

reinforcement group, it was 1.00 GTS points, and for the no reinforcement group, it was 0.50 GTS points. Finally, the own-control change was at the .05 level (one-tailed test) for the positive-personal reinforcement group $(t = 1.83)$, whereas it was not significant $(t = 0.34$ and $0.15)$ for the other two groups.

Clinically, these results may be presented in the following manner: Five of the 10 subjects in the positive-personal reinforcement group gained 10 or more GTS points; whereas 2 of the 10 subjects in the impersonal-unstructured reinforcement group gained this much, and only 1 of the 10 subjects in the no reinforcement group gained 10 or more GTS points.

DISCUSSION

The results of this study will be discussed in terms of hypotheses that are basic to interpreting psychotherapeutic interactions. One of these hypotheses is that the effect of such an interaction is measurable in an independent criterion situation. The frequency of use in projective situations of the verbal class conditioned in this study, emotional words, had previously been demonstrated to be significantly correlated with GTS scores (Ullmann

[3] The time between pre- and postratings averaged 14.80 days with a standard deviation of 3.31 days.

& McFarland, 1957). The relevance of the use of emotional words to group therapy ratings may explain why positive results were obtained in this study. Further, the evidence for the validity of the criterion used in this study (Finney, 1954) and the fact that the ratings depended on actual interpersonal behavior add to the pertinence of the criterion as a measure of the effectiveness of interpersonal interactions.

In terms of amount of change, it is interesting to note the relatively brief period of time (80 minutes) involved in the experiment itself. In addition, these results were obtained within an ongoing hospital treatment program which may well have increased within-group variance.[4] Despite this evidence for the therapeutic effectiveness of verbal conditioning, however, there are considerations that limit the generalizations to be drawn. On the one hand, the technique is not pertinent to regressed patients who cannot tell stories. Such patients are ones who might have been successfully approached by motor operant conditioning techniques (King et al., 1957; Lindsley & Skinner, 1954). With highly verbal or more "normal" subjects—college students, for example—it is possible to hypothesize that the practice of speech in general and emotional words in particular would be less effective because these subjects have less need for additional practice in emotional expressiveness. It is therefore hypothesized that the effectiveness of verbal conditioning as a "therapeutic" technique may well be useful only with people in a particular segment of the continuum of mental health.

The results of this study also lend support to the proposition that the changes in criterion measures ascribed to psychotherapy may be associated with specifiable therapist behaviors. Evidence for this concept stems from the three experimental groups used. In both the no reinforcement and the impersonal-unstructured reinforcement groups, the amount of additional personal contact with the patients matched that of the positive-personal reinforcement group. The use of the clicker-counter in the impersonal-unstructured reinforcement group matched the additional attention called to emotional words. Such additional cuing, by itself, did not yield a significant gain in group therapy scale ratings. Therefore, within the limits of the present design, there is evidence that positive-personal reinforcing behavior of the examiner was an important factor associated with the significant change in group therapy scores.

It is possible to hypothesize that the amount and direction of change measured by the criterion should be positively correlated with change in the experimental situation in the use of the reinforced verbal class. The design of the present study did not permit a test of this hypothesis. All experimental trials were reinforced, that is, there were no nonreinforced

---

[4] An idea of the uncontrolled variation present within an ongoing treatment program may be obtained by considering why subjects on whom pre-experimental ratings had been made did not complete the experiment: Eight of the men either failed to come to appointments, or when they came, were not cooperative in story-telling; four moved to different wards; three left the hospital; two men underwent extensive and painful dental work that interfered with story-telling; two were lost to the study when the group therapist moved to a different ward, and procedures were not completed with one man because the examiner broke her leg. In terms of the criterion pre-experimental ratings, these 20 men were not significantly different from the 30 who did complete the experiment. The average GTS rating of the 20 men who did not complete the experiment was 61.4 with a standard deviation of 20.9.

operant trials. This was done to avoid the extinction effect on schizophrenics of unreinforced trials which might have decreased the chance of obtaining change on the dependent measure. Other reasons for the decision made in this study were the failure of Rogers (1960) and Williams (1959) to obtain generalization effects after having obtained significant conditioning, and the attempt to design an analogue of psychotherapy in which the therapist is likely to give immediate reinforcement to the patient's first emission of the desired verbal behavior. Finally, the hypothesis of the positive correlation between change in use of the verbal class during experimental sessions and change on the criterion may be oversimplified. It may well be that the important thing learned was the permissibility of spontaneously using emotional words in an interpersonal situation rather than practice in the use of the words per se.

Beyond the evidence for specific hypotheses which underlie psychotherapy, the present paper illustrates the use of verbal conditioning as a miniature situation for the study of interpersonal behavior (Krasner, 1955). Verbal conditioning may be used both as a dependent variable to measure the effects of various experimental conditions on responsiveness to reinforcement, or, as in this study, as the independent variable. In either case, the verbal conditioning situation permits the reduction and isolation of interpersonal variables with a resultant increase in the opportunity for their systematic study.

SUMMARY

This study used a verbal conditioning situation to investigate hypotheses relevant to psychotherapeutic interactions. Neuropsychiatric patients who were receiving group therapy participated in four story-telling sessions during which emotional words were reinforced in one of the following three ways: a positive-personal manner, an impersonal-unstructured manner, and not reinforced at all. Ratings made by group therapists before and after the experimental story-telling sessions indicated a significant gain in adequacy of interpersonal relationships in group therapy for the group receiving positive-personal reinforcement. There was no significant gain for the other two groups on this criterion measure. The results support the hypotheses that one person can influence another person in a positive way and that this change may be measurable by an independent criterion situation. Further, this change in the subject's behavior may be demonstrated to be associated with specific behavior on the part of the experimenter.

REFERENCES

Berg, I. Measures before and after therapy. *J. clin. Psychol.*, 1952, 8, 46–50.

Brown, C. C. Changes in avoidance conditioning following psychotherapeutic treatment. *J. nerv. ment. Dis.*, 1957, 125, 487–489.

Fairweather, G. W., Simon, R., Gebhard, M. E., Weingarten, E., Holland, J. L., Sanders, R., Stone, G. B., & Reahl, J. Relative effectiveness of psychotherapeutic programs: A multicriteria comparison of four programs for three different patient groups. *Psychol. Monogr.*, 1960, 74(5, Whole No. 492).

FINNEY, B. C. A scale to measure interpersonal relationships in group therapy. *Group Psychother.*, 1954, **7**, 52–66.

GROSSMAN, D. An experimental investigation of a psychotherapeutic technique. *J. consult. Psychol.*, 1952, **16**, 325–331.

GUREL, L., & ULLMANN, L. P. Quantitative differences in response to TAT cards: The relationship between transcendence score and number of emotional words. *J. proj. Tech.*, 1958, **22**, 399–401.

KEET, C. D. Two verbal techniques in a miniature counseling situation. *Psychol. Monogr.*, 1948, **62**,(7, Whole No. 294).

KING, G. F., MERRELL, D. W., LOVINGER, E., & DENNY, M. R. Operant motor behavior in acute schizophrenics. *J. Pers.*, 1957, **25**, 317–326.

KRASNER, L. The use of generalized reinforcers in psychotherapy research. *Psychol. Rep.*, 1955, **1**, 19–25.

KRASNER, L. Studies of the conditioning of verbal behavior. *Psychol. Bull.*, 1958, **55**, 148–170.

KRASNER, L., & ULLMANN, L. P. Variables in the verbal conditioning of schizophrenic subjects. *Amer. Psychologist,* 1958, **13**, 358. (Abstract)

LEARY, T., & HARVEY, JOAN S. A methodology for measuring personality changes in psychotherapy. *J. clin. Psychol.*, 1956, **12**, 123–132.

LINDSLEY, O. R., & SKINNER, B. F. A method for the experimental analysis of the behavior of psychotic patients. *Amer. Psychologist,* 1954, **9**, 419–420. (Abstract)

MILLER, J. G. Criteria and measurement of change during psychiatric treatment. *Bull. Menninger Clin.*, 1954, **18**, 130–137.

PETERS, H. N. An experimental evaluation of learning vs. therapy in schizophrenia. *Amer. Psychologist,* 1952, **7**, 354. (Abstract)

PETERS, H. N., & JENKINS, R. L. Improvement of chronic schizophrenic patients with guided problem-solving motivated by hunger. *Psychiat. Quart. Suppl.*, 1954, **28**, 84–101.

ROGERS, C. R., & DYMOND, ROSALIND F. (Eds.) *Psychotherapy and personality change.* Chicago: Univer. Chicago Press, 1954.

ROGERS, J. M. Operant conditioning in a quasi-therapy setting. *J. abnorm. soc. Psychol.*, 1960, **60**, 247–252.

RUBINSTEIN, E. A., & PARLOFF, M. B. (Eds.) *Research in psychotherapy.* Washington, D.C.: American Psychological Association, 1959.

SALZINGER, K. Experimental manipulation of verbal behavior: A review. *J. gen. Psychol.*, 1959, **61**, 65–94.

SARASON, BARBARA R. The effects of verbally conditioned response classes on post-conditioning tasks. *Dissertation Abstr.*, 1957, **12**, 679. (Abstract)

TILTON, J. R. The use of instrumental motor and verbal learning techniques in the treatment of chronic schizophrenics. Unpublished doctoral dissertation, Michigan State University, 1957.

ULLMANN, L. P. Productivity and the clinical use of TAT cards. *J. proj. Tech.*, 1957, **21**, 399–403. (a)

ULLMANN, L. P. Selection of neuropsychiatric patients for group psychotherapy. *J. consult. Psychol.*, 1957, **21**, 277–280. (b)

ULLMANN, L. P. Clinical correlates of facilitation and inhibition of response to emotional stimuli. *J. proj. Tech.*, 1958, **22**, 341–347.

ULLMANN, L. P., & McFARLAND, R. L. Productivity as a variable in TAT protocols: A methodological study. *J. proj. Tech.*, 1957, **21**, 80–87.

WEISS, R. L., KRASNER, L., & ULLMANN, L. P. Responsivity to verbal conditioning as a function of emotional atmosphere and pattern of reinforcement. *Psychol. Rep.*, 1960, **6**, 415–426.

WILLIAMS, R. I. Verbal conditioning in psychotherapy. *Amer. Psychologist,* 1959, **14**, 388. (Abstract)

PART ELEVEN

Commitment and

Conformity

Imagine driving an automobile into a crowded parking lot. You start to back the car into an empty stall, and as you look through the rear window you see two things: your rear fender looks as if it is about to hit the car parked next to you, yet the lot attendant continues to wave you on. What do you do? Do you back up further or pull out of the slot? The answer, of course, will depend on many factors—your driving skill, your confidence in the attendant's judgment, the age of your car, whether the stall was the last empty one, and so on. The example has some interesting aspects, but the general case is even more intriguing. People are often in situations where others ask them to do or say things with which they don't agree; when do they listen to the others and when do they rely on their own judgment? This question is one of many that fall into the general study of conformity.

There is a long history of speculation and analysis concerning the nature of man's social relations. It is only quite recently, however, that social psychologists have sought to isolate and explore, one by one, the factors that shape social influence. The pioneering studies in this field were reported by Muzafer Sherif in 1935.[1] He capitalized on the phenomenon of the auto-kinetic effect, where a small stationary light in an otherwise dark room appears to move. Sherif asked subjects, alone or in groups, to estimate how far the light was "moving." He found that when people in groups estimated the movements, they tended to consolidate on a norm, and that the group's influence affected the individuals' judgments even after the group disbanded.

Asch's studies continued the investigation of group influence on judgment, but they differed from Sherif's. Instead of asking subjects to decide on the extent of apparent light movements, Asch had his subjects make a clear-cut unambiguous decision about the length of lines. Asch's experiments served several purposes. They provided a straightforward way of assessing a group's power over its members. They attempted to answer the question, "Will people defer to a group's judgment even if it means denying the testimony of their senses?" Asch found that although the question was simple,

[1] Muzafer Sherif, "A Study of Some Social Factors in Perception," *Archives of Psychology*, New York, 1935, No. 187.

the answer was complicated. Many people did yield; but no one yielded all the time, and a sizable proportion of the subjects remained totally independent.

This quantitative demonstration of group influence would have been a milestone in itself, but Asch's work went further. The critical subjects in the Asch experiments were limited in their choice of responses on any trial. They could agree with the group, moderately disagree, or strongly disagree. Whatever their choice, however, it could have been made for a variety of reasons. By carefully interviewing each subject after the group-pressure session, Asch was able to categorize and delimit several styles of response. These patterns or styles, it should be noted, are not hard and fast. They represent, after the fact, Asch's reasoned reconstructions based on the subjects' recollections and reports. Whether the subjects resisted or yielded for the reasons they verbalized can never be known, but the fruitfulness of Asch's speculations can be seen almost immediately. Since it is almost axiomatic that a single study cannot resolve an issue, the investigator must have some guide to the next step. The styles or patterns reported by the critical subjects provided Asch with these clues, and the rest of his paper reports the results of some of his subsequent studies testing the implications of the first experiment.

Asch's studies were interesting in their own right. Even more, they provided a technique for the study of conformity which permitted the easy incorporation of many additional variables. In point of fact, many additional variables have been studied with Asch's technique or its variations. So many variables have been investigated that we will limit the rest of the section to considerations of one factor, the degree to which the conforming subject is committed to his response.

Deutsch and Gerard approach the problem of influence and commitment by distinguishing two major reasons why people may agree with a group judgment: They may be using the group as a source of authority and evidence about the task (informational influence), or they may be complying to group pressures (normative influence). Although both of these processes may be operating on subjects in an Asch situation at any one time, the authors point out that the two sources of influence may not be uniform in their effects upon the yielding of the subjects. Their formulations incorporate the extent to which each subject is committed to his belief. In particular, Deutsch and Gerard are able to derive six hypotheses stemming from this distinction and test the first five of these by conducting an experiment with eight different groups of subjects which can be schematically illustrated as follows:

	No Commitment	Self-Commitment (regular pad)	Public Commitment (signed pad)
Face-to-Face	Condition 1	Condition 2	Condition 3
Anonymous	Condition 4	Condition 5	Condition 6
Anonymous	Condition 7— Group subjects were made to feel that they were a group.	Condition 8— Subjects used a "magic" pad instead of a regular one.	

In their results, Deutsch and Gerard find that group influence does, in fact, influence agreement with the group. But equally as striking is the way in which commitment affects the subjects. Public commitment to a response greatly reduces agreement with the group, and even private (self-commitment) has an appreciable effect upon group agreement.

The type of commitment discussed by Deutsch and Gerard was one in which subjects were committed, in writing, either to themselves or to the experimenter about a judgment on a particular trial. Gerard, however, wished to explore the effects of another aspect of commitment—commitment to behavioral consistency. As an Asch-type experimental session progresses, the critical subjects, by their responses, are declaring themselves to be either yielders or independents. This very declaration, which is established by the pattern of their responses, evokes a commitment from the subject. He has established justifications for his original pattern of responses, and he cannot easily change this pattern without sapping these justifications. In addition, he may wish to "save face" by maintaining his original stand; for to change it would be an admission that it was incorrect. This hypothesized tendency of people to remain consistent in their behavior should itself be affected by other factors. Gerard points out the ways in which public (face-to-face) versus private (anonymous) behavior evokes these consistency tendencies and presents an experiment which demonstrates these effects.

In the latter part of his paper, Gerard notes the resemblance of his consistency theorizing to similar ideas presented by experimenters in *cognitive dissonance*. The last paper in this section, by Festinger and Carlsmith, looks at consistency and compliance from a dissonance framework. Asch's work showed that, under social pressure, people could be influenced to make counterfactual statements; Gerard and Deutsch's following work explored the nature of this yielding and its relationship to commitment. Festinger and Carlsmith move one step forward in time and ask, "If we can force a subject to make a counterfactual response, what happens to his belief system as a result of his complying?" Although the immediate background of their study does not stem from Asch-type experiments, their experiment is certainly relevant to Asch-type findings.

Asch's technique is a useful one for analytically determining who complies and why. But Festinger and Carlsmith are not interested in producing experimental conditions in which subjects show differential compliance. Rather they wish to have conditions in which all subjects comply, but under different circumstances. Consequently, instead of using group pressures, they used a combination of money and subtle prodding by the experimenter to elicit from their subjects a job description that was patently untrue. The theory of cognitive dissonance led Festinger and Carlsmith to believe that the size of the inducement was one important variable on the effects of compliance. This variable provides the basis for their experimental arrangements, and their results show the operation of this factor.

The social nature of the conformity and compliance experiments lends itself to facile extrapolations—but these extensions are not unequivocal. Asch found that although many people yielded to the group, many others didn't. Deutsch and Gerard point out group pressures are far from being the only factor producing compliance. Gerard demonstrates that, under pressure, people may become more, rather than less, independent. Festinger and Carlsmith show that compliance produces belief change only when the compliance is elicited under certain specific, and in some ways surprising, circumstances. The conclusion at the end of the section is not the cynical, glib, and incorrect, "Every man has his price," but the realization that conformity and compliance, like most other psychological phenomena, although complex and not fully understood, are capable of rigorous and systematic investigation.

STUDY QUESTIONS

1. Asch states that the group is trying to pressure subjects into making a judgment that is counter to fact. How can Asch determine if subjects could make the correct judgments in the absence of group pressure? What would be the implications if the subjects could not make these judgments?
2. How does Asch's "late arrival of a 'true partner'" variation relate to and set the stage for Gerard's commitment study?
3. What are the differences between the face-to-face and anonymous conditions in the Deutsch and Gerard study? What did they test by establishing these conditions?
4. In the self-commitment conditions, why do Deutsch and Gerard feel the "magic pad" subjects responded differently from the regular pad subjects? How and why do the self-commitment subjects differ from the no-commitment subjects?
5. How does Gerard's use of the concept of commitment differ from the earlier use by Deutsch and Gerard? In what ways are the concepts similar?
6. How does the magnitude of the reward affect the person's dissonance after he has complied in making counterfactual statements?
7. Between what cognitions is there dissonance for the subjects in Festinger and Carlsmith's control condition? In the $1.00 condition? In the $20.00 condition? How do subjects in each condition reduce their dissonance?
8. The opposite of conformity is sometimes called deviance and sometimes, independence. In each of the first three studies, are the non-yielders deviates or independents? Are Festinger and Carlsmith's compliers conforming? If so, to what?

Effects of Group Pressure Upon the

Modification and Distortion of Judgments

S. E. Asch

Department of Psychology and Education, Swarthmore College

We shall here describe in summary form the conception and first findings of a program of investigation into the conditions of independence and submission to group pressure. This program is based on a series of earlier studies conducted by the writer while a Fellow of the John Simon Guggenheim Memorial Foundation. The earlier experiments and the theoretical issues which prompted them are discussed in a forthcoming work by the writer on social psychology.

Our immediate object was to study the social and personal conditions that induce individuals to resist or to yield to group pressures when the latter are perceived to be *contrary to fact*. The issues which this problem raises are of obvious consequence for society; it can be of decisive importance whether or not a group will, under certain conditions, submit to existing pressures. Equally direct are the consequences for individuals and our understanding of them, since it is a decisive fact about a person whether he possesses the freedom to act independently, or whether he characteristically submits to group pressures.

The problem under investigation requires the direct observation of certain basic processes in the interaction between individuals, and between individuals and groups. To clarify these seems necessary if we are to make fundamental advances in the understanding of the formation and reorganization of attitudes, of the functioning of public opinion, and of the operation of propaganda. Today we do not possess an adequate theory of these central psycho-social processes. Empirical investigation has been predominantly controlled by general propositions concerning group influence which have as a rule been assumed but not tested. With few exceptions investigation has relied upon descriptive formulations concerning the operation of suggestion and prestige, the inadequacy of which is becoming increasingly obvious, and upon schematic applications of stimulus-response theory.

The bibliography lists articles representative of the current theoretical and empirical situation. Basic to the current approach has been the axiom

Reprinted from H. Guetzkow (ed.), *Groups, Leadership, and Men* (Pittsburgh: Carnegie, 1951), 177–190.

that group pressures characteristically induce psychological changes *arbitrarily*, in far-reaching disregard of the material properties of the given conditions. This mode of thinking has almost exclusively stressed the slavish submission of individuals to group forces, has neglected to inquire into their possibilities for independence and for productive relations with the human environment, and has virtually denied the capacity of men under certain conditions to rise above group passion and prejudice. It was our aim to contribute to a clarification of these questions, important both for theory and for their human implications, by means of direct observation of the effects of groups upon the decisions and evaluations of individuals.

THE EXPERIMENT AND FIRST RESULTS

To this end we developed an experimental technique which has served as the basis for the present series of studies. We employed the procedure of placing an individual in a relation of radical conflict with all the other members of a group, of measuring its effect upon him in quantitative terms, and of describing its psychological consequences. A group of eight individuals was instructed to judge a series of simple, clearly structured perceptual relations—to match the length of a given line with one of three unequal lines. Each member of the group announced his judgments publicly. In the midst of this monotonous "test" one individual found himself suddenly contradicted by the entire group, and this contradiction was repeated again and again in the course of the experiment. The group in question had, with the exception of one member, previously met with the experimenter and received instructions to respond at certain points with wrong—and unanimous—judgments. The errors of the majority were large (ranging between ½″ and 1¾″) and of an order not encountered under control conditions. The outstanding person—the critical subject—whom we had placed in the position of a *minority of one* in the midst of a *unanimous majority*—was the object of investigation. He faced, possibly for the first time in his life, a situation in which a group unanimously contradicted the evidence of his senses.

This procedure was the starting point of the investigation and the point of departure for the study of further problems. Its main features were the following: (1) The critical subject was submitted to two contradictory and irreconcilable forces—the evidence of his own experience of an utterly clear perceptual fact and the unanimous evidence of a group of equals. (2) Both forces were part of the immediate situation; the majority was concretely present, surrounding the subject physically. (3) The critical subject, who was requested together with all others to state his judgments publicly, was obliged to declare himself and to take a definite stand vis-à-vis the group. (4) The situation possessed a self-contained character. The critical subject could not avoid or evade the dilemma by reference to conditions external to the experimental situation. (It may be mentioned at this point that the forces generated by the given conditions acted so quickly upon the critical subjects that instances of suspicion were rare.)

The technique employed permitted a simple quantitative measure of the "majority effect" in terms of the frequency of errors in the direction of the distorted estimates of the majority. At the same time we were concerned from the start to obtain evidence of the ways in which the subjects perceived the group, to establish whether they became doubtful, whether they were tempted to join the majority. Most important, it was our object to establish the grounds of the subject's independence or yielding—whether, for example, the yielding subject was aware of the effect of the majority upon him, whether he abandoned his judgment deliberately or compulsively. To this end we constructed a comprehensive set of questions which served as the basis of an individual interview immediately following the experimental period. Toward the conclusion of the interview each subject was informed fully of the purpose of the experiment, of his role and of that of the majority. The reactions to the disclosure of the purpose of the experiment became in fact an integral part of the procedure. We may state here that the information derived from the interview became an indispensable source of evidence and insight into the psychological structure of the experimental situation, and in particular, of the nature of the individual differences. Also, it is not justified or advisable to allow the subject to leave without giving him a full explanation of the experimental conditions. The experimenter has a responsibility to the subject to clarify his doubts and to state the reasons for placing him in the experimental situation. When this is done most subjects react with interest and many express gratification at having lived through a striking situation which has some bearing on wider human issues.

Both the members of the majority and the critical subjects were male college students. We shall report the results for a total of fifty critical subjects in this experiment. In Table 1 we summarize the successive comparison trials and the majority estimates.

The quantitative results are clear and unambiguous.

1. There was a marked movement toward the majority. One-third of all the estimates in the critical group were errors identical with or in the direction of the distorted estimates of the majority. The significance of this finding becomes clear in the light of the virtual absence of errors in control groups the members of which recorded their estimates in writing. The relevant data of the critical and control groups are summarized in Table 2.

2. At the same time the effect of the majority was far from complete. The preponderance of estimates in the critical group (68 per cent) was correct despite the pressure of the majority.

3. We found evidence of extreme individual differences. There were in the critical group subjects who remained independent without exception, and there were those who went nearly all the time with the majority. (The maximum possible number of errors was 12, while the actual range of errors was 0–11.) One-fourth of the critical subjects was completely independent; at the other extreme, one-third of the group displaced the estimates toward the majority in one-half or more of the trials.

The differences between the critical subjects in their reactions to the given conditions were equally striking. There were subjects who remained completely confident throughout. At the other extreme were those who

TABLE 1

LENGTHS OF STANDARD AND COMPARISON LINES

Trials	Length of Standard Line (in inches)	Comparison Lines (in inches)			Correct Response	Group Response	Majority Error (in inches)
		1	2	3			
1	10	8¾	10	8	2	2	—
2	2	2	1	1½	1	1	—
3	3	3¾	4¼	3	3	1*	+ ¾
4	5	5	4	6½	1	2*	−1.0
5	4	3	5	4	3	3	—
6	3	3¾	4¼	3	3	2*	+1¼
7	8	6¼	8	6¾	2	3*	−1¼
8	5	5	4	6½	1	3*	+1½
9	8	6¼	8	6¾	2	1*	−1¾
10	10	8¾	10	8	2	2	—
11	2	2	1	1½	1	1	—
12	3	3¾	4¼	3	3	1*	+ ¾
13	5	5	4	6½	1	2*	−1.0
14	4	3	5	4	3	3	—
15	3	3¾	4¼	3	3	2*	+1¼
16	8	6¼	8	6¾	2	3*	−1¼
17	5	5	4	6½	1	3*	+1½
18	8	6¼	8	6¾	2	1*	−1¾

* Starred figures designate the erroneous estimates by the majority.

became disoriented, doubt-ridden, and experienced a powerful impulse not to appear different from the majority.

For purposes of illustration we include a brief description of one independent and one yielding subject.

Independent. After a few trials he appeared puzzled, hesitant. He announced all disagreeing answers in the form of "Three, sir; two, sir"; not so with the unanimous answers. At trial 4 he answered immediately after the first member of the group, shook his head, blinked, and whispered to his neighbor: "Can't help it, that's one." His later answers came in a whispered voice, accompanied by a deprecating smile. At one point he grinned embarrassedly, and whispered explosively to his neighbor: "I always disagree—darn it!" During the questioning, this subject's constant refrain was: "I called them as I saw them, sir." He insisted that his estimates were right without, however, committing himself as to whether the others were wrong, remarking that "that's the way I see them and that's the way they see them." If he had to make a practical decision under similar circumstances, he declared, "I would follow my own view, though part of my reason would tell me that I might be wrong." Immediately following the experiment the majority engaged this subject in a brief discussion. When they pressed him to say whether the entire group was wrong and he alone right, he turned upon them defiantly, exclaiming: "You're *probably* right,

TABLE 2

DISTRIBUTION OF ERRORS IN EXPERIMENTAL AND CONTROL GROUPS

Number of Critical Errors	Critical Group* (N = 50)	Control Group (N = 37)
	F	F
0	13	35
1	4	1
2	5	1
3	6	
4	3	
5	4	
6	1	
7	2	
8	5	
9	3	
10	3	
11	1	
12	0	
Total	50	37
Mean	3.84	0.08

* All errors in the critical group were in the direction of the majority estimates.

but you may be wrong!" To the disclosure of the experiment this subject reacted with the statement that he felt "exultant and relieved," adding, "I do not deny that at times I had the feeling: 'to heck with it, I'll go along with the rest.'"

Yielding. This subject went with the majority in 11 out of 12 trials. He appeared nervous and somewhat confused, but he did not attempt to evade discussion; on the contrary, he was helpful and tried to answer to the best of his ability. He opened the discussion with the statement: "If I'd been the first I probably would have responded differently"; this was his way of stating that he had adopted the majority estimates. The primary factor in his case was loss of confidence. He perceived the majority as a decided group, acting without hesitation: "If they had been doubtful I probably would have changed, but they answered with such confidence." Certain of his errors, he explained, were due to the doubtful nature of the comparisons; in such instances he went with the majority. When the object of the experiment was explained, the subject volunteered: "I suspected about the middle —but tried to push it out of my mind." It is of interest that his suspicion was not able to restore his confidence and diminish the power of the majority. Equally striking is his report that he assumed the experiment to involve an "illusion" to which the others, but not he, were subject. This assumption too did not help to free him; on the contrary, he acted as if his divergence from the majority was a sign of defect. The principal impression this subject produced was of one so caught up by immediate difficulties that he lost clear reasons for his actions, and could make no reasonable decisions.

A FIRST ANALYSIS OF INDIVIDUAL DIFFERENCES

On the basis of the interview data described earlier, we undertook to differentiate and describe the major forms of reaction to the experimental situation, which we shall now briefly summarize.

Among the *independent* subjects we distinguished the following main categories:

(1) Independence based on *confidence* in one's perception and experience. The most striking characteristic of these subjects is the vigor with which they withstand the group opposition. Though they are sensitive to the group, and experience the conflict, they show a resilience in coping with it, which is expressed in their continuing reliance on their perception and the effectiveness with which they shake off the oppressive group opposition.

(2) Quite different are those subjects who are independent and *withdrawn*. These do not react in a spontaneously emotional way, but rather on the basis of explicit principles concerning the necessity of being an individual.

(3) A third group of independent subjects manifest considerable tension and *doubt*, but adhere to their judgments on the basis of a felt necessity to deal adequately with the task.

The following were the main categories of reaction among the *yielding* subjects, or those who went with the majority during one-half or more of the trials.

(1) *Distortion of perception* under the stress of group pressure. In this category belong a very few subjects who yield completely, but are not aware that their estimates have been displaced or distorted by the majority. These subjects report that they came to perceive the majority estimates as correct.

(2) *Distortion of judgment.* Most submitting subjects belong to this category. The factor of greatest importance in this group is a decision the subjects reach that their perceptions are inaccurate, and that those of the majority are correct. These subjects suffer from primary doubt and lack of confidence; on this basis they feel a strong tendency to join the majority.

(3) *Distortion of action.* The subjects in this group do not suffer a modification of perception nor do they conclude that they are wrong. They yield because of an overmastering need not to appear different from or inferior to others, because of an inability to tolerate the appearance of defectiveness in the eyes of the group. These subjects suppress their observations and voice the majority position with awareness of what they are doing.

The results are sufficient to establish that independence and yielding are not psychologically homogeneous, that submission to group pressure (and freedom from pressure) can be the result of different psychological conditions. It should also be noted that the categories described above, being based exclusively on the subjects' reactions to the experimental conditions, are descriptive, not presuming to explain why a given individual responded in one way rather than another. The further exploration of the basis for the individual differences is a separate task upon which we are now at work.

EXPERIMENTAL VARIATIONS

The results described are clearly a joint function of two broadly different sets of conditions. They are determined first by the specific external conditions, by the particular character of the relation between social evidence and one's own experience. Second, the presence of pronounced individual differences points to the important role of personal factors, of factors connected with the individual's character structure. We reasoned that there are group conditions which would produce independence in all subjects, and that there probably are group conditions which would induce intensified yielding in many, though not in all. Accordingly we followed the procedure of *experimental variation*, systematically altering the quality of social evidence by means of systematic variation of group conditions. Secondly, we deemed it reasonable to assume that behavior under the experimental social pressure is significantly related to certain basic, relatively permanent characteristics of the individual. The investigation has moved in both of these directions. Because the study of the character-qualities which may be functionally connected with independence and yielding is still in progress, we shall limit the present account to a sketch of the representative experimental variations.

THE EFFECT OF NONUNANIMOUS MAJORITIES

Evidence obtained from the basic experiment suggested that the condition of being exposed *alone* to the opposition of a "compact majority" may have played a decisive role in determining the course and strength of the effects observed. Accordingly we undertook to investigate in a series of successive variations the effects of *nonunanimous* majorities. The technical problem of altering the uniformity of a majority is, in terms of our procedure, relatively simple. In most instances we merely directed one or more members of the instructed group to deviate from the majority in prescribed ways. It is obvious that we cannot hope to compare the performance of the same individual in two situations on the assumption that they remain independent of one another. At best we can investigate the effect of an earlier upon a later experimental condition. The comparison of different experimental situations therefore requires the use of different but comparable groups of critical subjects. This is the procedure we have followed. In the variations to be described we have maintained the conditions of the basic experiment (e.g., the sex of the subjects, the size of the majority, the content of the task, and so on) save for the specific factor that was varied. The following were some of the variations we studied:

1. *The presence of a "true partner."* (a) In the midst of the majority were *two* naive, critical subjects. The subjects were separated spatially, being

seated in the fourth and eighth positions, respectively. Each therefore heard his judgment confirmed by one other person (provided the other person remained independent), one prior to, the other subsequently to announcing his own judgment. In addition, each experienced a break in the unanimity of the majority. There were six pairs of critical subjects. (b) In a further variation the "partner" to the critical subject was a member of the group who had been instructed to respond correctly throughout. This procedure permits the exact control of the partner's responses. The partner was always seated in the fourth position; he therefore announced his estimates in each case before the critical subject.

The results clearly demonstrate that a disturbance of the unanimity of the majority markedly increased the independence of the critical subjects. The frequency of pro-majority errors dropped to 10.4 per cent of the total number of estimates in variation (a), and to 5.5 per cent in variation (b). These results are to be compared with the frequency of yielding to the unanimous majorities in the basic experiment, which was 32 per cent of the total number of estimates. It is clear that the presence in the field of *one other* individual who responded correctly was sufficient to deplete the power of the majority, and in some cases to destroy it. This finding is all the more striking in the light of other variations which demonstrate the effect of even small minorities provided they are unanimous. Indeed, we have been able to show that a unanimous majority of three is, under the given conditions, far more effective than a majority of eight containing one dissenter. That critical subjects will under these conditions free themselves of a majority of seven and join forces with one other person in the minority is, we believe, a result significant for theory. It points to a fundamental psychological difference between the condition of being alone and having a minimum of human support. It further demonstrates that the effects obtained are not the result of a summation of influences proceeding from each member of the group; it is necessary to conceive the results as being relationally determined.

2. *Withdrawal of a "true partner."* What will be the effect of providing the critical subject with a partner who responds correctly and then withdrawing him? The critical subject started with a partner who responded correctly. The partner was a member of the majority who had been instructed to respond correctly and to "desert" to the majority in the middle of the experiment. This procedure permits the observation of the same subject in the course of transition from one condition to another. The withdrawal of the partner produced a powerful and unexpected result. We had assumed that the critical subject, having gone through the experience of opposing the majority with a minimum of support, would maintain his independence when alone. Contrary to this expectation, we found that the experience of having had and then lost a partner restored the majority effect to its full force, the proportion of errors rising to 28.5 per cent of all judgments, in contrast to the preceding level of 5.5 per cent. Further experimentation is needed to establish whether the critical subjects were responding to the sheer fact of being alone, or to the fact that the partner abandoned them.

3. *Late arrival of a "true partner."* The critical subject started as a minority of one in the midst of a unanimous majority. Toward the conclusion of the experiment one member of the majority "broke" away and began announcing correct estimates. This procedure, which reverses the order of conditions of the preceding experiment, permits the observation of the transition from being alone to being a member of a pair against a majority. It is obvious that those critical subjects who were independent when alone would continue to be so when joined by another partner.

The variation is therefore of significance primarily for those subjects who yielded during the first phase of the experiment. The appearance of the late partner exerts a freeing effect, reducing the level to 8.7 per cent. Those who had previously yielded also became markedly more independent, but not completely so, continuing to yield more than previously independent subjects. The reports of the subjects do not cast much light on the factors responsible for the result. It is our impression that having once committed himself to yielding, the individual finds it difficult and painful to change his direction. To do so is tantamount to a public admission that he has not acted rightly. He therefore follows the precarious course he has already chosen in order to maintain an outward semblance of consistency and conviction.

4. *The presence of a "compromise partner."* The majority was consistently extremist, always matching the standard with the most unequal line. One instructed subject (who, as in the other variations, preceded the critical subject) also responded incorrectly, but his estimates were always intermediate between the truth and the majority position. The critical subject therefore faced an extremist majority whose unanimity was broken by one more moderately erring person. Under these conditions the frequency of errors was reduced but not significantly. However, the lack of unanimity determined in a strikingly consistent way the *direction* of the errors. The preponderance of the errors, 75.7 per cent of the total, was moderate, whereas in a parallel experiment in which the majority was unanimously extremist (*i.e.*, with the "compromise" partner excluded), the incidence of moderate errors was reduced to 42 per cent of the total. As might be expected, in a unanimously moderate majority, the errors of the critical subjects were without exception moderate.

THE ROLE OF MAJORITY SIZE

To gain further understanding of the majority effect, we varied the size of the majority in several different variations. The majorities, which were in each case unanimous, consisted of 16, 8, 4, 3, and 2 persons, respectively. In addition, we studied the limiting case in which the critical subject was opposed by one instructed subject. Table III contains the means and the range of errors under each condition.

TABLE 3

ERRORS OF CRITICAL SUBJECTS WITH UNANIMOUS MAJORITIES
OF DIFFERENT SIZE

Size of majority	Control	1	2	3	4	8	16
N	37	10	15	10	10	50	12
Mean number of errors	0.08	0.33	1.53	4.0	4.20	3.84	3.75
Range of errors	0–2	0–1	0–5	1–12	0–11	0–11	0–10

With the opposition reduced to one, the majority effect all but disappeared. When the opposition proceeded from a group of two, it produced a measurable though small distortion, the errors being 12.8 per cent of the total number of estimates. The effect appeared in full force with a majority of three. Larger majorities of four, eight, and sixteen did not produce effects greater than a majority of three.

The effect of a majority is often silent, revealing little of its operation to the subject, and often hiding it from the experimenter. To examine the range of effects it is capable of inducing, decisive variations of conditions are necessary. An indication of one effect is furnished by the following variation in which the conditions of the basic experiment were simply reversed. Here the majority, consisting of a group of sixteen, was naive; in the midst of it we placed a single individual who responded wrongly according to instructions. Under these conditions the members of the naive majority reacted to the lone dissenter with amusement and disdain. Contagious laughter spread through the group at the droll minority of one. Of significance is the fact that the members lack awareness that they draw their strength from the majority, and that their reactions would change radically if they faced the dissenter individually. In fact, the attitude of derision in the majority turns to seriousness and increased respect as soon as the minority is increased to three. These observations demonstrate the role of social support as a source of power and stability, in contrast to the preceding investigations which stressed the effects of withdrawal of social support, or to be more exact, the effects of social opposition. Both aspects must be explicitly considered in a unified formulation of the effects of group conditions on the formation and change of judgments.

THE ROLE OF THE STIMULUS-SITUATION

It is obviously not possible to divorce the quality and course of the group forces which act upon the individual from the specific stimulus-conditions. Of necessity the structure of the situation moulds the group forces and determines their direction as well as their strength. Indeed, this was the reason that we took pains in the investigations described above to center the issue between the individual and the group around an elementary and fundamental matter of fact. And there can be no doubt that the resulting reactions were directly a function of the contradiction between the objectively grasped relations and the majority position.

These general considerations are sufficient to establish the need of varying the stimulus-conditions and of observing their effect on the resulting group forces. We are at present conducting a series of investigations in which certain aspects of the stimulus-situation are systematically altered.

One of the dimensions we are examining is the magnitude of discrepancies above the threshold. Our technique permits an easy variation of this factor, since we can increase or decrease at will the deviation of the majority from the given objective conditions. Hitherto we have studied the effect of a relatively moderate range of discrepancies. Within the limits of our procedure we find that different magnitudes of discrepancy produce approximately the same amount of yielding. However, the quality of yielding alters: as the majority becomes more extreme, there occurs a significant increase in the frequency of "compromise" errors. Further experiments are planned in which the discrepancies in question will be extremely large and small.

We have also varied systematically the structural clarity of the task, including in separate variations judgments based on mental standards. In agreement with other investigators, we find that the majority effect grows stronger as the situation diminishes in clarity. Concurrently, however, the disturbance of the subjects and the conflict-quality of the situation decrease markedly. We consider it of significance that the majority achieves its most pronounced effect when it acts most painlessly.

SUMMARY

We have investigated the effects upon individuals of majority opinions when the latter were seen to be in a direction contrary to fact. By means of a simple technique we produced a radical divergence between a majority and a minority, and observed the ways in which individuals coped with the resulting difficulty. Despite the stress of the given conditions, a substantial proportion of individuals retained their independence throughout. At the same time a substantial minority yielded, modifying their judgments in accordance with the majority. Independence and yielding are a joint function of the following major factors: (1) The character of the stimulus situation. Variations in structural clarity have a decisive effect: with diminishing clarity of the stimulus-conditions the majority effect increases. (2) The character of the group forces. Individuals are highly sensitive to the structural qualities of group opposition. In particular, we demonstrated the great importance of the factor of unanimity. Also, the majority effect is a function of the size of group opposition. (3) The character of the individual. There were wide, and indeed, striking differences among individuals within the same experimental situation. The hypothesis was proposed that these are functionally dependent on relatively enduring character differences, in particular those pertaining to the person's social relations.

BIBLIOGRAPHY

1. ASCH, S. E. Studies in the principles of judgments and attitudes: II. Determination of judgments by group and by ego-standards. *J. soc. Psychol.*, 1940, 12, 433–465.
2. ———. The doctrine of suggestion, prestige and imitation in social psychology. *Psychol. Rev.*, 1948, 55, 250–276.
3. ASCH, S. E., BLOCK, H., and HERTZMAN, M. Studies in the principles of judgments and attitudes. I. Two basic principles of judgment. *J. Psychol.*, 1938, 5, 219–251.
4. COFFIN, E. E. Some conditions of suggestion and suggestibility: A study of certain attitudinal and situational factors influencing the process of suggestion. *Psychol. Monogr.*, 1941, 53, No. 4.
5. LEWIS, H. B. Studies in the principles of judgments and attitudes: IV. The operation of prestige suggestion. *J. soc. Psychol.*, 1941, 14, 229–256.
6. LORGE, I. Prestige, suggestion, and attitudes. *J. soc. Psychol.*, 1936, 7, 386–402.
7. MILLER, N. E. and DOLLARD, J. *Social Learning and Imitation.* New Haven: Yale University Press, 1941.
8. MOORE, H. T. The comparative influence of majority and expert opinion. *Amer. J. Psychol.*, 1921, 32, 16–20.
9. SHERIF, M. A study of some social factors in perception. *Arch. Psychol.*, N.Y., 1935, No. 187.
10. THORNDIKE, E. L. *The Psychology of Wants, Interests, and Attitudes.* New York: D. Appleton-Century Company, Inc., 1935.

A Study of Normative and Informational

Social Influences upon Individual Judgment

Morton Deutsch and Harold B. Gerard[1]

Research Center for Human Relations, New York University

By now, many experimental studies (e.g., 1, 3, 6) have demonstrated that individual psychological processes are subject to social influences. Most investigators, however, have not distinguished among different kinds of social influences; rather, they have carelessly used the term "group" influence to characterize the impact of many different kinds of social factors. In fact, a review of the major experiments in this area—e.g., those by Sherif (6), Asch (1), Bovard (3)—would indicate that the subjects (Ss) in these experiments as they made their judgments were *not* functioning as *members* of a group in any simple or obvious manner. The S, in the usual experiment in this area, made perceptual judgments in the physical presence of others after hearing their judgments. Typically, the S was *not* given experimental instructions which made him feel that he was a member of a group faced with a common task requiring cooperative effort for its most effective solution. If "group" influences were at work in the foregoing experiments, they were subtly and indirectly created rather than purposefully created by the experimenter.

HYPOTHESES

The purpose of this paper is to consider two types of social influence, "normative" and "informational," which we believe were operative in the experiments mentioned above, and to report the results of an experiment bearing upon hypotheses that are particularly relevant to the former influence. We shall define a *normative social influence* as an influence to con-

---

Reprinted from *Journal of Abnormal and Social Psychology*, 1955, 51, 629–636.

[1] Dr. Gerard is now at the University of Buffalo. This research was conducted under a grant from the Office of Naval Research, Contract No. NONR 285(10).

form with the positive expectations[2] of another.[3] An *informational social influence* may be defined as an influence to accept information obtained from another as *evidence* about reality. Commonly these two types of influence are found together. However, it is possible to conform behaviorally with the expectations of others and say things which one disbelieves but which agree with the beliefs of others. Also, it is possible that one will accept an opponent's beliefs as evidence about reality even though one has no motivation to agree with him, per se.

Our hypotheses are particularly relevant to normative social influence upon individual judgment. We shall not elaborate the theoretical rationales for the hypotheses, since they are for the most part obvious and they follow from other theoretical writings (e.g., 4, 5).

Hypothesis I. Normative social influence upon individual judgments will be greater among individuals forming a group than among an aggregation of individuals who do not compose a group.[4]

That is, even when susceptibility to informational social influence is equated, we would predict that the greater susceptibility to normative social influence among group members would be reflected in the greater group influence upon individual judgment. This is not to say that individuals, even when they are not group members, may not have some motivation to conform to the expectations of others—e.g., so as to ingratiate themselves or so as to avoid ridicule.

Hypothesis II. Normative social influence upon individual judgment will be reduced when the individual perceives that his judgment cannot be identified or, more generally, when the individual perceives no pressure to conform directed at him from others.

Hypothesis III. Normative social influence to conform to one's own judgment will reduce the impact of the normative social influence to conform to the judgment of others.

Hypothesis IV. Normative social influence to conform to one's own judgment from another as well as from oneself will be stronger than normative social influence from oneself.

Normative social influence from oneself to conform to one's own judgment may be thought of as an internalized social process in which the indi-

---

[2] By positive expectations we mean to refer to those expectations whose fulfillment by another leads to or reinforces positive rather than negative feelings, and whose nonfulfillment leads to the opposite, to alienation rather than solidarity; conformity to negative expectations, on the other hand, leads to or reinforces negative rather than positive feelings.

[3] The term *another* is being used inclusively to refer to "another person," to a "group," or to one's "self." Thus, a normative social influence can result from the expectations of oneself, or of a group, or of another person.

[4] Generally one would also expect that group members would be more likely to take the judgments of other group members as trustworthy evidence for forming judgments about reality and, hence, they would be more susceptible to informational social influence than would nongroup members. The greater trustworthiness usually reflects more experience of the reliability of the judgments of other members and more confidence in the benevolence of their motivations. However, when group members have had no prior experience together and when it is apparent in both the group and nongroup situations that the others are motivated and in a position to report correct judgments, there is no reason to expect differential susceptibility to informational social influence among group and nongroup members.

vidual holds expectations with regard to his own behavior; conforming to positive self-expectations leads to feelings of self-esteem or self-approval while nonconformity leads to feelings of anxiety or guilt. In general, one would expect that the strength of these internalized self-expectations would reflect the individual's prior experiences with them as sources of need satisfaction—e.g., by conforming to his own judgments or by self-reliance he has won approval from such significant others as his parents. As Hypothesis IV indicates, we believe that contemporaneous social pressure to conform to one's own judgment may supplement, and perhaps be even stronger than, the individual's internalized pressure to conform to his own judgment.

Two additional hypotheses, dealing with the effect of difficulty of judgment, are relevant to one of the experimental variations. They follow: *Hypothesis V.* The more uncertain the individual is about the correctness of his judgment, the more likely he is to be susceptible to both normative and informational social influences in making his judgment.

Hypothesis VI. The more uncertain the individual is about the correctness of the judgment of others, the less likely he is to be susceptible to informational social influence in making his judgment.[5]

METHOD

Subjects. One hundred and one college students from psychology courses at New York University were employed as Ss. The study was defined for the Ss as an experimental study of perception.

Procedure. We employed the experimental situation developed by Asch (1) with certain modifications and variations which are specified below. For detailed description of the procedures utilized by Asch and replicated in this experiment, Asch's publication should be consulted. The basic features of the Asch situation are: (a) the Ss are instructed that they are participating in a perceptual experiment, wherein they have to match accurately the length of a given line with one of three lines; (b) correct judgments are easy to make; (c) in each experimental session there is only one *naive S*, the other participants, while ostensively Ss, are in fact "stooges"

[5] Although we have no data relevant to this hypothesis, we present it to qualify Hypothesis V and to counteract an assumption in some of the current social psychological literature. Thus, Festinger (5) has written that where no physical reality basis exists for the establishment of the validity of one's belief, one is dependent upon social reality (i.e., upon the beliefs of others). Similarly, Asch (2) has indicated that group influence grows stronger as the judgmental situation diminishes in clarity. The implication of Hypothesis VI is that if an individual perceives that a situation is objectively difficult to judge—that others as well as he experience the situation in the same way (i.e., as being difficult and as having uncertainty about their judgments)—he will not trust their judgments any more than he trusts his own. It is only as his confidence in their judgments increases (e.g., because he deems that agreement among three uncertain judges provides more reliable evidence than one uncertain judge) that the judgments of others will have informational social influence. However (at any particular level of confidence in the judgment of others), one can predict that as his confidence in his own judgment decreases he will be more susceptible to normative social influence. With decreasing self-confidence there is likely to be less of a commitment to one's own judgment and, hence, less influence not to conform to the judgments of others.

who carry out the experimenter's instructions; (d) each participant (i.e., the naive S and the stooges) has to indicate his judgments publicly; (e) on 12 of the 18 perceptual judgments the stooges announce wrong and unanimous judgments, the errors of the stooges are large and clearly in error; (f) the naive S and the stooges are in a face-to-face relationship and have been previously acquainted with one another.[6]

To test the hypotheses set forth in the foregoing section, the following experimental variations upon Asch's situation were employed:

1. *The face-to-face situation.* This was an exact replication of Asch's situation except for the following minor modifications: (a) Only three stooges, rather than eight, were employed;[7] (b) the S and the stooges were unacquainted prior to the experiment; and (c) two series of 18 judgments were employed. In one series (the visual series), the lines were physically present when the S and the stooges announced their judgments; in the other series (the memory series), the lines were removed before any one announced his judgment. In the memory series, approximately three seconds after the lines were removed the first stooge was asked to announce his judgment. The sequences of visual and memory series were alternated so that approximately half the Ss had the memory series first and half had the visual series first.

2. *The anonymous situation.* This situation was identical with the face-to-face situation except for the following differences: (a) Instead of sitting in the visual presence of each other, the Ss were separated by partitions which prevented them from talking to each other or seeing one another; (b) Instead of announcing their judgments by voice, the Ss indicated their judgments by pressing a button; (c) No stooges were employed. Each S was led to believe he was Subject No. 3, and the others were No. 1, No. 2, and No. 4. He was told that when the experimenter called out "Subject No. 3" he was to indicate his judgment by pressing one of three buttons (A, B, or C) which corresponded to what he thought the correct line was. When an S pressed a given button, a corresponding bulb lit on his own

---

[6] Inspection of the Asch situation would suggest that informational social influence would be strongly operative. As Asch has put it (2, p. 461):

The subject knows (a) that the issue is one of fact; (b) that a correct result is possible; (c) that only one result is correct; (d) that the others and he are oriented to and reporting about the same objectively given relations; (e) that the group is in unanimous opposition at certain points with him.

He further, perceives that the others are motivated to report a correct judgment. In such a situation, the subject's accumulated past experience would lead him to expect that he could rely on the judgments of others, especially if they all agreed. That is, even if his eyes were closed he might feel that he could safely risk his life on the assumption that the unanimous judgments of the others were correct. This is a strong informational social influence and one would expect it to be overriding except for the fact that the subject has his eyes open and receives information from a source which he also feels to be completely trustworthy—i.e., from his own perceptual apparatus. The subject is placed in strong conflict because the evidences from two sources of trustworthy information are in opposition.

In the Asch situation, it is apparent that, in addition to informational social influence, normative social influence is likely to be operating. The naive S is in a face-to-face situation with acquaintances and he may be motivated to conform to their judgments in order to avoid being ridiculed, or being negatively evaluated, or even possibly out of a sense of obligation. While it may be impossible to remove completely the impact of normative social influence upon any socialized being, it is evident that the Asch situation allows much opportunity for this type of influence to operate.

[7] Asch found that three stooges were about as effective in influencing the Ss as eight.

panel and on a hidden master panel. Presumably the appropriate bulb also lit on the panels of each of the other Ss, but, in fact, the bulbs on any S's panel were not connected to the buttons of the other Ss. When the experimenter called for the judgments of Subject No. 1, of Subject No. 2, and of Subject No. 4, a concealed accomplice manipulated master switches which lit bulbs on each of the S's panels that corresponded to judgments presumably being made by these respective Ss. Subjects No. 1, No. 2, and No. 4 were, in effect, "electrical stooges" whose judgments were indicated on the panels of the four naive Ss (all of whom were Subject No. 3) by an accomplice of the experimenter who manipulated master switches controlling the lights on the panels of the naive Ss. The pattern of judgments followed by the "electrical stooges" was the same as that followed by the "live stooges" in the face-to-face situation. (d) In providing a rationale for being labeled Subject No. 3 for each of the naive Ss, we explained that due to the complicated wiring setup, the S's number had no relation to his seating position. Implicitly, we assumed that each S would realize that it would be impossible for the others to identify that a judgment was being made by him rather than by any of two others. However, it is apparent from post-experiment questionnaires that many of the Ss did not realize this. It seems likely that if we had made the anonymous character of the judgments clear and explicit to the Ss, the effects of this experimental variation would have been even more marked.

3. *The group situation.* This situation was identical to the anonymous situation except that the subjects were instructed as follows:

This group is one of twenty similar groups who are participating in this experiment. We want to see how accurately you can make judgments. We are going to give a reward to the five best groups—the five groups that make the fewest errors on the series of judgments that you are given. The reward will be a pair of tickets to a Broadway play of your own choosing for each member of the winning group. An error will be counted any time one of you makes an incorrect judgment. That is, on any given card the group can make as many as four errors if you each judge incorrectly or you can make no errors if you each judge correctly. The five groups that make the best scores will be rewarded.

4. *The self-commitment variation.* This variation was employed in both the face-to-face and anonymous situations. In it, each S was given a sheet of paper on which to write down his judgment before he was exposed to the judgments of the others. He was told not to sign the sheet of paper and that it would not be collected at the end of the experiment. After the first series of 18 judgments, the Ss threw away their sheets. The Ss did not erase their recorded judgments after each trial as they did in the Magic Pad self-commitment variation.

4A. *The Magic Pad self-commitment variation.* This variation was employed in the anonymous situation. In it, each S was given a Magic Writing Pad on which to write down his judgment before he was exposed to the judgments of the others. After each S had been exposed to the judgment of the others and had indicated his own judgment, he erased his judgment on the Magic Writing Pad by lifting up the plastic covering. It was made convincingly clear to the S that only he would ever know what he had written down on the pad.

5. *The public commitment variation.* This variation was employed in both the face-to-face situation and in the anonymous situation. In it, the Ss followed the same procedure as in the self-commitment variation except that they wrote down their initial judgments on sheets of paper which they signed and which they knew were to be handed to the experimenter after each series of 18 judgments.

RESULTS

The primary data used in the analysis of the results are the errors made by the Ss which were in the direction of the errors made by the stooges. We shall present first the data which are relevant to our hypotheses; later we shall present other information.

Hypothesis I. The data relevant to the first hypothesis are presented in Table 1. The table presents a comparison of the anonymous situation in

TABLE 1

MEAN NUMBER OF SOCIALLY INFLUENCED ERRORS IN INDIVIDUAL
JUDGMENT AMONG GROUP MEMBERS AND AMONG NONMEMBERS

Experimental Treatment	N	Memory Series	Visual Series	Total
Group, anonymous, no commitment	15	6.87	5.60	12.47
Nongroup, anonymous, no commitment	13	3.15	2.77	5.92
			p values*	
		.01	.05	.001

* Based on a *t* test, using one tail of the distribution.

which the individuals were motivated to act as a group with the anonymous situation in which there was no direct attempt to induce membership motivation; in both situations, no self or public commitment was made. The data provide strong support for the prediction that the normative social influence upon individual judgments will be greater among individuals forming a group than among individuals who do not compose a group. The average member of the group made more than twice as many errors as the comparable individual who did not participate in the task as a member of a group.

Qualitative data from a postexperimental questionnaire, in which we asked the S to describe any feelings he had about himself or about the others during the experiment, also support Hypothesis I. Seven out of the fifteen Ss in the "group" condition spontaneously mentioned a felt obligation to the other group members; none of the individuals in the non-group condition mentioned any feeling of obligation to go along with the others.

Hypothesis II. To test the second hypothesis, it is necessary to compare the data from the face-to-face and anonymous situations among the individuals who were otherwise exposed to similar experimental treatments. Tables 2 and 3 present the relevant data. It is apparent that there was less social influence upon individual judgment in the anonymous as compared with the face-to-face situation. This lessening of social influence is at the .001 level of statistical confidence even when the comparisons include the "commitment variations" as well as both the visual and the memory series of judgments. The interaction between the commitment variations and the anonymous, face-to-face variations, which is statistically significant, is such

TABLE 2

MEAN NUMBER OF SOCIALLY INFLUENCED ERRORS IN INDIVIDUAL JUDGMENT
IN THE ANONYMOUS AND IN THE FACE-TO-FACE SITUATIONS

Situation	No Commitment				Self-Commitment				Public Commitment			
	Vis-ual	Mem-ory	Total	N	Vis-ual	Mem-ory	Total	N	Vis-ual	Mem-ory	Total	N
Face-to-face	3.00	4.08	7.08	13	.92	.75	1.67	12	1.13	1.39	2.52	13
Anonymous	2.77	3.15	5.92	13	.64	.73	1.37	11	.92	.46	1.38	13

as to reduce the over-all differences between the anonymous and face-to-face situation; the differences between the face-to-face and the anonymous situations are most strongly brought out when there is no commitment. Similarly, if we compare the anonymous and face-to-face situations, employing the memory rather than the visual series, the effect of the normative influence upon judgments in the face-to-face situation is increased somewhat, but not significantly. That is, as we eliminate counter-normative influences (i.e., the "commitment") and as we weaken reality restraints (i.e., employ the "memory" rather than "visual" series), the normative influences in the face-to-face situation operate more freely.

The support for Hypothesis II is particularly striking in light of the fact that, due to faulty experimental procedure, the "anonymous" character of the anonymous situation was not sufficiently impressed on some of the Ss. For these Ss, the anonymous situation merely protected them from the immediate, visually accessible pressure to conform arising from the lifted eyebrows and expressions of amazement by the stooges in the face-to-face situation. Complete feeling of anonymity would probably have strengthened the results.

TABLE 3

p VALUES* FOR VARIOUS COMPARISONS OF SOCIALLY INFLUENCED ERRORS
IN THE ANONYMOUS AND FACE-TO-FACE SITUATIONS

Comparison	Total Errors
A vs. F	.001
A vs. F, no commitment	.001
A vs. F, self-commitment	.10
A vs. F, public commitment	.001
Interaction of commitment with A-F	.01

* p values are based on t tests, using one tail of distribution, derived from analyses of variation.

Hypotheses III and IV. Tables 4, 5, and 6 present results showing the influence of the different commitment variations. The public and the self-commitment variations markedly reduce the socially influenced errors in both the face-to-face and anonymous situations. In other words, the data provide strong support for Hypothesis III which asserts that normative social influence to conform to one's own judgment will reduce the impact of the normative influence to conform to the judgment of others.

The data with regard to the influence of self-commitment are ambigu-

TABLE 4

p VALUES* FOR VARIOUS COMPARISONS OF SOCIALLY INFLUENCED
ERRORS IN THE DIFFERENT COMMITMENT TREATMENTS

Comparison	Total Errors	Errors on Visual Series	Errors on Memory Series
No commitment vs. public commitment, F	.001	.01	.001
No commitment vs. self-commitment, F	.001	.01	.001
Self-commitment vs. public commitment, F	.01	NS	NS
No commitment vs. self-commitment, A	.001	.01	.01
No commitment vs. public commitment, A	.001	.01	.002
Self-commitment vs. public commitment, A	NS	NS	NS

* p values are based on t tests, using one tail of the distribution, and derived from the analyses of variation.

ous in implication since the results of the two self-commitment variations—i.e., the "Magic Pad self-commitment" and the "self-commitment"—are not the same. The first self-commitment variation produced results which are essentially the same as the public commitment variation, markedly reducing socially influenced errors. The Magic Pad self-commitment variation produced results which were different from the no commitment variation, reducing the errors to an extent which is statistically significant; however, unlike the first self-commitment variation, the Magic Pad self-commitment was significantly less effective than the public commitment in reducing socially influenced errors.

Our hunch is that the Ss in the first self-commitment variation perceived the commitment situation as though it were a public commitment and that this is the explanation of the lack of differences between these two variations. That is, writing their judgments indelibly supported the belief that "others can see what I have written." The Ss in the Magic Pad self-commitment variation, on the other hand, were literally wiping their initial judgments away in such a manner that they would be inaccessible to anyone. Hence, in the Magic Pad variation, the normative influences to conform to one's own judgment had to be sustained by the S himself. Normative influences from the S's self (to be, in a sense, true to himself) were undoubtedly also operating in the noncommitment variation. What the Magic Pad did was to prevent the S from distorting his recollection of his independent judgment after being exposed to the judgments of the others. Further, there is a theoretical basis for assuming that the commitment to a judgment or decision is increased following the occurrence of behavior based upon it. Hence, the behavior of writing one's judgment down on the Magic Pad makes the original decision less tentative and less subject to change. However, it is apparent that this internally sustained influence to conform with

TABLE 5

MEAN NUMBER OF SOCIALLY INFLUENCED ERRORS IN JUDGMENTS IN THE ANONYMOUS SITUATION AS AFFECTED
BY THE COMMITMENT VARIATIONS

| | No Commitment | | | Magic Pad Self-Commitment | | | | Self-Commitment | | | | Public Commitment | | |
Visual	Memory	Total	N	Visual	Memory	Total	N	Visual	Memory	Total	N	Visual	Memory	Total	N
2.77	3.15	5.92	13	1.63	2.27	3.90	11	.64	.73	1.37	11	.92	.46	1.38	13

TABLE 6

p VALUES* FOR VARIOUS COMPARISONS OF SOCIALLY INFLUENCED
ERRORS IN THE DIFFERENT COMMITMENT VARIATIONS

Comparison	Total Errors	Errors on Visual Series	Errors on Memory Series
No commitment vs. Magic Pad self-commitment	.05	NS	NS
Magic Pad self-commitment vs. self-commitment	.005	NS	.05
Magic Pad self-commitment vs. public commitment	.001	NS	.01

* p values are based on t tests using one tail of the distribution.

one's own judgment was not as strong as the combination of external and self-motivated influences. These results support our fourth hypothesis.

Hypothesis V. Table 7 presents a comparison of the errors made on the visual and on the memory series of judgments. It is apparent that the Ss were less influenced by the judgments of others when the judgments were made on a visual rather than on a memory basis. It is also evident from the data of Table 2 that the differences between the visual and memory series were reduced or disappeared when the Ss wrote down their initial, independent judgments. These results support our fifth hypothesis which asserts that the more uncertain the individual is about the correctness of his judgment, the more likely he is to be susceptible to social influences in making his judgment. Further support comes from the questionnaire data. Out of the 90 Ss who filled out questionnaires, 51 indicated that they were more certain of their judgment when the lines were visually present, 2 were more certain when they were absent, and 39 were equally certain in both instances.

TABLE 7

SOCIALLY INFLUENCED ERRORS IN INDIVIDUAL JUDGMENTS AS
AFFECTED BY THE STIMULUS TO BE JUDGED (VISUAL OR MEMORY)

	N	Mean Number of Errors	"p" value
Errors on visual series	99	2.20	.005*
Errors on memory series	99	2.60	
Total errors when visual series was first	51	4.12	.005
Total errors when memory series was first	48	5.71	

* Based on a t test of differences between visual and memory series for each subject.

Being exposed first to the memory series rather than the visual series had the effect of making the Ss more susceptible to social influence upon their judgments throughout both series of judgments. In other words, an S was more likely to make socially influenced errors on the memory series and, having allowed himself to be influenced by the others on this first series of judgments, he was more likely to be influenced on the visual series than if he had not previously participated in the memory series. It is as though once having given in to the social influence (and it is easier to give in when one is less certain about one's judgment), the S is more susceptible to further social influences.

DISCUSSION

A central thesis of this experiment has been that prior experiments which have been concerned with "group" influence upon individual judgment have, in fact, only incidentally been concerned with the type of social influence most specifically associated with groups, namely "normative social influence." Our results indicate that, even when normative social influence in the direction of an incorrect judgment is largely removed (as in the anonymous situation), more errors are made by our Ss than by a control group of Ss making their judgments when alone.[8] It seems reasonable to conclude that the S, even if not normatively influenced, may be influenced by the others in the sense that the judgments of others are taken to be a more or less trustworthy source of information about the objective reality with which he and the others are confronted.

It is not surprising that the judgments of others (particularly when they are perceived to be motivated and competent to judge accurately) should be taken as evidence to be weighed in coming to one's own judgment. From birth on, we learn that the perceptions and judgments of others are frequently reliable sources of evidence about reality. Hence, it is to be expected that if the perceptions by two or more people of the same objective situation are discrepant, each will tend to re-examine his own view and that of the others to see if they can be reconciled. This process of mutual influence does not necessarily indicate the operation of normative social influence as distinct from informational social influence. Essentially the same process (except that the influence is likely to be unilateral) can go on in interaction with a measuring or computing machine. For example, suppose one were to judge which of two lines is longer (as in the Müller-Lyer illusion) and then were given information that a measuring instrument (which past experience had led one to believe was infallible) came up with a different answer; certainly one might be influenced by this information. This influence could hardly be called a normative influence except in the most indirect sense.

While the results of prior experiments of "group" influence upon perception can be largely explained in terms of non-normative social influence, there is little doubt that normative influences were incidentally operative.

[8] Asch (2) reports that his control group of Ss made an average of considerably less than one error per S.

However, these were the casual normative influences which can not be completely eliminated from any human situation, rather than normative influences deriving from specific group membership. Our experimental results indicate that when a group situation is created, even when the group situation is as trivial and artificial as it was in our groups, the normative social influences are grossly increased, producing considerably more errors in individual judgment.

The implications of the foregoing result are not particularly optimistic for those who place a high value on the ability of an individual to resist group pressures which run counter to his individual judgment. In the experimental situation we employed, the S, by allowing himself to be influenced by the others, in effect acquiesced in the distortion of his judgment and denied the authenticity of his own immediate experience. The strength of the normative social influences that were generated in the course of our experiment was small; had it been stronger, one would have expected even more distortion and submission.

Our findings, with regard to the commitment variations, do, however, suggest that normative social influences can be utilized to buttress as well as to undermine individual integrity. In other words, normative social influence can be exerted to help make an individual be an individual and not merely a mirror or puppet of the group. Groups can demand of their members that they have self-respect, that they value their own experience, that they be capable of acting without slavish regard for popularity. Unless groups encourage their members to express their own, independent judgments, group consensus is likely to be an empty achievement. Group process which rests on the distortion of individual experience undermines its own potential for creativity and productiveness.

SUMMARY AND CONCLUSIONS

Employing modifications of the Asch situation, an experiment was carried out to test hypotheses concerning the effects of normative and informational social influences upon individual judgment. The hypotheses received strong support from the experimental data.

In discussion of our results, the thesis was advanced that prior studies of "group" influence upon individual judgment were only incidentally studies of the type of social influence most specifically associated with groups—i.e., of normative social influence. The role of normative social influence in buttressing as well as undermining individual experience was considered.

REFERENCES

1. ASCH, S. E. Effects of group pressure upon the modification and distortion of judgments. In H. Guetzkow (Ed.), *Groups, leadership and men.* Pittsburgh: Carnegie Press, 1951. Pp. 177–190.
2. ASCH, S. E. *Social psychology.* New York: Prentice-Hall, 1952.
3. BOVARD, E. W. Group structure and perception. *J. abnorm soc. Psychol,* 1951, **46**, 398–405.

4. DEUTSCH, M. A theory of cooperation and competition. *Hum. Relat.*, 1949, **2**, 129–152.

5. FESTINGER, L. Informal social communication. *Psychol. Rev.*, 1950, **57**, 271–282.

6. SHERIF, M. A study of some social factors in perception. *Arch. Psychol.*, 1935, **27**, No. 187.

Conformity and Commitment to the Group

Harold B. Gerard

University of California, Riverside

As reported by Asch (1956), an individual who asserts his independence at the outset, in the face of successive disagreement with others, tends, over time, to remain independent. This tendency, it was hypothesized here, is due to the commitment to one's stand when confronting the others publicly. Data were examined from an experiment in which the individual experienced the same sequence of discrepant judgments used by Asch either with or without public confrontation. These data indicate that continued adamance occurs only with public confrontation. Also, with confrontation, the individual who tends to yield to the others does so with greater frequency as compared with the no confrontation situation. This bimodal reaction occurring with confrontation, it was suggested, offers evidence for the effects of a stronger commitment to behavior in a public situation.

Processes involving an individual's tendency to yield or maintain his independence when confronted with disagreement from others have been the subject of some intensive investigation. One of the workers in the field, Asch (1956), devised a situation, the features of which are as follows. The subjects, who are seated side by side, are instructed that they are participating in a perception experiment in which they have to match, by inspection at a distance, the length of a given line with one of three comparison lines. In each experimental session there is only one naive subject. The other participants, while ostensibly subjects, are in fact paid participants who carry out the experimenter's instructions. Each participant (that is, the naive subject and each paid participant) has to announce his judgments publicly and in full view of the others. On 12 of the 18 judgmental trials the paid participants, who always agree with one another, announce judgments which are clearly wrong. The task itself is perceptually unambiguous, that is, in the absence of the false consensus, subjects make no errors.

Asch found that if a subject was independent of the others at the outset, that is, did not yield his judgment in favor of theirs, he tended to

Reprinted from *Journal of Abnormal and Social Psychology*, 1964, 68, 209–211.

remain independent to the end of the series of judgments. Since the amount of evidence disconfirming the subject's own judgments increases with successive disagreement we would expect his confidence in his ability to decrease and his tendency to yield, therefore, to increase over time. Thus, a subject who was adamant at the outset would tend to relent with continued confrontation of discrepant judgments. The fact that this did not occur in Asch's work is puzzling.

We propose that the key to understanding this apparent lack of an increase in the tendency to yield to the group consensus over time lies in the nature of a face-to-face confrontation. Where the individual can be personally identified with his judgments he is responding not only to the apparent discrepancy in information about the stimulus but also to what he believes are the expectations of the others as to what his response should be. In a face-to-face situation an avowal of a discrepant stand is a public commitment to the group of one's stalwartness. Any change in this behavior in the direction of yielding would violate this image not only to oneself but to the group. We would therefore expect that an individual who started out deviating publicly in Asch's experiment would, as Asch discovered, continue to do so in the face of continued disagreement. If, however, we assume that the individual's confidence decreases with successive disagreement we would expect that where the individual *has not* been identified publicly with a deviant stand he would tend, with successive disagreement, to yield his own judgments and adopt those of the others.

In a previous experiment by Deutsch and Gerard (1955), which was stimulated by Asch's work, a situation was created in which to test the above derivation by comparing the effects of discrepant information with and without a public commitment to the group.[1] We therefore decided to take a new look at these old data.

Four subjects at a time (a naive one and three paid participants) were run in the standard face-to-face situation utilized by Asch. The subjects responded serially on each trial with the naive subject always in the third position. Other subjects responded anonymously. This latter condition, which has been used in a great deal of research since, was identical with the face-to-face situation except for the following differences. The four subjects sat in adjoining cubicles and were not able to see or talk to each other. They pressed a button to indicate their choice. No paid participants were employed since each subject was led to believe that he was Subject "3," and that the others were "1," "2," and "4." Each subject was told that when the experimenter called for the choice of Subject 3 he was to indicate his judgment by pressing one of three buttons (labeled A, B, or C) depending upon which of the three lines (also labeled A, B, and C) he believed to be correct. Judgments were called for in numerical sequence and the choices were displayed on a panel of lights. The pre-programed choices for the bogus Subjects 1, 2, and 4, were displayed to the subject at the appropriate time. The subject's own choices registered only on his panel and were recorded in the control room. In both the anonymous and face-to-face condi-

---

[1] Self-commitment and commitment to the experimenter were varied in the original experiment. Here we are considering commitment to the discrepant majority.

tions 36 trials were administered as two identical series of the 18 used by Asch.

There is some evidence in the post experimental questionnaire, not reported in the original article, which indicates that compared with the anonymous condition, the face-to-face condition was both more stressful and produced greater ego involvement. One question asked the subjects to estimate the number of times he disagreed with the others. An average of 19.8 disagreements were perceived in the face-to-face treatment as compared with 15.8 in the anonymous treatment ($p < .02$ by t). Since under both treatments the others deviated from the correct answer on the same number of trials, the perception of a greater number of disagreements may be taken as evidence of a more pronounced effect of the disagreement. The difference cannot be explained away on the basis of the number of disagreements existing taking into account the number of yielding responses since, as reported in the original paper, there was more yielding in the face-to-face treatment.

Another question asked the subject to indicate if at any time he had ever answered as the others did against his own first choice even though he thought the others wrong. In the anonymous treatment approximately one in four of the subjects indicated that they did so whereas not a single subject in the face-to-face situation said that he did. This is so again despite the greater number of yielding responses produced in the face-to-face treatment. This tendency for the subjects in the face-to-face treatment to deny that he yielded to the others suggests either a greater tendency to maintain "face" or an actual change in his perceptions due to public pressure.

During the first series of 18 trials, 25 of the 75 subjects[2] turned in an errorless performance; 13 in the anonymous and 12 in the face-to-face treatment. During the second series only 4 of these remained adamant in the anonymous treatment as compared with 9 in the face-to-face treatment ($p < .05$ by chi square). Thus, confidence in one's initial choice does appear to decrease with continued disagreement. In corroboration of Asch's results, this manifests to a lesser extent in the face-to-face treatment. The questionnaire data suggest that this is not due to any decrease in the perceived discrepancy (more likely an increase) but rather to the effects of public commitment.

How does this greater adamance in the face-to-face treatment square with the fact that, on the average, there was also more yielding there than in the anonymous treatment? Table 1 reveals the answer. Indicated are the

TABLE 1

TOTAL NUMBER OF ERRORS FOR BOTH SERIES

	0 errors	1–4 errors	5 or more errors
Anonymous	4	25	8
Face-to-face	9	11	18

[2] There were 101 subjects in the original experiment, however, 26 of these were in treatments which were not counterbalanced for the present purposes.

number of completely adamant subjects (those making no errors), those who yielded a few times (1–4 errors), and those yielding a relatively large number of times (5 or more errors). The break between 4 and 5 errors produced the best median split for the 62 subjects making at least 1 error. There is a preponderance of subjects in both the "0" and "5 or more" categories in the face-to-face as compared with the anonymous condition ($p < .01$ by chi square). Thus, there is both greater adamance and greater yielding with public confrontation. In line with our hypothesis, there is greater commitment to the behavior in a public situation be it yielding or independence. This commitment presumably involves the individual's concern with the estimate of himself he sees reflected in the attitudes of the others toward him. The individual assumes that the others prefer that he agree with them and is, therefore, concerned with possible censure. The yielder in the face-to-face situation is presumably motivated by these considerations. This was discussed fully in the original article.

In their recent review and critique of work on dissonance theory, Brehm and Cohen (1962) stress the importance of commitment for the arousal of dissonance. When two sets of cognitions held by the individual are not consistent with one another dissonance will arise to the extent that one of these sets is resistant to change. Commitment to a behavior serves to fix the cognitions associated with it. Subsequent dissonance reduction results in a weakening of the cognitions for which there was no strong commitment. This further affirms and supports the behavior to which the individual had initially committed himself. In our situation publicity produces a commitment. A person who tended to be independent would be more so in public. Similarly, a person who tends to conform would conform more in public. In terms of our interpretation above, taking either an independent or a conforming stand in public tends to fix the stand due to the negative consequences attendant on changing it.

REFERENCES

Asch, S. E. Studies of independence and conformity: I. A minority of one against a unanimous majority. *Psychol. Monogr.* 1956, **70**, (9 Whole No. 416).

Brehm, J. W., & Cohen, A. R. *Explorations of cognitive dissonance.* New York: Wiley, 1962.

Deutsch, M., & Gerard, H. B. A study of normative and informational social influences upon individual judgment. *J. abnorm. soc. Psychol.*, 1955, **51**, 629–636.

Cognitive Consequences of Forced Compliance

Leon Festinger and James M. Carlsmith[1]

Stanford University

What happens to a person's private opinion if he is forced to do or say something contrary to that opinion? Only recently has there been any experimental work related to this question. Two studies reported by Janis and King (1954; 1956) clearly showed that, at least under some conditions, the private opinion changes so as to bring it into closer correspondence with the overt behavior the person was forced to perform. Specifically, they showed that if a person is forced to improvise a speech supporting a point of view with which he disagrees, his private opinion moves toward the position advocated in the speech. The observed opinion change is greater than for persons who only hear the speech or for persons who read a prepared speech with emphasis solely on elocution and manner of delivery. The authors of these two studies explain their results mainly in terms of mental rehearsal and thinking up new arguments. In this way, they propose, the person who is forced to improvise a speech convinces himself. They present some evidence, which is not altogether conclusive, in support of this explanation. We will have more to say concerning this explanation in discussing the results of our experiment.

Kelman (1953) tried to pursue the matter further. He reasoned that if the person is induced to make an overt statement contrary to his private opinion by the offer of some reward, then the greater the reward offered, the greater should be the subsequent opinion change. His data, however, did not support this idea. He found, rather, that a large reward produced less subsequent opinion change than did a smaller reward. Actually, this finding by Kelman is consistent with the theory we will outline below but, for a number of reasons, is not conclusive. One of the major weaknesses of the data is that not all subjects in the experiment made an overt statement contrary to their private opinion in order to obtain the offered reward. What is more, as one might expect, the percentage of subjects who complied increased as the size of the offered reward increased. Thus, with self-selection of who did and who did not make the required overt statement and

Reprinted from *Journal of Abnormal and Social Psychology*, 1959, 58, 203–210.

[1] The experiment reported here was done as part of a program of research supported by a grant from the National Science Foundation to the senior author. We wish to thank Leonard Hommel, Judson Mills, and Robert Terwilliger for their help in designing and carrying out the experiment. We would also like to acknowledge the help of Ruth Smith and Marilyn M. Miller.

with varying percentages of subjects in the different conditions who did make the required statement, no interpretation of the data can be unequivocal.

Recently, Festinger (1957) proposed a theory concerning cognitive dissonance from which come a number of derivations about opinion change following forced compliance. Since these derivations are stated in detail by Festinger (1957, Ch. 4), we will here give only a brief outline of the reasoning.

Let us consider a person who privately holds opinion "X" but has, as a result of pressure brought to bear on him, publicly stated that he believes "not X."

1. This person has two cognitions which, psychologically, do not fit together: one of these is the knowledge that he believes "X," the other the knowledge that he has publicly stated that he believes "not X." If no factors other than his private opinion are considered, it would follow, at least in our culture, that if he believes "X" he would publicly state "X." Hence, his cognition of his private belief is dissonant with his cognition concerning his actual public statement.

2. Similarly, the knowledge that he has said "not X" is consonant with (does fit together with) those cognitive elements corresponding to the reasons, pressures, promises of rewards and/or threats of punishment which induced him to say "not X."

3. In evaluating the total magnitude of dissonance, one must take account of both dissonances and consonances. Let us think of the sum of all the dissonances involving some particular cognition as "D" and the sum of all the consonances as "C." Then we might think of the total magnitude of dissonance as being a function of "D" divided by "D" plus "C."

Let us then see what can be said about the total magnitude of dissonance in a person created by the knowledge that he said "not X" and really believes "X." With everything else held constant, this total magnitude of dissonance would decrease as the number and importance of the pressures which induced him to say "not X" increased.

Thus, if the overt behavior was brought about by, say, offers of reward or threats of punishment, the magnitude of dissonance is maximal if these promised rewards or threatened punishments were just barely sufficient to induce the person to say "not X." From this point on, as the promised rewards or threatened punishment become larger, the magnitude of dissonance becomes smaller.

4. One way in which the dissonance can be reduced is for the person to change his private opinion so as to bring it into correspondence with what he has said. One would consequently expect to observe such opinion change after a person has been forced or induced to say something contrary to his private opinion. Furthermore, since the pressure to reduce dissonance will be a function of the magnitude of the dissonance, the observed opinion change should be greatest when the pressure used to elicit the overt behavior is just sufficient to do it.

The present experiment was designed to test this derivation under controlled, laboratory conditions. In the experiment we varied the amount of reward used to force persons to make a statement contrary to their private views. The prediction [from 3 and 4 above] is that the larger the reward given to the subject, the smaller will be the subsequent opinion change.

PROCEDURE

Seventy-one male students in the introductory psychology course at Stanford University were used in the experiment. In this course, students are required to spend a certain number of hours as subjects (Ss) in experiments. They choose among the available experiments by signing their names on a sheet posted on the bulletin board which states the nature of the experiment. The present experiment was listed as a two-hour experiment dealing with "Measures of Performance."

During the first week of the course, when the requirement of serving in experiments was announced and explained to the students, the instructor also told them about a study that the psychology department was conducting. He explained that, since they were required to serve in experiments, the department was conducting a study to evaluate these experiments in order to be able to improve them in the future. They were told that a sample of students would be interviewed after having served as Ss. They were urged to cooperate in these interviews by being completely frank and honest. The importance of this announcement will become clear shortly. It enabled us to measure the opinions of our Ss in a context not directly connected with our experiment and in which we could reasonably expect frank and honest expressions of opinion.

When the S arrived for the experiment on "Measures of Performance" he had to wait for a few minutes in the secretary's office. The experimenter (E) then came in, introduced himself to the S and, together, they walked into the laboratory room where the E said:

This experiment usually takes a little over an hour but, of course, we had to schedule it for two hours. Since we have that extra time, the introductory psychology people asked if they could interview some of our subjects. [Offhand and conversationally.] Did they announce that in class? I gather that they're interviewing some people who have been in experiments. I don't know much about it. Anyhow, they may want to interview you when you're through here.

With no further introduction or explanation the S was shown the first task, which involved putting 12 spools onto a tray, emptying the tray, refilling it with spools, and so on. He was told to use one hand and to work at his own speed. He did this for one-half hour. The E then removed the tray and spools and placed in front of the S a board containing 48 square pegs. His task was to turn each peg a quarter turn clockwise, then another quarter turn, and so on. He was told again to use one hand and to work at his own speed. The S worked at this task for another half hour.

While the S was working on these tasks, the E sat, with a stop watch in his hand, busily making notations on a sheet of paper. He did so in order to make it convincing that this was what the E was interested in and that these tasks, and how the S worked on them, was the total experiment. From our point of view the experiment had hardly started. The hour which the S spent working on the repetitive, monotonous tasks was intended to provide, for each S uniformly, an experience about which he would have a somewhat negative opinion.

After the half hour on the second task was over, the E conspicuously set the stop watch back to zero, put it away, pushed his chair back, lit a cigarette, and said:

O.K. Well, that's all we have in the experiment itself. I'd like to explain what this has been all about so you'll have some idea of why you were doing this. [E pauses.] Well, the way the experiment is set up is this. There are actually two groups in the experiment. In one, the group you were in, we bring the subject in and give him essentially no introduction to the experiment. That is, all we tell him is what he needs to know in order to do the tasks, and he has no idea of what the experiment is all about, or what it's going to be like, or anything like that. But in the other group, we have a student that we've hired that works for us regularly, and what I do is take him into the next room where the subject is waiting—the same room you were waiting in before—and I introduce him as if he had just finished being a subject in the experiment. That is, I say: "This is so-and-so, who's just finished the experiment, and I've asked him to tell you a little of what it's about before you start." The fellow who works for us then, in conversation with the next subject, makes these points: [The E then produced a sheet headed "For Group B" which had written on it: It was very enjoyable, I had a lot of fun, I enjoyed myself, it was very interesting, it was intriguing, it was exciting. The E showed this to the S and then proceeded with his false explanation of the purpose of the experiment.] Now, of course, we have this student do this, because if the experimenter does it, it doesn't look as realistic, and what we're interested in doing is comparing how these two groups do on the experiment—the one with this previous expectation about the experiment, and the other, like yourself, with essentially none.

Up to this point the procedure was identical for Ss in all conditions. From this point on they diverged somewhat. Three conditions were run, Control, One Dollar, and Twenty Dollars, as follows:

CONTROL CONDITION

The E continued:

Is that fairly clear? [Pause.] Look, that fellow [looks at watch] I was telling you about from the introductory psychology class said he would get here a couple of minutes from now. Would you mind waiting to see if he wants to talk to you? Fine. Why don't we go into the other room to wait? [The E left the S in the secretary's office for four minutes. He then returned and said:] O.K. Let's check and see if he does want to talk to you.

ONE AND TWENTY DOLLAR CONDITIONS

The E continued:

Is that fairly clear how it is set up and what we're trying to do? [Pause.] Now, I also have a sort of strange thing to ask you. The thing is this. [Long pause, some confusion and uncertainty in the following, with a degree of embarrassment on the part of the E. The manner of the E contrasted strongly with the preceding unhesitant and assured false explanation of the experiment. The point was to make it seem to the S that this was the first time the E had done this and that he felt unsure of himself.] The fellow who normally does this for us couldn't do it today—he just phoned in, and something or other came up for him—so we've been looking around for someone that we could hire to do it for us. You see, we've got another subject waiting [looks at watch] who is supposed to be in that other condition. Now Professor ———, who is in charge of this experiment, suggested that perhaps we could take a chance on your doing it for us. I'll tell you what we had in mind: the thing is, if you could do it for us now, then of course you would know how to do it, and if something like this should ever come up again, that is, the regular fellow couldn't make it, and we had a subject scheduled, it would be very reassuring to us to know that we had somebody else we could call on who knew how to do it. So, if you would be willing to do this for us, we'd like to hire you to do it now and then be on call in the future, if something like this should ever happen again. We can pay you a dollar (twenty dollars) for doing this for us, that is, for doing it now and then being on call. Do you think you could do that for us?

If the S hesitated, the E said things like, "It will only take a few minutes," "The regular person is pretty reliable; this is the first time he has missed," or "If we needed you we could phone you a day or two in advance; if you couldn't make it, of course, we wouldn't expect you to come." After the S agreed to do it, the E gave him the previously mentioned sheet of paper headed "For Group B" and asked him to read it through again. The E then paid the S one dollar (twenty dollars), made out a handwritten receipt form, and asked the S to sign it. He then said:

O.K., the way we'll do it is this. As I said, the next subject should be here by now. I think the next one is a girl. I'll take you into the next room and introduce you to her, saying that you've just finished the experiment and that we've asked you to tell her a little about it. And what we want you to do is just sit down and get into a conversation with her and try to get across the points on that sheet of paper. I'll leave you alone and come back after a couple of minutes. O.K.?

The E then took the S into the secretary's office where he had previously waited and where the next S was waiting. (The secretary had left the office.) He introduced the girl and the S to one another saying that the S had just finished the experiment and would tell her something about it. He then left saying he would return in a couple of minutes. The girl, an undergraduate hired for this role, said little until the S made some positive remarks about the experiment and then said that she was surprised because a friend of hers had taken the experiment the week before and had told her that it was boring and that she ought to try to get out of it. Most Ss responded by saying something like "Oh, no, it's really very interesting. I'm sure you'll enjoy it." The girl, after this, listened quietly, accepting and agreeing to everything the S told her. The discussion between the S and the girl was recorded on a hidden tape recorder.

After two minutes the E returned, asked the girl to go into the experimental room, thanked the S for talking to the girl, wrote down his phone number to continue the fiction that we might call on him again in the future and then said: "Look, could we check and see if that fellow from introductory psychology wants to talk to you?"

From this point on, the procedure for all three conditions was once more identical. As the E and the S started to walk to the office where the interviewer was, the E said: "Thanks very much for working on those tasks for us. I hope you did enjoy it. Most of our subjects tell us afterward that they found it quite interesting. You get a chance to see how you react to the tasks and so forth." This short persuasive communication was made in all conditions in exactly the same way. The reason for doing it, theoretically, was to make it easier for anyone who wanted to persuade himself that the tasks had been, indeed, enjoyable.

When they arrived at the interviewer's office, the E asked the interviewer whether or not he wanted to talk to the S. The interviewer said yes, the E shook hands with the S, said good-bye, and left. The interviewer, of course, was always kept in complete ignorance of which condition the S was in. The interview consisted of four questions, on each of which the S was first encouraged to talk about the matter and was then asked to rate his opinion or reaction on an 11-point scale. The questions are as follows:

1. Were the tasks interesting and enjoyable? In what way? In what way were they not? Would you rate how you feel about them on a scale from −5 to +5 where −5 means they were extremely dull and boring, +5 means they were extremely interesting and enjoyable, and zero means they were neutral, neither interesting nor uninteresting.

2. Did the experiment give you an opportunity to learn about your own ability to perform these tasks? In what way? In what way not? Would you rate how you feel about this on a scale from 0 to 10 where 0 means you learned nothing and 10 means you learned a great deal.

3. From what you know about the experiment and the tasks involved in it, would you say the experiment was measuring anything important? That is, do you think the results may have scientific value? In what way? In what way not? Would you rate your opinion on this matter on a scale from 0 to 10 where 0 means the results have no scientific value or importance and 10 means they have a great deal of value and importance.

4. Would you have any desire to participate in another similar experiment? Why? Why not? Would you rate your desire to participate in a similar experiment again on a scale from −5 to +5, where −5 means you would definitely dislike to participate, +5 means you would definitely like to participate, and 0 means you have no particular feeling about it one way or the other.

As may be seen, the questions varied in how directly relevant they were to what the S had told the girl. This point will be discussed further in connection with the results.

At the close of the interview the S was asked what he thought the experiment was about and, following this, was asked directly whether or not he was suspicious of anything and, if so, what he was suspicious of. When the interview was over, the interviewer brought the S back to the experimental room where the E was waiting together with the girl who had posed as the waiting S. (In the control condition, of course, the girl was not there.) The true purpose of the experiment was then explained to the S in detail, and the reasons for each of the various steps in the experiment were explained carefully in relation to the true purpose. All experimental Ss in both One Dollar and Twenty Dollar conditions were asked, after this explanation, to return the money they had been given. All Ss, without exception, were quite willing to return the money.

The data from 11 of the 71 Ss in the experiment had to be discarded for the following reasons:

1. Five Ss (three in the One Dollar and two in the Twenty Dollar condition) indicated in the interview that they were suspicious about hav-

ing been paid to tell the girl the experiment was fun and suspected that that was the real purpose of the experiment.

2. Two Ss (both in the One Dollar condition) told the girl that they had been hired, that the experiment was really boring but they were supposed to say it was fun.

3. Three Ss (one in the One Dollar and two in the Twenty Dollar condition) refused to take the money and refused to be hired.

4. One S (in the One Dollar condition), immediately after having talked to the girl, demanded her phone number saying he would call her and explain things, and also told the E he wanted to wait until she was finished so he could tell her about it.

These 11 Ss were, of course, run through the total experiment anyhow and the experiment was explained to them afterwards. Their data, however, are not included in the analysis.

SUMMARY OF DESIGN

There remain, for analysis, 20 Ss in each of the three conditions. Let us review these briefly: 1. *Control condition.* These Ss were treated identically in all respects to the Ss in the experimental conditions, except that they were never asked to, and never did, tell the waiting girl that the experimental tasks were enjoyable and lots of fun. 2. *One Dollar condition.* These Ss were hired for one dollar to tell a waiting S that tasks, which were really rather dull and boring, were interesting, enjoyable, and lots of fun. 3. *Twenty Dollar condition.* These Ss were hired for twenty dollars to do the same thing.

RESULTS

The major results of the experiment are summarized in Table 1 which lists, separately for each of the three experimental conditions, the average rating which the Ss gave at the end of each question on the interview. We will discuss each of the questions on the interview separately, because they

TABLE 1

AVERAGE RATINGS ON INTERVIEW QUESTIONS FOR EACH CONDITION

Question on Interview	Experimental Condition		
	Control (N = 20)	One Dollar (N = 20)	Twenty Dollars (N = 20)
How enjoyable tasks were (rated from −5 to +5)	−.45	+1.35	−.05
How much they learned (rated from 0 to 10)	3.08	2.80	3.15
Scientific importance (rated from 0 to 10)	5.60	6.45	5.18
Participate in similar exp. (rated from −5 to +5)	−.62	+1.20	−.25

were intended to measure different things. One other point before we proceed to examine the data. In all the comparisons, the Control condition should be regarded as a baseline from which to evaluate the results in the other two conditions. The Control condition gives us, essentially, the reactions of Ss to the tasks and their opinions about the experiment as falsely explained to them, without the experimental introduction of dissonance. The data from the other conditions may be viewed, in a sense, as changes from this baseline.

HOW ENJOYABLE THE TASKS WERE

The average ratings on this question, presented in the first row of figures in Table 1, are the results most important to the experiment. These results are the ones most directly relevant to the specific dissonance which was experimentally created. It will be recalled that the tasks were purposely arranged to be rather boring and monotonous. And, indeed, in the Control condition the average rating was −.45, somewhat on the negative side of the neutral point.

In the other two conditions, however, the Ss told someone that these tasks were interesting and enjoyable. The resulting dissonance could, of course, most directly be reduced by persuading themselves that the tasks were, indeed, interesting and enjoyable. In the One Dollar condition, since the magnitude of dissonance was high, the pressure to reduce this dissonance would also be high. In this condition, the average rating was +1.35, considerably on the positive side and significantly different from the Control condition at the .02 level[2] ($t = 2.48$).

In the Twenty Dollar condition, where less dissonance was created experimentally because of the greater importance of the consonant relations, there is correspondingly less evidence of dissonance reduction. The average rating in this condition is only −.05, slightly and not significantly higher than the Control condition. The difference between the One Dollar and Twenty Dollar conditions is significant at the .03 level ($t = 2.22$). In short, when an S was induced, by offer of reward, to say something contrary to his private opinion, this private opinion tended to change so as to correspond more closely with what he had said. The greater the reward offered (beyond what was necessary to elicit the behavior) the smaller was the effect.

DESIRE TO PARTICIPATE IN A SIMILAR EXPERIMENT

The results from this question are shown in the last row of Table 1. This question is less directly related to the dissonance that was experimentally created for the Ss. Certainly, the more interesting and enjoyable they felt the tasks were, the greater would be their desire to participate in a similar experiment. But other factors would enter also. Hence, one would expect the results on this question to be very similar to the results on "how enjoyable the tasks were" but weaker. Actually, the results, as may be seen in the table, are in exactly the same direction, and the magnitude of the mean differences is fully as large as on the first question. The variability is greater, however, and the differences do not yield high levels of statistical significance. The difference between the One Dollar condition (+1.20) and

2 All statistical tests referred to in this paper are two-tailed.

the Control condition (−.62) is significant at the .08 level ($t = 1.78$). The difference between the One Dollar condition and the Twenty Dollar condition (−.25) reaches only the .15 level of significance ($t = 1.46$).

THE SCIENTIFIC IMPORTANCE OF THE EXPERIMENT

This question was included because there was a chance that differences might emerge. There are, after all, other ways in which the experimentally created dissonance could be reduced. For example, one way would be for the S to magnify for himself the value of the reward he obtained. This, however, was unlikely in this experiment because money was used for the reward and it is undoubtedly difficult to convince oneself that one dollar is more than it really is. There is another possible way, however. The Ss were given a very good reason, in addition to being paid, for saying what they did to the waiting girl. The Ss were told it was necessary for the experiment. The dissonance could, consequently, be reduced by magnifying the importance of this cognition. The more scientifically important they considered the experiment to be, the less was the total magnitude of dissonance. It is possible, then, that the results on this question, shown in the third row of figures in Table 1, might reflect dissonance reduction.

The results are weakly in line with what one would expect if the dissonance were somewhat reduced in this manner. The One Dollar condition is higher than the other two. The difference between the One and Twenty Dollar conditions reaches the .08 level of significance on a two-tailed test ($t = 1.79$). The difference between the One Dollar and Control conditions is not impressive at all ($t = 1.21$). The result that the Twenty Dollar condition is actually lower than the Control condition is undoubtedly a matter of chance ($t = 0.58$).

HOW MUCH THEY LEARNED FROM THE EXPERIMENT

The results on this question are shown in the second row of figures in Table 1. The question was included because, as far as we could see, it had nothing to do with the dissonance that was experimentally created and could not be used for dissonance reduction. One would then expect no differences at all among the three conditions. We felt it was important to show that the effect was not a completely general one but was specific to the content of the dissonance which was created. As can be readily seen in Table 1, there are only negligible differences among conditions. The highest t value for any of these differences is only 0.48.

DISCUSSION OF A POSSIBLE ALTERNATIVE EXPLANATION

We mentioned in the introduction that Janis and King (1954; 1956) in explaining their findings, proposed an explanation in terms of the self-convincing effect of mental rehearsal and thinking up new arguments by the person who had to improvise a speech. Kelman (1953), in the previously mentioned study, in attempting to explain the unexpected finding that the persons who complied in the moderate reward condition changed their opinion more than in the high reward condition, also proposed the same kind of explanation. If the results of our experiment are to be taken as strong corroboration of the theory of cognitive dissonance, this possible alternative explanation must be dealt with.

Specifically, as applied to our results, this alternative explanation would maintain that perhaps, for some reason, the Ss in the One Dollar condition worked harder at telling the waiting girl that the tasks were fun and enjoyable. That is, in the One Dollar condition they may have rehearsed it more mentally, thought up more ways of saying it, may have said it more convincingly, and so on. Why this might have been the case is, of course, not immediately apparent. One might expect that, in the Twenty Dollar condition, having been paid more, they would try to do a better job of it than in the One Dollar condition. But nevertheless, the possibility exists that the Ss in the One Dollar condition may have improvised more.

Because of the desirability of investigating this possible alternative explanation, we recorded on a tape recorder the conversation between each S and the girl. These recordings were transcribed and then rated, by two independent raters, on five dimensions. The ratings were, of course done in ignorance of which condition each S was in. The reliabilities of these ratings, that is, the correlations between the two independent raters, ranged from .61 to .88, with an average reliability of .71. The five ratings were:

1. The content of what the S said *before* the girl made the remark that her friend told her it was boring. The stronger the S's positive statements about the tasks, and the more ways in which he said they were interesting and enjoyable, the higher the rating.

2. The content of what the S said *after* the girl made the above-mentioned remark. This was rated in the same way as for the content before the remark.

3. A similar rating of the over-all content of what the S said.

4. A rating of how persuasive and convincing the S was in what he said and the way in which he said it.

5. A rating of the amount of time in the discussion that the S spent discussing the tasks as opposed to going off into irrelevant things.

The mean ratings for the One Dollar and Twenty Dollar conditions, averaging the ratings of the two independent raters, are presented in Table 2. It is clear from examining the table that, in all cases, the Twenty Dollar condition is slightly higher. The differences are small, however, and only on the rating of "amount of time" does the difference between the two conditions even approach significance. We are certainly justified in concluding that the Ss in the One Dollar condition did not improvise more nor act more convincingly. Hence, the alternative explanation discussed above cannot account for the findings.

SUMMARY

Recently, Festinger (1957) has proposed a theory concerning cognitive dissonance. Two derivations from this theory are tested here. These are:

1. If a person is induced to do or say something which is contrary to

his private opinion, there will be a tendency for him to change his opinion so as to bring it into correspondence with what he has done or said.

TABLE 2

AVERAGE RATINGS OF DISCUSSION BETWEEN SUBJECT AND GIRL

| | Condition | | |
Dimension Rated	One Dollar	Twenty Dollars	Value of t
Content before remark by girl (rated from 0 to 5)	2.26	2.62	1.08
Content after remark by girl (rated from 0 to 5)	1.63	1.75	0.11
Over-all content (rated from 0 to 5)	1.89	2.19	1.08
Persuasiveness and conviction (rated from 0 to 10)	4.79	5.50	0.99
Time spent on topic (rated from 0 to 10)	6.74	8.19	1.80

2. The larger the pressure used to elicit the overt behavior (beyond the minimum needed to elicit it) the weaker will be the above-mentioned tendency.

A laboratory experiment was designed to test these derivations. Subjects were subjected to a boring experience and then paid to tell someone that the experience had been interesting and enjoyable. The amount of money paid the subject was varied. The private opinions of the subjects concerning the experiences were then determined.

The results strongly corroborate the theory that was tested.

REFERENCES

FESTINGER, L. A theory of cognitive dissonance. Evanston, Ill.: Row Peterson, 1957.

JANIS, I. L., & KING, B. T. The influence of role-playing on opinion change. J. abnorm. soc. Psychol., 1954, 49, 211–218.

KELMAN, H. Attitude change as a function of response restriction. Hum. Relat., 1953, 6, 185–214.

KING, B. T., & JANIS, I. L. Comparison of the effectiveness of improvised versus non-improvised role-playing in producing opinion changes. Hum. Relat., 1956, 9, 177–186.

Index